ASP.NET v. 2.0—
The Beta Version

Microsoft .NET Development Series

John Montgomery, *Series Advisor*
Don Box, *Series Advisor*
Martin Heller, *Series Editor*

The **Microsoft .NET Development Series** is supported and developed by the leaders and experts of Microsoft development technologies including Microsoft architects and DevelopMentor instructors. The books in this series provide a core resource of information and understanding every developer needs in order to write effective applications and managed code. Learn from the leaders how to maximize your use of the .NET Framework and its programming languages.

Titles in the Series

Brad Abrams, *.NET Framework Standard Library Annotated Reference, Volume 1*, 0-321-15489-4

Keith Ballinger, *.NET Web Services: Architecture and Implementation*, 0-321-11359-4

Bob Beauchemin, Niels Berglund, Dan Sullivan, *A First Look at SQL Server 2005 for Developers*, 0-321-18059-3

Don Box with Chris Sells, *Essential .NET, Volume 1: The Common Language Runtime*, 0-201-73411-7

Mahesh Chand, *Graphics Programming with GDI+*, 0-321-16077-0

Anders Hejlsberg, Scott Wiltamuth, Peter Golde, *The C# Programming Language*, 0-321-15491-6

Alex Homer, Dave Sussman, Mark Fussell, *A First Look at ADO.NET and System.Xml v. 2.0*, 0-321-22839-1

Alex Homer, Dave Sussman, Rob Howard, *A First Look at ASP.NET v. 2.0*, 0-321-22896-0

James S. Miller and Susann Ragsdale, *The Common Language Infrastructure Annotated Standard*, 0-321-15493-2

Fritz Onion, *Essential ASP.NET with Examples in C#*, 0-201-76040-1

Fritz Onion, *Essential ASP.NET with Examples in Visual Basic .NET*, 0-201-76039-8

Ted Pattison and Dr. Joe Hummel, *Building Applications and Components with Visual Basic .NET*, 0-201-73495-8

Chris Sells, *Windows Forms Programming in C#*, 0-321-11620-8

Chris Sells and Justin Gehtland, *Windows Forms Programming in Visual Basic .NET*, 0-321-12519-3

Paul Vick, *The Visual Basic .NET Programming Language*, 0-321-16951-4

Damien Watkins, Mark Hammond, Brad Abrams, *Programming in the .NET Environment*, 0-201-77018-0

Shawn Wildermuth, *Pragmatic ADO.NET: Data Access for the Internet World*, 0-201-74568-2

Paul Yao and David Durant, *.NET Compact Framework Programming with C#*, 0-321-17403-8

Paul Yao and David Durant, *.NET Compact Framework Programming with Visual Basic .NET*, 0-321-17404-6

For more information go to www.awprofessional.com/msdotnetseries/

ASP.NET v. 2.0 — The Beta Version

■ Alex Homer
Dave Sussman
Rob Howard

♣ Addison-Wesley

Boston • San Francisco • New York • Toronto • Montreal
London • Munich • Paris • Madrid
Capetown • Sydney • Tokyo • Singapore • Mexico City

The publisher offers discounts on this book when ordered in quantity for bulk purchases and special sales. For more information, please contact:

U.S. Corporate and Government Sales
(800) 382-3419
corpsales@pearsontechgroup.com

For sales outside of the U.S., please contact:

International Sales
(317) 581-3793
international@pearsontechgroup.com

Visit Addison-Wesley on the Web:
www.awprofessional.com

Library of Congress Cataloging-in-Publication Data
Homer, Alex.
    ASP.NET v. 2.0 : the beta version/ Alex Homer, Dave Sussman, Rob Howard.—1st ed.
        p. cm.
    Includes bibliographical references and index.
    ISBN 0-321-25727-8
    1. Active server pages. 2. Microsoft.NET. 3. Web site development. 4. Internet programming. I Howard, Rob, 1973– II. Sussman, David, 1966–. III. Title.

    TK5105.8885.A26H65975 2005
    005.2'76—dc22

                                                2004012167

ISBN: 0-321-25727-8
Text printed on recycled paper
1 2 3 4 5 6 7 8 9 10—CRS—0807060504
First printing, July 2004

Contents

Figures

Tables

Foreword

ASP.NET IS THE FASTEST-GROWING Web development platform in the world today. It powers some of the biggest Web sites and applications in the world—a shortlist of well-known customers includes Dell Computer, Merrill Lynch, the London Stock Exchange, NASDAQ, JetBlue Airways, USA TODAY, Home Shopping Network, Weight Watchers, Bank One, and Century 21.

Every day thousands of new developers begin learning ASP.NET for the first time—supported by an incredible developer community of books (170+ different ASP.NET books have been printed), user groups (more than 150+ worldwide), forums (450,000+ registered users on the www.asp.net public forums), e-mail–based listservs, and Web logs.

Our goal while building ASP.NET version 2.0 has been not only to develop a product that makes this developer community proud but also to build a platform that defines a new level of rich features and functionality against which all Web development is measured.

Specifically, we've focused our work on ASP.NET 2.0 around three core themes.

Developer productivity: Our goal with ASP.NET 2.0 is to enable developers to build full-featured Web applications faster than ever before. We've spent countless hours talking with developers and looking at existing applications to identify the common features, patterns, and code that Web developers build over and over today. We've then worked to componentize and include these features as built-in functionality of ASP.NET.

For example, ASP.NET 2.0 now includes built-in support for Membership (username/password credential storage) and Role Manager services out of the box. The new Personalization service enables quick storage and retrieval of user settings and preferences—facilitating rich customization with minimal code. Use of master pages allows flexible page UI inheritance across sites. The navigation system helps developers quickly build menu-associated link structures. Themes enable flexible UI skinning of controls and pages. And the new Web Parts framework offers rich portal-style layout and end-user customization features that would otherwise require writing tens of thousands of lines of code.

Augmenting all these great infrastructure features are more than 50 new server controls in version 2.0 that enable powerful declarative support for data access, security, wizard navigation, menus, tree views, portals, and more. For example, building a page with a `DataGrid` in ASP.NET 1.0 bound to a three-tier business object that was filtered using a drop-down list, while also supporting paging and sorting and editing, would have required approximately 100 lines of code (and probably a few trips to the help documentation). In ASP.NET 2.0, this scenario can be accomplished without requiring a single line of procedural code (the new data controls do all the work)—and literally can be built in seconds using the new edition of Visual Studio development tools.

The collective arsenal of features now available to developers in ASP.NET 2.0 is truly awesome. With it, projects that used to take days or weeks can now be done in as little as a few hours.

Administration and management: Our goal with ASP.NET 2.0 is to ensure that administrators love ASP.NET as much as developers do. This means building features that further enhance the deployment, management, and operations of ASP.NET servers.

In ASP.NET 2.0 we've built new configuration management APIs, enabling users to programmatically build programs or scripts that create, read, and update `web.config` and `machine.config` configuration files. We've provided a new comprehensive administration tool that plugs into the existing IIS Administration MMC and enables an administrator to graphically read or change any setting within our XML configuration files. We've also added support for encrypting settings within `web.config` files, allowing you to easily save and manage sensitive settings like connection strings and passwords.

ASP.NET 2.0 will ship with a new application deployment utility that will enable both developers and administrators to pre-compile a dynamic ASP.NET application prior to deployment. This pre-compilation automatically identifies any compilation issues anywhere within the site and also enables ASP.NET applications to be deployed without any source being stored on the server (even the content of `.aspx` files is removed as part of the compile phase).

We are also providing new health monitoring support so that administrators can be automatically notified when an application on a server starts to experience problems. New tracing features will help administrators capture runtime and request data from a production server to better diagnose issues.

Speed and performance: ASP.NET is already the world's fastest Web application server. Our goal with ASP.NET 2.0 is to make it even faster.

ASP.NET 2.0 is now 64-bit enabled, meaning it can take advantage of the full memory address space of new 64-bit processors and servers. Developers can copy existing 32-bit ASP.NET applications onto a 64-bit ASP.NET 2.0 server and have them automatically be JIT compiled and executed as native 64-bit applications (no source code changes or manual recompile are required).

ASP.NET 2.0 also now includes automatic database server cache invalidation. This powerful and easy-to-use feature allows developers to aggressively output cache database-driven page and partial page content within a site—and have ASP.NET automatically invalidate these cache entries and refresh the content whenever the back-end database changes.

At the same time that we've focused efforts on making ASP.NET even better, we have also made major improvements to the Web development support within Visual Studio. This includes much better WYSIWYG designer support—to avoid any HTML reformatting of source, to provide full XHTML compliance of markup, and to provide a WYSIWYG designer for the new ASP.NET 2.0 Master Pages feature. It includes major project system enhancements—FrontPage Server Extensions are no longer required to create, edit, and run applications (just point at a file system directory and you can begin editing). It includes improvements to the code editing and code separation models, making code-behind much more elegant and robust. It includes built-in support for Section 508 and WCAG accessibility validation. It includes localization support to enable developers to easily build Web applications that can dynamically target a variety of languages and cultures. And it includes rich support for data access—leveraging the new ASP.NET 2.0 data controls to enable easy and powerful data UI generation against three-tier business objects with no code required. The combination of ASP.NET 2.0 and the new Visual Studio development tool features complement each other perfectly, enabling developers to quickly and easily build applications like never before.

This book provides an excellent guide for developers exploring and learning the amazing functionality that will be available with this new generation of Microsoft Web products. You'll be able to use this book as a valuable resource to gain insight into the new features—and to learn just how much easier and better Web development will be when ASP.NET 2.0 is released.

Scott Guthrie
Product Unit Manager
Web Platform and Tools Teams
Microsoft Corporation

Preface

DYNAMIC WEB PAGE GENERATION techniques have been around for many years, but ASP.NET took the world by storm when it was released in February 2002. The advent of a new page and postback architecture, server controls, and the whole .NET Framework made it easier to build Web sites and Web applications that performed better while reducing the amount of work required by the developer.

So, it comes as no surprise to see a new version of the .NET Framework, and with it version 2.0 of ASP.NET, starting to appear on the horizon. Sometime in 2005 we should have the final release of version 2.0 of the .NET Framework, together with new versions of Visual Studio and other tools. In the meantime, Microsoft is following its usual policy of involving developers as early in the process as possible, giving them the chance to provide feedback on the new product.

So, with the final release of version 2.0 still some way off, why would you be interested in it now? The simple answer is, of course, that as a developer you need to keep abreast of what's going on in your industry. And more than that, being aware of what's coming in the future might well influence what you do today, in the overall design of your applications and the preparations and plans you make for upcoming products and applications.

This book will help by introducing you to the new features that will be in version 2.0 of ASP.NET and how they can benefit your Web site and Web application development. And perhaps you don't actually intend to install the early releases of version 2.0, but you just want to know more about what it offers. No problem—that's OK with us as well!

Versions and Release Schedules

Before you read any further, it's important that you understand what this book covers and how it relates to the future and final releases of ASP.NET version 2.0.

The first public beta of version 2.0 of the .NET Framework arrives in mid-2004. There will probably be another beta release later in 2004, followed by a final release. However, there are unlikely to be any significant changes between the first beta release and the finished product because this phase of the development cycle concentrates on moving from "code complete" status though fine-tuning and bug fixing to final release.

This book covers the first beta release, and as such the class interface listings and code samples you see here cannot be guaranteed to work in exactly the same way right through to the final release version. However, the principles and general syntax are unlikely to differ by anything more than minor details.

What This Book Covers

This is not just a reference book but also a feature-packed exploration of version 2.0 of ASP.NET. It covers the changes between ASP.NET 1.x and ASP.NET 2.0 that make it even easier to build efficient, attractive, and interactive Web sites and Web applications using the new features in ASP.NET, while considerably reducing developer effort and code requirements.

The first chapter presents an overview of the new version and also lays out the roadmap for the remainder of the book. The following chapters discuss how the common requirements of developers have been addressed, starting with the ubiquitous need to access data from your pages and then progressing through to a detailed look at the new configuration and management features that version 2.0 provides.

Along with the final release of ASP.NET 2.0 we will, of course, see a new version of Visual Studio and other tools. While we do include some details of the new version of Visual Studio, called Visual Studio 2005, the book does not concentrate on this area. Many developers will be writing ASP.NET pages using other tools (including, we suspect, a text editor) while Visual Studio 2005 is still under development.

What You Need to Use This Book

The main thing you need to use this book is the beta release of version 2.0 of the .NET Framework. Other than that, you'll need something to transfer your creative efforts into ASP.NET files on disk. We still prefer a text editor, though early experiments with Visual Studio 2005 suggest that Windows Notepad will be seeing the light of day a lot less often in the future. However, it doesn't really matter which tool or editor you use as long as it can generate text files with the `.aspx` file extension.

Finally, you'll need to be prepared to change the way you think about building code for your Web pages because in many cases you don't actually have to write any code at all in version 2.0. See Chapter 1 for more details, and get ready to be more productive!

Obtaining and Running the Sample Files

Most of the examples you see in the book are provided for download so that you can experiment with them yourself, on your own server. We have also installed many of them on our server, where you can run them online to see the results, without having to download them. For more details, go to http://www.daveandal.net/books/ and follow the link to this book.

Acknowledgments

This book couldn't have been completed without help from many people.

First, we thank Appan Annamalai for his contribution on localization and resources. Rarely do you find someone who has never written before, volunteers to write, does so in double-quick time, and provides content that needs no editing and fits straight into the chapter. Thank you. Next time we'll have room for you to expand on this topic in much more depth.

Thank you to everyone on the ASP.NET team for their efforts, not only for getting a product ready to ship but also for taking time out to answer questions. In particular, thanks go to Stefan Schackow, Bradley Millington, Lance Olson, Doug Purdy, Shanku Niyogi, Erik Olson, Mike Volodarsky, Brian Goldfarb, Nikhil Kothari, Andres Sanabria, and last, but by no means least, Scott Guthrie.

Thanks are also due to Elizabeth Zdunich for managing the project, Chrysta Meadowbrooke for taking the gibberish we authors write and turning it into something resembling English (well, American English!), and Vicki Hochstedler for making the book look good.

And thanks to the reviewers, especially Ken Cox, who worked right up until the last minute to turn around chapters.

This book is dedicated to two people who are moving on in their careers. First is Stacey Giard, who for many years has been the author liaison with the ASP.NET team. She finally got fed up with us and is moving into a different role at Microsoft. We thank you for all of the hard work you've put into looking after us.

Second is Rob Howard, who moved back to Texas about a year ago and has finally decided that regular commuting between his home in Texas and work in Seattle doesn't leave him enough time for hockey. He has now left the ASP.NET team and started a training and consultancy business focusing on .NET.

We wish them both well in their new roles.

1

An Introduction to ASP.NET 2.0

W HEN MICROSOFT RELEASED the .NET Framework 1.0 Technology
Preview in July 2000, it was immediately clear that Web development was going to change. The company's then current technology, Active
Server Pages 3.0 (ASP), was powerful and flexible, and it made the creation of dynamic Web sites easy. ASP spawned a whole series of books, ar-
ticles, Web sites, and components, all to make the development process
even easier. What ASP didn't have, however, was an application framework; it was never an enterprise development tool. Everything you did in
ASP was code oriented—you just couldn't get away with not writing code.

ASP.NET was designed to counter this problem. One of its key design
goals was to make programming easier and quicker by reducing the
amount of code you have to create. Enter the declarative programming
model, a rich server control hierarchy with events, a large class library, and
support for development tools from the humble Notepad to the high-end
Visual Studio .NET. All in all, ASP.NET was a huge leap forward.

What's Wrong with ASP.NET 1.x?

So if ASP.NET 1.0 and 1.1 are so great, what's wrong with them? Well,
nothing, actually; but when developing software, there is always a trade-
off between how much can be done, how many resources you have, and

how much time you have to do it. There is an almost never-ending supply of features you can add, but at some stage you have to ship the product. You cannot doubt that ASP.NET 1.0 shipped with an impressive array of features, but the ASP.NET team members are ambitious, and they not only had plans of their own but also listened to their users.

ASP.NET 2.0 addresses the areas that both the development team and users wanted to improve. The aims of the new version are listed below.

- **Reduce the number of lines of code required by 70%.** The declarative programming model freed developers from having to write reams of code, but there are still many scenarios where this cannot be avoided. Data access is a great example, where the same `Connection`, `DataAdapter/DataSet`, and `Command/DataReader` code is used regularly.

- **Increase developer productivity.** This partly relates to reducing the amount of code required but is also affected by more server controls encompassing complex functionality, as well as providing better solutions for common Web site scenarios (such as portals and personalized sites).

- **Use a single control set for all devices.** Mobile devices are becoming more pervasive, with an increasing number of new devices. Many of the server controls render appropriately for small screens, but there are two major problems with the current support for mobile devices: (1) having a separate set of server controls purely for mobile devices is not only confusing but also costly, and (2) adding support for new devices requires additional development work and maintenance. ASP.NET 2.0 will provide a single set of controls and an extensible architecture to allow them (and other controls) to support multiple devices.

- **Provide the fastest Web server platform.** Although ASP.NET 1.0 offers a fast server platform, ASP.NET 2.0 will improve areas such as application start-up times and provide better application tracing and performance data. Innovative caching features will enhance application performance, especially when SQL Server is used.

- **Provide the best hosting solution.** With the large number of Internet applications being hosted, it's important to provide better solutions for hosters. For example, better management features to identify and stop rogue applications will give hosters more control over their current environment. More control can also be given to hosted companies by use of the new Web-based administration tool, allowing users to easily control the configuration of applications remotely.

- **Provide easier and more sophisticated management features.** Administration of ASP.NET applications under version 1.x required manual editing of the XML configuration file, which is not a great solution for administrators. Version 2.0 brings a graphical user interface–based administration tool that is integrated with the Internet Information Services (IIS) administration tool.

- **Ease implementation of entire scenarios.** The better management features are built on top of a management application programming interface (API), allowing custom administration programs to be created. Along with application packaging this will provide support for easily deployable applications, with or without source.

Even from this broad set of aims you can see that ASP.NET 2.0 is a great advance from 1.x for both developers and administrators.

New Features

This chapter isn't an in-depth look at any specific feature—instead we are going to give you a taste of what's to come so you can see how much easier Web development is going to be. For this outlook we've broken down the new features into rough end-to-end scenarios.

Templates for a Consistent Look and Feel

ASP.NET 1.x provides an easy way to develop Web sites, but one thing that has become apparent is the lack of an architecture for applying a consistent look and feel. Several workaround techniques emerged:

- Creating a custom class object that inherits from `Page` and having this custom page preload controls
- Creating a templated server control, where the templates provide the layout areas for each page, and using this control on every page
- Having User Controls for common areas of the site, such as headings, menus, and footers

Of these, the first two require knowledge of creating server controls, and although this is a topic most ASP.NET developers could master, it may not be one they've had experience with. Therefore a solution using custom server controls tends to be avoided. The last option, though, is a simple solution, easy to create and implement. User Controls were created to provide reusable functionality, and this is a great use for them. However, to apply a consistent look and feel you need to first place the User Controls on each page, then ensure that they are placed in the same place on each page. In other words, you really need a page template, and in reality this manifests itself as an ASP.NET file that you simply copy for each new page. The danger of this approach is that it's too easy to modify a page and change the layout for that single page.

To provide a templating solution, ASP.NET 2.0 has the concept of **master pages**, which provide a template for the look and implementation of a page. A master page is an ASP.NET page that provides a template for other pages, giving shared page-level layout and functionality. The master page defines placeholders for the content, which can be overridden by child pages. The resultant page is a combination of the master page and the child page, as shown in Figure 1.1.

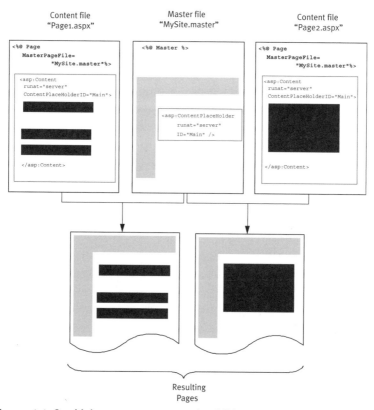

FIGURE 1.1. Combining a master page and a child page

Master pages are covered in Chapters 2 and 5.

Styles for Controls

The second major feature of ASP.NET 2.0 that deals with the look and feel of a site is that of **themes**. Theming, or skinning, has become very popular, allowing users to create a customized look for applications. On the Windows desktop two of the most popular themed applications are audio players (Winamp and Windows Media Player), and with some additional software, even Windows XP can be themed.

The popularity of theming is due to the nature of humans—we like to choose the way things look, and we like to express our individuality. This is easy on the desktop, where users generally have a single machine each. With Web sites, however, theming becomes a more difficult issue because of the number of users. Tracking which users have which themes and managing those themes becomes an overhead that site administrators don't want to get involved with.

Some Web sites provide forms of theming, but these are relatively limited in terms of customization, perhaps allowing only a choice of color scheme. Other sites provide a selection of stylesheets for users to pick from, assuming their browsers support this feature, or alternatively change the stylesheet on the server. This allows not only color schemes to be selected but also complete style choices, such as fonts, style of borders, and so on.

In ASP.NET 2.0 the goals for theming are quite simple.

- Make it simple to customize the appearance of a site or page, using the same design tools and methods used when developing the page itself. This means there's no need to learn any special tools or techniques to add themes to a site.
- Allow themes to be applied to controls, pages, and even entire sites. For example, this allows users to customize parts of a site while ensuring that other parts (such as corporate identity) aren't customized.
- Allow all visual properties to be customized, thus ensuring that when themed, pages and controls can achieve a consistent style.

The implementation of this in ASP.NET 2.0 is built around two areas: skins and themes. A **skin** is a set of properties and templates that can be applied to controls. A **theme** is a set of skins and any other associated files (such as images or stylesheets). Skins are control specific, so for a given theme there could be a separate skin for each control within that theme. Any controls without a skin inherit the default look. There are two types of themes.

- **Customization themes** override control definitions, thus changing the look and feel of controls. Customization themes are applied with the `Theme` attribute on the `Page` directive.
- **Stylesheet themes** don't override control definitions, thus allowing the control to use the theme properties or override them. Stylesheet themes are applied with the `StylesheetTheme` attribute on the `Page` directive.

The implementation is simple because a skin uses the same definition as the server control it is skinning, and themes are just a set of files in a directory under the application root. For example, consider the sample directory structure shown below:

```
default.aspx
\Themes
  \MyTheme
    MySkin.skin
  \YourTheme
    YourSkin.skin
```

Each theme consists of a directory under the `Themes` directory. Within each theme there is a file with a `.skin` suffix, which contains the skin details for that theme. For example, `MySkin.skin` might contain:

```
<asp:Label SkinID="Normal" runat="server"
  Font-Bold="True" BackColor="#FFC080" />
<asp:Label SkinID="Comic" runat="server"
  Font-Italic="True" Font-Names="Comic Sans MS" />
```

This defines two skins for the `Label` control, each with different visual properties. The theme can be chosen by setting the appropriate page-level property, and the skin is chosen by setting a control-level property, as demonstrated in the following code snippets.

```
<%@ Page Theme="MyTheme" %>

<form runat="server">
```

```
  <asp:Label SkinID="Comic" Text="A Label" />

</form>
```

or

```
<%@ Page StylesheetTheme="MyTheme" %>

<form runat="server">

  <asp:Label SkinID="Comic" Text="A Label" />

</form>
```

Both of these can be set at runtime as well as design time, so this provides an extremely powerful solution, especially when connected with the new Personalization features.

> Personalization and themes are covered in Chapter 7.

Securing Your Site

With the large amount of business being done on the Web, security is vitally important for protecting not only confidential information such as credit card numbers but also users' personal details and preferences. Thus you have to build into your site features to authenticate users. This was easy to do in ASP.NET 1.x, although you still had to write code. Security was created by picking your preferred security mechanism (most often Forms Authentication) and then adding controls to your page to provide the login details—username, password, "remember me" checkbox, and so on. There was no built-in mechanism for storing personal details, so this was a roll-it-yourself affair.

With ASP.NET 2.0, the pain has been taken out of both areas. For login functionality, there is now

- A Login control, providing complete functionality for logging into a site
- A LoginStatus control, which indicates the login status and can be configured to provide automatic links to login and logout pages
- A LoginName control to display the current (or anonymous) name

- A `LoginView` control, providing templated views depending on the login status
- A `CreateUser` wizard, to allow simple creation of user accounts
- A `PasswordRecovery` control, encompassing the "I forgot my password" functionality

For example, to add login features to your page all you need to do is add the following code:

```
<form runat="server">
  <asp:Login runat="server" />
</form>
```

This gives us the simple interface shown in Figure 1.2.

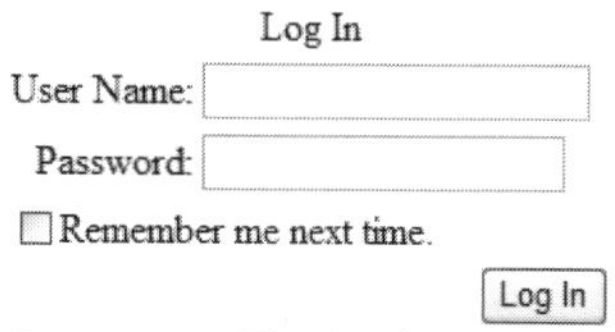

Log In

User Name:	
Password:	
☐ Remember me next time.	
	Log In

FIGURE 1.2. The Login control

This could be achieved easily in previous versions of ASP.NET, but not with such simplicity. You needed labels, text entry boxes, buttons, and validation, whereas now it's all rolled into one control. Sure it looks plain, but this is the basic unformatted version. Using the design tool Visual Studio .NET (more on that in Chapter 2), you can auto-format this for a better look. You can also skin the interface, as shown in Figure 1.3, or even template it to provide your own customized look. Along with the other login controls you get a complete solution for handling user logins.

The user interface isn't the only part of logging into a site; there's also the code needed to validate the user against a data store. With ASP.NET 1.x this required not only code to be written but also knowledge of what that

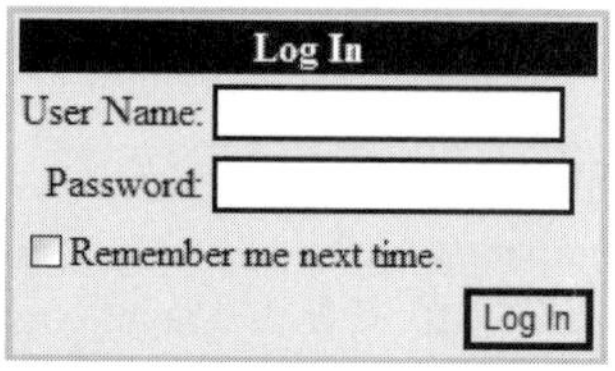

Log In

User Name:	
Password:	
☐ Remember me next time.	
	Log In

FIGURE 1.3. A skinned Login control

data store was and how it stored data. ASP.NET 2.0 introduces a new Membership API, whose aim is to abstract the required membership functionality from the storage of the member information. For example, validation of user credentials can now be replaced with the code shown in Listing 1.1.

LISTING 1.1. Validating User Credentials

```
If Membership.ValidateUser(Email.Text, Password.Text) Then
   ' user is valid
Else
   ' user is not valid
End If
```

What's even better is that when using the `Login` control you don't even have to do this—the control handles it for you.

The great strength of the Membership API is that it is built on the idea of Membership Providers, with support for Microsoft SQL Server and Access supplied by default. To integrate custom membership stores you simply need to provide a component that inherits from the Membership base class and add the new provider details to the configuration file.

The Membership API has some simple goals.

• Offer an easy solution for authenticating and managing users, requiring no knowledge of the underlying storage mechanism.

• Provide support for multiple data providers, allowing data stored about users to come from different data stores.

• Provide comprehensive user management in a simple-to-use API, giving an easy way for developers to store and access user details.

• Give users a unique identity, allowing integration with other services such as the Personalization and Role Manager features.

Security, membership, and role management are covered in Chapter 6.

Personalizing Your Site

One of the areas driving changes on the Internet is that of communities. People like to belong, and the Internet is a big, lonely place. Community sites give you a home, a sense of belonging. Part of that comes from being in contact with like-minded people, and part comes from the features some of these sites offer. Our houses are decorated to our style, and many of us customize our Windows desktop, so why shouldn't our favorite Web sites offer the same opportunity?

Hand in hand with the Membership API lie the Personalization features. These provide a simple programming model for storing user details (including those of anonymous users), with easy customization. Like Membership, Personalization can be configured to work with multiple data providers and provides an easy way to define custom properties for each user. This leads to a user profile with strong types, allowing easy access within ASP.NET pages. For example, you can create a profile with Name, Address, and Theme as properties and a page that allows the user to update them, as shown in Listing 1.2.

LISTING 1.2. Using the Profile Custom Properties

```
<script runat="server">

  Sub Page_Load(Sender As Object, E As EventArgs)

    Name.Text = Profile.Name
    Address.Text = Profile.Address
    UserTheme.Text = Profile.Theme

  End Sub

  Sub Update_Click(Sender As Object, E As EventArgs)

    Profile.Name = Name.Text
    Profile.Address = Address.Text
    Profile.Theme = UserTheme.Text

  End Sub

</script>

<form runat="server">
  Name:     <asp:TextBox id="Name" runat="server" /> <br />
  Address:  <asp:TextBox id="Address" runat="server" /> <br />
  Theme:    <asp:TextBox id="UserTheme" runat="server" /> <br />
  <asp:Button Text="Update" onClick="Update_Click" runat="server" />
</form>
```

The simplicity of this method means we only have to deal with the user profile. We don't need to know how it stores the data—we just deal with the properties each profile has. This personalization also allows us to easily use the theming capabilities, changing the theme when the page is created, as demonstrated below.

```
Sub Page_PreInit(Sender As Object, E As EventArgs)

    Me.Theme = Profile.Theme

End Sub
```

To ensure that the theme customization is applied before the controls are created we use the new `PreInit` event.

Personalization is covered in Chapter 7.

Creating Portals

As if customization of a site's look weren't enough, ASP.NET 2.0 also brings a way to alter the structure with its new portal framework.

The success of the ASP.NET IBuySpy portal application and its offshoots shows that customized sites are popular. The issue has always been how to provide a consistent look while still allowing user customization, not only of the style but also of the content and placement of content. Microsoft has already implemented solutions to provide this functionality, including SharePoint Server and Outlook Web Parts.

In ASP.NET 2.0, Web Parts become the underlying technology for all Microsoft portal applications, providing a single easy-to-use, extensible framework. The concept revolves around two key sets of controls—a set of zone controls and a range of different Web Part controls. The zone identifies areas on the page in which the appearance or behavior of the content is consistent (e.g., the colors, styles, and layout orientation), and the Web Parts identify the individual content areas or modules within each zone. There are different types of Web Part controls for different purposes, for example:

* `GenericWebPart`, which is used to reference assemblies or user controls that contain the content that is normally visible on the page
* A range of catalog parts, which display parts that are not currently on the page but are available to be added
* A range of editor parts such as the `AppearanceEditorPart` and the `LayoutEditorPart`, which allow customization of the visible parts

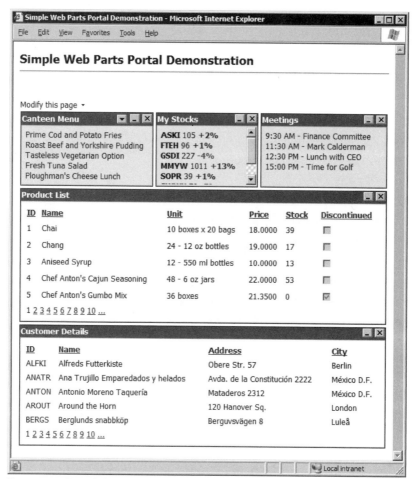

FIGURE 1.4. Sample intranet site using the portal framework

For example, consider an intranet site that needs a selection of areas of content, such as events and company information. Figure 1.4 shows a sample page.

This page has two main areas of content—the top area containing the three Web Parts named Canteen Menu, My Stocks, and Meetings, and the lower area containing two Web Parts named Product List and Customer Details. Each of these main areas is a WebPartZone control, and the content within them is made up of individual user controls that are declared and referenced in the <ZoneTemplate> section of the relevant WebPartZone. The code for the top WebPartZone control appears in Listing 1.3.

LISTING 1.3. Sample Intranet Site Using Web Parts

```
<asp:WebPartZone id="EventsZone" runat="server"
     PartChromeType="TitleAndBorder"
     VerbButtonType="Image"
     MenuPopupImageUrl="images/clickdown.gif"
     MinimizeVerb-ImageUrl="images/minimize.gif"
     RestoreVerb-ImageUrl="images/restore.gif"
     CloseVerb-ImageUrl="images/close.gif"
     EditVerb-ImageUrl="images/edit.gif"
     HelpVerb-ImageUrl="images/help.gif"
     LayoutOrientation="Horizontal"
     EmptyZoneText="Events Zone"
     HeaderText="Today's Events"
     SelectedPartChromeStyle-BorderStyle="Solid"
     SelectedPartChromeStyle-BorderWidth="5"
     SelectedPartChromeStyle-BorderColor="#ff3300"
     MenuStyle-BorderWidth="1"
     MenuStyle-BorderColor="#000000"
     MenuStyle-BorderStyle="Solid">
  <PartTitleStyle BackColor="#2254B1" ForeColor="White"
          Font-Bold="True" />
  <PartStyle CellSpacing="0" BackColor="#C0FFC0"
          BorderColor="#81AAF2" BorderStyle="Solid"
          BorderWidth="1px" />
  <ZoneTemplate>
    <ahh:Canteen id="pCanteen" runat="server"
        Title="Canteen Menu" />
    <ahh:Stocks id="pStocks" runat="server"
        Title="My Stocks" />
    <ahh:Meetings id="pMeetings" runat="server"
        Title="Meetings" />
  </ZoneTemplate>
</asp:WebPartZone>
```

At first glance this doesn't look like much improvement over existing layout methods such as user controls—in fact, it looks more complex. However, the framework on which Web Parts is built is great for developers and users alike. Developers only have to drop user controls or server controls into a `ZoneTemplate` to automatically receive Web Parts functionality.

For example, the Personalization features allow each Web Part to be moved to another location within its zone or to a different zone. Moving a Web Part is simply a matter of drag and drop, as shown in Figure 1.5, where the My Stocks section is being moved to the lower zone.

Editing of Web Part controls is also part of the portal framework. You can use a control called the `WebPartPageMenu` to automatically provide a drop-down list where users can change the mode that the page is viewed

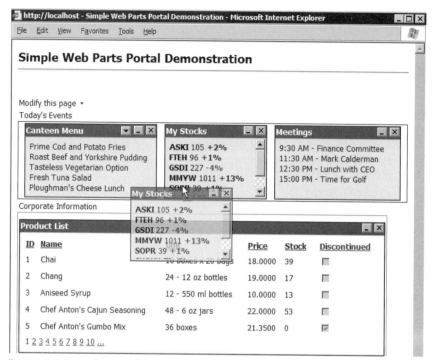

FIGURE 1.5. Dragging a Web Part to another location

in and then edit the properties of the individual Web Parts. By default the user can alter a range of layout and appearance properties, such as the title, height, and width (see Figure 1.6).

Web Parts can also be exported and imported using a standard XML-based dialect. This allows you to share Web Parts between applications. The built-in Catalog features automatically provide a section that allows you to import Web Parts into the current page (see Figure 1.7).

Other features of the Web Parts framework allow you to add Help pop-ups to each Web Part, expose custom properties from Web Parts and allow the user to edit these properties, and connect Web Parts together so they can interact. Web Parts is still an evolving technology, and you can expect to see even more features and improvements in the final release of ASP.NET 2.0.

The portal framework is covered in Chapter 8.

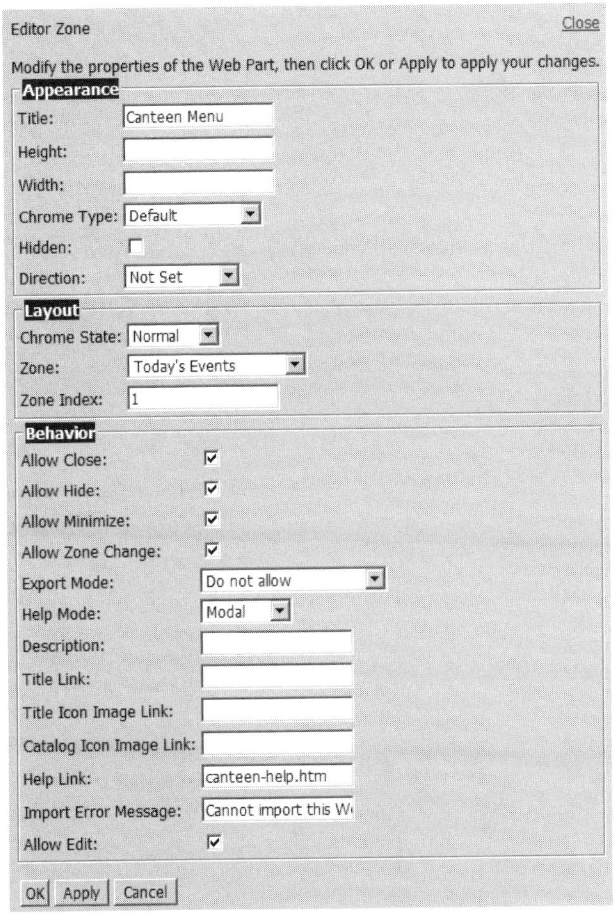

FIGURE 1.6. The built-in editing features for a Web Part

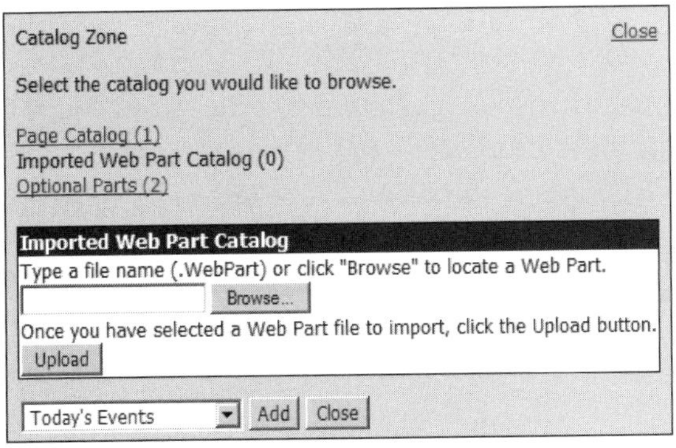

FIGURE 1.7. Importing a Web Part into the page

Setting Up and Managing Your Site

ASP.NET 1.x made deployment of Web sites easy with its xcopy deployment model. This removed the need for some administrative tasks, such as registering COM components, but still left other tasks, such as site administration, as more manual affairs. The XML-based configuration file obeyed the xcopy rule, but there are three major problems with it. First, there is no easy-to-use administration tool, meaning you must have knowledge of the XML schema before you can modify it. Second, you need some way to actually fetch the file, edit it, and then upload it. This is a problem particularly for hosted scenarios, where users are always remote, and administration of many sites can become a management nightmare. Finally, you cannot create a Web Application, which is required for sites that require security.

Three features in ASP.NET 2.0 help solve these issues. The first is the Microsoft Management Console (MMC) Snap-in for configuration, as shown in Figure 1.8.

The second feature is a Management API, providing a programmable interface to manage a site. For example, Listing 1.4 sets the authorization mode using the API.

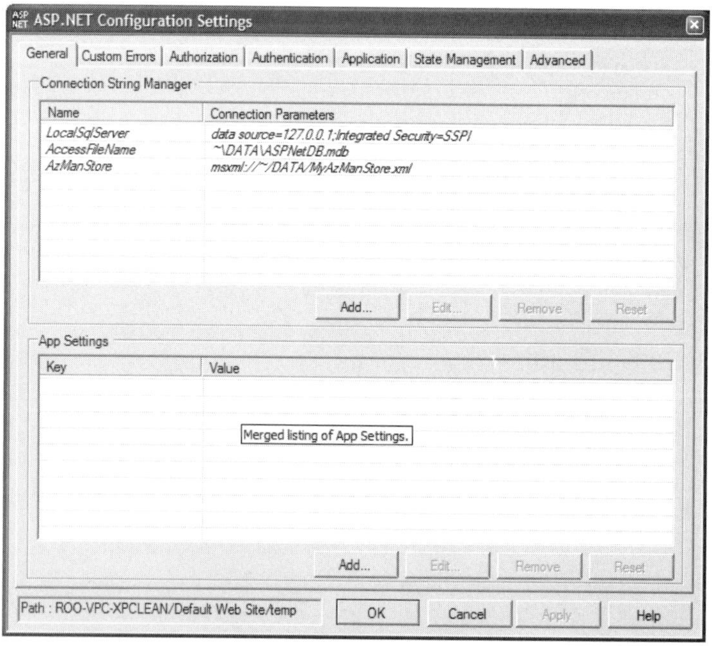

FIGURE 1.8. ASP.NET Configuration MMC Snap-in

LISTING 1.4. Setting the Authorization Mode

```
Dim cfg As System.Configuration.Configuration
Dim authSection As AuthenticationSection

cfg = Configuration.GetWebConfiguration(Request.ApplicationPath)
authSection = CType(cfg.GetSection("system.web/authentication"), _
                    AuthenticationSection)

authSection.Mode = AuthenticationMode.Windows
cfg.Update()
```

The Management API provides access to all areas of the configuration, both at the machine level (`machine.config`) and the application level (`web.config`). This allows utilities to be written not only to manage a single site but also to manage all sites.

The third aspect of site management is the creation of a Web-based tool, wrapping much of the Management API. This provides a simple way to remotely administer a site, as shown in Figure 1.9.

Here you have a simple Web interface that allows configuration of all aspects of a site. The interface is designed to be customized, so corporations and hosts can give it a company look.

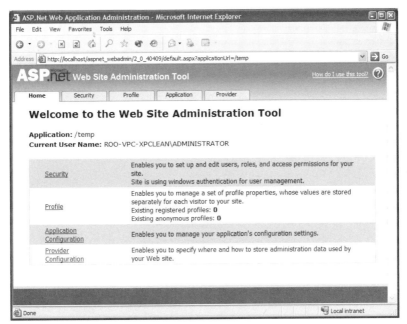

FIGURE 1.9. The Web Site Administration Tool

Administration is covered in Chapter 13.

Using Images on Your Site

Using images isn't a particularly difficult area of site design, but their use has been eased with two new server controls. First, the `ImageMap` control provides easy support for image maps, as demonstrated in the next code sample.

```
<asp:ImageMap runat="server"
    onClick="Map_Click"
    ImageUrl="images/states.jpg">
  <asp:CircleHotSpot X="100" Y="100" Radius="25"
      PostBackValue="Other State" />
  <asp:RectangleHotSpot Top="200" Left="150"
      Right="200" Bottom="150"
      PostBackValue="More State"/>
  <asp:PolygonHotSpot Coordinates="3,4, 15,18, 45,18, 15,70, 3,4"
      PostBackValue="State 1" />
</asp:ImageMap>
```

The detection of the hot spot is handled in the postback event:

```
Sub Map_Click(Sender As Object, E As ImageMapEventArgs)

  Select Case e.PostBackValue
  Case "State 1"
    ' ...
  Case "Other State"
    ' ...
  Case "More States"
    ' ...
  End Select

End Sub
```

The second new image-handling feature is that of dynamic images, designed specifically to render images appropriate to the calling browser. This is necessary because images displayed in Web browsers generally aren't suitable for smaller devices, such as PDAs or phones. The new `DynamicImage` control uses an `HttpHandler` to sniff the browser type and render the appropriate image. For example, consider the following code:

```
<form runat="server">
  <asp:DynamicImage ImageType="Automatic"
                    ImageFile="car.gif" runat="server" />
</form>
```

For a standard Web browser the image is rendered as expected, but for a Wireless Access Protocol (WAP) phone, the image is rendered as a Wireless Bitmap (WBMP). This removes any need for the developer to specifically target images to browser types.

Images are covered in Chapter 10.

Using Data on Your Site

It's probably no exaggeration to say that most, if not all, Web sites use some form of data to drive them. Whether XML files, a database, or another dynamic form of storage, the data allows a site to respond to the user and to be up-to-date. ASP.NET 1.x provided some great data binding capabilities, but they always involved code, often the same code used over and over. One of the key goals of ASP.NET 2.0 is to reduce code and to ease the use of databases, especially for beginner programmers. To achieve this a new set of data controls has been introduced, removing the need for in-depth knowledge of ADO.NET.

Data source controls provide a consistent and extensible method for declaratively accessing data from Web pages. There are several data source controls, including `AccessDataSource`, `SqlDataSource`, `XmlDataSource`, and `ObjectDataSource`, and it's likely that others (perhaps for Excel and Exchange Server) will appear as ASP.NET 2.0 nears release, along with third-party data sources. The use of data controls is simple, as shown below.

```
<asp:SqlDataSource id="ds1" runat="server"
  ConnectionString="server=.;database=pubs;Trusted_Connection=True"
  SelectCommand="SELECT * FROM authors"/>

<asp:DataGrid DataSourceId="ds1" runat="server" />
```

This just encapsulates the code everyone used to put in the `Page_Load` event—it connects to the database, fetches the data, and binds the grid. The contents of the `SelectCommand` can be a stored procedure as well as a

SQL command, thus preserving the separation of data access from the page itself. There are commands for updating, inserting, and deleting.

This model is extended by use of a parameter collection, allowing parameters to be passed into the command from a variety of sources. For example, the code in Listing 1.5 automatically takes the value from the `TextBox` control `txtState` and feeds this into the parameter `@state`.

LISTING 1.5. Using a ControlParameter

```
<asp:SqlDataSource id="ds1" runat="server"
  ConnectionString="server=.;database=pubs;Trusted_Connection=True"
  SelectCommand="SELECT * FROM authors WHERE state=@state">
  <SelectParameters>
    <asp:ControlParameter name="@state" ControlID="txtState"
      PropertyName="Text" />
  </SelectParameters>
</asp:SqlDataSource>

<asp:TextBox id="txtState" runat="server" />

<asp:DataGrid DataSourceId="ds1" runat="server" />
```

There are also other parameter types, allowing parameter information to be taken directly from Session variables, Cookies, the Request (QueryString), and the HTML Form.

Data Binding

Data binding in ASP.NET 1.x was simple, but it did cause confusion in some areas. For example, should you use early binding, for which you have to know the underlying data structure? Or should you take the development shortcut and use late binding, like this:

```
<%# DataBinder.Eval(Container.DataItem, "au_lname") %>
```

With ASP.NET 2.0 this syntax has been simplified:

```
<%# Eval("au_lname") %>
```

There is also an equivalent XPath syntax for XPath expressions when binding to XML documents:

```
<%# XPath("@au_lname") %>
```

Binding to Objects

One of the most requested features has been the ability to bind data directly to objects. Good design dictates that you separate your data access layer from your presentation layer, and this is often done as a set of classes. The new `ObjectDataSource` allows you to simply bind directly to existing objects, such as classes, thus allowing you to have a strongly typed data layer but still participate in the easy data binding that ASP.NET 2.0 brings.

Binding to Configuration Settings

A similar binding syntax is used to allow declarative access to certain configuration parameters, such as application settings, connection strings, and resources. Here is the syntax for these:

```
<%$ section: key %>
```

For example:

```
<%$ ConnectionStrings: pubs %>
```

Data source controls and data binding are covered in Chapter 3.

Internationalization

Building Web sites that support multiple languages is important because Web sites are used by more and more people for whom English is a secondary language. In ASP.NET 2.0 support for multiple languages is extremely simple, based around global resources (sometimes called shared resources) and local page resources. Global resources live in the `Resources` folder underneath the application root and consist of XML-based resource files (`.resx`) containing keys and content for those keys. Global resources can be accessed by any page in the application. For example, consider a file called `shared.resx`, which among the meta-data might have a key like this:

```
<data name="SharedResource">
  <value>English Label from shared resource file</value>
</data>
```

There might also be a French language resource file, `shared.fr-fr.resx`:

```
<data name="SharedResource">
  <value>French shared resource</value>
</data>
```

Binding to these resources declaratively can be done in the same way as binding to configuration resources, for example:

```
<asp:Label runat="server" id="MyLabel"
    Text="%<$ Resources: SharedResource %> />
```

At page compilation time the browser language is detected and the resource selected from the appropriate file.

Another way to fetch this resource is to use a meta-attribute on the label:

```
<asp:Label runat="server" id="MyLabel"
    meta:resourcekey="Shared:SharedResource"/>
```

In this case the first part of the `meta` value identifies the name of the file, and the second part (after the colon) identifies the key.

Local resources are only accessible to individual pages. Like global resources they are stored in `.resx` files, but this time under a `LocalResources` directory, where the name of the resource file is the ASP.NET page with the `.resx` extension applied. Thus for a page supporting two languages there would be two local resource files: `LocalResources\UsingResources.aspx.resx` and `LocalResources\ UsingResources.aspx.fr-fr.resx`. Either of the binding formats works for local resources, but generally the `meta` one is used because Visual Studio 2005 can automatically process ASP.NET pages, adding the meta-attribute and building a resource file.

Resources are covered in Chapter 9.

Adding Mobility Support

Mobile devices are becoming more pervasive. It seems everyone has a mobile phone, many people have PDAs, and some great devices now combine the functionality of both. From the development perspective the problem with these devices is their screen size and rendering capabilities. Not only do many of them not accept HTML, but with their tiny screens some also can't display images, tables, and so on.

In ASP.NET 1.x, the Microsoft Mobile Internet Toolkit (MMIT in version 1.0 and ASP.NET Mobile Controls in version 1.1) provided this support, including separate controls for building Web pages suitable for small-screen browsers. In ASP.NET 2.0, the MMIT is no longer required because mobile support is built into all controls. This reduces the amount of code required as well as the need for specialist knowledge about mobile platforms. This might seem relatively unimportant while the number of sites that target mobile browsers is small, but this is bound to increase as the features of small devices improve and prices drop.

The really important part of the changes is to the infrastructure of the ASP.NET server controls. All controls are now built on a control adapter architecture, where there is an adapter for each specific device. The adapters have knowledge of each device and perform the rendering appropriate for its markup language and screen size. Because the controls are derived from adapters, they don't need to perform any special action to choose what to render—the adapter intelligently renders the appropriate content based on the calling device. New devices are easily supported because they require only the addition of an adapter, which the controls can then take advantage of.

Device Filters

This architecture is taken further by allowing adapter-specific attributes for controls, enabling the page designer to provide different content for specific devices. For example, the following code shows how different text and cascading style sheet (CSS) styling can be defined for a mobile device.

```
<asp:Label id="MyLabel" runat="server"
        Text="Welcome to our site"
        Nokia:Text="Time to upgrade your Nokia phone!"
        cssClass="StandardStyleClass"
        Nokia:cssClass="SpecialNokiaStyleClass" />
```

Device Templates

Along with modified attributes, we also have the ability to provide templates for specific devices. We know that mobile devices have a small screen size, so repeated controls such as grids and lists either aren't appropriate or need different output. By using specific templates for devices we can now provide different content to different devices, as shown in Listing 1.6.

LISTING 1.6. Filtered Templates for Mobile Devices

```
<asp:Repeater runat="server" ..>

  <HtmlBrowsers:HeaderTemplate>
    <table>
      <tr><td>UserName</td><td>Address</td><td>Phone</td></tr>
  </HtmlBrowsers:HeaderTemplate>

  <HtmlBrowsers:ItemTemplate>
    <tr>
      <td><%# Container.DataItem("UserName") %></td>
      <td><%# Container.DataItem("Address") %></td>
      <td><%# Container.DataItem("Phone") %></td>
    </tr>
  </HtmlBrowsers:ItemTemplate>

  <WmlBrowsers:ItemTemplate>
    <asp:Panel runat="server">
      <%# Container.DataItem("UserName") %>
      <%# Container.DataItem("Phone") %>
    </asp:Panel>
  </WmlBrowsers:ItemTemplate>

  <HtmlBrowsers:FooterTemplate>
    </table>
  </HtmlBrowsers:FooterTemplate>

</asp:Repeater>
```

These mechanisms provide a way for developers to override the built-in rendering for mobile devices. Along with automatic mobile support with the standard controls, there are controls specifically designed for mobile devices, such as PhoneLink (to launch a phone call) and Pager (to provide paging support). Standard controls also support the SoftKeyLabel attribute to allow specific text to be targeted to soft keys on phones.

> Mobility is covered in Chapter 10.

Compilation and Deployment

Since the release of ASP.NET 1.0 there's been a fairly standard approach to Web site architecture. In general there has been a separation of business logic into separate assemblies, often in a separate directory with a make file. Using Visual Studio .NET 1.0 and 2003 for this approach is fine since it provides the compilation step for you, but stand-alone tools (such as Web Matrix) don't, so you have to handcraft a batch file to make your assemblies.

ASP.NET 2.0 provides automatic compilation for satellite code by supporting a `code` directory. All files within this directory will be compiled on the first run, thus removing the need for separate compilation scripts. Files within the `code` directory don't have to be just pure code, such as Visual Basic .NET or C# files. Support is also included for Web Services Description Language (WSDL) files and strongly typed data sets (XSD) files. For WSDL files the proxy will automatically be created, and for XSD files the appropriate classes will be created.

Along with automatic compilation comes pre-compilation—an entire site (Web pages and code) can be pre-compiled. This not only provides a way to deploy compiled applications but also removes the performance hit taken by the compilation process on the first run. In addition, because only compiled files are deployed, intellectual property is protected.

Another automatic feature is that of resources, such as those used for globalization. The `resources` directory provides a place for these, which are included as part of the compilation process.

Compilation is covered in Chapter 2.

Development Tools

Having a whole raft of new features in ASP.NET is great, but what about design tools? Version 2.0 of the .NET Framework will introduce the latest version of Visual Studio .NET—Visual Studio 2005. When ASP.NET 1.0 was released, it quickly became apparent that a development tool targeted at Web developers was required. Visual Studio .NET provides great project and design features targeted at corporate developers. Web Matrix was released to appeal to ASP.NET developers who don't have access to Visual Studio .NET. It's a small stand-alone tool, specifically targeted at ASP.NET development, and provides some features that aren't in Visual Studio .NET.

With ASP.NET 2.0, Visual Studio 2005 has undergone some major enhancements and now provides a far superior environment for developing Web applications than previous versions. While the design environment is very familiar, the feature set has improved, making it a premier Web development tool.

Key design features for Visual Studio 2005 include the following:

- Traditional inline coding approach, plus a new code-behind model
- Support for all managed languages
- Ability to edit any file anywhere (FTP, File System, Front Page Server Extensions, and so on)
- Support for data controls, drag and drop, and database access, with a rich design surface
- Support for visual inheritance through master pages
- No project files, allowing projects to be manipulated outside of the tool
- Integrated Web Site Administration Tool
- IntelliSense included
- Support for internationalization
- Debugging support
- No "build" step—ability to compile on first run

This feature set is really a combination of features from Visual Studio .NET and Web Matrix. As well as Visual Studio 2005 there is a stand-alone development tool targeted specifically at Web developers: Visual Web Developer Express Edition.

> Visual Studio 2005 and Visual Web Developer Express Edition are covered in Chapter 2.

SUMMARY

Of course, there are many changes within ASP.NET 2.0—too many to mention in this introduction, although some highlights were covered in this chapter. The remainder of the book covers these changes (including items such as changes to existing controls, changes to page attributes, new controls, and so on) in detail.

It's important to remember that this is a beta technology, still evolving and still in testing. Despite that, the feature set is extremely impressive and provides a leap in productivity for Web site developers.

2

Tools and Architecture

IN THE PREVIOUS CHAPTER we gave a brief outline of some of the new and exciting features in ASP.NET 2.0, and now it's time to dig into them a bit deeper. In this chapter we're going to look at how development has been eased in two main areas. The first is the design time experience. With ASP.NET 1.x you had the choice of Visual Studio .NET or Web Matrix for development. With ASP.NET 2.0 this is still the case, but Visual Studio 2005 is greatly improved for ASP.NET developers.

In addition to the full version of Visual Studio .NET, there is also Visual Web Developer Express Edition, a lightweight, streamlined edition of Visual Studio 2005 targeted specifically at Web developers learning or evaluating ASP.NET and available as a separate product. The full version of Visual Studio 2005 is aimed at professional and corporate developers, while the Express Edition is targeted primarily at nonprofessionals and therefore doesn't contain the complete set of features that the full product has. However, it shouldn't be dismissed entirely as a hobbyist product because its feature set is still impressive. We'll look at the differences between the two products, but by and large most of what we present throughout the book will work in both products. To avoid excessive use of acronyms and repeated product names, we'll refer to only a single product: Visual Studio 2005. Where specific features aren't supported in the Express Edition, we will make that clear.

The second main area we'll cover is compilation. It may not seem like much of a burden in the current release, especially when using Visual Studio 2005, but there are several ways in which compilation has been improved, including a better model for code separation, centralized code directories with automatic compilation, and pre-compilation of sites to improve speed and deployment.

Visual Studio 2005

You may wonder about the confusion over development tools and which tool a developer should use for which purpose. After all, no matter what type of development is being done, many of the requirements are the same. However, there are differences in the ways developers work in different types of applications, especially Web applications. To understand those differences you have to look at both the history of ASP development and the current tools. ASP rapidly rose to success, with a very diverse set of developers, ranging from corporate teams to home hobbyists. Despite its widespread use there was no dedicated development tool. There were plenty of editors with which ASP could work (Visual InterDev, Front Page, and so on), but nothing specific. Visual Studio was purely a Windows development tool.

With the release of .NET 1.0, Visual Studio became Visual Studio .NET and was enhanced to allow Web development. The real trouble with this approach wasn't with Visual Studio .NET itself but more with the completely different way of working that was previously used by most ASP developers. For example, the code-behind model was alien to ASP scripters, who were used to having all of their code within the same file, and the whole idea of a project didn't relate well with people who were used to just dealing with files in a directory.

Another issue was that Visual Studio .NET is a professional development tool and therefore commands a professional price. A large amount of Web development is done by amateurs, for whom the price of this tool is too high. Enter Web Matrix, a small, easy-to-use, and (most importantly) free development tool. Web Matrix is aimed only at ASP.NET developers and also has become a test bed for new ideas and features that weren't in Visual Studio .NET. There wasn't a tool that had everything a developer needed—until now.

The latest version, Visual Studio 2005, is not only a combination of the best bits of both Visual Studio .NET 2003 and Web Matrix but also the next step upward. Along with great design features such as support for drag and drop, Visual Studio 2005 also brings the following benefits.

- There are no project files, thus existing sites can simply be opened from their locations.
- Support for code inline, or the improved code-behind model, allows files created with other editors to be easily imported.
- Multiple ways to access Web sites, such as through the file system, IIS, FTP, and SharePoint (Front Page Server Extensions), are available. This also includes publishing to remote Web sites.
- The Server Explorer integrates a data editing tool and allows drag and drop of tables onto the design grid. This is called the Data Explorer in Visual Web Developer Express Edition, but we'll use the term Server Explorer in this chapter.
- Support for the new data binding models allows easy design of data-driven pages.
- Visual inheritance with master pages eases site design.
- Full IntelliSense in HTML and code views enables quicker code development.
- Support for accessibility; checks ensure Web sites conform to government regulations for accessibility like Section 508 and Web Content Accessibility Guidelines (WCAG).
- An improved designer surface, supporting the enhanced Web Control Designer Framework.
- A built-in Web Server allows development and testing without IIS and without administrator privileges.
- The ability to import and export user settings allows you to easily configure other installations of Visual Studio 2005 with your favorite preferences.
- Starter kits help developers create out-of-the-box sites with little or no extra work required.

In this chapter we'll look at some of these features and see how some of the new architectural changes to ASP.NET integrate with Visual Studio 2005 and make development easier. Note that the following features are not included in Visual Web Developer Express Edition:

- Accessibility checker
- Source code control integration
- Pre-compilation and MSI deployment

- Extensibility, such as add-ins, macros, and VSIP
- Remote data
- Full-featured Server Explorer
- Class designer
- XSLT debugging
- Remote debugging
- Windows Forms
- Class library creation

Many of these features are mostly high-end professional features, so for many people who specialize in simpler Web site development they won't be missed. However, because the express and full editions are built from the same code, the upgrade path is seamless. Let's now look at the features in more detail.

Project-less Development

There are two very good reasons why moving to a project-less system is a good choice. First, it makes team development simpler. For teams using a source code control system the project file becomes a blocking point. All files checked into and out of the project require the project file to be checked in and out. With multiple people editing multiple files, the project file can easily be locked by another person. Second, a project-less system is easier for sites designed with other development tools—the absence of a project system means sites can be easily accessed directly. For example, Figure 2.1 shows the Open Web Site dialog when selecting FTP as the mechanism.

If an existing site was not created with Visual Studio 2005, it will be upgraded in place, so be careful if you plan to open existing Web sites. (You will see a warning.) Whichever method of opening a site you use, or when creating new sites, you will see a familiar layout (Figure 2.2).

Although this is a new tool, you can see it looks very similar to both Visual Studio .NET 2002/2003 and Web Matrix, thus ensuring that developers can work in a familiar environment. When you work within it, though, you will soon realize that there are many more features.

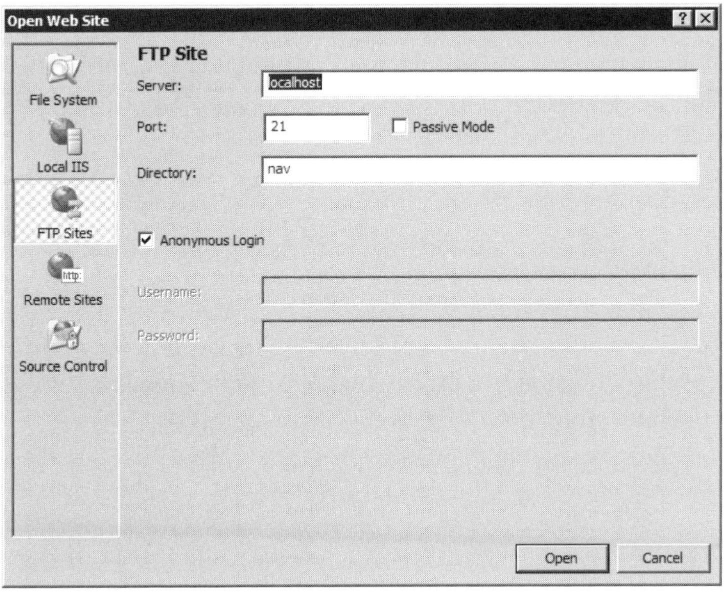

FIGURE 2.1. Opening a Web site via FTP

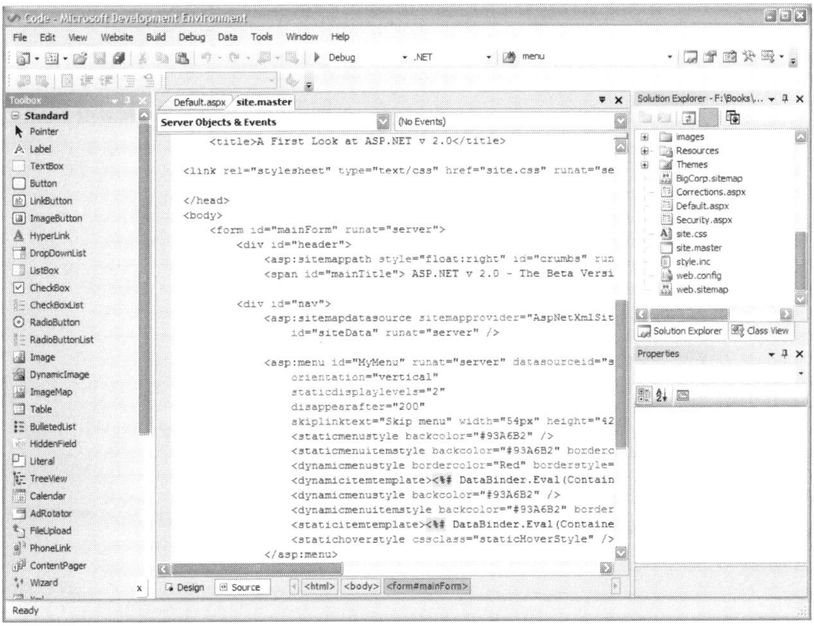

FIGURE 2.2. The Visual Studio 2005 main windows

The Solution Explorer

The Solution Explorer is almost the same as in previous versions of Visual Studio .NET, although it has been simplified. There are no longer two buttons for opening Web pages, one for design view and one for code view. (How often did you double-click to open the file only to have it open in design view rather than code view?) Visual Studio 2005 supports both inline code and the new code-separation model, where files show in the Solution Explorer as two files (Figure 2.3).

FIGURE 2.3. The Solution Explorer

Here you can see that both the user-interface (UI) file and the code-behind file are separate items. Double-clicking opens the file in the design window.

The Toolbox

The Toolbox is the same as in previous versions of Visual Studio .NET, although there are more tabs, with controls split into logical groups:

- Standard, for the core server controls such as TextBox, Label, and so on
- Data, for the DataSource and grid controls
- Validation, for the field validator controls
- Navigation, for navigation controls, such as Menu and SiteMapPath
- Login, for the login controls
- Web Parts, for the WebPart controls
- HTML, for the HTML controls

Of course, the Toolbox is customizable, not only by adding local components but also by adding components from Web sites by use of the Control Gallery.

The Design Window

The design window is similar to that in previous versions of Visual Studio .NET, although there are a number of important differences. The first thing

FIGURE 2.4. The design window

to note is that the default layout mode is flow, not absolute; the second is the different views you get within the editor. Figure 2.4 shows the source code editor window.

At the bottom of this window there are two buttons to switch between the design view and the source code view. Both of these apply to the same file but show a different view.

- **Design** is the standard design surface.
- **Source** is the entire source code for the file, including the UI section and inline code.

Whether using code-inline or code-behind for your source code, the views seen by using the Design and Source buttons for an ASP.NET page point to the same file; they are just two different views of it. When using code-behind you have to watch for which file you are in when creating code because it's perfectly legal to have code in both. However, the environment is sensible, so that when you're using code-behind and you double-click a button to create an event procedure, the code is created in the code-behind file.

The other noteworthy point about the source view is the HTML tags shown along the bottom. These follow the cursor and give you an indication of where you are within the hierarchy of controls. Editing has also been improved by great IntelliSense support and simple features such as the highlighting of start and end tags, again allowing you to easily see controls.

Another addition to the source view is that the Toolbox isn't disabled; drag and drop is fully supported in the source editor. This prevents having to switch to the design view to add new controls—they can simply be dragged from the Toolbox and dropped into the source file. Better support for the code editor has also been provided by enabling the Properties window to track the cursor so that the properties reflect the object the cursor is currently on. Both of these features are attractive to developers who prefer to work in source view rather than design view. Added to this is selection preservation when switching between views, so you can select a control in one view and have the same control selected when views are switched.

The Design Surface

The design surface works exactly the same as in previous versions of Visual Studio .NET, except that it's more context sensitive. For example, consider Figure 2.5, where a GridView has been added to the page. Selecting the GridView shows an additional icon, like a Smart Tag in Office. Upon selecting this icon, a Tasks panel is displayed showing the most common tasks applicable to the object. This panel pops up automatically on creation of the control and remains open until selection is lost, bringing greater discoverability for the features of a control.

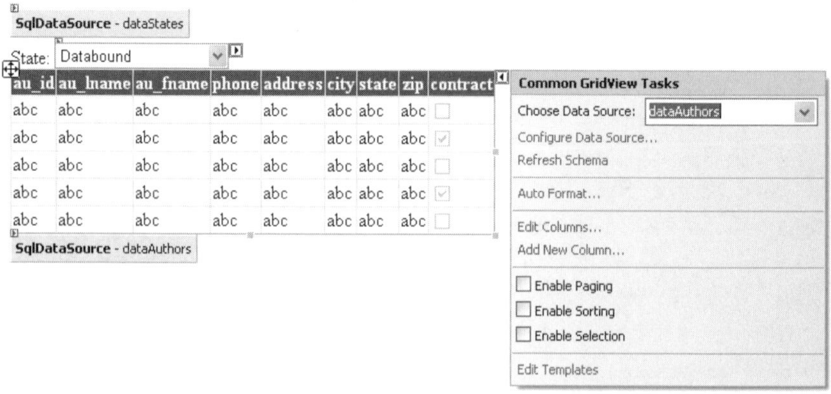

FIGURE 2.5. Viewing common tasks for a GridView

The Server Explorer

A new feature that comes from Web Matrix is the Server Explorer, which allows connections to data stores to be set up. For example, Figure 2.6 shows a connection to a SQL Server.

Once connected, you have a great range of features to control your data source—in fact, the Server Explorer is almost a mini SQL Server Enterprise Manager. For example, you can create new objects (including database diagrams and functions), edit existing ones, edit data, export data, and so on. The great advantage of having so much power in the Server Explorer is that you don't have to load an additional tool—everything you need is right within your development environment. In fact, it's better than Enterprise Manager because the stored procedure editor isn't modal!

Another great feature links two windows, allowing you to drag tables from the Server Explorer and drop them onto the design surface. When you do this, SqlDataSource and a GridView controls are automatically created and formatted, as shown in Figure 2.7, where the authors table has been dropped onto the page.

The SqlDataSource is automatically configured, and the commands used to fetch, update, insert, and delete data are populated. To edit the properties of the DataSource control you can select Configure DataSource from the Common Tasks menu, which displays the window shown in Figure 2.8. Here you see the currently selected connection (from the Server Explorer) and the provider details. These cannot be changed here, but if you do need to edit them (e.g., to pick another provider), you can edit the connection details manually in the properties for the DataSource.

Clicking the Next button allows you to specify the table and columns or select the data, as shown in Figure 2.9.

You can fine-tune the command by selecting the WHERE, ORDER BY, and Advanced Options... buttons. If you select the option to build

au_id	au_lname	au_fname	phone	address	city	state	zip	contract
abc	abc	abc	abc	abc	abc	abc	abc	☐
abc	abc	abc	abc	abc	abc	abc	abc	☑
abc	abc	abc	abc	abc	abc	abc	abc	☐
abc	abc	abc	abc	abc	abc	abc	abc	☑
abc	abc	abc	abc	abc	abc	abc	abc	☐

SqlDataSource - dataAuthors

FIGURE 2.6. The Server Explorer

FIGURE 2.7. A database table dropped onto a page

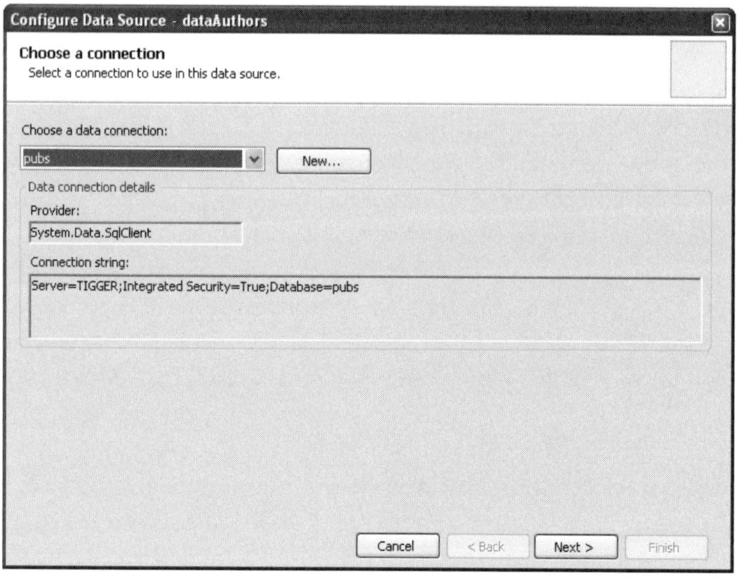

FIGURE 2.8. Configuring a DataSource Control

the queries (for the SELECT, UPDATE, INSERT, and DELETE statements) yourself, as shown in Figure 2.10.

Pressing Next from this screen allows you to add parameters and specify the source of the parameter—in this case it's set to the value of a drop-

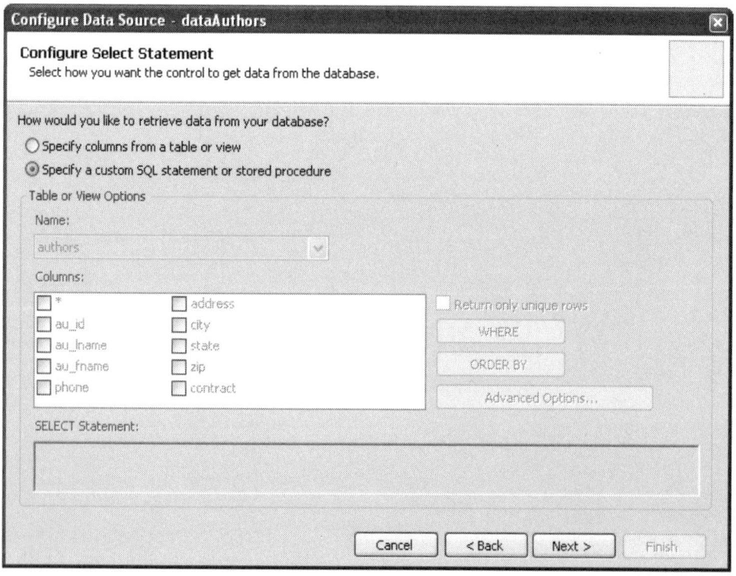

FIGURE 2.9. Editing DataSource SQL statements

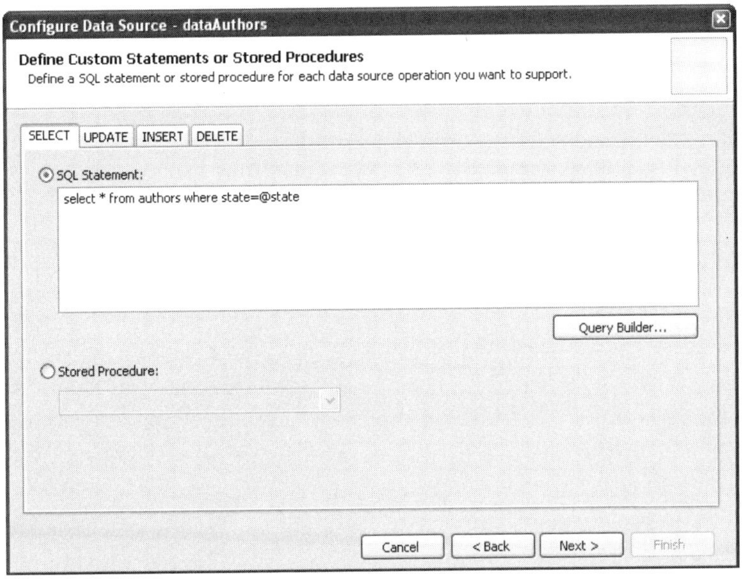

FIGURE 2.10. Configuring the SELECT command

down list, as shown in Figure 2.11. This allows you to easily build commands based on values external to the data source, such as control values, form fields, query string values, and so on. This technique allows you to build powerful pages without any code at all.

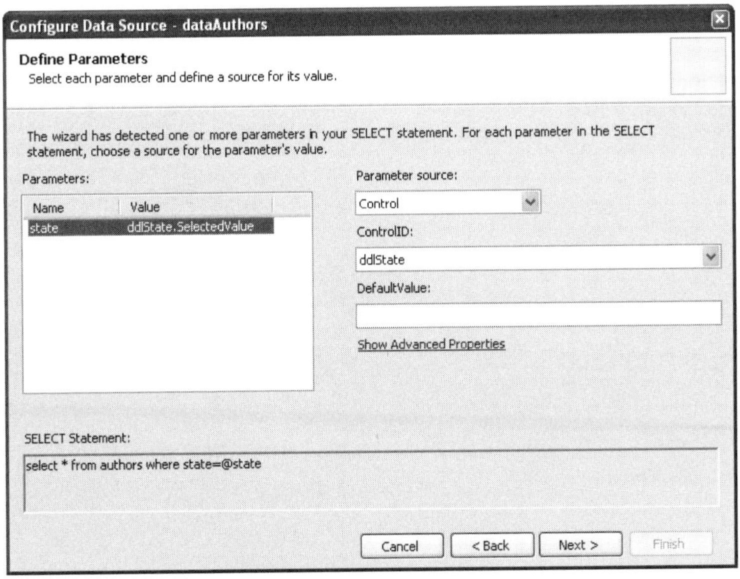

FIGURE 2.11. Configuring the command parameters

Visual Inheritance

In Chapter 1 we briefly looked at how a single style could be applied to all or a selection of pages in a site through the use of master pages. Visual Studio 2005 supports this model for master pages defined in a content page (it supports master pages defined in configuration but doesn't display the master page's contents). It allows the creation of master pages and the linking of standard pages to a master, and it shows the visual inheritance of the master. For example, Figure 2.12 shows a master page that defines the menu on the left and the title and current page details along the top.

The important aspect of this page is the `ContentPlaceHolder`, which defines the area where child pages can add their content, as shown in Figure 2.13. Here all of the content from the master page shows on the screen but is disabled (the menu in the screenshot doesn't show correctly because this is a pre-release version). Thus you can edit content only in the area allowed by the master page.

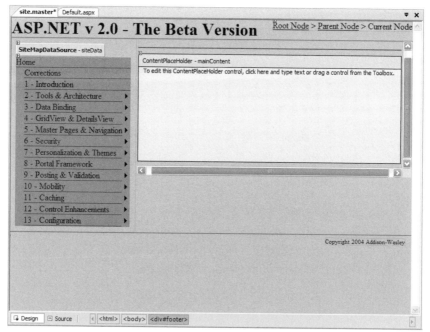

FIGURE 2.12. A master page

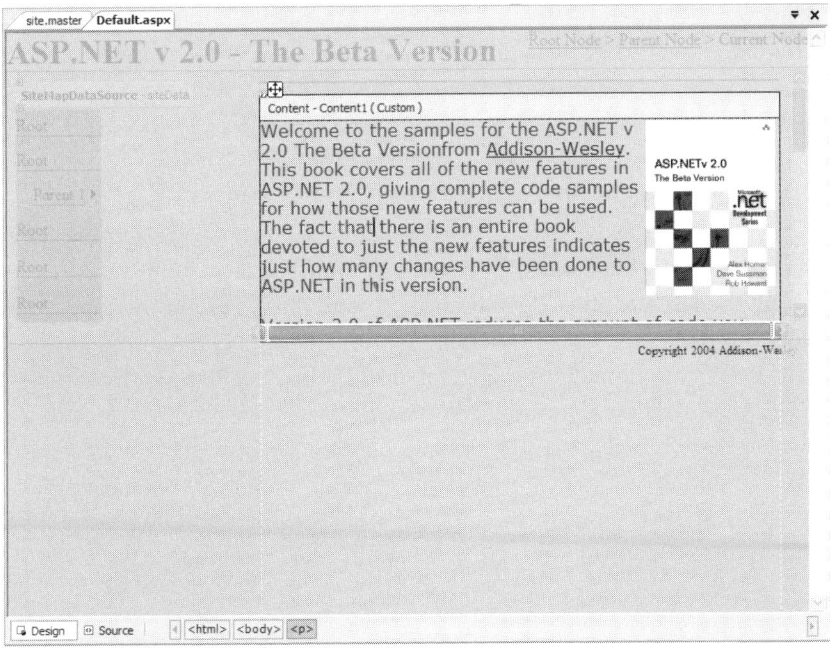

FIGURE 2.13. A child page that uses a master

Master pages are covered in more detail in Chapter 5.

Built-in Administration

Administration of Web sites has been improved by building in support for the Web Site Administration Tool. From the Website menu there is an ASP.NET Configuration option, which launches the Web Site Administration Tool in your browser.

This same menu also provides the capability to publish an entire site to a remote location, by way of the Copy Web Site menu item, allowing you to easily work on a local copy and deploy it when ready. This launches a window within the design area, as shown in Figure 2.14. Here the local site is shown in the left, with the target site (in this case an FTP site) on the right. You have the opportunity to synchronize the entire site or just copy individual files.

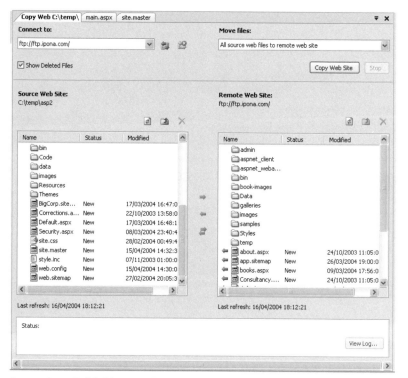

FIGURE 2.14. Publishing a Web site to an FTP location

The Web Site Administration Tool is covered in more detail in Chapter 13.

Code Separation

We saw earlier that files created with code separation now show in Visual Studio 2005 as two files. In ASP.NET versions 1.0 and 1.1, the code-behind model allowed separation of code from content, and in ASP.NET 2.0 this model has been changed to simplify development. Instead of the content page inheriting from the code-behind page, we now specify which code-behind file is to be compiled with the content file. That may seem like just a change in semantics, but it's actually a more fundamental change, made at the Common Language Runtime (CLR) level.

Version 2.0 of the CLR provides support for **partial classes,** where the same class can span multiple files. This allows the code-separation page to be far simpler than in previous versions because it can be part of the same class as the content page, meaning no more protected variables are required to reference the controls on a page, and the Designer does not need to write code into the code-behind file.

The implementation of this is easy. Consider the page for `Authors.aspx` (Listing 2.1).

Listing 2.1. Using Code Separation—the ASP.NET Page

```
<%@ Page compileWith="Authors.aspx.vb"
        className="ASP.authors_aspx" %>

<form runat="server">

  <asp:Button runat="server" onClick="button_Click" />
  <asp:Label runat="server" id="Message" />

</form>
```

Because of partial classes, the code-separation file (`Authors.aspx.vb`) is simple, as shown in Listing 2.2.

Listing 2.2. Using Code Separation—the Code-Behind File

```
Namespace ASP

  Partial Class Authors_asp

    Sub button_Click(Sender As Object, E As EventArgs)
      Message.Text = "You pressed the button"
    End Sub

  End Class

End Namespace
```

Partial classes have introduced the new `Partial` keyword, indicating that this class is not self-contained and is part of the `Authors_asp` class. For the content page, the `compileWith` attribute defines the physical file containing the code to compile along with the content page, and the `className` attribute indicates the name (including the namespace) of the class. When the `className` attribute of the content file and the namespace and class of the code file match, code for both files is compiled into a single class.

Dynamic Compilation

ASP.NET 1.x already supports **dynamic compilation** of pages and user controls (.aspx and .ascx files), eliminating the need for an explicit compilation step. Pages are compiled the first time they are requested by a user, when they are changed, or when any of their dependencies (such as web.config or global.asax) are changed. Files with no explicit dependency, however, do not trigger this compilation. This includes components (assemblies in the \bin folder and their source), resource files, Web Services, and so on. They do not trigger their target ASP.NET pages to be compiled, and they aren't compiled automatically. They require a manual compilation stage, which invariably means a batch file to compile them or the use of a make system.

ASP.NET 2.0 improves dynamic compilation by supporting an increased number of files. Stand-alone classes, Web Services, typed data sets, master pages, resource files, and themes are now automatically compiled without the need for manual intervention. There are two real benefits to this approach. First, developers can concentrate on just coding. Saving your files to the appropriate folder means your Web applications will always be up-to-date. Second, when using Visual Studio 2005 there's no need for an intermediate compile stage—you don't have to build the application to use it, you can just hit the Refresh button in the browser.

New Folders for Dynamic Compilation

Developers tend to follow the same style for laying out the folders in Web applications—an \Images folder for all of the site images, perhaps a \Components folder to store user controls or source for data layers, and so on. The expansion of dynamic compilation introduces the following reserved folders, which you should avoid using in current ASP.NET projects to prevent potential upgrade problems.

- The **\Code** folder is for storage of class files (.cs or .vb), WSDL files (.wsdl), and typed data sets (.xsd). Placing files of these types in the \Code folder will enable them for automatic compilation.

- The **\Resources** folder is for storage of application-wide resources (.resx and .resources). Resource files can also be stored in the \Code folder.

- The **\LocalResources** folder is for storage of page-level resources (.resx and .resources).

- The \Themes folder is for storing themes and skins (.skin).
- The \Data directory stores personalization databases.

Using these fixed folders allows the ASP.NET compilation process to automatically compile files as part of its normal compilation of ASP.NET pages.

Using the \Code Folder in Visual Studio 2005

The \Code folder is fully supported in Visual Studio 2005, and its use is simply a matter of creating the folder. Code classes can be added, as shown in Figure 2.15.

FIGURE 2.15. Creating classes in the \Code folder

A great use of the \Code folder's automatic compilation is for placement of business objects. For example, consider Listing 2.3, which shows a class to handle data from an authors table (Authors.vb).

Listing 2.3. A Simple Business Component

```
Imports System
Imports System.Web
Imports System.Data
Imports System.Data.SqlClient

Namespace Pubs
  Public Class Authors

    Public Function GetAuthors() As DataSet
      Dim conn As New _
       SqlConnection( _
ConfigurationSettings.ConnectionStrings("pubs").ConnectionString)
      Dim da As New SqlDataAdapter("select * from authors", conn)
      Dim ds As New DataSet

      da.Fill(ds, "Authors")

      Return ds
    End Function
  End Class
End Namespace
```

We can simply use this code from within our existing pages, perhaps by using an `ObjectDataSource` to bind directly to the class, and then by using a grid to bind to the data source, as shown in Figure 2.16.

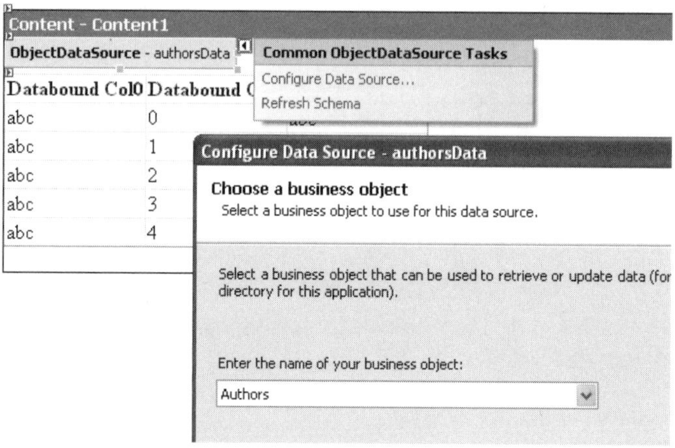

FIGURE 2.16. Binding an ObjectDataSource

Folder Hierarchy

The hierarchy of these folders can be configured depending on requirements, but there are some rules. At the top level the names cannot change, and they must be underneath the application root. Within the folders, though, there are some options.

The \Code Folder

There is no restriction on creating subfolders to organize your code. For example, consider the following application structure:

```
c:\Inetpub\wwwroot
  Default.aspx
  \Code
    Authors.vb
    \Utilities
      Tools.vb
```

Here we have `Authors.vb` at the top level of the `\Code` folder and `Tools.vb` under the `\Utilities` folder. Both files will be dynamically compiled and linked to the target assembly. This means that types within these classes are automatically available from any other page within the application. You therefore don't have to use namespaces and import them in your ASP.NET pages, meaning new code files can just be dropped into the `\Code` folder for them to become available for use.

Supporting Multiple Languages. By default the \Code folder supports only a single language (because everything is compiled into a single assembly), no matter what the hierarchy of subfolders. However, this behavior can be configured through the application configuration file, as demonstrated in Listing 2.4.

Listing 2.4. Configuring Compilation Directories

```xml
<?xml version="1.0" encoding="UTF-8" ?>

<configuration>
  <system.web>
    <compilation>
      <codeSubDirectories>
        <add directoryName="vb_code" />
        <add directoryName="cs_code" />
      </codeSubDirectories>
    </compilation>
  </system.web>
</configuration>
```

This instructs the compilation system to produce separate assemblies for files under the two directories, and therefore they can contain different languages (although they are still restricted to a single language per directory). For example, our folder hierarchy could now become

```
c:\WebSites\MySite
  Default.aspx
  \Code
    \vb_code
      Authors.vb
      \Utilities
        Tools.vb
    \cs_code
      Interop.cs
```

Folders added to the codeSubDirectories section of the configuration file are only a single layer deep. Thus you cannot code

```
<add directoryName="vb_code\utilities" />
```

You can, however, have a deep hierarchy underneath the top level, but all code files will be built into a single assembly for that folder.

The assemblies created are not placed in the \bin directory—indeed, with this system there is no need for a \bin folder, although the \bin folder is still supported and should be used for scenarios where dynamic compilation is not required or supported. Automatically compiled assemblies are placed in a folder managed by ASP.NET, so you don't even have to worry about where they are. If deployment is intended, then pre-compilation is required, and that is covered a little later in the chapter.

Web Services. In ASP.NET 1.x, Web Service proxies had to be manually created, usually by using the `wsdl.exe` tool or by including a reference in Visual Studio .NET. In ASP.NET 2.0, Web Services are catered for by including WSDL files in the `\Code` folder. With automatic compilation, a proxy class is automatically built from the WSDL file and linked to the default assemblies, and the service can be called directly from ASP.NET pages.

Typed Data Sets. Typed data sets provide strongly typed access to data, from either XML files or `DataSets`. Like Web Services, in version 1.x these had to be manually generated (using `xsd.exe`), but they follow the same pattern as WSDL files in version 2.0. All that s required is for the XSD file to be placed in the `\Code` directory, and the proxy will be generated automatically.

The \Resources Folder

The `\Resources` folder allows for easy globalization of applications. Under ASP.NET 1.x, resource files were manually compiled and placed in the `\bin` folder, under subfolders named for the culture of the resource.

In ASP.NET 2.0, shared or application resources can be placed into the `\Resources` folder, where they are then compiled as part of dynamic compilation. Page-level resources are stored in the `\LocalResources` directory.

Resources are covered in detail in Chapter 9.

The \Themes Folder

As mentioned in Chapter 1, themes provide a way to supply different UI styles to controls. Because themes can be set at runtime, they are later compiled when required. A local themes file is used only for local themes; site-wide themes, such as those available to all applications, are held in a central location.

Themes are covered in detail in Chapter 7.

Configuring Compilation Options

The dynamic compilation system allows configuration through `web.config`. Earlier we talked about the `codeSubDirectories` section allowing configuration of folders and target assemblies. Table 2.1 shows that there are also batch options available as attributes to the `compilation` element.

Table 2.1. Compilation Configuration Options

Attribute	Default Value	Description
`batch`	true	Indicates whether or not batch compilation takes place.
`batchTimeout`	15	The number of seconds for compilation to take place. An exception is thrown if this time is exceeded.
`maxBatchSize`	1000	The maximum number of pages/classes compiled into a single batch.
`maxBatchGeneratedFileSize`	3000	The maximum size (in kilobytes) of an assembly.

Custom Builds. Like much of ASP.NET, the build process is extensible, using build providers targeted at specific file extensions. These are configured by default in `machine.config` and can be added there or within `web.config`. For example, the `<compilation>` section could have a `<buildProviders>` section that looks like Listing 2.5.

Listing 2.5. Configuring Build Providers

```
<configuration>
  ...
  <buildProviders>
    <add extension="*.aspx" appliesTo="Web"
        type="System.Web.Compilation.PageBuildProvider" />
    <add extension="*.wsdl" appliesTo="Code"
        type="System.Web.Compilation.WsdlBuildProvider" />
  </buildProviders>
</configuration>
```

Build providers are also inferred from the `<compilers>` section of the `<system.codedom>` configuration, so there are no explicit build providers for code files. The `extension` applies to the folder in which dynamic compilation applies. The `appliesTo` attribute indicates the folder in which the build provider applies, where Web indicates general Web folders. Multiple folders for build providers are supported by simply separating the folders in the appliesTo attribute with a comma.

This system allows custom providers to be built for types not known to ASP.NET, allowing specification of selected directories for those files.

Build Order and Life Cycle. Dynamic compilation builds automatically; therefore, understanding the build order is important to ensure that dependencies are not missed. The build order is as follows:

- The \Resources folder and other resource files
- The \Code folder and other code files
- Global.asax
- Resource files outside of the \Resources and \Code folders
- Individual Web files, such as ASP.NET pages or Web Services

The life cycle of pages and the application is also affected by dynamic compilation because updating a file can result in more than just a single page hit.

Pre-compilation of Applications

Dynamic compilation is targeted at reducing the number of manual steps developers have to perform while constructing a site. **Pre-compilation,** on the other hand, targets two issues with ASP.NET 1.x: (1) the compilation delay when first hitting a site or page, and (2) the hosting scenario, where source code must be present on the server. For intellectual property reasons this isn't always an acceptable situation.

Both of these issues are tackled individually by a pre-compilation system.

In-place Pre-compilation

Although ASP.NET performs extremely well, the hit taken while a site initially compiles can be quite large. To avoid this, some developers have built tools to hit every page to ensure it is compiled. In ASP.NET there is support for in-place compilation, which does just that—it compiles every file within an application root. This mechanism is done by navigating to the special URL:

http://applicationDirectory/precompile.axd

The precompile.axd URL is handled by an HttpHandler, which precompiles the entire site, thus avoiding the compile delay during the first hit. There is no overhead if the URL is called multiple times because only changed files are recompiled. Global dependencies, such as changes to global.asax and web.config, are obeyed, and all source files will be marked as out-of-date, triggering a complete compilation if requested.

Errors that occur during pre-compilation will halt the entire process. These appear in the browser window exactly as they would if the page in error had been hit directly.

Pre-compilation for Deployment without Source

Being able to pre-compile to a target directory without the source is a great way to not only deploy ready-to-go applications but also to protect intellectual property. Pre-compilation is achieved by use of the aspnet_compiler.exe tool, whose syntax is shown below:

```
aspnet_compiler.exe
      [-m metabasePath | -v virtualPath | [-p physicalDir]]
      [targetDir]
```

where:

- metabasePath is the full IIS metabase path of the application.
- virtualPath is the virtual path of the application.
- physicalDir is the physical path of the application.
- targetDir is the target directory for the fully compiled application.

If the target directory is not supplied, the application is pre-compiled in place and the source is left where it is. When a target directory is specified, the target will contain no source code after the compilation. A text file is placed at the top-level directory indicating that the site has been pre-compiled. All of the source files are compiled into assemblies, and the source files have all content removed and remain simply as markers so that IIS can find the physical files.

Pre-compilation does not compile static files, such as HTML files, web.config, XML files, and so on. These are just copied to the target directory. If you wish to keep the contents of HTML files from being readable in the target directory, you could rename them to .aspx so they will take part in the pre-compile. This isn't recommended, however, because it loses the benefits of IIS being able to serve HTML pages efficiently, and the performance loss may not be acceptable. Assemblies in the \bin directory of the source application are also preserved and copied directly to the target directory.

Once an application has been pre-compiled in this manner, changes (e.g., additions to the source directory) will not trigger a recompilation. Compilable files (such as `.aspx` files) cannot be added to the target directory once it has been generated. They must be added to the source directory and recompiled to the target.

Pre-compilation for Deployment with Source

As mentioned earlier, dynamic files cannot exist in a pre-compiled target directory, so it is not possible to deploy a pre-compiled application with the source intact. This is a feature that is being investigated for later releases, but for the time being the standard deployment and in-place pre-compilation is a great model to work with.

The Compilation API

The technology underlying the pre-compilation system is the `ClientBuildManager`, which also provides an API, allowing custom tools to be built. Listing 2.6 shows how this can be achieved.

Listing 2.6. Using the Compilation API

```
Imports System.Web.Compilation

Public Sub BuildApplication

  Dim src As String = "C:\Development\WebSites\MySite"
  Dim vdir As String = "/MySite"
  Dim tgt As String = "C:\InetPub\WWWRoot\MySite"

  Dim bmgr As New ClientBuildManager(src, vdir, tgt, Nothing)

  bmgr.PrecompileApplication()

End Sub
```

The `System.Web.Compilation` namespace has other classes to help with build tools, such as data binding and expression builders, ways of managing dependencies, and events to hook into the existing build system. All in all there's a lot of power that can be exploited.

Creating Custom Build Providers

Creating your own build providers to integrate into the ASP.NET 2.0 build system is simply a matter of creating the appropriate class and adding the configuration details to web.config. All build providers inherit from the abstract class BuildProvider (in System.Web.Compilation), which has the signature shown in Listing 2.7.

Listing 2.7. The BuildProvider Abstract Class

```
Public Abstract Class BuildProvider

  Public ReadOnly Property CodeCompilerType As CompilerType
  Public ReadOnly Property VirtualPathDependencies As ICollection

  Public Sub GenerateCode(builder As AssemblyBuilder)
  Public Function GetCustomString(results As CompilerResults) As
String
  Public Function GetGeneratedType(results As CompilerResults) As Type
  Public Function GetResultFlags(results As CompilerResults) _
                                   As BuildProviderResultsFlag

End Class
```

At minimum you need to implement the GenerateCode method and provide a way to actually compile or create the code from your custom definition.

For expression builders, such as those used by resources or connection strings, you inherit from the ExpressionBuilder base class, which has the signature shown in Listing 2.8.

Listing 2.8. The ExpressionBuilder Abstract Class

```
Public Abstract Class ExpressionBuilder

  Public ReadOnly Property SupportsEvaluate As Boolean

  Public Function EvaluateExpression(target As Object, _
          entry As BoundPropertyEntry, parsedData As Object, _
          context As ExpressionBuilderContext) As Object
  Public Function GetCodeExpression(entry As BoundPropertyEntry, _
          parsedData As Object, _
          context As ExpressionBuilderContext) As CodeExpression
  Public Function ParseExpression( _
          context As ExpressionBuilderContext) As Object

End Class
```

The implementation of these build providers is outside the scope of this book, but the documentation will contain more details.

SUMMARY

In this chapter we've looked at the new design tool, Visual Studio 2005, and some of the great features it offers, including some data binding scenarios, support for master pages, connections to databases, and so on. Rather than list all of the new features, we've concentrated on the ones that will have the most dramatic effect on development, making sites easier and quicker to construct.

The second topic of this chapter was compilation and the underlying changes to ASP.NET. We've seen how the compilation system can free you from the "make file nightmare," allowing you to just save files and browse the application. Pre-compilation brings improvements in two areas: (1) performance, by compiling in-place to avoid the first-hit compilation, and (2) protection of intellectual property, by removing the source code.

Now it's time to start looking in depth at the ASP.NET 2.0 features, starting with data source controls and binding.

3

Data Source Controls and Data Binding

O NE OF THE FEATURES of ASP.NET 1.0 that so excited developers was the introduction of server-side data binding. This had probably the greatest effect of all the new features in reducing the code required to build data-driven pages, when compared with previous versions of ASP (and other dynamic Web page technologies). No longer do you need to write masses of intermingled markup, literal text, and code to build HTML tables in your pages to display data. And, as an added advantage, data binding usually provides improved performance as well.

ASP.NET 2.0 continues the process of reducing the requirements for code and developer effort. It provides new controls that remove the need to write those almost identical chunks of data access code that fetch the data you need from the data store. And it also considerably simplifies the previously cumbersome syntax for server-side data binding.

In this chapter and the next, we look at the main areas where ASP.NET 2.0 changes the data access, data binding, and data output models used in ASP.NET 1.x. In this chapter we'll cover the following:

- An overview of "code-free" data binding and data updating techniques
- The new data source controls that expose data without requiring any data access code

Another new feature in the .NET Framework can be useful when working with data in your Web pages and applications: a facility to add data source connection strings to a new section of a `web.config` file, which allows them to be encrypted for security purposes. This topic is covered, along with other configuration topics, in Chapter 13.

Meanwhile, we start off in this chapter with a brief "wow factor" look at just how easy it is to display and edit data using the combination of a data source control and a `GridView` control. This will also give you a good overview of the new controls and techniques that are explained in more detail throughout the rest of this chapter and the next.

Code-Free Data Binding

One of the major goals of ASP.NET since version 1.0 has been to allow developers to achieve more while writing less code. Server controls such as the `DataGrid`, as well as the rest of the ASP.NET page architecture and postback mechanism, remove the need for code that iterates through rowsets, generates HTML table elements, and manages the values of controls between postbacks.

However, one area that seems to have been ignored until now is data access. In ASP.NET 1.x, you still have to create functions or routines that connect to the data store, extract the rows or values, and then expose them to the server controls in the page. OK, so that's generally not difficult, and it does provide plenty of flexibility. But it's still effort you have to put in when building the pages.

In ASP.NET 2.0, Microsoft has added new controls that take away the need for this code. Data source controls allow declarative definition of all the information required to extract the data from the data source, and they react to events within the page framework to fetch this data and display it in other data-bound controls to which they are attached.

Displaying Data with a Data Source Control

As a simple example and a dramatic indication of how easy it is to do, Listing 3.1 shows the complete declaration of the `<form>` section of a page that displays rows from a database. This is all you need—there is no server-side code in the page at all.

LISTING 3.1. Displaying Data with a Data Source Control

```
<form runat="server">

<asp:SqlDataSource id="ds1" runat="server"
  ConnectionString="server=localhost;database=Northwind;uid=x;pwd=x"
```

```
SelectCommand="SELECT ProductID, ProductName, QuantityPerUnit,
              UnitPrice, UnitsInStock, Discontinued FROM Products"
/>

<asp:GridView id="grid1" DataSourceID="ds1" runat="server" />

</form>
```

The `SqlDataSource` control uses a connection string and a SQL statement (or a stored procedure name), plus sensible default settings, to connect to a database and extract the data rows. It reacts to the page-level events that occur when the page is requested and internally builds the usual ADO.NET objects it needs (either a `Connection`, `DataAdapter`, and `DataSet` or a `Connection`, `Command`, and `DataReader`). If you think about it, when you create these objects yourself all you start out with is the connection string and a SQL statement!

The other control, the `GridView`, displays the data. The `GridView` is a new version of the `DataGrid` from ASP.NET 1.0, enhanced with a lot of new features. Notice how it is connected to the data source control using the `DataSourceID` attribute. All ASP.NET server controls that support data binding expose this attribute in version 2.0, so they can be used interchangeably with any data source control.

The screenshot in Figure 3.1 shows the result of the code in Listing 3.1. You can see that it looks rather like the output you would get from the

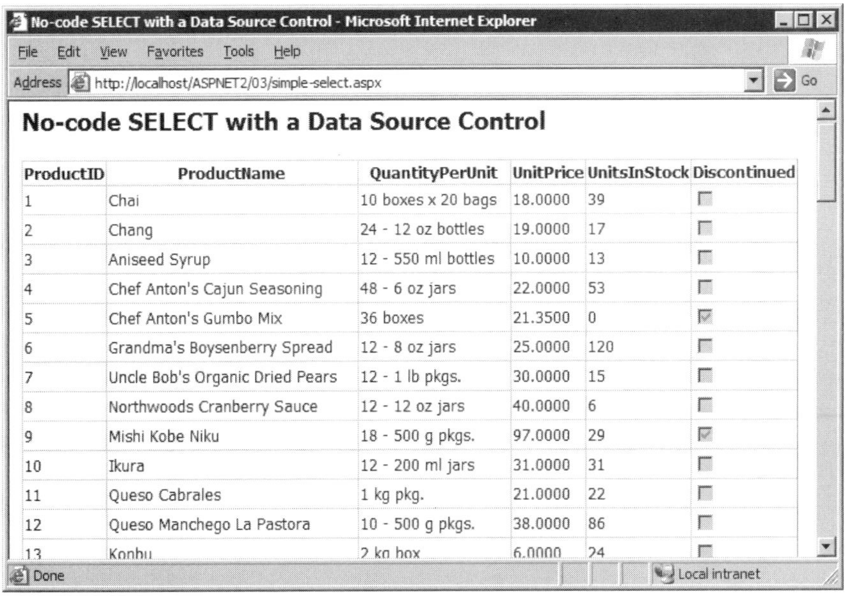

FIGURE 3.1. Displaying data with a data source control

version 1.0 `DataGrid` control. It displays all the rows from the Products table in the Northwind database, just as specified in the SQL statement. Notice the Discontinued column, however. This is a `Boolean` field in the table, and the control automatically displays it using read-only (disabled) checkboxes.

Adding Row Sorting Capabilities

Another example of the power of the `GridView` control can be seen when you want to allow the user to sort the rows in the grid. In ASP.NET 1.0, with the `DataGrid`, this was relatively easy. It meant adding a couple of attributes to the control declaration and writing a dozen or so lines of code. However, with the `GridView`, all you need to do is add the `AllowSorting` attribute to the control declaration:

```
<asp:GridView id="grid1" DataSourceID="ds1" runat="server"
         AllowSorting="True" />
```

There's no code to write, no events to handle, and nothing more to do. The control looks after everything for you. Of course, you can provide custom sorting features if you want, but it's not a requirement.

Adding Row Paging Capabilities

Another common requirement, which was a little more difficult to do in version 1.0 with the `DataGrid`, is to add "paging" so that only a specific number of rows are shown each time and the display provides links to go to other pages. Again, with the `GridView`, it's just a matter of adding one attribute to the control declaration:

```
<asp:GridView id="grid1" DataSourceID="ds1" runat="server"
         AllowSorting="True"
         AllowPaging="True" />
```

As before, there's no code to write. It just works. The screenshot in Figure 3.2 shows the result of adding the attributes that enable sorting and paging to the basic `GridView` declaration.

You can see that only ten rows are displayed by default, and the paging controls at the bottom of the window provide links to the other pages. Also notice that the column headings are hyperlinks—the grid now supports sorting as well. The screenshot in Figure 3.3 shows the result of clicking the ProductName heading. Repeated clicks alternate between ascending and descending sort order.

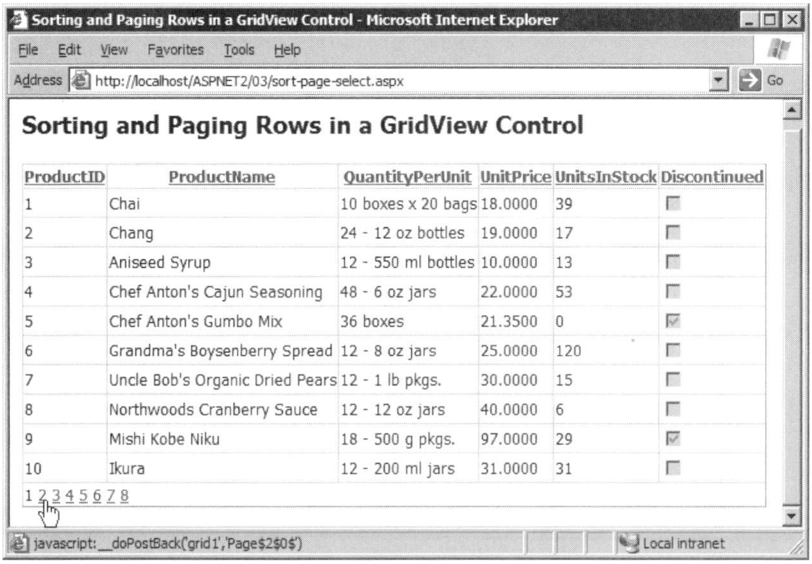

FIGURE 3.2. Paging with a GridView control

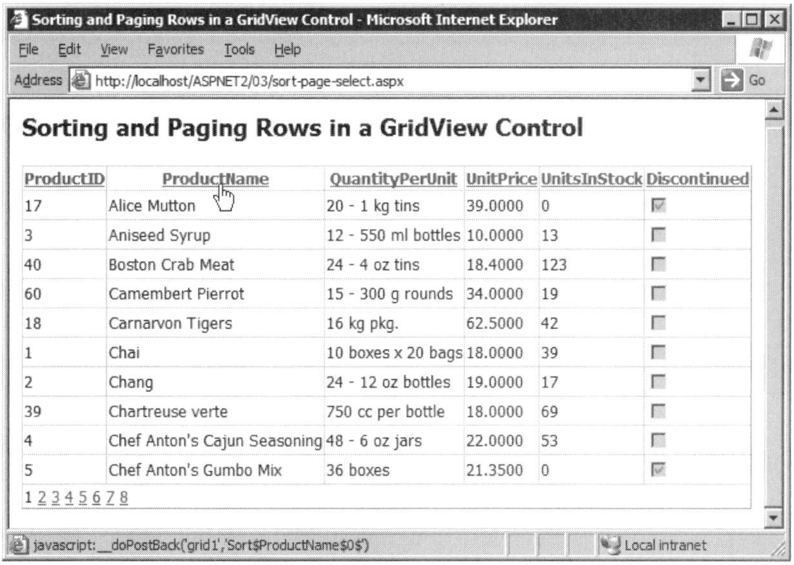

FIGURE 3.3. Sorting with a GridView control

Built-in Small-Screen and Mobile Device Support

The GridView control is part of the unified control architecture we discuss in more detail in Chapter 10, using an adapter to generate the appropriate device-dependent markup for clients that load the page. Tables and grids are notoriously difficult for small-screen devices to display, and Microsoft has addressed this issue by creating two different modes for displaying data in a table: summary view and details view.

The GridView control supports this approach automatically. If you open the page shown in Figure 3.2 in a suitable mobile device or device emulator, you'll see that the control renders the content using these two views. Figures 3.4 and 3.5 show the kind of output you can expect, though it does of course differ depending on the device.

In Figure 3.4 the grid is in summary view. You can see the ProductName column heading and below it the values from that column. All of these are links. Selecting the column heading link causes the data to be sorted on the values in the column. Each product name below the column heading provides a link to display more details about that product (the other values from that row in the table). And, if paging is enabled for the GridView control, there is a set of links to the other pages at the bottom of the list, just as when the page is viewed in an ordinary Web browser.

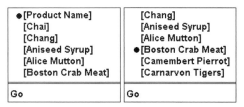

FIGURE 3.4. Mobile device output in summary view

Figure 3.5 shows the output after selecting a product in the previous screen. The grid is now in details view, and the values of the selected product are shown. Notice that the checkbox for the Discontinued column is represented in a way that suits the device. Following all the values are the links to switch back to summary view or to move to the next or previous row.

Boston Crab Meat 40 24 - 4 oz Tins 18.4000 123 [X]	123 [X] ● [Summary View] [Next Row] [Previous Row]
Go	Go

FIGURE 3.5. Mobile device output in details view

Specifying the Summary View Column

All this output is created automatically and does not require any developer effort. However, one point worth bearing in mind is that by default the summary view will display the first column. In the figures we showed the second column (the product name) as the summary column. To achieve this, just add the `SummaryViewColumn` attribute to the declaration of the `GridView` control and specify the column name:

```
<asp:GridView id="grid1" DataSourceID="ds1" runat="server"
    AllowSorting="True"
    AllowPaging="True"
    SummaryViewColumn="ProductName" />
```

It's worth adding this attribute every time you use a `GridView` so that small-screen devices see the most useful column. It doesn't affect the display for nonmobile devices in any way.

Linking Page Controls and Data Source Control Parameters

A regular requirement for pages that display data is to include one or more controls that can be used to select or filter the rows displayed. For example, you may display a list of countries and then show only the rows from a table of customer details for that country. The data source controls can be used to fill both the list of countries and the rows for a particular country when the user makes a selection.

The example in Listing 3.2 uses two data source controls. The first, with ID value `ds1`, retrieves a list of the countries in the rows of the Customers table using the `DISTINCT` keyword in the SQL statement. These rows are then displayed in an ASP.NET `DropDownList` control by assigning the data source control to the `DataSourceID` property of that control and specifying the column to be displayed as the `DataTextField` attribute. Notice also that the `DropDownList` control has `AutoPostback` set to `True`, so selecting a country will cause a postback to the server.

LISTING 3.2. Linking Data Source Control Parameters

```
<asp:SqlDataSource id="ds1" runat="server"
  ConnectionString="server=localhost;database=Northwind;uid=x;pwd=x;"
  SelectCommand="SELECT DISTINCT Country FROM Customers
                 ORDER BY Country"
  EnableCaching="True" CacheDuration="300" />

<asp:DropDownList id="lstCountry" DataSourceID="ds1"
  DataTextField="Country" AutoPostback="True" runat="server" />
...
```

One extremely useful feature of the data source controls is the ability to cache the data they retrieve, thus reducing server loading and improving performance in cases where the data is not expected to change between postbacks. The `EnableCaching` and `CacheDuration` attributes are discussed later in this chapter in the SqlDataSource Control section, along with the ability to link the cache to the original data source so that changes to the data will invalidate the cache.

Specifying and Using the Country Parameter

The next section of code declares the second data source control and the `GridView` control (see Listing 3.3). The data source control `ds2` has a SQL statement for the `SelectCommand` attribute that contains the parameter `WHERE Country = @Country`. There is also a `SelectParameters` section within the data source control declaration. This declares a `ControlParameter` named `Country` that takes its value from the `SelectedValue` property of the control named `lstCountry` (the data-bound `DropDownList` populated with the country names that is declared in Listing 3.2). Finally, a `GridView` control is bound to the `ds2` data source.

LISTING 3.3. Linking Data Source Control Parameters

```
. . .
<asp:SqlDataSource id="ds2" runat="server"
   ConnectionString="server=localhost;database=Northwind;uid=x;pwd=x;"
   SelectCommand="SELECT CompanyName, Address, City, PostalCode,
              Country FROM Customers WHERE Country = @Country">

  <SelectParameters>
    <asp:ControlParameter Name="Country" ControlID="lstCountry"
                     PropertyName="SelectedValue" />
  </SelectParameters>

</asp:SqlDataSource>

<asp:GridView id="grid1" DataSourceID="ds2" runat="server" />
```

When the page is executed, the `ControlParameter` is populated with the value currently selected in the `DropDownList` control, and then this parameter is added to the data source control's `Parameters` collection before the SQL statement is executed. All this happens automatically, and no code is required. The data source control then selects only the rows that satisfy

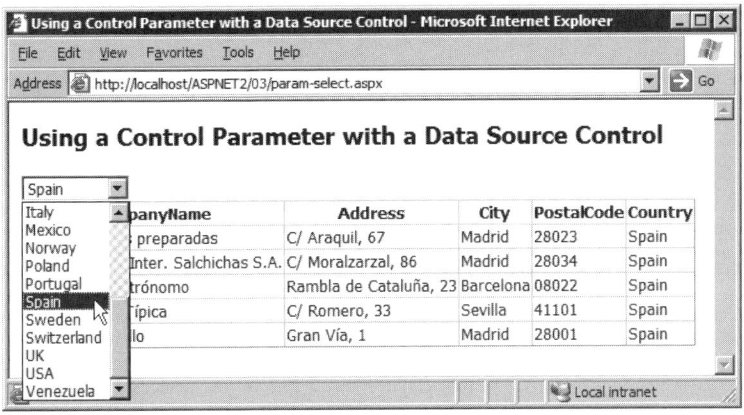

FIGURE 3.6. Using control parameters with a data source control

the parameter value and displays these in the `GridView` control. You can see the result in the screenshot in Figure 3.6.

Editing Data with a GridView and a Data Source Control

As a final example of the power of the new combination of data source controls and the `GridView` control, this section looks at inline editing of the data within a `GridView` control. And, like all of the previous examples, no code is required to make it work.

> In fact, there is a small section of code in this example, which we discuss when we look at how you can react to events raised by the `GridView` control in Chapter 4, but this is not usually required for the simple editing and deleting of rows demonstrated here.

To enable inline editing of rows, the declaration of the data source control must include a value for the `UpdateCommand` attribute, and to allow rows to be deleted, the `DeleteCommand` attribute must be defined. In Listing 3.4, both are SQL statements including parameters that will be populated from the `GridView` control automatically in response to `Update` and `Delete` commands. The automatic parameter population also gives a useful extra benefit by helping to protect against SQL scripting attacks that can occur if you use values typed in by users.

The `GridView` control declaration also requires a few "extra" attribute values to be defined. You must specify the `DataKeyNames` attribute value as a comma-delimited list of primary key column names so that the control can locate the correct values for the key in the table and prevent editing of the key values. In this case it is just `ShipperID`. And, so that the Edit, Update, and Delete links will appear in the grid, you must set the `AutoGenerateEditButton` and `AutoGenerateDeleteButton` attributes to True.

LISTING 3.4. A Data Source Control with Edit Commands

```
<asp:SqlDataSource id="ds1" runat="server"
  ConnectionString="server=localhost;database=Northwind;uid=x;pwd=x;"
  SelectCommand="SELECT * FROM Shippers"
  UpdateCommand="UPDATE Shippers SET CompanyName=@CompanyName,
                Phone=@Phone WHERE ShipperID=@ShipperID"
  DeleteCommand="DELETE FROM Shippers WHERE ShipperID=@ShipperID" />

<asp:GridView id="grid1" DataSourceID="ds1" runat="server"
  DataKeyNames="ShipperID"
  AutoGenerateEditButton="True"
  AutoGenerateDeleteButton="True" />
```

And that is all that is required to make it work. The screenshot in Figure 3.7 shows the grid with all the rows in normal mode, as it appears when first loaded. The Edit and Delete links appear in the first column.

Clicking an Edit link switches that row in the grid to edit mode, and the value of the non-key columns can be edited (see Figure 3.8). Notice that the ShipperID column, the primary key specified in the `DataKeyNames` attribute, is not editable.

After editing the values, the Update link pushes the changes back into the database using the SQL statement specified for the `UpdateCommand`, while the Cancel link just switches the row back to normal mode without

FIGURE 3.7. Selecting a row to edit with a data source control

FIGURE 3.8. Updating a row with a data source control

persisting the changes to the row values. Likewise, the Delete link uses the SQL statement specified as the `DeleteCommand` to remove the row that contains the link.

> However, because the table has linked child rows in the Products table, you can't actually delete a row with this example. Instead, the page handles the delete action and displays a message. You'll see more about this in Chapter 4 in the subsection Handling a GridView Event.

The DetailsView Control

All of the examples shown previously in this chapter use a `GridView` control to display the data rows. The `GridView` provides the ubiquitous "grid" layout that is so familiar with controls such as the `DataGrid` in version 1.x. However, often you want to display data so that only one "row" or "record" is visible, allowing users to scroll through the rows—and perhaps edit the values as well. The second of the new data-bound controls in ASP.NET, the `DetailsView` control, does just that.

We'll be looking in more depth at the `GridView`, `DetailsView`, and another similar control named `FormView` in Chapter 4. However, just to complete this first look at the controls, the screenshot in Figure 3.9 shows the `DetailsView` control in action. You'll see how this works in the next chapter.

So, having seen just how powerful this new approach to data access, display, and editing is, and how easy it is to achieve, the remaining sections of this chapter and all of the next chapter look in more depth at the controls themselves and the more advanced techniques that you can take advantage of when working with them.

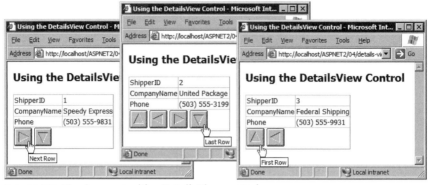

FIGURE 3.9. Viewing rows with a DetailsView control

Data Source Controls

In essence, a data source control simply replaces the data access code you create in ASP.NET 1.x to generate the rowset of data that you want to use in your page. Instead of writing a function that returns (for example) a `DataSet` loaded with the data rows you want to display, you just place a data source control on the page and set the properties to define the data you want. When a control such as a `GridView` or a `DropDownList` renders the data, it uses the data source control to fetch the data and expose it for data binding.

Therefore, when adding a control that supports data binding to the page, you don't have to write any code at all. And the new `GridView` and `DetailsView` controls can automatically provide features to update the data as well—again without requiring you to write any code. Meanwhile, you *can* still write code to interact with the controls if you want to, and you can perform customized data binding or manipulate the data directly. However, in the vast majority of cases the controls will do all the work for you.

The aims of the data source controls (combined with the new `GridView`, `DetailsView`, and `FormView` controls and data binding) are to provide the following.

- **Data binding without requiring any code to be written.** You can display, edit, and sort data with little or no code required. A data source control has the same kind of simple declarative persistence format, using HTML-like elements, as other ASP.NET server controls. Where code is required, the data source controls make it intuitive and concise.

- **A consistent declarative programming model,** regardless of the type of data source or data provider. Developers use the same syntax irrespective of the data source, and control authors have a common interface to implement in their custom data source controls.

- **A self-describing interface** that makes it easy to discover the capabilities of the control. `Boolean` properties indicate whether `SELECT`, `INSERT`, `UPDATE`, `DELETE`, and sorting operations are supported for the data source. Code in the page can test for these capabilities, and custom control authors can implement automatic behavior when certain capabilities are available.

- **A richer design time experience.** Development tools can make it easier to generate instances of the controls and the data binding statements, perhaps using drag-and-drop design techniques. The controls can use a schema to display the data at design time in a way that more closely resembles the runtime appearance.

- **The same flexibility as in version 1.0,** by allowing developers to take full control of the data binding process and react to events (though there should be far less need to do so).

- **Performance equal to or exceeding that of version 1.0** when retrieving data and displaying it through data binding.

To connect a data source control to a server control that will display the data, you use the `DataSourceID` attribute of the data-bound server control—setting it to the `id` attribute value of the data source control. All the controls in the `System.Web.UI.WebControls` and `System.Web.UI.HtmlControls` namespaces that already support server-side data binding now accept the `DataSourceID` attribute.

Types of Data Source Controls

Data source controls fall into different classes, depending on the type of data source they will be used to access. All data source controls live in the `System.Web.UI.WebControls` namespace of the .NET Framework class library and are descended from the base classes `DataSourceControl` or `HierarchicalDataSourceControl`. The data source controls provided with the beta release of ASP.NET 2.0 are listed below.

- The `SqlDataSource` control is the one you'll use for most of your relational database access requirements. It can be used with a database through the SQL Server provider (using the classes from the `SqlClient` namespace), through OLE-DB, or through ODBC.

- The `AccessDataSource` control makes it easy to connect to a Microsoft Access database. This is just one of the database-specific controls; other types of data sources can be accessed through specific data source controls that are under development at the time of writing.

- The `XmlDataSource` control can expose hierarchical XML documents and XML data for binding to controls such as a `TreeView`, as well as exposing the data as an `XmlDataDocument`.

- The `DataSetDataSource` control exposes nonhierarchical XML as a rowset for data binding, as well as exposing the data as an ADO.NET `DataSet`.

- The `SiteMapDataSource` control uses a hierarchical XML file to provide a data source for the special controls in ASP.NET that implement menus and other site navigation features. This control is discussed in depth in Chapter 5.

- The `ObjectDataSource` control allows developers to interact with a data access layer consisting of suitable classes, rather than directly with the database.

In forthcoming releases of ASP.NET you can expect to see more new data source controls such as the `WebServiceDataSource`, `ExcelDataSource`, and `IndexServiceDataSource`. A list of the proposed data source controls appears near the end of this chapter. Here, we'll look at each of the data source controls in the beta version individually. We'll start with the `SqlDataSource` control and then see how the other data source controls differ from it.

The SqlDataSource Control

For most relational database access tasks, the `SqlDataSource` control is the obvious choice. By default it will use a SQL Server–specific connection, but by simply changing the connection string and `ProviderName` property you can use any of the databases for which a provider is available, without having to rewrite your code or change the page in any other way.

Declaring a SqlDataSource Control

All data source controls can be instantiated through declarative elements in the page, and their properties set using attributes, just as you declare any other ASP.NET server control. The complete set of attributes you can use in a SqlDataSource control declaration is shown in Listing 3.5.

LISTING 3.5. Declaring a SqlDataSource Control

```
<asp:SqlDataSource id="String" runat="server"
  ConnectionString="String"
  ProviderName="String"
  DataSourceMode="[DataSet|DataReader]"
  SelectCommand="String"
  SelectCountCommand="String"
  CancelSelectOnNullParameter="[True|False]"
  InsertCommand="String"
  UpdateCommand="String"
  UpdateMode="[Optimistic|Pessimistic]"
  DeleteCommand="String"
  DeleteMode="[Optimistic|Pessimistic]"
  FilterExpression="String"
  SortParameterName="String"
  OldValuesParameterFormatString="String"
  EnableSqlPaging="[True|False]"
  EnableCaching="[True|False]"
  CacheDuration="Integer"
  CacheKeyDependency="String"
  SqlCacheDependency="String"
  CacheExpirationPolicy="[Absolute|Sliding]"
  OnSelecting="SqlDataSourceSelectingEventHandler"
  OnSelected="SqlDataSourceStatusEventHandler"
  OnUpdating="SqlDataSourceCommandEventHandler"
  OnUpdated="SqlDataSourceStatusEventHandler"
  OnInserting="SqlDataSourceCommandEventHandler"
  OnInserted="SqlDataSourceStatusEventHandler"
  OnDeleting="SqlDataSourceCommandEventHandler"
  OnDeleted="SqlDataSourceStatusEventHandler">

    <SelectParameters>
        [<System.Web.UI.WebControls.Parameter...>]
    </SelectParameters>
    <UpdateParameters>
        [<System.Web.UI.WebControls.Parameter...>]
    </UpdateParameters>
    <InsertParameters>
        [<System.Web.UI.WebControls.Parameter...>]
    </InsertParameters>
    <DeleteParameters>
        [<System.Web.UI.WebControls.Parameter...>]
    </DeleteParameters>
    <FilterParameters>
        [<System.Web.UI.WebControls.Parameter...>]
    </FilterParameters>

</asp:SqlDataSource>
```

The attributes in the opening element tag correspond in a one-to-one fashion to the properties of the control listed in the next subsection, which details the complete control interface. The **content** of the `<asp:SqlDataSource>` element is a series of parameter declarations that define how the control should select and filter the data and how it will update the data when changes are pushed back into the database. We'll look at these parameter declarations later in this chapter.

Like all server controls, the `SqlDataSource` exposes an interface that you can access programmatically. When the control is inserted into the page, ASP.NET instantiates the control and uses the attributes you specify to set the properties without requiring any code to be written in the page. Of course, you can read and set the properties in code as required.

SqlDataSource Properties and Attributes

Table 3.1 lists the properties and attributes shown in the declaration of the control in Listing 3.5. In general, you must set at least the `ConnectionString` and `SelectCommand`. If you are *not* accessing SQL Server, you must also set the `ProviderName` to the namespace of the classes in the .NET Framework library that correspond to the type of data source and data access method you are using.

TABLE 3.1. The SqlDataSource Class Properties and Attributes

Property/Attribute	Description
`ConnectionString`	Sets or returns the connection string that the control uses to access the database as a `String` value. The format of the string must match the requirements of the database provider specified for the `ProviderName`. If no `ProviderName` is specified, the control assumes that SQL Server TDS will be used. For security reasons, the `ConnectionString` property is not stored in the viewstate of the page.
`ProviderName`	Sets or returns the namespace that contains the data provider used by the control as a `String`. The default is `System.Data.SqlClient`. The providers that are available are listed in the `<DbProviderFactories>` section of the `<system.data>` element in `machine.config`.
`DataSourceMode`	Sets or returns the type of object that the control will use to access the database as a value from the `SqlDataSourceMode` enumeration. The available values are `DataSet` and `DataReader`. A `DataReader` provides better performance but does not allow for caching, filtering, or sorting within the control. The default is `SqlDataSourceMode.DataSet`.

TABLE 3.1. The SqlDataSource Class Properties and Attributes (continued)

Property/Attribute	Description
SelectCommand	Sets or returns a String that specifies the SQL statement or stored procedure name that will be used to extract the data from the database. Parameters are passed to the SQL statement or stored procedure by using a <SelectParameters> element or by assigning values at runtime to the SelectParameters property (discussed later in this chapter).
SelectCountCommand	Sets or returns a String that specifies the SQL statement or stored procedure name that will be used to return a count of the total number of available rows. Selection and filtering can be applied in the usual way with parameters.
CancelSelectOnNullParameter	Sets or returns a Boolean value that, when True, specifies that the Select process will not take place if any of the parameters have a Null value. This can be useful in preventing errors.
InsertCommand	Sets or returns a String that specifies the SQL statement or stored procedure name that will be used to insert rows into the database. Parameters are passed to the SQL statement or stored procedure by using an <InsertParameters> element or by assigning values at runtime to the InsertParameters property (discussed later in this chapter).
UpdateCommand	Sets or returns a String that specifies the SQL statement or stored procedure name that will be used to update existing rows within the database. Parameters are passed to the SQL statement or stored procedure by using an <UpdateParameters> element or by assigning values at runtime to the UpdateParameters property (discussed later in this chapter).
UpdateMode	Sets or returns a value from the DataSourceOperationMode enumeration that specifies whether the data access will take place in Optimistic or Pessimistic mode. In Pessimistic mode, the original values of the columns in each row are checked against the values in the database to prevent concurrency errors, while in Optimistic mode they are not.

continues

TABLE 3.1. The SqlDataSource Class Properties and Attributes (continued)

Property/Attribute	Description
DeleteCommand	Sets or returns a String that specifies the SQL statement or stored procedure name that will be used to delete rows from the database. Parameters are passed to the SQL statement or stored procedure by using a `<DeleteParameters>` element or by assigning values at runtime to the DeleteParameters property (discussed later in this chapter).
DeleteMode	See the UpdateMode property.
FilterExpression	Sets or returns a String that contains the expression to be used to filter the data specified in the SelectCommand property. It is valid only when the DataSourceMode is DataSet. The syntax of the filter expression is the same as that used in the RowFilter property of an ADO.NET DataView. Parameters should be prefixed with the @ character (or a character specific to the database). For example: `"FieldName1=value1, FieldName2='value2'"` `"FieldName=@param"`
SortParameterName	Sets or returns a String that contains the name of the stored procedure parameter that will be used to sort the rows. It applies only if the SelectCommand property specifies the name of a stored procedure and not a SQL statement.
OldValuesParameterFormatString	When the UpdateMode or DeleteMode is set to Pessimistic, the old values must be passed to the Update or Delete method. The format string stored in this property determines the names for these parameters. The default is `"orig_{0}"`.
EnableSqlPaging	Sets or returns a Boolean value that specifies whether the control will take advantage of ADO.NET database paging features. When True, and if the database supports it, the control will use the new features of the ADO.NET 2.0 Command object to extract only the rows required for the current page.

TABLE 3.1. The SqlDataSource Class Properties and Attributes (continued)

Property/Attribute	Description
EnableCaching	Sets or returns a `Boolean` value that specifies whether caching will be applied to the data selected in the control. It is valid only when the `DataSourceMode` is `DataSet`. When `True`, the data is cached and used in subsequent `Select` operations. The default is `False`.
CacheDuration	Sets or returns the number of seconds that data is cached when `EnableCaching` is `True`, as an `Integer`. The `CacheExpirationPolicy` property determines whether this is an absolute or sliding window value. If not specified, the data is cached for all subsequent `Select` operations.
CacheKeyDependency	Sets or returns a `String` that is a reference to a user-defined cache key name. When this key is expired, any cached data held by this data source is expired.
SqlCacheDependency	Sets or returns an optional cache dependency as a `String`, such as: `connection:table1;connection:table2`. The `connection` refers to a named entry within the `<sqlCacheDependency>` section of the `<caching>` section of `machine.config` or `web.config`. The `table` refers to the name of the table in the database. Multiple dependencies are delimited with a semicolon as shown above. The database must be configured to support SQL cache invalidation.
CacheExpirationPolicy	Sets or returns a Boolean value that specifies whether the control will take advantage of the database paging features that are slated for inclusion in the final release of ADO.NET 2.0. When True and if the database supports it, the control will use the new features of the ADO.NET 2.0 Command object to extract only the rows required for the current data page.

Specifying Parameters for the SqlDataSource Control

To be able to use a control to access (and update) data, there has to be a way to pass parameter values to the SQL statements or stored procedures it uses under the hood. Otherwise the value of the `SelectCommand` would need to be changed each time the control is required to extract a different set of rows (or to perform different updates to the database tables).

So that you don't have to write code to set these parameter values, the `SqlDataSource` control exposes the parameters in a way that allows them to be set declaratively by referencing dynamic values that are part of the page request or the control tree.

For a stored procedure, parameters are defined as part of the procedure definition within the database itself. For a SQL statement, parameters are specified using placeholders, for example:

```
"SELECT * FROM Customers WHERE Country=@Country"
```

At runtime, the control replaces the @Country placeholder with the specific value of the parameter. The values that are passed to the SQL statement or stored procedure can be taken directly from

- The value of a server control within the page, using a ControlParameter control
- A name/value pair that appears in the Request.QueryString collection, using a QueryStringParameter control
- A value from a control that appears in the Request.Form collection, using a FormParameter control
- A value stored in the user's ASP.NET session, using a SessionParameter control
- A value in a cookie sent by the browser with the request, using a CookieParameter control
- A user-specific value stored within the ASP.NET Personalization system, using a ProfileParameter control. More details of the Personalization features of ASP.NET can be found in Chapter 7.

These controls are declared within the SqlDataSource control element as a set of optional nested elements. As well as the parameters for the Select, Update, Insert, and Delete operations, there is an optional element that can be used to filter the rows returned by a Select operation (see Listing 3.6).

LISTING 3.6. Parameter Outline for a SqlDataSource Control

```
<asp:SqlDataSource id="String" runat="server"
   ... >

   <SelectParameters>
      ... one or more xxxParameter elements here ...
   </SelectParameters>

   <UpdateParameters>
      ... one or more XXXParameter elements here ...
   </UpdateParameters>
```

```
<InsertParameters>
   ... one or more XXXParameter elements here ...
</InsertParameters>

<DeleteParameters>
   ... one or more XXXParameter elements here ...
</DeleteParameters>

<FilterParameters>
   ... one or more XXXParameter elements here ...
</FilterParameters>

</asp:SqlDataSource>
```

At runtime, ASP.NET creates a separate `ParameterCollection` for each of the sections that appear within the declaration of the control and populates these collections using the `Parameter` elements in each section. The `ParameterCollection` instances are then applied to the properties of the `SqlDataSource` control. These properties are shown in Table 3.2.

TABLE 3.2. The ParameterCollection Class Properties

Property	Description
SelectParameters	Returns a reference to the `ParameterCollection` containing the parameters for the `Select` operation.
UpdateParameters	Returns a reference to the `ParameterCollection` containing the parameters for the `Update` operation.
InsertParameters	Returns a reference to the `ParameterCollection` containing the parameters for the `Insert` operation.
DeleteParameters	Returns a reference to the `ParameterCollection` containing the parameters for the `Delete` operation.
FilterParameters	Returns a reference to the `ParameterCollection` containing the parameters used to filter the rows returned by a `Select` operation.

Parameter Properties and Attributes.   The six types of parameters that you can use within the parameter sections of the `SqlDataSource` control are descended from the common base class `System.Web.UI.WebControls.Parameter`. This class exposes five properties that are inherited by all of the parameter types (see Table 3.3).

TABLE 3.3. The Parameter Class Properties and Attributes

Property/Attribute	Description
Name	Sets or returns the name of the parameter as a `String`, corresponding to the parameter in the SQL statement or stored procedure to which it will be applied. Note that the `@` prefix should not be included in the name.
Direction	Sets or returns the "direction" for the parameter, as a value from the `System.Data.ParameterDirection` enumeration. Valid values are: • `Input`: The parameter carries an input value for the query. • `Output`: The parameter collects an output value from the query. • `InputOutput`: The parameter carries an input value for the query and returns with the value updated by the query. • `ReturnValue`: The parameter carries the value specified by a `RETURN` statement in a stored procedure.
DefaultValue	Sets or returns the default value of the parameter as a `String` representation of that value.
Type	Sets or returns the data type that the value and the `DefaultValue` represent, using a standard .NET `TypeCode` value such as `String`, `Int16`, or `Decimal`.
ConvertEmptyStringToNull	Sets or returns a `Boolean` value that indicates whether an empty `String` for the value will be treated as `Null` when the SQL statement or stored procedure is executed.

The six specific parameter classes expose at least one additional `String` property, depending on the parameter type (see Table 3.4). These properties are used to specify how the value for the parameter is selected from all the values available in the set of controls on the page, in the `QueryString` or `Form` collection, in the session, in the cookies sent from the client, or from a value in the current user's Personalization store.

Listing 3.7 shows an example of the ways that the parameter controls can be used. Each of the properties of the `SqlDataSource` can be set with any of the six different parameter types or with a mixture of different types.

TABLE 3.4. The Six Parameter Section Types

Parameter Control	Properties
ControlParameter	ControlID: The id of the control containing the value to use. PropertyName: The name of the control property that contains the value, for example, Text for the Text property of a TextBox control.
QueryStringParameter	QueryStringField: The name of the name/value pair that contains the value to use, for example, UserID, where the query string contains UserID=smithron.
FormParameter	FormField: The name of the control on the page that contains the value to use. It does not have to be a server control. Corresponds to the name attribute of the control within the HTML source of the page.
SessionParameter	SessionField: The name of the key used to store the value in the user's ASP.NET session, for example, UserID, where the value was stored using Session("UserID") = "smithron".
CookieParameter	CookieName: The name of the key used to store the value in the cookie.
ProfileParameter	PropertyName: The name of the property within the Personalization system.

LISTING 3.7. Parameter Details for a SqlDataSource Control

```
<asp:SqlDataSource id="String" runat="server"
  ... >

  <SelectParameters>
    <asp:ControlParameter Name="UserID"
        ControlID="txtUserID" PropertyName="Text" />
    <asp:ControlParameter Name="UserName"
        ControlID="lstName" PropertyName="SelectedValue" />
  </SelectParameters>

  <UpdateParameters>
    <asp:FormParameter Name="State" FormField="StateList" />
    <asp:ProfileParameter Name="Country" PropertyName="UserCountry" />
  </UpdateParameters>

  <InsertParameters>
    <asp:QueryStringParameter Name="UID" QueryStringField ="uid" />
    <asp:SessionParameter Name="Page" SessionField ="PageName" />
  </InsertParameters>

  <DeleteParameters>
```

continues

```
    <asp:ControlParameter Name="UserID"
        ControlID="txtUserID" PropertyName="Text" />
    <asp:FormParameter Name="Country" FormField="CountryBox" />
    <asp:CookieParameter Name="CheckVal" CookieName="CheckSum" />
</DeleteParameters>
```

```
</asp:SqlDataSource>
```

Remember that you need to set only the `SqlDataSource` properties that correspond to the operations you'll be carrying out. In other words, if you are just displaying data—and not updating it—you can omit the `UpdateParameters`, `InsertParameters`, and `DeleteParameters` sections.

Applying a Dynamic Filter Expression with Parameters. The same approach is taken if you want to specify a filter that will be applied to the results of the `SelectCommand`. For example, the code in Listing 3.8 specifies the `Text` value of a `TextBox` control that has the ID `txtFilterExpr`. This value is used as a filter against the column named *table-column-name* within the results set—in effect setting the `FilterExpression` to *table-column-name=value-of-textbox*.

LISTING 3.8. Using FilterParameters with a SqlDataSource Control

```
    . . .
    <FilterParameters>
      <asp:ControlParameter Name="table-column-name"
          ControlID="txtFilterExpr" PropertyName="Text" />
    </FilterParameters>
    . . .
```

Working with the SqlDataSource Control at Runtime

The combination of the `SqlDataSource` control and data-bound controls (such as the new `GridView` and `DetailsView` controls) is designed to remove the need for you to write runtime code to create output in the page. However, there are still occasions where you may want to interact with a data source control directly, for example, to modify the output based on the content of the data rows by reacting to an event that the control (or some other control on the page) raises. The next subsections list the remaining members of the interface for the `SqlDataControl`.

SqlDataSource Control Methods. As well as the `DataBind` method that is inherited from the base class `Control`, the `SqlDataSource` control exposes four methods that you can call to perform data access operations through the control. Each method uses the appropriate command specified in the `SelectCommand`, `DeleteCommand`, `InsertCommand`, or `UpdateCommand` properties of the control and takes into account any parameters defined for the `SelectParameters`, `DeleteParameters`, `InsertParameters`, or `UpdateParameters` properties, respectively. Table 3.5 lists the four methods.

TABLE 3.5. The SqlDataSource Control Methods

Method	Description
Select(args)	Returns all the rows specified by the `SelectCommand` and the values in the `SelectParameters` collection from the data source or from the cached `DataSourceView` that contains the rows. Returns a `DataView` instance if the `DataSourceMode` property is set to `DataSet`, or a `DataReader` if the `DataSourceMode` property is set to `DataReader`. The `DataReader` must be explicitly closed after use. The `args` parameter is a reference to a `DataSourceSelectArguments` instance that instructs the method to perform specific actions such as retrieving a fixed number of rows, sorting the rows, or counting the total number of rows available. It also returns information such as the row count. Use `Nothing` (null in C#) if the extra features are not required.
Delete()	Deletes the row(s) specified by the `DeleteCommand` and the values in the `DeleteParameters` collection from the data source. Returns an `Integer` that is the number of rows deleted from the data source.
Insert()	Inserts a new row into the data source using the `InsertCommand` and the values in the `InsertParameters` collection. Returns an `Integer` that is the number of rows inserted into the data source table.
Update()	Updates rows in the data source using the `UpdateCommand` and the values in the `UpdateParameters` collection. Returns an `Integer` that is the number of rows updated in the data source.

SqlDataSource Control Events. The `SqlDataSource` control raises various events as it operates on the data source or when its methods are called. The event handlers that will respond to these events can be specified within the declaration of the `SqlDataSource` control or added to the control at runtime by using the `AddHandler` method in Visual Basic .NET or by appending them to the event property in C# in the usual way. Table 3.6 lists the events.

TABLE 3.6. The SqlDataSource Control Events

Event	Description
Selecting	Raised before the `Select` method is executed. A `SqlDataSourceSelectingEventArgs` instance passed to the event handler exposes four properties: • `Command`: Returns a reference to the `Command` (`System.Data.IDbCommand`) instance that will be used to execute the operation on the rows in the database. • `Arguments`: Returns a reference to the `DataSourceSelectArguments` instance that was passed to the `Select` method. • `ExecutingSelectCount`: Returns a `Boolean` value that is `True` if the current operation is one that will return only a count of the rows available or `False` if it will return a rowset. • `Cancel`: A `Boolean` property that can be set to `True` to cancel the current operation.
Selected	Raised after the `Select` method completes. A `SqlDataSourceStatusEventArgs` instance passed to the event handler exposes four properties: • `Command`: Returns a reference to the `Command` (`System.Data.IDbCommand`) instance that was used to execute the operation on the rows in the database. • `Exception`: Returns an `Exception` instance if the data access process currently being executed fails. A reference to the actual exception that was raised by the object can be obtained from the `InnerException` property of this current exception. • `ExceptionHandled`: A `Boolean` value that you can set to `True` after handling any exception raised by the data access process to indicate that this exception should *not* be raised to the code that called this method. • `RowsAffected`: Returns the number of data rows affected by this operation as an `Integer`.
Deleting	Raised before the `Delete` method is executed. A `SqlDataSourceCommandEventArgs` instance passed to the event handler exposes two properties: • `Command`: Returns a reference to the `Command` (`System.Data.IDbCommand`) instance that will be used to execute the operation on the rows in the database. • `Cancel`: Returns a `Boolean` property that can be set to `True` to cancel the current operation.
Deleted	Raised after the `Delete` method completes. A `SqlDataSourceStatusEventArgs` instance is passed to the event handler. (See the `Selected` event for details.)

TABLE 3.6. The SqlDataSource Control Events (continued)

Event	Description
Inserting	Raised before the `Insert` method is executed. A `SqlDataSourceCommandEventArgs` instance is passed to the event handler. (See the `Deleting` event for details.)
Inserted	Raised after the `Insert` method completes. A `SqlDataSourceStatusEventArgs` instance is passed to the event handler. (See the `Selected` event for details.)
Updating	Raised before the `Update` method is executed. A `SqlDataSourceCommandEventArgs` instance is passed to the event handler. (See the `Deleting` event for details.)
Updated	Raised after the `Update` method completes. A `SqlDataSourceStatusEventArgs` instance is passed to the event handler. (See the `Selected` event for details.)

SqlDataSource Constructors. You can create an instance of a `SqlDataSource` control and add it to the `Controls` collection of the page by using one of the constructors. You also need to set the property values and then call any methods you require (such as `Select` or `Update`). The constructors are shown in Table 3.7.

TABLE 3.7. The SqlDataSource Constructors

Constructor	Description
`SqlDataSource()`	Creates a new `SqlDataSource` instance with the default values for all the properties.
`SqlDataSource (connect-string, select-command)`	Creates a new `SqlDataSource` instance with the specified values for the `ConnectionString SelectCommand` properties. All other properties are set to the default value. As the `ProviderName` property defaults to `SqlClient`, this only allows access to SQL Server via TDS unless you set this property to another provider namespace.
`SqlDataSource (provider-name, connect-string, select-command)`	Creates a new `SqlDataSource` instance with the specified values for the `ProviderName`, `ConnectionString`, and `SelectCommand` properties. All other properties are set to the default value.

The Parameter and ParameterCollection Interfaces. A parameter for use with the `SqlDataSource` control can be created using one of the constructors shown in Table 3.8. The `Parameter` class has a single method, also shown in Table 3.8.

TABLE 3.8. The Parameter Class Interface

Constructor	Description
`Parameter()`	Creates a new `Parameter` instance with the default values for all the properties.
`Parameter(name)`	Creates a new `Parameter` instance with the specified value for the `Name` property (as a `String`).
`Parameter(name, type)`	Creates a new `Parameter` instance with the specified value for the `Name` property (as a `String`) and the specified data type (as a value from the `TypeCode` enumeration).
`Parameter(name, type, default-value)`	Creates a new `Parameter` instance with the specified value for the `Name` property (as a `String`), the specified data type (as a value from the `TypeCode` enumeration), and the specified `default-value` (as a `String`).
Method	
`ToString()`	Returns the value of the `Parameter` as a `String`. If the value is specified as representing a different data type, the `String` representation of the value is returned.

It's also possible to create a copy of an existing `Parameter` instance using the `Clone` method or to create a new `Parameter` instance with the same values using the constructor: `Parameter(existing-param-instance)`.

The `ParameterCollection` class holds a collection of `Parameter` instances, as assigned to one of the *xxx*Parameters properties of the `SqlDataSource` control (e.g., the `SelectParameters` or `FilterParameters` property)—see Table 3.9.

TABLE 3.9. The ParameterCollection Class Interface

Constructor	Description
`ParameterCollection()`	Creates a new empty `ParameterCollection`.
Property	
`Count`	Returns the number of parameters in the collection as an `Integer`.
`Item(name)`	Returns a reference to a parameter within the collection specified by its name as a `String`.
`Item(index)`	Returns a reference to a parameter within the collection specified by its index as an `Integer`.
Method	
`Add(param)`	Adds the specified `Parameter` instance to the collection. Returns the index of the parameter within the collection as an `Integer`.
`Add(name, value)`	Adds a `Parameter` with the specified (`String`) name and specified (`String`) value to the collection. Returns the index of the parameter within the collection as an `Integer`.
`Add(name, type, value)`	Adds a `Parameter` with the specified (`String`) name, the specified (`TypeCode`) data type, and the specified (`String`) value to the collection. Returns the index of the parameter within the collection as an `Integer`.
`Clear()`	Removes all Parameter instances from the `ParameterCollection`.
`Contains(parameter)`	Returns a `Boolean` value indicating whether the specified `Parameter` instance is in this `ParameterCollection`.
`GetValues(context, section)`	Returns an ordered dictionary containing the name/value pairs for the parameters for a specified section of the `SqlDataSource` control, for example, the `SelectParameters` or `UpdateParameters` section.
`IndexOf(parameter)`	Returns an `Integer` value indicating that the index of the specified parameter within the `ParameterCollection`.
`Insert(index, param)`	Inserts the specified `Parameter` instance into the collection at the specified zero-based `Integer` index. No return value.
`Remove(param)`	Removes the specified `Parameter` instance from the collection. No return value.

continues

TABLE 3.9. The ParameterCollection Class Interface (continued)

Constructor	Description
RemoveAt (*index*)	Removes the parameter at the specified zero-based Integer index position within the collection. No return value.
UpdateValues (*section*)	Updates the parameters for a specified section of the SqlDataSource control with the values returned by executing the operation for that section. No return value.
Event	
ParametersChanged	Raised when the value of a parameter in the collection changes (e.g., following a Select method call), when a value is changed in code, or when a parameter is added to or removed from the collection.

The SqlDataSourceView Interface

Every data source control exposes the data it selects from its corresponding data store as a DataSourceView. The SqlDataSource control exposes a SqlDataSourceView instance. The data-bound controls in the page then consume the SqlDataSourceView and display the data rows it contains.

Of course, if you are simply declaring the SqlDataSource and GridView controls on your page and not interacting with them in code, you don't need to worry about the SqlDataSourceView itself. However, it is useful when you want to access rows and individual values in, say, an event handler. The SqlDataSourceView has a single constructor (see Table 3.10) and exposes broadly the same set of properties, methods, and events as the SqlDataSource control itself.

TABLE 3.10. The SqlDataSourceView Constructor

Constructor	Description
SqlDataSourceView (*owner, name, context*)	Creates a new instance of a SqlDataSourceView for the SqlDataSource instance specified as the owner, with the specified (String) value for the name, and within the HttpContext provided as the third parameter. This replaces the existing SqlDataSourceView for the specified SqlDataSource control.

SqlDataSourceView Properties. The `SqlDataSourceView` exposes the same `SelectCommand`, `SelectCountCommand`, `SelectParameters`, `UpdateCommand`, `UpdateParameters`, `UpdateMode`, `InsertCommand`, `InsertParameters`, `DeleteCommand`, `DeleteParameters`, `DeleteMode`, `SortParameterName`, `FilterExpression`, `FilterParameters`, and `OldValuesParameterFormatString` properties as the `SqlDataSource` control. Additionally there are properties that provide information about the `SqlDataSourceView`'s capabilities, set the sorting order, and expose the name of the `SqlDataSourceView` instance (see Table 3.11).

TABLE 3.11. The SqlDataSourceView Properties

Property	Description
Name	Returns the name of this `SqlDataSourceView` instance as a `String`.
CanDelete	Returns a `Boolean` value that indicates whether rows can be deleted from this `SqlDataSourceView` instance. Returns `False` if the `DeleteCommand` property is empty.
CanInsert	Returns a `Boolean` value that indicates whether rows can be inserted into this `SqlDataSourceView` instance. Returns `False` if the `InsertCommand` property is empty.
CanUpdate	Returns a `Boolean` value that indicates whether rows can be updated within this `SqlDataSourceView` instance. Returns `False` if the `UpdateCommand` property is empty.
CanSort	Returns a `Boolean` value that indicates whether the rows in this `SqlDataSourceView` instance can be sorted. Returns `False` if the `DataSourceMode` property of the owning `SqlDataSource` control property is not set to `DataSet`.
CanPage	Returns a `Boolean` value that indicates whether the output can be processed as separate pages within this `SqlDataSourceView` instance. Reflects the setting of the `EnableSqlPaging` property of the parent `SqlDataSource` instance.
CanRetrieveTotalRowCount	Returns a `Boolean` value that indicates whether the total number of rows can be determined. Returns `True` if the `SelectCountCommand` property of the parent `SqlDataSource` instance is set, or if the `DataSourceMode` is set to `DataSet` and paging is not enabled.

continues

TABLE 3.11. The SqlDataSourceView Properties (continued)

Property	Description
SortExpression	Sets or returns a String that defines the sort order for the rows in this SqlDataSourceView instance. This is a comma-delimited list of column names, each optionally suffixed with DESC for a descending sort. This property applies only when the DataSourceMode property of the owning SqlDataSource control is set to DataSet.

SqlDataSourceView Methods. The SqlDataSourceView exposes the same Select method as the SqlDataSource control, plus three methods that operate directly on rows within this SqlDataSourceView instance (see Table 3.12).

TABLE 3.12. The SqlDataSourceView Methods

Method	Description
Delete(*parameters*)	Deletes row(s) using the parameters specified as a dictionary of name/value pairs. Returns the number of rows deleted as an Integer.
Insert(*values*)	Inserts a new row using the values specified as a dictionary of name/value pairs. Returns the number of rows inserted as an Integer.
Update(*parameters*, *values*)	Updates row(s) using the parameters specified as a dictionary of name/value pairs, and the values specified as a dictionary of name/value pairs. Returns the number of rows updated as an Integer.

SqlDataSourceView Events. The SqlDataSourceView exposes the same Selected, Selecting, Updated, Updating, Deleted, Deleting, Inserted, and Inserting events as the SqlDataSource control.

The AccessDataSource Control

The AccessDataSource control inherits from SqlDataSource and carries a slightly changed set of interface members to make it easier to work with Access database files. Listing 3.9 shows an abridged declaration of the control.

LISTING 3.9. Declaring an AccessDataSource Control

```
<asp:AccessDataSource id="String" runat="server"
  DataFile="String"
  DataSourceMode= "[DataSet|DataReader]"
  SelectCommand="String"
  InsertCommand="String"
  UpdateCommand="String"
  DeleteCommand="String"
  ...
  OnSelecting="SqlDataSourceCommandEventHandler"
  ...
  OnDeleted="SqlDataSourceStatusEventHandler">

    <SelectParameters>
        [<System.Web.UI.WebControls.Parameter ...>]
    </SelectParameters>
    <UpdateParameters>
        [<System.Web.UI.WebControls.Parameter ...>]
    </UpdateParameters>
    <InsertParameters>
        [<System.Web.UI.WebControls.Parameter ...>]
    </InsertParameters>
    <DeleteParameters>
        [<System.Web.UI.WebControls.Parameter ...>]
    </DeleteParameters>
    <FilterParameters>
        [<System.Web.UI.WebControls.Parameter ...>]
    </FilterParameters>

  ...
</asp:AccessDataSource>
```

Table 3.13 shows the two constructors of the `AccessDataSource` control, and the differences between the properties of the `AccessDataSource` control and its base class the `SqlDataSource` control.

TABLE 3.13. The AccessDataSource Control Interface

Property	Description
`AccessDataSource()`	Creates a new `AccessDataSource` instance with the default values for all the properties.
`AccessDataSource` `(datafile, select)`	Creates a new `AccessDataSource` instance with the specified values for the `DataFile` and `SelectCommand` properties. All other properties are set to the default value.

continues

TABLE 3.13. The AccessDataSource Control Interface (continued)

Property	Description
DataFile	Sets or returns the relative path to the .mdb database file as a String and is used in place of the ConnectionString property in the control declaration. The value is passed to the Server.MapPath method to convert it to a full physical path before appending it to the ConnectionString.
ConnectionString	The OLE-DB connection string for the source Access database, including the value of the DataFile property.
ProviderName	Inherited from the SqlDataSource base class, but not supported and cannot be set or retrieved in the AccessDataSource control.
SqlCacheDependency	Inherited from the SqlDataSource base class, but not supported and cannot be set or retrieved in the AccessDataSource control.

As with the SqlDataSource control, the AccessDataSource control exposes its data through an AccessDataSourceView instance. This inherits from SqlDataSourceView, with the only difference being that the constructor accepts an AccessDataSource as the first parameter (see Table 3.14).

TABLE 3.14. The AccessDataSourceView Constructor

Constructor	Description
AccessDataSourceView (owner, name, context)	Creates a new instance of an AccessDataSourceView for the AccessDataSource instance specified as the owner, with the specified (String) value for the name, and within the HttpContext provided as the third parameter. This replaces the existing AccessDataSourceView for the specified AccessDataSource control.

The Base Classes for the Data Source Controls

The data source controls we've looked at so far connect to a relational database and extract data as a series of rows and columns. However, it's becoming increasingly common to encounter data that is persisted or exposed as XML. This data can be a simple "flat" representation of, for example, a relational database table. However, XML data is often hierarchical in nature.

In order to be able to handle these two types of XML data formats, the data source controls available in ASP.NET are descended for two different base classes.

- The DataSourceControl class is the base class for the data source controls that are designed to handle only flat data. This includes the SqlDataSource control we looked at earlier in this chapter and the AccessDataSource control that descends from it. The DataSourceControl class is also the base class for the DataSetDataSource control and the ObjectDataSource control, which we'll look at in more detail later in this chapter.

- The HierarchicalDataSourceControl class is the base class for the two data source controls that can handle hierarchical XML data. These are the XmlDataSource control and the SiteMapDataSource control. We look at the XmlDataSource control in the next subsection. The SiteMapDataSource control is discussed in Chapter 5.

The XmlDataSource Control

The XmlDataSource control loads an XML document and exposes the data it contains. If the XML has nested elements, giving a hierarchical structure, the control exposes the data in this way. The result is that data cannot then be bound to controls that accept only flat data structures such as a table or an array—for example, the ordinary "list" controls. However, controls such as the TreeView expect to receive hierarchical data, and for these the XmlDataSource control is the obvious choice. Listing 3.10 shows how you can bind hierarchical XML data to a TreeView control using an XmlDataSource control.

LISTING 3.10. Using an XmlDataSource Control to Populate a TreeView Control

```
<asp:XmlDataSource id="ds1" runat="server"
                   DataFile="XmlDataSource.xml" />

<asp:TreeView id="tv1" DataSourceID="ds1" runat="server">
  <DataBindings>
    <asp:TreeNodeBinding DataMember="Manufacturer" TextField="Make" />
    <asp:TreeNodeBinding DataMember="Car" TextField="Model" />
    <asp:TreeNodeBinding DataMember="Package" TextField="Trim" />
  </DataBindings>
</asp:TreeView>
```

Figure 3.10 shows the results of the code in Listing 3.10, where the XML file contains a list of car models and the fictional types of accessory packs that might be available for them. Listing 3.11 shows the actual XML file, with some repeated elements removed for clarity.

LISTING 3.11. The XML Source File for the XmlDataSource Control Example

```
<Automobiles>
  <Manufacturer Make="Audi">
    <Car Model="A4" Id="02347">
      <Package Trim="Sport" />
      <Package Trim="Luxury" />
      <Package Trim="Cold Weather" />
    </Car>
    <Car Model="A6" Id="02932">
      <Package Trim="Sport" />
      <Package Trim="Luxury" />
      <Package Trim="Cold Weather" />
    </Car>
    <Car Model="A8" Id="09381">
      <Package Trim="Sport" />
      <Package Trim="Luxury" />
      <Package Trim="Cold Weather" />
    </Car>
  </Manufacturer>
  ... more <Manufacturer> elements here ...
</Automobiles>
```

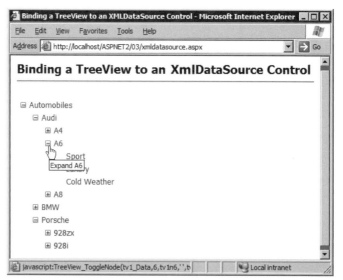

FIGURE 3.10. Binding a TreeView to an XmlDataSource control

Declaring an XmlDataSource Control

Although they inherit from different base classes, the XmlDataSource class exposes many of the same interface members as the SqlDataSource control. This means that attributes you use with the SqlDataSource control (such as EnableCaching and CacheDuration) apply equally to the XmlDataSource control. However, the control can access an XML document as a disk file (or as a resource that dynamically creates and returns XML), so there are different attributes that specify how to load the XML document, plus a series of nested elements that allow the source data to be declared inline (see Listing 3.12).

LISTING 3.12. Declaring an XmlDataSource Control

```
<asp:XmlDataSource id="String" runat="server"
  DataFile="String"
  SchemaFile="String"
  TransformFile="String"
  AutoSave="[True|False]"
  ReadOnly="[True|False]"
  XPath="String"
  EnableCaching="[True|False]"
  CacheDuration="Integer"
  CacheExpirationPolicy="[Absolute|Sliding]"
  CacheKeyDependency="String"
  OnTransforming="EventHandler" >

    <Data>
      [...Inline XML Data...]
    </Data>
    <Schema>
      [...Inline XML Schema...]
    </Schema>
    <Transform>
      [...Inline XSL/XSLT Transform...]
    </Transform>

</asp:XmlDataSource>
```

The attributes set in bold type in Listing 3.12 are those that have not been discussed previously in this chapter. The others behave exactly as described earlier for the SqlDataSource control.

The XmlDataSource Control Interface

The attributes and nested elements shown in bold type in Listing 3.12 correspond to the properties in Table 3.15. The Transforming event, specified by the OnTransforming attribute, is described in Table 3.17.

TABLE 3.15. The XmlDataSource Control Properties

Property	Description
DataFile	Sets or returns the relative or absolute path to the XML data file to use as input. This property accepts a String value.
SchemaFile	Sets or returns the relative or absolute path to a schema that defines the structure of the XML. This property accepts a String value.
TransformFile	Sets or returns the relative or absolute path to an XSL or XSLT document that will be used to transform the XML data before it is exposed by the control. This property accepts a String value.
AutoSave	Sets or returns a Boolean value that indicates whether changes to the data will be saved back to the XML disk file automatically, as soon as a change is made. The default is True. When set to False, the Save method must be called to update the XML disk file. This can be used to reduce disk accesses. It applies only when the XML document is specified using the DataFile property and not as inline data in the <Data> section or as a String specified for the Data property.
ReadOnly	Sets or returns a Boolean value that indicates whether the XML document will be opened in read-only mode. The default is True. When set to False, the XML document is opened in read/write mode and the CanInsert, CanUpdate, and CanDelete properties of the XmlDataSourceView will return True.
XPath	Sets or returns a String containing an XPath statement that filters or selects elements from the source document. It has the same kind of effect as applying a FilterExpression with the SqlDataSource control.
Data	Sets or returns the XML content that will be used as the source data, as a String. This property can be set declaratively using the Data child element within the main XmlDataSource element. The DataFile property must be empty in this case.
Schema	Sets or returns the schema content that defines the data structure, as a String. This property can be set declaratively using the Schema child element within the main XmlDataSource element. The SchemaFile property must be empty in this case.
Transform	Sets or returns the XSL or XSLT document that will be used to transform the data before it is exposed by the control, as a String. This property can be set declaratively using the Transform child element within the main XmlDataSource element. The TransformFile property must be empty in this case.

TABLE 3.15. The XmlDataSource Control Properties (continued)

Property	Description
TransformArgumentList	Sets or returns a reference to an `XsltArgumentList` instance containing the arguments that will be used in the transformation process when using the `TransformFile` or `Transform` properties to specify an XSLT stylesheet. This property should be set in the `OnTransforming` event to ensure that the arguments are available when the transformation is applied.

The `XmlDataSource` control exposes two methods you can use to interact with the control at runtime (see Table 3.16).

TABLE 3.16. The XmlDataSource Control Methods

Method	Description
GetXmlDataDocument()	Returns a reference to an `XmlDataDocument` instance that contains the XML representation of the source data from the control.
Save()	Persists the current values in the control to the XML disk file.

Finally, there is a single event you can handle to interact with the process (see Table 3.17).

TABLE 3.17. The XmlDataSource Control Event

Event	Description
Transforming	Raised before the control applies any XSL or XSLT stylesheet to the XML source data. Useful if you need to provide an `XsltArgumentList` reference to the control before the data is bound to other controls in the page.

As with all the data source controls, the data for the `XmlDataSource` control is exposed through an `XmlDataSourceView` instance. Because the various *xxx*DataSourceView classes all descend from the base class `DataSourceView`, the functionality they expose is fundamentally the same, even if the internal implementation of the interface members differs. This is the case with the `XmlDataSourceView`, which overrides the `Select` method.

The DataSetDataSource Control

The second data source control designed to handle XML data is the DataSetDataSource control, which works only with flat (nonhierarchical) formatted XML. One interesting possibility for manipulating XML data is to store it in and expose it through a DataSet. More than that, the nature of the DataSet allows it to move between a relational and an XML-based view of that data.

In effect, the DataSetDataSource control provides an interface to an instance of a DataSet and implements the same processes as other data source controls such as the SqlDataSource to support automated server-side data binding, as well as features that allow the XML source data to be updated. The DataSetDataSource also allows runtime code to access the data directly as a DataSet, giving almost ultimate flexibility in working with the data.

Declaring a DataSetDataSource Control

The declaration of the DataSetDataSource control is similar to that of the XmlDataSource control. However, as there is no facility to apply XSLT transformations to the data, properties related to that ability are not provided (see Listing 3.13).

LISTING 3.13. Declaring a DataSetDataSource Control

```
<asp:DataSetDataSource id="String" runat="server"
  DataFile="String"
  SchemaFile="String"
  AutoSave="[True|False]"
  ReadOnly="[True|False]"
  EnableCaching="[True|False]"
  CacheDuration="Integer"
  CacheExpirationPolicy="[Absolute|Sliding]"
  CacheKeyDependency="String"

    <Data>
      [...Inline XML Data...]
    </Data>
    <Schema>
      [...Inline XML Schema...]
    </Schema>

</asp:DataSetDataSource>
```

The DataSetDataSource Control Interface

The DataSetDataSource control implements the same set of properties as the XmlDataSource control, with the exception of the Transform, TransformFile, XPath, and TransformArgumentList properties.

The DataSetDataSource control does not implement the GetXmlDocument method of the XmlDataSource control, but it does implement the same Save method. There is also one method available for the DataSetDataSource that is not implemented by the XmlDataSource control. This method can be used to directly access and manipulate the DataSet that is holding the source data (see Table 3.18). This means that you can, for example, sort and filter the rows displayed in the bound control by setting the Sort and RowFilter properties of the default DataView for the tables in the DataSet.

TABLE 3.18. The DataSetDataSource Control Method

Method	Description
GetDataSet()	Returns a reference to the DataSet that is the source of the data from the control.

The DataSetDataSource control is unique among the data source controls in that it can reference more than one DataSetDataSourceView instance. This is because the DataSet it references can contain more than one table, so there will be a DataSetDataSourceView instance for each table.

Updating Data with an XmlDataSource or a DataSetDataSource Control

Both the XmlDataSource control and the DataSetDataSource control can be used to update the XML data they are referencing. However, there are some limitations to this feature.

- The ReadOnly property of the control must be set to False.
- The XML document must be referenced through the DataFile property and not declared inline within the control declaration (in other words, it can't be declared in the <Data> section).
- For the XmlDataSource control, there cannot be any XSLT transformation specified.
- For the DataSetDataSource control, there must be a schema loaded into the control, which fully defines the structure of the XML data and specifies a primary key field or column within the data.

If the `AutoSave` property is `False`, you can save the changes to the XML by calling the `Save` method of the control. Caching is enabled by default for the `XmlDataSource` and the `DataSetDataSource` controls and set to `Infinite`, so changes will be lost if you do not use the `AutoSave` feature or call the `Save` method after updating the XML content.

The ObjectDataSource Control

All of the data source controls covered so far encourage a "two-tier architecture" approach to building applications. They directly access the data store (the data layer), be it a relational database or an XML document. However, the `ObjectDataSource` control allows developers to work with three-tier or *n*-tier architectures by exposing data access layer and/or custom business objects in a way suited to declarative server-side data binding. Like the other data source controls, simply declaring the `ObjectDataSource` control on the page and linking it to a suitable data-bound control can provide "no-code" data binding—and even editing capabilities.

The only limitations are that the objects the `ObjectDataSource` control will access must be stateless, must expose a default constructor, and must have methods that can be directly and individually mapped to the `Select`, `Update`, `Insert`, and `Delete` actions of the control (although a subset of these can be supported if not all types of update actions are required, e.g., an application may be designed to support inserting of objects but not updates to them).

Data access to objects revolves around methods that the objects expose, so ordinary SQL statements cannot be used to select or update them. Instead, the objects themselves take care of extracting values from their own data store, exposing the values, and persisting changes where appropriate. This means that a data source control that accesses objects has to provide an interface that can be used to define the processes required to extract and update data. It does this by referencing the methods within the objects that perform these processes.

As a simple example, Listing 3.14 shows a custom business object class named `Products`, implemented within a Visual Basic file named `Products.vb` that exposes a single method named `ByCategory`, which returns a `DataSet` populated with a subset of rows from the sample Northwind database.

LISTING 3.14. A Class File That Defines a Simple Business Object

```
Imports System.Data
Imports System.Data.SqlClient
Imports System.Configuration

Public Class Products

  Public Sub New()
    MyBase.New()
  End Sub

  Public Function ByCategory(ByVal CategoryID As Integer) As DataSet
    Dim sConnect As String = ConfigurationSettings.ConnectionStrings _
                              ("nwind").ConnectionString
    Dim sSQL As String = "SELECT CategoryID, ProductName, " _
      & "UnitPrice, UnitsInStock, Discontinued FROM Products " _
      & "WHERE CategoryID = @CategoryID"
    Dim oConn As New SqlConnection(sConnect)
    Dim oDA As New SqlDataAdapter(sSQL, oConn)
    oDA.SelectCommand.Parameters.Add("CategoryID", SqlDbType.Int)
    oDA.SelectCommand.Parameters("CategoryID").Value = CategoryID
    Dim oDS As New DataSet()
    oDA.Fill(oDS, "Products")
    Return oDS
  End Function

End Class
```

ASP.NET 2.0 uses a special folder named `Code`, within the root folder of an application, to identify code that will be automatically compiled when the application runs. By simply placing the `Products.vb` file shown in Listing 3.14 into this folder, it will be compiled and made available to pages in the application automatically, just as if it had been pre-compiled and placed in the `\bin` folder.

Listing 3.15 shows the declaration of an `ObjectDataSource` that uses the custom business object shown in Listing 3.14 to extract the data and display it in a `GridView` control, based on the category value selected in a drop-down list. The overall approach is identical to that of using the `SqlDataSource` control (as demonstrated earlier in this chapter), with a `ControlParameter` control contained within the `ObjectDataSource` declaration to select the appropriate set of values. Figure 3.11 shows the result.

LISTING 3.15. Using an ObjectDataSource Control to Extract and Display Data through Business Objects

```
Select Category:
<asp:dropdownlist id="lstCategory" autopostback="True" runat="server">
  <asp:ListItem text="1" value="1" />
  <asp:ListItem text="2" value="2" />
  <asp:ListItem text="3" value="3" />
  <asp:ListItem text="4" value="4" />
  <asp:ListItem text="5" value="5" />
</asp:dropdownlist>

<asp:ObjectDataSource id="ds1" TypeName="Products"
    SelectMethod="ByCategory" runat="server">
  <SelectParameters>
    <asp:ControlParameter Name="CategoryID" ControlID="lstCategory"
        Type="Int32" PropertyName="SelectedValue" />
  </SelectParameters>
</asp:ObjectDataSource>

<asp:GridView id="grid1" DatasourceID="ds1" runat="server" />
```

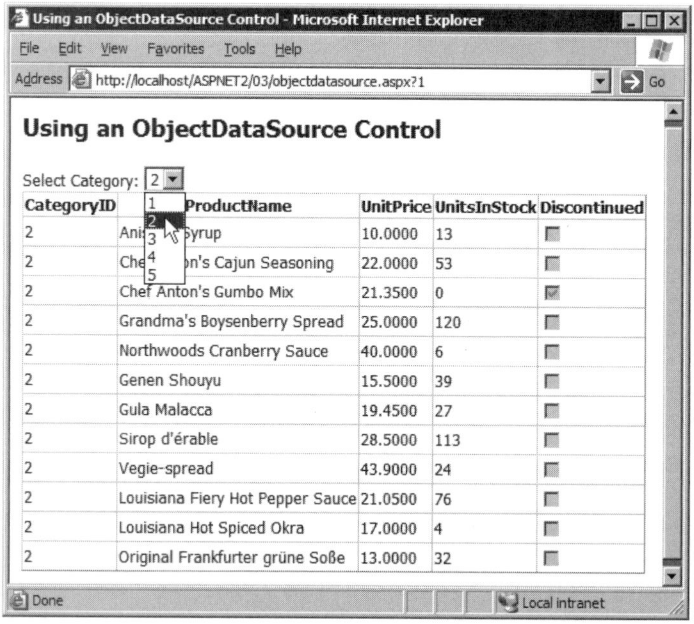

FIGURE 3.11. Using an ObjectDataSource control

Parameters are matched to the object method's parameters by name. In Listing 3.15 the parameter name is identified by the `Name` attribute. For methods that take several parameters, such as those that update data, an alternative to using a parameter for each value that needs updating is to use a strongly typed object. For example, consider a `Product` object, with data access methods like these:

```
Public Class Products
    Public Function ByCategory(CategoryID As Integer) As DataSet
    Public Function Update(updatedProduct As Product) As DataSet
    Public Function Insert(updatedProduct As Product) As DataSet
    Public Function Delete(updatedProduct As Product) As DataSet
```

In this case the `TypeName` would still be `Products`, but the `DataObjectTypeName` could be set to `Product`. When the appropriate method is called by the `ObjectDataSource`, the type identified by `DataObjectTypeName` is instantiated and the parameters are matched to the public properties of the object.

Declaring an ObjectDataSource Control

The `ObjectDataSource` control exposes many of the same properties as the `SqlDataSource` control we examined earlier in this chapter. The main difference is that the operations on the data must be specified as methods of the objects referenced by the control (as demonstrated in Listing 3.15). The differences in the declaration of the `ObjectDataSource` control compared to the `SqlDataSource` control are set in bold in Listing 3.16.

LISTING 3.16. Declaring an ObjectDataSource Control

```
<asp:ObjectDataSource id="String" runat="server"
    DataObjectTypeName="String"
    TypeName="String"
    SelectMethod="String"
    SelectCountMethod="String"
    UpdateMethod="String"
    InsertMethod="String"
    DeleteMethod="String"
    EnablePaging="[True|False]"
    StartRecordParameterName="String"
    MaxRecordsParameterName="String"
    UpdateMode="[Optimistic|Pessimistic]"
    DeleteMode="[Optimistic|Pessimistic]"
    FilterExpression="String"
    SortParameterName="String"
    OldValuesParameterFormatString="String"
    EnableCaching="[True|False]"
```

continues

```
CacheDuration="Integer"
CacheExpirationPolicy="[Absolute|Sliding]"
CacheKeyDependency="String"
SqlCacheDependency="String"
OnSelecting="ObjectDataSourceSelectingEventHandler"
OnSelected="ObjectDataSourceStatusEventHandler"
OnUpdating="ObjectDataSourceMethodEventHandler"
OnUpdated="ObjectDataSourceStatusEventHandler"
OnInserting="ObjectDataSourceMethodEventHandler"
OnInserted="ObjectDataSourceStatusEventHandler"
OnDeleting="ObjectDataSourceMethodEventHandler"
OnDeleted="ObjectDataSourceStatusEventHandler"
OnObjectCreating="ObjectDataSourceObjectEventHandler"
OnObjectCreated="ObjectDataSourceObjectEventHandler"
OnObjectDisposing="ObjectDataSourceDisposingEventHandler" >

   <SelectParameters>
     [<System.Web.UI.WebControls.Parameter ...>]
   </SelectParameters>
   <UpdateParameters>
     [<System.Web.UI.WebControls.Parameter ...>]
   </UpdateParameters>
   <DeleteParameters>
     [<System.Web.UI.WebControls.Parameter ...>]
   </DeleteParameters>
   <InsertParameters>
     [<System.Web.UI.WebControls.Parameter ...>]
   </InsertParameters>
   <FilterParameters>
     [<System.Web.UI.WebControls.Parameter ...>]
   </FilterParameters>

</asp:ObjectDataSource>
```

The ObjectDataSource Control Interface

The boldfaced lines in Listing 3.16 of the ObjectDataSource control show the attributes, and hence the properties, that differ from those for the SqlDataSource control, as described in Table 3.19.

TABLE 3.19. The ObjectDataSource Control Properties

Property	Description
DataObjectTypeName	A String that contains the type name of the object to be used as the parameter type for the Insert, Update, and Delete methods.
TypeName	A String that contains the type name of the object to create. This can be a partially qualified name such as MyClass or a fully qualified name such as MyNamespace.MyClass.

TABLE 3.19. The ObjectDataSource Control Properties (continued)

Property	Description
SelectMethod	The method of the object to invoke for a SELECT operation. Any parameters required can be defined as the SelectParameters property or in the nested SelectParameters element of the control declaration.
SelectCountMethod	The method of the object to invoke to return a count of the total number of available objects. Selection and filtering can be applied in the usual way with parameters.
UpdateMethod	The method of the object to invoke for an UPDATE operation. Any parameters required can be defined as the UpdateParameters property or in the nested UpdateParameters element of the control declaration.
InsertMethod	The method of the object to invoke for an INSERT operation. Any parameters required can be defined as the InsertParameters property or in the nested InsertParameters element of the control declaration.
DeleteMethod	The method of the object to invoke for a DELETE operation. Any parameters required can be defined as the DeleteParameters property or in the nested DeleteParameters element of the control declaration.
EnablePaging	A Boolean value that specifies whether paging will be enabled within the control. When set to True, the StartRecordParameterName and MaxRecordsParameterName property values are used to specify the rows or objects retrieved.
StartRecordParameterName	The name of the value in the InputParameters collection that defines the index of the first row or object to return when paging is enabled.
MaxRecordsParameterName	The name of the value in the InputParameters collection that defines the maximum number of rows or objects to return when paging is enabled.

The ObjectDataSource has the same four methods as the SqlDataSource control, namely Select, Insert, Update, and Delete. Two constructors, listed in Table 3.20, can be used to create an instance of the control at runtime.

TABLE 3.20. The ObjectDataSource Control Constructors

Constructor	Description
ObjectDataSource()	Creates a new instance of an ObjectDataSource with the default values for all its properties.
ObjectDataSource (type, select)	Creates a new instance of an ObjectDataSource with the specified (String) value for the TypeName and SelectMethod properties.

The ObjectDataSource exposes the same set of events as the SqlDataSource, though these accept different types of "argument" classes. There are also three extra events for the ObjectDataSource, which are invoked before and after an instance of the class that the data source will use is created, and before it is disposed. Table 3.21 summarizes all the events and the argument types for the ObjectDataSource control.

TABLE 3.21. The ObjectDataSource Control Events

Event	Description
ObjectCreating	Raised immediately before the object specified by TypeName/DataObjectTypeName is created. An ObjectDataSourceEventArgs instance passed to the event handler exposes a single property: • ObjectInstance: A reference to the instance of the object on which the current operation is taking place.
ObjectCreated	Raised immediately after the object specified by TypeName/DataObjectTypeName has been created. An ObjectDataSourceEventArgs instance is passed to the event handler. (See the ObjectCreating event for details.)
ObjectDisposing	Raised just before the object specified by TypeName/DataObjectTypeName is disposed. An ObjectDataSourceDisposingEventArgs instance passed to the event handler exposes two properties: • ObjectInstance: A reference to the instance of the object on which the current operation is taking place. • Cancel: A Boolean property that can be set to True to cancel the current operation.

TABLE 3.21. The ObjectDataSource Control Events (continued)

Event	Description
Selecting	Raised before the `Select` method is executed. An `ObjectDataSourceSelectingEventArgs` instance passed to the event handler exposes two properties: • `InputParameters`: A reference to an ordered dictionary (`IDictionary`) that is used to hold any values that need to be passed to the current method of the `ObjectDataSource`. • `ExecutingSelectCount`: A Boolean value that is `True` if the current operation is one that will return only a count of the object instances available or `False` if it will return a collection of object instances.
Selected	Raised after the `Select` method completes. An `ObjectDataSourceStatusEventArgs` instance passed to the event handler exposes four properties: • `OutputParameters`: A reference to an ordered dictionary (`IDictionary`) that contains the values that were passed to the current method of the `ObjectDataSource`. • `ReturnValue`: Returns a reference (as an `Object` data type) to the object that was returned by the current method, or `Nothing` (`null` in C#) if the current method does not have a return value. • `Exception`: Returns an `Exception` instance if the method currently being executed fails. A reference to the actual exception that was raised by the object can be obtained from the `InnerException` property of this current exception. • `ExceptionHandled`: A Boolean value that you can set to `True` after handling any exception raised by the object to indicate that this exception should *not* be raised to the code that called this method.
Deleting	Raised before the `Delete` method is executed. An `ObjectDataSourceMethodEventArgs` instance passed to the event handler exposes a single property: • `InputParameters`: A reference to an ordered dictionary (`IDictionary`) that is used to hold any values that need to be passed to the current method of the `ObjectDataSource`.
Deleted	Raised after the `Delete` method completes. An `ObjectDataSourceStatusEventArgs` instance is passed to the event handler. (See the `Selected` event for details.)
Inserting	Raised before the `Insert` method is executed. An `ObjectDataSourceMethodEventArgs` instance is passed to the event handler. (See the `Deleting` event for details.)
Inserted	Raised after the `Insert` method completes. An `ObjectDataSourceStatusEventArgs` instance is passed to the event handler. (See the `Selected` event for details.)

continues

TABLE 3.21. The ObjectDataSource Control Events (continued)

Event	Description
Updating	Raised before the Update method is executed. An ObjectDataSourceMethodEventArgs instance is passed to the event handler. (See the Deleting event for details.)
Updated	Raised after the Update method completes. An ObjectDataSourceStatusEventArgs instance is passed to the event handler. (See the Selected event for details.)

Possible Forthcoming Data Source Controls

More data source controls are planned for future releases of ASP.NET, and the following may well find their way into the final release version:

- A WebServiceDataSource control to allow you to work with data exposed by Web Services
- An ExcelDataSource control to allow access to Excel worksheet files
- An OracleDataSource control to allow manipulation of data in an Oracle database without using OLE-DB or ODBC directly
- An IndexServiceDataSource control that will allow the Indexing Service catalog to be queried
- A SharePointDataSource control that will allow interaction with the database of resources maintained in Microsoft SharePoint

SUMMARY

This is the first of two related chapters that look at how ASP.NET 2.0 changes the way data can be accessed, displayed, and updated—without requiring any code to be written (or at least considerably reducing the code requirements). The combination of a data source control and server-side data binding, especially when matched up with a GridView or DetailsView control, provides a powerful new technique for working with data in your Web pages and Web applications.

In this chapter we started off with a brief look at what the new controls can achieve. The "no-code" examples we used show just how powerful the new approach is and how quickly and easily you can build pages that are attractive and highly interactive.

Then we moved on to look in more depth at the data source controls that power the process. The most commonly used is likely to be the `SqlDataSource` control, and we concentrated mainly on this in the chapter and the examples. However, we also looked at the other data source controls that are included in the beta release, and those that might be added as the product moves toward final release.

In the next chapter we continue on the same theme and complete the discussion of accessing, displaying, and manipulating data through the new controls. In particular, we look in depth at the new `GridView`, `DetailsView`, and `FormView` controls and the new simplified syntax for data binding.

4

The GridView, DetailsView, and FormView Controls

THIS IS THE SECOND in a two-chapter look at the new approach to accessing, displaying, and manipulating data introduced with ASP.NET 2.0. This new approach is based around the concept of data source controls and the new GridView, DetailsView, and FormView bound controls. The previous chapter gave a brief overview of the process, demonstrated the ease with which it can be accomplished, and examined the data source controls in depth.

In this chapter we'll build on what you've seen so far by looking in more detail at the new controls for displaying rowset data. These powerful yet easy-to-use controls include a wide range of features that make building even the most complex types of data-bound pages a lot easier than in ASP.NET 1.x.

The topics we'll be covering include the following:

- The new GridView control for displaying rowset data as a table
- The new DetailsView control for displaying rowset data as individual pages
- The new FormView control that provides a fully templated interface
- The simplified syntax for data binding expressions and the new XML binding syntax

We start with a detailed look at the `GridView` control. You saw some examples of this control at the start of Chapter 3, but here you'll see how flexible it is and how easily it can be declared and used in even quite complex scenarios.

The GridView Control

One of the most useful controls introduced with ASP.NET 1.0 was the `DataGrid`. This control makes it easy to display rowsets of data, provides plenty of opportunities for formatting the output, and even supports inline editing of the data. However, to use a `DataGrid` you still have to write code that generates the rowset and then binds it to the `DataGrid` control at runtime.

As you saw in Chapter 3, the new data source controls in ASP.NET 2.0 remove the need to write data access code and can also expose various kinds of data as rowsets suitable for data binding to any of the ASP.NET server controls. However, to take maximum advantage of these data source controls, Microsoft has added a new grid control in version 2.0. The `GridView` control enables data to be displayed, sorted, and edited without having to write any code at all. It can even provide a paging facility and—when combined with the `DetailsView` control that you'll read more about later in this chapter—enables you to create pages that allow new data rows to be inserted.

An Overview of the GridView Control

In basic terms, the `GridView` is similar to the version 1.0 `DataGrid` (which is, of course, still provided within the .NET Framework). It exposes many of the same features for formatting the data content using style attributes and templates. However, it adds a few extra features, such as support for multiple primary keys, extra opportunities for customizing the appearance, and new column types and templating options. There is also a new model for handling or canceling events. The aims of the `GridView`, `DetailsView`, and `FormView` controls are the following:

- To support the new data source controls by exposing a binding model that allows developers to display data without the need to write any code

- To provide features such as sorting, paging, editing, and updating of the data without requiring any code to be written

- To support the adaptive page rendering approach used in other controls in version 2.0, providing output that is compatible with mobile devices and other user agents
- To add features requested by users of the version 1.0 DataGrid control, such as multiple-field primary keys, hyperlink columns that have more than one data field, columns with checkboxes, and columns with standard buttons
- To provide better templating options to support custom paging and better support for null values

While the GridView control does have an object model similar to that of the DataGrid, it is not 100% backward compatible. You can't just switch from a DataGrid to a GridView in your pages without some reworking of the attributes and code. In general, you may find that it's better to use the GridView when you build new pages that take advantage of its capabilities, rather than trying to retrofit it into existing pages. Also note that the GridView does not support automatic insert operations for new rows—the associated DetailsView control is used to provide this feature.

Declaring a GridView Control

The GridView is obviously quite a complex control and has a correspondingly large number of properties and events. Listing 4.1 shows the general declaration of a GridView control and the types of values used for the attributes. The tables in the following subsections list and describe all of the properties, except for the generic styling properties (which are familiar from the DataGrid control).

LISTING 4.1. The General Declaration of a GridView Control

```
<asp:GridView id="String" runat="server"
  DataSourceID="String"
  DataKeyNames="[column-name[,column-name]]"
  AutoGenerateColumns="[True|False]"
  RowStyle-[PropertyName]="[value]"
  AlternatingRowStyle-[PropertyName]="[value]"
  AllowSorting="[True|False]"
  AllowPaging="[True|False]"
  PageSize="Integer"
  PageIndex="Integer"
  PagerStyle-[PropertyName]="[value]"
  AutoGenerateSelectButton="[True|False]"
  SelectedIndex="Integer"
  SelectedRowStyle-[PropertyName]="[value]"
  AutoGenerateDeleteButton="[True|False]"
```

continues

```
AutoGenerateEditButton="[True|False]"
EditIndex="Integer"
EditRowStyle-[PropertyName]="[value]"
EmptyDataRowStyle-[PropertyName]="[value]"
EmptyDataText="String"
ShowHeader="[True|False]"
UseAccessibleHeader="[True|False]"
HeaderStyle-[PropertyName]="[value]"
ShowFooter="[True|False]"
FooterStyle-[PropertyName]="[value]"
RowHeaderColumn="String"
SummaryViewColumn="String"
SummaryTitleStyle-[PropertyName]="[value]"
DetailNextRowText="String"
DetailPreviousRowText="String"
DetailSummaryText="String"
DetailLinkStyle-[PropertyName]="[value]"
DetailTitleStyle-[PropertyName]="[value]"
BackImageUrl="String"
CellPadding="Integer"
CellSpacing="Integer"
Caption="String"
CaptionAlign="[Bottom|Top|Left|Right|NotSet]"
GridLines="[Both|Horizontal|Vertical|None]"
HorizontalAlign="[Center|Justify|Left|Right|NotSet]"
EnableSortingAndPagingCallbacks="[True|False]"
OnRowDeleting="GridViewDeleteEventHandler"
OnRowDeleted="GridViewDeletedEventHandler "
OnRowUpdating="GridViewUpdateEventHandler"
OnRowUpdated="GridViewUpdatedEventHandler"
OnRowEditing="GridViewEditEventHandler"
OnRowCancelingEdit="GridViewCancelEditEventHandler"
OnPageIndexChanging="GridViewPageEventHandler"
OnPageIndexChanged="EventHandler"
OnSelectedIndexChanging="GridViewSelectEventHandler"
OnSelectedIndexChanged="EventHandler"
OnSorting="GridViewSortEventHandler"
OnSorted="EventHandler"
OnRowCommand="GridViewCommandEventHandler"
OnRowCreated ="GridViewRowEventHandler"
OnRowDataBound="GridViewRowEventHandler" >

  <[...TableItemStyle...] />
  ...See The Nested TableItemStyle Elements...

  <[...Style...] />
  ...See The Nested Style Elements...

  <PagerStyle />
  <PagerSettings />
  ...See The Nested PagerStyle and PagerSettings Elements...
```

```
<PagerTemplate />

<EmptyDataTemplate />

<ColumnFields>
  <...[column-definition]... />
  ...See Defining the Columns in a GridView Control...
</ColumnFields>
```

```
</asp:GridView>
```

As with the `DataGrid` control, the `GridView` contains nested elements that further define the appearance and behavior of the control. The `PagerTemplate` section is used to declare the content and controls that will be displayed in the pager row of the `GridView` control when you turn off automatic generation of the pager elements. The `EmptyDataTemplate` is used to declare the content (and controls if required) that will be displayed instead of the HTML table that the `GridView` normally generates when the data source to which it is bound is empty (in other words, it contains no data rows).

The other nested elements in Listing 4.1 are examined in more detail later in this chapter. The relevant section names are shown in the listing to help you locate them.

The Properties and Attributes of the GridView Control

The attributes shown in Listing 4.1 are documented in Tables 4.1, 4.2, and 4.3. These attributes set the corresponding properties of the control, though (as with other server controls) you can read and set these properties at run-time as well. Table 4.1 lists the properties that correspond to the attributes in the same order as in the control declaration shown in Listing 4.1. (Note that style-related properties and attributes are not included in this table.)

The attributes shown in Listing 4.1 that do not appear in Table 4.1, such as `RowStyle-[PropertyName]` and `PagerStyle-[PropertyName]`, are used to specify the style of various sections of the output generated by the `GridView`. As with other Web Forms controls, the attribute sets a property of the object that generates that specific section of the output. For example, the following code sets the foreground color of the rows in the output to red:

```
RowStyle-ForeColor="Red"
```

The `GridView` also supports theming, so it accepts attributes and exposes properties such as `SkinID` and `EnableTheming` that you can use to specify the theme for the control. See Chapter 7 for more details of the Themes feature in ASP.NET 2.0.

TABLE 4.1. The Properties and Attributes of the GridView Control

Property/Attribute	Description
DataSourceID	Sets or returns a `String` value that is the ID of the data source control that supplies the data for the `GridView` and through which any updates will be processed.
DataKeyNames	Sets or returns a `String Array` that specifies the primary key fields/columns for the rows. It is set in a control declaration attribute as a comma-delimited list. These keys are used to uniquely identify each row when performing updates or deletes in the source data. By default, the specified columns are displayed as read-only when in edit mode.
AutoGenerateColumns	Sets or returns a `Boolean` value that specifies whether the control should create columns based on the structure of the source rows (`True`, the default) or use the column definitions declared in a `<ColumnFields>` element (`False`).
AllowSorting	Sets or returns a `Boolean` value that indicates whether the grid will support sorting and will display the column headings as hyperlinks. The default is `False`. If the `CanSort` property of the data source is `True`, the sorting process is handled automatically.
AllowPaging	Sets or returns a `Boolean` value that indicates whether the grid will support paging and will display controls for navigating from one page to another. The default is `False`. A `SqlDataSource` must have its `DataSourceMode` property set to `DataSet` for this to work.
PageSize	Sets or returns an `Integer` value that indicates the number of rows to be displayed on each page when paging is enabled.
PageIndex	Sets the current page number for the grid to display, or returns the current page number as an `Integer` value, when paging is enabled for the grid. This is the ordinal index of the page, starting from `0`.

TABLE 4.1. The Properties and Attributes of the GridView Control (continued)

Property/Attribute	Description
`AutoGenerateSelectButton`	Sets or returns a `Boolean` value that indicates whether a column containing a Select button will appear in the output.
`SelectedIndex`	Sets or returns the index of the row that will be displayed in selected mode as an `Integer` value.
`AutoGenerateDeleteButton`	Sets or returns a `Boolean` value that indicates whether a column containing a Delete button will appear in the output.
`AutoGenerateEditButton`	Sets or returns a `Boolean` value that indicates whether a column containing an Edit button will appear in the output.
`EditIndex`	Sets or returns the index of the row that will be displayed in edit mode as an `Integer` value.
`EmptyDataText`	Sets or returns a `String` value that will appear in the output of the control where a null value occurs in the source data.
`ShowHeader`	Sets or returns a `Boolean` value that indicates whether a header row will be included in the output of the control.
`UseAccessibleHeader`	Sets or returns a `Boolean` value that indicates whether the HTML rendering of the `<th>` elements that display the column headings will include the `scope` attribute to assist nonvisual page reader applications and specialist user agents.
`ShowFooter`	Sets or returns a `Boolean` value that indicates whether a footer row will be included in the output from the control.
`RowHeaderColumn`	Sets or returns a `String` value that indicates the column to be used as the row header. This helps nonvisual page readers and specialist user agents to correctly identify the heading column for a row.
`SummaryViewColumn`	Sets or returns a `String` value that indicates the name of the column that will be shown when the control renders output to a mobile device. By default this is the first column. See Chapter 3 for more details of how tables are displayed on mobile devices.

continues

TABLE 4.1. The Properties and Attributes of the GridView Control (continued)

Property/Attribute	Description
DetailNextRowText	Sets or returns a String value that is the text to display for the link to the next column when the control renders output to a mobile device. The default is "Next Row".
DetailPreviousRowText	Sets or returns a String value that is the text to display for the link to the previous column when the control renders output to a mobile device. The default is "Previous Row".
DetailSummaryText	Sets or returns a String value that is the text to display for the link from details view back to summary view when the control renders output to a mobile device. The default is "summary view".
BackImageUrl	Sets or returns a String value that specifies the path to a graphics file that will be displayed as the background of the GridView control.
CellPadding	Sets or returns the number of pixels (as an Integer) between the content and border of each cell in the rendered HTML table that the GridView control generates.
CellSpacing	Sets or returns the number of pixels (as an Integer) between each cell in the rendered HTML table that the GridView control generates.
Caption	Sets or returns a String value that is the caption to display for the GridView control.
CaptionAlign	Sets or returns a value from the TableCaptionAlign enumeration that defines how the caption will be aligned with the GridView. Possible values are NotSet (the default), Bottom, Top, Left, and Right.
GridLines	Sets or returns a value from the GridLines enumeration that defines whether the borders of the cells that make up the GridView control output will be visible. Possible values are Both (the default), Horizontal, Vertical, and None.
HorizontalAlign	Sets or returns a value from the HorizontalAlign enumeration that defines how the GridView control will be horizontally aligned within the page. Possible values are NotSet (the default), Center, Justify, Left, and Right.

TABLE 4.1. The Properties and Attributes of the GridView Control (continued)

Property/Attribute	Description
EnableSortingAndPagingCallbacks	Sets or returns a `Boolean` value that, when `True`, causes client-side script to be injected into the page that initiates a callback to the server after the grid has been sorted or a different page of rows has been selected.

Declarative and Dynamic Version 1.x–Style Data Source Assignment. Two properties of the `GridView` control can be used to specify data binding to a rowset that you generate in code, in the same way that you had to do with the `DataGrid` and other list controls in ASP.NET 1.x (see Table 4.2). You won't use these properties if you take advantage of the "no-code" approach to displaying data—you'll just use the `DataSourceID` instead.

TABLE 4.2. The Data Binding Properties and Attributes of the GridView Control

Property/Attribute	Description
DataSource	Sets or returns a `String` value that indicates the specific item within the specified `DataSource` that will be used as the data source for the control. Sets or returns a reference to an `Object` that exposes the data rows or collection members that the `GridView` control will display.
DataMember	Sets or returns a `String` value that indicates the specific item within an `IListSource` instance that will be used as the data source for the control. For example, when the `DataSource` is a `DataSet` (which could contain more than one table), this property is the table name.

Read-Only Properties. The `GridView` control exposes a series of properties that are read-only at runtime and can be used to get information about the control or to get a reference to the various objects that together generate the control output (see Table 4.3). Again, if you use the no-code approach you won't need to access these properties.

TABLE 4.3. The Read-Only Properties of the GridView Control

Property/Attribute	Description
DataKeys	Returns a `DataKeyArray`, which is a collection of `DataKey` instances, one for each row in the `GridView`. Each `DataKey` instance contains a name/value pair for each key listed in the `DataKeyNames` property and the corresponding value for the current row. In other words, it exposes the primary key value(s) for each row in the grid.
SelectedDataKey	Returns a `DataKey` instance that exposes the primary key values for the row that is in selected mode.
SelectedValue	Returns an `Object` containing the current value of the `DataKey` for the current row.
SortExpression	Returns a `String` value that contains the current sort expression for the control.
SortDirection	Returns a value from the `SortDirection` enumeration that indicates the direction of the current sort expression. Valid values are `Ascending` and `Descending`.
PageCount	Returns an `Integer` value that indicates the number of pages available when paging is enabled, based on the number of rows in the data source and the setting of the `PageSize` property.
ColumnFields	Returns a `DataControlFieldCollection` that represents all of the columns (all the *xxx*`Fields`) in the grid control.
Rows	Returns a `GridViewRowCollection` that represents all of the data-bound rows in the grid control, excluding any header, footer, or pager rows and excluding the null row if the data source returns no rows.
SelectedRow	Returns a reference to the `GridViewRow` instance that represents the row in the grid control output that is currently in selected mode.
HeaderRow	Returns a reference to the `GridViewRow` instance that represents the header row of the grid control output.
FooterRow	Returns a reference to the `GridViewRow` instance that represents the footer row of the grid control output.
TopPagerRow	Returns a reference to the `GridViewRow` instance that represents the row at the top of the grid control output that contains the pager controls.

TABLE 4.3. The Read-Only Properties of the GridView Control (continued)

Property/Attribute	Description
BottomPagerRow	Returns a reference to the `GridViewRow` instance that represents the row at the bottom of the grid control output that contains the pager controls.
PagerSettings	Returns a reference to the `PagerSettings` instance that represents the appearance of the pager rows. The `PagerSettings` options are described later in this chapter.

The DataBind Method of the GridView Control

When a data source control and a `GridView` are combined (as shown in Chapter 3), there is no need to write code to initiate data binding, as you would with other data-bound controls such as the `DataGrid`. The `DataBind` method of the `GridView` is called automatically. However, this method is also declared as `Public` and so is exposed for use in your own code if required. If you bind a `GridView` to a source of data other than a data source control, using the `DataSource` and `DataMember` properties, you must call the `DataBind` method yourself.

The Events of the GridView Control

The `GridView` control raises a series of events as it binds to a data source, generates the output, and responds to user interaction (see Table 4.4). You can handle these events to provide custom output, interact with the output process, and execute code in response to user actions.

TABLE 4.4. The Data Binding Events of the GridView Control

Event	Description
PageIndexChanging	Raised when a pager navigation control is activated, before the grid changes to the new page. Passes a `GridViewPageEventArgs` instance to the event handler, which exposes the following properties: • `NewPageIndex`: An `Integer` that is the ordinal index of the page that will be shown next. • `Cancel`: A `Boolean` property that can be set to `True` to prevent changes to the page.
PageIndexChanged	Raised when a pager navigation control is activated, after the grid has displayed the new page. Passes a standard `EventArgs` instance to the event handler.

continues

TABLE 4.4. The Data Binding Events of the GridView Control (continued)

Event	Description
RowCancelingEdit	Raised when the Cancel command is activated for a row that is in edit mode. Passes a GridViewCancelEditEventArgs instance to the event handler, which exposes the following properties:
	• RowIndex: An Integer value indicating the index of the row within the data source.
	• Cancel: A Boolean property that can be set to True to prevent the edit operation from being canceled.
RowCommand	Raised when a control in the rows of the grid causes a postback. This command may be one of the predefined buttons such as Edit, Cancel, Delete, or Update, or it may be a custom command. Passes a GridViewCommandEventArgs instance to the event handler, which exposes the following properties:
	• CommandSource: A reference to the control that raised the event.
	• CommandArgument: The value of the CommandArgument property of the control that raised the event.
	• CommandName: The value of the CommandName property of the control that raised the event.
RowCreated	Raised when a new row is created in the source rowset for the grid. Passes a GridViewRowEventArgs instance to the event handler, which exposes the following property:
	• Row: Returns a reference to the current row.
RowDataBound	Raised for each row in the grid after it has been bound to its data source row, allowing the output for the row to be modified. Passes a GridViewRowEventArgs instance to the event handler (see the RowCreated event).
RowDeleting	Raised before the data source control deletes a row in the data source. Passes a GridViewDeleteEventArgs instance to the event handler, which exposes the following properties:
	• Keys: An IOrderedDictionary instance containing the primary key values for the row.
	• Values: An IOrderedDictionary instance containing the non-key values currently in the row.
	• RowIndex: An Integer value indicating the index of the row within the data source rowset.
	• Cancel: A Boolean property that can be set to True to cancel the delete operation.

TABLE 4.4. The Data Binding Events of the GridView Control (continued)

Event	Description
RowDeleted	Raised after the data source control has deleted a row from the data source. Passes a `GridViewDeletedEventArgs` instance to the event handler, which exposes the following properties: • `Keys`: An `IOrderedDictionary` instance containing the primary key values for the row. • `Values`: An `IOrderedDictionary` instance containing the non-key values from the deleted row. • `AffectedRows`: An `Integer` value that indicates the number of rows that were deleted. • `Exception`: An `Exception` instance returned if the delete process fails. A reference to the actual exception that was raised by the database can be obtained from the `InnerException` property of this current exception. • `ExceptionHandled`: A `Boolean` value that you can set to `True` after handling any exception raised by the delete process to indicate that this exception should *not* be raised to the code that called this method.
RowEditing	Raised when an `Edit` command in the grid is activated, before a row changes into edit mode. Passes a `GridViewEditEventArgs` instance to the event handler, which exposes the following properties: • `NewEditIndex`: An `Integer` you can set to the index of the row that will be placed in edit mode, or `-1` if no row will be in edit mode. • `Cancel`: A `Boolean` property that can be set to `True` to prevent the row from entering edit mode.
RowUpdating	Raised before the data source control updates a row in the data source. Passes a `GridViewUpdateEventArgs` instance to the event handler, which exposes the following properties: • `Keys`: An `IOrderedDictionary` instance containing the primary key values for the row. • `NewValues`: An `IOrderedDictionary` instance containing the values that will be placed into the row. • `OldValues`: An `IOrderedDictionary` instance containing the values currently in the row. • `RowIndex`: An `Integer` value indicating the index of the row within the data source rowset. • `Cancel`: A `Boolean` property that can be set to `True` to cancel the update operation.

continues

TABLE 4.4. The Data Binding Events of the GridView Control (continued)

Event	Description
RowUpdated	Raised after the data source control has updated a row in the data source. Passes a `GridViewUpdatedEventArgs` instance to the event handler, which exposes the following properties: • `Keys`: An `IOrderedDictionary` instance containing the primary key values for the row. • `NewValues`: An `IOrderedDictionary` instance containing the updated non-key values currently in the row. • `OldValues`: An `IOrderedDictionary` instance containing the non-key values that were in the row before the update process was executed. • `AffectedRows`: An `Integer` value that indicates the number of rows that were updated. • `KeepInEditMode`: A `Boolean` value that you can set to indicate whether the current row control should remain in edit mode or return to normal mode. • `Exception`: An `Exception` instance returned if the update process fails. A reference to the actual exception that was raised by the database can be obtained from the `InnerException` property of this current exception. • `ExceptionHandled`: A `Boolean` value that you can set to `True` after handling any exception raised by the update process to indicate that this exception should *not* be raised to the code that called this method.
SelectedIndexChanging	Raised when a `Select` command in the grid is activated, before the row is placed into selected mode. Passes a `GridViewSelectEventArgs` instance to the event handler, which exposes the following properties: • `NewSelectedIndex`: An `Integer` you can set to the index of the row that will be placed in selected mode, or –1 if no row will be in selected mode. • `Cancel`: A `Boolean` property that can be set to `True` to prevent the row from being placed into selected mode.
SelectedIndexChanged	Raised after a row has been placed into selected mode. Passes a standard `EventArgs` instance to the event handler.
Sorting	Raised when a column heading is activated to sort the rows in the grid. Passes a `GridViewSortEventArgs` instance to the event handler, which exposes the following properties: • `SortExpression`: A `String` containing the sort expression that will be applied. • `Cancel`: A `Boolean` property that can be set to `True` to prevent the sort.

TABLE 4.4. The Data Binding Events of the GridView Control (continued)

Event	Description
Sorted	Raised after the sorting process has completed. Passes a standard EventArgs instance to the event handler.

Handling a GridView Event.   The example of editing rows shown at the start of Chapter 3 (Listing 3.4) contains a Delete link for each row displayed in the GridView control. However, in the sample Northwind database that the page uses, rows cannot be deleted from the Shippers table because there are related child rows in other tables. As an example of handling the events raised by the GridView control, the page prevents these existing rows from being deleted by checking the value of the primary key.

The declaration of the GridView includes the OnRowDeleting attribute, which specifies that an event handler named CheckDelete will be executed when the RowDeleting event is raised (see Listing 4.2). This occurs just before the GridView control instructs the data source control to delete the row. There is also a Label control on that page where the event handler will display any error message.

LISTING 4.2. Using the RowDeleting Event

```
<asp:GridView id="grid1" DataSourceID="ds1" runat="server"
    DataKeyNames="ShipperID"
    AutoGenerateEditButton="True"
    AutoGenerateDeleteButton="True"
    OnRowDeleting="CheckDelete" />

<asp:Label id="lblError" EnableviewState="False" runat="server" />
```

The event handler is shown in Listing 4.3. It simply extracts the value of the primary key from the Keys array passed to the event handler within the GridViewDeleteEventArgs instance—there is only one column in the primary key, so the code just accesses Keys(0). Then, if this key value is less than 4 (in other words, this is one of the existing rows in the table), it sets the Cancel property to True to prevent the GridView from continuing with the delete operation, and it displays a message in the Label control.

LISTING 4.3. The Event Handler for the RowDeleting Event

```
<script runat="server">
Sub CheckDelete(oSender As Object, oArgs As GridViewDeleteEventArgs)
  Dim iKey As Integer = CType(oArgs.Keys(0), Integer)
```

continues

```
If iKey < 4 Then
  oArgs.Cancel = True
  lblError.Text = "Cannot delete the original rows from the table"
End If
End Sub
</script>
```

Figure 4.1 shows the result. An attempt to delete the second row causes the event handler to display the error message below the grid. If you want to try deleting a row, use Enterprise Manager or type a SQL statement into Query Analyzer to insert a new row into the Shippers table, then run the page to delete the new row.

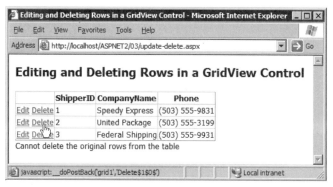

FIGURE 4.1. Handling the RowDeleting event for a GridView control

The Nested TableItemStyle Elements

You can optionally include, within the declaration of a `GridView` control, nested elements that define the style for various sections of the output generated as HTML table rows. Listing 4.4 shows the general declaration of these elements.

LISTING 4.4. The Nested TableItemStyle Elements

```
<[TableItemStyle]
  BackColor="Color"
  BorderColor="Color"
  BorderStyle="[Solid|Dashed|Dotted|Double|Groove|
               Ridge|Inset|Outset|None|NotSet]"
  BorderWidth="Unit"
  CssClass="String"
  Font-[Bold|Italic|Name|Names|Overline|Size|
        Strikeout|Underline]="[value]"
  ForeColor="Color"
  Height="Unit"
```

```
Width="Unit"
HorizontalAlign="[Center|Justify|Left|Right|NotSet]"
VerticalAlign="[Bottom|Middle|Top|NotSet]"
Wrap="[True|False]" />
```

The types of elements you can use (replacing [*TableItemStyle*] in Listing 4.4) are shown in Table 4.5.

TABLE 4.5. The TableItemStyle Element Types

TableItemStyle	Description
RowStyle	Sets the style and appearance for the data-bound rows within the grid.
AlternatingRowStyle	Sets the style and appearance for alternate data-bound rows within the grid.
SelectedRowStyle	Sets the style and appearance for the selected row within the grid.
EditRowStyle	Sets the style and appearance for the row that is in edit mode within the grid.
EmptyDataRowStyle	Sets the style and appearance for the row that will be displayed if there are no data rows in the source rowset.
HeaderStyle	Sets the style and appearance for the header row of the grid.
FooterStyle	Sets the style and appearance for the footer row of the grid.
PagerStyle	Sets the style and appearance for the row of the grid that contains the pager controls.

The Nested Style Elements

Another type of nested element that you can optionally include within the declaration of a GridView control is one that defines the style for the text and links that appear only when the grid is rendered on a small-screen or mobile device, where the output is displayed as separate summary and details views. Listing 4.5 shows the general declaration of these elements.

LISTING 4.5. The Nested Style Elements

```
<[TextStyle]
  BackColor="Color"
  BorderColor="Color"
  BorderStyle="[Solid|Dashed|Dotted|Double|Groove|
```

continues

```
                    Ridge|Inset|Outset|None|NotSet]"
BorderWidth="Unit"
CssClass="String"
Font-[Bold|Italic|Name|Names|Overline|Size|
                    Strikeout|Underline]="[value]"
ForeColor="Color"
Height="Unit"
Width="Unit" />
```

The three types of elements you can use (replacing [TextStyle] in Listing 4.5) are shown in Table 4.6.

TABLE 4.6. The Style Element Types

TextStyle	Description
SummaryTitleStyle	Sets the style and appearance of the title text displayed when the grid is displaying the data in summary view.
DetailTitleStyle	Sets the style and appearance of the title text displayed when the grid is displaying one of the rows in details view.
DetailLinkStyle	Sets the style and appearance of the links included in each row when the grid is displaying the data in summary view.

How the GridView Appears on Small-Screen and Mobile Devices. As you will surmise from the previous subsections, the GridView control automatically changes the way it renders the data when viewed on a small-screen or mobile device. When the page first loads, only the column specified by name as the SummaryViewColumn property is displayed. Each value in this single column is a link that changes the display to show all the column values for just that row (see Figure 4.2). These are the summary view and details view mentioned in the property descriptions in this chapter and demonstrated at the start of Chapter 3.

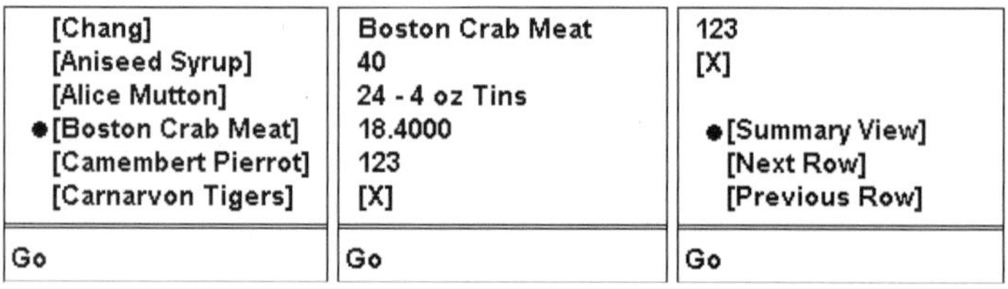

[Chang]	Boston Crab Meat	123
[Aniseed Syrup]	40	[X]
[Alice Mutton]	24 - 4 oz Tins	
●[Boston Crab Meat]	18.4000	●[Summary View]
[Camembert Pierrot]	123	[Next Row]
[Carnarvon Tigers]	[X]	[Previous Row]
Go	Go	Go

FIGURE 4.2. The GridView control on small-screen devices

The Nested PagerStyle and PagerSettings Elements

If you specify that the `GridView` will support paging by including the `AllowPaging="True"` attribute in the declaration, you can optionally specify in more detail how the section of the output that includes the page navigation controls will appear. You include a nested `PagerStyle` element, and/or a nested `PagerSettings` element, within the declaration of the `GridView` control.

The `PagerStyle` element is identical to the *TableItemStyle* elements shown earlier, with one extra attribute supported that indicates where row(s) containing the pager controls will appear:

```
Position="[Bottom|Top|TopAndBottom]"
```

The `PagerSettings` element defines the appearance of the paging controls in more detail. It allows you to use images, text links, or page numbers for the navigation controls. Listing 4.6 shows the general declaration of this element.

LISTING 4.6. The PagerSettings Element

```
<PagerSettings
  Mode="[NextPrevious|NextPreviousFirstLast|Numeric|NumericFirstLast]"
  FirstPageText="String"
  PreviousPageText="String"
  NextPageText="String"
  LastPageText="String"
  FirstPageImageUrl="url"
  PreviousPageImageUrl="url"
  NextPageImageUrl="url"
  LastPageImageUrl="url"
  PageButtonCount="Integer" />
```

Defining the Columns in a GridView Control

The `GridView` control can automatically generate the columns required to display the contents of the source data rows, just as the ASP.NET 1.0 `DataGrid` control does. The default for the `AutoGenerateColumns` property is `True`, indicating that an `AutoGeneratedField` bound column will be generated for each column in the data rows.

However, as with the `DataGrid`, you can set this property to `False` and specify the columns you want instead. This is useful if you want to use any of the special column types, other than the default type that displays the value as a text string (or in a `TextBox` control when the row is in edit mode) or as a `CheckBox` control (if the data is a `Boolean` or bit field).

Compared with the DataGrid control, there are some interesting new column types available for the GridView control.

The GridView Column Types

The GridView control supports a range of column types, allowing you to display the data within each column in a range of ways. Note that the controls are named as *xxx*Field. This is in order to differentiate them from the *xxx*Column controls used in a DataGrid control and because they are used to define the rows in a DetailsView control (as you'll see later in this chapter).

- The AutoGeneratedField column, the default column type, is used when the AutoGenerateColumns property is set to True. It acts like both a BoundField column and a CheckBoxField column. If the data is Boolean, a disabled CheckBox control appears with its Checked property signifying the value of the data. When the row is in edit mode, the CheckBox becomes enabled and the user can check or uncheck the CheckBox to change its value. If the data is of any other type, the value is displayed as text (in a TextBox control when in edit mode). However, note that the AutoGeneratedField column type should *not* be declared directly and is used only when the AutoGeneratedFields property is True for the GridView control. It also has one specific property that the other field types do not: DataType, which sets or returns the .NET type for the data that the column will display.

- The BoundField column works like that in the existing version 1.x DataGrid control. It displays the value from this column for each row as a text string (or in a TextBox control when the row is in edit mode).

- The ButtonField column displays a Button control in each row of this column. It can be rendered as a standard HTML button, a text LinkButton, or a clickable image. The caption, text, or URL can be set to the value from this column for each current row.

- The CheckBoxField column displays a CheckBox control in this column of each row. This column type is usually bound to a column in the data source that contains Boolean or bit values, and the CheckBox sets or reflects the value of this column for each row.

- The HyperLinkField column displays a HyperLink control in this column of each row. The value of the column, or other static values, can be used to set the `Text` and `NavigateUrl` properties of each `HyperLink` control.

- The `TemplateField` column provides a free-form section where the developer specifies all the details of the required user interface. A range of templates can be specified to display different controls depending on the current mode of the row. This type of column is useful when you need to include validation controls as well as interactive UI controls.

- The `CommandField` column displays a series of text links, HTML buttons, or clickable images used to change the mode of the current row for editing. Depending on the current mode and the property settings for the column, these buttons can include Select, Edit, Delete, Insert, and Cancel (or equivalent images provided by the developer).

Declaring a BoundField Column

In a `BoundField` column, the value in the column is displayed as text, except when the row is in edit mode, in which case it is displayed in a standard ASP.NET `TextBox` control. The `DataFormatString` property takes a `String` value that includes the placeholder `{0}` where the value should be inserted. And you can add one of the standard formatting characters, for example, using `{0:C}` to display the value as currency. Listing 4.7 shows the outline declaration of a `BoundField` column.

LISTING 4.7. Declaring a BoundField Column

```
<asp:BoundField
  DataField="String"
  DataFormatString="String"
  ApplyFormatInEditMode="[True|False]"
  TreatEmptyStringAsNull="[True|False]"
  NullDisplayText="String"
  HtmlEncode="[True|False]"
  ReadOnly="[True|False]"
  Visible="[True|False]"
  SortExpression="String"
  ShowHeader="[True|False]"
  HeaderText="String"
  AccessibleHeaderText="String"
  HeaderStyle-[PropertyName]="[value]"
  HeaderImageUrl="String"
  ItemStyle-[PropertyName]="[value]"
  FooterText="String"
  FooterStyle-[PropertyName]="[value]" />
```

The attributes shown in Listing 4.7 correspond to the properties in Table 4.7.

TABLE 4.7. The Properties and Attributes of the BoundField Control

Property/Attribute	Description
DataField	Sets or returns a String that is the name of the column in the source rows that will provide the data to display in this column of the grid.
DataFormatString	Sets or returns a String that contains the formatting details for the value displayed in this column.
ApplyFormatInEditMode	Sets or returns a Boolean value that indicates whether the formatting applied by the DataFormatString property when in normal mode will also be applied in edit mode; for example, displaying a currency symbol and trailing zeros in the text box in edit mode rather than just the numeric value.
TreatEmptyStringAsNull	Sets or returns a Boolean value that indicates whether an empty string in this column should be treated as null. This is useful when editing the data if the data source expects null values to be used when no value is present.
NullDisplayText	Sets or returns a String that is the text to display in the grid for rows that have a null value in this column.
HtmlEncode	Sets or returns a Boolean value that indicates whether the values in this column will be HTML-encoded before they are inserted into the output generated by the GridView control.
ReadOnly	Sets or returns a Boolean value that indicates whether the values in this column can be edited. If True, the column will not display a text box in edit mode.
Visible	Sets or returns a Boolean value that indicates whether this column is visible within the output generated by the grid control.
SortExpression	Sets or returns a String that defines the sort expression for this column, as a comma-delimited list of column names.
ShowHeader	Sets or returns a Boolean value that indicates whether the header for this column will be displayed.

TABLE 4.7. The Properties and Attributes of the BoundField Control (continued)

Property/Attribute	Description
HeaderText	Sets or returns a String that is the text to display in the header row for this column.
AccessibleHeaderText	Sets or returns a String that sets the value of the HTML abbr attribute of the <th> elements that display the column headings when this column is rendered. Nonvisual page reader applications and specialist user agents use the abbr attribute to assist in determining the layout of a table.
HeaderStyle	Returns a reference to a TableItemStyle instance that describes the style and formatting of the header for this column. The TableItemStyle properties were described earlier in this chapter.
HeaderImageUrl	Sets or returns a String that is the relative or absolute URL of an image to display in the header row for this column.
ItemStyle	Returns a reference to a TableItemStyle instance that describes the style and formatting of the values in the data-bound rows in this column.
FooterText	Sets or returns a String that is the text to display in the footer row for this column.
FooterStyle	Returns a reference to a TableItemStyle instance that describes the style and formatting of the footer for this column.

Declaring a ButtonField Column

A ButtonField is used when you want each row in the output to include a button or a clickable link that causes a postback, perhaps to display more details of the row or to open an image or other resource. It can display the link as a standard HTML button control (an <input type="submit"> element), a clickable image (an <input type="image"> element), or a text link (an <a> element with some client-side script to submit the page). Listing 4.8 shows the outline declaration of a ButtonField column.

LISTING 4.8. Declaring a ButtonField Column

```
<asp:ButtonField
   ButtonType="[Button|Image|Link]"
   CommandName="String"
   DataTextField="String"
   DataTextFormatString="String"
   CausesValidation="[True|False]"
   ValidationGroup="String"
   Text="String"
   ImageUrl="String"
   ApplyFormatInEditMode="[True|False]"
   HtmlEncode="[True|False]"
   Visible="[True|False]"
   SortExpression="String"
   ShowHeader="[True|False]"
   HeaderText="String"
   AccessibleHeaderText="String"
   HeaderStyle-[PropertyName]="[value]"
   HeaderImageUrl="String"
   ItemStyle-[PropertyName]="[value]"
   FooterText="String"
   FooterStyle-[PropertyName]="[value]" />
```

The attributes shown in bold in Listing 4.8 correspond to the properties in Table 4.8. The rest are the same as those listed for the `BoundField` control in Table 4.7.

TABLE 4.8. The Properties and Attributes of the ButtonField Control

Property/Attribute	Description
ButtonType	Sets or returns a value from the ButtonType enumeration (Button, Image, or Link) that specifies the type of control to create in each row for this column. The default is Link.
CommandName	Sets or returns a String value that is the CommandName property of the button in each row of the output.
DataTextField	Sets or returns a String that indicates the name of the column within the source data that will supply the value for the Text property of the control (the caption of a button or the text of a link).
DataTextFormatString	Sets or returns a String that contains the formatting information for the value in the row. Uses the same syntax as the DataFormatString property described for the BoundField control, using {0} as a placeholder.

TABLE 4.8. The Properties and Attributes of the ButtonField Control (continued)

Property/Attribute	Description
CausesValidation	Sets or returns a `Boolean` value that indicates whether the button will cause any validation controls in the page to validate their values and report any errors. The default is `True`.
ValidationGroup	Sets or returns a `String` that is the name of the group of validation controls that this button will be a member of. See Chapter 9 for more details about validation groups.
Text	Sets or returns a `String` that will be used in place of `DataTextField`, in other words, the static value for the caption or text of the link that is the same for every row.
ImageUrl	Sets or returns a `String` that is the relative or absolute URL of the image to display when the `ButtonType` property is set to `Image`.

Declaring a CheckBoxField Column

A `CheckBoxField` is used when you want every row to display a checkbox in this column, with the checkbox setting reflecting the value in the row. Because an HTML checkbox can be only on or off, this column type really only works with columns in the source data rows that contain `Boolean` or `bit` values. Listing 4.9 shows the outline declaration of a `CheckBoxField` column.

LISTING 4.9. Declaring a CheckBoxField Column

```
<asp:CheckBoxField
  DataField="String"
  ReadOnly="[True|False]"
  Text="String"
  ApplyFormatInEditMode="[True|False]"
  HtmlEncode="[True|False]"
  InsertVisible="[True|False]"
  Visible="[True|False]"
  SortExpression="String"
  ShowHeader="[True|False]"
  AccessibleHeaderText="String"
  HeaderText="String"
  HeaderStyle-[PropertyName]="[value]"
  HeaderImageUrl="String"
  ItemStyle-[PropertyName]="[value]"
  FooterText="String"
  FooterStyle-[PropertyName]="[value]" />
```

The two attributes shown in bold in Listing 4.9 correspond to the properties in Table 4.9. The rest are the same as those listed for the `BoundField` control in Table 4.7.

TABLE 4.9. The Properties and Attributes of the CheckBoxField Control

Property/Attribute	Description
Text	Sets or returns a `String` that will be used as the `Text` property of the `CheckBox` control.
InsertVisible	Sets or returns a `Boolean` value that indicates whether the `CheckBox` control will be visible when inserting a new row, when this column type is used in a `DetailsView` control. Not applicable when this column type is used in a `GridView` control.

Declaring a HyperLinkField Column

A `HyperLinkField` is used to display a clickable link in each row by inserting a standard `<a>` element into the output. The control allows you to set the text content of the `<a>` element and the `href` attribute as either static values or as values from the source data row. You can also specify a value for the target window name, though this can be only static text and not a bound value. Listing 4.10 shows the outline declaration of a `HyperLinkField` column.

LISTING 4.10. Declaring a HyperLinkField Column

```
<asp:HyperLinkField
  DataTextField="String"
  DataTextFormatString="String"
  Text="String"
  DataNavigateUrlFields="String[,String]"
  DataNavigateUrlFormatString="String"
  NavigateUrl="String"
  Target="String"
  ApplyFormatInEditMode="[True|False]"
  HtmlEncode="[True|False]"
  Visible="[True|False]"
  SortExpression="String"
  ShowHeader="[True|False]"
  HeaderText="String"
  AccessibleHeaderText="String"
  HeaderStyle-[PropertyName]="[value]"
  HeaderImageUrl="String"
  ItemStyle-[PropertyName]="[value]"
  FooterText="String"
  FooterStyle-[PropertyName]="[value]" />
```

The attributes shown in bold in Listing 4.10 correspond to the properties in Table 4.10. The rest are the same as those listed for the `BoundField` control in Table 4.7.

TABLE 4.10. The Properties and Attributes of the HyperLinkField Control

Property/Attribute	Description
`DataTextField`	Sets or returns a `String` that indicates the name of the column within the source data that will supply the value for the `Text` property of the control (the visible text of the link).
`DataTextFormatString`	Sets or returns a `String` that contains the formatting information for the bound value that is applied to the `Text` property of the link.
`Text`	Sets or returns a `String` that will be used in place of `DataTextField`, in other words, the static value for the text of the link that is the same for every row.
`DataNavigateUrlFields`	Sets or returns a `String Array` that specifies the names of the columns within the source data that will supply values for the `NavigateUrl` property of the control (the `href` attribute of the resulting `<a>` element). Use a comma-delimited list of column names when declaring the control. This means that you can use values from different columns for hyperlinks. See the Using the DataNavigateUrlFields Property section.
`DataNavigateUrlFormatString`	Sets or returns a `String` that contains the formatting information for the bound values that will be applied to the `NavigateUrl` property.
`NavigateUrl`	Sets or returns a `String` that will be used in place of `DataNavigateUrlFields`, in other words, the static value for the `href` of the links that is the same for every row.
`Target`	Sets or returns a `String` that is the name of the target window for the link and will be used as the `target` attribute of the resulting `<a>` element.

Using the DataNavigateUrlFields Property

New in the beta release of ASP.NET 2.0 is the ability to specify more than one column for the `DataNavigateUrlFields` property or attribute of a grid-type control. When the GridView binds a HyperLinkField to its source data, all the columns declared for the DataNavigateUrlFields property can be used within the DataTextFormatString property to provide more than one href value for the hyperlinks. For example, you can declare a HyperLinkField like this:

```
<asp:HyperLinkField DataTextField="ProductName"
    DataNavigateUrlFields="ProductID,ProductName"
    DataNavigateUrlFormatString=
        "http://www.mysite.com/products?product={0}" />
```

In this case, for a row containing the product named Chang with ProductID value 2, the href value will appear as

```
http://www.mysite.com/products?product=2
```

However, you can also declare the DataNavigateUrlFormatString as

```
DataNavigateUrlFormatString=
    "http://www.mysite.com/products?product={1}" />
```

In this case, the href value for the same row will appear as:

```
http://www.mysite.com/products?product=Chang
```

The same effect can be obtained, of course, by changing the value of the DataNavigateUrlFormatString property at runtime in the ItemDataBound event, just as you would with one of the version 1.x grid or list controls.

However, the most useful feature of all, one that many users requested, is that the DataNavigateUrlFormatString can now contain more than one placeholder, for example:

```
DataNavigateUrlFormatString=
    "http://www.mysite.com/products?product={0}&amp;name={1}" />
```

The href value for the same row will now appear as

```
http://www.mysite.com/products?product=2&name=Chang
```

This gives you the opportunity to easily create href values that contain multiple query string parameters. Just remember to use the HTML-encoded ampersand (&) to concatenate them, as shown above.

Declaring a TemplateField Column

When you need to provide output that is not supported by any of the standard column types, you can use a `TemplateField`. This works just as in the `DataGrid` from version 1.0 of ASP.NET, and it is the same approach to generating list output used by other controls such as the `Repeater` and `DataList`. You specify all the content you want to be output for the column within one or more templates nested in the `TemplateField` declaration (or added at runtime in code). The control selects the appropriate template depending on which mode the row is currently in. Listing 4.11 shows the outline declaration of a `TemplateField` column.

LISTING 4.11. Declaring a TemplateField Column

```
<asp:TemplateField
  ApplyFormatInEditMode="[True|False]"
  HtmlEncode="[True|False]"
  Visible="[True|False]"
  SortExpression="String"
  ShowHeader="[True|False]"
  HeaderText="String"
  AccessibleHeaderText="String"
  HeaderStyle-[PropertyName]="[value]"
  HeaderImageUrl="String"
  ItemStyle-[PropertyName]="[value]"
  FooterText="String"
  FooterStyle-[PropertyName]="[value]" >

    <HeaderTemplate>...</HeaderTemplate>
    <ItemTemplate>...</ItemTemplate>
    <AlternatingItemTemplate>...</AlternatingItemTemplate>
    <EditItemTemplate>...</EditItemTemplate>
    <FooterTemplate>...</FooterTemplate>

</asp:TemplateField>
```

All the attributes of the control are the same as those listed for the `BoundField` control in Table 4.7. The five kinds of templates you can specify, set in bold in Listing 4.11, are documented in Table 4.11.

TABLE 4.11. The Templates of the TemplateField Control

Template	Description
HeaderTemplate	The markup, text, controls, and other content required to generate the entire content for the header of this column of the grid.

continues

TABLE 4.11. The Templates of the TemplateField Control (continued)

Template	Description
`ItemTemplate`	The markup, text, controls, and other content required to generate the entire content for this column in data-bound rows within the grid.
`AlternatingItemTemplate`	The markup, text, controls, and other content required to generate the entire content for this column in alternating data-bound rows within the grid.
`EditItemTemplate`	The markup, text, controls, and other content required to generate the entire content for this column in the row within the grid that is in edit mode.
`FooterTemplate`	The markup, text, controls, and other content required to generate the entire content for the footer of this column of the grid.

Declaring a CommandField Column

The final column type for the `GridView` control is the `CommandField` column. This is used to switch the row between modes and to confirm updates to the values. When the row is not in edit mode, the column displays one or more of the Select, Insert, Edit, and Delete buttons, depending on the values you've specified for the Show*xxx*Button properties of the `GridView` control. When the row is in edit mode, it displays Update and Cancel buttons, again depending on the property settings you make for the `GridView` control.

Clicking on the buttons raises an event that is automatically handled by the data source control to which the `GridView` is connected, though you can also respond to the events in code yourself by handling the `RowCommand` event. Listing 4.12 shows the outline declaration of a `CommandField` column.

LISTING 4.12. Declaring a CommandField Column

```
<asp:CommandField
  ButtonType="[Button|Image|Link]"
  UpdateText="String"
  UpdateImageUrl="String"
  ShowCancelButton="[True|False]"
  CancelText="String"
  CancelImageUrl="String"
  ShowSelectButton="[True|False]"
  SelectText="String"
  SelectImageUrl="String"
```

```
ShowEditButton="[True|False]"
EditText="String"
EditImageUrl="String"
ShowDeleteButton="[True|False]"
DeleteText="String"
DeleteImageUrl="String"
CausesValidation="[True|False]"
ValidationGroup="String"
Visible="[True|False]"
SortExpression="String"
ShowHeader="[True|False]"
HeaderText="String"
AccessibleHeaderText="String"
HeaderStyle-[PropertyName]="[value]"
HeaderImageUrl="String"
ItemStyle-[PropertyName]="[value]"
FooterText="String"
FooterStyle-[PropertyName]="[value]" />
```

The attributes shown in bold in Listing 4.12 correspond to the properties in Table 4.12. The rest are the same as those listed for the `BoundField` control in Table 4.7.

TABLE 4.12. The Properties and Attributes of the CommandField Control

Property/Attribute	Description
ButtonType	Sets or returns a value from the ButtonType enumeration (Button, Image, or Link) that specifies the type of controls to create in each row of this column. The default is Link.
UpdateText	Sets or returns a String value that is the caption for the button that causes an update process to occur. The default is Update.
UpdateImageUrl	Sets or returns a String that is the relative or absolute URL of the image to display in place of a text Update link.
ShowCancelButton	Sets or returns a Boolean value that indicates whether a Cancel button will be displayed in this column when the row is in edit mode.
CancelText	Sets or returns a String value that is the caption for the button that cancels an update process. The default is Cancel.
CancelImageUrl	Sets or returns a String that is the relative or absolute URL of the image to display in place of a text Cancel link.

continues

TABLE 4.12. The Properties and Attributes of the CommandField Control (continued)

Property/Attribute	Description
ShowSelectButton	Sets or returns a Boolean value that indicates whether a Select button will be displayed in this column.
SelectText	Sets or returns a String value that is the caption for the button that causes the row to be shown in selected mode. The default is Select.
SelectImageUrl	Sets or returns a String that is the relative or absolute URL of the image to display in place of a text Select link.
ShowEditButton	Sets or returns a Boolean value that indicates whether an Edit button will be displayed in this column.
EditText	Sets or returns a String value that is the caption for the button that causes the row to be shown in edit mode. The default is Edit.
EditImageUrl	Sets or returns a String that is the relative or absolute URL of the image to display in place of a text Edit link.
ShowDeleteButton	Sets or returns a Boolean value that indicates whether a Delete button will be displayed in this column.
DeleteText	Sets or returns a String value that is the caption for the button that deletes a row. The default is Delete.
DeleteImageUrl	Sets or returns a String that is the relative or absolute URL of the image to display in place of a text Delete link.
CausesValidation	Sets or returns a Boolean value that indicates whether the button will cause any validation controls in the page to validate their values and report any errors. The default is True.
ValidationGroup	Sets or returns a String that is the name of the group of validation controls that this button will be a member of. See Chapter 9 for more details about validation groups.

Using a Mixture of Column Types

To demonstrate some of the column types available for the DataGrid control, Listing 4.13 shows a GridView control that extracts some rows from the Northwind database Products table and displays them with sorting and paging enabled. The data source control declaration contains the commands required to allow updating of the data in the table and caches the data for five minutes to improve performance when just reading the rows.

LISTING 4.13. Using a Mixture of Column Types

```
<asp:SqlDataSource id="ds1" runat="server"
  ConnectionString="server=localhost;database=Northwind;uid=x;pwd=x;"
  SelectCommand="SELECT ProductID, ProductName, QuantityPerUnit,
                 Discontinued, UnitPrice FROM Products"
  UpdateCommand="UPDATE Products SET QuantityPerUnit=@QuantityPerUnit,
                 Discontinued=@Discontinued
                 WHERE ProductID=@ProductID"
  DeleteCommand="DELETE FROM Products WHERE ProductID=@ProductID"
  EnableCaching="True" CacheDuration="300" />

<asp:GridView id="grid1" runat="server" DataSourceID="ds1"
  AllowSorting="True" AllowPaging="True" PageSize="5"
  DataKeyNames="ProductID"
  AutoGenerateColumns="False" OnRowCommand="ShowDetails">

  <ColumnFields>
    ...column definitions shown later...
  </ColumnFields>

</asp:GridView>

<asp:Label id="lblInfo" EnableViewState="False" runat="server" />
```

The RowCommand event is raised when any control in the grid (including the standard Edit, Delete, Update, and Cancel links and any pager links) causes a postback. Code in the page will handle this event and display details about a row in a Label control (declared at the end of Listing 4.13) when a button in that row is clicked. The screenshot in Figure 4.3 shows

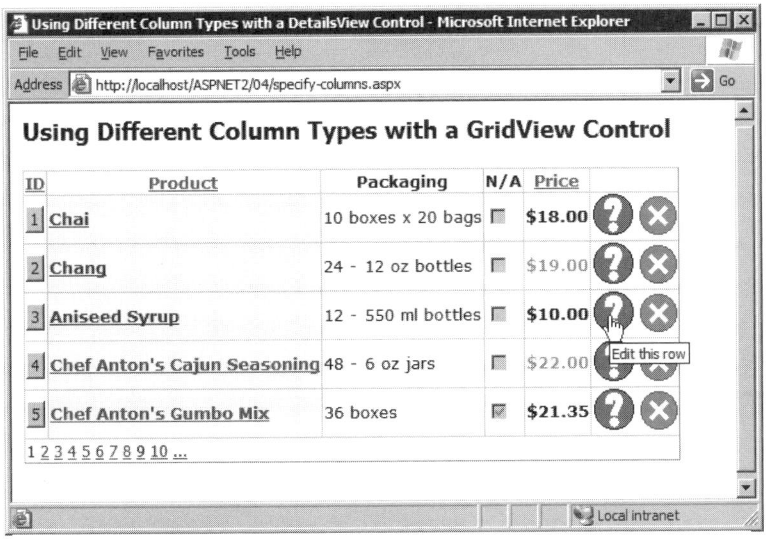

FIGURE 4.3. Using a mixture of column types

the result; the custom column declarations the GridView uses are discussed in the subsections that follow.

The GridView control shown in Listing 4.13 and Figure 4.3 contains the attribute AutoGenerateColumns="False", so it will not automatically generate the columns based on the structure of the data rows. The columns are declared individually within the <ColumnFields> element. The next subsections describe each of the columns we've used.

The ButtonField Column

The first column is a ButtonField column that displays a button with the row ID as the caption. The DataTextField attribute causes the values from the ProductID column to be used for the Text property of the button in each row, and the SortExpression attribute allows the rows to be sorted using the values in this column (see Listing 4.14). A header row is displayed for this column, containing the text "ID", and it is styled as bold Verdana font. Finally, the CommandName attribute causes the CommandName property of each button to be set to MyRoutine. This is required to be able to identify which control caused the postback when we handle the RowCommand event.

LISTING 4.14. Declaring the ButtonField Column

```
<asp:ButtonField ButtonType="Button" DataTextField="ProductID"
    SortExpression="ProductID" ShowHeader="True" HeaderText="ID"
    CommandName="MyRoutine" HeaderStyle-Font-Name="Verdana"
    HeaderStyle-Font-Bold="True" />
```

The HyperLinkField Column

The next column is a HyperLinkField, bound to the ProductName column. The Text property of each hyperlink is set to the value in each row of the ProductName column by the DataTextField attribute (see Listing 4.15). The NavigateUrl (href) of each hyperlink is set to a string value such as http://www.mysite.com/products?product=2&name=Chang by the combination of the DataNavigateUrlFields attribute (which specifies the ProductID and ProductName columns) and the DataNavigateUrlFormatString attribute (which supplies the format string with the placeholders {0} and {1} for the value from each row).

LISTING 4.15. Declaring the HyperLinkField Column

```
<asp:HyperLinkField DataTextField="ProductName"
    ShowHeader="True" HeaderText="Product"
    DataNavigateUrlFields="ProductID,ProductName"
    DataNavigateUrlFormatString=
        "http://www.mysite.com/products?product={0}&amp;name={1}"
    SortExpression="ProductName" HeaderStyle-Font-Name="Verdana"
    HeaderStyle-Font-Bold="True" ItemStyle-Font-Name="Verdana"
    ItemStyle-Font-Bold="True" ItemStyle-BackColor="Yellow" />
```

The BoundField Column

Next comes a `BoundField` column, bound to the `QuantityPerUnit` column. It, too, has a header, and both this and the "item" rows are styled using attributes in the column declaration (see Listing 4.16).

LISTING 4.16. Declaring the BoundField Column

```
<asp:BoundField DataField="QuantityPerUnit" ShowHeader="True"
    HeaderText="Packaging" HeaderStyle-Font-Name="Verdana"
    HeaderStyle-Font-Bold="True" ItemStyle-Font-Name="Verdana" />
```

The CheckBoxField Column

The `Discontinued` column in the data rowset is a `Boolean` type, so the ideal representation is a checkbox. This is the default for this type of data column anyway. The `CheckBoxField` column is bound to the `Discontinued` column in the data rows and the header "N/A" (not available) declared for it (see Listing 4.17).

LISTING 4.17. Declaring the CheckBoxField Column

```
<asp:CheckBoxField DataField="Discontinued" ShowHeader="True"
    HeaderText="N/A" HeaderStyle-Font-Name="Verdana"
    HeaderStyle-Font-Bold="True" />
```

The TemplateField Column

The most complex column type is the `TemplateField`, and this cannot be bound directly to a column in the source data rowset. Instead, it contains individual templates that define the output to be displayed depending on the row location and which mode the row is in. You can see that the example contains an `ItemTemplate` and an `AlternatingItemTemplate`, each containing a `Label` control that displays the value from the `UnitPrice` column in each row—and with alternating foreground colors (see Listing 4.18).

LISTING 4.18. Declaring the TemplateField Column

```
<asp:TemplateField ShowHeader="True" HeaderText="Price"
    SortExpression="UnitPrice" HeaderStyle-Font-Name="Verdana"
    HeaderStyle-Font-Bold="True" ItemStyle-Font-Name="Verdana"
    ItemStyle-Font-Bold="True">
  <ItemTemplate>
    <asp:Label runat="server"
               Text='<%# Eval("UnitPrice", "${0:F2}") %>' />
  </ItemTemplate>
  <AlternatingItemTemplate>
    <asp:Label runat="server" ForeColor="DarkGray"
               Text='<%# Eval("UnitPrice", "${0:F2}") %>' />
  </AlternatingItemTemplate>
</asp:TemplateField>
```

It's possible to include an `EditItem` template that defines the appearance of the row when it is in edit mode. However, because this column type cannot be bound directly to a column in the source data, a different type of data binding syntax is required. We examine this in the section Two-Way Data Binding Syntax for Templated Controls at the end of this chapter. An alternative is to write code that is executed in response to the `RowUpdating` event and add the value(s) of the fields in the `TemplateField` to the `NewValues` dictionary of the `GridViewUpdateEventArgs` instance.

The CommandField Column

The final column displays the images for switching to edit mode, updating a row, canceling the changes, and deleting the row. The `CommandField` column declaration specifies that the links should be images and also declares the relative URL of the images and the text to use as the `alt` attribute of these images (see Listing 4.19).

LISTING 4.19. Declaring the CommandField Column

```
<asp:CommandField ButtonType="Image"
    UpdateImageUrl="i.gif" UpdateText="Apply these changes"
    ShowCancelButton="True" CancelImageUrl="s.gif"
    CancelText="Cancel this update"
    ShowEditButton="True" EditImageUrl="q.gif"
    EditText="Edit this row"
    ShowDeleteButton="True" DeleteImageUrl="x.gif"
    DeleteText="Delete this row" />
```

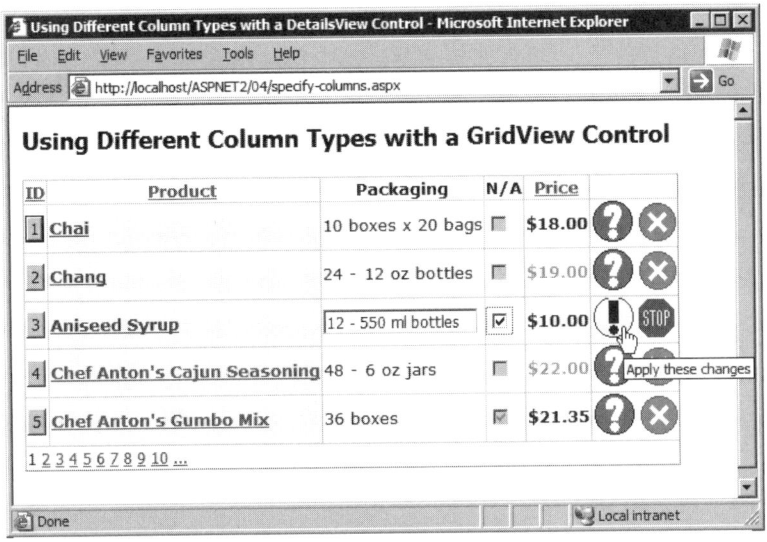

FIGURE 4.4. Editing a row with custom column types

As we've seen earlier, the GridView control manages all the mode switching and updates automatically, without requiring any code to be written. The screenshot in Figure 4.4 shows the grid with the third row in edit mode. Notice that the HyperLinkField column does not allow the value to be edited, while the BoundField column does. The CheckBoxField column automatically enables the checkbox in this row to allow the value to be changed. Meanwhile the CommandField column displays the Update and Cancel images. All this happens automatically with the column declarations we used, without any code required.

Handling the RowCommand Event

The first column (a ButtonField column) contains buttons that raise the RowCommand event when clicked. The declaration of the GridView control includes the attribute OnRowCommand="ShowDetails", which will execute the only code in the page—an event handler named ShowDetails (see Listing 4.20)—when any one of the buttons is clicked.

LISTING 4.20. The Event Handler for the RowCommand Event

```
Sub ShowDetails(oSender As Object, oArgs As GridViewCommandEventArgs)
   If oArgs.CommandName = "MyRoutine" Then
     lblInfo.Text = "More details here for product " _
               & oArgs.CommandSource.Text
   End If
End Sub
```

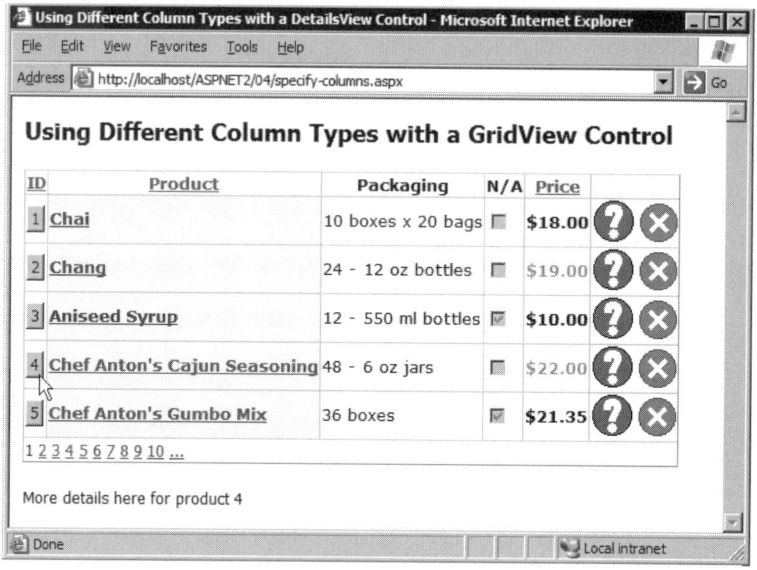

FIGURE 4.5. Handling the RowCommand event

However, the RowCommand event is also raised for some other actions that cause a postback, including the pager links at the bottom of the grid. So, before processing the row values, the event handler has to check whether it was in fact a button in the first column that caused the postback. The ButtonField column declaration contains the attribute CommandName ="MyRoutine", so the event handler can check the CommandName property of the GridViewCommandEventArgs instance passed to it. If this is a button from the first column, a reference to it is obtained from the CommandSource property of the GridViewCommandEventArgs instance, and the Text property contains the value from the current row.

The code in Listing 4.20 simply displays the text "More details here for product x" but could easily go off and query the database or fetch an image of the product to display more information as required. Figure 4.5 shows the result of clicking one of the buttons in the first column.

The DetailsView Control

The GridView control we examined in the previous section is designed to display data as a table, with each row containing one data row (one record). However, sometimes it's useful to be able to display data one row at a time, especially when there is a large number of columns or when you want to be able to edit the values of each column without using the rather cramped inline editing mode of the GridView.

To provide a one-row-per-page feature for displaying and editing data, ASP.NET 2.0 includes the new DetailsView control. It can be used in stand-alone mode where paging controls that allow the user to scroll through the rows are provided. Alternatively it can be combined with a GridView control to provide a master-detail display. In fact, you have already seen DetailsView-like rendering in action in the previous section of this chapter. When serving a page containing a GridView to a small-screen or mobile device, ASP.NET automatically uses such rendering to create the details page containing all the columns from the current row.

Using a Stand-Alone DetailsView Control

The declaration and attribute set for the DetailsView control is similar to that of the GridView. When used on its own, however, you need to either enable the paging feature in order to display the paging controls or add your own custom paging feature so that users can navigate through the rows.

Listing 4.21 shows a declaration of a DetailsView control that turns on the paging features and specifies that the mode should be NextPreviousFirstLast so that the usual four links are displayed (the default mode is Numeric, where a numbered link is displayed for each row). The declaration also specifies the relative URLs of the images to display for the paging controls and the text to use as the alt attribute of each one.

LISTING 4.21. An Example of Using a DetailsView Control

```
<asp:DetailsView id="details1" DataSourceID="dvs1" runat="server"
  DataKeyNames="ShipperID" AllowPaging="True"
  PagerSettings-Mode="NextPreviousFirstLast"
  PagerSettings-FirstPageImageUrl="f.gif"
  PagerSettings-FirstPageText="First Row"
  PagerSettings-PreviousPageImageUrl="p.gif"
  PagerSettings-PreviousPageText="Previous Row"
  PagerSettings-NextPageImageUrl="n.gif"
  PagerSettings-NextPageText="Next Row"
  PagerSettings-LastPageImageUrl="l.gif"
  PagerSettings-LastPageText="Last Row" />

<asp:SqlDataSource id="dvs1" runat="server"
  ConnectionString="server=localhost;database=Northwind;uid=x;pwd=x"
  SelectCommand="SELECT ShipperID,CompanyName,Phone FROM Shippers">
</asp:SqlDataSource>
```

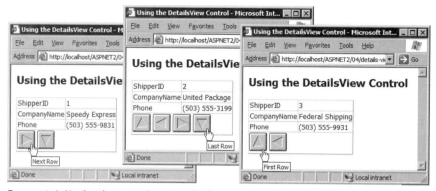

FIGURE 4.6. Navigating rows in a DetailsView control

After the DetailsView control comes the declaration of the data source control. You can see that this is identical to the way it is used with a GridView control. The compound screenshot in Figure 4.6 shows the result, with the paging controls and the alternate text captions visible.

The DetailsView control accepts basically the same set of styling attributes as the GridView control, so you can improve the appearance from the default shown here. You can also turn off automatic generation of the fields (by setting the AutoGenerateRows attribute to False) and then specify the fields you want to display as well as their appearance and behavior.

Note that the DetailsView control uses a <RowFields> section in place of the <ColumnFields> section of the GridView control, but the same types of fields are used within it as in the GridView. You can declare your own sequence of BoundField, ButtonField, CheckBoxField, HyperLinkField, TemplateField, and CommandField controls within the <RowFields> section.

The other main difference is in the names of the nested styling elements you can place within a DetailsView control declaration. Instead of ItemStyle, AlternatingItemStyle, and EditItemStyle, you use RowStyle, AlternatingRowStyle, and EditRowStyle. There is also a CommandRowStyle that sets the style of the row containing the Edit, Update, and Cancel links when editing is enabled in a DetailsView control. Other differences between the attributes and properties of the GridView and DetailsView controls are listed in Table 4.13 later in this chapter.

Creating a Master-Detail Page with GridView and DetailsView Controls

For rowsets that have a large number of columns, the one-row-per-page approach provided by the DetailsView control is useful. However, it does make it harder to navigate through and generally scan the data by eye. For that, the table layout provided by the GridView control is better. The ideal is to combine the two so that a few selected columns are displayed in the GridView, and the user can select a row to see it displayed with all the fields visible in the DetailsView.

The two controls provide features that link them together declaratively, without requiring any code to be written. Listing 4.22 shows how this works. In this example, the GridView is bound to a data source control named dgs1, and the DataKeyNames attribute specifies that the ShipperID column in the rowset exposed by that data source control is the primary key for each row. The AutoGenerateSelectButton attribute is set to True to display a Select link in each row.

LISTING 4.22. Master-Detail Pages: The GridView and SqlDataSource Controls

```
<asp:GridView id="grid1" DataSourceID="dgs1" runat="server"
    DataKeyNames="ShipperID" SelectedIndex="0"
    AutoGenerateSelectButton="True" />

<asp:SqlDataSource id="dgs1" runat="server"
  ConnectionString="server=localhost;database=Northwind;uid=x;pwd=x"
  SelectCommand="SELECT ShipperID,CompanyName,Phone FROM Shippers" />
...
```

The DetailsView control is declared next (see Listing 4.23). It is bound to the second data source control on the page, named dvs1, and again has the primary key column identified by the DataKeyNames attribute. The data source control has the same SelectCommand as the previous one, though it doesn't have to—if you display a different selection of columns in the two controls, you can select just the columns you need.

LISTING 4.23. Master-Detail Pages with a DetailsView and Filtered SqlDataSource

```
...
<asp:DetailsView id="details1" DataSourceID="dvs1" runat="server"
    DataKeyNames="ShipperID" />

<asp:SqlDataSource id="dvs1" runat="server"
  ConnectionString="server=localhost;database=Northwind;uid=x;pwd=x"
```

continues

```
SelectCommand="SELECT ShipperID,CompanyName,Phone FROM Shippers"
FilterExpression="ShipperID=@ShipperID">

<FilterParameters>
  <asp:ControlParameter Name="ShipperID" ControlID="grid1"
                        PropertyName="SelectedValue" />
</FilterParameters>

</asp:SqlDataSource>
```

The link between the two data source controls, which ensures that the row selected in the GridView is displayed in the DetailsView control, is the addition of a filter to the second data source control. The FilterExpression declares a parameter @ShipperID, and the <FilterParameters> section of the control contains a ControlParameter that is bound to the SelectedValue property of the GridView control.

By default, the first data row in the source rowset is selected when the page loads. As the user selects rows in the GridView control, the SelectedValue is automatically set to the ID of that row and thus filters the data source control that powers the DetailsView control on that ID value.

Figure 4.7 shows the result. A Select link appears in each row of the GridView control, and clicking one displays that row in the DetailsView control below it.

FIGURE 4.7. Selecting a row in a master-detail page

Inserting and Editing Rows with a DetailsView Control

A task that is regularly required when working with data rows, one that is quite complex to achieve in ASP.NET 1.0, is inserting a new row into the source data table. In ASP.NET 2.0, with a `GridView` control, you can do this by using a `DetailsView` control instance declared separately on the page. The technique is very similar to that just seen for creating a master-detail page. First, a `GridView` control is declared together with the associated data source control that supplies the data (see Listing 4.24).

LISTING 4.24. Inserting and Editing Rows with a GridView and SqlDataSource

```
<asp:GridView id="grid1" DataSourceID="dgs1" runat="server"
  DataKeyNames="ShipperID" SelectedIndex="0"
  AutoGenerateSelectButton="True" />

<asp:SqlDataSource id="dgs1" runat="server"
 ConnectionString="server=localhost;database=Northwind;uid=x;pwd=x"
 SelectCommand="SELECT ShipperID,CompanyName,Phone FROM Shippers" />
...
```

Enabling Editing in a DetailsView Control

To enable row edits, row deletes, and/or row inserts in a `DetailsView` control, you just add the relevant attributes to the control declaration. The first four attributes set in bold in Listing 4.25 turn on display of the Insert, Edit, Delete, and Cancel links, respectively (the Update link always appears when editing is enabled). For the automatic no-code updates to work, you also have to provide the relevant SQL statements or stored procedures. The other attributes set in bold for the data source control in Listing 4.25 show the UPDATE, DELETE, and INSERT statements that will push changes to the rows back into the database.

LISTING 4.25. Inserting and Editing Rows with a DetailsView and SqlDataSource

```
...
<asp:DetailsView id="details1" DataSourceID="dvs1" runat="server"
    DataKeyNames="ShipperID"
    AutoGenerateInsertButton="True" AutoGenerateEditButton="True"
    AutoGenerateDeleteButton="True" AutoGenerateCancelButton="True"
    OnItemDeleting="CheckDelete" />

<asp:SqlDataSource id="dvs1" runat="server"
  ConnectionString="server=localhost;database=Northwind;uid=x;pwd=x"
  SelectCommand="SELECT ShipperID,CompanyName,Phone FROM Shippers"
  UpdateCommand="UPDATE Shippers SET CompanyName=@CompanyName,
                 Phone=@Phone WHERE ShipperID=@ShipperID"
  DeleteCommand="DELETE FROM Shippers WHERE ShipperID=@ShipperID"
  InsertCommand="INSERT INTO Shippers (CompanyName, Phone)
                 VALUES (@CompanyName, @Phone)"
  FilterExpression="ShipperID=@ShipperID" >
```

continues

```
<FilterParameters>
  <asp:ControlParameter Name="ShipperID" ControlID="grid1"
                        PropertyName="SelectedValue" />
</FilterParameters>

</asp:SqlDataSource>

<asp:Label id="lblError" EnableviewState="False" runat="server" />
```

The screenshot in Figure 4.8 shows two views of the process of editing a row. The `DetailsView` displays the Edit, Delete, and New links. Clicking the Edit link switches the `DetailsView` into edit mode, and the values of the non-key fields can be edited.

It's also possible to insert a row by clicking the New link, entering the values, and then clicking the Insert link (see Figure 4.9). Notice that the

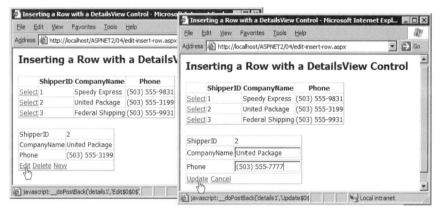

FIGURE 4.8. Editing a row with a DetailsView control

FIGURE 4.9. Inserting a row with a DetailsView control

primary key is displayed as a text box so that the user can enter an appropriate value.

In our case, however, the primary key column within the database table is auto-generated (an IDENTITY column). You don't need to enter a value, and the INSERT statement declared for the InsertCommand property of the data source control does not attempt to apply any value that you might enter anyway. You could create the fields for the DetailsView control manually, by setting the AutoGenerateRows attribute to False and using a BoundField with the InsertVisible property set to False, or by using a TemplateField, so that the value is not editable.

Handling DetailsView Control Events

The declaration of the DetailsView control shown in Listing 4.25 (and repeated in Listing 4.26 for convenience) includes an attribute that specifies the event handler that will be executed in response to the ItemDeleting event.

LISTING 4.26. The OnItemDeleting Event Attribute Declaration

```
<asp:DetailsView id="details1" DataSourceID="dvs1" runat="server"
    DataKeyNames="ShipperID"
    AutoGenerateInsertButton="True" AutoGenerateEditButton="True"
    AutoGenerateDeleteButton="True" AutoGenerateCancelButton="True"
    OnItemDeleting="CheckDelete" />
```

The ItemDeleting event occurs just before a row is deleted in the DetailsView control, and the page handles this to prevent attempts to delete the existing rows in the table (as shown earlier for the GridView control). Other than the fact that this event handler takes a DetailsViewDeleteEventArgs instance as the second argument, rather than the GridViewDeleteEventArgs instance used in the earlier example, the code is identical (see Listing 4.27).

LISTING 4.27. The Event Handler for the ItemDeleting Event

```
<script runat="server">
Sub CheckDelete(oSender As Object, _
                oArgs As DetailsViewDeleteEventArgs)
  Dim iKey As Integer = oArgs.Keys(0)
  If iKey < 4 Then
    oArgs.Cancel = True
    lblError.Text = "Cannot delete the original rows from the table"
  End If
End Sub
</script>
```

Another situation where event handling might be useful is to highlight the current row in the `GridView` control when the user navigates through the rows using the `DetailsView` pager controls. The `GridView` would need to have a different style defined for the selected row (using the `SelectedItemTemplate`). Code that handles the `DataItemIndexChanged` event for the `DetailsView` would just set the `SelectedIndex` property of the `GridView` to the appropriate row index. This automatically displays the new row in the appropriate way.

The DetailsView Control Interface

As noted earlier, and as you've seen from the earlier examples, the `DetailsView` control interface is similar to that of the `GridView`. This isn't surprising because they both do effectively the same thing—display rows of data. The main difference is that the `GridView` displays the rows horizontally as a table, with the fields in columns, while the `DetailsView` displays each row as a separate page with the fields laid out vertically. However, for completeness, the following sections list the members of the `DetailsView` that are not found in the `GridView`.

Properties Specific to the DetailsView Control

The `DetailsView` control does not support sorting and thus has none of the properties associated with this feature that apply to the `GridView` control. And the different ways that the rows are displayed mean that there is no concept of a selected row in a `DetailsView`, so there is no `AutoGenerateSelectButton` or selected row style properties. Properties that are available for the `DetailsView` control, and not for the `GridView` control, include those listed in Table 4.13.

The TemplateField in the DetailsView Control

Although the types of field controls you can use in a `DetailsView` control are the same as those you use in a `GridView` control, the `TemplateField` control has some extra properties when used in a `DetailsView` control. This is because the `DetailsView` control allows new rows to be inserted, which the `GridView` control does not. The extra properties are detailed in Table 4.14. For the same reason, the `DetailsView` also allows you to include a nested `<InsertItemTemplate>` section within a `TemplateField` declaration.

TABLE 4.13. The Properties Specific to the DetailsView Control

Property	Description
AutoGenerateRows	Sets or returns a `Boolean` value that indicates whether the control will automatically generate fields for each column in the source data rowset.
AutoGenerateInsertButton	Sets or returns a `Boolean` value that indicates whether the control will automatically generate a New button for each row.
DataKey	Returns a `DataKey` instance containing the keys and values corresponding to the key names specified by the `DataKeyNames` attribute.
DataItemIndex	Sets or returns an `Integer` value that is the zero-based index of the `DataItem` (row) currently displayed.
DataItemCount	Returns an `Integer` value that is the total number of rows in the underlying data source bound to the control.
DefaultMode	Sets or returns a value from the `DetailsViewMode` enumeration that specifies how the fields are displayed when the page loads and after Cancel, Update, Delete, or New is pressed. Valid values are `ReadOnly` (the default), Edit, and `Insert`.
CurrentMode	Returns a value from the `DetailsViewMode` enumeration that indicates the current mode of the `DetailsView`.
InsertVisible	Sets or returns a `Boolean` value that indicates whether this field will be displayed when inserting a new row into the source rowset.
HeaderText	Sets or returns a `String` that is the text to be displayed immediately above the fields in the output generated by the control.
Rows	Contains a `DetailsViewRow` object for each row in the `DetailsView`.
RowFields	Returns a `DataControlFieldCollection` instance that is a collection of all the `DataControlField` objects that generate the output for the control.

Note that if you want to be able to perform updates to the source data from a `TemplateField` column when using a data source control to populate the `DetailsView` control, you must use the new two-way data binding syntax. See the Two-Way Data Binding Syntax for Templated Controls section near the end of this chapter for more details.

TABLE 4.14. The TemplateField Properties Specific to the DetailsView

Property	Description
ShowInsertButton	Sets or returns a `Boolean` value that indicates whether an Insert button will be displayed in this column.
NewText	Sets or returns a `String` value that is the caption for the button that adds an empty row to the rowset and displays this empty row in edit mode with the Insert and Cancel buttons visible. The default caption for this button is `New`.
NewImageUrl	Sets or returns a `String` that is the relative or absolute URL of the image to display in place of a text New link.
InsertText	Sets or returns a `String` value that is the caption for the button that inserts the new row into the grid after the user has filled in the values. The default is `Insert`.
InsertImageUrl	Sets or returns a `String` that is the relative or absolute URL of the image to display in place of a text Insert link.

Events Specific to the DetailsView Control

The `DetailsView` control has the same `DataBinding` and `DataBound` events as the `GridView`, but the remaining events are specific to the `DetailsView` control (see Table 4.15).

TABLE 4.15. The Events of the DetailsView Control

Event	Description
DataItemIndexChanging	Raised before the `DetailsView` control changes from one row to the next. Passes a `DetailsViewItemEventArgs` instance to the event handler, which exposes the following properties: • `Cancel`: A `Boolean` property that can be set to `True` to prevent the control from changing to the new row. • `NewDataItemIndex`: The zero-based `Integer` index of the row that will be displayed next.

TABLE 4.15. The Events of the DetailsView Control (continued)

Event	Description
DataItemIndexChanged	Raised after the DetailsView control changes from one row to the next. Passes a standard EventArgs instance to the event handler.
ItemCommand	Raised when any control in the DetailsView causes a postback. Passes a DetailsViewCommandEventArgs instance to the event handler, which exposes the following properties:
	• CommandArgument: The value of the CommandArgument property of the button that raised the event.
	• CommandName: The CommandName property of the control that caused the postback as a String.
	• CommandSource: An Object reference to the control that caused the postback.
ItemCreated	Raised when a new row is created in the DetailsView control. Passes a standard EventArgs instance to the event handler.
ItemDeleting	Raised before the data source control bound to the DetailsView deletes a row. Passes a DetailsViewDeleteEventArgs instance to the event handler, which exposes the following properties:
	• Cancel: A Boolean property that can be set to True to cancel the delete operation.
	• Keys: An IOrderedDictionary instance containing the primary key values for the row.
	• Values: An IOrderedDictionary instance containing the non-key values currently in the row.
	• RowIndex: An Integer value indicating the index of the row within the data source rowset.
ItemDeleted	Raised after the data source control bound to the DetailsView deletes a row. Passes a DetailsViewDeletedEventArgs instance to the event handler, which exposes the following properties:
	• Keys: An IOrderedDictionary instance containing the primary key values for the row.
	• Values: An IOrderedDictionary instance containing the non-key values from the deleted row.
	• AffectedRows: The number of rows that were deleted.
	• Exception: An Exception instance returned if the delete process fails. A reference to the actual exception that was raised by the database can be obtained from the InnerException property of this current exception.

continues

TABLE 4.15. The Events of the DetailsView Control (continued)

Event	Description
	• ExceptionHandled: A Boolean value that you can set to True after handling any exception raised by the delete process to indicate that this exception should *not* be raised to the code that called this method.
ItemInserting	Raised before the data source control bound to the DetailsView inserts a new row. Passes a DetailsViewInsertEventArgs instance to the event handler, which exposes the following properties: • Cancel: A Boolean property that can be set to True to cancel the insert operation. • CommandArgument: The value of the CommandArgument property of the control that raised the event. • Values: An IOrderedDictionary instance containing the values for the new row.
ItemInserted	Raised after the data source control bound to the DetailsView inserts a new row. Passes a DetailsViewInsertedEventArgs instance to the event handler, which exposes the following properties: • Values: An IOrderedDictionary instance containing the non-key values in the new row. • AffectedRows: The number of rows that were deleted. • KeepInInsertMode: A Boolean value that you can set to indicate whether the current row control should remain in insert mode or return to normal mode. • Exception: An Exception instance returned if the insert process fails. A reference to the actual exception that was raised by the database can be obtained from the InnerException property of this current exception. • ExceptionHandled: A Boolean value that you can set to True after handling any exception raised by the insert process to indicate that this exception should *not* be raised to the code that called this method.
ItemUpdating	Raised before the data source control bound to the DetailsView updates a row. Passes a DetailsViewUpdateEventArgs instance to the event handler, which exposes the following properties: • Cancel: A Boolean property that can be set to True to cancel the update operation. • CommandArgument: The value of the CommandArgument property of the button that raised the event. • Keys: An IOrderedDictionary instance containing the primary key values for the row. • NewValues: An IOrderedDictionary instance containing the non-key values that will be placed into the row.

TABLE 4.15. The Events of the DetailsView Control (continued)

Event	Description
	•OldValues: An IOrderedDictionary instance containing the non-key values currently in the row.
ItemUpdated	Raised after the data source control bound to the DetailsView has updated a row. Passes a DetailsViewUpdatedEventArgs instance to the event handler, which exposes the AffectedRows property indicating the number of rows affected by the update operation. •Keys: An IOrderedDictionary instance containing the primary key values for the row. •NewValues: An IOrderedDictionary instance containing the non-key values that will be placed into the row. •OldValues: An IOrderedDictionary instance containing the non-key values currently in the row. •AffectedRows: The number of rows that were updated. •KeepInEditMode: A Boolean value that you can set to indicate whether the current row control should remain in edit mode or return to normal mode. •Exception: An Exception instance returned if the update process fails. A reference to the actual exception that was raised by the database can be obtained from the InnerException property of this current exception. •ExceptionHandled: A Boolean value that you can set to True after handling any exception raised by the update process to indicate that this exception should *not* be raised to the code that called this method.
ModeChanging	Raised before the DetailsView changes from one mode to another (ReadOnly, Edit, or Insert). Passes a DetailsViewModeEventArgs instance to the event handler, which exposes the following properties: •Cancel: A Boolean property that can be set to True to prevent the control changing to the new mode. •CancelingEdit: A Boolean value that is True if the mode change was caused by the user clicking the Cancel button while in edit mode. •NewMode: The new mode as a value from the DetailsViewMode enumeration. The value can be changed to display a different mode.
ModeChanged	Raised after the DetailsView has changed from one mode to another (ReadOnly, Edit, or Insert). Passes a standard EventArgs instance to the event handler.

The FormView Control

The third new list control in ASP.NET version 2.0 is the `FormView` control. At first sight, it seems to be remarkably similar to the `DetailsView` control. In fact, the interface is almost identical, and virtually all of the techniques, syntax, and methods for using it are the same. The difference lies in the way it generates the appearance and content of the user interface.

The `DetailsView` control uses *fields* to define the content. The `RowFields` collection of the control is a reference to a `DataControlFieldCollection` that contains references to a mixture of the various types of fields that can be used in a `GridView` or `DetailsView` control. This includes the `BoundField`, `CheckBoxField`, `HyperLinkField`, and so on.

The `FormView` control is different in that it does not support any predefined column types at all. It is a completely templated control, in the same way as the existing `Repeater` control in ASP.NET 1.x. Unless you specify the user interface you want, inside the appropriate templates, you get no output at all from the control.

You can liken this to the differences between the version 1.x `DataGrid` and `Repeater` controls. Although a `DataGrid` can create the complete output itself, automatically generating the appropriate set of columns, you always have to provide a template for a `Repeater` control.

In most other ways, however, the `FormView` control behaves just like the `DetailsView` control. It displays rows from the data source one at a time, rather than in the grid format of the `GridView` and `DataGrid` controls. It also modifies its output automatically to suit small-screen and mobile devices, in the same way as you saw for the `GridView` control earlier in this chapter.

Declaring a FormView Control

The `FormView` control declaration is similar to that of the `DetailsView`, except that you use templates for the user interface rather than declaring a series of fields (or just relying on the appropriate fields to be created automatically). Because the `FormView` is fully templated (with no header or footer rows), there are just three templates you can use. Listing 4.28 shows these three templates within an outline view of the `FormView` control declaration.

LISTING 4.28. An Outline Declaration of a FormView Control

```
<asp:FormView id="fview1" DataSourceID="dvs1" runat="server"
    DataKeyNames="ShipperID" AllowPaging="True"
```

```
    PagerSettings-Mode="Numeric">

  <ItemTemplate>
    ...UI content for displaying row values goes here...
  </ItemTemplate>

  <EditItemTemplate>
    ...UI content for editing rows goes here...
  </EditItemTemplate>

  <InsertItemTemplate>
    ...UI content for adding new rows goes here...
  </InsertItemTemplate>

</asp:FormView>
```

In most cases, you'll want to enable paging (as shown in Listing 4.28) so that users can scroll through the rows, and you'll want to specify the DataKeyNames so that the key values from each row are stored in the DataKeys array. In fact, the only attributes/properties of the DetailsView control not available for the FormView control are the following:

- AutoGenerateRows
- AutoGenerateDeleteButton
- AutoGenerateEditButton
- AutoGenerateInsertButton
- EnablePagingCallbacks
- RowFields

Declaring Templates for a FormView Control

The templates you declare for a FormView control must contribute the entire UI content, including any command buttons or links you need. The advantage is that you can create almost any layout and appearance. As an example, Listings 4.29, 4.30, and 4.31 show three templates that use ordinary HTML tables to generate the required appearance and layout of the controls.

The ItemTemplate, shown in Listing 4.29, contains an Image control in the left-hand cell of the table, which displays the logo of each shipping company as you scroll through the rows. The right-hand cell contains the company name, phone number, and the links to switch the FormView control into edit mode for the current row or to switch it into insert mode to add a new row.

The `Image` control uses the new simplified data binding syntax for the `Eval` method to bind the `ImageUrl` and `AlternateText` attributes to columns in the data source row, and to insert the company name and phone number into the right-hand table cell. The image displayed in the `Image` control comes from a disk file whose name matches the ID values for each shipping company, for example, `2.gif` for the shipping company whose `ShipperID` value is 2. (The new data binding syntax in ASP.NET 2.0, as demonstrated by the use of the `Eval` method here, is covered in more detail later in this chapter.)

To switch modes, the only requirement is that the links or buttons have the correct values for their `CommandName` properties. The permissible values are `"Edit"`, `"Update"`, `"Delete"`, `"New"`, `"Add"`, and `"Cancel"`. In this example we've used `LinkButton` controls, but you can use the ordinary `Button` control, or use the `ImageButton` control if you want to display the commands as clickable images.

LISTING 4.29. The ItemTemplate Declaration for a FormView Control

```
<ItemTemplate>
  <table border="0" cellpadding="5">
  <tr>
    <td>
      <asp:Image Width="100" Height="123"
          runat="server"
          ImageUrl='<%# Eval("ShipperID", "{0}.gif") %>'
          AlternateText='<%# Eval("CompanyName", "{0} Logo") %>' />
    </td>
    <td>
      <b><%#Eval("CompanyName")%></b><p />
      <%#Eval("Phone")%><p />
      <asp:LinkButton id="btnEdit" runat="server"
          CommandName="Edit" Text="Edit Details" /><br />
      <asp:LinkButton id="btnInsert" runat="server"
          CommandName="New" Text="Add New Shipper" />
    </td>
  </tr>
  </table>
</ItemTemplate>
```

Listing 4.30 shows the declaration of the `EditItemTemplate` in this example. Again an HTML table is used. The ID of the shipping company is shown as text; however, it is required to populate the `@ShipperID` parameter of the SQL `UPDATE` statement that will be executed to push the changed values back into the database. This means that we must use a server control with a unique ID, along with the `Bind` method, to expose this value for use as a parameter. Meanwhile the company name and phone number are displayed in `TextBox` controls so they can be edited, again using the `Bind` method (instead of the `Eval` method) so that their values will be available as parameters for the SQL `UPDATE` statement.

LISTING 4.30. The EditItemTemplate Declaration for a FormView Control

```
<EditItemTemplate>
  <table border="0" cellpadding="5">
    <tr>
      <td align="right">ShipperID:</td>
      <td>
        <asp:Label runat="server" id="lblEditID"
             Text='<%# Bind("ShipperID") %>' /></td>
    </tr>
    <tr>
      <td align="right">Company Name:</td>
      <td>
        <asp:TextBox id="txtEditName" runat="server"
             Text='<%# Bind("CompanyName") %>' />
      </td>
    </tr>
    <tr>
      <td align="right">Phone:</td>
      <td>
        <asp:TextBox id="txtEditPhone" runat="server"
             Text='<%# Bind("Phone") %>' />
      </td>
    </tr>
    <tr>
      <td colspan="2">
        <asp:LinkButton id="btnUpdate" CommandName="Update"
             Text="Update" runat="server" />
        <asp:LinkButton id="btnCancel" CommandName="Cancel"
             Text="Cancel" runat="server" />
      </td>
    </tr>
  </table>
</EditItemTemplate>
```

The final template is the `InsertItemTemplate`, shown in Listing 4.31. This is very similar to the `EditItemTemplate` seen in Listing 4.30. However, the `ShipperID` is an `IDENTITY` (or `AutoNumber`) column in the database, so it does not appear in the SQL `INSERT` statement. As there is no need to populate a parameter for the `ShipperID`, there is no requirement for a control where the user would enter a value. However, you would have to insert it if the column were not an `IDENTITY` type.

Of course, the company name and phone number are required, and two `TextBox` controls are provided for this. These `TextBox` controls use the

Bind method, so as to populate the two matching parameters in the INSERT statement.

The only other differences between the InsertItemTemplate and the EditItemTemplate are the selection of command buttons that are declared in the right-hand cell. When adding new rows, you need only the Insert command and the Cancel command.

LISTING 4.31. The InsertItemTemplate Declaration for a FormView Control

```
<InsertItemTemplate>
  <table border="0" cellpadding="5">
    <tr>
      <td align="right">Company Name:</td>
      <td>
        <asp:TextBox id="txtInsertName" runat="server"
            Text='<%# Bind("CompanyName") %>' />
      </td>
    </tr>
    <tr>
      <td align="right">Phone:</td>
      <td>
        <asp:TextBox id="txtInsertPhone" runat="server"
            Text='<%# Bind("Phone") %>' />
      </td>
    </tr>
    <tr>
      <td colspan="2">
        <asp:LinkButton id="btnAdd" CommandName="Insert"
            Text="Add" runat="server" />
        <asp:LinkButton id="btnAbandon" CommandName="Cancel"
            Text="Cancel" runat="server" />
      </td>
    </tr>
  </table>
</InsertItemTemplate>
```

Listings 4.28 through 4.31 show all the code required to declare a complete FormView control that can provide attractive customized output that doesn't look like the standard GridView or DetailsView controls. The remaining task is to add a data source control to the page, with the appropriate settings for the SelectCommand, UpdateCommand, and InsertCommand, as shown in Listing 4.32. This data source control is connected to the FormView control through the DataSourceID property of the FormView, and no other code is required to make it all work. Figure 4.10 shows the results, with the page in normal mode, edit mode, and insert mode.

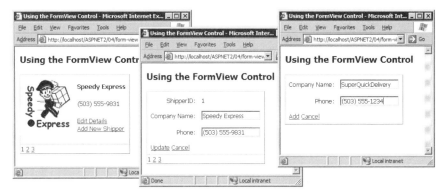

FIGURE 4.10. The FormView control in normal, edit, and insert modes

LISTING 4.32. The Declaration of the SqlDataSource Control for the FormView

```
<asp:SqlDataSource id="dvs1" runat="server"
  SelectCommand="SELECT ShipperID, CompanyName, Phone FROM Shippers
  UpdateCommand="UPDATE Shippers SET CompanyName=@CompanyName,
                Phone=@Phone WHERE ShipperID=@ShipperID"
  InsertCommand="INSERT INTO Shippers (CompanyName, Phone)
                VALUES (@CompanyName, @Phone)" />
```

The New and Simplified Data Binding Syntax

You may have noticed that the code we used in the examples earlier in this chapter takes advantage of a simplified syntax for the data binding expressions. ASP.NET 2.0 fully supports the previous (version 1.0) syntax but adds a couple of new features as well. There is the simplified syntax for binding to nonhierarchical data (rows and columns), plus new techniques that allow binding to hierarchical data such as XML documents.

The ASP.NET 1.0 Syntax for Data Binding

In ASP.NET 1.0, there are two ways to bind to data in a control that supports data binding. One choice is to use the early-bound approach that references the container directly:

```
<%# Container.DataItem("expression") %>
```

The *expression* is usually a column name from the rowset, though it can be the name of a property or field exposed by the object bound to the control.

The alternative, which is useful if you want to format the value, is the late-bound approach using the `Eval` method of the `DataBinder` that is responsible for carrying out the data binding:

```
<%# DataBinder.Eval(Container.DataItem, _
           "expression"[, "format"]) %>
```

In this case, the optional *format* string can be used to output markup and literal content, with the value inserted into the string at the point where a {0} placeholder is located. The placeholder can also include a standard format string character to format the value at the same time, for example:

```
<%# DataBinder.Eval(Container.DataItem, _
           "TotalPrice", "Total Price: {0:C}") %>
```

You can see one of the issues that come into play here. The statement is verbose, and yet the majority is exactly the same in every occurrence. Moreover, because the content is executable code (the `Eval` method), line continuation characters are required in Visual Basic. Yet this is the only way to exert any real control over the format and content of the output.

Simplified ASP.NET 2.0 Syntax for Nonhierarchical Data Binding

In version 2.0, the most obvious simplification is that `DataBinder` is now the default context for data binding expressions, so the `Eval` method can be used like this:

```
<%# Eval("expression"[, "format"]) %>
```

The preceding example then becomes just

```
<%# Eval("TotalPrice", "Total Price: {0:C}") %>
```

And, if no formatting of the value is required, you can use

```
<%# Eval("TotalPrice") %>
```

Simplified ASP.NET 2.0 Syntax for Hierarchical (XML) Data Binding

ASP.NET 2.0 introduces new data source controls that can expose hierarchical data from XML documents. When a control is bound to such a data source control, the data is exposed to the control as a hierarchical structure that cannot be bound using the existing data binding syntax.

Instead, a development on the existing techniques is used, based on a new XPathBinder object exposed by the list control when bound to XML data. The XPathBinder exposes two methods named Eval and Select. Both take an instance of an object that exposes the IXPathNavigable interface (such as the container for a data source control bound to an XML document). The second parameter is an XPath expression that selects one or more nodes from the source data.

The Eval (XPath) Method

The Eval method returns a single value from the current "row" (a single element value) and can optionally format it using the same approach as described for nonhierarchical data in the previous section:

```
<%# XPathBinder.Eval(Container.DataItem, _
            "expression"[, "format"]) %>
```

However, the simplified syntax is the obvious choice here, using an override of the Eval method named XPath:

```
<%# XPath("expression"[, "format"]) %>
```

The *expression* is an XPath that returns a single node (element or attribute) from the fragment or XML document to which the control is bound. The *format* is the same as you use with the Eval method for non-hierarchical (rowset) data.

The Select (XPathSelect) Method

With hierarchical data, each node can be a collection of other nodes. For example, in an XML document, each <employee> element in a list of employees is likely to be the parent of several other nodes (see Listing 4.33).

LISTING 4.33. A Sample XML File for Data Binding

```
<employee-list>
  <employee id="1">
    <name>Mike</name>
    <department>Sales</department>
    <phone>3867</phone>
  </employee>
  <employee id="2">
    <name>Nikita</name>
    <department>Marketing</department>
    <phone>1442</phone>
  </employee>
  <employee id="3">
    ... etc. ...
  </employee>
<employee-list>
```

In this case, a control bound to the data can use the XPath approach to select a specific employee name:

```
<%# XPath("employee[@id='2']/name") %>
```

However, a useful feature would be to bind a nested list control to each employee element so that it can display the details of each employee. In this case, the data binding statement must return a collection of nodes. The `Select` method of the `XPathBinder` does just this:

```
<%# XPathBinder.Select(Container.DataItem, _
                "expression") %>
```

Again, there is a simplified approach that uses an override of the `Select` method called `XPathSelect`. (There is no format parameter because the method returns a collection and not a single value.)

```
<%# XPathSelect("expression") %>
```

As an example, the following statement will return all the child elements of the `<employee>` element that has an `id` attribute with the value 2:

```
<%# XPathSelect("employee[@id='2']") %>
```

Two-Way Data Binding Syntax for Templated Controls

The new `GridView`, `DetailsView`, and `FormView` controls that are added to ASP.NET in version 2.0 support automatic no-code data binding to a data source control. This process also supports editing the data and automatically pushes changes such as inserts, deletes, and updates back into the original data source. In the `GridView` and `DetailsView` controls, this works because the standard field controls used to generate the columns or fields can connect the individual edit controls in each column with the appropriate data columns in the original data source.

However, when you use templates to generate the user interface, the controls cannot perform this automatic linking of UI control to data source column. In this case, you must use another form of data binding syntax specifically designed to support two-way data binding. Instead of the `Container.DataItem` or `Eval` approaches, you use the `Bind` method. Like `Eval`, it has two overloads. Effectively, this means that the format string (the second parameter) is optional:

```
<%# Bind("expression"[, "format"]) %>
```

Therefore, if formatting of a column value is required, you can use something like this:

```
<%# Bind("UnitPrice", "{0:C}") %>
```

If no formatting of the value is required, you just use the column name:

```
<%# Bind("UnitPrice") %>
```

There are some issues to be aware of when using the `Bind` method.

- The `Bind` method automatically populates the parameters declared within the SQL statements used for the `InsertCommand`, `UpdateCommand`, and `DeleteCommand` properties of the attached data source control. Therefore, you must include a server control (with a unique ID property value) for every parameter used in the relevant SQL statement and then use the `Bind` method with this control. In other words, in an `EditItemTemplate`, you must include a control that uses the `Bind` method for every parameter in the SQL `UPDATE` statement. In an `InsertItemTemplate` you must include a control that uses the `Bind` method for every parameter in the SQL `INSERT` statement.
- It should be used only where values can be edited, for example, in an `EditItemTemplate` and `InsertItemTemplate`, not in an `ItemTemplate`, `AlternatingItemTemplate`, or `SelectedItemTemplate`.
- It can be used only in a data-bound container control, not at `Page` level or in other controls.
- The list control must be populated by a data source control connected to it through the `DataSourceID` property or attribute. It cannot be used for controls that use the `DataSource` property.
- The UI control that uses the `Bind` method must have a unique user-declared value for its `id` property.
- The `Bind` method cannot be used in a `DataList` or `Repeater` control. Effectively, the only controls to which it applies are `GridView`, `DetailsView` and `FormView`. A new `ListView` control is proposed to replace `DataList`, but this is not implemented in the current beta release.

New and Simplified Data Binding Syntax Options

In summary, you now have six types of data binding expressions:

A: `<%# Container.DataItem("[column|property|field]") %>`

B: `<%# DataBinder.Eval("[column|property|field]"[, "format"]) %>`

C: `<%# Eval("[column|property|field]"[, "format"]) %>`

D: `<%# Bind("[column|property|field]"[, "format"]) %>`

E: `<%# XPath("xpath-expression"[, "format"]) %>`

F: `<%# XPathSelect("xpath-expression") %>`

Table 4.16 shows how and where they can be used.

TABLE 4.16. Availability of Data Binding Options

	Nonhierarchical (Rowset) Data	Hierarchical (XML) Data	Returns a Single Value	Returns a Collection	Supports Formatting	Two-Way Templated Binding
A	✓	✗	✓	✗	✗	✗
B	✓	✗	✓	✗	✓	✗
C	✓	✗	✓	✗	✓	✗
D	✓	✗	✓	✗	✓	✓
E	✗	✓	✓	✗	✓	✗
F	✗	✓	✗	✓	✗	✗

Building Data-Bound Pages with Visual Studio 2005

In this and the previous chapter, we've concentrated on the new controls in ASP.NET 2.0 that make it easy to build data-bound pages that can display and update data. We showed you how easy it is to declare the controls you need and how to add attributes to change the appearance or behavior of the controls. But the main focus has been to help you understand what the controls do and how they are used as part of the overall page design process.

However, it is even easier to build these kinds of pages using a suitable development tool or environment. We introduced Microsoft's Visual Studio 2005 tool in Chapter 2, and you saw how comprehensive it is. It is ideal for building data-bound pages—you can open a connection to a database in the Server Explorer window and then simply drag a table onto the design surface. This automatically creates the appropriate `SqlDataSource` and `GridView` controls and sets the relevant properties (see Figure 4.11).

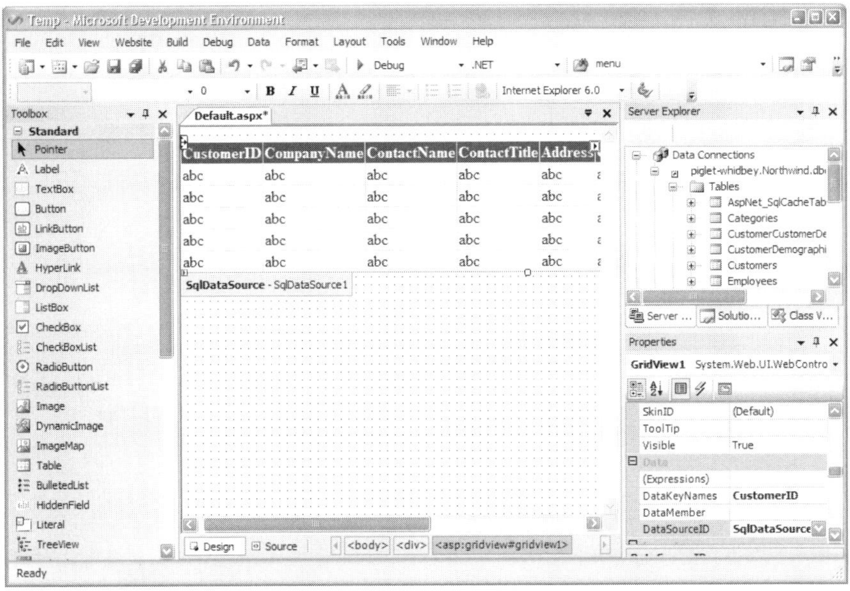

FIGURE 4.11. Creating a data-bound page with Visual Studio 2005

The resulting page displays all the rows from that table, as shown in Figure 4.12. You can then use the Common Tasks menus or the Properties window to configure the GridView and SqlDataSource controls, apply formatting, add sorting and paging, and so on.

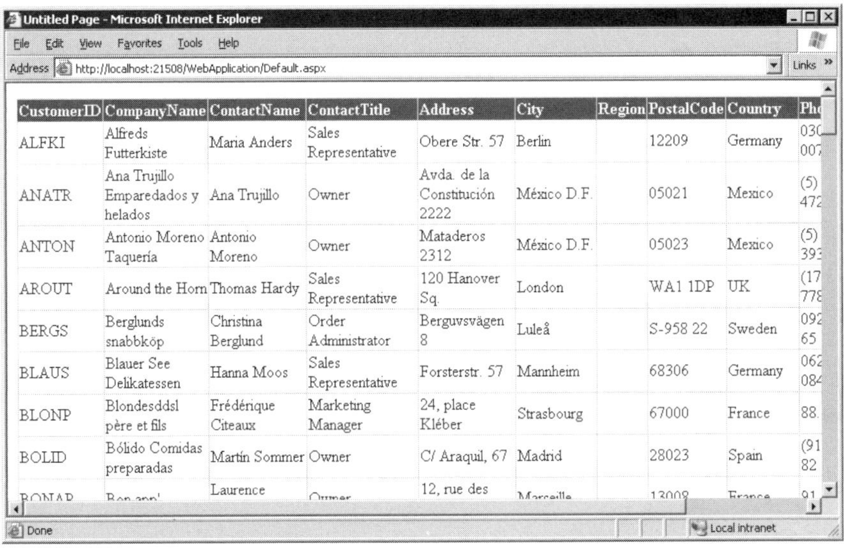

FIGURE 4.12. Viewing the results

Note that, by default, Visual Studio 2005 changes the `ProviderName` property of the `SqlDataSource` control from the default of `System.Data.SqlClient` to `System.Data.OleDb` in order to provide maximum compatibility with all types of relational databases.

SUMMARY

In this and the previous chapters we've looked at the new aspects of ASP.NET 2.0 that are perhaps the most vital in business or commercial Web sites and Web applications—the presentation and manipulation of data stored in a database or other type of data store.

A whole new approach to extracting data from a data store and pushing updates back into a data store has been added in version 2.0. In 2002, Microsoft released a free development tool called ASP.NET Web Matrix, which pioneered the concept of data source controls and grid controls that require no code to be written when displaying data.

Building on that, ASP.NET 2.0 includes a whole raft of data source controls, with more on the way, allowing no-code data binding to be performed against almost any data source. And, even better, most of these data source controls also support updates, allowing changes to the data and the addition of new rows to be pushed back into the data store automatically.

In this chapter, we looked in depth at the new `GridView`, `DetailsView`, and `FormView` controls. We also discussed the simplified syntax for data binding and the new XML binding syntax, as well as a quick overview of using Visual Studio 2005 to build data-bound pages.

You'll see more discussion of using data-bound controls in the next chapter, where—along with the use of the new Master Pages feature in ASP.NET—we'll look at other controls that are designed to work with data and how we can use them for page and site navigation purposes.

■ 5 ■

Master Pages and Navigation

T HE LOOK AND FEEL OF A SITE can be its savior or its downfall, and plenty of books and Web sites instruct readers in design and usability. This chapter discusses not site design but how ASP.NET 2.0 aids in the design and consistency of sites. From the development perspective, generating a site that is consistent isn't so hard and can be achieved in plenty of ways. However, these are all custom solutions, not part of the underlying .NET Framework. ASP.NET 2.0 brings a solution that not only improves ways of providing UI reuse but also aids in maintenance of the site.

Likewise, providing navigation within a site can be achieved easily, but you nearly always have to write code or buy a custom solution. ASP.NET 2.0 has a new framework that provides a simple and extensible solution for providing navigation.

Master Pages in Detail

In Chapter 1 we had a brief look at the idea of master pages, showing how they provide a template for all content pages. This provides a way to create a consistent look for a site, because the look is defined in the master page. Let's refresh ourselves about how this works.

Figure 5.1 shows an example of two content pages using a master page. The master page defines the page layout—that is, the shared user interface and code plus any default content. In this case it is the light shaded content at

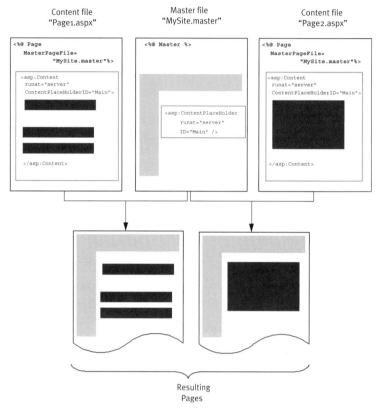

Figure 5.1. Master pages in action

the top and left, representing menus and other navigation features. The master page defines content areas using the `ContentPlaceHolder` control, and it is into these areas that content pages place their content (shown as dark shaded areas in the figure). Pages that use a master page to define the layout can place content only in the areas defined by the `ContentPlaceHolder`, thus enabling a consistent site design.

Creating Master Pages

In Visual Studio 2005, creating master pages is simply a matter of selecting Master Page from the Add New Item dialog. The newly created master page is just an ASP.NET page with a different file extension (`.master`), so it fits with your existing knowledge. You don't have to learn any new techniques, apart from the use of the `ContentPlaceHolder` control. Listing 5.1, for example, shows the contents of a master page newly added to a site.

Listing 5.1. A Simple Master Page

```
<%@ Master language="VB" %>

<script runat="server">

</script>

<html>
<head runat="server">
  <title>Untitled Page</title>
</head>

<body>
  <form runat="server">
    <asp:ContentPlaceHolder
        id="ContentPlaceHolder1" runat="server">
    </asp:ContentPlaceHolder>
  </form>
</body>
</html>
```

You can see that this looks similar to existing ASP.NET pages and contains simple HTML and ASP.NET controls. The main difference between this page and a standard ASP.NET page is the use of the `Master` directive and the file suffix `.master`. The critical point is the use of the `ContentPlaceHolder` control, which dictates where content pages can insert content. The `id` attribute uniquely identifies the placeholder so that more than one placeholder can be in a master page. The master page can have code as well as content, allowing the master page to be dynamic.

Turning this empty master page into one that defines the look and feel of a site is simply a matter of adding controls to get the required look. Figure 5.2,

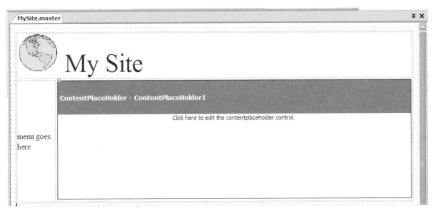

Figure 5.2. The master page in design view

for example, shows the addition of a table to define the page layout, with an area at the top where the logo and site description sit and a region down the left for the menu. In the middle we have the ContentPlaceHolder, which is the area we are leaving for content pages to fill in.

Using a Master Page

To create a page that uses the master page, you pick Web Form from the Add New Item dialog and tick the Select master page checkbox. When you click the Add button, you get the opportunity to pick which master page you wish the content page to inherit from, as shown in Figure 5.3.

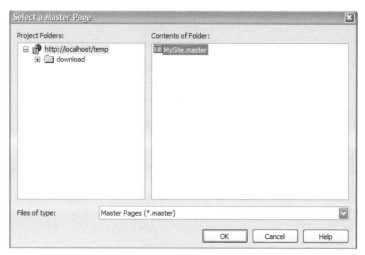

Figure 5.3. Picking a master page for a content page

When first created, the content page contains a single line of code (wrapped here to make it easier to read):

```
<%@ Page language="VB" masterpagefile="~/mysite.master"
        Title="untitled page" %>
```

Figure 5.4 shows this content page in design view. Notice how the content defined in the master is grayed out and disabled; the only area allowed for editing is that defined by the Content control.

The confusing thing here is that this Content control doesn't seem to exist in the file—remember there was only a single line, the Page directive. This is because at design time the content of the master page is rendered, but our page defines no content, so an empty region is displayed where the

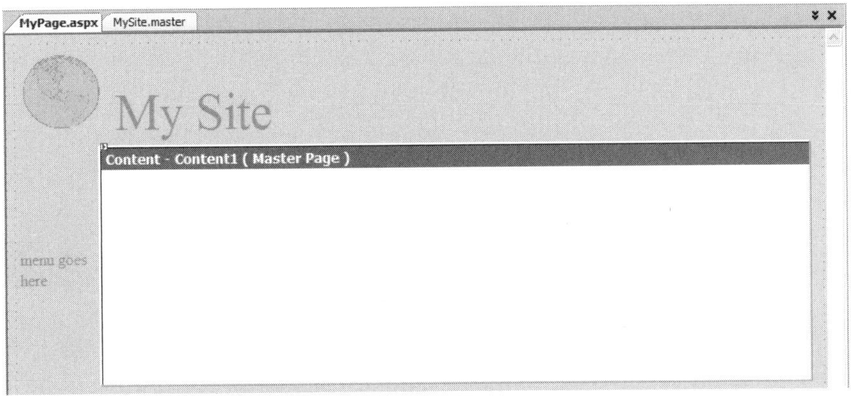

Figure 5.4. A content page with an attached master

Designer can prompt you to add the Content control. This can be done either by selecting the Create Empty Content option from the Common Tasks menu or by simply dragging controls from the Toolbox into this region.

Listing 5.2 shows the source view for a content page with a couple of controls added.

LISTING 5.2. Using a Master Page (MyPage.aspx)

```
<%@ Page Language="VB" MasterPageFile="MySite.master" %>

<asp:Content id="Content1"
    ContentPlaceHolderId="ContentPlaceHolder1"
    runat="server">
  <asp:Button id="Button1" runat="server" text="Button" />
  <asp:ListBox id="ListBox1" runat="server">
  </asp:ListBox">
</asp:Content>
```

The local content is within the Content control—content in a page that has a master page cannot be outside a Content control. This ensures that all content pages using a master have a consistent look. Because master pages can contain multiple content areas, the id of the ContentPlaceHolder control is used to link the Content control to the ContentPlaceHolder control in the master page. When the page is constructed, ASP.NET first adds all of the content from the master page. Then it loops through the ContentPlaceHolder controls and, for each, looks in the content page for a Content control where the ContentPlaceHolderId matches the id of the ContentPlaceHolder. This ensures that the correct content is placed in the correct holder.

Default Content

Along with layout and code that applies to all pages, the master page can also supply default content, which can be overridden by content pages or displayed if not overridden. This is achieved by simply inserting the content within the `ContentPlaceHolder` element. For example, our `MySite.master` page could have the following default content:

```
<asp:ContentPlaceHolder
    id="ContentPlaceHolder1" runat="server">

  <h2>Welcome</h2>
  Welcome to my site, where you'll find
  lots of interesting stuff.
</asp:ContentPlaceHolder>
```

Creating a new content file based on this master would give us the following line of code:

```
<%@ Page Language="VB" masterpagefile="~/MySite.master" %>
```

Because we haven't specified a `Content` control, all content is provided by the master page, as shown in Figure 5.5.

Figure 5.5. A content page with no content other than default content

Nested Master Pages

Master pages aren't limited to a single master and content pages; the architecture allows for nested master pages, where a master page can have a master page. This is particularly useful for sites that require some overall branding and look but that also have subsites whose look must be consistent. For example, consider a corporation with group intranets—perhaps one for the sales department and one for research. The company wishes to have an overall look, including menus between the subsites, but allows the departments to design their parts of the site to fit their business needs. In this situation you could have three master pages—the top-level master defining the corporate site image, a submaster for the sales department, and a submaster for the research department. The sales and research submaster pages would define the corporate master as their master page. The inheritance rules of master pages mean that any page using one of the submaster pages receives content from all master pages in the hierarchy (see Figure 5.6).

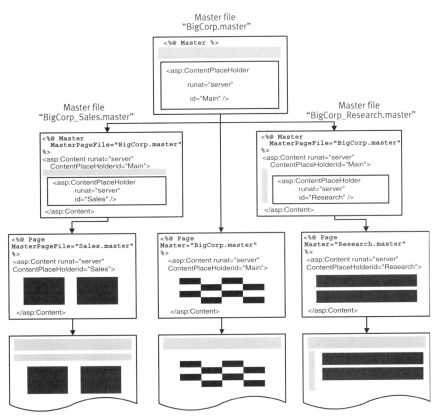

Figure 5.6. Using nested master pages

Notice that you can inherit from any level of the hierarchy—you aren't limited to using the bottom level. This allows you to provide generic content pages that apply to the whole site, as well as pages that apply to individual site areas. Let's take a look at the code that makes this possible, starting with the site master as shown in Listing 5.3.

LISTING 5.3. The Site Master Page (BigCorp.master)

```
<%@ Master %>

<html>
<head>
  <link rel="stylesheet" type="text/css" href="MySite.css">
</head>

<body>
<form runat="server">
  <table width="100%" border="0">
    <tr>
      <td>
        <asp:Hyperlink ImageUrl="home.gif" runat="server"
            NavigateUrl="BigCorp_Default.aspx" />
      </td>
      <td>
        <h1>Big Corp Intranet</h1>
      </td>
      <td>
        <a href="BigCorp_SalesDefault.aspx">Sales</a>
      </td>
      <td>
        <a href="BigCorp_ResearchDefault.aspx">Research</a>
      </td>
    </tr>
  </table>
  <asp:ContentPlaceHolder runat="server"
    id="MainContentRegion">
    Welcome to Big Corp. Please use the menus above
    to select the required department.
  </asp:ContentPlaceHolder>
</form>
</body>
</html>
```

This simple master page, containing some content and a placeholder, is shown in design view in Figure 5.7.

Now consider Listing 5.4, which shows a submaster page that inherits from the first master page.

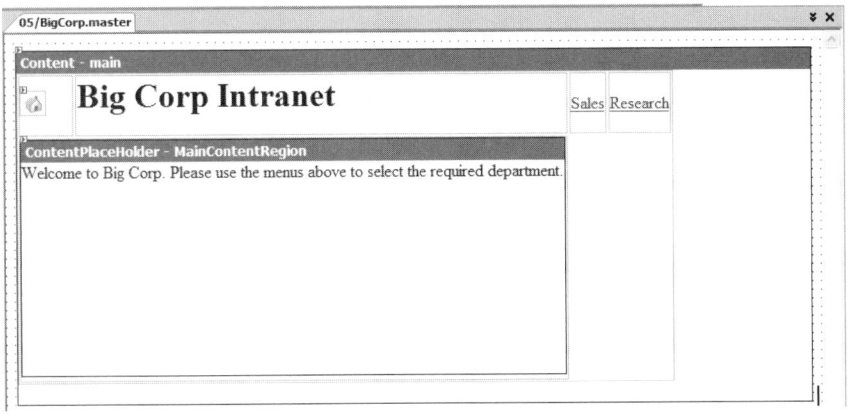

Figure 5.7. The site-wide master page (BigCorp.master)

LISTING 5.4. A Submaster Page (BigCorp_Sales.master)

```
<%@ Master MasterPageFile="BigCorp.master"%>

<asp:Content ContentPlaceHolderId="MainContentRegion"
    runat="server">
<table border="0" width="100%">
  <tr>
    <td>
      <h2>Big Corp Sales</h2>
    </td>
  </tr>
  <tr>
    <td>
      <table border="0" width="100%">
        <tr>
          <td><a href="sales/page1.aspx" Menu 1</a></td>
          <td><a href="sales/page2.aspx" Menu 2</a></td>
          <td><a href="sales/page3.aspx" Menu 3</a></td>
          <td><a href="sales/page4.aspx" Menu 4</a></td>
        </tr>
      </table>
    </td>
  </tr>
  <tr>
    <td>
      <asp:ContentPlaceHolder runat="server"
          id="SalesContentRegion" />
    </td>
  </tr>
</table>
</asp:Content>
```

Because this page inherits from a master page, all content must be within a `Content` control, with a `ContentPlaceHolderId` matching that of the master `ContentPlaceHolder`. However, we can also include `ContentPlaceHolder` controls in this master, allowing content pages to add content to our content.

> Showing nested master pages, or content pages whose master is nested, in design view is not supported by Visual Studio 2005. Instead you must use the source code view to edit the nested master page. This is also true of master pages defined in the configuration files, where the content from the master page is not shown.

Using the nested master page is the same as creating any other content page. For example, Listing 5.5 shows a content page using `BigCorp_Sales.master`.

LISTING 5.5. A Content Page Using a Nested Master Page

```
<%@ Page MasterPageFile="BigCorp_Sales.master" %>

<script runat="server">

    Sub Page_Load(sender As Object, e As EventArgs)

    End Sub

</script>

<asp:Content ContentPlaceHolderId="SalesContentRegion"
    runat="server">
  Welcome to the Big Corp Sales Intranet
</asp:Content>
```

Here the `ContentPlaceHolderId` matches the immediate parent, and because the parent inherits from another page, the ultimate result is a combination of both master pages and the child ASP.NET content page. So, if we have two child content pages, one for the sales division and one for the research division, we'll end up with a site as shown in Figure 5.8.

In Figure 5.8 you can see that although both departments have chosen a different style of menu (one vertical and one horizontal), the top of the page remains constant because it is defined in the top-level master.

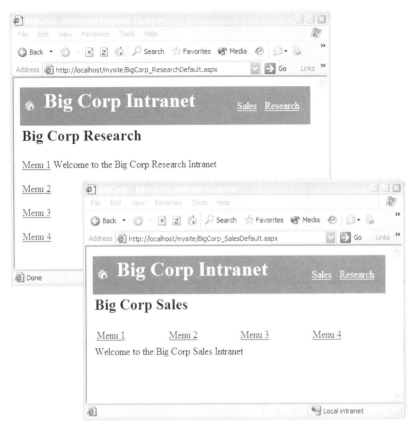

Figure 5.8. Using nested master pages

Master Page Configuration

Attaching a master page directly to a page provides great flexibility but does have a downside. Not only must developers know the name of the master but they are also free to not use it, which could result in pages not fitting with the overall site design. To ensure that a master page cannot be omitted, master pages can be attached globally by modifying the Web configuration file, as shown in the following fragment:

```
<configuration>
  <system.web>

    <pages masterPageFile="BigCorp.master" />

  </system.web>
</configuration>
```

A master page attached locally via the `MasterPageFile` attribute, however, overrides any global master pages defined in `web.config`.

Device-Specific Master Pages

ASP.NET has a new architecture for detecting and rendering content to mobile devices, and this control architecture has also been implemented by the master page processing, enabling different master pages to be used for different devices. For example, it would be possible to supply different master pages for Internet Explorer and Mozilla. This is achieved by creating separate master pages and then in the page prefixing the `MasterPageFile` attribute with the name of the device, as shown below:

```
<%@ Page MasterPageFile="default.master"
         Mozilla:MasterPageFile="mozilla.master" %>
```

When this page is accessed by a Mozilla browser, `mozilla.master` is used. All other browsers use the default master page. The results can be seen in Figure 5.9, where the content simply differs for each browser. This technique comes into its own when used to support multiple devices, such as small-screen devices, where your master page might need to be very different, perhaps to incorporate a different menu structure. Device-specific

Figure 5.9. Device-specific master pages

support is also available on the `Content` control, where the device-specific content could be used like this:

```
<asp:Content runat="server"
    ContentPlaceHolderId="HeaderContent"
    Mozilla:ContentPlaceHolderId="HeaderMoz">
    . . .
</asp:Content>
```

Support for mobile devices is covered in more detail in Chapter 10.

> Like the rest of the device-specific features, the list of devices can be found in the CONFIG directory under the .NET Framework installation directory. These device capability files detail the exact features of each browser.

Event Ordering

Because events can be present in both the master and content pages, the event order follows that of User Controls. So, for events that are captured twice, such as the `Page_Load` event, the content page event is fired first.

Setting the Master Page Programmatically

In addition to being set at the page level or the application level, the master page can be set at runtime. Because the master is compiled as part of the page, this needs to be done in the `PreInit` event of the page, before the control tree is constructed. For example:

```
Protected Overrides Sub OnPreInit(E As EventArgs)

  MyBase.OnPreInit(e)

  Me.MasterPageFile = "site.master"

End Sub
```

Accessing the Master Page

Content pages that have a master have a property, `Master`, allowing access to the master page. The `Master` property returns an instance of `Page` (from `System.Web.UI`), and thus you can access all of the properties and methods in the same way as for other pages. Strong typed access to the master page is enabled by using the `MasterType` page directive (this can be used on any page that inherits from a master page). For example, to access a control from the master page you can do one of two things, both described in this section.

The first option is to expose the control through a public property on the master page (Listing 5.6) and access that property from the content page (Listing 5.7).

LISTING 5.6. Exposing Master Page Properties (MySite.master)

```
<%@ Master %>
<script runat="server">

Public ReadOnly Property Home() As Hyperlink
  Get
    Return homeUrl
  End Get
End Property

</script>

<form runat="server">

  <asp:Hyperlink id="homeUrl"
     NavigateUrl="default.aspx" />

</form>
```

LISTING 5.7. Accessing Exposed Master Page Properties (MyPage.aspx)

```
<%@ Page MasterPageFile="MySite.master" %>
<%@ MasterType virtualPath="MySite.Master" %>
<script runat="server">

Sub Page_Load(sender As Object, e As EventArgs)

  Dim Url As String = Master.Home.NavigateUrl

End Sub

</script>
```

Listing 5.6 shows a master page with a control exposed as a `Public Property`, and Listing 5.7 shows a content page accessing that control through the exposed property. Without the `MasterType` directive the `Home` property would not be accessible because the `Master` reference would be to the default type `MasterPage` rather than the instance of the actual master page. The `MasterType` directive can use one of the `virtualPath` or `typeName` attributes, but not both.

The second approach is to access the controls late bound and use the `FindControl` method to find the controls, as shown in Listing 5.8.

LISTING 5.8. Accessing Master Page Contents Late Bound

```
<%@ Page MasterPageFile="MySite.master" %>
<script runat="server">

Sub Page_Load(sender As Object, e As EventArgs)

  Dim Url As String = _
   CType(Master.FindControl("homeUrl"), _
       Hyperlink).NavigateUrl

End Sub

</script>
```

Although the first solution does require you to expose controls as properties, you have to do this only for controls that are needed external to the master page. This approach does provide a more efficient solution than the late-bound approach.

Remember that controls in a `Content` region replace controls in the associated `ContentPlaceHolder` region on the master. Therefore, if each of the `Content` and `ContentPlaceHolder` controls contain a `Label` control, accessing that `Label` from server code in the content page will actually access the `Label` from the content page and not the master page.

Navigation

The importance of good navigation on a site cannot be underestimated. It doesn't matter how great your site looks or how well it was developed—if it's hard to navigate, users won't like using it. It's easy to see how seriously navigation is taken just by looking at the number of menu controls that have been written since ASP.NET 1.0 was released. There are now controls that use tree views, vertical expansion, horizontal layouts, flashy graphics, and so on.

Providing a good menu isn't the end of site navigation because it's important to ensure visitors know where they are within the site hierarchy. Too often we see sites with pages three or four levels deep within the menu structure, but when we navigate to those pages there's no indication of where we are. We are left wondering how to navigate back up the structure; at worst, we have to go back to the home page to navigate down again.

Site Maps

There are plenty of ways to implement navigation on a site, but none are an intrinsic part of ASP.NET 1.x. With ASP.NET 2.0, new controls and configuration files provide a set way to define site structure and techniques for displaying the navigation information and extracting the current navigation path.

Like the rest of ASP.NET, the architecture for navigation has been broken down into logical parts, allowing customization. First, there is a configurable provider supplying the site map information, and then a set of controls that can take advantage of the data supplied by the provider. The provider not only exposes the site structure to other controls but also keeps track of the current navigation, allowing pages to identify where in the hierarchy they are. The entire structure and the current details can be exposed to users by binding controls to the provider. This pluggable architecture means that data defining the structure of a site can come from any data source—the site map provider is the link between the data and the navigation within a site.

Site Map Providers

A **site map provider** is a data provider that exposes the site structure by way of a set interface. Site maps are pluggable within the application configuration file, within the `<system.web>` section. The syntax for this section is shown in Listing 5.9.

LISTING 5.9. Site Map Configuration Syntax

```
<siteMap
    defaultProvider="String"
    enabled="[true|false]">
  <providers>
    <add
        type="String"
        name="String"
        description="String"
        provider-specific-configuration />
    <remove
```

```
        name="String" />
    <clear>
  </providers>
</siteMap>
```

The attributes for the `siteMap` element are shown in Table 5.1. The attributes for the `providers` element are shown in Table 5.2.

With the beta release of ASP.NET 2.0, the only provider is the `XmlSiteMapProvider` (in `System.Web`), allowing site navigation structure to be stored in an XML file. For a full description of the `type` attribute, see the `machine.config` file. The `XmlSiteMapProvider` has one provider-specific attribute, as shown in Table 5.3.

With the beta release of ASP.NET 2.0, the only provider is the `XmlSiteMapProvider` (in `System.Web`), allowing site navigation structure to be stored in an XML file. For a full description of the type attribute, see the `machine.config` file. The `XmlSiteMapProvider` has one provider-specific attribute, as shown in Table 5.3.

TABLE 5.1. siteMap Configuration

Attribute	Description
defaultProvider	The name of the default provider. This should match one of the names supplied in the `providers` section.
enabled	A `Boolean` value indicating whether or not site maps are enabled.

TABLE 5.2. siteMap providers Configuration

Attribute	Description
name	The name of the site map provider.
description	A description of the provider.
type	A string containing the full .NET type of the provider.

TABLE 5.3. XmlSiteMapProvider-Specific Attribute

Attribute	Description
siteMapFile	The name of the XML file containing the site structure. The filename is configured as `web.SiteMap`.

The pluggable architecture makes it extremely easy to add support for additional methods of site map storage. For example, you could write a Front Page Server Extensions site map provider to read the site structure from the format used by Microsoft Front Page, or perhaps one to build the structure from the file system, directly reading the names of the files and directories. To write your own site map provider you need to inherit from the abstract class `SiteMapProvider`. A discussion of this is outside the scope of the book, but details of the class can be found in the documentation.

Site Map Configuration Files

The `XmlSiteMapProvider` defines a set schema for the `web.SiteMap` file, as shown in Listing 5.10.

LISTING 5.10. XmlSiteMapProvider Schema

```
<xs:schema xmlns:xs="http://www.w3.org/2001/XMLSchema"
           elementFormDefault="qualified">
  <xs:element name="siteMap">
    <xs:complexType>
      <xs:sequence>
        <xs:element ref="siteMapNode"
                    maxOccurs="unbounded"/>
      </xs:sequence>
    </xs:complexType>
  </xs:element>
  <xs:element name="siteMapNode">
    <xs:complexType>
      <xs:sequence>
        <xs:element ref="siteMapNode" minOccurs="0"
                    MaxOccurs="unbounded"/>
      </xs:sequence>
      <xs:attribute name="url" type="xs:string"/>
      <xs:attribute name="title" type="xs:string"/>
      <xs:attribute name="description" type="xs:string"/>
      <xs:attribute name="roles" type="xs:string"/>
      <xs:attribute name="SiteMapFile" type="xs:string"/>
      <xs:attribute name="Provider" type="xs:string"/>
    </xs:complexType>
  </xs:element>
</xs:schema>
```

This defines a structure consisting of a root `siteMap` element, with the site structure being contained by `siteMapNode` elements. There has to be one top-level `siteMapNode` element, and within that can be any number of `siteMapNode` elements of any depth. The attributes for the `siteMapNode` element are shown in Table 5.4.

TABLE 5.4. siteMapNode Attributes

Attribute	Description
url	The URL to be used to navigate to the node. This must be unique within the entire site map file.
title	The title of the node.
description	A description of the node.
roles	A list of roles allowed to view the node. Multiple roles can be separated by semicolons (;) or commas (,).
SiteMapFile	An external file containing additional siteMap nodes.
Provider	The name of the site map provider that will supply additional nodes specified in SiteMapFile.

The use of SiteMapFile allows the site map information to be split among different sources. This is especially useful when different divisions supply sections of a corporate site—each part of the site map can be authored independently and even stored in different providers.

Listing 5.11 shows a sample site map file. To create one within Visual Studio 2005 you simply create a new XML file and call it web.SiteMap—there isn't a template for this.

LISTING 5.11. Sample web.SiteMap File

```xml
<?xml version="1.0" encoding="utf-8" ?>
<siteMap>
  <siteMapNode title="Home" url="sitemaps.aspx">
    <siteMapNode title="A" url="sitemapsA.aspx">
      <siteMapNode title="1" url="sitemapsA1.aspx" />
      <siteMapNode title="2" url="sitemapsA2.aspx" />
      <siteMapNode title="3" url="sitemapsA3.aspx" />
    </siteMapNode>
    <siteMapNode title="B" url="sitemapsB.aspx">
      <siteMapNode title="4" url="sitemapsB4.aspx">
        <siteMapNode title="a" url="sitemapsB4a.aspx" />
        <siteMapNode title="b" url="sitemapsB4b.aspx" />
      </siteMapNode>
      <siteMapNode title="5" url="sitemapsB5.aspx" />
      <siteMapNode title="6" url="sitemapsB6.aspx" />
    </siteMapNode>
    <siteMapNode title="C" url="sitemapsC.aspx" />
  </siteMapNode>
</siteMap>
```

This provides the following structure for the site:

```
Home
  A
      1
      2
      3
  B
      4
          a
          b
      5
      6
  C
```

Using a Site Map File

Once the structure of your site is defined in the site map file, you need a way to make use of it. For this you use a `SiteMapDataSource` control, which provides data access to the site map data, and then a control to display that data. From within Visual Studio 2005 you can just drag a `SiteMapDataSource` control onto the design surface—there's no need to set any properties because it defaults to using `web.SiteMap` as its data source. You can then drag a `TreeView` or `Menu` control onto the page and set the `DataSourceId` property to the `id` of the `SiteMapDataSource` control. Figure 5.10, for example, shows how our Big Corp site could be constructed using a single menu.

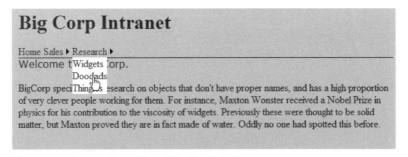

Figure 5.10. A menu bound to a SiteMapDataSource

Other controls can be bound to site map data, but in the beta release, the `Menu` and `TreeView` controls provide the best option because of their hierarchical display.

Site Maps in Depth

At its simplest, the use of site maps needs nothing more than what we just discussed, but there's actually more to them. Adding a `SiteMapDataSource` control to a page provides all that's needed for site map handling, but there are properties that allow for more control over how the data is supplied from the `SiteMapDataSource` to controls. For example, Listing 5.12 shows the syntax of the `SiteMapDataSource` control.

LISTING 5.12. SiteMapDataSource Syntax

```
<asp:SiteMapDataSource id="String" runat="server"
  SiteMapProvider="String"
  ShowStartingNode="[true|false]"
  StartFromCurrentNode="[true|false]"
  StartingNodeOffset="Integer"
  StartingNodeUrl="String"
/>
```

Table 5.5 lists the attributes.

TABLE 5.5. SiteMapDataSource Attributes

Attribute	Description
`SiteMapProvider`	Specifies the name of the provider supplying the site map data.
`ShowStartingNode`	Indicates whether or not the starting node is shown. The default value is `True`.
`StartFromCurrentNode`	Indicates whether or not the data exposed starts from the current node. The default value is `False`.
`StartingNodeOffset`	Specifies the node depth at which to start representing data. The default is `0`, which is the first node.
`StartingNodeUrl`	Specifies the URL of the node at which to start representing data.

The effects of some of these properties may not be immediately obvious; the best way to understand them is to walk through an example that allows setting of the properties, as shown in Figure 5.11. This scenario uses the site map code shown earlier in Listing 5.11. There are two navigation controls, a `TreeView` and a `Menu`, and for clarity all nodes are made visible.

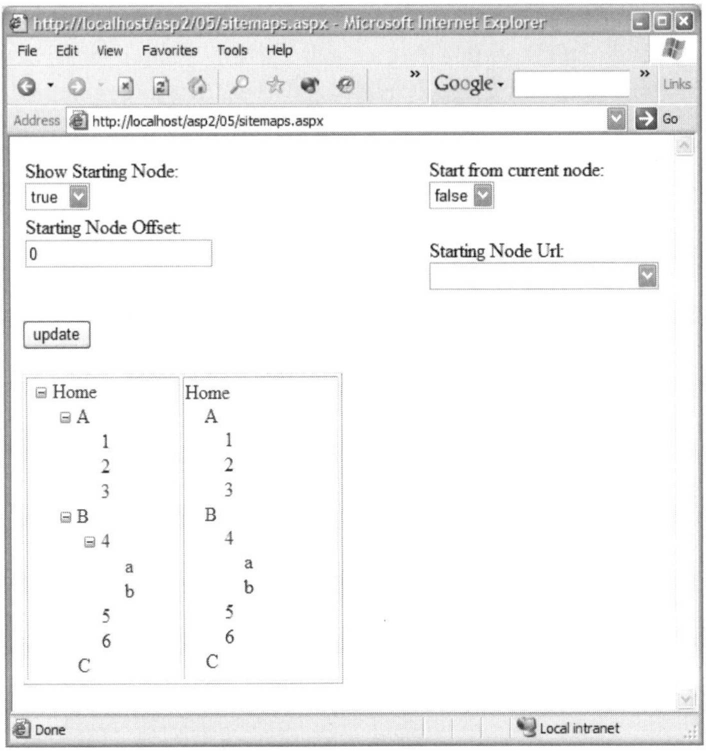

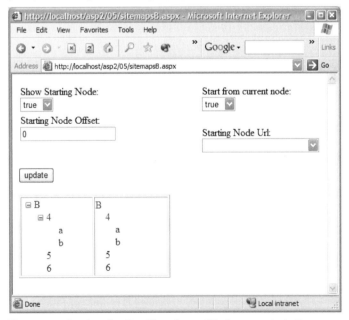

Figure 5.11. Setting the site map's properties

Figure 5.12. Setting the StartFromCurrentNode property to True

Starting from the Current Node

The StartFromCurrentNode property indicates whether the data exposed from the site map starts at the currently selected node. For example, in Figure 5.12 the StartFromCurrentNode property has been set to True, and we have navigated to page B. We can see that for both navigation controls only the nodes from the current node are shown.

Disabling the Starting Node

Setting the ShowStartingNode property to False means that the starting node isn't shown. It's important to remember that this doesn't mean the root node; it's the node from which navigation starts. For example, Figure 5.13 shows this property set to False when the StartFromCurrentNode property is also set to False. The current page is B, but notice that B doesn't show in the navigation because it is the starting node.

Setting the Starting Node Offset

The StartingNodeOffset property defines the offset from the starting node and can be a positive or negative number. For example, Figure 5.14 shows a StartingNodeOffset of -2 with navigation on page B4a. You'd expect the navigation controls to show only siblings of the a node (because the StartFromCurrentNode property is also True), but the offset of -2 pushes the node up two levels. A positive number would push the navigation down levels in the hierarchy.

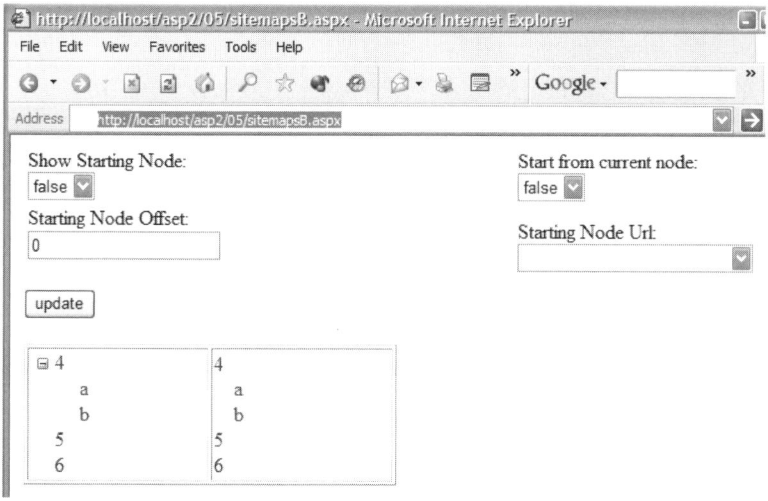

Figure 5.13. Setting the ShowStartingNode property to False

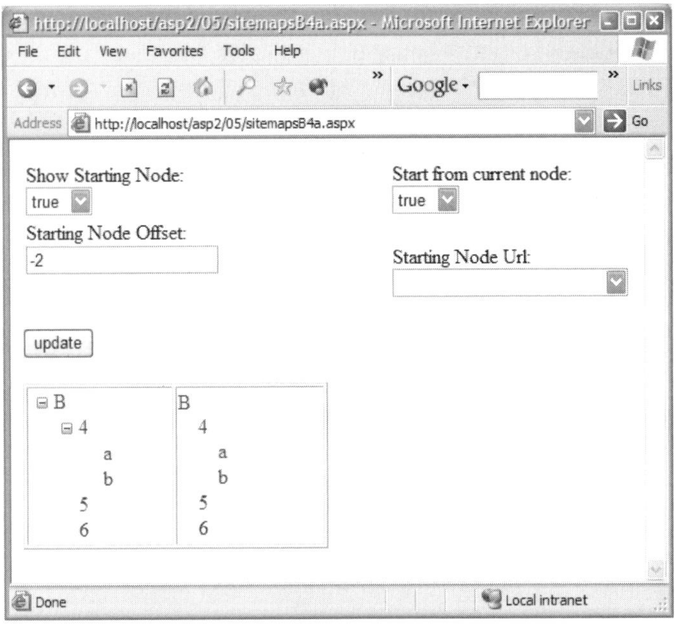

Figure 5.14. Setting the StartingNodeOffset Property

Setting the Starting Node URL

The StartingNodeUrl property allows us to set the starting point, given the URL of a page. Since URLs in the site map file must be unique, this allows us to navigate to a given node knowing only the URL, rather than its location in the hierarchy.

Showing a Navigation Path

When a site map provides the navigational architecture for a site, it's easy to add features that take advantage of this. With a hierarchy three deep or more, it has always been hard for users to remember where they are within that structure, so the idea of breadcrumbs came about, laying a trail of the path back to the root of the site.

With ASP.NET 2.0 this is simple. We have the SiteMapPath control, which automatically hooks into the site map architecture, so all you have to do is drop it on a page, as shown in Figure 5.15.

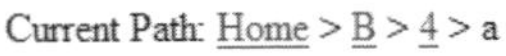

Current Path: Home > B > 4 > a

Figure 5.15. The SiteMapPath control

This figure shows the default implementation, just from adding the following line of code to our page:

```
<asp:SiteMapPath ID="SiteMapPath1" runat="server" />
```

To use the `SiteMapPath` control you don't need a `SiteMapDataSource` control because it works directly with the site map provider.

The current node is shown as simple text, and parent nodes are shown as hyperlinks, allowing quick navigation up the tree. The text for the tooltip is set to the `description` attribute from the site map file.

There are plenty of ways to customize this control to fit it to your site. The syntax is shown in Listing 5.13.

LISTING 5.13. SiteMapPath Syntax

```
<SiteMapPath id="String" runat="server"
  CurrentNodeStyle="Style"
  CurrentNodeTemplate="Template"
  HoverNodeStyle="Style"
  NodeStyle="Style"
  NodeTemplate="Template"
  ParentLevelsDisplayed="Integer"
  PathDirection="[CurrentToRoot|RootToCurrent]"
  PathSeparator="String"
  PathSeparatorStyle="Style"
  PathSeparatorTemplate="Template"
  RenderCurrentNodeAsLink="Boolean"
  RootNodeStyle="Style"
  RootNodeTemplate="Template"
  ShowToolTips="Boolean"
  SiteMapProvider="String"
  />
```

These are just the unique properties for this control, described in Table 5.6. All other properties are inherited and are described in the documentation.

TABLE 5.6. SiteMapPath Properties

Property	Description
CurrentNodeStyle	Sets or returns the `Style` object that defines how the current node is displayed.
CurrentNodeTemplate	Sets a `Template`, allowing customization of how the current node is displayed.

continues

TABLE 5.6. SiteMapPath Properties (continued)

Property	Description
HoverNodeStyle	Sets or returns the `Style` to be used when hovering over nodes.
NodeStyle	Sets or returns the `Style` to be used for nodes.
NodeTemplate	Sets a `Template`, allowing customization of how a node is displayed.
ParentLevelsDisplayed	Sets or returns the number of parent levels displayed. By default all parent levels are displayed.
PathDirection	Gets or sets the direction in which the nodes are displayed. This can be one of the `PathDirection` enumerations, whose values are • `CurrentToRoot`: The current node is shown on the left, and parent nodes are shown on the right. • `RootToCurrent`: The parent node is shown on the left, and parent nodes are shown on the right. This is the default value. Setting the direction has no effect on the separator between nodes.
PathSeparator	Sets or returns a `String` to be used as a separator between nodes. This is replaced by the contents of the `PathSeparatorTemplate` if present. The default is >.
PathSeparatorStyle	Sets or returns the `Style` to be used for the `PathSeparator` string.
PathSeparatorTemplate	Sets a `Template`, allowing customization of the node separator.
RenderCurrentNodeAsLink	Sets or returns a `Boolean` that indicates whether or not the current node is rendered as a hyperlink. The default value is `False`.
RootNodeStyle	Sets or returns the `Style` to be used for the root node. Any `Style` values set here override those set in the `NodeStyle` property.
RootNodeTemplate	Sets a `Template`, allowing customization of the root node.
ShowToolTips	Sets or returns a `Boolean` indicating whether or not tooltips are shown on hyperlinks.
SiteMapProvider	Sets or returns a `String` indicating the site name of the provider supplying the site map data.

These properties give a great deal of flexibility in how the navigation path is shown. For example, consider the code shown in Listing 5.14.

LISTING 5.14. Setting the SiteMapPath Properties

```
<asp:SiteMapPath ID="SiteMapPath1" runat="server"
    NodeStyle-Font-Names="Franklin Gothic Medium"
    NodeStyle-Font-Underline="true"
    NodeStyle-Font-Bold="true"
    RootNodeStyle-Font-Names="Symbol"
    RootNodeStyle-Font-Bold="false"
    CurrentNodeStyle-Font-Names="Verdana"
    CurrentNodeStyle-Font-Size="10pt"
    CurrentNodeStyle-Font-Bold="true"
    CurrentNodeStyle-ForeColor="red"
    CurrentNodeStyle-Font-Underline="false">
  <PathSeparatorTemplate>
      <asp:Image runat="server" ImageUrl="arrow.gif"/>
  </PathSeparatorTemplate>
</asp:SiteMapPath>
```

This defines styles for the nodes and a separator that uses a custom image. The results are shown in Figure 5.16.

Notice that the root node is underlined even though it wasn't specified as part of the `RootNodeStyle`—the underlining was inherited from the `NodeStyle`.

Current Path: _Home_ ⇒ **Β** ⇒ **4** ⇒ a

Figure 5.16. A customized SiteMapPath control

SiteMapPath Events

The `SiteMapPath` is built dynamically from the data held by the underlying site map provider. As the tree of nodes is traversed, each item in the path, from the root node to the current node, is added to the `Controls` collection of the `SiteMapPath` control. Like other collection controls (such as the `DataList` or `DataGrid`), two events are fired when items are either created (`ItemCreated`) or bound (`ItemDataBound`) to the `SiteMapPath`. The signature for these events is the same:

```
Sub eventName(Sender As Object, E As SiteMapNodeItemEventArgs)
```

`SiteMapNodeItemEventArgs` has one property, `Item`, which returns an object of type `SiteMapNodeItem`, which in turn has three properties, as described in Table 5.7.

TABLE 5.7. SiteMapNodeItem Properties

Property	Description
ItemIndex	The zero-based index number of the item being added.
ItemType	The type of node being added, which can be one of the `SiteMapNodeItemType` enumerations: • `Current`: Indicates the current node (page) within the navigation path. • `Parent`: Indicates a parent of the current node. All nodes between the current node and the root node are parent nodes. • `PathSeparator`: Indicates a separator between nodes. • `Root`: Indicates the root node of the navigation path.
SiteMapNode	The `SiteMapNode` that represents the node being added to the `SiteMapPath`.

Intercepting the `ItemCreated` and `ItemDataBound` events gives you a chance to change the default behavior as the items are created.

The SiteMapNode Object

When the site map is constructed from the data provider, each of the items is built into a `SiteMapNode` object. These in turn are added to a `SiteMapNodeCollection`, which therefore represents all pages within a Web site. The `SiteMapNode` object provides links to nodes up, down, and next to it in the hierarchy and thus can be used to build a treelike structure. The `ItemCreated` event of the `SiteMapPath` object allows access to the `SiteMapNode`, which has the properties detailed in Table 5.8.

TABLE 5.8. SiteMapNode Properties

Property	Description
Attributes	Returns a collection of additional attributes applicable to the node. For the XmlSiteMapProvider, the list of attributes maps to existing properties, namely Title, Description, Url, Attributes, Roles, and Keywords.
ChildNodes	If applicable, returns a SiteMapNodeCollection containing child nodes of the current node.
Description	Returns the description of the current node.
HasChildNodes	Indicates whether or not the current node has any child nodes.
NextSibling	Returns the next node on the same level as the current node, or returns null (Nothing in Visual Basic) if there is no next node.
ParentNode	Returns the parent node of the current node, or returns null (Nothing in Visual Basic) if there is no parent node (i.e., the current node is the root node).
PreviousSibling	Returns the previous node on the same level as the current node, or returns null (Nothing in Visual Basic) if there is no previous node.
Roles	Returns an IList containing the roles applicable to the current node.
RootNode	Returns the root node.
Title	Returns the title of the current node.
Url	Returns the URL of the current node.

There are three methods for the `SiteMapNode` object, as described in Table 5.9.

TABLE 5.9. SiteMapNode Methods

Method	Description
GetAllNodes	Returns a `SiteMapNodeCollection` containing all child nodes of the current node.
GetDataSourceView	Returns a `SiteMapDataSourceView`, which is a view of the underlying site map data. This is useful for control developers who wish to interface to the site map architecture.
IsDescendantOf	Indicates whether or not the current node is a descendant of a supplied node.

Accessing the Site Map at Runtime

So far we've seen the site map be used by controls, but it can also be accessed directly because it is exposed through a static page property called `SiteMap`. For example, to access the current node within the site map, you can use the following code:

```
Dim currNode As SiteMapNode

currNode = SiteMap.CurrentNode
```

This means that even if you aren't using a `SiteMapPath` control, you can easily build links pointing back to the hierarchy, as shown in Listing 5.15.

LISTING 5.15. Using the SiteMap Property of the Page

```
<script runat="server">

Sub Page_Load(Sender As Object, E As EventArgs)

  ParentLink.NavigateUrl = SiteMap.CurrentNode.ParentNode.Url

End Sub

</script>

<form runat="server">

  <asp:HyperLink id="ParentLink" Text="Go Back" />

</form>
```

Table 5.10 details the properties of the `SiteMap` class.

TABLE 5.10. SiteMap Class Properties

Property	Description
CurrentNode	Returns a `SiteMapNode` object representing the current page.
Provider	Returns the site map provider.
Providers	Returns a collection (`SiteMapProviderCollection`) of all site map providers.
RootNode	Returns a `SiteMapNode` object representing the root node.

These properties give you access to the site map details and allow you to interface into it at the programmatic level, in case more flexibility is required than the standard server controls provide.

Navigation Controls

The two primary controls for navigation are the `TreeView` and `Menu`, both of which can be bound to a `SiteMapDataSource` control. Both of these controls provide a great deal of options for customization, supporting the standard AutoFormat options for easy styling, as well as support for styles and templates. For this support there are a number of style properties for the controls, which can be added either to the control declaration or as subelements. Both controls support a variety of these style elements to allow fine-grained customization of the control.

Styling the TreeView Control

The `TreeView` control allows styles to be defined for various types of nodes as well as for the level at which the node appears. For example, consider Listing 5.16, which shows the use of some of these style elements. Notice that the `LevelStyles` element is a collection of `TreeNodeStyle` elements; these are assigned to consecutive levels in the tree, so the first level gets a red background and the second a green one.

Listing 5.16. Styling a TreeView Control

```
<asp:TreeView id="TreeView1" runat="server">
  <LevelStyles>
    <asp:TreeNodeStyle BackColor="Red" />
    <asp:TreeNodeStyle BackColor="Green" />
  </LevelStyles>
  <HoverNodeStyle Font-Underline="True" />
</asp:TreeView>
```

Table 5.11 shows the allowed style elements.

Table 5.11. TreeView LevelStyles Elements

Element	Description
HoverNodeStyle	Defines the format for when the cursor is hovering over a node.
LeafNodeStyle	Defines the style for a leaf node, that is, a node with no children.
LevelStyles	Defines a collection of TreeNodeStyle elements, each of which matches to a level in the tree.
NodeStyle	Defines the general style for a node, unless overridden by another style.
ParentNodeStyle	Defines the style for a node that contains children, unless overridden by another style.
RootNodeStyle	Defines the style for the root node, unless overridden by another style.
SelectedNodeStyle	Defines the style for a selected node.

Additional properties are Nodes, which defines a collection of TreeNode elements for declarative assignment of nodes, and Bindings, which defines a collection of TreeNodeBinding elements to bind to data sources. The default bindings when used with a data source control are the following.

- The title is shown as the text of the node.
- The description is shown as the tooltip text of the node.
- The URL is the navigation path of the node.

Styling the Menu Control

Like the TreeView, the Menu control also supports the notion of style elements, but these are a little more complex. This is because the Menu can be either a static or a dynamic Menu, or a combination of both. By default only the first node is static, always appearing on the page; all other nodes are dynamic and appear as fly-out windows. The StaticDisplayLevels property can be set to define the number of levels that appear statically, and these by default are indented so the hierarchical structure is not lost. To cater to this mixed mode of operation there are style elements for the static and dynamic portions of the menu, as well as the individual items that appear on those menus. For example, consider Listing 5.17, which defines style elements for submenus. Notice that the first submenu doesn't override any style values already set; it is simply a placeholder to allow styles to be set for the second and third submenu items.

Listing 5.17. Styling a Menu Control

```
<asp:Menu id="menu1" runat="server" staticDisplayLevels="2">
  <LevelSubMenuStyles>
    <asp:SubMenuStyle />
    <asp:SubMenuStyle BackColor="green" />
    <asp:SubMenuStyle BackColor="red" />
  </LevelSubMenuStyles>
  <StaticHoverStyle ForeColor="White" BackColor="#990000" />
</asp:Menu>
```

Table 5.12 defines the style properties in more detail.

Table 5.12. Menu Style Elements

Element	Description
DynamicHoverStyle	Defines the style used when hovering over dynamic menu items.
DynamicMenuItemStyle	Defines the style for individual menu items on a dynamic menu.
DynamicMenuStyle	Defines the style for a dynamic menu.
DynamicSelectedStyle	Defines the style for a selected item in a dynamic menu.
LevelMenuItemStyles	Defines a collection of MenuItemStyle elements that define the style for each menu item.
LevelSelectedStyles	Defines a collection of MenuItemStyle elements that define the style for selected menu items.
LevelSubMenuStyles	Defines a collection of SubMenuStyle elements that define the style for the submenu as a whole.
StaticHoverStyle	Defines the style used when hovering over static menu items.
StaticMenuItemStyle	Defines the style for individual menu items on a static menu.
StaticMenuStyle	Defines the style for a static menu.
StaticSelectedStyle	Defines the style for selected items on a static menu.

Similar to the TreeView, the Menu can also have items defined declaratively, via the Items element, which contains a collection of MenuItem elements. Explicit binding can be done via the DataBindings collection.

SUMMARY

In this chapter we've looked at two very important topics: how the look and feel of sites can be implemented in ASP.NET 2.0 and how navigation around those sites can be implemented.

We've seen how a great deal of time-consuming work has been removed by the introduction of master pages, allowing the site layout and default implementation to be easily centralized. This makes it easier to develop individual pages, and because layout and code can be centrally contained, it also eases maintenance and reduces potential errors.

Next we discussed how ASP.NET 2.0 supplies a comprehensive architecture for site navigation. The introduction of the `SiteMapDataSource` and the underlying flexibility of providers allow site structure to be easily defined and used within Web pages. By placing this navigation within a master page you also have to define the navigation in only a single place.

Now it's time to move on to another important topic—security, and how to identify users and control what they can do once they reach your site.

■ 6 ■

Security

VERSION 1.1 OF ASP.NET provided many built-in security services for developers to take advantage of. A common favorite is Forms-based authentication.

Forms-based authentication allows Web developers to easily build applications that require authentication to access secured resources. However, rather than relying on Windows Authentication, Forms-based authentication allows us to author a simple ASP.NET login page. ASP.NET is then configured so that any unauthenticated requests are redirected to the login page (see Figure 6.1).

The login page is a simple ASP.NET page used to collect and verify the user's credentials. It is the responsibility of the login page to determine whether the user credentials are valid; typically this information is stored in a database.

Listing 6.1 shows an example of a login page written in ASP.NET 1.1.

LISTING 6.1. Example Login Page

```
<%@ Page Language="VB" %>
<%@ import namespace="System.Data" %>
<%@ import namespace="System.Data.SqlClient" %>

<script runat="server">

  Public Sub Login_Click(ByVal sender As Object, ByVal e As EventArgs)
```

continues

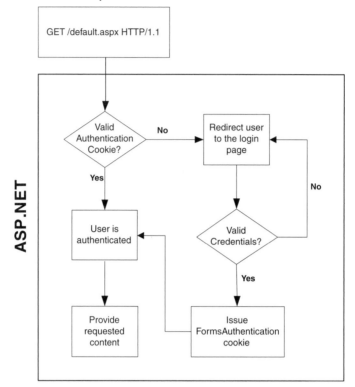

FIGURE 6.1. Forms Authentication

```
Dim userId As Integer
Dim reader As SqlDataReader
Dim connectionString = _
    ConfigurationSettings.ConnectionStrings("MyConnectionString")
Dim conn As New SqlConnection(connectionString)
Dim command As New SqlCommand("dbo.Authenticate", conn)

' Set the command type to stored procedure
command.CommandType = CommandType.StoredProcedure

' Set @Username and @Password
command.Parameters.Add("@Username", _
      SqlDbType.NVarChar, 256).Value = Username.Text
command.Parameters.Add("@Password", _
      SqlDbType.NVarChar, 256).Value = Password.Text

' Open the connection and execute the reader
conn.Open()
reader = command.ExecuteReader()
```

```
    ' Read the value we're looking for
    reader.Read()

    userId = Integer.Parse(reader("UserId"))

    ' Close connections
    reader.Close()
    conn.Close()

    ' Did we find a user?
    If (userId > 0) Then
        FormsAuthentication.RedirectFromLoginPage(Username.Text, _
                                                  False)

    Else
      Status.Text = "Invalid Credentials: Please try again"

    End If

  End Sub

</script>

<html>
  <body style="FONT-FAMILY: Verdana">

  <H1>Enter your username/password</H1>

  <form id="Form1" runat="server">
    Username: <asp:textbox id="Username" runat="server" />
    <br>
    Password: <asp:textbox id="Password" runat="server" />
    <p>
    <asp:button id="Button1"
                text="Check if Member is Valid"
                onclick="Login_Click" runat="server"/>
  </form>

  <font color="red" size="6">
    <asp:label id="Status" runat="server"/>
  </font>

  </body>
</html>
```

In this sample the login page raises the `Login_Click` event, connects to a database, calls a stored procedure to verify the submitted username and password, and then either uses the `FormsAuthentication` APIs to log the user in or tells the user that the credentials are invalid.

The ASP.NET `FormsAuthentication` class is used to encrypt the username and store it securely in an HTTP cookie. On subsequent requests this HTTP cookie, with its encrypted contents, is decrypted and the user automatically reauthenticated.

Forms Authentication is definitely a great feature, but what makes it even better is the reduction in the amount of code developers must write. Forms Authentication isn't something new introduced by ASP.NET. Rather, ASP.NET is simply providing an easier way to solve the problem; in the past, most developers would have needed to author this code plus infrastructure on their own.

One of the things you may have noticed about the ASP.NET team members: They are always looking for ways to make things easier. They want developers to solve problems without writing hundreds of lines of code. For ASP.NET 2.0 they're again tackling many security-related problems and providing new features to make things simpler.

In this chapter we're going to examine some of the security infrastructure and controls that have been added in ASP.NET 2.0. We'll start by looking at the new Membership feature. Membership solves the user credential storage problem, a problem most developers solved themselves in ASP.NET 1.0.

Membership

After Microsoft released ASP.NET 1.0, the team members immediately started looking for areas where they could simplify. One area was the management of user credentials, personalization, and user roles. These problems could be solved in ASP.NET 1.1, but the team wanted to make the process better and easier!

The Membership feature of ASP.NET does just that—makes it better and easier. Membership provides secure credential storage with simple, easy-to-use APIs. Rather than requiring you to repeatedly develop infrastructure features for authenticating users, it is now part of the platform. More importantly, it's a pluggable part of the platform through the new provider pattern, allowing you to easily extend the system (e.g., to add support for LDAP or existing corporate user account systems).

Forms Authentication and Membership complement one another. However, they can also act independently; that is, you don't have to use them together. The code sample in Listing 6.2 demonstrates how Membership is used with Forms Authentication.

LISTING 6.2. Using the Membership API

```
<script runat="server">

  Public Sub Login_Click(sender As Object, e As EventArgs e)

    ' Is the user valid?
    If (Membership.ValidateUser (Username.Text, Password.Text)) Then

      FormsAuthentication.RedirectFromLoginPage (Username.Text, false)

    Else

      Status.Text = "Invalid Credentials: Please try again"

    End If

  End Sub

</script>

<html>
    <body style="FONT-FAMILY: Verdana">

    <H1>Enter your username/password</H1>

    <form id="Form1" runat="server">
      Username: <asp:textbox id="Username" runat="server" />
      <br>
      Password: <asp:textbox id="Password" runat="server" />
      <p>
      <asp:button id="Button1"
                  text="Check if Member is Valid"
                  onclick="Login_Click" runat="server"/>
    </form>

    <font color="red" size="6">
      <asp:label id="Status" runat="server"/>
    </font>

    </body>
</html>
```

As you can see, our custom code to validate the credentials is now replaced with a single call to the static `Membership.ValidateUser()`
method. The code is also much cleaner and more readable as a result—and
much more concise!

The `Membership` class contains only static methods. You don't have to
create an instance of the class to use its functionality; for example, you
don't have to `new` the `Membership` class to use it. Behind the scenes the

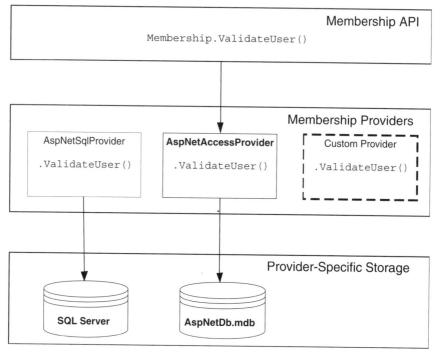

FIGURE 6.2. The provider model

Membership class is forwarding the calls through a configured provider. The provider in turn knows which data source to contact and how to verify the credentials (see Figure 6.2).

Providers are a new design pattern introduced with ASP.NET 2.0. Providers are pluggable data abstraction layers used within ASP.NET. All ASP.NET 2.0 features that rely on data storage expose a provider layer. The provider layer allows you to take complete control over how and where data is stored.[1]

Membership Providers

The beauty of the provider model is the abstraction that it affords the developer. Rather than being pigeonholed into a particular data model or fixed API behavior, the provider pattern allows you to determine how and where the actual data storage takes place and the behavior of the API itself.

---

1. For more details on providers, see Chapter 7. Also, the provider specification is published on MSDN at http://msdn.microsoft.com/library/default.asp?url=/library/en-us/dnaspnet/html/asp02182004.asp.

ASP.NET 2.0 will ship with several providers for Membership (not a complete list):

- Access
- SQL Server
- Active Directory[2]

You can easily author your own provider and plug it in. The provider design pattern allows for one common API that developers can familiarize themselves with, such as Membership, but under the covers you still have control over what exactly is happening. For example, if you had all of your customer information stored in an AS/400, you could write a provider for Membership. Users would call the familiar Membership APIs, but the work would actually be handled by the configured AS/400 provider.

The goal of Membership is to simplify managing and storing user credentials while still allowing you to control your data, but it does much more. Let's dig deeper.

Setting Up Membership

Setting up Membership is easy: It just works. By default all the providers that ship with ASP.NET 2.0 use a Microsoft Access provider and will use the default `AspNetDB.mdb` file created in the `\data\` directory of your application.[3]

If the `\data\` directory of your application does not exist, ASP.NET will attempt to create it. If ASP.NET is unable to create the `\data\` directory or the `AspNetDB.mdb` file because of the security policy on the machine, an exception is thrown detailing what needs to be done.

Before we can begin using Membership for its most common task—validating user credentials—we need to have users to validate!

Creating a New User

The Membership API exposes two methods for creating new users:

---

2. Not available with the beta release of ASP.NET 2.0.
3. Access is the configured default since it works without requiring the user to perform any further setup. SQL Server is the recommended provider for large applications.

```
CreateUser(username As String, password As String)

CreateUser(username As String, password As String,
           email As String)
```

These two APIs are somewhat self-explanatory. We call them to create a user with a username and password, optionally also providing the e-mail address. Both of these methods return a `MembershipUser` instance, which we'll look at later in this chapter.

Which of these two methods you use is determined by the Membership configuration settings. We can examine the settings in `machine.config` for the defaults (see Listing 6.3, where the line in bold indicates whether or not an e-mail address must be unique).[4]

LISTING 6.3. Membership Configuration

```
<configuration>
  <system.web>

    <membership defaultProvider="AspNetAccessProvider"
              userIsOnlineTimeWindow="15">
      <providers>

        <add
          name="AspNetAccessProvider"
          type="System.Web.Security.AccessMembershipProvider,
              System.Web,
              Version=2.0.3600.0,
              Culture=neutral, PublicKeyToken=b03f5f7f11d50a3a"
          connectionStringName="AccessFileName"
          enablePasswordRetrieval="false"
          enablePasswordReset="true"
          requiresQuestionAndAnswer="false"
          applicationName="/"
          requiresUniqueEmail="false"
          passwordFormat="Hashed"
          description="Stores and retrieves membership data from
                      the local Microsoft Access database file"/>

      </providers>
    </membership>

  </system.web>
</configuration>
```

---

4. You can also define these settings or change the defaults in the `web.config` file of your application.

Table 6.1 shows an explanation of the various configuration settings.

TABLE 6.1. Configuration Elements for the Membership Provider

Attribute	Description
`connectionStringName`	Names the key within the `<connectionStrings />` configuration section where the connection string is stored. The default value for the Access provider is `AccessFileName`, and for the SQL Server provider it is `LocalSqlServer`.
`enablePasswordRetrieval`	Controls whether or not the password can be retrieved through the Membership APIs. When set to `false`, the password cannot be retrieved from the database. The default value is `false`.
`enablePasswordReset`	Allows the password to be reset. For example, although the password may not be retrieved, the APIs will allow for a new random password to be created for the user. The default value is `true`.
`requiresQuestionAndAnswer`	Allows the use of a question and answer to retrieve the user's password. Only valid when the `passwordFormat` setting is not `Hashed` and `enablePasswordRetrieval` is `true`. The default value is `false`.
`applicationName`	Indicates the application to which the Membership data store belongs. Multiple applications can share the same Membership data store by specifying the same `applicationName` value. The default value is `/`.
`requiresUniqueEmail`	Requires that a given e-mail address can be used only once. This attribute can be used to prevent users from creating multiple accounts. Note that the uniqueness is constrained to the `applicationName` the user is created within. The default value is `false`.
`passwordFormat`	Controls how the password is stored in the data store. `Hashed` is the most secure but does not allow password retrieval. Additional valid values include `Encrypted` and `Clear`. The default value is `Hashed`.
`description`	Describes the provider. This is an optional attribute; when present, tools capable of working with providers can optionally display this description string.

Knowing what the defaults are, we can write a simple page for creating new users (see Listing 6.4).

LISTING 6.4. Creating Users with the Membership API

```vb
<%@ Page Language="VB" %>

<script runat="server">

  Public Sub CreateUser_Click (sender As Object, e As EventArgs)

    Try

      ' Attempt to create the user
      Membership.CreateUser(Username.Text, Password.Text)

      Status.Text = "Created new user: " & Username.Text

    Catch ex As MembershipCreateUserException

      ' Display the status if an exception occurred
      Status.Text = ex.ToString()

    End Try


  End Sub

</script>
<html>
  <head>
  </head>

  <body style="FONT-FAMILY: Verdana">

    <H1>Create a new user</H1>

    <hr />

    <form runat="server">
    Desired username: <asp:TextBox id="Username" runat="server"/>
    <br>
    Password: <asp:TextBox id="Password" runat="server" />
    <p>
    <asp:button Text="Create Member"
                OnClick="CreateUser_Click" runat="server"/>
    </form>

    <font color="red" size="6">
    <asp:Label id="Status" runat="server" />
    </font>

  </body>
</html>
```

The code in Listing 6.4 calls the `Membership.CreateUser()` method, which accepts a username and a password.[5] If there is a problem creating the user, a `MembershipCreateUserException` is thrown. If there are no problems, the new user is created.

Once we've created some users, we can test the `Membership.ValidateUser()` method.

Validating User Credentials

The primary purpose for Membership is to validate credentials. This is accomplished through the static `ValidateUser()` method:

```
ValidateUser(username As String,
             password As String) As Boolean
```

We can use this method, as seen earlier, along with Forms Authentication to validate user credentials. Here is a partial code example:

```
If (Membership.ValidateUser (Username.Text, Password.Text)) Then

    FormsAuthentication.RedirectFromLoginPage (Username.Text, False)

Else

    Status.Text = "Invalid Credentials: Please try again"

End If
```

Apart from `ValidateUser()`, most of the remaining Membership APIs are used for retrieving a user or users.

Retrieving a User

There are a few ways you can retrieve users that have already been created:

```
GetUser() As MembershipUser

GetUser(userIsOnline As Boolean) As MembershipUser

GetUser(username As String) As MembershipUser

GetUser(username As String,
        userIsOnline As Boolean) As MembershipUser
```

---

5. You may already wonder what we do with additional user data, such as first names. Membership is not used to store this type of data. Instead, the new Personalization feature is used to store user data—Membership is used only for storing user credentials used in authentication. Personalization is covered in Chapter 7.

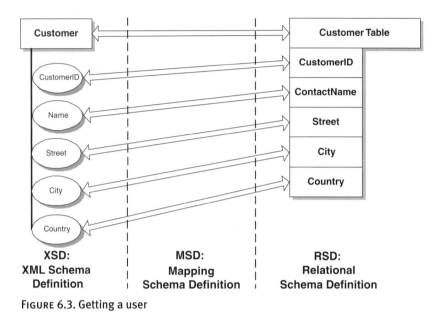

FIGURE 6.3. Getting a user

The first two methods that don't have a `username` parameter will attempt to return the currently logged-on user. The parameter `userIsOnline`, when set to `True`, will update a timestamp in the data store indicating the date/time the user was last requested. This timestamp can then be used to calculate the total number of users online.[6] The remaining methods will perform similar operations but on a specified user.

Figure 6.3 shows an example of getting the `MembershipUser` class for the currently logged-on user.

Listing 6.5 provides the code used for this page.

LISTING 6.5. Fetching the Logged-on User

```
<%@ Page Language="VB" %>

<script runat="server">

  Public Sub Page_Load()
```

---

6. This functionality is similar to that used on the ASP.NET forums (http://www.asp.net
/Forums/). All users have a timestamp that can be updated. The number of users
online is calculated by finding all users whose timestamps fall within a calculated
window of time. This time window is configured in the `<membership>` configuration setting `userIsOnlineTimeWindow`.

```
    Dim user As MembershipUser

    ' Get the currently logged-on user and
    ' update the user's online timestamp
    user = Membership.GetUser(True)

    UserName.Text = user.Username

  End Sub

</script>

<html>

  <body style="FONT-FAMILY: Verdana">

  <H1>Get User</H1>

  <hr />

    <form runat="server">
      The currently logged-on user is:
      <asp:literal id="UserName" runat="server" />
  </form>

  </body>
</html>
```

If we want to find a user but don't have the username (e.g., the user forgot his or her username), we can use the GetUserNameByEmail() method:

```
GetUserNameByEmail(email As String) As String
```

Once we have the username, we can then look up the user with one of the GetUser() methods listed earlier.

We can additionally get multiple users with the following method:

```
Membership.GetAllUsers() As MembershipUserCollection
```

Membership.GetAllUsers() simply returns a MembershipUserCollection, which we can use to enumerate users or bind to a server control, such as a Repeater or DataGrid (see Figure 6.4).

Listing 6.6 shows the code.

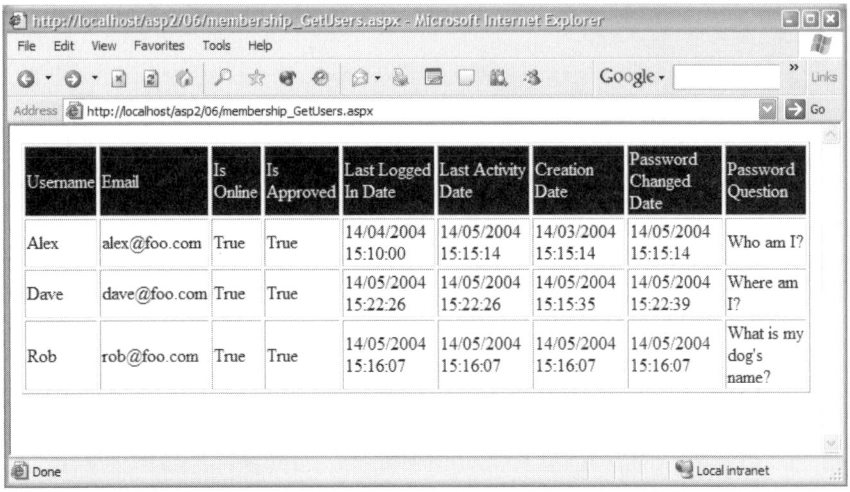

FIGURE 6.4. Getting all users

LISTING 6.6. Displaying All Users

```vb
<%@ Page Language="VB" %>

<script runat="server">

  Public Sub Page_Load()

    Users.DataSource = Membership.GetAllUsers()
    Users.DataBind()

  End Sub

</script>

<html>
  <head>
  </head>

  <body style="FONT-FAMILY: Verdana">

    <H1>Users in Membership Database</H1>

    <hr />

    <asp:repeater id="Users" runat="server">
      <headertemplate>
        <table border="1">
          <tr>
            <td bgcolor="black" style="color:white">
                Username
            </td>
```

```
        <td bgcolor="black" style="color:white">
            Email
        </td>

        <td bgcolor="black" style="color:white">
            Is Online
        </td>

        <td bgcolor="black" style="color:white">
            Is Approved
        </td>

        <td bgcolor="black" style="color:white">
            Last Logged In Date
        </td>

        <td bgcolor="black" style="color:white">
            Last Activity Date
        </td>

        <td bgcolor="black" style="color:white">
            Creation Date
        </td>

        <td bgcolor="black" style="color:white">
            Password Changed Date
        </td>

        <td bgcolor="black" style="color:white">
            Password Question
        </td>
    </tr>
</headertemplate>

<itemtemplate>
  <tr>
    <td>
      <%# Eval("Username") %>
    </td>

    <td>
      <%# Eval("Email") %>
    </td>

    <td>
      <%# Eval("IsOnline") %>
    </td>

    <td>
      <%# Eval("IsApproved") %>
    </td>
```

```
      <td>
        <%# Eval("LastLoginDate") %>
      </td>

      <td>
        <%# Eval("LastActivityDate") %>
      </td>

      <td>
        <%# Eval("CreationDate") %>
      </td>

      <td>
        <%# Eval("LastPasswordChangedDate") %>
      </td>

      <td>
        <%# Eval("PasswordQuestion") %>
      </td>
    </tr>
  </itemtemplate>

  <footertemplate>
    </table>
  </footertemplate>
 </asp:repeater>


 </body>
</html>
```

The `GetAllUsers()` method now also supports paging for working with large sets of users. This overloaded version expects `pageIndex`, `pageSize`, and `totalRecords` out parameters, where `pageIndex` is the location within the result set and `pageSize` controls the number of records returned per page. For example, a `pageIndex` of 2 with a `pageSize` of 25 in a system with 2,000 records would return users 26–50.

Now that we've looked at how to create users and retrieve named users, let's look at the `MembershipUser` class, which allows us to set and retrieve extended properties for each user.

The MembershipUser Class

The `MembershipUser` class represents a user stored in the Membership system. It provides the following methods for performing user-specific operations, such as retrieving or resetting a user's password.

```
GetPassword() As String

GetPassword(answer As String) As String

ChangePassword(oldPassword As String,
               newPassword As String) As Boolean

ChangePasswordQuestionAndAnswer(password As String,
                                question As String,
                                answer As String) As Boolean

ResetPassword() As String

ResetPassword(answer As String) As String
```

Note that if a question and answer are being used, the overloaded GetPassword(answer As String) method requires the case-insensitive question answer.

The ChangePassword() method allows changes to the user's password, and the ChangePasswordQuestionAndAnswer() method allows changes to the user's password question and answer. The code in Listing 6.7 allows the currently logged-on user to change his or her password question and answer.[7]

LISTING 6.7. Changing a Password

```
<%@ Page Language="VB" %>

<script runat="server">

  Public Sub Page_Load()

    If Not Page.IsPostBack Then
      DisplayCurrentQuestion()
    End If

  End Sub

  Public Sub SetQandA_Click(sender As Object, e As EventArgs)

    Dim u As MembershipUser = Membership.GetUser()
```

continues

---

7. When the <membership /> configuration's requiresQuestionAndAnswer is set to true, the GetPassword(answer As String) and ResetPassword(answer As String) methods must be used to either retrieve or reset the user's password. (The *answer* value is the answer to the user's question.)

```
      u.ChangePasswordQuestionAndAnswer(CurrentPassword.Text, _
                                       Question.Text, _
                                       Answer.Text)

    Membership.UpdateUser(u)

    DisplayCurrentQuestion()
  End Sub

  Public Sub DisplayCurrentQuestion()

    Status.Text = Membership.GetUser().PasswordQuestion

  End Sub

</script>

<html>
  <body style="FONT-FAMILY: Verdana">

  <H1>Set Question Answer</H1>

  <hr />

  <form id="Form1" runat="server">
    Current Password: <asp:textbox id="CurrentPassword"
                                   runat="server" />
    <p></p>
    Question: <asp:textbox id="Question" runat="server" />
    <p></p>
    Answer:   <asp:textbox id="Answer" runat="server" />
    <p></p>
    <asp:button id="Button1" text="Set Question/Answer"
             onclick="SetQandA_Click" runat="server"/>
  </form>

  <font size="6"> Your new password question is:
  <asp:label id="Status" runat="server"/>
  </font>

</html>
```

The ResetPassword() methods are similar to the GetPassword() methods. However, rather than retrieving the user's password, they reset and then return a random password for the user.

Keep in mind that the ability to retrieve, change, or reset the user's password is determined by the settings within the configuration.

In addition to password management, the MembershipUser class has some useful properties that provide us some details about how and when the user last logged in, last changed passwords, and so on (see Table 6.2).

TABLE 6.2. MembershipUser Properties

Property	Description
LastLoginDate	Sets or returns a timestamp for the last time `ValidateUser()` was called for the current `MembershipUser`.
CreationDate	Sets or returns a timestamp value set when the user was first created.
LastActivityDate	Sets or returns a timestamp value set when the user authenticates or is retrieved using the overloaded `GetUser()` method that accepts a `userIsOnline` parameter.
LastPasswordChangedDate	Sets or returns a timestamp value set when the user last changed his or her password.
Email	Sets or returns the e-mail address, if set, of the user.
IsApproved	Sets or returns a value that indicates whether or not the user is approved. Users whose `IsApproved` property is set to `false` cannot log in, even when the specified credentials are valid.
PasswordQuestion	Returns the question used in question/answer retrieval.
Provider	Returns an instance (of type `MembershipProvider`) of the current provider used to manipulate the data store.
UserName	Returns the username of the current user.

Updating a User's Properties

When changes are made to the user, for example, updating the user's e-mail address, we need to use the `Membership.UpdateUser(user As MembershipUser)` method to save the values.[8] For example, in Listing 6.7 earlier, the `SetQandA_Click` event (repeated here for convenience) shows an example of `Membership.UpdateUser()`:

---

8. The goal of this design is to allow multiple values to be changed without requiring multiple round-trips to the data store. By using the `UpdateUser()` method, all updates are batched together.

```
Public Sub SetQandA_Click(sender As Object, e As EventArgs)

  Dim u As MembershipUser = Membership.GetUser()

  u.ChangePasswordQuestionAndAnswer(CurrentPassword.Text,
                                    Question.Text,
                                    Answer.Text)

  Membership.UpdateUser(u)

  DisplayCurrentQuestion()
End Sub
```

So far we've learned how to create and update users, but what about removing users from the Membership system?

Deleting a User

Deleting a user from Membership is easy. Membership supports a single method for removing users:

```
DeleteUser(username As String) As Boolean
```

We simply need to name the user we wish to delete. If the operation is successful, the method returns True. If the delete operation fails, for example, if the user doesn't exist, False is returned.

Listing 6.8 shows a code example that allows us to specify a user to be removed from the Membership system.

LISTING 6.8. Deleting a User

```
<%@ Page Language="VB" %>

<script runat="server">

  Public Sub DeleteUser_Click(sender As Object, e As EventArgs)

    If (Membership.DeleteUser(Username.Text)) Then
      Status.Text = Username.Text & " deleted"
    Else
      Status.Text = Username.Text & " not deleted"
    End If

  End Sub

</script>
<html>
  <head>
  </head>
```

```
<body style="FONT-FAMILY: Verdana">


  <H1>Delete a user</H1>

  <hr />

  <form runat="server">
    Username to delete: <asp:TextBox id="Username"
                                     runat="server"/>
    <p>
    <asp:button Text="Delete User"
                OnClick="DeleteUser_Click" runat="server"/>
  </form>

  <font color="red" size="6">
  <asp:label id="Status" runat="server" />
  </font>

</body>
</html>
```

Figure 6.5 shows how this page looks.

While the Membership APIs definitely simplify day-to-day tasks, there is also an alternative to using programmatic APIs: security server controls. In many cases we can use these server controls and never have to write code that uses the Membership APIs!

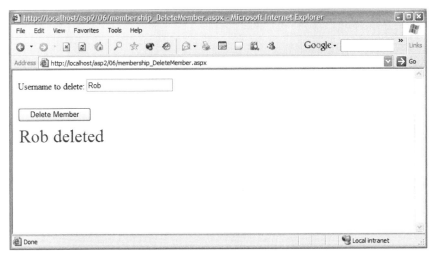

FIGURE 6.5. Deleting a user

Security Server Controls

The new Membership infrastructure feature of ASP.NET simplifies the management and storage of user credentials. Using APIs, such as `Membership.ValidateUser()`, for Forms Authentication definitely makes things easy. However, some techniques are made even easier through the use of several new security-related server controls. For example, you can author your own login page with zero lines of code by using the new `Login` control or create users using the new `CreateUserWizard` control.

The CreateUserWizard Control

Earlier in the chapter we showed the code required to create a new user. In the alpha version of ASP.NET (then code-named "Whidbey") this was the only way to create new users. In the beta version the new `CreateUserWizard` control can be used instead for a no-code alternative.

The `CreateUserWizard` control, `<asp:CreateUserWizard runat= "server" />`, uses the new `Wizard` control and allows for multiple steps to be defined during the user creation process. Figure 6.6 shows the `CreateUserWizard` control in design time. As you can see, the options

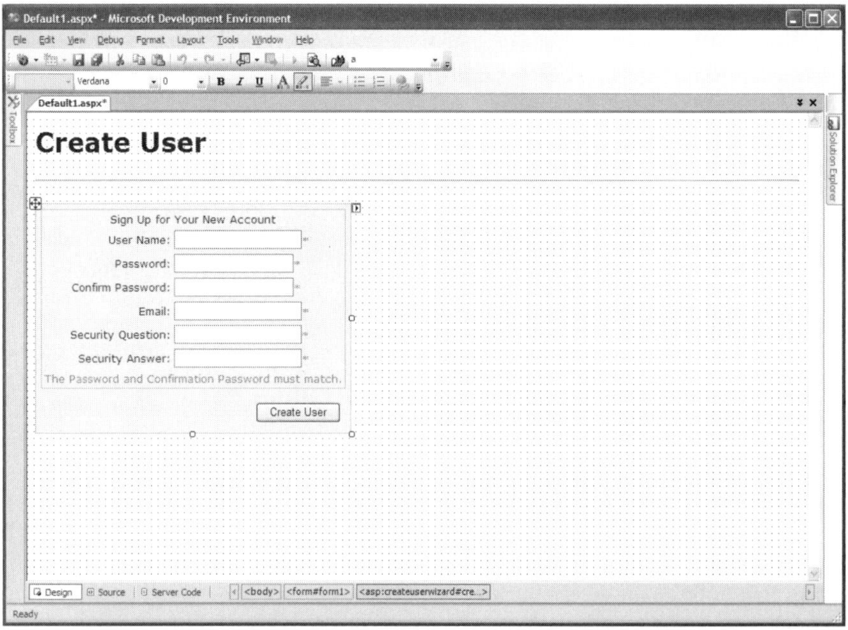

FIGURE 6.6. The CreateUserWizard control

available are specific to Membership, but we could just as easily add another step to the control for collecting more user information, such as first name, last name, and so on. Listing 6.9 shows the source to the `control_createuser.aspx` page.

LISTING 6.9. Using the CreateUserWizard Control

```html
<html>

  <body style="FONT-FAMILY: Verdana">

    <H1>Validate Credentials</H1>
    <hr />
    <form id="Form1" runat="server">

      <asp:CreateUserWizard runat="server" />

    </form>

  </body>

</html>
```

The Login Control

Figure 6.7 shows a `control_login.aspx` page that authenticates the user's credentials against the default Membership provider and uses the new `<asp:Login runat="server" />` control. As you can see in Figure 6.7, it looks nearly identical to the login page we built with the Membership APIs. Listing 6.10 shows the source to the `control_login.aspx` page.

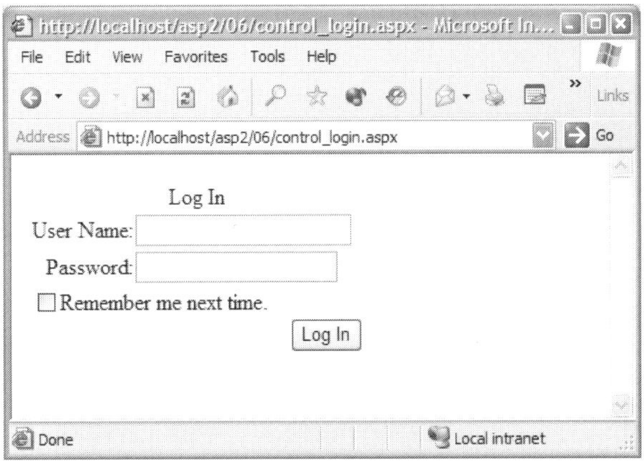

FIGURE 6.7. The login control

LISTING 6.10. Using the Login Control

```
<html>

  <body style="FONT-FAMILY: Verdana">

    <H1>Validate Credentials</H1>
    <hr />
    <form id="Form1" runat="server">

      <asp:Login id="Login1" runat="server" />

    </form>

  </body>

</html>
```

When the username and password are entered, this control will automatically attempt to log in the user by calling `Membership .ValidateUser()`. If successful, the control will then call the necessary `FormsAuthentication.RedirectFromLoginPage` API to issue a cookie and redirect the user to the page he or she was attempting to access. In other words, all the code you would have needed to write in ASP.NET 1.1 is now neatly encapsulated in a single server control!

The `<asp:Login runat="server" />` control automatically hides itself if the user is logged in. This behavior is determined by the `AutoHide` property, set to `True` by default. If the login control is used with Forms Authentication and hosted on the default login page (specified in the configuration for Forms Authentication) the control will not auto-hide itself.

We can further customize the login control's UI. To preview one UI option—we can't cover all of them in depth in this book—right-click on the login control within Visual Studio 2005 and select Auto Format. This will bring up the dialog box shown in Figure 6.8.

Once you've chosen an auto-format template, such as Classic, you can see the changes in the login control (see Listing 6.11).

LISTING 6.11. A Formatted Login Control

```
<asp:Login id="Login1"
           runat="server"
           font-names="Verdana"
           font-size="10pt"
           bordercolor="#999999"
           borderwidth="1px"
           borderstyle="Solid"
```

```
                backcolor="#FFFFCC">
  <TitleTextStyle Font-Bold="True"
                  ForeColor="#FFFFFF"
                  BackColor="#333399">
  </TitleTextStyle>
</asp:Login>
```

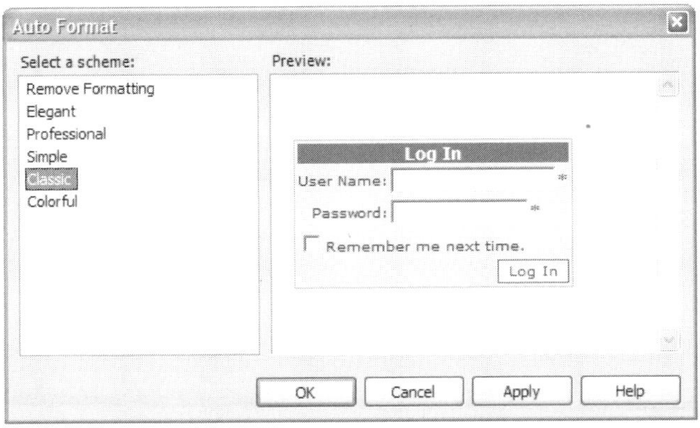

FIGURE 6.8. The Auto Format dialog

If you desire more control over the display of the control, right-click on the control, or from the Common Tasks dialog, select Convert to Template. You'll see no changes in the rendered UI of the control. However, you will see a notable difference in the declarative markup generated for the control. For brevity we are not including the updated markup.[9] What you will see is a series of templates that allow you to take 100% control over the UI rendering of the control. Note that it is important that the IDs of the controls within these templates remain because the control expects to find these IDs.

While the login control simplifies authoring the login page, several other controls help us display content to users based on their login status. Let's take a look at the login status control first.

The Login Status Control

The login status control, `<asp:LoginStatus runat="server" />`, is used to display whether the user is logged in or not. When the user is not logged in, the status displays a Login link (see Figure 6.9). When the user is logged in, the status displays a Logout link (see Figure 6.10).

---

9. One of the nice features in the Designer is a Reset feature. When you change your mind about using the template layout of the login control, you can simply select Reset from the Common Tasks menu.

FIGURE 6.9. The login status control when the user is not logged in

FIGURE 6.10. The login status control when the user is logged in

Listing 6.12 shows the code required.

LISTING 6.12. The Login Status Control

```
<html>

  <body style="FONT-FAMILY: Verdana">

  <h1>Login Status</h1>

  <hr />

  <form runat="server">
    <asp:LoginStatus id="LoginStatus1" runat="server" />
  </form>

  </body>

</html>
```

By default the text displayed for the link is "Login" when the user is not logged in and "Logout" when the user is logged in.[10] However, this text can easily be changed; you simply need to change the `LoginText` or `LogoutText` properties of the control:

```
<asp:LoginStatus id="Loginstatus1" runat="server"
                LoginText="Please log in"
                LogoutText="Please log out" />
```

Other properties can also be set to control the behavior of this control. For example, you can use the `LoginImageUrl` and the `LogoutImageUrl` to use images rather than text for displaying the login status. Finally, there are two properties for controlling the behavior upon logout:

- `LogoutAction`: This property specifies the behavior when the logout button is clicked. Options include `Refresh`, `Redirect`, and `RedirectToLoginPage`.
- `LogoutPageUrl`: When the `LogoutAction` is set to `Redirect`, the `LogoutPageUrl` is the location to which the browser is redirected.

Whereas `<asp:LoginStatus runat="server" />` provides an easy way for the user to log in and log out, another server control, `<asp:LoginView runat="server" />`, allows us to easily determine what content is shown to the user based on his or her login status.

The Login View Control

The `<asp:LoginView runat="server" />` server control is used to display different output depending on the login status of the user. Furthermore, the control can also be used to display different content based on the role(s) the user belongs to. Figure 6.11 shows an example of what the control might display for an anonymous user. The code that generates this page appears in Listing 6.13.

LISTING 6.13. Using the Login View Control

```
<html>

  <body style="FONT-FAMILY: Verdana">
```

continues

---

10. Note the handy feature in Visual Studio 2005 in the Tasks dialog, Views, which allows you to select the view of the control in the Designer.

FIGURE 6.11. The login view for an anonymous user

```
<h1>Login View and Login Name Controls</h1>

<hr />

<form runat="server">

  <asp:LoginView id="Loginview1" runat="server">
    <anonymoustemplate>
      Unknown user please <asp:LoginStatus runat="server"
                                     logintext="login" />
    </anonymoustemplate>

    <rolegroups>
      <asp:rolegroup roles="Admin">
        <contenttemplate>
          This is admin only content!
        </contenttemplate>
       </asp:rolegroup>
     </rolegroups>

    <loggedintemplate>
      You are logged in as: <asp:LoginName id="LoginName1"
                                     runat="server" />
    </loggedintemplate>
   </asp:LoginView>
 </form>

 </body>

</html>
```

In this code you can see that two templates are defined for the `<asp:LoginView runat="server" />` control:

- `<anonymoustemplate />` is used to control the displayed content when the user is not logged in.

- `<loggedintemplate />` is used to control the displayed content when the user is logged in.

In addition to the templates, there is also a special `<rolegroups />` section that allows us to create different templates that are displayed if the user is in a corresponding role or roles. If the user is logged in but no roles apply, the `<loggedintemplate />` is used.[11]

You'll notice that we also made use of another control in Listing 6.13: `<asp:LoginName runat="server" />`. This control simply displays the name of the logged-in user. If the user is not logged in, the control does not render any output.

The last security-related server control is `<asp:PasswordRecovery runat="server" />`, which is used to help users obtain their forgotten passwords.

The Password Recovery Control

The `<asp:PasswordRecovery runat="server" />` control works in conjunction with the Membership system to allow users to easily recover their passwords.[12]

The `<asp:PasswordRecovery runat="server" />` control relies on the `<smtpMail />` configuration options to be correctly set to a valid SMTP server—the control will mail the password to the user's e-mail address. By default, the `<smtpMail />` section will have the SMTP mail server set to `localhost` and the port set to `25` (the default SMTP port).

Similar to `<asp:Login runat="server" />`, this control supports auto-format and full template editing. Assuming we select an auto-format template, such as Classic, and use the default Membership settings, we should see the page shown in Figure 6.12.

Listing 6.14 presents the code that generates this page (auto-formatting removed).

---

11. Template evaluation for `rolegroups` is done top to bottom. The first matched role group is used. If no match is found, the `<loggedintemplate />` is used.
12. For this server control to work, your Membership configuration must be set up to allow for password recovery.

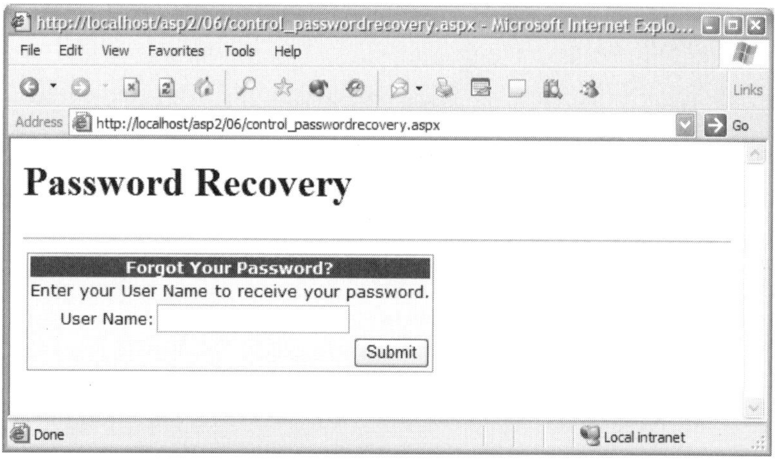

FIGURE 6.12. Password recovery

LISTING 6.14. Using the Password Recovery Control

```
<html>
  <body style="FONT-FAMILY: Verdana">

    <H1>
      Password Recovery
      <hr />
    </H1>
    <form id="Form1" runat="server">
      <asp:PasswordRecovery runat="server">
        <maildefinition from="admin@mywebsite.com" />
      </asp:PasswordRecovery>
    </form>

  </body>

</html>
```

If we attempt to use the control with the default Membership settings—which do not allow password recovery—we will receive the following error:

"Your attempt to retrieve your password was not successful. Please try again."

To allow us to recover the password, we need to change some of the default membership settings. Below are the necessary changes to the `<membership />` configuration settings to allow for password recovery:

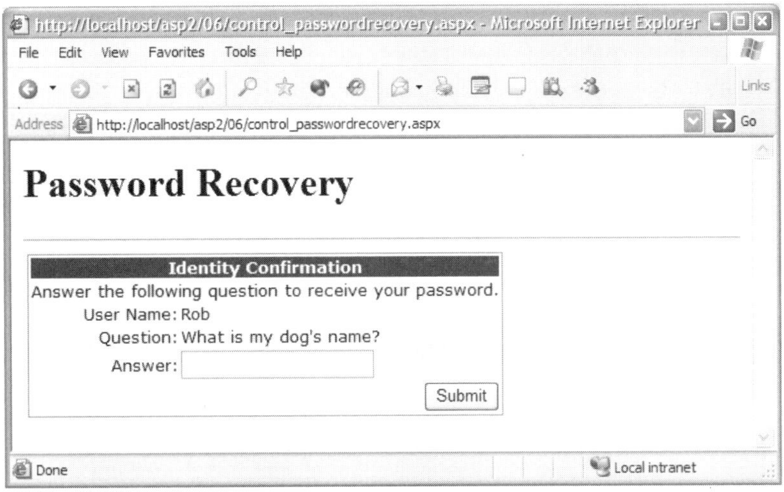

FIGURE 6.13. Password recovery with question and answer

- `enablePasswordRetrieval="True"`
- `passwordFormat="Clear"`

The `enablePasswordRetrieval` attribute must be set to `True` to allow for password retrieval, and the `passwordFormat` attribute must be set to either `Clear` or `Encrypted`.[13] Another alternative is that when `enable PasswordReset` is set to `True`, the new password can be e-mailed to the user.

In addition to configuring the `<membership />` configuration settings, we must specify the `<maildefinition />` element of the `<asp:PasswordRecovery runat="server" />` control. The `<maildefinition />` names the address from whom e-mails are sent.

Finally, we can also use the `<asp:PasswordRecovery runat="server" />` control to retrieve the user's password using the question/answer support of Membership (see Figure 6.13). The control still requires that we enter the username first, but before simply mailing the password it will first also request the answer to the user's question.

---

13. The default `passwordFormat` value, `Hashed`, can be best thought of as one-way encryption; thus it is impossible to retrieve the original value once the value is hashed. The hashed value is also salted (combined with random characters) to further obscure the password.

This behavior is forced by setting the `<membership />` configuration setting `requiresQuestionAndAnswer` to `true` (the default is `false`).[14] Note that this configuration change is in addition to changing the `enablePasswordRetrieval` to `true` and setting the `passwordFormat` to a value other than `Hashed`.

Managing and storing user credentials are only one part of securely controlling access to resources within your site. In addition to validating who the user is, you need to determine whether the user is allowed to access the requested resource. The process of validating credentials is known as *authentication*; *authorization* is the process of determining whether the authenticated user is allowed to access a particular resource.

ASP.NET 1.x already provides authorization facilities, but just as we have shown with Membership, there is more simplification to be done.

Role Manager

The ASP.NET Role Manager feature is designed to simplify managing roles and the users that belong to those roles. After authentication, when Role Manager is enabled, ASP.NET will automatically add the users to the role(s) he or she belongs to. When ASP.NET authorization occurs, the user is either allowed or denied access to the requested resource based on his or her role(s).[15]

URL-based role authorization is a feature of ASP.NET 1.0. We can control what users are allowed to access by specifying access permissions within `configuration` (see Listing 6.15).

LISTING 6.15. Configuring Roles

```
<configuration>

  <system.web>
    <authorization>
      <deny users="?" />
    </authorization>
  </system.web>
```

---

14. You will also need to ensure that the user set a question and answer when his or her account in the Membership system was created.
15. Authorization always occurs after authentication; that is, first the user's credentials are validated, and if the credentials are valid, then the determination is made whether the user is allowed to access the requested resource.

```
<location path="PremiumContent.aspx">
  <system.web>
    <authorization>
      <allow roles="Premium" />
      <deny users="*" />
    </authorization>
  </system.web>
</location>

</configuration>
```

The above web.config file could be added to any application. It states that anonymous users are denied access to all resources. Furthermore, only users in the role Premium are allowed access to PremiumContent.aspx. All other users are denied access.

Before we can control access to resources through roles, we need to create some roles and then add users to them. Let's look at how we can do this with the new Role Manager feature.

Setting Up Role Manager

Similar to Membership, Role Manager relies on a provider to store data and thus allow us to create roles and associations between users and their roles.[16] Unlike Membership, Role Manager is not enabled by default. Therefore, before we can use the Role Manager API, we need to enable the feature in its configuration settings.

Similar to Membership configuration settings, Role Manager configuration settings are defined in machine.config and can be overridden or changed within an application's web.config file. Listing 6.16 shows a sample web.config enabled for Role Manager.

LISTING 6.16. Configuring Role Manager

```
<configuration>
  <system.web>

    <roleManager enabled="true"
                 cacheRolesInCookie="true"
                 cookieName=".ASPXROLES"
                 cookieTimeout="30"
```

continues

---

16. This is identical to how Membership uses a provider. The difference is that a different set of providers exists for the Role Manager feature. Different providers are used to avoid making Role Manager providers dependent on Membership.

```
                          cookiePath="/"
                          cookieRequireSSL="false"
                          cookieSlidingExpiration="true"
                          cookieProtection="All"
                          defaultProvider="AspNetAccessProvider" >
            <providers>
              <add name="AspNetAccessProvider2"
                   type="System.Web.Security.AccessRoleProvider, System.Web"
                   connectionStringName="AccessFileName"
                   applicationName="/"
                   description="Stores and retrieves roles data from
                                the local Microsoft Access database file" />
            </providers>
          </roleManager>

        </system.web>
     </configuration>
```

Table 6.3 shows an explanation of the various configuration settings.

TABLE 6.3. Role Manager Configuration Settings

Attribute	Default Value	Description
enabled	false	Controls whether or not the Role Manager feature is enabled. By default it is disabled because enabling breaks backward compatibility with ASP.NET 1.0.
cacheRolesInCookie	true	Allows for the roles to be cached within an HTTP cookie. When the roles are cached within a cookie, a lookup for the roles associated with the user does not have to be done through the provider.
cookieName	.ASPXROLES	Sets the name of the cookie used to store the roles when cookies are enabled.
cookieTimeout	30	Sets the period of time for which the cookie is valid. If cookieSlidingExpiration is true, the cookie timeout is reset on each request within the cookieTimeout window.
cookiePath	/	Sets the path within the application within which the cookie is valid.
cookieRequireSSL	false	Specifies whether or not the cookie must be sent over an SSL channel.

TABLE 6.3. Role Manager Configuration Settings (continued)

Attribute	Default Value	Description
cookieSlidingExpiration	true	Sets the cookie timeout. When `true`, the cookie timeout is automatically reset each time a request is made within the `cookieTimeout` window, effectively allowing the cookie to stay valid until the user's session is complete.
cookieProtection	All	Controls how the data stored within the cookie is secured.
defaultProvider	*string*	Sets the friendly name of the provider to use for `roleManager`. By default this is `AspNetAccessProvider`.

Now that we've seen how to configure the settings of Role Manager, let's create some roles.

Creating Roles

The `Roles` API supports a single method for creating roles:

```
CreateRole(rolename As String)
```

This API is used to create the friendly role name, such as Administrators, used to control access to resources. Listing 6.17 provides sample code for creating roles in an ASP.NET page.

LISTING 6.17. Creating and Viewing Roles

```
<script runat="server">

  Public Sub Page_Load (sender As Object, e As EventArgs)

    If Not Page.IsPostBack Then
      DataBind()
    End If

  End Sub


  Public Sub CreateRole_Click(sender As Object, e As EventArgs)

    Try

      ' Attempt to create the role
      Roles.CreateRole (Rolename.Text)
```

continues

```
        Catch ex As Exception

          ' Failed to create the role
          Status.Text = ex.ToString()

        End Try

        DataBind()

      End Sub

      Public Overrides Sub DataBind()

        RoleList.DataSource = Roles.GetAllRoles()
        RoleList.DataBind()

      End Sub

    </script>


    <html>
      <body style="FONT-FAMILY: Verdana">

      <H1>Create Role</H1>
      Below is a list of the current roles:
      <asp:datagrid id="RoleList" runat="server" />

      <hr />

      <form runat="server">

        Rolename to create: <asp:TextBox id="Rolename" runat="server" />
        <asp:button Text="Create Role"
                    OnClick="CreateRole_Click" runat="server"/>

      </form>

      <font color="red" size="6">
      <asp:Label id="Status" runat="server"/>
      </font>

      </body>
    </html>
```

This code sample allows us to enter a role name, which is then created using the `Roles.CreateRole()` API. If the role already exists, an exception is thrown. Finally, all of the available roles are enumerated through a `DataGrid` using the `Roles.GetAllRoles()` API, discussed shortly.

Now that we can create roles, let's add some users to the roles.

Adding Users to Roles

Membership and Role Manager are not rigidly coupled. They are designed to work together, but you do not have to use one to use the other. Both use the authenticated username as the only shared piece of data. For example, it is possible to add a user to a role even if the user is not created through the Membership system.[17]

Adding users to roles is accomplished by using the following methods supported by the `Roles` API:

```
AddUserToRole(username As String, rolename As String)

AddUserToRoles(username As String, rolenames() As String)

AddUsersToRole(usernames() As String, rolename As String)

AddUsersToRoles(usernames() As String, rolenames() As String)
```

These various methods allow for adding users to roles in bulk or individually. Listing 6.18 demonstrates `Roles.AddUserToRole()`.

LISTING 6.18. Adding Users to Roles

```vb
<%@ Page Language="VB" %>

<script runat="server">

  Public Sub Page_Load(ByVal sender As Object, ByVal e As EventArgs)

    DataBind()

  End Sub

  Public Sub AddUserToRole_Click(sender As Object, e As EventArgs)

    Roles.AddUserToRole(Username.Text, _
                    RoleList.SelectedItem.Value)

    DataBind()

  End Sub
```

continues

---

17. This flexible design allows using various providers for data storage. For example, you could have an AS/400 Membership provider and an Access Role Manager provider.

```
Public Overrides Sub DataBind()

  RoleList.DataSource = Roles.GetAllRoles()
  RoleList.DataBind()

End Sub

</script>

<html>
  <body style="FONT-FAMILY: Verdana">

  <H1>Add User to Role</H1>

  <form runat="server">
    User: <asp:TextBox id="Username" runat="server" />
    Role to add user to: <asp:DropDownList id="RoleList"
                                            runat="server" />
    <asp:button Text="Add User To Role"
             OnClick="AddUserToRole_Click" runat="server"/>
  </form>

  <font size="6" color="Red">
  <asp:Label id="StatusCheck" runat="server"/>
  </font>

  </body>

</html>
```

This code sample data binds the results of `Roles.GetAllRoles()` to a `DropDownList` control and then allows us to enter a user to add to a role.[18] The `Roles.AddUserToRole()` API is then used to add the user to the role.

When adding multiple users to roles or a user to multiple roles, the addition occurs within the context of a transaction. Either all updates succeed or all fail.

We can now use another `Roles` API to determine to what roles a particular user belongs.

Returning a User's Roles

To return a list of the roles to which a user belongs, we can simply use one of the following APIs:

---

18. You could also data-bind to a list of the Members from the Membership system.

```
GetRolesForUser() As String()

GetRolesForUser(username As String) As String()

GetUsersInRole(rolename As String) As String()
```

The `Roles.GetRolesForUser()` method will return a string array of all the roles that the current user is in. The overloaded version of this method that accepts a `username` parameter allows us to specify for which user we want a listing of roles. The last method, `Roles.GetUsersInRole()`, allows us to get a string array listing of usernames that belong to the specified role.

Listing 6.19 demonstrates the overloaded version of `Roles.GetRolesForUser()`.

LISTING 6.19. Finding the Roles for a User

```
<script runat="server">

  Public Sub GetRolesForUser_Click(sender As Object, e As EventArgs)

    RolesForUser.DataSource = Roles.GetRolesForUser(Username.Text)
    RolesForUser.DataBind()

  End Sub

</script>

<html>
  <body style="FONT-FAMILY: Verdana">

  <H1>Roles user is in</H1>
  <hr />

  <form runat="server">
    Username: <asp:TextBox id="Username" runat="server" />
    <asp:button Text="Roles User Is In"
                OnClick="GetRolesForUser_Click" runat="server"/>
  </form>

  User is in roles:

  <asp:DataGrid runat="server" id="RolesForUser" />

  </body>
</html>
```

This code sample simply asks for the name of a user. When the page is posted back, the `Roles.GetRolesForUser()` API is called, passing in the name of the specified user. The results are then data-bound to a `DataGrid`.

Checking Whether a User Is in a Role

Access to resources can be controlled by which roles the user belongs to. As shown in the beginning of this section, it is possible to control access to URLs based on settings made in the configuration file. In addition to this declarative security access control, we can also perform programmatic checks for the role the user belongs to.

ASP.NET 1.1 allowed for programmatic checks for determining whether the user was in a role through `User.IsInRole(`*username* `as String)`; the result of this method returned `True` or `False`. The `Roles` API supports a similar `Roles.IsUserInRole(`*rolename* `As String)` API:

```
IsUserInRole(rolename As String) As Boolean

IsUserInRole(username As String, rolename As String) As Boolean
```

Now that we've seen how to add users to roles and check whether users are in a particular role, let's look at how we can remove a user from a role.

Removing Users from Roles

Similar to the methods used for adding a user to roles, we have four different methods for removing users from roles:

```
RemoveUserFromRole(username As String, rolename As String)

RemoveUserFromRoles(username As String, rolenames() As String)

RemoveUsersFromRole(usernames() As String, rolename As String)

RemoveUsersFromRoles(usernames() As String, rolenames() As String)
```

Again, similar to adding users to roles, when the process of removing users from roles is transacted, either all succeed or all fail.

Deleting a Role

Roles can be deleted easily by using the `Roles.DeleteRole(`*rolename* `As String)` method. Listing 6.20 shows a sample ASP.NET page that demonstrates how to use this API.

LISTING 6.20. Deleting a Role

```vb
<%@ Page Language="VB" %>

<script runat="server">

  Public Sub Page_Load()

    If Not Page.IsPostBack Then
      DataBind()
    End If

  End Sub

  Public Sub DeleteRole_Click(sender As Object, e As EventArgs)

    Try
      Roles.DeleteRole(Rolename.Text)
    Catch ex As Exception
      StatusCheck.Text = "There was an error removing the role(s)"
    End Try

    DataBind()

  End Sub

  Public Overrides Sub DataBind()
    RoleList.DataSource = Roles.GetAllRoles()
    RoleList.DataBind()

  End Sub

</script>

<html>
  <body style="FONT-FAMILY: Verdana">

  <H1>Delete Role</H1>
  Below is a list of the current roles:
  <asp:datagrid id="RoleList" runat="server" />

  <hr />

  <form runat="server">
    Rolename to delete: <asp:TextBox id="Rolename" runat="server" />
    <asp:button Text="Delete Role" OnClick="DeleteRole_Click"
                runat="server"/>
  </form>

  <font color="red" size="6">
```

continues

```
<asp:Label id="StatusCheck" runat="server"/>
</font>

</body>

</html>
```

This code lists all the available roles by binding the result of `Roles.GetAllRoles()` to a `DataGrid`. It then allows for a specific role to be named and deleted using the `Roles.DeleteRole()` method, as shown in Figure 6.14. There is a second form of `DeleteRoles` that takes two parameters: the first is the role name and the second a Boolean to indicate whether an exception should be thrown if the role being deleted has users.

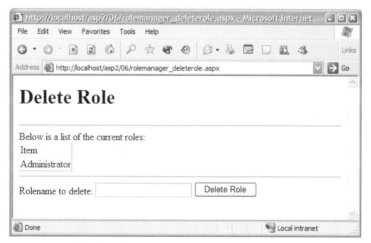

FIGURE 6.14. Deleting roles

Role Manager uses a provider to write back to and read from a data store in which the roles and user-to-role mapping is done. Rather than reading/writing to this database on each request—since a list of the roles the user belongs to must be obtained—a cookie can optionally be used to cache roles, as described in the next subsection.

Role Caching

Role caching is a feature of Role Manager that enables user-to-role mappings to be performed without requiring a lookup to the data store on each request.[19] Instead of looking up the user-to-role mapping in the data store, the roles the user belongs to are stored, encrypted, within an HTTP cookie. If the user does not have the cookie, a request is made against the provider to retrieve the roles the user belongs to. The roles are then encrypted and stored within a cookie. On subsequent requests the cookie is decrypted and the roles obtained from the cookie.

Internally, in cases where there are more roles than can fit in the cookie, the cookie is marked as an incremental role cookie. That is, the cookie stores as many roles as possible but likely not all the roles. When role checking is performed, and the user is not in one of the roles being checked for, ASP.NET will call the `Roles` API and check whether the user belongs to that role. If not, access is denied. If the user is in the role and the role is not currently stored in the cookie, the last role stored within the cookie is removed and the requested role is added. Thereby, in cases where the user has more roles than can fit in the cookie, the cookie over time will contain a list of the most frequently accessed roles.

Cookieless Forms Authentication

ASP.NET 1.0 introduced the Forms Authentication feature to allow developers to easily author ASP.NET applications that rely on an authentication mechanism they could control. Forms Authentication exposed a set of APIs that developers can simply call to authenticate the user, such as

```
FormsAuthentication.RedirectFromLoginPage(Username.Text, False)
```

Forms Authentication in ASP.NET 1.0 would then take the username, encrypt it, and store it within an HTTP cookie. The cookie would be presented on subsequent requests and the user automatically reauthenticated.

One of the common feature requests the ASP.NET team continually received was the ability for Forms Authentication to support cookieless authentication, that is, to not require an HTTP cookie. This is just what the team has provided in ASP.NET 2.0.

Enabling Cookieless Forms Authentication

Cookieless Forms Authentication is enabled within the `machine.config` file or the `web.config` file of your application by setting the new `cookieless` attribute (see Listing 6.21).

---

19. This implementation is similar to what is done within all the ASP.NET Starter Kits.

LISTING 6.21. Default Configuration for Forms Authentication

```
<configuration>
  <system.web>
    <authentication mode="Forms">
      <forms name=".ASPXAUTH"
             loginUrl="login.aspx"
             protection="All"
             timeout="30"
             path="/"
             requireSSL="false"
             slidingExpiration="true"
             defaultUrl="default.aspx"
             cookieless="UseCookies" />
    </authentication>
  </system.web>
</configuration>
```

The cookieless attribute has four possible values:[20]

- UseUri: Forces the authentication ticket to be stored in the URL.
- UseCookies: Forces the authentication ticket to be stored in the cookie (same as ASP.NET 1.0 behavior).
- AutoDetect: Automatically detects whether the browser/device does or does not support cookies.
- UseDeviceProfile: Chooses to use cookies or not based on the device profile settings from machine.config.

If we set the cookieless value to UseUri within web.config and then request and authenticate with Forms Authentication, we should see something similar to what Figure 6.15 shows within the URL of the requested page.

Below is the requested URL—after authentication—in a more readable form:

http://localhost/Whidbey/GrocerToGo/(A(AcNzj7rSUh84OWViZTcwMioxNWYyLTQ5
ODAtYjU2NCoyYTg3MjEzMzRhY2Y`)F(uoG1wsK16NJFs7e2TJo2yNZ6eAZ8eoU9T8rSXZX
LEPPM8STwp6EONVtt4YCqEeb-9XDrrEpIHRpOOlKh8rO9foAhP6AXWwL*obM bxYcfZ
c`))/default.aspx

---

20. In case you forget the values, an incorrect value set for cookieless will cause an ASP.NET error page to be generated that lists the acceptable values.

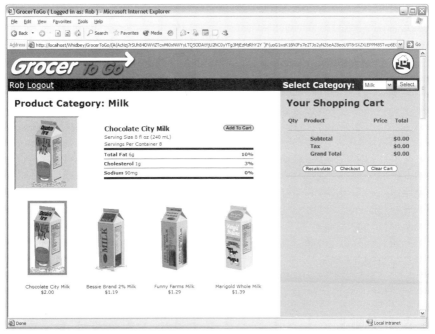

FIGURE 6.15. Cookieless Forms Authentication

The Web Site Administration Tool

Administration of ASP.NET applications has always been easy, although diving into the XML-based configuration file isn't the most user-friendly way to do it. For the 2.0 release of ASP.NET, there is the Web Site Administration Tool, which allows configuration of a Web application via an easy browser interface.

The Web Site Administration Tool is useful for two main reasons. First, it abstracts the XML configuration into an easy-to-use interface, and second, it provides administration features via a browser. This means that for remote sites (such as those provided by a hosting company), it's easy to administer an application without having to edit the configuration file (e.g., to add new security credentials) and then upload it.

The Web Site Administration Tool is available for each directory configured as an application, by way of a simple URL:

http://website/WebAdmin.axd

This presents you with a home page and menu consisting of five main options.

The Home Page

The Home page, shown in Figure 6.16, details the current application and security details, as well as links to the other main sections.

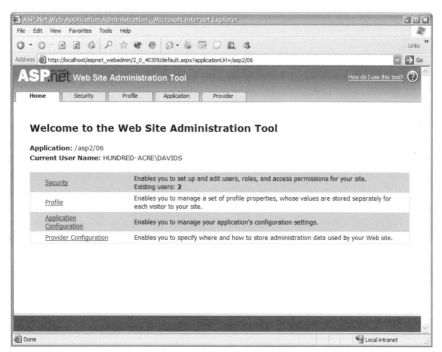

FIGURE 6.16. The Web Site Administration Tool Home page

The Security Page

The Security page, shown in Figure 6.17, offers two options for configuring security. The first is a wizard that takes you through the following steps:

1. **Select Access Method,** which defines whether the application is available from the Internet (in which case Forms Authentication is used) or from the LAN (in which case Windows Authentication is used)

2. **Specify Data Source,** where you can specify the database (Access or SQL Server) that will store the user credentials and what details are required (e.g., unique e-mail address, allow password retrieval, and so on)

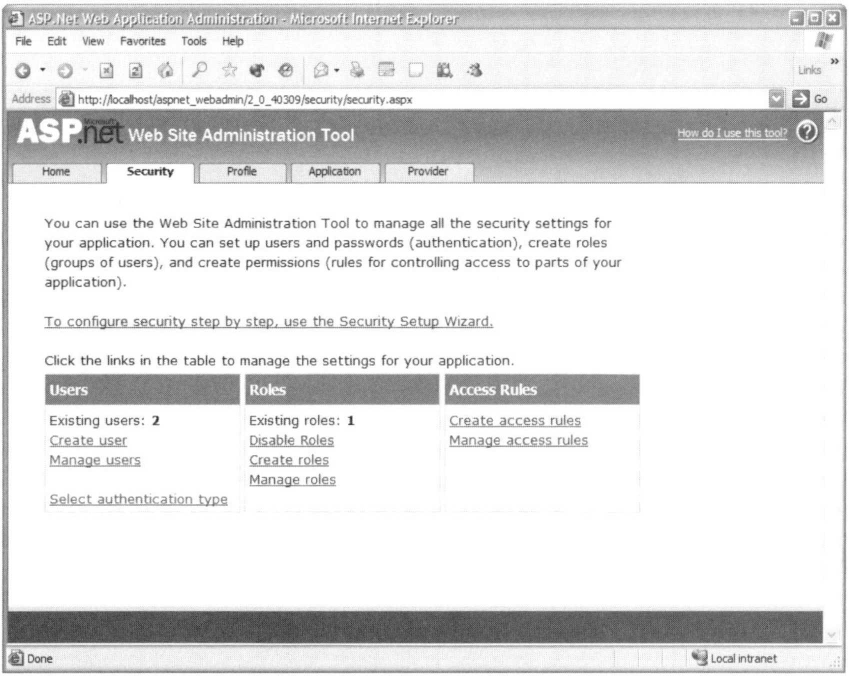

FIGURE 6.17. The Web Site Administration Tool Security page

3. **Define Roles,** where you can optionally specify Authorization roles
4. **Add New Users,** which allows addition of new users and allocation to roles
5. **Add New Access Rules,** which defines which files and folders users and roles have permissions for
6. **Complete,** to indicate that the security settings have been configured

The second option is for configuration of security that has already been enabled. If configured, the details are shown at the bottom of the main security page (see the following subsection for more information).

Security Management

Once you have initially set up security (or selected the second option titled Security Management on the main Security page), the Security page allows management of users, roles, and permissions without the use of the wizard.

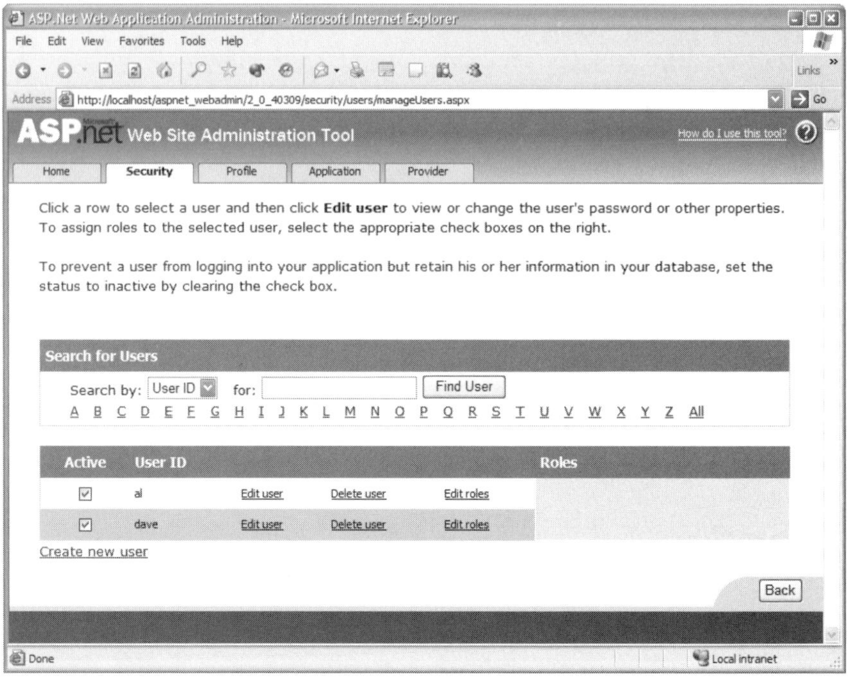

FIGURE 6.18. Web Site Administration Tool user configuration

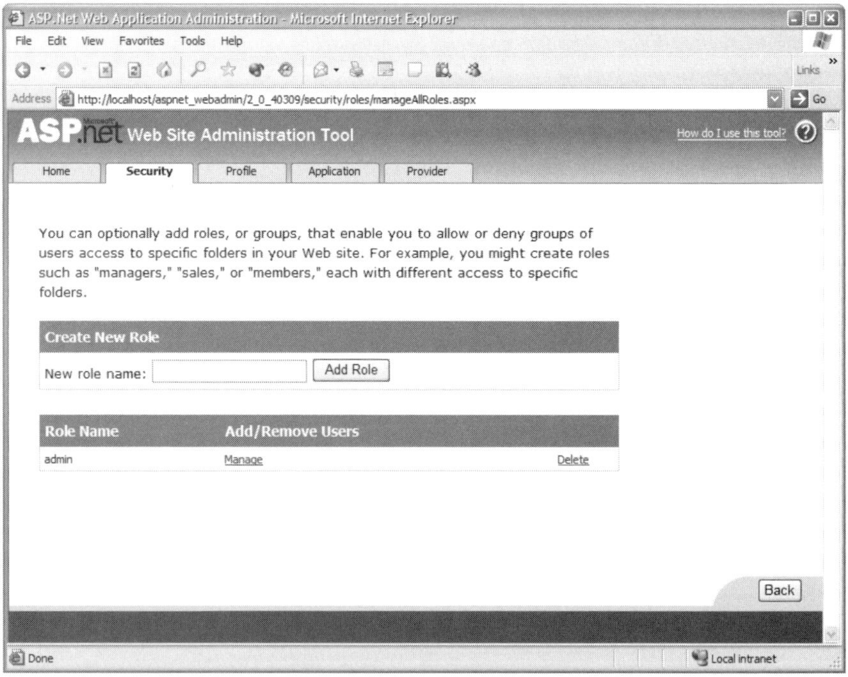

FIGURE 6.19. Web Site Administration Tool role configuration

For example, consider the users added earlier in the chapter. If we select the Manage Users options, we see the User Management features shown in Figure 6.18.

Likewise, selecting Manage Roles allows you to customize roles and members, as shown in Figure 6.19.

Other Pages

Three other pages are used in the Web Site Administration Tool:

- **Profile**, which allows configuration of the Personalization Profile (see Chapter 7)
- **Application**, which allows configuration of application settings, site and page counters, SMTP settings, and debugging and tracing (see Chapter 13)
- **Provider**, which allows configuration of the data provider or providers to be used in the application (see Chapter 13)

SUMMARY

We've sampled only some of the new security capabilities in ASP.NET 2.0. The Membership and Role Manager features are specifically designed to solve problems the ASP.NET team saw developers addressing over and over again. Although both complement and can be used easily with Forms Authentication, they were also designed to work independently—independently of one another and independently of Forms Authentication. Furthermore, both support the provider design pattern. This design pattern allows you to take complete control over how and where the data used for these features is stored. The provider design pattern gives you ultimate control and flexibility, because you can control the business logic, while developers can learn a simple, friendly, and easy-to-use API.

Although writing code using Membership has become more concise, there are also now cases where no code is required. The new security server controls make many scenarios, such as login or password recovery, much easier to implement. The other security-related server controls simply save you the time formerly required to write code to perform simple tasks such as checking who is logged in.

The cookieless support for Forms Authentication means you don't have to require the use of cookies for authenticating users—something many of you have been requesting.

Finally, the Web Site Administration Tool provides a simple way to administer site security without building custom tools.

Now it's time to extend the topic of users interacting with a site and look at how sites can be personalized.

7

Personalization and Themes

IN CHAPTER 6 WE DISCUSSED the new infrastructure feature of Membership. Membership is used to store user credentials and offers APIs for validating those credentials as well as managing users. A common question that comes up when discussing Membership is how additional user details are stored; for example, your application may want to associate first and last names with the user or store a theme.

Although Membership does store some user information, such as when the user last logged on, the logon username, and so on, it is not specifically designed to store additional user characteristics such as first and last names. Storing additional user data is the responsibility of the new Personalization feature.

Personalization is a persistent user storage system for storing any data related to the user of your application. Several good examples that we'll use to demonstrate Personalization in this chapter include the following:

- Common user characteristics such as first and last names
- User application properties such as a shopping cart
- Application-specific data, such as the personalization settings used by the ASP.NET Forums (http://www.asp.net/forums)
- UI properties, such as the look and feel of controls

The Personalization services feature of ASP.NET 2.0 was designed with several specific goals in mind. Understanding these goals will help you successfully use Personalization in your application.

1. *Strongly typed access*: Unlike features such as `Cache`, `Session`, or `Application`, which require a key to retrieve a value from a dictionary, Personalization uses strongly typed properties, meaning that properties are easier to discover and use. For example, you may replace `Session` code with Personalization for storing the user's first name, as shown below:

```
Dim firstName As String

' First name retrieved from Session
firstName = Session("FirstName")

' First name retrieved from Profile
firstname = Profile.FirstName
```

2. *On-demand lookup*: Unlike Session state, which looks up the values of `Session` on each request regardless of whether or not the data is used, Personalization retrieves data only when it is requested.

3. *Extensible data store*: Personalization implements the new provider model design pattern. This design pattern exists to allow you to abstract the data access layer away from the Personalization APIs. For example, if you have data stored in an AS/400, you could use Personalization to access that data by authoring a provider to communicate with the AS/400. Later in this chapter we're going to look at a provider for the ASP.NET Forums to demonstrate how easy it is to author a provider. Providers can be configured as the default or set at runtime.

4. *Partitioned data access*: Properties stored in the `Profile` API can be partitioned across data providers. Thus while `Firstname`, `Lastname`, and `ZipCode` may come from a Microsoft SQL Server data store, other data such as `CustomerHistory` can come from a completely separate provider such as Oracle.

Below are the topics we're going to explore in this chapter:

- Storing and retrieving user personalization data
- Anonymous identification
- Anonymous personalization

- The provider model design pattern
- Authoring a customer Personalization provider
- Customizing the look of a site through themes

As we'll see, Personalization is a very powerful new feature of ASP.NET 2.0. It has been designed to integrate seamlessly with the new Membership services feature—but it can work independently as well.

Storing and Retrieving User Personalization Data

My first experience with a Personalization system was with the Site Server 3.0's Personalization and Membership feature. One of the frustrating aspects with Site Server's Personalization model, as well as all other commercially available Personalization systems, is that they are dictionary based. For example, were you to store or retrieve a value such as "John" as the first name of the user using ASP.NET's `Session` APIs, you would use code like this:

```
' Store the user's first name value
Session("FirstName") = "John"

. . .

' Retrieve the user's first name
string firstName = Session("FirstName")
```

Using key/value pairs is a very common pattern. In fact, this type of data storage and retrieval is used for `Application` state, `Session` state, `ViewState`, `Cache`, and so on. While this technique is both common and a very acceptable approach for storing data work, there are two problems.

1. *Key-based access*: The developer who writes the application must remember the key `FirstName` used to retrieve the value from the dictionary. While this isn't problematic for simple values, for large applications and complex items this can be quite a lot to remember. It is common for these items to be defined as constant strings within the application.
2. *Not strongly typed*: In addition to remembering the key of what was stored, the developer also must recall the data type the value was stored as. Values retrieved from the dictionary are returned as type `Object` for complex types, such as a business class `ShoppingCart`; a cast is required to coerce the `Object` back to the appropriate type.

Following is an example of non–strongly typed code that could be used to access a `ShoppingCart` class instance's `CartID` property from an instance of the `ShoppingCart` stored in `Session` state:

```
Dim cartID As Integer
Dim cart As ShoppingCart

' First get the Shopping Cart
cart = CType(Session("MyCart"), ShoppingCart)

' Next, get the cart id
cartID = cart.CartID
```

The key `MyCart` is used to retrieve the object from `Session` state. We then cast the returned object to the appropriate type `ShoppingCart`.

Using the new ASP.NET 2.0 Personalization feature, this same code is written as:

```
Dim cartID As Integer

' Get the cart id
cartID = Profile.Cart.CartID
```

Rather than accessing the value with a key, `Cart` is a property of type `ShoppingCart` and the `cartID` property can be used directly. No casts and no keys to remember—and a nice side effect is that you get statement completion within your development environment too!

The ASP.NET 2.0 Personalization system can store any data type, from simple scalar values such as integers and strings to complex user data types such as shopping carts. The option of storing any data type gives you a great degree of flexibility in your applications.

You may be wondering how the `Cart` property became available on the `Profile` class. The `Profile` class is a special class dynamically compiled with your ASP.NET application. The addition of the `Profile` class is done automatically—without your needing to do anything.

Properties on the `Profile` class are added through the ASP.NET configuration system within a new `<profile/>` section of the configuration file.

Configuring Personalization

Personalization properties are defined within the ASP.NET configuration system in the new `<profile/>` section. Listing 7.1 is a sample `web.config` containing `<property/>` settings.

LISTING 7.1. Configuring Personalization

```
<configuration>
  <system.web>

    <profile>

      <properties enabled="true"
                  defaultProvider="AspNetAccessProvider"
                  inherits="System.Web.Profile.HttpProfileBase,
                            System.Web,
                            Version=2.0.3600.0,
                            Culture=neutral,
                            PublicKeyToken=b03f5f7f11d50a3a" >

        <property name="FirstName" />

        <property name="TotalPosts"
                  type="System.Int32"
                  defaultValue="0" />

        <property name="LastPostDate"
                  type="System.DateTime" />

        <property name="Cart"
                  allowAnonymous="true"
                  type="Market.ShoppingCart, market"
                  serializeAs="Binary" />
      </properties>
    </profile>

  <system.web>
</configuration>
```

> **Note:** The configuration has changed from the Technology Preview, where `profile` was called `personalization`, and `properties` was called `profile`.

The `<profile/>` section follows the same provider design pattern used by Membership, Role Manager, and other ASP.NET 2.0 features that require data storage services. We'll cover the provider model in detail later in this chapter.

Within the `<profile/>` element of the machine configuration file the `defaultProvider` is set to `AspNetAccessProvider`—the Access Personalization provider is therefore configured as the default. You can easily change the default by specifying a different provider from those available in the `<providers/>` element. We'll come back to the `<providers/>` section shortly. We can also specify whether or not the Profile feature is enabled and finally the base class the Profile inherits from.

The `<properties/>` section is where individual properties are specified. These properties are then made available automatically through the `Profile` class in the `Page`. In the configuration sample above we created four properties:

- `FirstName`: Property used to store the first name value.
- `TotalPosts`: Property of type `Integer`, with a default value of `0`, used to store the total posts the user has made, for example, within the ASP.NET Forums application.
- `LastPostDate`: Property of type `DateTime`, used to store the last post date for a sample application such as the ASP.NET Forums.
- `Cart`: Property of type `ShoppingCart`. The property allows anonymous personalization, has a serialization type determined by the provider, and uses the `ShoppingCart` to retrieve and store data. The `ShoppingCart` is a custom type defined either in an assembly or defined in a class in the `Code` directory.

The default data type for `Profile` properties is `String`. Programmatically these properties are accessed as shown in Listing 7.2.

LISTING 7.2. Setting the Properties of a Profile

```
Dim totalPosts As Integer

' Set the user's first name
Profile.FirstName = "Rob"

' Access the user's total posts
totalPosts = Profile.TotalPosts

' DataBind to the user's cart and
' display items in his/her basket
DataGrid1.DataSource = Profile.Cart.Basket
DataGrid1.DataBind
```

If you want to take more control over how the data within the `Profile` object is organized, you can control the object model structure that is created in the `Profile`.

For example, if we wished to store personalization data from the ASP.NET Forums (http://www.asp.net/forums), we may wish for it to be organized logically together. This can be accomplished using a special `<group/>` element within `<properties/>` (see Listing 7.3).

LISTING 7.3. Configuring a Personalization Group

```
<properties>
  <property name="FirstName" />
  <property name="LastPostDate" type="System.DateTime" />

  <group name="Forums">
    <property name="TotalPosts" type="System.Int32"/>
    <property name="Location" />
    <property name="AllowAvatar" type="System.Boolean" />
    <property name="AvatarURL" />
  </group>

</properties>
```

Values within a group are accessed as follows:

```
Dim location As String

' Get the user's location
location = Profile.Forums.Location
```

As you can probably tell, the `<property/>` element is key to setting up Personalization properties. The `<group/>` element simply provides an easy way to logically organize these properties.

In these examples, we've shown several of the different attributes the `<property/>` element supports. Let's take a closer look at all these attributes.

Configuring Personalization Properties

The `<property/>` element is what you use to add properties to the programmatic `Profile` API—when ASP.NET compiles your page, the default `Profile` class is replaced with a class instance that contains the properties you define. This all happens under the covers; all you need to know is how to specify the property.

The simplest use of `<property/>` is to declare a new Personalization property with only the `name` attribute defined:

```
<properties>
  <property name="FirstName" />
</properties>
```

This instructs the Personalization system to add a property named `FirstName` of type `String` with no default value, to not allow anonymous personalization, and to store/retrieve the value from the default Personalization provider.

When defining properties, the only required attribute is `name`; this is used to access the property from the programmatic `Profile` in the page. All other attributes, while important, are optional.

Table 7.1 lists all the `<property/>` attributes.

TABLE 7.1. Personalization Property Attributes

Attribute	Description
name	Sets the name of the Personalization property. This is used as the key to access the data and also as the name of the property exposed on the programmatic `Profile` API. It is the only required attribute of the `<property/>` element.
readOnly	Specifies that the property is read-only and cannot have values set. This is useful for assigning values, such as `DisplayName`, that are not configurable but are specific to each user. If not specified, it defaults to `false`.
serializeAs	Determines how the data stored within Personalization properties, such as first name or shopping cart, is stored. Valid values include: ● `String`: Attempt to convert the value to a string. ● `XML`: Serialize the data as XML. ● `Binary`: Serialize the data as binary. ● `ProviderSpecific`: Store the data as the provider determines. No serialization of the data occurs. It is the responsibility of the provider to determine how to store the data. The default is `String`.
provider	Names the provider used for setting and retrieving data for the property. If not specified, the default provider is used. We'll look at a sample later in the chapter that demonstrates how you can author your own provider.
defaultValue	Allows for a default value to be specified. For example, a default theme could be specified if the user has not already selected one.

TABLE 7.1. Personalization Property Attributes (continued)

Attribute	Description
type	Specifies the type of the property. The default is String; however, this can be set to any data type.
allowAnonymous	When set to true, allows anonymous unauthenticated users to store data in the Personalization system. This also requires the anonymous identification feature to be enabled. If not specified, the default value is false. This attribute is discussed in more detail in the Anonymous Personalization section of this chapter.

Accessing Other Users' Personalization Data

The Profile API within your ASP.NET application will automatically be set to retrieve the personalization data for the authenticated user. However, if you wish to retrieve data for a different user, you can retrieve the user's profile using the Profile.GetProfile(username) API. You simply specify the username as a string and you can access that user's personalization data.

Now that we've looked at how to set up the required configuration properties and how to access other users' personalization data, let's look at how to configure the databases required to store the personalization data.

Setting Up the Databases for Personalization

Two Personalization providers ship with ASP.NET 2.0:

1. Microsoft Access: Recommended for development or prototyping
2. Microsoft SQL Server: Recommended for production

By default Personalization is set to use the Microsoft Access Personalization provider, defined in the class AccessPersonalizationProvider. This provider is found in the namespace System.Web.Personalization in the System.Web.dll assembly.

Personalization is instructed to use the Access provider through the configuration settings. The defaultProvider attribute on the <profile/> element controls what the default provider is:

```
<profile defaultProvider="AspNetAccessProvider">
```

The provider itself is then defined within the <providers/> section of <profile/> (see Listing 7.4).

LISTING 7.4. Configuring the Access Personalization Provider

```
<add name="AspNetAccessProvider"
     type="System.Web.Personalization.
           AccessPersonalizationProvider,
           System.Web,
           Version=2.0.3600.0,
           Culture=neutral,
           PublicKeyToken=b03f5f7f11d50a3a"
     connectionStringName="AccessFileName"
     applicationName="/"
     description="Stores and retrieves personalization
                  data from the local Microsoft Access
                  database file" />
```

As mentioned, there is also a Personalization provider for Microsoft SQL Server (see Listing 7.5).

LISTING 7.5. Configuring the SQL Server Personalization Provider

```
<add name="AspNetSqlProvider"
     type="System.Web.Personalization.
           SqlPersonalizationProvider,
           System.Web,
           Version=2.0.3600.0, Culture=neutral,
           PublicKeyToken=b03f5f7f11d50a3a"
     connectionStringName="LocalSqlServer"
     applicationName="/"
     description="Stores and retrieves personalization
                  data from the local Microsoft
                  SQL Server database" />
```

Table 7.2 gives you an idea of which provider to use depending on your application.

TABLE 7.2. Personalization Providers' Supported Security Models

	SQL	Access
Windows Authentication	✗	✗
Small intranet (non-domain-based)	✗	✗
Internet (enterprise)	✗	
Internet (personal/hobby)	✗	✗

The ASP.NET team specifically recommends using SQL Server for production applications.

Let's take a look at both providers in more detail and see how we set them up.

Using the Access Personalization Provider and the \data\ Directory

The Microsoft Access database used by ASP.NET Personalization is the same Microsoft Access database used by other Access providers, such as Membership. To use Microsoft Access as your database, ASP.NET must have read/write permission on the actual Microsoft Access file.

If you create your project using the Visual Studio 2005 tool, the tool will attempt to grant the necessary permission for ASP.NET to have read/write access. In fact, what will happen is that a new directory, \data\, will be created within your application, and a copy of an existing template Access file containing all the necessary tables and procedures will be copied from `ASPNetdb_Template.mdb` in the Framework installation directory. This file is created in your project as `\data\AspNetDB.mdb`.

If you receive a security error when attempting to use any of the features that utilize the Access provider, you will need to manually add the necessary permissions.

Granting Permissions to the Access Database. To grant ASP.NET permissions to the Microsoft Access database, follow these steps:

1. Open Windows Explorer and navigate to your Web application directory.
2. Create a `\data\` directory if it does not already exist.
3. Right-click on the `\data\` directory and select Properties.
4. Within the Properties dialog, select the Security tab (see Figure 7.1).
5. Click the Add button and add one of the following accounts:
   * If you are running Windows XP or Windows Server 2000 (and hence IIS 5), you need to add the user ASPNET.
   * If you are running Windows Server 2003 (and hence IIS 6), you need to add the group IIS_WPG.
6. Once the user or group is visible in the list of users and groups—as in Figure 7.1—select the user or group and check the Full Control Allow checkbox.

This grants permission to either the ASP.NET worker process or the IIS 6.0 worker process to have read/write permissions on the `\data\` directory, allowing ASP.NET to modify the Access database.

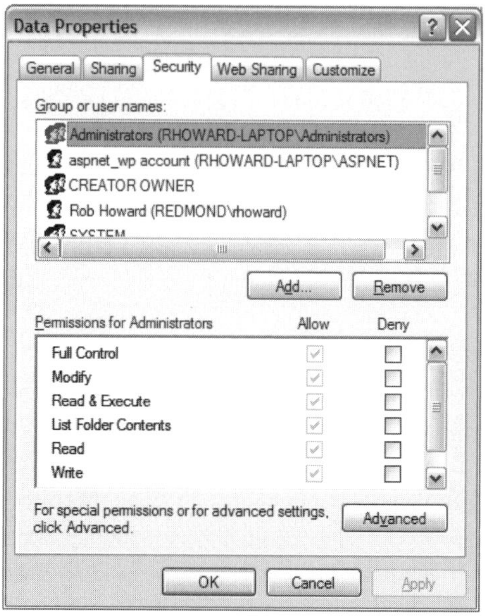

FIGURE 7.1. Configuring permissions on the database

Specifying Which Access Database to Use.   You'll notice that the actual filename of the Access database to use for the Personalization provider is not named. Instead only the following reference exists:

```
connectionStringName="AccessFileName"
```

All connection string information is now stored in the new connection string manager section of web.config. Data stored in the connection string manager section can be encrypted so if your web.config file were compromised, your connection strings would be safe.

Listing 7.6 shows the entry from machine.config for the new connection string manager feature.

LISTING 7.6. Configuring Connection Strings

```
<system.web>
  <connectionStrings>
    <add name="LocalSqlServer"
      connectionString="data source=127.0.0.1;
                        Integrated Security=SSPI" />
    <add name="AccessFileName"
      connectionString="~\DATA\ASPNetDB.mdb" />
  </connectionStrings>
</system.web>
```

All connection strings used by providers are stored within `<connectionStrings/>`.

By default all Access providers will attempt to use the `\Data\AspNetDb.mdb` file relative to the current application—specified by the tilde (~). You can easily change this to use an Access file from a different location. For example, you may want all your applications to share one `AspNetDB.mdb` file. To do this, specify an absolute path, or each application's `web.config` could set its own value.

Using the SQL Server Personalization Provider

Microsoft Access is a great storage solution for small Web sites or intranet applications. However, as we stated earlier, Microsoft SQL Server is the recommended data storage location for enterprise-level Internet applications.

While providers that use Microsoft Access "just work," a bit of setup needs to take place in order to use Microsoft SQL Server. There are several different options for configuring Microsoft SQL Server for ASP.NET services:

* The Web Site Administration Tool: As discussed in Chapter 6, you can use the Web Site Administration Tool to set up SQL Server databases for ASP.NET.
* The ASP.NET SQL Server Setup Wizard: This command-line and GUI tool can be used to set up a SQL Server for ASP.NET features.
* The `.sql` scripts: Use SQL Server tools to run the `.sql` files to configure features.

Let's look at how we can set up a SQL Server database for the ASP.NET Personalization feature using the ASP.NET SQL Server Setup Wizard.

ASP.NET SQL Server Setup Wizard. The ASP.NET SQL Server Setup Wizard is both a command-line and GUI-based utility. It is used to configure SQL Server to support the various application services (such as Membership, Personalization, and so on) used by ASP.NET.

The tool, `aspnet_regsql.exe`, can be found in `\Windows\Microsoft.NET\Framework\v2.0.40419\`. Note that the directory number corresponds to the version of .NET Framework installed. You will likely have a directory different from `\v2.0.40419\`.

The tool supports two modes: command-line and GUI. The command-line mode gives you the most control over what is going to be set up, while the GUI tool simply installs or removes all features.

To run in command-line mode, first open a command shell, navigate to the directory where the `aspnet_regsql.exe` tool is located, and type

```
aspnet_regsql.exe /?
```

This will give you a listing of the command-line capabilities of this tool. In Figure 7.2 you can see some of the output in command-line mode. Instructions for using the tool as well as the various switches are also listed. In future books we'll go into more detail on how all these command-line options work. For now we're going to focus on the GUI mode.

To run the `aspnet_regsql.exe` tool in GUI mode, type

```
aspnet_regsql.exe
```

with no parameters, or double-click on the file from Explorer. This will open the wizard and display the welcome screen (see Figure 7.3).

Click Next to select the setup options (see Figure 7.4). From this screen you have only two options.

1. Configure SQL Server for application services: Runs the necessary `.sql` scripts. These scripts exist within the same directory as the `aspnet_regsql.exe` tool. There are scripts for both installing and uninstalling the features.

2. Remove application services information from an existing database: Runs the uninstall scripts on the specified database.

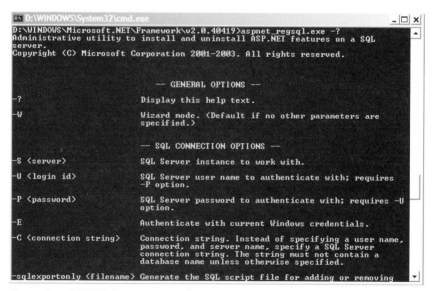

FIGURE 7.2. ASP.NET SQL Server configuration tool command line

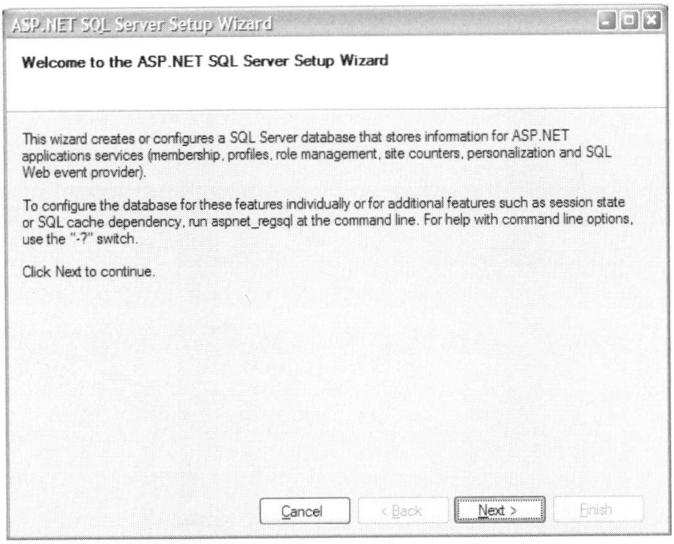

FIGURE 7.3. ASP.NET SQL Server configuration tool wizard

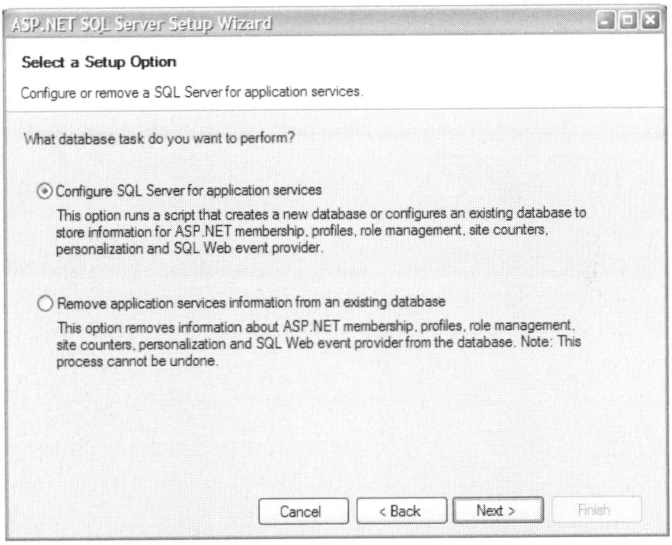

FIGURE 7.4. Using the ASP.NET SQL Server configuration tool, step 1

(In later beta releases you will be able to configure database cache invalidation—see Chapter 12—from the tool as well.) If you select to configure SQL Server, the tool will run all .sql scripts required for SQL Server support for all ASP.NET services.

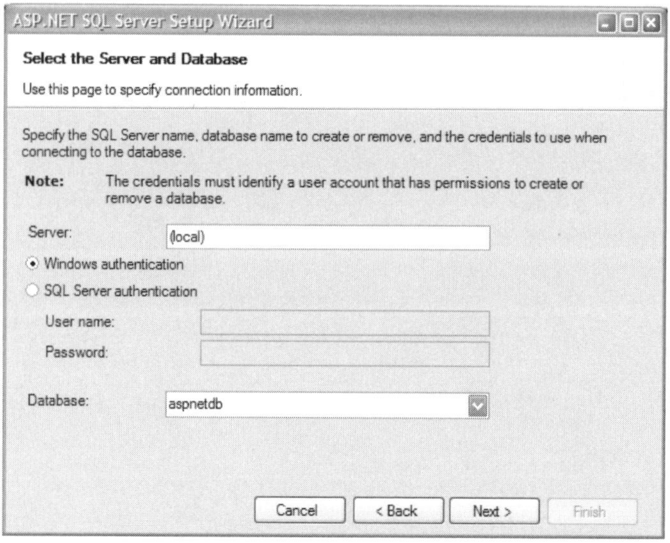

FIGURE 7.5. Using the ASP.NET SQL Server configuration tool, step 2

The next screen (see Figure 7.5) will ask which SQL Server and database to execute these scripts on. You will need to select both the server and the database to install to. If a database does not exist, you can specify a new database by simply typing in the database name.

After clicking Next you will see a screen to confirm your selections, and installation will begin. Once complete, you will see a screen indicating success or failure, and you can then exit the wizard.

Finally, you will need to modify the `<connectionStrings/>` section of the configuration file to specify the username and password to access SQL Server. By default the connection string is set to use Windows Integrated Authentication.

Windows Integrated Authentication will attempt to log into SQL Server using the credentials of the process running ASP.NET (assuming impersonation is not enabled). This identity is either the `ASPNET` user for Windows Server 2000 or Windows XP or a user within the `IIS_WPG` group for Windows Server 2003. Alternatively you can specify a SQL username and password in the connection string.

Data Access Optimizations

When designing the Personalization system, the ASP.NET team took great care to ensure the system is flexible for storing and accessing data but at the same time smart and performance-focused about how data is accessed.

Personalization versus Session State

Many people may initially confuse Personalization and Session state. Although they are similar in that both features store data for users, they are very distinct in how they operate on that data and how data is maintained.

Session state is for temporary user session data. When the user's session expires, the data stored in Session state is removed. Session state also is auto-populated on each request to the application. Whether you use it or not, you are likely paying the cost for Session state—which is even more costly when the Session state data is stored out-of-process.

Personalization is for long-lived data. Whereas with Session state the data is created and then, if the session is not active for a period of time, automatically removed, data created through Personalization—in theory—exists forever. For example, if you stored a `ShoppingCart` in Session state, the contents of the cart would be lost when the session ended. However, with Personalization the contents of the cart could be persisted indefinitely.

The last and major difference between personalization and session state is the manner in which data is both retrieved and saved. Session state makes use of the two application events:

```
Application_OnAcquireRequestState
```
and
```
Application_OnReleaseRequestState.
```

When the request is starting, the `OnAcquireRequestState` event is raised, and the Session state module contacts the session store and retrieves all session data for the current user. It also then places a lock on this data in the session store to prevent other threads from modifying the data. Lastly, once the request is complete the `OnReleaseRequestState` event is raised, the Session state data is updated—or left unchanged—and the lock is released.

If two requests, as in a frame-based Web application, both attempt to change a value in Session state, the lock would prevent one of the threads from accessing the data until the other request first fully completes. This locking and reading of Session state occurs on each request, no matter if Session state data is even used. This can be controlled through page- and application-level directives such as `EnableSession`, but nevertheless this approach can be inefficient.

Personalization, on the other hand, is designed to be very smart about how it accesses and saves data. Data stored in Personalization is not retrieved until it is requested. Unlike Session, which populates the Session dictionary each time, Personalization waits until the user requests a property. Then, when Personalization does need to retrieve data, it will retrieve the data for the requested property and all related properties within the same provider. For example, the configuration for Personalization shown in Listing 7.7 adds a new `AspNetForums` provider—which we'll create later in the chapter—and specifies that all properties in the Forums group use this provider.

LISTING 7.7. Configuring a New Personalization Provider

```
<configuration>
  <system.web>
    <profile enabled="true"
                    defaultProvider="AspNetSqlProvider" >
      <providers>
        <add name="AspNetForums"
             type="AspNetForums.SqlDataProvider" />
      </providers>

      <properties>
        <property name="FirstName" />
        <property name="LastName" />
        <property name="ZipCode" />

        <group name="Forums">
          <property name="TotalPosts" type="System.Int32"
                    provider="AspNetForums"/>
          <property name="Location" provider="AspNetForums"/>
          <property name="AllowAvatar" type="System.Boolean" />
                    provider="AspNetForums"/>
          <property name="AvatarURL" provider="AspNetForums"/>
        </group>
      </properties>
    </profile>
  </system.web>
</configuration>
```

When using Personalization and requesting the `FirstName` property, the values for `LastName` and `ZipCode` are also retrieved since they all come from the default provider:

```
Dim firstName As String

' Get the user's first name
firstName = Profile.FirstName
```

However, values for `TotalPosts`, `Location`, `AllowAvatar`, and `AvatarURL` are not retrieved. These properties belong to a different provider, and their values will not be retrieved until the value of one of those properties is requested. This means that you can easily partition your data into multiple providers and make intelligent decisions about when to retrieve what data, unlike Session, which would simply retrieve everything. As you'll see later in the chapter, creating providers was designed to be easy. In fact, the ASP.NET team fully expects you to create providers for your data.

Finally, when values are set using the Profile API, the data store is updated when the page completes execution.

Membership and Personalization

Personalization stores data by associating the data with the authenticated username as the key. While Membership provides services to authenticate the user and set the authentication username, Membership is not required to use Personalization. In fact, any authentication mechanism will work. As long as a value is set for User.Identity.Name, personalization data can be stored.

For anonymous users, that is, users accessing the application who might not necessarily be authenticated, the User.Identity.Name value will not be set. To store anonymous personalization data, you need to enable the new anonymous identification feature.

Anonymous Identification

Anonymous identification is another new feature in ASP.NET 2.0. The goal of the feature is to provide a unique identification to users who are not authenticated. The feature is not tied in any way to security but is rather a simple mechanism to assign a guaranteed unique ID to anonymous users. After authentication, the anonymous ID is removed from the request.

Anonymous identification is not enabled by default. To enable it you must either add an entry to your web.config file or modify machine.config. Below is a web.config that enables the anonymous identification feature:

```
<configuration>
  <system.web>
    <anonymousIdentification enabled="true" />
  </system.web>
</configuration>
```

Enabling the feature is simple. There are, however, several other attributes that can be set, as shown in Listing 7.8.

continues

LISTING 7.8. Configuring Anonymous Identification

```
<configuration>
  <system.web>
    <anonymousIdentification
        enabled="true"
        cookieName=".ASPXANONYMOUS"
        cookieTimeout="100000"
        cookiePath="/"
        cookieRequireSSL="false"
        cookieSlidingExpiration="true"
        cookieProtection="None"
        cookieless="UseCookies"
    />
  </system.web>
</configuration>
```

As you can see, a `Boolean`-enabled attribute is used to enable the feature. When enabled, anonymous identification will use a cookie to store the anonymous ID. If you do not wish to use a cookie or do not know if the end user browser supports cookies, you can also set one of the following values for `cookieless`:

- `UseUri`: Store the anonymous ID within the address of the application. (This is similar to what is done in ASP.NET 1.0 with cookieless Session support.)

- `AutoDetect`: Automatically detect whether cookies are supported or not. When cookies are supported, use them. If not, store the anonymous ID in the URL.

- `UseDeviceProfile`: Use the configured profile for the device making the request.

However, `UseCookies` (shown in Listing 7.8) is the recommended choice. This option is less intrusive; that is, the ID is not embedded in the URL, and nearly all users accept cookies. When using the `AutoDetect` option, keep in mind that ASP.NET will need to test the incoming request to see whether cookies are supported.

Once anonymous identification is enabled, unauthenticated requests are assigned an anonymous ID. This is different than the `Session` ID. The `Session` ID is a relatively small identifier and is guaranteed to be unique only for the duration of the session; the anonymous ID value is a GUID and is guaranteed to be globally unique.

The anonymous ID is accessed through the new `Request.AnonymousId` property. Although the anonymous ID is a GUID, the ASP.NET team decided to make the return value type `string`—more users are familiar with working with `string` than GUIDs.

Anonymous Identification Events

Two events are raised by anonymous identification.

1. `AnonymousIdentification_OnCreate`: Raised when the anonymous ID is created. The `EventArgs` of the event delegate must be of type `AnonymousIdentificationEventArgs`. That type exposes an `AnonymousId` property that can be set. If you desire to change the auto-generated anonymous ID, you must change the value within this event.

2. `AnonymousIdentification_OnRemove`: Raised when the request is authenticated but an anonymous ID is still present. This event allows you to perform any cleanup with the anonymous ID before it is removed. Once a request is authenticated, the anonymous ID is no longer available.

As we'll see shortly, the `AnonymousIdentification_OnRemove` event is important since we use it in conjunction with Personalization to allow for the migration of anonymous personalization data.

Anonymous Personalization

Anonymous personalization refers to any personalization performed for users who are not already authenticated. By default Personalization is configured to not allow anonymous personalization; this was done for the following reasons.

- Anonymous personalization data can easily fill a database, and you need to have a strategy in place for managing this data.
- Personalization, by default, relies on the username value of the authenticated users to store/associate personalization data for a user.

To use anonymous personalization you must take two steps.

1. Enable anonymous identification, which is disabled by default.
2. Specify which Personalization properties can be set for anonymous users.

Specifying which Personalization properties can be used by anonymous users is done by adding the `allowAnonymous` attribute to your Personalization property. For example, Listing 7.9 shows how to allow anonymous users to use the `Cart` property.

LISTING 7.9. Configuring Anonymous Personalization

```
<configuration>
  <system.web>

    <anonymousIdentification enabled="true" />

    <profile>

      <properties>
        <property name="FirstName" />
        <property name="LastName" />
        <property name="Cart"
                allowAnonymous="true"
                type="Market.ShoppingCart, market"
                serializeAs="Binary" />
      </properties>
    </profile>
  </system.web>
</configuration>
```

Anonymous users browsing the site can now add items to the shopping cart without being required to first authenticate—a behavior most sites want to support! Personalization data for the user is then automatically keyed off the value of the anonymous ID.

While anonymous personalization is desirable, at some point the user may either authenticate or create an account on the system. For example, in an e-commerce site you would want the user to create an account before checking out. Giving the user an account would allow you to capture more specific data about the user required for fulfilling the order, such as the shipping address.

As discussed earlier in the Anonymous Identification section, when an authenticated user signs in, the anonymous ID is removed. With anonymous personalization this would orphan any anonymous data. When switching from an anonymous user to an authenticated user, you will potentially need to migrate anonymous personalization data to the authenticated user's profile.

Migrating from Anonymous to Authenticated Users

The migration strategy from anonymous to authenticated is designed to allow the developer to make the decisions through code as to which data is migrated and which data is not migrated (as opposed to automatically migrating all data). This design allows you to make intelligent decisions. For example, if you have a shopping cart populated by an anonymous user who then authenticates, you may find that the authenticated user's profile also has items within the shopping cart. Ideally you would add the anonymous shopping cart items rather than replacing them.

Migration is accomplished through a special event raised by Personalization:

```
Profile_OnMigrateAnonymous
```

This event is raised after the `AnonymousIdentification_OnRemove` event is raised and can be trapped as an application event in `global.asax`. Any migration code needs to exist within the `Profile_OnMigrateAnonymous` event. The event allows you to access the anonymous profile through the `ProfileMigrateEventArgs.AnonymousId` property, and by using this property you can retrieve the profile of the anonymous user as well as values (see Listing 7.10).

LISTING 7.10. Migrating Anonymous Users

```
<%@ Application %>
<%@ Import Namespace="System.Security.Principal" %>

<script runat="server">

  Public Sub Profile_OnMigrate (sender As Object,
                                e As ProfileMigrateEventArgs)

    ' Migrate the shopping Cart
    Profile.Cart = Profile.GetProfile(e.AnonymousId).Cart

    End Sub

</script>
```

The anonymous migration strategy provides you with the most flexibility since you make all the decisions about what data is migrated and what data is no longer needed.

The Provider Design Pattern

The provider design pattern exists to allow you to extend features of ASP.NET by swapping out the standard ASP.NET providers with yours. A provider is both a data abstraction layer and a business logic layer class that you create and plug into ASP.NET. When features such as Personalization are used, instead of calling one of the ASP.NET providers to retrieve or store user data, your class can be called, and within that class you can make decisions on how to operate on and store that data. Developers continue using the familiar APIs supported by ASP.NET, but it's your code that is running.

The beauty of the provider design is that it allows developers to learn to program to a well-known API, while internally the API can behave differently (e.g., SQL Server versus Oracle data stores).

Providers are based on the common object-oriented principles of abstraction. A class derives from an abstract base class and applications can then depend on the functionality of the base class instead of directly on the derived class. Internally the functionality can be completely different from class to class, but the object model is the same. For example, ASP.NET Personalization supports a name/value table for storing personalization data. If you wished to use your own data structure, as shown later in this chapter, you would author a provider.

The provider design pattern is comprised of the following:

* Configuration
* Derivation from the feature-specific base class

In the Technology Preview release the abstract classes were interfaces.

Configuration

All ASP.NET features that implement the provider model require a configuration section where providers are added. Additionally the feature requires a defaultProvider attribute to identify which provider is the default.

Listing 7.11 demonstrates how this is used in the <profile/> section.

LISTING 7.11. Configuring a Default Personalization Provider

```
<configuration>
  <system.web>

    <profile defaultProvider="AspNetAccessProvider">

      <providers>
        <add name="AspNetAccessProvider"
             type="System.Web.Personalization.
                   AccessPersonalizationProvider,
                   System.Web,
                   Version=2.0.3600.0,
                   Culture=neutral,
                   PublicKeyToken=b03f5f7f11d50a3a"
             connectionStringName="AccessFileName"
             applicationName="/"
             description="Stores and retrieves personalization
                          data from the local Microsoft Access
                          database file" />
        <add name="AspNetSqlProvider"
             type="System.Web.Personalization.
                   SqlPersonalizationProvider,
                   System.Web,
                   Version=2.0.3600.0, Culture=neutral,
                   PublicKeyToken=b03f5f7f11d50a3a"
             connectionStringName="LocalSqlServer"
             applicationName="/"
             description="Stores and retrieves personalization
                          data from the local Microsoft
                          SQL Server database" />
      </providers>

    </profile>

  </system.web>
</configuration>
```

Implementers of providers should have a `defaultProvider` attribute on the main `<profile/>` section. If a default provider is not specified, the first item in the collection is considered the default.

Managing Providers in Configuration

The `<providers/>` configuration section contains one or more `<add>`, `<remove>`, or `<clear/>` elements. The following rules apply when processing these elements.

- It is not an error to declare an empty `<providers/>` element.
- Providers inherit items from parent configuration `<add/>` statements.

- It is an error to redefine an item using `<add/>` if the item already exists or is inherited.
- It is an error to remove a nonexistent item.
- It is not an error to add, remove, and then add the same item again.
- It is not an error to add, clear, and then add the same item again.
- `<clear/>` removes all inherited items and items previously defined (e.g., an `<add/>` declared before a `<clear/>` is removed, but an `<add/>` declared after a `<clear/>` is not removed).

Table 7.3 lists the elements of `<providers/>`.

TABLE 7.3. Provider Elements

Element	Description
`<add/>`	Adds a data provider. Supports the following attributes: • `name`: The friendly name of the provider. • `type`: A class that implements the required provider interface. The value is a fully qualified reference to an assembly. • Other name/value pairs: Additional name/value pairs may be present, such as `connectionStringName` for the default ASP.NET SQL Personalization Provider implementation. All name/value pairs are the responsibility of the provider to understand.
`<remove/>`	Removes a named data provider. Supports the following attribute: • `name`: The friendly name of the provider to remove.
`<clear/>`	Removes all inherited providers.

Implementation of the ProviderBase Base Class

All base providers are required to derive from the `ProviderBase` base class (see Listing 7.12).

LISTING 7.12. The ProviderBase Base Class

```
namespace System.Configuration.Providers {
  public class ProviderBase {

    // Methods
    public virtual void Initialize(string name,
                                   NameValueCollection config);

    // Properties
    public virtual string Name { get; }
  }
}
```

The `ProviderBase` base class is used by ASP.NET to enforce a standard way to initialize providers. The `Initialize()` method should set the name of the provider from the `name` attribute of the `<add/>` element within the configuration file, and `config` is a collection of attributes and values specified in the `<add/>` section of the provider. This collection would contain any additional properties needed by the provider, such as a connection string for connecting to the database.

Implementation of the Feature-Specific Interface

All ASP.NET features that support providers will also support feature-specific base classes. Table 7.4 lists features as well as their base classes.

Table 7.4. Feature Base Classes

Feature	Base Class
Membership	`System.Web.Security.MembershipProvider`
Role Manager	`System.Web.Security.RoleProvider`
Personalization	`System.Web.ProfileProvider`
Page Personalization	`System.Web.UI.WebControls.WebParts.Personalization Provider`
Site Map	`System.Web.SiteMapProvider`
Site Counters	`System.Web.SiteCountersProvider`
Health Monitoring	`System.Web.Management.WebEventProvider`

Features that implement providers will derive from their feature-specific base class, which in turn derives from `ProviderBase`.

Writing a Personalization Provider

When the ASP.NET team members set out to build the ASP.NET Personalization system, the most challenging aspect of the design was the data model. They wanted to allow for the maximum amount of flexibility and extensibility. They initially examined several approaches with schemas within the database to describe properties and their types but found that this created very deep tables that couldn't efficiently be used without an intimate knowledge of the schema. They were also concerned that this approach would not perform well. They ideally desired for the data model to use the columns for each type of data, for example, a `FirstName` column of type `nvarchar(256)`. Although this gave them the best performance, it was the most difficult to extend; extensibility would have consisted of adding columns and tables.

They decided on an approach that gave the end developer the most flexibility. Hence the provider design pattern was created. The provider pattern allows you to store or use data in any shape and use the friendly, easy-to-use Personalization APIs. In fact, the team wants you to write providers. Most developers already have lots of user data. Rather than forcing you to use a new data model, the provider pattern allows the data to remain in whatever format you desire, but at the same time you can easily expose that data through the Personalization APIs.

All providers must derive from the feature-specific base class (e.g., `ProfileProvider` for the Profile features). For Profile this is `System.Web.Profile.ProfileProvider`. Earlier in the chapter we discussed a Personalization provider for the ASP.NET Forums; Listing 7.13 shows a simple implementation of that Personalization provider.

LISTING 7.13. Sample Personalization Provider

```
Imports System
Imports System.Web
Imports System.Collections
Imports System.Collections.Specialized
Imports System.Web.Profile
Imports System.Configuration.Provider
Imports System.Data
Imports System.Data.SqlClient


Namespace Forums

    Public Class ForumsPersonalizationProvider
        Inherits ProfileProvider

        Public Overrides Sub Initialize(ByVal name As String, _
                    ByVal config As NameValueCollection)
            ' Used to set the name and any
            ' config data from configuration
        End Sub

        Public Overrides ReadOnly Property Name() As String
            Get
                Return "ForumsProvider"
            End Get
        End Property

        Public Overrides Property ApplicationName() As String
```

```
        Get
            Return "/"
        End Get
        Set(ByVal Value As String)
        End Set
    End Property

    Public Overrides Sub SetPropertyValues( _
ByVal context As System.Configuration.SettingsContext, _
ByVal ppvc As System.Configuration.SettingsPropertyValueCollection)
        ' Not implemented
    End Sub

    Public Overrides Function DeleteInactiveProfiles( _
ByVal authenticationOption As ProfileAuthenticationOption, _
ByVal userInactiveSinceDate As Date) As Integer
        ' Not implemented
        Return 0
    End Function

    Public Overrides Function GetAllInactiveProfiles( _
ByVal authenticationOption As ProfileAuthenticationOption, _
ByVal userInactiveSinceDate As Date, ByVal pageIndex As Integer, _
ByVal pageSize As Integer, ByRef totalRecords As Integer) _
As System.Web.Profile.ProfileInfoCollection
        ' Not implemented
        Return Nothing
    End Function

    Public Overrides Function FindProfilesByUserName( _
ByVal authenticationOption As ProfileAuthenticationOption, _
ByVal usernameToMatch As String, ByVal pageIndex As Integer, _
ByVal pageSize As Integer, ByRef totalRecords As Integer) _
As System.Web.Profile.ProfileInfoCollection
        ' Not implemented
        Return Nothing
    End Function

    Public Overrides Function FindInactiveProfilesByUserName( _
ByVal authenticationOption As ProfileAuthenticationOption, _
ByVal usernameToMatch As String, ByVal userInactiveSinceDate As Date, _
ByVal pageIndex As Integer, ByVal pageSize As Integer, _
ByRef totalRecords As Integer) _
As System.Web.Profile.ProfileInfoCollection
        ' Not implemented
        Return Nothing
    End Function

    Public Overrides Function DeleteProfiles( _
ByVal profiles As ProfileInfoCollection) As Integer
        ' Not implemented
        Return 0
```

continues

```vbnet
        End Function

        Public Overrides Function DeleteProfiles( _
ByVal usernames() As String) As Integer
            ' Not implemented
            Return 0
        End Function

        Public Overrides Function GetNumberOfInactiveProfiles( _
ByVal authenticationOption As ProfileAuthenticationOption, _
ByVal userInactiveSinceDate As Date) As Integer
            ' Not implemented
            Return 0
        End Function

        Public Overrides Function GetAllProfiles( _
ByVal authenticationOption As ProfileAuthenticationOption, _
ByVal pageIndex As Integer, ByVal pageSize As Integer, _
ByRef totalRecords As Integer) _
As System.Web.Profile.ProfileInfoCollection
            ' Not implemented
            Return Nothing
        End Function

        Public Overrides Function GetPropertyValues( _
ByVal context As System.Configuration.SettingsContext, _
ByVal ppc As System.Configuration.SettingsPropertyCollection) _
As System.Configuration.SettingsPropertyValueCollection
            Dim connection As SqlConnection
            Dim command As SqlCommand

            connection = New SqlConnection("connection string")
            command = New SqlCommand("SELECT * FROM Users " _
            & "WHERE Username = '" _
            & userName & "'", connection)
            Dim reader As SqlDataReader

            connection.Open()

            reader = command.ExecuteReader()

            While reader.Read()
                ppc("Email").DefaultValue = reader("Email")
                ppc("FakeEmail").DefaultValue = reader("FakeEmail")
                ppc("Trusted").DefaultValue = reader("Trusted")
                ppc("DateCreated").DefaultValue = _
                                    reader("DateCreated")
                ppc("TotalPosts").DefaultValue = _
                                    reader("TotalPosts")
            End While

            connection.Close()
```

```
        End Function

    End Class

End Namespace
```

Once compiled, we can use this provider by specifying it in our web.config, as demonstrated in Listing 7.14.

LISTING 7.14. Adding the Custom Provider

```
<configuration>
  <system.web>
    <profile>
      <providers>
        <add name="ForumsProvider"
             type="Forums.ForumsPersonalizationProvider,
                   ForumsPersonalizationProvider"
             applicationName="/" />
      </providers>
      <properties>
        <property name="FirstName"/>
        <property name="LastName" />
        <property name="Email" provider="ForumsProvider" />
        <property name="FakeEmail" provider="ForumsProvider" />
        <property name="Trusted" type="System.Boolean"
                  provider="ForumsProvider" />
        <property name="DateCreated" type="System.DateTime"
                  provider="ForumsProvider" />
        <property name="TotalPosts" type="System.Int32"
                  provider="ForumsProvider" />
      </properties>
    </profile>
  </system.web>
</configuration>
```

Finally, we can then write pages that display the property values (see Listing 7.15).

LISTING 7.15. Using the Custom Provider

```
Your email address is: <% =Profile.Email %>
<P>
Your fake email address is: <% =Profile.FakeEmail %>
<P>
Your total posts are: <% =Profile.TotalPosts %>
<P>
Your account was created:
<% =Profile.DateCreated.ToString("MM/dd/yy mm:ss")%>
```

Providers allow you to fully plug into the APIs exposed by ASP.NET. You can take full control over what happens when those APIs are used within your application.

Configuring Profile Properties

The Web Site Administration Tool can be used to configure the `<profile/>` section, as shown in Figure 7.6.

There are three main sections to Profile management. The first allows enabling or disabling of the Profile for known and anonymous users. The second allows configuration of the Profile properties or property groups, as shown in Figure 7.7.

Here you can see the list of existing properties, the group they belong to, and the data type. Editing an existing property or creating a new property allows you to change all attributes, such as setting the data type (including custom types) and default values and allowing the property to be available for anonymous users.

The third section of Profile management allows the removal of values from the Profile store, as shown in Figure 7.8.

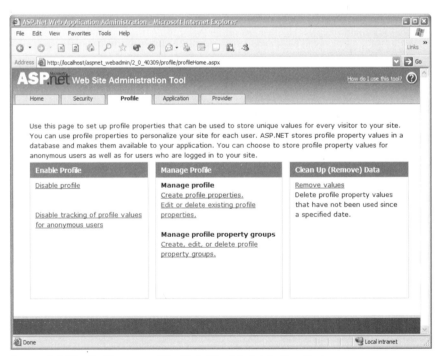

FIGURE 7.6. The Profile page of the Web Site Administration Tool

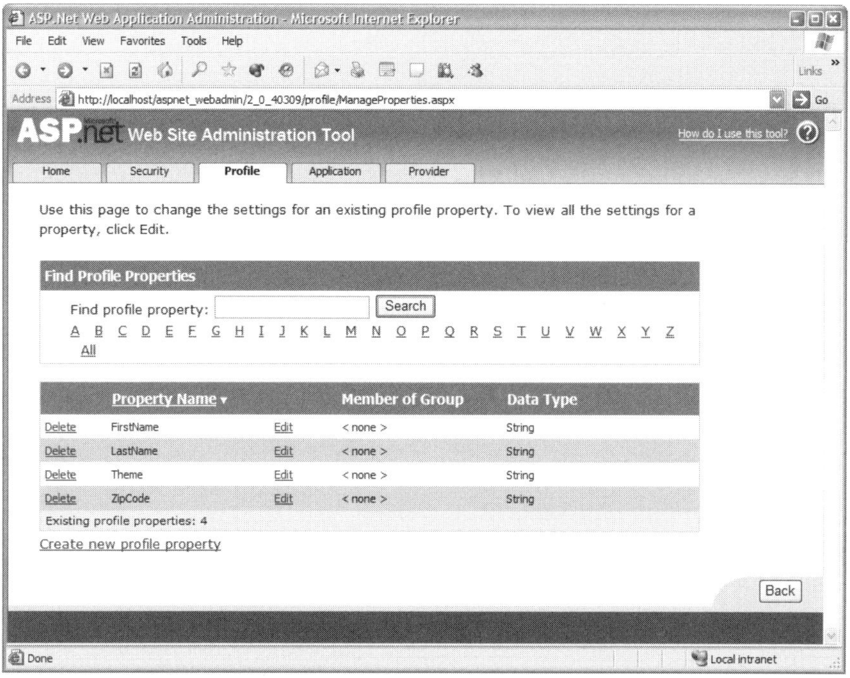

FIGURE 7.7. Configuring Profile properties

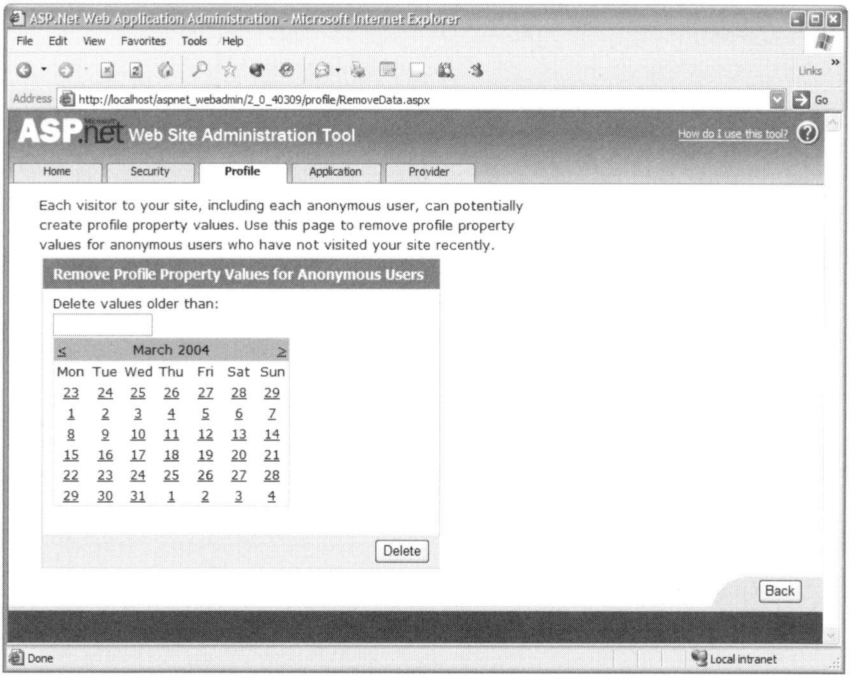

FIGURE 7.8. Removing Profile property values

Here you have the opportunity to enter a date beyond which all property values are deemed to be stale, giving the ability to clean out the property store of redundant data.

Themes

The Profile provides a simple way to store customized data about users, but often you need to provide this ability to the look of the site as well. Themes provide a way to customize the look and feel of your site, including graphics, CSS styles, properties, and so on. Not only does this provide a way for you, the developer, to provide a consistent style, but it also allows the users to select the style. Although this may not be required in every Web site, using themes does allow for consistency among pages and controls, giving an easy way to change the look of the site even if this isn't a user requirement.

The great beauty of the way themes work is that there are very few changes required to an ASP.NET page for them to be used. This means that from the development perspective, the work involved is minimal. Once theme support is included in a site or page, the addition, change, or removal of themes is simple because themes are stored external to the pages themselves. To understand themes you have to understand the terminology and how it is applied within ASP.NET.

Themes and Skins

The theme architecture defines two terms—**themes** and **skins.** A skin defines the visual style applied to a control, such as the stylesheet attributes, images, colors, and so on. A theme is a collection of skins and applies to an ASP.NET page. Themes are stored under the `Themes` directory under the application root, with a directory for each theme. Within the directory for a theme there is a skin file for each skin in the theme (containing the skin details for each control), stylesheets, and any images required for controls (e.g., images for the `TreeView` control).

Each theme can have a default look, where no skin is specified, or there can be multiple skins within each theme. This allows you to have themes that are distinct from each other and have multiple looks. For example, you could have a theme called `Pastel` and within it skins called `Pink` and `Blue`.

A theme doesn't have to provide a skin for every server control. Any controls that have no skin within the theme file will use the default look supplied by the browser (or as overridden by a stylesheet). For consistency, however, it is better to provide a skin for each control you use. Setting the skin for a control where no skin exists for that control type will generate an error.

You can use skins to do more than provide just a single look for the entire site. Skins are uniquely identified by the SkinID property applied to the control in a skin file, allowing the same control to be duplicated in the skin file with different SkinID values. This allows, for example, the same type of control to be used on different pages but to have a different look on each page. Theming can also be disabled at both the page and control levels, so page developers aren't forced to use themes.

Customization Themes and Stylesheet Themes

There are two types of themes: those that impose structure (**customization themes**) and those that suggest structure (**stylesheet themes**). Both use the same directory and file layout. A customization theme imposes its look upon the page and controls, and the properties cannot be overridden at the control or page level. A stylesheet theme suggests its look to the page and control and can be overridden at the page or control level. In this way stylesheet themes are synonymous with CSS stylesheets, where controls can override properties defined in the stylesheet.

Because there are three places where properties can be set, the properties are applied first from the stylesheet theme, then from the control, and finally from the customization theme.

The use of themes is simply dependent on using either the Theme attribute (for a customization theme) or the StyleSheetTheme attribute (for a stylesheet theme) on the Page directive.

Global Themes

In addition to theme support on a local application level, the Framework supports global themes, which are available to all applications. These can be installed in the Web root (Inetpub\wwwroot\aspnet_client\{version}\Themes). Local themes with the same name as a global theme replace the global theme in its entirety—no merging with or inheritance from the global theme takes place. The structure of global themes follows the same as local themes.

Creating Themes

To create local themes, you simply create a directory called Themes under your application root, then create a directory for each theme. For example, consider Figure 7.9, where a theme called `Basic` has been created. The skin details for the theme are in the file called `Basic.skin`.

The name of the skin file doesn't have to match that of the theme, although for the default skin this makes

FIGURE 7.9. The directory and file for a simple theme

sense. Any images relating to this theme can be placed either in the `Themes` directory itself or in a separate directory, as shown in Figure 7.9. URLs in the skin file to external resources should be relative and will be rebased when the page is compiled.

The contents of the skin file are simply control declarations. For example, the default skin for `Basic` has the following code:

```
<asp:Label runat="server"
    ForeColor="#FFFFFF" BackColor="#660000" />
```

This simply defines a single control, with white text on a red background. When the theme of a page is set to `Basic`, all `Label` controls will inherit this style. Because no other controls are defined in this skin, they will use either the default HTML settings or those supplied by a stylesheet.

Creating Skins

An explicitly named skin is created by supplying a `SkinID` property on the controls in the skin file. For example:

```
<asp:Label runat="server" SkinID="Red"
    ForeColor="#FFFFFF" BackColor="#660000" />
```

Here the `SkinID` is set to `Red`. This wouldn't, therefore, be part of the default skin (which has no `SkinID`), and its look has to be explicitly set on a control within a page.

`SkinID`s must be unique for each control, so you cannot have the same `SkinID` for the same control type with the same value. A compile error is generated if this occurs.

Creating Multiple Skins

Multiple skins can be supplied in one of two ways. The first method is to supply all of the skins within the same file. For example, to provide a default skin plus a red skin, the skin file could contain these lines:

```
<asp:Label runat="server"
     ForeColor="#000000" BackColor="#FFFFFF" />

<asp:Label runat="server" SkinID="Red"
     ForeColor="#FFFFFF" BackColor="#660000" />
```

Here you just add all of the controls and create duplicates for those that require multiple skins, setting the `SkinID` for each duplicate to a different name.

The second method is to split the skins into separate files. For example, consider the provision of a `Basic` theme, with default controls, and two skins—`Red` and `Blue`. We could use the structure shown in Figure 7.10.

FIGURE 7.10. Multiple skin files

In this example there is a skin file for each distinct skin. This method is easier to maintain because the skins are completely separate from each other, and it allows more skins to be created by simply copying an existing file and modifying it.

A theme directory can contain other resources, which can be accessed from skin files with relative paths. For example, Figure 7.10 shows an `Images` directory, allowing skin files to include specific images. This is especially useful for the `TreeView` control; separate images can be used per theme. For example, consider the following fragment:

```
<%@ Page Theme="Basic" %>

<asp:TreeView SkinID="Basic"
     LeafNodeImage="images\MyTheme_Skin_LeafNode.gif" ...
```

In this example the `LeafNodeImage` property identifies the image to use for leaf nodes of the `TreeView`. Since this control is skinned, the images are taken from the `Images` directory under the theme.

Using Stylesheets in Themes

Skin files can also use stylesheets, allowing a greater separation of styling features. Any stylesheet within the theme directory is automatically used if the theme is used. For this to work, the ASP.NET page must have a server-based `<head>` tag:

```
<head runat="server" />
```

This is required because the stylesheet is injected into the `<head>` tag at compile time. URLs used within styles and stylesheets are rebased to take account of the actual directory at runtime.

Setting a Page Customization Theme

To use a customization theme on a page, you simply set the `Theme` property of the page. This can be done either declaratively as an attribute of the `Page` directive:

```
<%@ Page Theme="Basic" %>
```

or within code:

```
Page.Theme = Request.QueryString("Theme")
Page.Theme = Profile.Theme
```

When setting the theme programmatically, it must be set within the new page-level `PreInit` event. For example:

```
Sub Page_PreInit(Sender As Object, E As EventArgs)

  Page.Theme = Profile.Theme

End Sub
```

This event must be used because the theme and skin details for controls need to be set before the controls are added to the page, and other events (such as `Init`, `PreRender`, `Load`, and so on) occur too late in the control creation chain.

Themes can also be filtered, for example:

```
<%@ Page Theme="BasicBlue" ie:Theme="SmokeAndGlass" %>
```

Setting a Page Stylesheet Theme

Using a stylesheet theme is similar to using a customization theme, except the property is called `StyleSheetTheme`. For example:

```
<%@ Page StyleSheetTheme="BasicBlue" %>
```

Unlike customization themes, the stylesheet theme isn't set in the `PreInit` event, but by overriding the `StyleSheetTheme` property of the page. For example:

```
Public Overrides Property StyleSheetTheme() As String
  Get
    Return "BasicBlue"
  End Get
  Set
  End Set
End Property
```

Setting a Skin

Skins apply to controls, so the `SkinID` property of the controls must be set. Like the page theme, this can be set in one of three ways. The first is declaratively:

```
<asp:Label SkinID="Red" Text="I'm Skinned" />
```

The second is programmatically:

```
Label.SkinID = "Red"
Label.SkinID = Profile.SkinID
```

The third is only for stylesheet themes, the skins of which can be set in the Designer by use of the Auto Format dialog on certain controls. For example, the `GridView` allows you to pick from a selected list of standard formats, but setting the `StyleSheetTheme` property for a page changes the list that Auto Format shows. For example, consider a `Pastel` theme with several skins. Figure 7.11 shows the Auto Format dialog when the `StyleSheetTheme` has been set to `Pastel`. You can see that along with the list of standard formats there is also a list of skins in the `Pastel` theme, and from here you can select the desired skin.

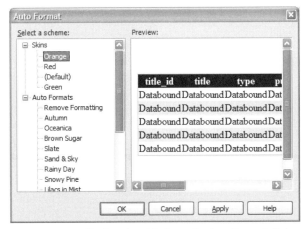

FIGURE 7.11. Selecting the skin from the AutoFormat dialog

Applying Skins to All Controls

The skin applies only to a single control and not to child controls. Thus setting the SkinID for a Panel that contains other controls only sets the SkinID for the Panel. If you wish to ensure that all controls on a page have a SkinID applied, you can recurse the Controls collection. For example, Listing 7.16 shows how the page theme and skin could be set for all controls, based on the details set in the user Profile.

LISTING 7.16. Setting the Skin for All Controls

```
Sub Page_PreInit(Sender As object, E As EventArgs)

  Page.Theme = Profile.Theme
  SkinControls(Profile.SkinID, Page.Controls)

End Sub

Private Sub SkinControls(Skin As String, ctls As ControlCollection)

  For Each ctl As Control In ctls
    If ctl.EnableTheming Then
      ctl.SkinID = Skin

      If ctl.HasControls Then
        SkinControls(Skin, ctl.Controls)
      End If
    End If
  Next

End Sub
```

One problem with this technique is that if a SkinID is not defined for a particular control type in use on the page, an exception is raised. For this reason it's better to explicitly set the skin for individual controls.

> Note that changing the SkinID property can be done only for a customization theme, not for stylesheet themes.

Applying Skins to Dynamically Created Controls

Controls dynamically added to a page will have the appropriate customization theme and skin applied by ASP.NET. For stylesheet themes, the theme needs to be applied to the control before it is added to the control tree, as shown in Listing 7.17.

LISTING 7.17. Applying a Stylesheet Theme to a Dynamically Added Control

```
<%@ Page StyleSheetTheme="Pastel" %>
Sub Page_Load(Sender As Object, E As EventArgs)

  Dim grid As New GridView()
  grid.DataSourceId = "gridData"
  grid.SkinID = "Red"
  grid.ApplyStyleSheetSkin(Me)
  placholder.Controls.Add(grid)

End Sub
```

Allowing User Selection of Skins

If your site supports multiple themes and skins, allowing users to select their preferred look is a great feature. It's relatively easy to do dynamically if you stick to a strict convention, keeping individual skins in separate files so you can then simply search for skin files. For example, you could build a theme browser similar to that shown in Figure 7.12, where the themes are shown at the top and some sample controls are shown below. Selecting a theme file could then apply that theme.

The big problem with this approach is the event ordering. Remember that themes and skins are applied before controls are added to the page, and in this example we set the details in the PreInit event, which is executed before the postback event. This means that when you select the theme or skin, the server-side postback event occurs after the skin details have been set in PreInit. Selecting the same theme or skin again is a workaround as the selected value will already be set from the previous postback and so would be available at the PreInit stage. Other options are to have an Apply button that causes a postback, either to itself or to another page, thus giving you the second postback, or using the Theme or Skin value directly from the form or query string in PreInit.

Using Personalization for Themes

Some of the code samples earlier showed the Profile being used to store the theme and skin names. Configuration of this simply requires the properties to be added to the <profile/> section in web.config (see Listing 7.18).

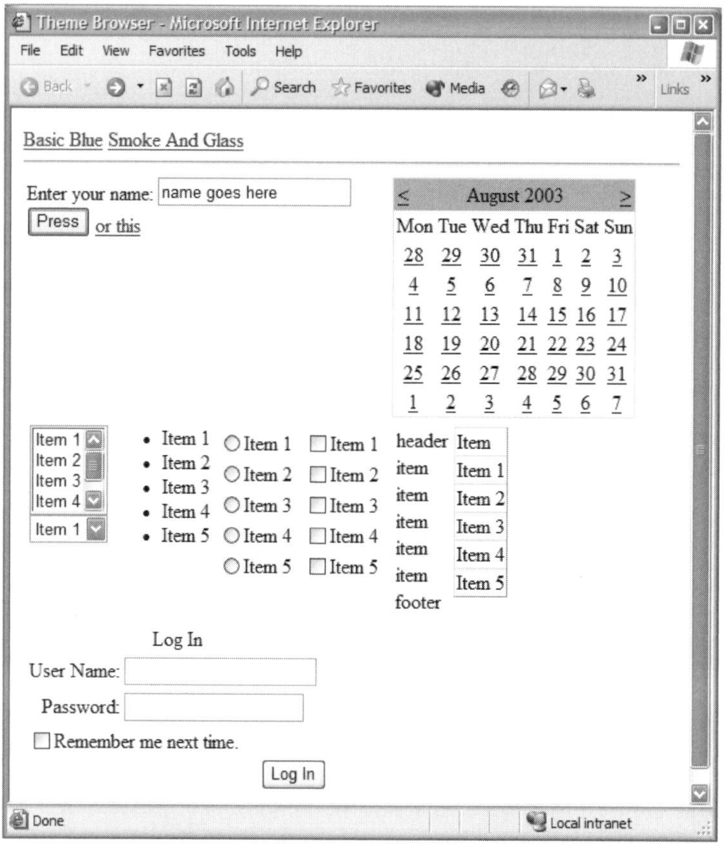

FIGURE 7.12. A theme browser

LISTING 7.18. Configuring Personalization to Store Theme Details

```
<configuration>
  <system.web>

    <profile>
      <properties>
        <add name="Theme" />
        <add name="StyleSheetTheme" />
        <add name="SkinID" />
      </properties>
    </profile>

  <system.web>
</configuration>
```

Now when storing the selected theme, perhaps from the theme browser shown earlier, you can simply store the user's selected theme in his or her profile when the user selects a particular theme from the appropriate link (see Listing 7.19).

LISTING 7.19. Storing the Theme in the Profile

```
<asp:LinkButton runat="server" Text="Basic Blue"
  onCommand="SetTheme" CommandName="BasicBlue" />
<asp:LinkButton runat="server" Text="Smoke and Glass"
  onCommand="SetThem" CommandName="SmokeAndGlass" />


<script runat="server">

Sub SetTheme(Sender As Object, E As CommandEventArgs)

  Profile.Theme = e.CommandName

End Sub

</script>
```

The theme details can then simply be ready from the `Profile` at any stage, especially during the `Page_PreInit` event where the theme can be set for the page.

Collections of Controls

Care has to be taken when skinning collections of controls because for customization themes the themed collection replaces a collection applied in a page. For example, consider the following themed control within `MyTheme.skin` (shown in Listing 7.20).

LISTING 7.20. A Themed Collection Control

```
<asp:RadioButtonList runat="server">
  <asp:ListItem value="1">Option 1</asp:ListItem>
  <asp:ListItem value="2">Option 2</asp:ListItem>
  <asp:ListItem value="3">Option 3</asp:ListItem>
  <asp:ListItem value="4">Option 4</asp:ListItem>
</asp:RadioButtonList>
```

Now consider the page created by Listing 7.21.

LISTING 7.21. Using a Themed Collection Control

```
<%@ Page Theme="MyTheme" %>

<form runat="server">
```

continues

```
<asp:RadioButtonList id="list" runat="server">
  <asp:ListItem value="5">Option 5</asp:ListItem>
  <asp:ListItem value="6">Option 6</asp:ListItem>
  <asp:ListItem value="7">Option 7</asp:ListItem>
  <asp:ListItem value="8">Option 8</asp:ListItem>
</asp:RadioButtonList>
</form>
```

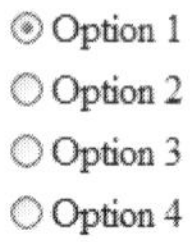

⦿ Option 1
◯ Option 2
◯ Option 3
◯ Option 4

FIGURE 7.13. A themed collection

The results of running this page are shown in Figure 7.13.

Notice that the collection from the theme (options 1 to 4) is used instead of the collection from the page (options 5 to 8). This is because the controls on the page are replaced by their equivalents in the theme file. To get around this you can change the values in the `Page_Load` event, either by manually deleting the collection entries and adding them or by data binding, in which case the collection from the theme is replaced. Alternatively you could use a stylesheet theme, so that the controls on the page override those in the theme.

Disabling Themes

Theming can be explicitly disabled on controls by setting the `EnableTheming` property to `False`. When the controls are added to the page, any controls (and their children) with this property set to `False` will not have the theme applied (see Listing 7.22).

LISTING 7.22. Disabling Theming on Controls

```
<%@ Page Theme="BasicBlue" %>

<asp:Panel runat="server" EnableTheming="False">
  <asp:Label id="WelcomeMessage" runat="server" />
  <br />
  <asp:DataGrid id="News" runat="server" />
</asp:Panel>
```

In this case the `Panel`, the `Label`, and the `DataGrid` will not have the theme applied because the `EnableTheming` property has been set to `False`. This is particularly useful when including third-party controls, such as search controls, that must conform to a set look.

Adding Themes to a Site

In addition to setting themes at the page level, you can set them globally by modifying the application configuration file, as shown in Listing 7.23.

LISTING 7.23. Configuring a Site-Wide Theme

```
<configuration>
  <system.web>
    <pages theme="BasicBlue" styleSheetTheme="SmokeAndGlass" />
  </system.web>
</configuration>
```

Like all page settings, this is overridden when set on individual pages.

Enabling Themes in Custom Controls

When building custom controls, theme support is automatically enabled if your control inherits from System.Web.UI.Control (either directly or indirectly). To disable theme support in your control, you can override the EnableTheming property, as shown in Listing 7.24.

LISTING 7.24. Disabling Theming in a Custom Control with Properties

```
Public Class MyControl
    Inherits System.Web.UI.Control

  Public Overrides Property EnableTheming() As Boolean
    Get
      Return False
    End Get
    Set(ByVal Value As Boolean)
      base.EnableTheming = Value
    End Set
  End Property
End Class
```

This property can also be set as an attribute on the entire class, to disable theme support for the control (see Listing 7.25).

LISTING 7.25. Disabling Theming in a Custom Control with Attributes

```
<EnableTheming(False)> _
Public Class MyControl
    Inherits System.Web.UI.Control

End Class
```

Individual properties can also have theme support disabled by use of an attribute (see Listing 7.26).

LISTING 7.26. Disabling Theming on a Property

```
Public Class MyControl
    Inherits System.Web.UI.Control

  Private _searchString As String

  <Themable(False)> _
  Public Property SearchString() As String
    Get
      Return _searchString
    End Get
    Set(ByVal Value As Boolean)
      _searchString = Value
    End Set
  End Property

End Class
```

SUMMARY

Personalization is a very powerful feature of ASP.NET 2.0. It gives you an easy, type-safe way to expose all sorts of user data. Personalization does require a database, but the ASP.NET team has tried hard to ensure that you can take full control over how this data is both operated on and stored. The provider model is the functionality that enables this, and we fully intend to publish more documentation on how providers are built.

ASP.NET ships with two providers: Microsoft SQL Server and Microsoft Access. Access is the default provider and when used, all personalization data is stored within an Access database located within the application. The ASP.NET team recommends using the Microsoft SQL Server provider for large enterprise applications.

In this chapter we built a simple provider for Personalization that allows ASP.NET Personalization to retrieve data from the ASP.NET Forums application. Building providers was designed to be simple, as demonstrated, and we fully expect you to write your own Personalization providers to control access to your data.

Finally, we looked at themes, one of the visual aspects of Personalization, which allow users to customize the look and feel of a site. Because this requires very few changes to existing pages and relies on some simple properties, it's ideal for storage as part of the Personalization `Profile`.

Now it's time to take Personalization to the next level by looking at the ASP.NET portal framework.

8

Web Parts and the Portal Framework

C USTOMIZATION IS A BIG TOPIC in application development. Users like to be able to change the layout, appearance, and behavior of their applications—fine-tuning them to better suit their business practices and working preferences. However, while this has become common in mainstream applications like the Microsoft Office programs and Windows itself, Web sites that support this type of feature are still quite rare (perhaps a notable exception is http://msn.com/, which has had personalized pages for some years).

But all that changes in ASP.NET 2.0, as you've seen with the Personalization features in earlier chapters. In this chapter, you'll see even more ways that users can customize their views of your Web applications and Web pages. We'll be looking at:

- The portal framework that is now a fundamental part of ASP.NET 2.0
- What Web Parts are and how you can use them in your pages
- Interacting with Web Parts using server-side code
- How Visual Web Developer and Visual Studio 2005 support these new features

We start with a look at what Web Parts and the portal framework actually are and how they relate to building portal-style applications with ASP.NET 2.0 (and on different software platforms as well).

The ASP.NET 2.0 Portal Framework

In reality, the home page of any Web site or Web application is a "portal" to that site or application. In general, the home page carries things like news, information, and of course links to the other pages that make up the content of the site or application. However, the term "portal" has increasingly become associated with pages that offer a modularized view of information. This is one of the main aims of Microsoft SharePoint and other similar content management systems.

The ASP.NET 2.0 Web Parts technology is designed to make this kind of page and application easy to build, often without requiring the developer to write any code. The screenshot in Figure 8.1 shows a simple example of

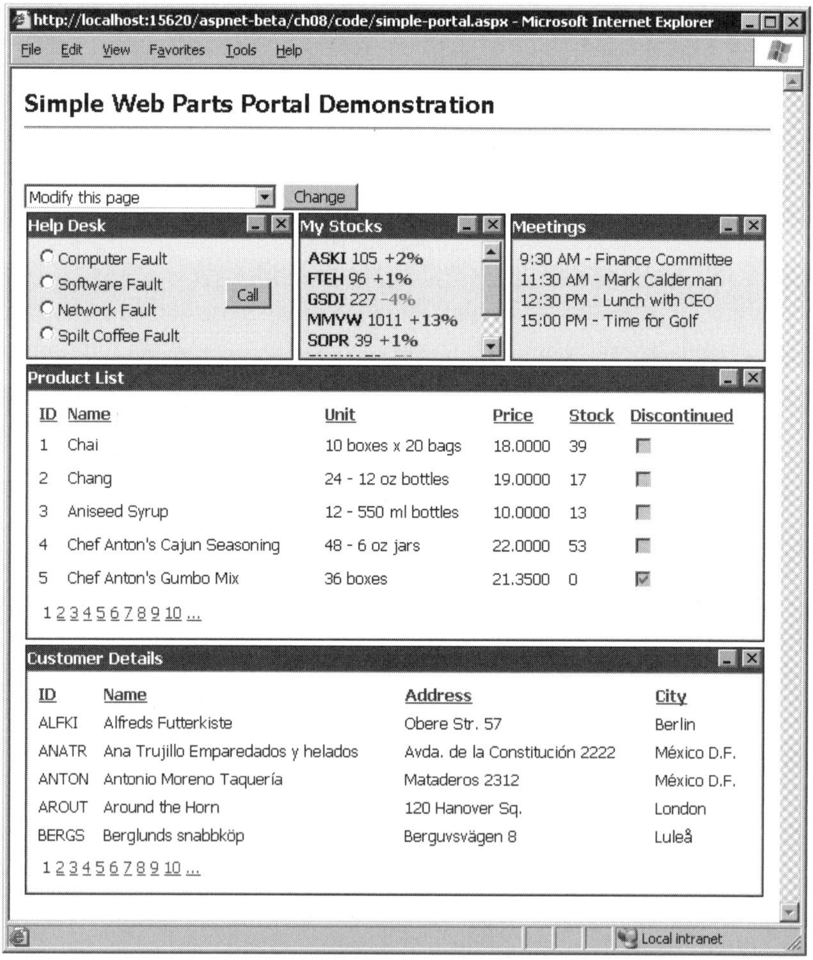

FIGURE 8.1. A simple demonstration of Web Parts and the portal framework

a portal page containing five Web Parts. They display different sets of information that would be useful for, say, a worker on the corporate intranet.

The Goals of the Portal Framework

Web Parts is not a brand-new technology, and in some ways it combines existing development efforts in an attempt to provide a general solution. The goals for the technology are to

- Provide a robust framework for Web pages and applications that support modular content and can be customized by end users
- Expose a programming model that is easy to understand and use and that requires no code to be written for most types of pages, while being capable of providing support for more complex scenarios as well
- Provide a rich user experience where this is supported by the client's software, plus safe fallback support for other clients
- Be easy to configure for individual users and groups of users, and to tie in with the underlying Personalization features of ASP.NET 2.0
- Support the growth in Web Parts technology that is happening outside ASP.NET, for example, in SharePoint, Content Management Server, and Office 2003, by establishing a foundation of a single portal technology for use across all Microsoft applications
- Provide full support and integration for third-party Web Parts and assemblies to be used, expose backward compatibility as far as possible, and offer a migration path for other existing technologies
- Meet the performance demands of portal applications, which often experience bursts of high usage (such as when a group of users all start work at the same time)

Integration with SharePoint and Office Web Parts

One important aim of the new ASP.NET Web Parts technology is to allow it to be extended within SharePoint and other Microsoft applications, as well as to provide support for existing Web Parts. Web Parts have been around for a few years, in products like the Digital Dashboard and Content Management Server.

It's hoped that all of these Web Parts will be usable directly within the ASP.NET portal framework. The ongoing Web Parts development process aims to expose an interface that can be used by other Microsoft applications and other third-party tools and environments. Web Parts can also be imported and exported using a standardized XML description.

Customization and Personalization

The Web Parts technology used to create the page shown in Figure 8.1 also provides built-in capabilities for customizing the display. This is integrated with the ASP.NET Personalization features so that the settings are persisted on a per-user basis and automatically retrieved when that user logs in again next time.

As an example of the customization features, the screenshot in Figure 8.2 shows how a rich client (Internet Explorer 6) allows the user to enter

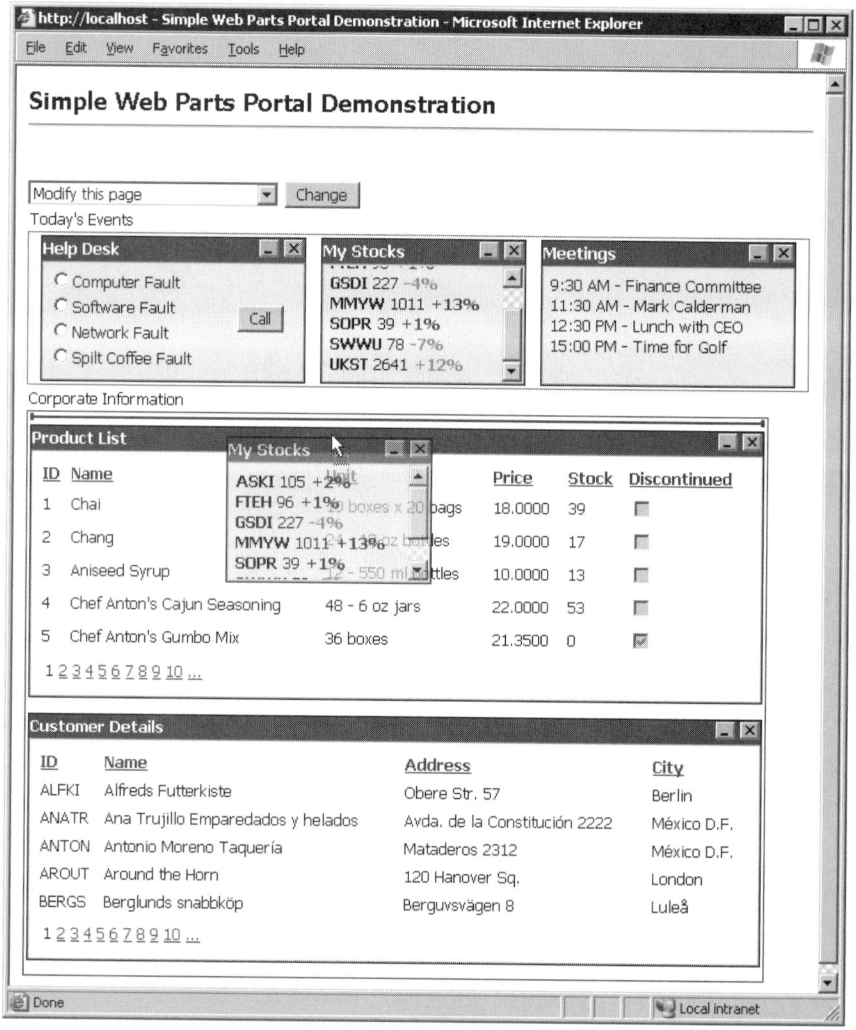

FIGURE 8.2. Changing the layout in Internet Explorer 6

design mode and change the layout of the modules on the page by simply dragging them from one place to another.

Web Parts technology implements all the customization processes automatically and many other features as well. You can minimize or "roll up" a Web Part so that only the title bar is visible. And, as you'll see in the example page shown in this chapter, you can easily expose features that allow the user to edit the appearance and behavior of individual Web Parts, open dedicated Help windows for each one, close or hide individual Web Parts, and add new Web Parts to the page.

It all looks like a complex process, and it certainly does produce a page containing features that would take considerable developer effort to achieve from scratch. Yet the example in Figure 8.2, which we'll discuss in more depth shortly, contains only declarative content (ASP.NET server controls) and requires no server-side or client-side code to be written.

About the Web Parts Framework

The Web Parts technology is exposed through a series of ASP.NET server controls. In combination, they work together to generate the kind of output and feature set you saw in the previous screenshots. Underneath, the source for the page builds up a structured hierarchy of objects from the server control declarations. Figure 8.3 shows that structure.

The Web Parts technology uses several terms whose meanings may not be immediately obvious. For example, the noncontent areas of a Web Part (the border, title bar, open/close/minimize buttons, and so on) are together referred to as the **chrome** of the window. The individual buttons and command links on the title bar of a Web Part, and the links available in a drop-down list from the title bar of each Web Part, execute actions that are implemented by the Web Parts technology. These buttons or links, their appearance, and the actions they execute are defined as a series of individual **verbs**. You'll meet these terms within the names of properties and classes throughout this chapter.

Every page that uses Web Parts must contain a single instance of the `WebPartManager` control. This control is responsible for binding all the other controls together, reacting to events in the page, handling dynamic connections between Web Parts, and calling the methods on each Web Part

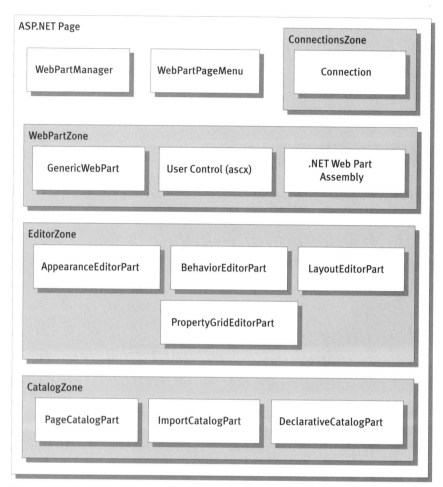

FIGURE 8.3. The object structure for a Web Parts portal page

to create the control tree for the page and generate the output. A WebPartManager requires only this simple declaration:

```
<asp:WebPartManager id="PartManager" runat="server" />
```

To allow users to switch modes, so that they can change the layout of the page, edit the properties of the individual Web Parts, or import other Web Parts, you can include a WebPartPageMenu control. As long as Personalization is enabled for the page, this automatically generates a drop-down menu with the caption Modify this page (as seen near the top of the pages in Figures 8.1 and 8.2) where users can select the actions they want to modify the page. A WebPartPageMenu requires only this simple declaration:

```
<asp:WebPartPageMenu id="PageMenu" runat="server" />
```

The remaining Web Parts features are declared within "zones" on the page (although other content for the page can, of course, be located outside the zones). Web Parts that appear when the page is first opened are referenced within a `WebPartZone`. In the example page, all the Web Parts you see are standard ASP.NET user controls, which are inserted into the page using the `Register` directive in the usual way. For example, the Canteen Menu Web Part is registered using the following code:

```
<%@ Register TagPrefix="ahh" TagName="Canteen" src="canteen.ascx" %>
```

Web Part Zones

It's possible to place a Web Part directly on an ASP.NET page, but in general you will place them within zones that are defined using a `WebPartZone` control. This is a templated control that references all the Web Parts for the current zone and synchronizes the layout, appearance, and colors of these Web Parts. An ASP.NET page can contain more than one `WebPartZone`—the example in Figures 8.1 and 8.2 contains two zones. One shows today's events, and the other shows corporate information such as the product and customer lists.

A `WebPartZone` declaration follows the same principles as most other familiar templated controls. It accepts attributes that define the behavior of the zone and all of the Web Parts within the zone, elements that define the style of specific sections of the output, and a `ZoneTemplate` that contains the declaration of the Web Parts that will appear in this zone by default (see Listing 8.1).

LISTING 8.1. Outline of a Simple WebPartZone Control Declaration

```
<asp:WebPartZone id="EventsZone" runat="server"
    HeaderText="Today's Events"
    LayoutOrientation="Horizontal"
    EmptyZoneText="Events Zone">
  <PartTitleStyle BackColor="#2254B1" ForeColor="White"
            Font-Bold="True" />
  <PartStyle CellSpacing="0" BackColor="#C0FFC0"
          BorderColor="#81AAF2" BorderStyle="Solid"
          BorderWidth="1px" />
  <ZoneTemplate>
    ... Web Parts for this zone are referenced here ...
  </ZoneTemplate>
</asp:WebPartZone>
```

Bear in mind that the layout of the Web Parts in the page may be different when the page is actually displayed. If this is a postback, and editing of the page layout is enabled, the user may have moved Web Parts from one zone to another. Likewise, if Personalization is enabled for the page, Web Parts may appear in a different zone from the original location. The following kinds of Web Parts can appear in a `WebPartZone`:

- Standard ASP.NET User Controls (referenced through a `Register` directive in the page), which can contain HTML, markup, dynamic content, or any other content available for use in a Web page
- Compiled .NET assemblies (referenced through a `Register` directive in the page), which generate the same kinds of content as a User Control or Web page

In the future, support will be extended to DLLs and components that do not run under the .NET Framework, to provide cross-application integration with Web Parts from other arenas.

A Simple Web Parts Example Page

The screenshots shown in Figures 8.1 and 8.2 (earlier in this chapter) are taken from a simple example page that demonstrates most of the features of the portal framework and Web Parts technologies. These screenshots, together with those you'll see in this section, show the appearance of the page at various stages of customization. You'll see how this page is constructed and the ways that the various attributes and control elements govern the behavior of the page.

An Overall View of the Example Page

Listing 8.2 shows the complete code for the example page. The user controls that implement the seven Web Parts we provide are registered at the start of the page, and a `WebPartManager` control and a `WebPartPageMenu` control are included in the server-side `<form>` that also contains the five zones used in the page.

- The `CatalogZone` contains a `PageCatalogPart` to display the Web Parts that are currently closed, an `ImportCatalogPart` to allow parts to be imported, and a `DeclarativeCatalogPart` that references two parts that are available for use on the page but are not displayed by default.

- The `EditorZone` contains three of the editor controls: `AppearanceEditorPart`, `LayoutEditorPart`, and `BehaviorEditorPart`.

- The `ConnectionsZone` is empty. This is where connections between the parts would be declared if the parts exposed properties and methods to support this. This feature is available only for compiled assemblies, not for user controls.

- The `EventsZone` is a `WebPartZone` control that references three user controls that implement the output for the three Web Parts at the top of the page: Help Desk, My Stocks, and Meetings.

- The `CorpInfoZone` is a `WebPartZone` control that references two user controls that implement the output for the two Web Parts toward the bottom of the page: Product List and Customer Details.

You can see some of the many attributes that can be added to the zone elements to specify the appearance and behavior of the individual Web Parts (as shown in Figure 8.4) in Listing 8.2. The attributes used for the two `WebPartZone` controls specify an appearance similar to an ordinary Windows dialog window, with images used for the Minimize and Close links in the title bar to reinforce this appearance.

LISTING 8.2. A Simple Web Parts Example Page

```
<%@Page Language="VB"%>

<%@ Register TagPrefix="ahh" TagName="Meetings"
            src="meetings.ascx" %>
<%@ Register TagPrefix="ahh" TagName="Stocks"
            src="stocks.ascx" %>
<%@ Register TagPrefix="ahh" TagName="Canteen"
            src="canteen.ascx" %>
<%@ Register TagPrefix="ahh" TagName="Products"
            src="products.ascx" %>
<%@ Register TagPrefix="ahh" TagName="Customers"
            src="customers.ascx" %>
<%@ Register TagPrefix="ahh" TagName="HelpDesk"
            src="helpdesk.ascx" %>
<%@ Register TagPrefix="ahh" TagName="PhoneBook"
            src="phonebook.ascx" %>
<html>
<head>
<title>Simple Web Parts Portal Demonstration</title>
</head>
<body>
<form runat="server">
```

continues

```
<asp:WebPartManager id="PartManager" runat="server"
    Personalization-Enabled="true"
    Personalization-InitialScope="Shared" /><br />

<asp:WebPartPageMenu ID="WebPartPageMenu1" Runat="server"
    MenuStyle-BorderColor="#000000" MenuStyle-BorderStyle="Solid"
    MenuStyle-BorderWidth="1" />

<asp:CatalogZone id="CatalogZone" runat="server"
    BackColor="LightGray"
    BorderWidth="1"
    BorderColor="Black"
    Style="padding:5px;margin-top:7px">
  <PartTitleStyle BackColor="Blue" ForeColor="White"
                  Font-Bold="True" />
  <PartStyle BackColor="White" />
  <ZoneTemplate>
    <asp:PageCatalogPart id="PageCatalogPart1" runat="server" />
    <asp:ImportCatalogPart id="ImportCatalogPart1" runat="server" />
    <asp:DeclarativeCatalogPart id="DeclarativeCatalogPart1"
        runat="server" Title="Optional Parts">
      <WebPartsTemplate>
        <ahh:Canteen id="pCanteen" runat="server"
            Title="Canteen Menu" />
        <ahh:PhoneBook id="pPhoneBook" runat="server"
            Title="Phone Book" />
      </WebPartsTemplate>
    </asp:DeclarativeCatalogPart>
  </ZoneTemplate>
</asp:CatalogZone>

<asp:EditorZone id="EditorZone" runat="server"
    BackColor="LightBlue"
    Style="padding:5px;margin-top:7px">
  <PartTitleStyle BackColor="Blue" ForeColor="White"
                  Font-Bold="True"/>
  <ZoneTemplate>
    <asp:AppearanceEditorPart id="AppearanceEditorPart1"
                    runat="server" />
    <asp:LayoutEditorPart id="LayoutEditorPart1"
                    runat="server" />
    <asp:BehaviorEditorPart id="BehaviorEditorPart1"
                    runat="server" />
  </ZoneTemplate>
</asp:EditorZone>

<asp:ConnectionsZone ID="ConnectionsZone1" Runat="server" />

<asp:WebPartZone id="EventsZone" runat="server"
    PartChromeType="TitleAndBorder"
    VerbButtonType="Image"
    MenuPopupImageUrl="images/clickdown.gif"
```

```
        MinimizeVerb-ImageUrl="images/minimize.gif"
        RestoreVerb-ImageUrl="images/restore.gif"
        CloseVerb-ImageUrl="images/close.gif"
        EditVerb-ImageUrl="images/edit.gif"
        HelpVerb-ImageUrl="images/help.gif"
        LayoutOrientation="Horizontal"
        EmptyZoneText="Events Zone"
        HeaderText="Today's Events"
        SelectedPartChromeStyle-BorderStyle="Solid"
        SelectedPartChromeStyle-BorderWidth="5"
        SelectedPartChromeStyle-BorderColor="#ff3300"
        MenuStyle-BorderWidth="1"
        MenuStyle-BorderColor="#000000"
        MenuStyle-BorderStyle="Solid">
    <PartTitleStyle BackColor="#2254B1" ForeColor="White"
                    Font-Bold="True" />
    <PartStyle CellSpacing="0"  BackColor="#C0FFC0"
               BorderColor="#81AAF2" BorderStyle="Solid"
               BorderWidth="1px" />
    <ZoneTemplate>
      <ahh:HelpDesk id="pHelpDesk" runat="server"
           Title="Help Desk" />
      <ahh:Stocks id="pStocks" runat="server"
          Title="My Stocks" />
      <ahh:Meetings id="pMeetings" runat="server"
          Title="Meetings" />
    </ZoneTemplate>
</asp:WebPartZone>

<asp:WebPartZone id="CorpInfoZone" runat="server"
        PartChromeType="TitleAndBorder"
        VerbButtonType="Image"
        MenuPopupImageUrl="images/clickdown.gif"
        MinimizeVerb-ImageUrl="images/minimize.gif"
        RestoreVerb-ImageUrl="images/restore.gif"
        CloseVerb-ImageUrl="images/close.gif"
        EditVerb-ImageUrl="images/edit.gif"
        HelpVerb-ImageUrl="images/help.gif"
        LayoutOrientation="Vertical"
        EmptyZoneText="Corporate Information Zone"
        HeaderText="Corporate Information"
        SelectedPartChromeStyle-BorderStyle="Solid"
        SelectedPartChromeStyle-BorderWidth="5"
        SelectedPartChromeStyle-BorderColor="#ff3300"
        MenuStyle-BorderWidth="1"
        MenuStyle-BorderColor="#000000"
        MenuStyle-BorderStyle="Solid">
    <PartTitleStyle BackColor="#2254B1"
                    ForeColor="White" Font-Bold="True"/>
    <PartStyle CellSpacing="0"  BackColor="LightYellow"
               BorderColor="#81AAF2" BorderStyle="Solid"
               BorderWidth="1px" />
```

continues

```
<ZoneTemplate>
  <ahh:Products id="pProducts" runat="server"
      Title="Product List" />
  <ahh:Customers id="pCustomers" runat="server"
      Title="Customer Details" />
</ZoneTemplate>
<HelpVerb ImageUrl="images/help.gif"></HelpVerb>
</asp:WebPartZone>

</form>
</body>
</html>
```

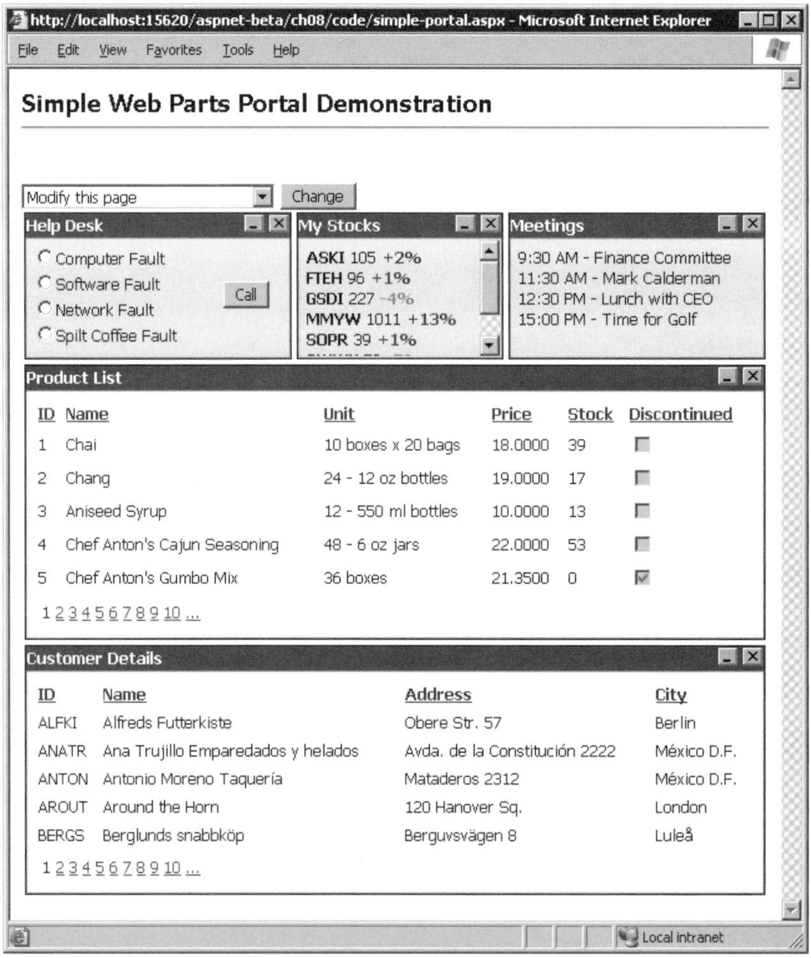

FIGURE 8.4. The example page, showing the view when first loaded

The default appearance of the page when first loaded is shown again in Figure 8.4 so that you can see the relationship between the control declarations and the output they generate.

The Events Zone Declaration

Zones contain one or more Web Parts and also control the layout and appearance of these Web Parts. The Events zone in this example displays three Web Parts, arranged horizontally by setting the LayoutOrientation attribute (see Listing 8.3). The zone attributes also define the text to display for the zone when in edit mode (HeaderText) and when there are no Web Parts in it (EmptyZoneText).

LISTING 8.3. Declaring the WebPartZone for the EventsZone

```
<asp:WebPartZone id="EventsZone" runat="server"
    LayoutOrientation="Horizontal"
    HeaderText="Today's Events"
    EmptyZoneText="Events Zone"
    PartChromeType="TitleAndBorder"
    VerbButtonType="Image"
    MenuPopupImageUrl="images/clickdown.gif"
    MinimizeVerb-ImageUrl="images/minimize.gif"
    RestoreVerb-ImageUrl="images/restore.gif"
    CloseVerb-ImageUrl="images/close.gif"
    EditVerb-ImageUrl="images/edit.gif"
    HelpVerb-ImageUrl="images/help.gif"
    SelectedPartChromeStyle-BorderStyle="Solid"
    SelectedPartChromeStyle-BorderWidth="5"
    SelectedPartChromeStyle-BorderColor="#ff3300"
    MenuStyle-BorderWidth="1"
    MenuStyle-BorderColor="#000000"
    MenuStyle-BorderStyle="Solid">
  <PartTitleStyle BackColor="#2254B1" ForeColor="White"
                Font-Bold="True" />
  <PartStyle CellSpacing="0"  BackColor="#C0FFC0"
           BorderColor="#81AAF2" BorderStyle="Solid"
           BorderWidth="1px" />
  ...
```

The PartChromeType attribute specifies whether the Web Parts within the zone will be displayed with title and border or just the title bar will be visible (equivalent to being minimized). The actions available for each Web Part can be displayed in the title bar as text links, buttons, or clickable images, depending on the value of the VerbButtonType attribute, and the following attributes reference the image files used in this example for the Help, Minimize, Restore, Close, and Edit buttons (by default they appear as hyperlinks).

When a part is selected for editing, the `SelectedPartChromeStyle` attribute values are used to display it. They should be set to values that make it easy to identify the part, and the example page does this by placing a 5-pixel-wide red border around the selected part. Web Parts can also provide a drop-down menu for the user to select edit mode or display a Help page, and there are a series of attributes that allow the appearance of this menu to be defined. The example page simply places a 1-pixel-wide black border around the menu.

The rest of the content of the `WebPartZone` element shown in Listing 8.3 is a `ZoneTemplate` that contains references to the Web Parts it will display by default (see Listing 8.4). The `Title` attribute specifies the title that will be displayed for that part. Each Web Part is a user control in this example, which is registered in the page in the usual way. However, you can mix user controls and Web Part assemblies, or any of the other types of Web Parts listed earlier as support for them is enabled.

LISTING 8.4. Declaring the ZoneTemplate and Content for the EventsZone

```
...
<ZoneTemplate>
  <ahh:HelpDesk id="pHelpDesk" runat="server"
      Title="Help Desk" />
  <ahh:Stocks id ="pStocks" runat="server"
      Title="My Stocks" />
  <ahh:Meetings id="pMeetings" runat="server"
      Title="Meetings" />
</ZoneTemplate>
</asp:WebPartZone>
```

The Web Part User Control Declarations

Web Parts can be implemented in a range of ways, as discussed at the beginning of this chapter. The example page uses only Web Parts that are implemented as user controls. Listing 8.5 shows two of the simple user controls, which implement the My Stocks and Help Desk parts seen in the screenshots of the example page.

LISTING 8.5. Two Simple Declarative User Control Web Parts

```
<%@ Control Language="VB" %>
<asp:Panel ID="Panel1" Runat="server" ScrollBars="Vertical"
        Width="160" Height="90" Wrap="False"
        Style="padding:5px">
  <b>ASKI</b> 105 <font color="blue"><b>+2%</b></font><br />
  <b>FTEH</b> 96 <font color="blue"><b>+1%</b></font><br />
  <b>GSDI</b> 227 <font color="red"><b>-4%</b></font><br />
```

```
    <b>MMYW</b> 1011 <font color="blue"><b>+13%</b></font><br />
    <b>SOPR</b> 39 <font color="blue"><b>+1%</b></font><br />
    <b>SWWU</b> 78 <font color="red"><b>-7%</b></font><br />
    <b>UKST</b> 2641 <font color="red"><b>+12%</b></font><br />
</asp:Panel>

<%@ Control Language="VB" %>
<asp:Panel Runat="server" id="Panel1"
          Width="210" Height="90" Wrap="False"
          Style="padding:3px">
<table border="0" cellpadding="0" cellspacing="0" width="100%">
  <tr>
    <td>
      <asp:RadioButtonList id="hdlist" runat="server"
          CellPadding="0" CellSpacing="0">
        <asp:ListItem Text="Computer Fault" />
        <asp:ListItem Text="Software Fault" />
        <asp:ListItem Text="Network Fault" />
        <asp:ListItem Text="Spilt Coffee Fault" />
      </asp:RadioButtonList>
    </td>
    <td>
      <asp:Button id="hdbtn" runat="server" Text=" Call " />
    </td>
  </tr>
</table>
</asp:Panel>
```

To maintain control over the size, border padding, and the presence of scroll bars, a useful approach is to enclose all the content in a `Panel` control. The user control for the Help Desk also includes an HTML table, which lays out the content in two columns. You can use any normal ASP.NET controls, HTML, and other content within a user control, with the usual exceptions of the `<html>` and `<body>` tags and server-side `<form>` elements.

The second zone on the page, named `CorpInfoZone`, contains the lists of products and customers. Notice that, unlike the parts in the first zone, these are fully interactive—you can sort the rows by clicking the column headings and page through the rows by using the links at the bottom of each list. In this zone the layout orientation is set to `Vertical`, but otherwise the attributes in the `WebPartZone` element are much the same as the first zone.

The two user controls for the lists of products and customers are extremely simple, despite the rich content they generate. They use a data source control and a `GridView` control (as demonstrated in Chapters 3 and 4). Notice that there is no `<form>` element in the control—one is already included in the main page. Listing 8.6 shows the entire code of the user control for the Product List part of the page.

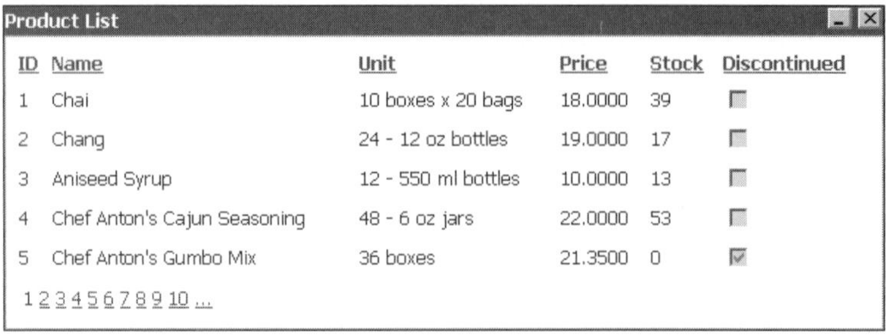

FIGURE 8.5. The output of the Product List user control

LISTING 8.6. Declaring the Product List User Control

```
<%@ Control Language="VB" debug="True" %>

<asp:SqlDataSource id="ds1" runat="server"
  ConnectionString="server=localhost;database=Northwind;uid=x;pwd=x;"
  SelectCommand="SELECT ID=ProductID, Name=ProductName,
                 Unit=QuantityPerUnit, Price=UnitPrice,
                 Stock=UnitsInStock, Discontinued FROM Products" />

<asp:GridView id="grid1" runat="server" DataSourceID="ds1"
    HeaderStyle-HorizontalAlign="Left" Width="100%"
    BorderWidth="0" CellPadding="3" SummaryViewColumn="ProductName"
    AllowSorting="True" AllowPaging="True" PageSize="5" />
```

The output of this simple declarative-only user control (shown in Figure 8.5) provides the content that is exposed as a Web Part, and the list of customers is generated in exactly the same way but (of course) with a different SQL statement.

Catalog Zones

By default, users can close a Web Part on the page by clicking the Close button or link in the title bar. They can later add this Web Part back to the page or add any other Web Parts you have associated with the page. The WebPartPageMenu control automatically provides a link to switch the page into catalog mode (see Figure 8.6), as long as Personalization is enabled for the application.

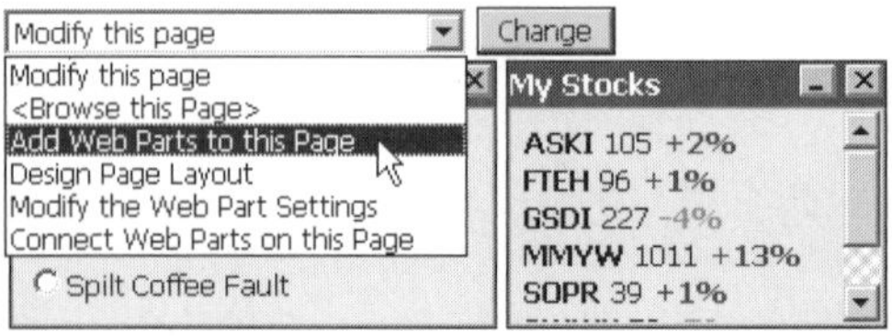

FIGURE 8.6. The drop-down menu created by the WebPartPageMenu control

Adding a new or closed Web Part to the page is achieved through controls declared within a `CatalogZone`. The `CatalogZone` and the `EditorZone` are not visible in the page by default; they appear only when the page is switched into catalog or edit mode from the `WebPartPageMenu` or when code in the page switches the `DisplayMode` property of the `WebPartManager` control. The lists of Web Parts that will be available in a `CatalogZone` are generated with any combination of `PageCatalogPart`, `ImportCatalogPart`, and one or more `DeclarativeCatalogPart` controls (see Listing 8.7).

LISTING 8.7. The CatalogZone Control Declaration

```
<asp:CatalogZone id="CatalogZone" runat="server"
    BackColor="LightGray"
    BorderWidth="1"
    BorderColor="Black"
    Style="padding:5px;margin-top:7px">
  <PartTitleStyle BackColor="Blue" ForeColor="White"
                  Font-Bold="True" />
  <PartStyle BackColor="White" />
  <ZoneTemplate>
    <asp:PageCatalogPart id="PageCatalogPart1" runat="server" />
    <asp:ImportCatalogPart id="ImportCatalogPart1" runat="server" />
    <asp:DeclarativeCatalogPart runat="server"
        id="DeclarativeCatalogPart1"
        Title="Optional Parts">
      <WebPartsTemplate>
        <ahh:Canteen id="pCanteen" runat="server"
            Title="Canteen Menu" />
        <ahh:PhoneBook id="pPhoneBook" runat="server"
            Title="Phone Book" />
      </WebPartsTemplate>
    </asp:DeclarativeCatalogPart>
  </ZoneTemplate>
</asp:CatalogZone>
```

At the top of the Catalog Zone dialog that this zone declaration creates are links to the three types of `CatalogPart` declared within the `CatalogZone` in Listing 8.7—the Page Catalog (the Web Parts that are currently closed, of which there is one available), the Imported Web Part Catalog (none have been imported), and the Optional Parts (the Web Parts referenced in the `DeclarativeCatalogPart` with this value for the `Title` property). If there is more than one `DeclarativeCatalogPart` in the `CatalogZone`, there will be entries for each one.

The left-hand screenshot in Figure 8.7 shows Page Catalog selected, and in this view the `PageCatalogPart` control generates a list of the Web Parts

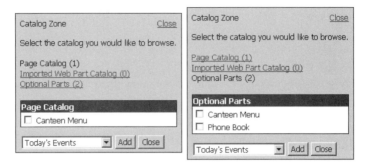

FIGURE 8.7. The modes of the CatalogZone control

for the page that are currently closed (i.e., Web Parts that the user has re-moved from the page by using the Close button on the title bar of that Web Part). It also generates UI elements where the user can specify which of these Web Parts should be shown again and which zone they should appear in.

The right-hand screenshot in Figure 8.7 shows the display when the Optional Parts section is selected. These are the Web Parts defined within the `WebPartsTemplate` section of the `DeclarativeCatalogPart` control shown in Listing 8.7. Notice how a part can appear in both lists if it has already been added to the page and then hidden.

The Imported Web Part Catalog link changes the display of the `CatalogZone` control to allow users to import Web Part definitions from appropriate XML files (see Figure 8.8).

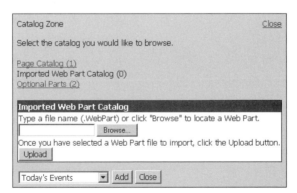

FIGURE 8.8. The import mode of the CatalogZone control

Editor Zones

Editor zones allow users or administrators (depending on the roles and permission settings of the application) to edit the behavior and appearance of individual Web Parts. An `EditorZone` is included in the page and can contain instances of one or more of the different types of editor controls (depending on which editing features you want to offer). The controls most commonly used within an `EditorZone` are the `AppearanceEditorPart`, `LayoutEditorPart,` and `BehaviorEditorPart` controls, as shown in Listing 8.8.

LISTING 8.8. Declaring an EditorZone Control

```
<asp:EditorZone id="EditorZone" runat="server"
    BackColor="LightBlue"
    Style="padding:5px;margin-top:7px">
  <PartTitleStyle BackColor="Blue" ForeColor="White"
                Font-Bold="True" />
  <ZoneTemplate>
    <asp:AppearanceEditorPart id="AppearanceEditorPart1"
                        runat="server" />
    <asp:LayoutEditorPart id="LayoutEditorPart1" runat="server" />
    <asp:BehaviorEditorPart id="BehaviorEditorPart1" runat="server" />
  </ZoneTemplate>
</asp:EditorZone>
```

It is possible to expose custom properties from a Web Part, a topic we're not covering here. However, in this case, you can include a `PropertyGridEditorPart` in the `EditorZone` as well, allowing users to set the values of these custom properties when that Web Part is in edit mode.

The screenshot in Figure 8.9 shows the output that these controls generate when the page is in edit mode and a single control is selected for editing. (At other times they do not appear in the output generated for the page.) You can, of course, provide just one or two of the different edit controls if you don't want users to be able to change all of the settings to which these controls provide access.

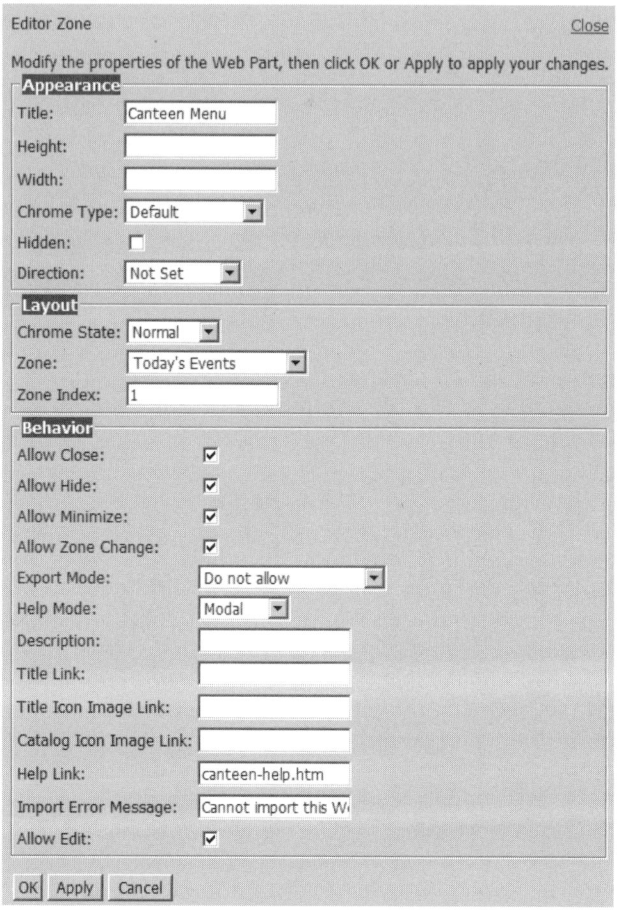

FIGURE 8.9. The EditorZone control in action

Page Design and Web Part Editing

Adding editing features to a page is extremely easy. As you've seen, the controls do all of the work for you pretty much automatically. All you have to do is enable Personalization for the application that contains the page and ensure that the WebPartManager control contains the Personalization-Enabled="true" attribute. The WebPartPageMenu control then enables the user to select either of the two edit modes using the drop-down menu it creates (see Figure 8.10).

Bear in mind that there are effectively two ways that users can edit a page that contains Web Parts. First, they can change the layout of the parts by selecting Design Page Layout. This causes the zone frames to be displayed, and users can drag controls to relocate them within the same zone

FIGURE 8.10. Switching to edit mode (left) and design mode (right)

or drag them from one zone to another. Figure 8.2, near the start of this chapter, shows an example of dragging a control.

Second, switching to edit mode also enables the drop-down menu in the title bar of each Web Part. By default, this is activated using a small down-pointing arrow. However, the zone declarations in our example replaced this with a custom image that resembles a drop-down button. When clicked, the drop-down menu appears for that Web Part, containing the Edit link (see Figure 8.11). Other entries can appear in this menu as well, depending on whether the Web Part has a Help page or exposes properties and methods that allow connections to be created between the parts.

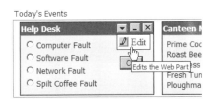

FIGURE 8.11. The Individual Web Part Drop-down Menu

The Editor Controls

When the user clicks the Edit link for a Web Part, the `SelectedPartChromeStyle` properties for the edited Web Part take effect. In our example page, these are set to produce a 5-pixel-wide red border around the part (see Listing 8.2), indicating which one is being edited. The three editing controls included in the declaration of the `EditorZone` in the example page also appear.

In the Appearance section (Figure 8.12), the user can specify the text of the title bar of the Web Part and its size on the page. The Chrome Type can be Default, Title and Border, Title Only, Border Only, or None. The Web Part can also be hidden within the page, and you can specify the layout direction (Left to Right, Right to Left, or Not Set).

For the Layout settings (also shown in Figure 8.12), you can specify the Chrome State (Normal or Minimized), the zone that the Web Part will appear in, and the index (position) within that zone.

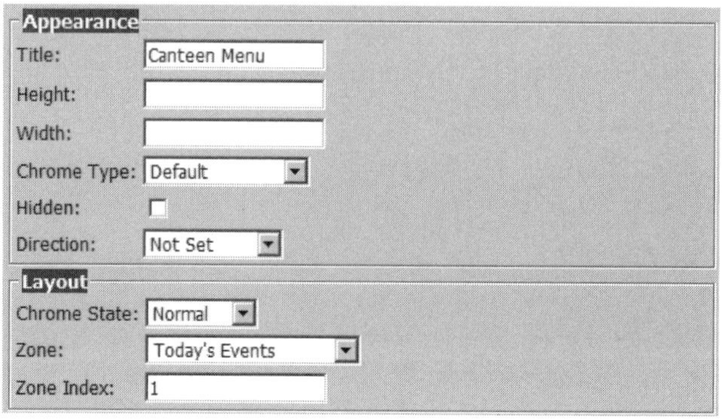

FIGURE 8.12. The Appearance and Layout sections of the EditorZone control

For the Behavior settings (see Figure 8.13), users or administrators can specify whether the Web Part can be closed (removed from the page), hidden, minimized, or moved to another zone. The Export Mode setting determines whether users will be able to export the definition and data for this part. The options are Do not allow, Export all data, and Non-sensitive data only.

Users or administrators can also specify the way that any help information will be displayed for a Web Part (in a modal or nonmodal window, or by navigating the current window to the Help page); the text for the alternate description of the Web Part; and the URL to open when a custom link or image in the title bar is clicked. This is followed by settings that specify the URLs of the image to show in the title bar and the image used when the Web Part is displayed in a catalog.

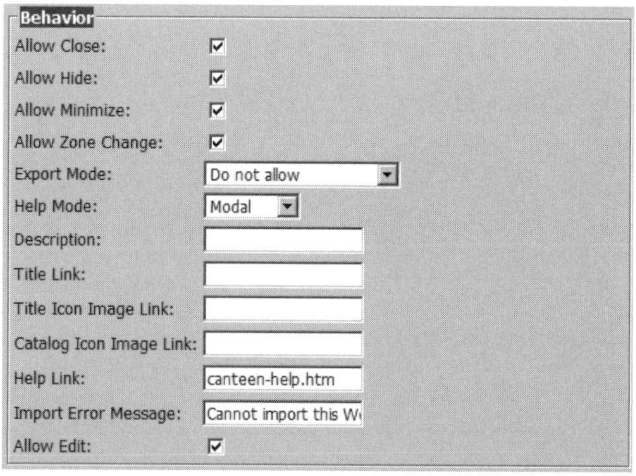

FIGURE 8.13. The Behavior section of the EditorZone control

Finally, there is the URL of the Help page for this Web Part, the error message to display when a user attempts to import this part when importing is not permitted, and a checkbox to enable or disable editing of the Web Part.

A Web Part developer can add custom properties to the Web Part and declare meta-data defining other entries that will appear when a `PropertyGridEditorPart` is included in the page (not shown in our example).

Help Features for Web Parts

One of the entries that can be added to the drop-down menu that appears in the title bar of a Web Part is the Help item. The URL of the Help page is specified in the Behavior section (see Figure 8.13), together with the window mode that will be used. If you add the Canteen Menu Web Part to the example page (from the Optional Parts section of the catalog, as shown earlier in Figure 8.7) and then specify canteen-help.htm for the Help Link when in edit mode, you'll see the Help item appear in the menu. When clicked, it opens the page shown in Figure 8.14. There is also a Help page named meetings-help.htm that you can specify for the Meetings part.

So, by using the edit and catalog features, users can customize the page to suit their requirements, displaying just the Web Parts they want to see and laying them out in the page as they require. Of course, the controls used to create this page expose their interfaces to code running in the page. So, while this example used no code, you can write code that interacts with the zone and Web Part controls and reacts to events in the page. We look briefly at this topic in the section Working with Web Parts in Code later in this chapter.

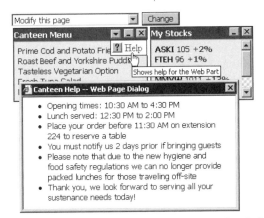

FIGURE 8.14. The Help menu link and pop-up Help window

Connecting Web Parts

As mentioned earlier in this chapter, it's possible to connect Web Parts. A Web Part can be configured as a provider, whereupon it exposes an instance of a custom class that can be consumed by another Web Part. The custom class implements an interface that itself defines the properties to be communicated between the Web Parts. Changes to the values of these properties in the provider are then transmitted to the consumer over the specified connection when the next page postback occurs.

We don't have room in this chapter to cover connections in full detail, but we do provide an example (`connections-portal.aspx`) in the sample files you can download for this book. It is a version of the simple portal page you've seen so far in this chapter, with two extra Web Parts added to it. These Web Parts, Address Details and Local Weather, appear in Figure 8.15.

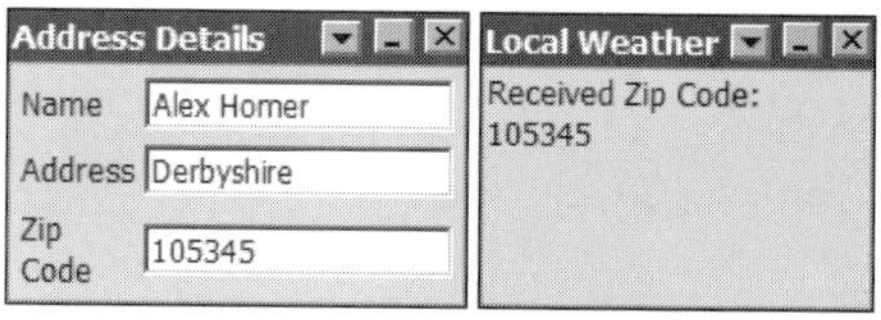

FIGURE 8.15. Two connected Web Parts

The Address Details Web Part exposes a class named `UserWebPart`, which implements an interface named `IZipCode`. This interface exposes a single read-only property named `ZipCode`:

```
Public Interface IZipCode
  ReadOnly Property ZipCode() As Integer
End Interface
```

Attributes are added to the public methods in the Web Parts that expose or consume the custom class, so that the Web Parts mechanism can discover them. For example, the method that is called within the Address Details Web Part to get the class instance is decorated with the `ConnectionProvider` attribute, which defines the "friendly name" for the interface (Zip Code) and the actual name (`ZipProvider`) that will be used to access this connection:

```
<ConnectionProvider("Zip Code", "ZipProvider")>
```

In a similar way, the consumer Web Part has a `ConnectionConsumer` attribute attached to the receiving method (named `ZipConsumer`) within the class definition.

Declaring Static Connections

To connect the two Web Parts together, the example page declares a static connection within the declaration of the `WebPartManager` control. This declaration, shown in Listing 8.9, specifies the ID of the Web Part that will act as the provider (`Zip1`) and the name declared in the `ConnectionProvider` attribute of the method that exposes the class instance (`ZipProvider`). It also specifies the ID of the Web Part that will act as the consumer (`Weather1`) and the name of the method that receives the class instance (`ZipConsumer`).

LISTING 8.9. Declaring Static Connections in a Page

```
<asp:WebPartManager id="WebPartManager1" runat="server"
                    Personalization-Enabled="True">
    <StaticConnections>
        <asp:Connection runat="server" ID="connection1"
            ProviderID="Zip1"
            ProviderConnectionPointID="ZipProvider"
            ConsumerID="Weather1"
            ConsumerConnectionPointID="ZipConsumer" />
    </StaticConnections>
</asp:WebPartManager>
```

Editing Web Part Connections

Providing that Personalization is enabled for the page, the drop-down list created by the `WebPartPageMenu` control will contain an entry to switch the page into a mode where connections between Web Parts can be edited. This causes the drop-down lists in the title bars of the individual Web Parts that can act as providers or consumers to display a Connect option. When this option is selected, the `ConnectionsZone` on the page displays details of the current connection between the selected Web Part and any other Web Parts. For example, Figure 8.16 shows the `ConnectionsZone` editor for the Local Weather Web Part, which indicates that it is acting as a consumer of the Zip Code interface (the friendly name declared in the `ConnectionConsumer` method attribute) where the provider is the Address Details Web Part.

If the selected Web Part is not already connected to another Web Part, the Connections Zone editor provides an interface that allows the user to select which Web Part on the page they want to connect it to. The options are, of course, limited by the interface(s) that the selected Web Part and other Web Parts on the page implement. In the example shown in Figure 8.17, the selected Web Part implements only the Zip Code interface, so there

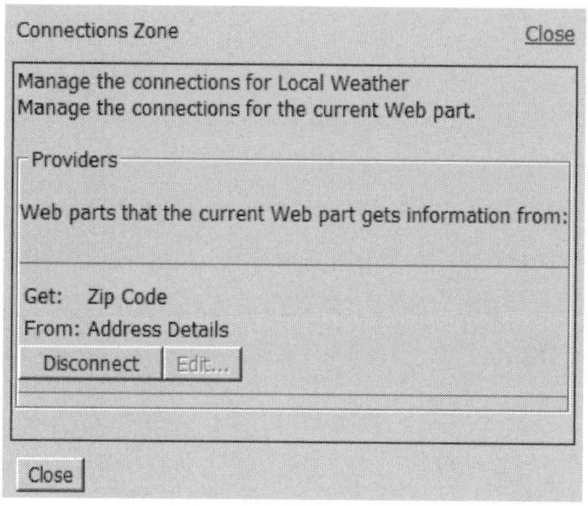

FIGURE 8.16. Editing an existing Web Parts connection

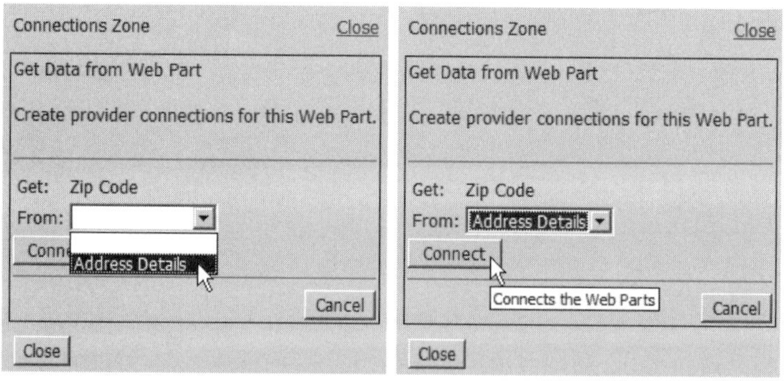

FIGURE 8.17. Connecting Web Parts dynamically

is no option to select a different one. And the only Web Part on the page that exposes this interface is the Address Details Web Part, so this is the only one that appears in the From list.

Working with Web Parts in Code

The controls used to generate portal pages are all ASP.NET server controls and become part of the control tree for the page when it is compiled and executed. So they can be accessed and manipulated using server-side code, and in some cases client-side code as well.

The hierarchy of classes used to represent Web Parts is quite complex. There is a single class used to implement the WebPartManager object, then a series of classes used to represent the different types of zone objects. The base class is the Zone class, and there are several intermediate classes. The

`Public` zone classes that you'll generally need to manipulate in code, or create instances of, are listed here.

- `WebPartZone`: This class implements the single object that controls all the Web Parts, zones, connections, and other objects used in the page.
- `CatalogZone`: This class implements a zone on the page that contains one or more of the `CatalogPart` objects, which are used to insert other Web Parts into the current page.
- `ConnectionsZone`: This zone is where you define the connections between Web Parts on the current page, so that a part can communicate and update its display in response to changes or user interaction in another part.
- `EditorZone`: This class implements a zone on the page that contains one or more of the `EditorPart` objects, which allow the user to customize the way that other parts on the current page appear and behave.

Figure 8.18 shows the hierarchy of classes used to implement the actual parts placed in the zones on the page. You can see that they all inherit from the standard ASP.NET `Panel` control and hence expose the same set of

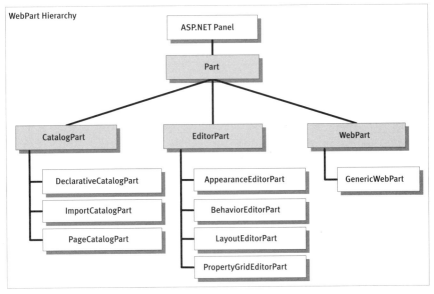

FIGURE 8.18. The Web Part Classes Hierarchy

properties as the `Panel` control. This includes properties that specify styling and appearance settings, plus the standard set of methods and events exposed by all ASP.NET Web Forms controls.

The classes shown with a shaded background in Figure 8.18 are abstract (`MustInherit` in Visual Basic .NET). The rest are `Public` classes from which instances can be created in code. You can see that this includes three different types of catalog parts, four different types of editor parts, and a single type of generic part. This last type is the one used to implement the actual Web Parts that are usually visible on the page and that contain the content the page will display in normal mode.

Still more classes are used to implement things like event handlers, connections between Web Parts, and the verbs that define the actions for the various types of buttons that can appear on the title bar of each part. In all there are over 80 different classes defined within the Web Parts framework, so we obviously don't have room to cover them all in detail in this book. Instead, we'll concentrate on the three basic types of classes that you'll use to build Web Parts pages—the `WebPartManager` class, the classes to implement zones, and the `GenericWebPart` class.

The WebPartManager Class

The `WebPartManager` is responsible for managing all the zones and Web Parts on the page. It exposes an interface that allows you to change the display mode, access and specify the behavior of zones and Web Parts, and react to events that occur within the page. The `WebPartManager` class is located in the `System.Web.UI.WebControls.WebParts` namespace (as are the majority of classes used with Web Parts), and it descends directly from `Control`.

The WebPartManager Constructor

`WebPartManager` has a single constructor, which returns a new instance ready to add to the `Controls` collection of the `Page` (see Table 8.1).

TABLE 8.1. The Constructor for the WebPartManager Class

Constructor	Description
WebPartManager()	Creates a new instance of the `WebPartManager` class with the default values for all its properties.

The Commonly Used Properties of the WebPartManager Class

The WebPartManager class exposes all the interface members of the Control class. In addition, several properties are specific to working with Web Parts. The ones you'll generally use are shown in Table 8.2.

TABLE 8.2. The Commonly Used Properties of the WebPartManager Class

Property	Description
DisplayMode	Sets or returns a WebPartDisplayMode value that changes the display mode for the page, or indicates the current display mode. The standard modes are Static properties of the WebPartManager class: NormalDisplayMode (0), ConnectDisplayMode (1), EditDisplayMode (2), CatalogDisplayMode (3), and DesignDisplayMode (4). You can define and add new modes by creating your own WebPartDisplayMode instances.
DisplayModes	Returns a reference to a WebPartDisplayModeCollection that lists all the display modes supported for the current page.
Zones	Returns a reference to a WebPartZoneCollection that contains all the zones in the page.
WebParts	Returns a reference to a WebPartCollection that contains all the Web Parts for the page.
Connections	Returns a reference to a ConnectionCollection instance that contains details of each connection between the Web Parts on the page.
Personalization	Sets or returns a reference to a WebPartPersonalization instance that defines the Personalization provider and permissions for the current page. See Chapter 7 for details of the ASP.NET 2.0 Personalization features.
SelectedWebPart	Returns a reference to the WebPart instance that is currently selected on the page, or Nothing (null in C#) if none is selected.
WebPartToEdit	Returns a reference to the WebPart instance that is currently being edited, or Nothing (null in C#) if none are selected for editing.
EnableClientScript	Sets or returns a Boolean value that specifies whether the page will use client-side script when dragging and positioning Web Parts on the page in the browser.

The Commonly Used Methods of the WebPartManager Class

The WebPartManager class allows you to mirror the client-side user actions of adding, moving, and closing Web Parts by calling the methods directly. There are also methods to manage connections and to import and export Web Parts (see Table 8.3).

TABLE 8.3. The Commonly Used Methods of the WebPartManager Class

Method	Description
AddWebPart (part, zone, index)	Adds a Web Part to a zone given a reference to the WebPart to add, a reference to the WebPartZone to add it to, and an Integer that is the zero-based index of the position of the new Web Part within the target zone. No return value.
MoveWebPart (part, zone, index)	Moves a Web Part to another zone or to another location within the same zone. Takes a reference to the WebPart to move, a reference to the WebPartZone to move it to, and an Integer that is the zero-based index of the new position of the Web Part within the target zone. No return value.
DeleteWebPart (part)	Removes the specified WebPart instance from the page. No return value.
BeginWebPartEditing (part)	Takes a reference to a WebPart instance and places it into edit mode. No return value.
EndWebPartEditing ()	Changes the state of the WebPart that is currently in edit mode back to normal mode. No return value.
BeginWebPartConnecting (part)	Takes a reference to a WebPart instance and places it into connect mode. No return value.
EndWebPartConnecting ()	Changes the state of the WebPart that is currently in connect mode back to normal mode. No return value.
ConnectWebParts (provider, providerConnectionPoint, consumer, consumerConnectionPoint)	Creates a connection between the two specified ConnectionPoint instances in two Web Parts (the provider and the consumer). Returns a reference to the new Connection instance.
DisconnectWebParts (connection)	Deletes the specified Connection instance. No return value.

TABLE 8.3. The Commonly Used Methods of the WebPartManager Class (continued)

Method	Description
Import(*reader*)	Imports the data for a Web Part from an XML file using the specified `XmlTextReader` instance, and returns a `String` containing any error message.
Export(*part, writer*)	Exports the specified Web Part to an XML file using an `XmlTextReader` instance. No return value.

The Commonly Used Events of the WebPartManager Class

The `WebPartManager` class exposes several events that are specific to Web Parts and can be used to interact with the various actions taken by users, in some cases allowing you to prevent actions they take from being carried out (see Table 8.4).

TABLE 8.4. The Events of the WebPartManager Class

Event	Description
DisplayModeChanging	Raised immediately before the current mode of the page changes. Passes an instance of a `WebPartDisplayModeCancelEventArgs` to the event handler, which has the following properties: • `Cancel`: A `Boolean` value that can be set to `True` to prevent changes to the display mode. • `NewDisplayMode`: A `WebPartDisplayMode` value that indicates the new display mode and can be changed to specify a different display mode.
DisplayModeChanged	Raised after the current mode of the page has changed. Passes an instance of a `WebPartDisplayModeEventArgs` to the event handler, which has the following property: • `OldDisplayMode`: A `WebPartDisplayMode` value that indicates the previous display mode.
WebPartAdded	Raised after a Web Part has been added to the page. Passes an instance of a `WebPartEventArgs` to the event handler, which has the following property: • `WebPart`: A reference to the Web Part that was added, selected, or deleted.
WebPartDeleted	Raised after a Web Part is closed or removed from the page. Passes an instance of a `WebPartEventArgs` to the event handler. (See the `WebPartAdded` event.)

continues

TABLE 8.4. The Events of the WebPartManager Class (continued)

Event	Description
SelectedWebPartChanging	Raised immediately before the currently selected Web Part becomes unselected. Passes an instance of a WebPartCancelEventArgs to the event handler, which has the following properties: • Cancel: A Boolean value that can be set to True to prevent the Web Part from being unselected. • WebPart: A reference to the Web Part that is currently selected.
SelectedWebPartChanged	Raised immediately after a Web Part becomes unselected. Passes an instance of a WebPartEventArgs to the event handler. (See the WebPartAdded event.)
WebPartsConnected	Raised when two Web Parts are connected. Passes an instance of a WebPartConnectionsEventArgs to the event handler, which has the following properties: • Connection: A reference to the Connection instance that joins the two Web Parts. • ProviderWebPart: A reference to the Web Part that will act as the source of communications. • ProviderConnectionPoint: A reference to the connection point within the provider Web Part that is the source of communications. Usually a method name within the component that implements the Web Part. • ConsumerWebPart: A reference to the Web Part that will receive communications. • ConsumerConnectionPoint: A reference to the connection point within the consumer Web Part that is the target of communications.
WebPartsDisconnected	Raised after two Web Parts have been disconnected. Passes an instance of a WebPartConnectionsEventArgs to the event handler (see the WebPartsConnected event).

The Zone Classes

Web Part zones are implemented through a series of classes. The Zone base class is inherited by WebPartZoneBase (from which descends the Public class WebPartZone) and ToolZone (from which descends the Public classes EditorZone, ConnectionsZone, and CatalogZone). Each class represents a zone within the page and is a member of the Zones collection of the current WebPartManager.

The next section describes the `WebPartZone` class, which is used to hold `GenericWebPart` instances and which exposes all the members of the `Zone` base class as well as those it adds or overrides itself. The tables in this sub-section summarize all the interface members that are relevant to working with Web Parts. Following that is a summary of the extra interface members of the `EditorZone`, `ConnectionsZone`, and `CatalogZone` classes.

The WebPartZone Constructor

The `WebPartZone` class has a single constructor, which creates a new `WebPartZone` that can be added to the `Zones` collection of the `WebPartManager` (see Table 8.5).

TABLE 8.5. The Constructor for the WebPartZone Class

Constructor	Description
`WebPartZone()`	Creates a new instance of a `WebPartZone` with the default values for all its properties.

The Behavior Properties of the WebPartZone Class

The `WebPartZone` has many properties, though we list only those that are specific to working with Web Parts and are relevant to the topics in this chapter (see Table 8.6).

TABLE 8.6. The Relevant Properties of the WebPartZone Class

Property	Description
`AllowLayoutChange`	Sets or returns a `Boolean` value that indicates whether the Web Parts in this zone can be moved to another zone or to another position within this zone. The default is `True`.
`DragHighlightColor`	Sets or returns a `Color` instance that specifies the color of the "target block" that will receive the Web Part. This "block" appears when a Web Part is dragged to another position, indicating the actual location it will take if dropped at that point.
`LayoutOrientation`	Sets or returns a value from the `Orientation` enumeration that indicates how the Web Parts in this zone will be laid out. Valid values are `Horizontal` and `Vertical`.

continues

TABLE 8.6. The Relevant Properties of the WebPartZone Class (continued)

Property	Description
PartChromeType	Sets or returns a value from the PartChromeType enumeration that specifies the default type of window or frame to display for each Web Part in this zone. Valid values are TitleAndBorder, TitleOnly, BorderOnly, None, and Default.
CloseVerb	Returns a reference to a WebPartVerb instance that describes the command verb that will be used to create the Close link or button for the Web Parts in this zone. Read-only. The WebPartVerb class is described in Table 8.9.
ConnectVerb	Returns a reference to a WebPartVerb instance that describes the command verb that will be used to connect Web Parts in this zone to other Web Parts. Read-only.
EditVerb	Returns a reference to a WebPartVerb instance that describes the command verb that will be used to create the Edit link or button for the Web Parts in this zone. Read-only.
ExportVerb	Returns a reference to a WebPartVerb instance that describes the command verb that will be used to export the data that defines Web Parts in this zone. Read-only.
HelpVerb	Returns a reference to a WebPartVerb instance that describes the command verb that will be used to create the Help link or button for the Web Parts in this zone. Read-only.
MinimizeVerb	Returns a reference to a WebPartVerb instance that describes the command verb that will be used to create the Minimize link or button for the Web Parts in this zone. Read-only.
RestoreVerb	Returns a reference to a WebPartVerb instance that describes the command verb that will be used to create the Restore link or button for the Web Parts in this zone. Read-only.
VerbButtonType	Sets or returns a value from the ButtonType enumeration that specifies the default control type for the command verbs that will appear in the title bars of the Web Parts in this zone. Valid values are Link (the default), Button, and Image.
Enabled	Sets or returns a Boolean value that indicates whether all of the Web Parts within this zone are enabled. The default is True.
Visible	Sets or returns a Boolean value that indicates whether the zone and its content will be visible. The default is True. When False, the zone and its constituent controls still appear in the control tree of the page.

TABLE 8.6. The Relevant Properties of the WebPartZone Class (continued)

Property	Description
HeaderText	Sets or returns a `String` that is the text to be used as part of the `DisplayTitle` at the top of the zone when the page is in catalog, design, or edit mode.
DisplayTitle	Returns a `String` that is a combination of the `HeaderText` and the title of the selected part when the page is in catalog, design, or edit mode.
HeaderAlignment	Sets or returns a value from the `HorizontalAlign` enumeration that indicates the default alignment of the `DisplayTitle` text for this zone. Valid values are `Left`, `Right`, `Center`, `Justify`, and `NotSet`.
EmptyZoneText	Sets or returns a `String` that is the text to display within the zone when it contains no Web Parts.
ShowTitleIcons	Sets or returns a `Boolean` value that indicates whether the image specified in the `TitleIconImageUrl` property of the Web Parts in this zone will be displayed at the left end of their title bars.
MenuLabelText	Sets or returns a `String` that is the text for a menu that can optionally be displayed in the title bar of a Web Part.
MenuCheckImageUrl	Sets or returns a `String` that is the URL of the image to display as a "tick" mark for the menu items.
MenuDropDownImageUrl	Sets or returns a `String` that is the URL of the image to display for the drop-down items in the menu.
MenuPopupImageUrl	Sets or returns a `String` that is the URL of the image to display for the pop-up items in the menu.
ZoneTemplate	Sets or returns a reference to an `ITemplate` class that represents the `ZoneTemplate` section of the declaration of this zone.

There are also about 20 properties that expose a standard `Style` object and can be used to apply specific style settings to each part of the zones and their content controls. These are not listed here but can be found in the .NET SDK reference section for the specific zone class. Some examples of these properties are `PartStyle`, `HeaderStyle`, `VerbStyle`, `MenuStyle`, and `EmptyZoneTextStyle`.

The Events of the WebPartZone Class

The WebPartZone class exposes a single event that is directly relevant to Web Parts (see Table 8.7).

TABLE 8.7. The Event of the WebPartZone Class

Event	Description
CreateVerbs	Raised when the zone creates the links for the title bars of each Web Part. Passes an instance of a WebPartVerbsEventArgs to the event handler, which exposes a WebPartVerbCollection instance that contains all the verbs for the Web Part.

The EditorZone, CatalogZone, and ConnectionsZone Classes

The three zone classes other than WebPartZone expose a range of extra properties related to the tasks that these zones must accomplish. The properties are summarized for each zone in Table 8.8.

TABLE 8.8. The Zone-Specific Properties of the EditorZone, CatalogZone, and ConnectionsZone Classes

Class	Description
EditorZone	Exposes properties for the buttons or links that will appear when EditorParts are displayed, such as ApplyVerb, CancelVerb, OKVerb, VerbButtonType, InstructionText, and a collection of the EditorParts that are displayed.
CatalogZone	Exposes properties for the buttons or links that will appear when CatalogParts are displayed, such as AddVerb, CloseVerb, InstructionText, ShowCatalogIcons, and a collection of the CatalogParts that are displayed.
ConnectionsZone	Exposes properties for the buttons or links that will appear when Connections are displayed, such as ConnectVerb, ConfigureVerb, DisconnectVerb, CloseVerb, and CancelVerb, plus a whole range of properties for the various instruction and information messages that this type of zone can display.

The WebPartVerb Class

The buttons, links, and menu items in the title bar of a Web Part are referred to as *verbs*. The *xxx*Verb properties shown in Tables 8.6 and 8.8 expose a reference to a WebPartVerb class instance, which itself defines the appearance and behavior of the command links or buttons in the title bar of each Web Part. Table 8.9 shows the properties of the WebPartVerb class.

TABLE 8.9. The Properties of the WebPartVerb Class

Property	Description
Text	Sets or returns a `String` value that is the name of the command verb, such as `Edit`.
Description	Sets or returns a `String` that is displayed as a tooltip or long description of the command, such as `"Closes the Web Part"`.
ImageUrl	Sets or returns a `String` that is the URL of the image to display for this command in the title bar of the Web Part when command links are shown as images.
Visible	Sets or returns a `Boolean` value that indicates whether this command link is displayed.
Enabled	Sets or returns a `Boolean` value that indicates whether the command is available.
Checked	Sets or returns a `Boolean` value that indicates whether a "tick" should appear in a menu containing this verb.
ServerClickHandler	Returns a reference to the `WebPartEventHandler` that will be executed when the command is carried out. Read-only.
ClientClickHandler	Returns a `String` value that is the name of the client-side function, or the client-side script code, that runs when the user executes the command. Read-only.

The GenericWebPart Class

The `GenericWebPart` class represents an individual Web Part on the page and is a member of the `WebParts` collection of the zone that contains this Web Part. Table 8.10 shows the two `Public` constructors for the `GenericWebPart` class.

TABLE 8.10. The Constructors for the GenericWebPart Class

Constructor	Description
GenericWebPart()	Creates a new instance of a `GenericWebPart` with the default values for all its properties.
GenericWebPart(control)	Creates a new instance of a `GenericWebPart` based on an existing Web Part or any other `Control` object instance.

The Commonly Used Properties of the GenericWebPart Class

Many of the properties of the GenericWebPart class are inherited from the base class Panel, as this is effectively how a Web Part is represented in the markup that is generated and sent to the client. However, a number of properties are specific to Web Parts, and these are documented in Table 8.11.

TABLE 8.11. The Commonly Used Properties of the GenericWebPart Class

Property	Description
AllowClose	Sets or returns a Boolean value that indicates whether the Web Part can be closed (i.e., removed from a zone). The default is True.
AllowEdit	Sets or returns a Boolean value that indicates whether the Web Part can be placed into edit mode. The default is True.
AllowHide	Sets or returns a Boolean value that indicates whether the Web Part can be hidden using the controls in an EditZone, so that it still remains in the zone but is not visible. The default is True.
AllowMinimize	Sets or returns a Boolean value that indicates whether the Web Part can be minimized or "rolled up" so that only the title bar is displayed. The default is True.
AllowZoneChange	Sets or returns a Boolean value that indicates whether the Web Part can be moved to another zone when the page is in design or edit mode. The default is True.
Caption	Returns a String that is a combination of the Title and any document name, making it easy to use several instances of the same Web Part in a page with each displaying different data or documents. Read-only.
CatalogIconImageUrl	Sets or returns a String that is the URL of the image to display for this Web Part when it appears in a CatalogZone list.
ChromeState	Sets or returns a value from the PartChromeState enumeration that specifies the way the Web Part will be displayed. Valid values are Normal (the default) and Minimized.
ChromeType	Sets or returns a value from the PartChromeType enumeration that specifies the type of frame to display around the Web Part. Valid values are TitleAndBorder, TitleOnly, BorderOnly, None, and Default.
Description	Sets or returns a String that is the description of the Web Part.
DisplayTitle	Sets or returns a String that is displayed as the title of the Web Part in an editor zone.

TABLE 8.11. The Commonly Used Properties of the GenericWebPart Class (continued)

Property	Description
ExportMode	Sets or returns a value from the `WebPartExportMode` enumeration that specifies whether the Web Part can be exported. Valid values are `All`, `NonSensitiveData`, and `None`.
HelpMode	Sets or returns a value from the `WebPartHelpMode` enumeration that indicates how the Help window will be displayed. Valid values are `Modal` (the default help content is displayed in a modal window if the client supports this feature or in a separate pop-up window if not), `Modeless` (help content is displayed in a separate pop-up window), and `Navigate` (the current browser instance navigates directly to the Help page).
HelpUrl	Sets or returns a `String` that is the URL of the Help page to display for this Web Part when the Help icon or link on the title bar is clicked.
Hidden	Sets or returns a `Boolean` value that indicates whether the user has hidden the Web Part using the options in the `EditorZone`. When hidden it remains within the current zone but is not displayed. The default is `False`.
ImportErrorMessage	Sets or returns a `String` that is the message to display if an error occurs when importing a Web Part.
IsExcludedByRoles	Sets or returns a `Boolean` value that indicates whether the current user is excluded from editing the Web Part by the Role Manager system.
IsShared	Returns a `Boolean` value that indicates whether this Web Part is shared between multiple users or is available only to the current user. Read-only.
Title	Sets or returns a `String` value that is the text to display in a catalog, as a tooltip, and in the title bar of the Web Part.
TitleIconImageUrl	Sets or returns a `String` that is the URL of the image to display at the left end of the title bar for the Web Part.
TitleUrl	Sets or returns a `String` that is the URL of a page containing more information about the Web Part. When set, a link appears in the title bar of the Web Part.
Verbs	Returns a reference to a `WebPartVerbCollection` that contains the verbs or commands that the user can execute for this Web Part, such as `Minimize`, `Edit`, `Close`, and `Help`. Read-only.

continues

TABLE 8.11. The Commonly Used Properties of the GenericWebPart Class (continued)

Property	Description
Visible	Sets or returns a `Boolean` value that indicates whether the Web Part is displayed. It remains as part of the control tree when not displayed. The default is `True`.
Zone	Returns a reference to the zone containing this Web Part as a `WebPartZoneBase` instance. Read-only.

Remember that, because the `GenericWebPart` class descends from the ASP.NET `Panel` class, all of the members of that class are available as well as those shown in Table 8.11. For example, you can set the `Height`, `Width`, `Scrollbars`, `Direction`, `Wrap`, and `Enabled` properties, plus all the usual style properties, just as you would for a `Panel` control.

The CatalogPart and EditorPart Classes

As well as the `GenericWebPart` class, there are four `CatalogPart` and three `EditorPart` classes that (like `GenericWebPart`) are ultimately descended from the base class `Part`. So, in general, these classes expose the same properties as the `GenericWebPart` class. However, a few extra properties and methods are specific to the various classes. These are summarized in Table 8.12.

TABLE 8.12. The Properties for the Other Web Part Classes

Class	Description
BehaviorEditorPart AppearanceEditorPart LayoutEditorPart	All three classes expose the `ApplyChanges` and `SyncChanges` methods that can be used to manually apply changes to the Web Parts.
PropertyGridEditorPart	Exposes the `SyncChanges` method and an `ErrorText` property.
PageCatalogPart	Exposes the `GetAvailableWebPartDescriptions` and `GetWebPart` methods that can be used to discover what Web Parts are available and get a reference to each one using its `Description`.
DeclarativeCatalogPart	Exposes the `GetAvailableWebPartDescriptions` and `GetWebPart` methods, plus a `WebPartsTemplate` property that is a reference to an `ITemplate` instance that contains the controls and content declared for this Web Part.

TABLE 8.12. The Properties for the Other Web Part Classes (continued)

Class	Description
ImportCatalogPart	Exposes the GetAvailableWebPartDescriptions and GetWebPart methods, plus properties that set the text to display when selecting a Web Part to import. These properties are UploadButtonText, UploadHelpText, BrowseHelpText, ImportedPartLabelText, and PartImportErrorLabelText.

Web Parts and Visual Studio 2005

While the overall structure of a portal framework page is not that difficult to grasp, the multiple nested layers of style elements and zone templates, and the Web Parts themselves declared within content templates, do make it quite taxing to create pages from scratch. However, as you'd expect, Visual Studio 2005 makes it all much easier.

Figure 8.19 shows the example page you saw earlier loaded into Visual Web Developer (part of the Visual Studio 2005 suite). Each zone control allows you to switch the display mode, so that you can see how the page will

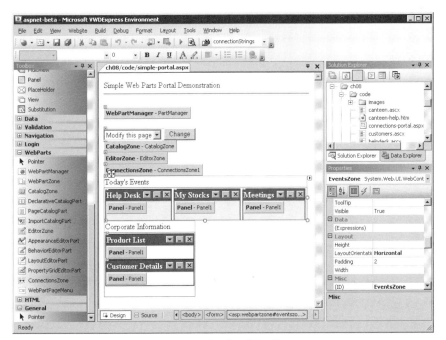

FIGURE 8.19. Building a Web Parts page in Visual Studio 2005

look in each mode. It also contains all the relevant controls in the Toolbox on the left, allowing you to drag them onto a page as required and simply set the properties in the lower right-hand section of the window.

SUMMARY

Building portal-style pages that contain multiple items of information and yet are neat, attractive, and—more important—customizable has been a complex task in the past. In ASP.NET 2.0, the new portal framework, which integrates Web Parts of different types into a single development model, makes it extremely easy to build these kinds of pages.

As we demonstrated in this chapter, by simply declaring a mix of several different types of `Zone` server controls plus a single `WebPartManager` instance and a `WebPartPageMenu` instance on the page, you can create complex interactive layouts that require no server-side code. This includes enabling features for changing the layout of the page sections using drag and drop; changing the behavior and appearance of individual Web Parts; rolling up, closing, and/or hiding individual controls; and even being able to add new Web Parts to the page.

Then, if you want to expand the capabilities of the page, you can write code that reacts to events in the page and interacts with the various controls that implement the zones and Web Parts. Although we didn't cover this topic in any detail, you can find lists of properties and methods in the SDK provided with ASP.NET or online.

We have not covered two features in depth, mainly due to lack of space:

- The ability to export and import Web Parts (as XML documents), allowing them to be moved from one page to another and one application to another
- The ability to expose custom properties from a Web Part, which can then be configured in a `PropertyGridEditorPart` control declared within the `EditorZone`

In the next chapter, we'll move on to look at how ASP.NET has evolved in version 2.0 to allow you to more easily accomplish some of the tasks that users found difficult in version 1.x. This includes things like cross-page posting and group validation.

9

Pages, Posting, Resources, and Validation

O NE OF THE GREATEST IMPROVEMENTS of ASP.NET over ASP is the post-back architecture, allowing client-side events to be linked to server code. Not only does it provide a richer programming model, but it also leads to more structured (and therefore more maintainable) code. This architecture is used whenever a control posts back to a page and there are times when you want to alter the default behavior. ASP.NET 2.0 provides support for directing where pages post to and how that posting takes place.

In this chapter we are going to look at several topics revolving around ASP.NET pages and the page architecture, in particular:

- How cross-page posting has been improved and simplified
- How validation has been improved by way of groups, allowing only controls within selected groups to participate in validation
- How to map pages to other pages with URL mapping
- What improvements have been made to client-side scripting support
- What new attributes for pages have been added
- How to localize pages to support multiple cultures
- How new events fit within the existing life cycle of control and page creation

Cross-Page Posting

The postback architecture of ASP.NET is undoubtedly good, but it can be confusing to many traditional ASP programmers. The problem people have is not with automatically posting back to the same page but with not being able to specify another page to post to. There are reasons both for (security) and against (big pages) posting to another page, and many people used `Server.Transfer` to move between pages. Content from the posting form was accessible only by ensuring the posting page was strongly typed or by storing it before posting (such as in the `Items` collection of the page). The biggest problem with `Server.Transfer` is that the original URL still shows in the browser.

ASP.NET 2.0 has made cross-page posting easier by allowing button controls to indicate the page they are posting to. This actually sets the `action` attribute on the form, but specifying this attribute manually will not work because it continues to be ignored. Security issues regarding the `ViewState` are not relevant; the post will instruct the receiving page to ignore it. The previous page can be accessed with the new page property `PreviousPage`.

Posting to Another Page

Let's consider two pages—Page1 (`Page1.aspx`) needs to post to Page2 (`Page2.aspx`). Page1 could look like the code shown in Listing 9.1.

LISTING 9.1. Posting to Another Page

```
<form runat="server">

  This is the first page
  <p />
  Please select a country:
  <asp:DropDownList id="Country" runat="server">
    <asp:ListItem text="USA" value="0" />
    <asp:ListItem text="Canada" value="1" />
    <asp:ListItem text="UK" value="2" />
  </asp:DropDownList>


  <p />
  <asp:Button id="Button1"
    Text="This button just posts back to itself"
    onClick="btn_click" runat="server" />
  <br />
  <asp:Button id="Button2"
    Text="This button posts to another page"
    PostBackUrl="Page2.aspx" runat="server" />

</form>
```

The important section is the one containing `Button2`, where you see the `PostBackUrl` attribute, which is set to the page being posted to. When the button is clicked, instead of posting back to the same page, the postback is redirected to the requested page, which can then access controls from Page1. However, controls on a page are protected, so they either have to be exposed on the previous page as a `Public Property` or accessed via `FindControl`. For example, we could add the following code to Page1 to expose the list of countries:

```
Public ReadOnly Property SelectedCountry() As DropDownList
  Get
    Return Country
  End Get
End Property
```

The exposed control doesn't have to be `ReadOnly`, but it works well for this example.

> In the Technology Preview release, `PostBackUrl` was called `PostTargetUrl`.

Accessing the Previous Page

Once the postback has been completed, you are now in the second page, and with the addition of the `PreviousPage` property, `Page2.aspx` now has the capability to access content from `Page1.aspx`. However, by default, the `PreviousPage` property is not strongly typed and will therefore be of type `Page`. To strongly type the page, use the `PreviousPageType` directive:

```
<%@ PreviousPageType VirtualPath="page_name.aspx" %>
```

or

```
<%@ PreviousPageType TypeName="type" %>
```

Only one of the attributes can be used at a time.

Now the exposed controls can be accessed easily. For example, consider Page2 (see Listing 9.2).

LISTING 9.2. Using a Strongly Typed Page

```
<%@ Page Language="VB" %>
<%@ PreviousPageType VirtualPath="Page1.aspx" %>

<script runat="server">

  Public Sub Page_Load()

    PrevMessage.Text = "On the previous page you selected: " & _
      PreviousPage.SelectedCountry.SelectedItem.Text

  End Sub

</script>

<form runat="server">

  This is the second page
  <p />

  <asp:Label id="PrevMessage" runat="server" />

</form>
```

Here you can see that the `PreviousPageType` directive indicates that `Page1.aspx` is the previous page—this ensures that the `PreviousPage` property will be strongly typed. From `Page1.aspx` the `DropDownList` is exposed via the `SelectedCountry` property.

You can have only one `PreviousPageType` directive on a page, although this doesn't prevent multiple pages from cross-posting to a single page. However, setting the `PreviousPageType` directive will mean that all pages will be strongly typed as the same type. Under these circumstances it's best to not use the `PreviousPageType` directive and instead access late-bound controls.

Transferring to Another Page in Code

Transferring execution to another page can also be achieved with `Server.Transfer`, and with ASP.NET 2.0 this has another overloaded method:

```
Server.Transfer(IHttpHandler, preserveForm)
```

This method has the following parameters.

- *IHttpHandler* indicates an object that implements the IHttpHandler interface (such as the Page object) and thus the PreviousPage property.
- *preserveForm* is a Boolean value indicating whether or not the form contents (i.e., ViewState) should be preserved across the transfer.

Detecting Cross-Page Posting

The question that naturally arises out of the preceding code concerns what happens if Page2 is accessed directly, without having been posted to from Page1.aspx, or perhaps if it posts back to itself. In addition to the PreviousPage property, there is an IsCrossPagePostBack property, which indicates whether or not a page is participating in a cross-page post-back. This property is True only for Page1 during its second instantiation, when accessed via the PreviousPage property of Page2. The following lists show what properties are set under what circumstances.

Page1 Posting Back to Itself

Page1.IsPostBack	True
Page1.PreviousPage	null (Nothing in Visual Basic .NET)
Page1.IsCrossPagePostBack	False

Page1 Cross-Posting to Page2

Page2.PreviousPage	Reference to Page1
Page1.IsCrossPagePostBack	True
Page1.IsPostBack	True
Page2.IsPostBack	False
Page2.IsCrossPagePostBack	False

Page1 Transfers to Page2 with Server.Transfer

Page2.PreviousPage	Reference to Page1
Page1.IsCrossPagePostBack	False
Page1.IsPostBack	False
Page2.IsPostBack	False
Page2.IsCrossPagePostBack	False

Here you can see that the existing ASP.NET 1.0 behavior isn't changed. When a page posts back to itself, the IsPostBack property is True, and the new properties are False. When posting to another page, however, the new properties are set. The use of these properties allows you to detect the stage of the postback.

The Page Life Cycle

It is important to understand the life cycle of the pages when posting across pages. The following list indicates what happens when Page1 posts to Page2, and in what order:

1. Page1 cross-posts to Page2 via a button with its `PostBackUrl` property set.
2. `ViewState` from Page1 is stored by Page2 but ignored.
3. The `PreviousPage` property is accessed in Page2.
4. Page1 is instantiated and the stored `ViewState` from Page1 is applied.
5. Page1 executes up to the `OnLoadComplete` event. For more details on which events will be fired, see Table 9.7 later in the chapter.

Understanding this life cycle ensures that you realize the implications of using cross-page posting. For example, posting from a page with a large amount of `ViewState` means the `ViewState` is stored and then reposted when the `PreviousPage` is accessed.

Posting to Another Application

Using the `PostBackUrl` property to post a page from one application to another application is possible, but the destination application will not have access to the `ViewState` of the first application and the `PreviousPage` property will be null.

Validation

One issue that was identified with the ASP.NET validation controls in version 1.x was that they all belonged to the same "group" within a page. For example, take a page that contains a login and password text box for existing users, plus a set of controls where new users can register their details instead. In Internet Explorer, the page cannot be submitted because the client-side validation checks will fail on the controls that have no values. In other browsers the page can be submitted, but the `Page.IsValid` property will return `False`.

One way around this is to arrange to disable the validators on the sets of controls for which users are not entering values, but this depends on knowing which sets of controls they will use. The other alternative is to disable all the validators, then enable the appropriate ones and call their `Validate` method in code when the page is submitted.

The ValidationGroup Property

In ASP.NET 2.0, the problem goes away courtesy of the new `ValidationGroup` property exposed by the `BaseValidator` control from which all the validation controls inherit. You assign the same `String` value to this property for all the validators that are in the same group, and different values for different groups. This is particularly useful for those scenarios where multiple forms are required or on pages that use the `Wizard` and `MultiView` controls.

The three controls you can use to submit a form (the `Button`, `LinkButton`, and `ImageButton` controls) also expose the `ValidationGroup` property, and you set this to the same value as the validators in the group that the button corresponds to. For example, in Figure 9.1, the page contains a Login and a Register section.

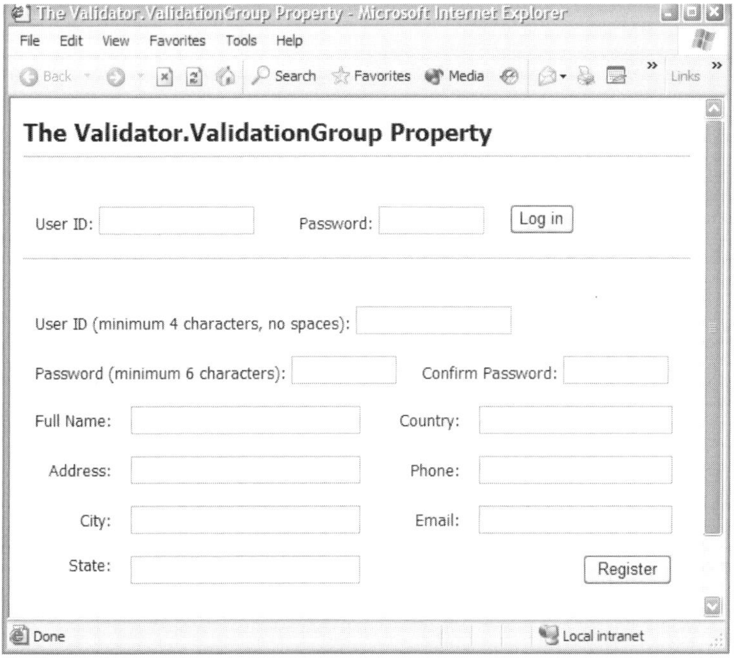

FIGURE 9.1. An ASP.NET page with two validation groups

All the validation controls in the Login section at the top carry the attribute `ValidationGroup="LoginGroup"`, as does the `Button` control labeled Log in. All the validation controls in the lower Register section carry the attribute `ValidationGroup="RegisterGroup"`, as does the `Button` control labeled Register.

When the page is submitted, an event handler defined in the `OnClick` attribute of the `Button` controls is executed. For example, the Log in button has the `OnClick="DoLogin"` attribute so the event handler named `DoLogin` runs. In it we check whether the user's values are valid by examining the `IsValid` property of the current `Page`:

```
If Page.IsValid Then
    ... code to run when valid values have been provided ...
Else
    ... code to run when the values provided are not valid ...
End If
```

In ASP.NET 2.0, the `IsValid` property now automatically takes into account the value of the `ValidationGroup` property, using the value set for this property on the button that caused the postback. So, if the user clicks the Log in button, which carries the attribute `ValidationGroup="LoginGroup"`, only the validation controls with the same value for their `ValidationGroup` property are checked. Validators and buttons with no `ValidationGroup` property set are regarded as being in the default group, so ASP.NET 1.x pages will continue to work as before under ASP.NET 2.0.

To go with the new `ValidationGroup` property are a couple of new or changed methods for the `Page` class (see Table 9.1). These allow you to interact with the validation controls in code at runtime.

TABLE 9.1. Page Validation Methods

Method	Description
`Page.GetValidators("group_name")`	Returns a collection of validation controls that have the specified value for their `ValidationGroup` property.
`Page.Validate("group_name")`	Performs validation for only the validation controls that have the specified value for their `ValidationGroup` property. Returns `True` if all these contain valid values, or returns `False` otherwise.

The SetFocusOnError Property

Another new feature of the validation controls is the ability to make the page more user-friendly by automatically setting the input focus to the first control that contains an invalid value. All the validation controls now expose the `SetFocusOnError` property, which you can set to `True` (in code or by adding an attribute when you declare the control) to turn on this feature. The default if not specified is `False`.

The ValidateEmptyText Property

When using a `CustomValidator`, an additional property, `ValidateEmpty Text`, indicates whether an empty value will be classed as being invalid (`True`), or not validated (`False`). This bypasses the need to call custom scripts for empty values and saves having to build checks for empty values into the validation code.

URL Mapping

With the increasing complexity of many sites, it's important to provide not only easy-to-use menu controls but also easy-to-remember URLs. For example, consider the ASP.NET community site at http://www.asp.net/, shown in Figure 9.2, which has a number of different tabs.

Although there are a number of tabs, all navigation goes through the `default.aspx` page, passing in the tab number as part of the query string. The hard-coding of these query string parameters means that if tabs are added, deleted, or reordered, bookmarked pages will potentially break.

To solve this problem, mapping URLs is now easy with a new section in the application configuration file, specifying the target URL and the actual URL. The syntax of the configuration section is shown here:

```
<urlMappings enabled="[true|false]">
  <add
    url="String"
    mappedUrl="String" />
  <remove
    url="String" />
</urlMappings>
```

FIGURE 9.2. The ASP.NET community site menu

The properties for urlMappings are detailed in Table 9.2.

TABLE 9.2. urlMappings Properties

Property	Description
enabled	Indicates whether or not the urlMappings service is enabled. The default is true.
url	Sets the displayed URL. This must be a relative URL starting with ~/.
mappedUrl	Sets the actual URL. This must be a relative URL starting with ~/.

As an example of urlMappings, consider the following code:

```
<urlMappings enabled="true">

  <add url="~/Home.aspx"
    mappedUrl="~/default.aspx?tab=0" />
  <add url="~/Forums/default.aspx"
    mappedUrl="~/default.aspx?tab=1" />

</urlMappings>
```

With the configuration shown here, any requests for Forums /default.aspx will result in default.aspx being called with the tab parameter set to 1, but Forums/default.aspx will still be displayed in the browser search bar.

Note that although a directory name alone can be included for the url attribute, no mapping will take place. This is because this is an ASP.NET service, and without a specified ASP.NET page, the URL mapping is not executed. For example, consider the following mapping:

```
<add url="~/Forums/"
  mappedUrl="~/default.aspx?tab=1" />
```

Although this is valid, ASP.NET never sees this request because it is for a directory; IIS sees there is no directory present and so issues a 404 error. Creating the directory doesn't work either because you'll then receive a Directory Listing Denied error or a directory listing if browsing is allowed. You can, however, create directories and empty ASP.NET pages purely to facilitate the mapping.

Client-Side Script Features

Although ASP.NET is a server-side programming environment, there are times when client-side script is required. This is especially true when dealing with smart browsers, such as Internet Explorer, where programming client-side can enhance the user experience. To improve this interaction ASP.NET 2.0 introduces improvements to registering script blocks and a way to allow script to perform callbacks to the server without a postback.

Registering Script Blocks

Programmatically adding client-side script to a page is achieved with `RegisterClientScriptBlock` and `RegisterStartupScript`, which both take a key and the script. This causes problems because it's not possible to use the same key for both a start-up script and another script block. To preserve compatibility, these methods still work, but a new `ClientScriptManager`, accessible from the `ClientScript` property of the page, provides enhanced features. For example:

```
Sub Page_Load(Sender As Object, E As EventArgs)

  Dim Script As String = "<script>" & _
                         alert('Morning everyone');" & _
                         "</script>"

  Page.ClientScript.RegisterClientScriptBlock(Me.GetType(), _
                         "FormValidation", Script)

End Sub
```

Another parameter has been added to allow the automatic insertion of the `<script>` tags. For example:

```
  Dim Script As String = alert('Morning everyone');"
  Page.ClientScript.RegisterClientScriptBlock(Me.GetType(), _
                         "FormValidation", Script, True)
```

Script Includes

In version 1.x of ASP.NET, to include a reference to an included script you had to do the following:

```
Sub Page_Load(Sender As Object, E As EventArgs)

  Dim URL As String = Page.ResolveUrl("~/Scripts/MyScript.js")
  Dim Script As String = "<script language='javascript'" & _
                         " src='" & URL & "'></script>"
```

```
Page.RegisterClientScriptBlock(Me.GetType(), _
                            "FormValidation", Script)

End Sub
```

With version 2.0 there is now a `RegisterClientScriptInclude` method to make this easier. For example:

```
Sub Page_Load(Sender As Object, E As EventArgs)

  Dim URL As String = "Scripts/MyScript.js"

  Page.ClientScript.RegisterClientScriptInclude( _
                            "FormValidation", URL)

End Sub
```

This will generate the following:

```
<script src="Scripts/MyScript.js" type="text/javascript"></script>
```

Client Callbacks

Client callbacks allow client-side script to call server-side events asynchronously, without causing a postback. This opens up a whole avenue for creating responsive interfaces, where data can be fetched or commands can run in the background.

ASP.NET 2.0 introduces the `CallBackManager`, which acts as an intermediary between client code and server code. It is responsible for accepting requests from the client, firing the appropriate server event, and then passing the results back to the client, as shown in Figure 9.3.

Several things are required for this process to work.

- The `CallBackManager` code must know the name of the client-side method that instantiates the callback. This is accomplished by using the `GetCallbackEventReference` method of the `Page`, which returns a string containing the client script required to initiate the callback.

- A client-side method must be created to handle the data returned by the `CallBackManager`.

- The browser must support XmlHTTP because that provides the client functionality to send requests to the server. To check for support, the `BrowserCaps` object has two new capabilities—`SupportsXmlHTTP`

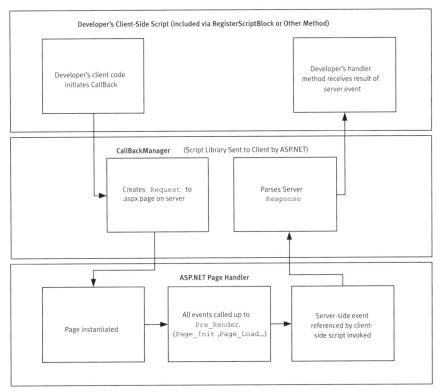

FIGURE 9.3. Client callback architecture

and `SupportsCallBacks`. In version 2.0 these will reflect the same capabilities, but having them separate allows for the callback implementation to be changed so that it is independent of XmlHTTP.

We'll look at the individual implementation details first, then look at a simple example.

Implementing the Callback Event Handler

If a page or control wishes to receive callback events, it must implement the `ICallbackEventHandler` interface. For a control developer this is simply a matter of adding the `Implements` keyword to the class definition:

```
Public Class MyControl
   Inherits WebControl
   Implements ICallbackEventHandler

End Class
```

For a Web page the `Implements` directive is used:

```
<%@ Page Language="VB" %>
<%@ Implements Interface="System.Web.UI.ICallbackEventHandler" %>
```

Implementing the interface is simple because it has only one method, the method that will be called from the client. Its signature is

```
Function RaiseCallbackEvent(eventArgument As String) As String
```

The single argument will contain data from the client, and the return value is returned back to the client. For example:

```
Function MyCallbackEvent(eventArgument As String) As String _
    Implements ICallbackEventHandler.RaiseCallbackEvent

  Return "The server saw " & eventArgument

End Function
```

Client-Side Script

On the client, there needs to be a minimum of two scripts—one to call the server, and one to act as the callback from the server. The latter of these must match the following signature:

```
<script>

  function MyCallback(result, context) { }

</script>
```

The return value from the server `RaiseCallbackEvent` will be passed into this function in the `result` parameter, and `context` is passed from the `context` parameter of `GetCallbackEventReference`, which is described in the next subsection.

There can also be a third script, of the same signature as the `MyCallback` script, which is run if an error occurs during the callback procedure.

Generating the Client Callback Code

For the client script to call back to the server, the client needs to know the control implementing the `ICallbackEventHandler` interface. For this the `GetCallbackEventReference` method is used (in much the same way that `GetPostbackEventReference` is used for controls responding to postbacks). The `GetCallbackEventReference` method is overloaded, having the signatures shown in Listing 9.3.

LISTING 9.3. GetCallbackEventReference Syntax

```
Public Function GetCallbackEventReference(
                control As Control,
                argument As String,
                clientCallback As String,
                context As String) As String

Public Function GetCallbackEventReference(
                control As Control,
                argument As String,
                clientCallback As String,
                context As String,
                clientErrorCallback As String) As String

Public Function GetCallbackEventReference(
                target As String,
                argument As String,
                clientCallback As String,
                context As String,
                clientErrorCallback As String) As String
```

Parameters for these signatures are shown in Table 9.3.

TABLE 9.3. Parameters for GetCallbackEventReference

Parameter	Description
control	The control that implements RaiseCallbackEvent.
argument	A value to be sent to the RaiseCallbackEvent via the eventArgument parameter.
clientCallback	The name of the client-side event handler that will receive the results of the server event if successful.
context	A value that will be passed back to the client-side event handler via the context parameter.
clientErrorCallback	The name of the client-side event handler that will receive the results of the server event if an error occurs.
target	The ID of the control to which the callback should be sent if the default control is not required.

Listing 9.4 shows how to get the reference and register it as a script block.

LISTING 9.4. Generating the Client Callback

```
Dim refscr As String = _
    Page.GetCallbackEventReference(Me, "arg", "MyCallBackHandler", _
                                "ctx", "null")

Dim scr As String = _
    "function CallTheServerCallBack(arg, ctx) {" _
    & refscr & "; }"

Page.ClientScript.RegisterClientScriptBlock(Me.GetType(), _
    "CallTheServerCallBack", scr, True)
```

The first line constructs the actual line of client script that will generate the callback. For example, if this is run from the `Page_Load` event of an ASP.NET page, it will generate the following line:

```
WebForm_DoCallback('__Page',arg,MyCallBackHandler,ctx,null)
```

The parameters are defined as follows.

* `__Page` is the current page.
* `arg` is the string to be passed into the server `RaiseCallbackEvent`.
* `MyCallBackHandler` is the name of a client script to receive the callback from the server.
* `ctx` is the string to be passed directly through to the `MyCallBackHandler` in the context parameter.
* `null` indicates that no error callback function is required.

This `WebForm_DoCallback` function needs to be hooked into a client-side event to trigger the callback. This can be either directly triggered (such as from the `onClick` event of a button) or wrapped in another function, which is what the following line does:

```
Dim scr As String = _
    "function CallTheServerCallBack(arg, ctx) {" _
    & refscr & "; }"
```

This simply turns the callback routine into

```
function CallTheServerCallBack(arg, ctx)
{
    WebForm_DoCallback('__Page',arg,MyCallBackHandler,ctx,null)
}
```

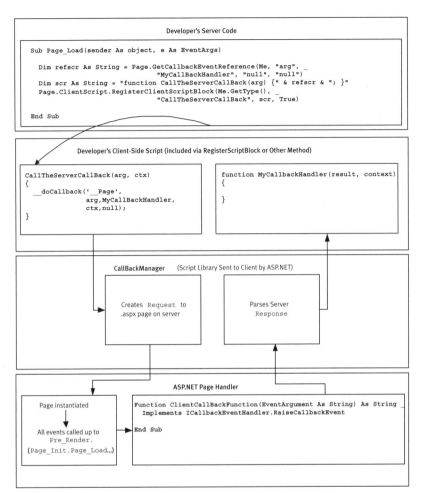

FIGURE 9.4. Client callback architecture with code

The final part of the required action is to register this block of client script:

```
Page.ClientScript.RegisterClientScriptBlock(Me.GetType(), _
    "CallTheServerCallBack", scr, True)
```

At this stage you now have a client script function that will perform the callback. The server implementation of `RaiseCallbackEvent` will process the argument and return its data back to `MyCallBackHandler`. Figure 9.4 shows a new copy of the client callback architecture diagram to make things clearer.

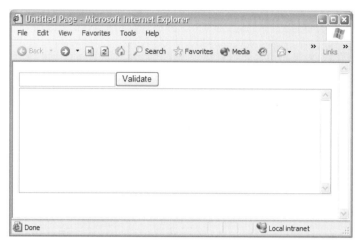

FIGURE 9.5. ClientSideCallback.aspx

Client Callbacks in Action

Because the code for this is confusing without a good example, let's look at the entire code for a page called `ClientSideCallback.aspx` (see Figure 9.5).

Entering a value into the top text box and pressing the button performs a client callback—in this case simulating the validation of a zip code. The results are displayed in the lower text area (see Figure 9.6).

The code for this is shown in Listing 9.5.

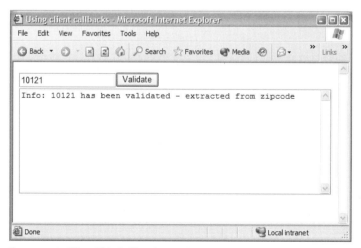

FIGURE 9.6. ClientSideCallback.aspx in action

LISTING 9.5. Using Client Callbacks

```
<%@ page language="VB" %>
<%@ implements interface="System.Web.UI.ICallbackEventHandler" %>


<script runat="server">

  Function ClientCallBackFunction(EventArgument As string) As String _
           Implements ICallbackEventHandler.RaiseCallbackEvent

    Return EventArgument & " has been validated"

  End Function

  Sub Page_Load(sender As object, e As EventArgs)

    Dim refscr As String = _
                Page.GetCallbackEventReference(Me, "arg", _
                "MyCallBackHandler", "ctx", "null")
    Dim scr As String = _
                "function CallTheServerCallBack(arg, ctx){ " _
                & refscr & "; }"
    Page.ClientScript.RegisterClientScriptBlock(Me.GetType(), _
                "CallTheServerCallBack", scr, True)

  End Sub

</script>

<html>
<head runat="server">
    <title>Untitled Page</title>
</head>
<body>
  <form runat="server">
    <script language="javascript">
      function CallTheServer()
      {
        var zc = document.forms[0].elements['zipcode'];
        CallTheServerCallBack(zc.value, zc.id);
      }
      function MyCallBackHandler(result, context)
      {
        l = document.forms[0].elements['resultlabel'];
        l.value = "Info: " + result
                  + ' - extracted from ' + context;
      }
    </script>
    <input type="text" id="zipcode" name="zipcode"></input>
    <button id="myBtn" onclick="CallTheServer()">Validate</button>
    <br />
    <textarea id="resultlabel" name="resultlabel"
```

continues

```
                    rows="10" cols="60"></textarea>
    </form>
</body>
</html>
```

The `Page_Load` event is exactly as we've discussed in earlier sections—it simply constructs the `CallTheServerBack` function, which wraps the `WebForm_DoCallback` function.

The server `ClientCallBackFunction` event simply returns a string—in a real application this perhaps would perform some sort of data lookup.

On the client side there is a button with an `onClick` event procedure, which takes the `value` from the top text box (`zipcode`) and the `id` and calls the server callback routine with those values. Giving the `CallTheServerCallBack` function two parameters allows for a flexible approach, where the value and context can be passed in. You could also do this for the callback functions if required.

Finally, the `MyCallBackHandler` function just accepts the `result` and `context` from the callback handler and displays them in the text area.

You can see that although there are several steps in this code, it's actually quite simple. This example uses an ASP.NET page, but it's just as easy to put the implementation into a custom server control. Although this technique relies on XmlHTTP, it is cross-browser friendly and works on Netscape Navigator (see Figure 9.7).

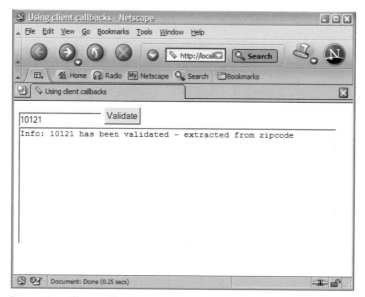

FIGURE 9.7. Client callbacks on Netscape Navigator

Uses for Client Callbacks

Client callbacks are perfect for those situations where you want to provide quick access to server functionality—this approach avoids the rendering phase for a page or control. This could be used for validation, preloading of data, or even timed execution of server code to simulate a push scenario.

Another perfect situation for the use of client callbacks is to solve a problem discussed earlier in the book, in Chapter 7's Allowing User Selection of Skins subsection. There we discussed the problem of a theme browser that would allow users to select a theme to see how it looks. The problem was that the server event procedure that resulted from the selection of the theme fires too late for the theme to be applied (remember that themes have to be applied in the `PreInit` event). With this new technique, selection of the theme can now perform a client callback that sets the theme, for example:

```
Function MyCallBackEvent(EventArgument As String) As String _
    Implements ICallbackEventHander.RaiseCallbackEvent

  Profile.Theme = EventArgument

End Function
```

The client callback function can then simply invoke a standard post-back:

```
<script language="javascript">

  function MyCallBackHandler(result,context)
  {
    __doPostBack('btnUpdate',,)
  }

</script>
```

The real postback will then run the `PreInit` event, at which stage the theme can be read from the `Profile`. Now a single selection can change the theme of a page.

New Form Capabilities

Several new features either directly or indirectly relate to the HTML form, including default focus and explicit focus setting.

Form Focus

To set the client-side focus, there are two new methods and an attribute on the form. Each control has a Focus method:

```
btn1.SetFocus()
```

The Page has a SetFocus method:

```
Page.SetFocus(btn1)
```

Finally, the form has an additional attribute (DefaultButton) to set the default button:

```
<form runat="server" DefaultButton="btn2">
```

These can be used as shown in Listing 9.6.

LISTING 9.6. Using the Focus and SetFocus Methods

```
<script runat="server">

  Sub btn1_click(sender As Object, E As EventArgs)
    btn3.Focus()
  End Sub

  Sub btn2_click(sender As Object, E As EventArgs)
    ...
  End Sub

  Sub btn3_click(sender As Object, E As EventArgs)
    Page.SetFocus(btn1)
  End Sub

</script>
<form runat="server" DefaultButton="btn2">
  <asp:Button id="btn1" Text="Button 1"
      onClick="btn1_click" runat="server" />
  <asp:Button id="btn2" Text="Button 2"
      onClick="btn2_click" runat="server" />
  <asp:Button id="btn3" Text="Button 3"
      onClick="btn3_click" runat="server" />
</form>
```

The default focus is applied only when no other focus methods are used.

Client Click Events

For server controls, the OnClick event refers to a server event. To hook a client-side event procedure into the click of a server button requires adding an attribute. To make this easier, ASP.NET 2.0 has the `OnClientClick` method:

```
<asp:Button runat="server" OnClientClick="ClientScript" />
```

The `onClientClick` event is supported by the `Button`, `ImageButton`, and `LinkButton` controls.

Submitting Disabled Controls

HTML by default doesn't submit controls that are disabled (that is, those with the `enabled` property set to `false`), and thus they don't appear as part of the form when posted to the server. If you need to receive the values of disabled controls as part of the form, you can set the `SubmitDisabledControls` attribute on the form element to `true`:

```
<form runat="server" SubmitDisabledControls="true">
```

This works by using a JavaScript postback system that enables all disabled controls, posts the form, and then disables the controls again.

This doesn't affect your ability to access disabled controls in server-side code, which works whether or not controls are disabled.

Changes to Page Directives

To cater to some of the new features in ASP.NET 2.0, new page-level directives and attributes apply to a variety of files. These new directives are listed here:

- `Async`, used to identify asynchronous pages
- `Image`, which applies to dynamic image files of type `.ASIX` (see Chapter 11)
- `MasterPageFile`, used to identify a master page
- `MasterType`, used to provide strong typing to the master page
- `PreviousPageType`, used to identify the previous page in a cross-page posting scenario
- `Reference`, used to point to a type that will be separately compiled and linked to the page assembly
- `Skin`, used to identify a skin file

Detailed explanation of master pages appears in Chapter 5, although the attributes are outlined later in this section.

The Page Directive

The Page directive has several new attributes, as shown in Table 9.4.

TABLE 9.4. New Attributes for the Page Directive

Attribute	Description
Async	A Boolean indicating whether or not the page is an asynchronous handler (i.e., it implements IHttpAsyncHandler). The default value is False.
CompileWith	A String indicating the path (relative or absolute) to the code-separation file. A Namespace is required for the code-beside file, and the ClassName attribute must also be specified.
EnableTheming	A Boolean indicating whether or not theming is enabled for the page. The default value is True.
LinePragmas	A Boolean indicating whether line pragmas are added to the compiled assembly.
MaintainScrollPositionOnPostBack	A Boolean indicating whether or not the current scroll position is retained over postbacks. The default value is True.
MasterPageFile	A String indicating the path (relative or absolute) to the master page.
PersonalizationProvider	The name of a Personalization provider, as detailed in the configuration file.
TargetSchema	This attribute is currently ignored and is intended for future releases.
Theme	The name of a theme.
Title	The page title.

The Master Directive

The Master directive can have the following attributes:

- AutoEventWireup
- CodeBehind
- CompileWith
- ClassName
- CompilerOptions
- Debug

- Description
- EnableViewState
- Inherits
- LinePragmas
- Src
- TargetSchema
- EnableTheming
- Explicit
- Language
- MasterPageFile
- Strict
- Title

All of these are similar to those for the Page directive, having either the functionality described in Table 9.4 for new attributes or the same functionality as in version 1.x of ASP.NET.

The MasterType Directive

The MasterType directive can take one of two attributes, as shown in Table 9.5. Only one of these can be used at a time—that is, you cannot specify both TypeName and VirtualPath.

TABLE 9.5. Attributes for the MasterType Directive

Attribute	Description
TypeName	The strong type of the master page. If this is not set, it defaults to type Page.
VirtualPath	The relative path of the master page.

The PreviousPageType Directive

The PreviousPageType directive is covered in more detail in the Cross-Page Posting section earlier in this chapter. This directive has two attributes, as shown in Table 9.6. Similar to the MasterType directive, you cannot specify both the TypeName and VirtualPath attributes at the same time for PreviousPageType.

TABLE 9.6. Attributes for the PreviousPageType Directive

Attribute	Description
TypeName	The strong type of the previous page. If this is not set, it defaults to type Page.
VirtualPath	The relative path of the ASP.NET page from which the request originated.

Changes to Page Headings

There is now an `HtmlHead` control that is equivalent to the `<head>` element on a page, allowing the header to be accessed in server code; this is exposed by the `Header` property of the `Page`. Alongside of this is the `HtmlTitle` control, which is equivalent to the `<title>` element, which is exposed by the `Title` property of the `Header`. This means that page titles can now be set like so:

```
Page.Header.Title = "My page"
```

The `Title` property and the `Title` attribute of the `Page` directive are the same, with the property set in code overwriting the title set declaratively.

To set the `Title` property in code, the `<head>` element must be defined with `runat="server"`. The `Title` property is set in the `Init` event; therefore, any changes to `Title` before this in the page life cycle will be lost.

xHTML Compliance

ASP.NET 2.0 has been designed to comply with the xHTML Transitional specification. Although this section is not going to explore xHTML in depth, some things are worth pointing out because they affect not only the output rendered to the browser but also the output from page templates. The major points are listed here.

- Client script tags are rendered without the `language` attribute and with the `type` attribute.
- Hidden fields, such as those used by `ViewState`, are rendered within a `div` whose display attribute is set to `none`.
- Input elements must be rendered within a block element; therefore, immediately inside the `form` element is a `div` element.
- The form `name` attribute is rendered only when the browser capability `W3CDomVersion.MajorVersion` is greater than `0`.
- Special characters (such as ampersands, apostrophes, and angle brackets) are now encoded in both attributes and query strings rendered by controls.

The Page and Control Life Cycle

There are several new events for an ASP.NET page.

- `LoadComplete` occurs when the page has finished handling post-back data.
- `PreInit` occurs before the `Init` event for controls on the page.
- `PreLoad` occurs before the `PreLoad` event for controls on the page.
- `PreRenderComplete` occurs after the `PreRender` event for all controls on the page.

The life cycle of events is shown in Table 9.7. This table covers both public and private events so that the interaction between page and control events can be seen. `Page` corresponds to a page event, and `Ctl` corresponds to a control event. New events are shown in bold. The phase and subphase items are logical and do not exist as physical events or phases—they are purely to show the stage in the life cycle. The Adapter Handling column indicates which phases involve the device adapter. (Device adapters are covered in Chapter 10.)

TABLE 9.7. The Page and Control Life Cycle

Phase	Subphase	Adapter Handling	Event/ Method	Notes
Start	Detect postback	Yes	`Page.DeterminePostbackMode`	If there is no `ViewState` or the `posteventSourceID` is empty, an initial request is assumed.
Initialization			**`Page.PreInit`**	The place to load Personalization and theme details.
			`Page.ApplyControlTheme`	
			`Page.ApplyPersonalization`	
		Yes	`Page.Init` `Ctl.Init`	`Ctl.Load`
	Begin tracking ViewState		`Ctl.TrackViewState`	

continues

TABLE 9.7. The Page and Control Life Cycle (continued)

Phase	Subphase	Adapter Handling	Event/ Method	Notes
			Page.InitComplete	
Load State	Load Control State		Ctl.LoadControlState	For controls that require private state.
	Load ViewState	Yes	Ctl.LoadViewStateRecursive Ctl.LoadViewState	Occurs for each control in the collection.
	Process post data	Yes	Page.ProcessPostData Ctl.LoadPostData	For controls that implement IPostBackDataHandler. First attempt for the RaisePostback event handler.
Load			**Page.PreLoad**	
		Yes	Ctl.LoadRecursive Ctl.Load	Occurs for each control in the collection.
	Process postback	Yes	Page.ProcessPostData Ctl.LoadPostData	For controls that implement IPostBackDataHandler. Second attempt for RaiseChanged events and PostBackEvent.
			RaiseCallbackEvent	If the page or control has a callback event handler.
	Postback events		RaiseChangedEvents RaisePostBackevent	
			Page.LoadComplete	
Pre-Render	Create child controls		Ctl.EnsureChildControls	
		Yes	Ctl.CreateChildControls	
			Page.PreRenderComplete Page.SavePersonalizationData	
Save State	Save Control State		Ctl.SaveControlState	

TABLE 9.7. The Page and Control Life Cycle (continued)

Phase	Subphase	Adapter Handling	Event/ Method	Notes
	Save ViewState		`Ctl.SaveViewStateRecursive`	Occurs for each control in the collection.
		Yes	`Ctl.SaveViewState`	
Render			`Page.CreateMarkupTextWriter` `Ctl.RenderControl` `Ctl.Render` `Ctl.RenderChildren`	
Unload			`Page.UnLoadRecursive` `Ctl.UnLoadRecursive` `Ctl.Unload`	Occurs for each control in the collection.
		Yes	`Page.UnLoad`	
	Dispose		`Ctl.Dispose`	

Site and Page Counters

Counting page hits is a requirement for many large Web sites and hosting companies, and some excellent commercial packages provide a range of services for tracking and analyzing data. However, there is often a need for a smaller, more localized set of services to track page hits or click-throughs.

This has been implemented in ASP.NET 2.0 with an easy-to-use Site Counters Service, which tracks clicks and hits in a configurable data provider (Access and SQL Server being the supplied providers). The Site Counters Service tracks a number of pieces of information, such as the current page, the target page, named counter groups and counters, and the application name. Each unique combination of these results, within a configurable time period, results in the creation of a new counter and a new row in the database. Subsequent instances cause the counter to be updated.

The database provides the columns shown in Table 9.8.

TABLE 9.8. Site Counters Database Columns

Column	Description
Id	A unique key, automatically generated.
Application	The name of the application, as configured in the IIS metabase.

continues

TABLE 9.8. Site Counters Database Columns (continued)

Column	Description
PageUrl	The URL of the source page.
CounterGroup	The group to which the counter belongs.
CounterName	The name of the counter.
CounterEvent	The event that generated the counter. This will either be `Click` or `View`, to indicate tracking of a click-through or a page view.
NavigateUrl	The URL of the target page, if navigating.
StartTime	The time when tracking started for this counter. This time is dependent on the number of rows per day and is the time the counter interval started, not the time the first page was tracked. For example, with a `RowsPerDay` value of `24`, the start time would always be on the hour.
EndTime	The time when tracking ended for this counter.
Total	The total number of clicks/hits for this counter for this interval.

The schema for these counters is shown in Table 9.9. Data will be truncated if it exceeds the lengths specified by the schema.

TABLE 9.9. Site Counters Database Schema

Column	Access Data Type	SQL Server Data Type
Id	`AutoNumber`	`int (Identity)`
Application	`Memo`	`nvarchar(256)`
PageUrl	`Memo`	`nvarchar(512)`
CounterGroup	`Memo`	`nvarchar(256)`
CounterName	`Memo`	`nvarchar(256)`
CounterEvent	`Memo`	`nvarchar(256)`
NavigateUrl	`Memo`	`nvarchar(512)`
StartTime	`Date/Time`	`datetime`
EndTime	`Date/Time`	`datetime`
Total	`Number (Long Integer)`	`int`

Using Site Counters

The underlying implementation of site counters is an easy-to-use API that can be used directly or built into controls. The following list shows which controls have built-in support for the Site Counters Service:

- AdRotator
- HyperLink
- Button
- ImageButton
- LinkButton
- PhoneLink
- ImageMap

Because these implement the service, they automatically have the option of exposing the properties shown in Table 9.10.

TABLE 9.10. Site Counter Properties Added to Controls

Property/Attribute	Description
CountClicks	Sets or returns a value that indicates whether or not the number of clicks is counted by site counters.
CountViews	Sets or returns a value that indicates whether or not the number of views is tracked (e.g., each time an ad is shown).
CounterGroup	Sets or returns the group name to which this counter belongs. If this is not specified, the default is the type of control being tracked.
CounterName	Sets or returns the name of the counter. If this is not specified, the default is the name of the control being tracked.
RowsPerDay	Sets or returns the maximum number of rows that will be stored in the logging database. The default value is 1, and the maximum value is 1440, indicating one row per minute.
SiteCountersProvider	Sets or returns the provider used to log site counter data. If not set, the default provider from the application configuration file will be used.
TrackApplicationName	Sets or returns a value that indicates whether or not the application name is tracked with the site counter details. The default value is True.

continues

TABLE 9.10. Site Counter Properties Added to Controls (continued)

Property/Attribute	Description
TrackNavigateUrl	Sets or returns a value that indicates whether or not the URL of the target page is tracked with the site counter details.
TrackPageUrl	Sets or returns a value that indicates whether or not the URL of the current page is tracked with the site counter details. The default value is True.

By default, tracking is disabled for these controls, but it's simple to enable. For example, at its simplest it's just a matter of setting the CountClicks property to True:

```
<asp:Hyperlink runat="server" NavigateUrl="products.aspx"
    Text="Product List" CountClicks="True" />
```

Every time this link is clicked, the details will be tracked. To add more details to the tracking, you can set more of the properties to differentiate different links:

```
<asp:Hyperlink runat="server" NavigateUrl="products.aspx"
    Text="Product List" CountClicks="True"
    CounterGroup="Products" CounterName="Overview"/>

<asp:Hyperlink runat="server"
    NavigateUrl="products.aspx?ProductID=123"
    Text="Special Offer" CountClicks="True"
    CounterGroup="Products" CounterName="Special"/>
```

Here both links have the same CounterGroup but a different CounterName, ensuring they are tracked as separate items. To track items with different URLs as though they are the same (e.g., all hits on products.aspx no matter what the query string or which page the URL is on), the same CounterName can be used. Any session information stored as part of the URL is stripped before being logged.

Using the Site Counters API

Access to the site counter data is available through an API exposed via the SiteCounters property on the Page. There are only two properties— Enabled, to indicate whether the service is enabled, and a SiteCountersProviderCollection, which is a collection of all available site counters. The methods of the API are detailed in Table 9.11.

TABLE 9.11. SiteCounter Methods

Method	Returns	Description
Flush		Flushes the tracking information for a given provider to the database, or all providers if no provider is specified.
FlushAll		Flushes the tracking information for all providers to the database.
GetGroupRows	DataSet	Returns the rows for a given CounterGroup.
GetNameRows	DataSet	Returns the rows for a given CounterName.
GetNavigateUrlRows	DataSet	Returns the rows for a given source page URL.
GetRedirectUrl	String	Returns the target URL given a selection of counter details.
GetRows	DataSet	Returns the rows for a selection of counter details.
GetTotalCount	Integer	Returns the total number of hits for a selection of counter details.
GetTotalGroupCount	Integer	Returns the total number of hits for a given CounterGroup.
GetTotalNameCount	Integer	Returns the total number of hits for a given CounterName.
GetTotalNavigateUrlCount	Integer	Returns the total number of hits for a given source page URL.
Write		Writes site counter details to the provider.

The Web Site Administration Tool (covered in Chapter 13) allows configuration of site statistics from the Application page, letting you update the configuration and viewing reports on the counters and page hits. The Get methods shown in Table 9.11 allow you to provide your own interface if required. The Write method allows you to control the tracking of hits from within code. For example, although site counters do not permit absolute URLs, you could implement tracking of these manually, as shown in Listing 9.7.

LISTING 9.7. Manually Adding URLs to the Site Counters Service

```
<script runat="server">

Sub NavigateAway(Sender As Object, E As EventArgs)

  SiteCounters.Write("Navigate", "Away", "Click", _
                     "http://www.asp.net/", True, True)
  Response.Redirect("http://www.asp.net/")

End Sub

</script>

<form runat="server">

  <asp:LinkButton runat="Server" onClick="NavigateAway"
     Text="ASP.NET" />

</form>
```

The `Write` method is overloaded and has several forms. See the documentation for complete details.

Configuring Site and Page Counters

The default installation of ASP.NET 2.0 ships with two providers for page tracking—one for Microsoft Access and one for Microsoft SQL Server—and these are configured in the application configuration file. Listing 9.8 shows the syntax.

LISTING 9.8. Site Counters Configuration

```
<siteCounters
  enabled="[true|false]"
  defaultProvider="String"
  handlerPath="String"
  handlerType="String"
  rowsPerDay="Integer"
  type="String">
    <providers>
      <add
        name="String"
        type="String"
        provider-specific-configuration />
      <remove
        name="String" />
      <clear/>
    </providers>
```

```
    <pageCounters
      enabled="[true|false]"
      defaultProvider="String"
      rowsPerDay="Integer"
      trackApplicationName="true|false"
      trackPageUrl="true|false"
      counterGroup="String"
      counterName="String">

        <pagesToCount>

          <add path="String" />
          <remove path="String" />
          <clear/>
        </pagesToCount>
    </pageCounters>
</siteCounters>
```

The configuration is broken down into two sections. The first (`<siteCounters/>`) defines the properties and providers for the Site Counters Service itself (see Table 9.12).

TABLE 9.12. Site Counters Configuration Properties

Property/Attribute	Description
enabled	Indicates whether or not the service is enabled. The default value is true.
defaultProvider	Indicates the provider to use if no explicit provider is named. The default is the Access provider.
handlerPath	Indicates the URL used to handle click-throughs. The default is ~/counters.axd, which is an HttpHandler that intercepts page clicks and tracks the data.
rowsPerDay	Defines the granularity with which data is logged to the provider. The default value is 1.
type	Indicates the full class name of the default provider.

The `<providers/>` element is where the actual site counter providers are added. The provider-specific configuration properties for the Access and SQL Server providers are the same (see Table 9.13).

TABLE 9.13. Site Counter Database Provider Properties

Property/Attribute	Description
name	The name of the provider.
type	The full class name of the provider.
connectionStringName	The name of the connection string, from the `<connectionStrings/>` configuration elements, that defines the connection details for the tracking database. This property is Access and SQL Server specific.
description	A description of the provider.
commitInterval	The interval, in seconds, between flushing the in-memory counters to the database. The default is 90.
commitTimeout	The time, in seconds, to wait before aborting the database command that writes the counters. The default is 60.

The attributes of the `<pageCounters/>` element map directly to the properties we have already discussed, although by default page counters are disabled.

The `<pagesToCount/>` element details which pages will have counter information logged. This supports wildcards, so a value of * indicates all pages, for example:

```
<pagesToCount>
  <add path="*" />
</pagesToCount>
```

Wildcards can also be included as part of the `path`, for example:

```
<pagesToCount>
  <add path="/*/default.aspx" />
</pagesToCount>
```

This ensures that only the `default.aspx` page is tracked, but only if one level down from the application root directory. There is no notion of excluding pages, so if only selected pages are required, the pages need to be added to the configuration.

Configuring the Counter Database

You don't need to do anything specific to start using site counters, even though they are logged to a database. Because the default provider is

Microsoft Access, when you first hit a page with site counters enabled, a new directory called DATA is created under your application directory if it doesn't already exist. Then a template database is copied into this directory and called ASPNetDB.mdb.

For SQL Server there is no automatic installation, but a SQL Script, called InstallSiteCounters.sql, is included in the .NET Framework's installation directory.

Resources and Localization

In ASP.NET v1.x, it was hard to use and manage resources, which made creating localized Web applications difficult and tedious. There was no declarative way to set control properties using resources because the resources were available only through the ResourceManager object. The localization feature therefore required a compilation step and satellite assemblies.

In ASP.NET 2.0, you will be able to set up a page or an entire Web application for localization by specifying the resources in the standard .resx file format. You can reference resources within an application in both declarative and programmatic ways. ASP.NET 2.0 has built-in support for culture identification. You can declaratively define resource keys for controls, subobjects, and their properties without writing any code. You can use page-level or application-level resources to localize an application without having to create and compile satellite assemblies. Finally, you can also use the new mechanism for inherent extensibility of resources to store and retrieve resources from databases or any other custom format.

In this section we'll look at an overview of "code-free" localization and multiple-culture handling techniques, before moving on to how to use the new expression types, resource types, and attributes to localize a page, again without writing any code.

Code-Free Localization

ASP.NET 2.0 helps achieve its overall promise of 60% less code by allowing you to localize a Web application without writing any code. Microsoft has provided built-in localization support in the .NET Framework and Visual Studio 2005.

You can localize an application by using a combination of implicit and/or explicit expressions and page-level and/or application-level resources. The following subsections explain these expression types and resource types with examples.

Using Implicit Expressions and Local Resources

Let us start with localization using implicit expressions, which is a kind of automatic way to apply resources to control properties. We'll create a simple Web page, `Sample.aspx`, as shown in Listing 9.9.

LISTING 9.9. A Sample Web Page to Illustrate Implicit Expressions

```
<%@ page language="VB" Title="English Page" %>
...
<asp:Button ID="Button1" Runat="server" Text="English Button" />
<asp:TextBox ID="TextBox1" Runat="server">
    English TextBox</asp:TextBox>
<asp:Label ID="Label1" Runat="server" Text="English Label">
</asp:Label>
```

The page contains a button, a text box, and a label. Create this page in Visual Studio 2005, switch to design view, and set the focus to design view. In the Tools menu, click the menu item Generate Local Resource. This command writes a resource key into each control and into the page directive in the Web page. In Listing 9.10, the resource key additions to the page appear in bold type.

LISTING 9.10. Sample Web Page with Resource Key Additions

```
<%@ page language="VB" Title="English Page"
    meta:resourceKey="PageResource1" %>
...
<asp:Button ID="Button1" Runat="server" Text="English Button"
    meta:resourcekey="ButtonResource1" />
<asp:TextBox ID="TextBox1" Runat="server"
    meta:resourcekey="TextBoxResource1">English TextBox</asp:TextBox>
<asp:Label ID="Label1" Runat="server" Text="English Label"
    meta:resourcekey="LabelResource1">
</asp:Label>
```

The `page` directive and each server control now have a resource key marked by the `meta:resourcekey` attribute. The combination of the `meta:resourcekey` attribute and the resource key is called an *implicit expression*.

The Generate Local Resource command also creates a `LocalResources` folder at the same folder level as the page. The `LocalResources` folder stores resource files that are page specific. The Generate Local Resource command also introduces a culture-neutral resource file, `Sample.aspx.resx`, in the `LocalResources` folder. The file is named after the source Web page, `Sample.aspx`. It contains resource values for keys declared in the page. To view the generated `.resx` file, double-click its name in the Solution Explorer to view its contents in the RESX editor. Figure 9.8 shows the contents.

Name	Value	Comment
▶ ButtonResource1.SoftkeyLabel		
ButtonResource1.Text	English Button	
ButtonResource1.ToolTip		
LabelResource1.Text	English Label	
LabelResource1.ToolTip		
PageResource1.Title	Untitled Page	
TextBoxResource1.Text	English TextBox	
TextBoxResource1.ToolTip		

Categories: Other ▾

Name	Type	Value	Comment
▶ ButtonResource1.Visible	System.Boolean	True	
LabelResource1.Visible	System.Boolean	True	
TextBoxResource1.Visible	System.Boolean	True	

FIGURE 9.8. Contents of culture-neutral resource file

The .resx file contains a resource key and value for each control property that is designated internally in the control as localizable. The design-time-only attribute is used by the designer as a pointer for properties to be pushed to the .resx file. It is not a runtime feature. The file also contains a key/value pair for the page directive. Each control can have different properties designated as localizable, although most text-based properties are marked localizable by default. As seen in Figure 9.8, the Button control's properties such as SoftKeyLabel, Text, ToolTip, and Visible are marked as localizable by default. Note that all strings are displayed in the Strings category and other types such as Boolean are displayed in the Other category in the RESX editor.

Next, let us create a new resource file that contains resource values in French culture. Change all occurrences of "English" to "French" in Sample.aspx.resx, and save the file as Sample.aspx.fr.resx. (Note the addition of fr in the filename, which is the standard abbreviation for "French.") The new file is added to the LocalResources folder and displayed in the Solution Explorer. You now have two .resx files, one for French and the original one, which is not marked with a language abbreviation. The unmarked file is used for any browser requests that don't explicitly request French. That is, the unmarked file is for the neutral culture, sometimes referred to as the fallback culture.

The last thing to do is to set UICulture for the page by adding a UICulture="auto" attribute in the page directive:

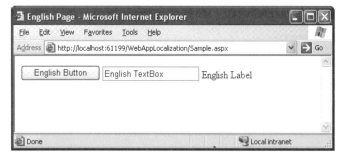

FIGURE 9.9. Results of running the localized page under the default culture

```
<%@ page language="VB" Title="English Page" UICulture="auto"
       meta:resourceKey="PageResource1" %>
```

The UICulture attribute is required so that ASP.NET will automatically read the culture information passed from the browser. That's it—we have localized a page without any code!

Figure 9.9 shows the result of running this page with the default culture.

At runtime, the .resx files are compiled to a binary and added to an assembly. The Resource Manager under the hood performs the resource lookup. To see how the culture-specific resources are used, you will need to set your browser's culture accordingly. You can set the browser's culture to French by following these steps.

1. In Microsoft Internet Explorer, choose Internet Options from the Tools menu.
2. In the General tab of the Internet Options dialog box, click the Languages button.
3. Click Add on the Language Preference dialog box.
4. From the list of languages, select French (France) [fr].
5. Click OK to close the Add Language dialog box.
6. In the Language Preference dialog box, select French (France) [fr] from the list of languages, and then click Move Up.
7. Click OK to close the Language Preference dialog box.
8. Click OK to close the Internet Options dialog box.

Once French is set as the browser's culture, the page will automatically read resource information from the Sample.aspx.fr.resx file, and French contents will be displayed when the page is refreshed in Internet Explorer. Figure 9.10 shows the result of running the page with the language set to

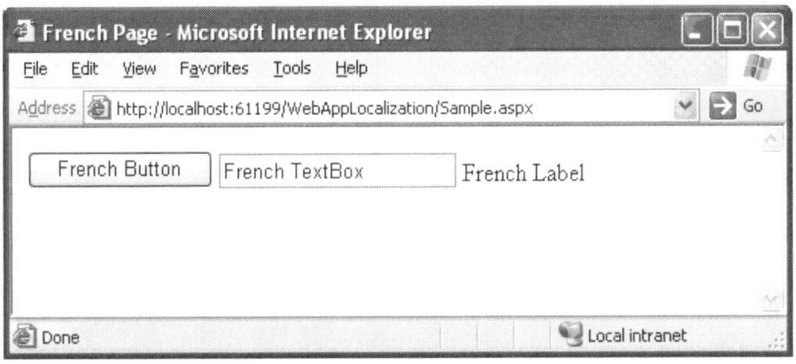

FIGURE 9.10. Results of running the localized page under the French culture

French culture. If you change the browser's language to any other language, the page will not find a corresponding .resx file and will revert to the culture-neutral .resx file (the file in English).

You can support more cultures by creating corresponding .resx files. You can then send the files to localizers along with a read-only version of the source Web page for context. When the files are translated, you can add the final .resx files to the LocalResources folder. You can then run the page under various browser settings to verify the localization.

Visual Studio 2005 greatly simplifies the localization of a page using implicit expressions, page-level or local-level resources, and declarative programming.

Note: Design view of a localized page always uses the culture-neutral resource file and reflects the ASP.NET runtime behavior. While the ASP.NET runtime supports application-level resources, Visual Studio 2005 does not provide WYSIWYG support of application-level resources at this time.

Using Explicit Expressions

In the previous subsection, we demonstrated localization using implicit expressions. Another way to localize Web pages is to take advantage of a new feature in ASP.NET 2.0 called *expressions*. Expressions allow you to declaratively assign values to just about any property of a control or subobject in a Web page. You can localize a control or a subobject on a per-property basis by using the new expression syntax:

```
<%$ Resources:
    [NameSpace, ClassName.]ResourceKey[, DefaultDesignerValue] %>
```

This expression type is called *explicit expression*. Explicit expressions are useful for localizing those properties that are not marked as localizable. For example, you can use explicit expression to localize the `BackColor` property of a button.

To localize a `BackColor` property value by using explicit expressions, you need to define a color resource. The new resource needs to be defined in all appropriate resource files, including the culture-neutral resource file.

Any resource key/value pair that is manually added to a culture-specific resource file should be added to the culture-neutral resource file as well.

Listing 9.11 shows how to add a color resource, `MyColor`, to the `.resx` files using data and value elements. The color in the culture-neutral resource file is set to `Teal`, and in the French file it is set to `Blue`.

LISTING 9.11. Additions to Resource Files to Support a Color Resource

```
Sample.aspx.resx
. . .
  <data name="MyColor">
    <value xml:space="preserve">Teal</value>
  </data>
</root>

Sample.aspx.fr.resx
. . .
  <data name="MyColor">
    <value xml:space="preserve">Blue</value>
  </data>
</root>
```

Note that `MyColor` is of type `System.String`. ASP.NET 2.0 will automatically type-convert the string value to the destination type as required.

This resource can now be used to change a color property of any control between cultures. In Visual Studio 2005, this resource can be applied by using the Expressions dialog box shown in Figure 9.11. You can display the Expressions dialog box by clicking on the Expand button in the Expressions box in the Property Browser for `Button1`.

Each localized property is indicated by a pink-colored icon. Clicking OK in the Expressions dialog box creates an explicit expression that assigns the resource to the property you are editing:

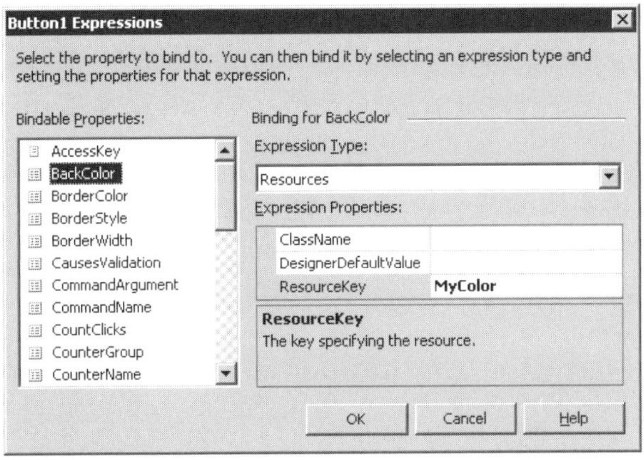

FIGURE 9.11. Setting the BackColor property by using the Expressions dialog box

```
<asp:Button ID="Button1"
    BackColor="<%$ Resources:MyColor %>"
    Runat="Server" Text="English Button"
    meta:resourceKey="ButtonResource1" />
```

This expression indicates that the `BackColor` property will use the `MyColor` resource. The exact value of the resource will be determined by what resource file the page selects, based on the browser's culture at runtime. ASP.NET 2.0 will convert the resource value to a value of `System.Drawing.Color` type and use it in Visual Studio 2005 and in the .NET Framework.

Once again, any property can be localized without writing any code, this time by using an explicit expression. Figure 9.12 displays the result under the French culture.

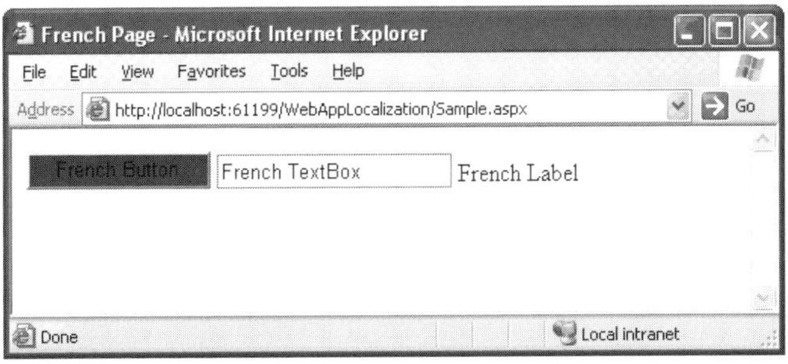

FIGURE 9.12. Results after using an explicit expression

As you might have guessed by now, you could have typed the explicit expression syntax in source view instead of using the Expressions dialog box. Expressions are not case sensitive.

Using Application Resources

Local resources are great for storing unique resource keys for individual Web pages. However, shared resources are best stored in a type of resources called *application resources*. All application-level resources are stored in a `Resources` folder at the Web application level. You can then use them by specifying the namespace and/or class name in explicit expression syntax.

Here is how to use a shared resource called `MySharedKey` in `Shared.resx` (or its culture variants) to set a button's `Text` property:

```
<asp:Button ID="Button1"
    BackColor="<%$Resources: MyColor%>" Runat="Server"
    Text="<%$Resources: Shared, MySharedKey, 'Sample Text'"
    meta:resourceKey="ButtonResource1" />
```

In this example, the `Text` property is set using an explicit expression. However, the expression uses an expanded syntax that includes the name of the resource file (`Shared`), the resource (`MySharedKey`), and a default designer value (`"Sample Text"`) that is used by the Visual Studio 2005 Designer if the resource cannot be found. By using this expanded syntax, you can point a property to resources in an application resource file, which in turn allows you to use the same resource file from multiple pages.

You can use both implicit and explicit expressions together as shown in the example. In such cases, implicit expressions have higher precedence over explicit expressions. In other words, the .NET Framework will use the value of `ButtonResource1.Text` instead of `MySharedKey.Text` to set the `Text` property.

In the example, the `SoftKeyLabel` and `Visible` properties of the button will use the `ButtonResource1` resource key from the local resource file. The `BackColor` property will use the `MyColor` resource from the local resource file, and the `Text` property will use the `MySharedKey` value in the application resource file named `Shared`. The default value, `"Sample Text"`, will be used if `MySharedKey` is not found. You can create as many culture-specific application resource files as needed. Note that you can programmatically access both page-level and application-level resources.

Localizing Static Content

ASP.NET 2.0 also supports localization of static text markup. It is as easy as enclosing the static contents in the new `<Localize>` element. Listing 9.12 shows a simple example.

LISTING 9.12. Localizing Static Content by Using the `<Localize>` Element

```
<p>
<localize Runat="server">This will be localized</localize>
While this will not be!
</p>
...
```

After you've enclosed the text to localize in a `<localize>` element, you can execute the Generate Local Resource command, as described earlier. The command will create a resource key for the `<localize>` element, encode the text enclosed by the `<localize>` element, and store the result as the value for the resource key in the page's culture-neutral resource file.

You can work with the `<localize>` element in source view only. The element can contain only static contents; don't enclose ASP.NET Web controls in the element. Any nonstatic content will be treated as static content and pushed to the resource file. Any HTML inside the element will be encoded and pushed to the resource file.

Exempting Controls from Localization

If you don't want to localize a control or `page` directive, all you need to do is set the `meta:localize` attribute to `false`:

```
<asp:Button ID="Button1" Runat="server"
            Text="Don't Localize Me!"
            meta:localize="false" />
```

The button will display the default text `"Don't Localize Me!"` for all cultures. When you use the Generate Local Resource command, no resource key will be generated for controls with the `meta:localize` attribute set to `false`.

Hiding Controls at Runtime

In some cases, instead of localizing the properties of a control, you might want to simply hide the control altogether for some cultures. For example, perhaps your Web page contains a graphic that you want to show for some cultures but not for others. To hide a control under a specific culture, set the resource value of the control's `Visible` property to `False`. In the first example, if you would like to hide the text box for the French culture, set the value of `TextBoxResource1.Visible` to `False` in the `Sample.aspx.fr.resx` file. It is as simple as that! The page will take care of the rest at runtime—the `TextBox` control will be hidden for French culture requests but displayed in all other cultures.

What Expression Type to Use, and When

In general, the ASP.NET team recommends using implicit expressions to localize a control or subobject. The shortened notation allows you to declare the resource key at the control level instead of having to define an expression for each property of the control. However, implicit expressions can be used only with local resources, meaning that you must have a set of `.resx` files for each separate page.

Remember that you will need to use explicit expressions to localize a property of a control or object using values from shared resources.

Either expression type can be used with the page directive. You can combine implicit and explicit forms of expressions for the same control. As you saw in one of the earlier examples, such a combination might be useful to localize a property that is not localized by default.

Table 9.14 outlines how to use different expression types with different resource types.

Table 9.14. Use of Different Expression and Resource Types

	Can Refer to Local Resources?	Can Refer to Application Resources?
Implicit expressions	Yes	No
Explicit expressions	Yes	Yes

User-Selectable Localization

There may be times when you prefer your users to be able to select the locale in which they want to view the site. Typical implementations have a page showing flags for the languages supported; selecting the appropriate flag will set the culture. In ASP.NET 2.0 this can be accomplished by using personalization and storing the selected culture as a property of the Profile. Setting the culture as each page loads, or in a master page, is not possible in the beta release, but there's an excellent solution using one of the application events. For example, consider Listing 9.13, where the CurrentCulture and CurrentUICulture for the CurrentThread are set to a culture defined in the Language property of the Profile.

LISTING 9.13. Setting Localization from Code

```
<%@ application language="VB" %>

<%@ import Namespace="System.Threading" %>
<%@ import namespace="System.Globalization" %>

<script runat="server">

  Sub Application_PostAcquireRequestState(ByVal sender As Object, _
                                  ByVal e As System.EventArgs)

    Dim ci As CultureInfo

    If Profile.Language Is Nothing Then
      ci = New CultureInfo("en-us")
    Else
      ci = New CultureInfo(Profile.Language)
    End If

    Thread.CurrentThread.CurrentUICulture = ci
    Thread.CurrentThread.CurrentCulture = ci

  End Sub

</script>
```

Programmatic Access of Resources

Local resources are not strongly typed, but you can programmatically access them through Resource Manager or a helper method, GetPageResourceObject. Application resources are strongly typed, and you can access them by using the Resources namespace or the GetAppResourceObject method. Listing 9.14 shows a simple example.

LISTING 9.14. Programmatically Accessing Local and Page Resources

```
<script runat="server">
  Sub Page_Load()

    Button1.Text = _
        GetPageResourceObject("ButtonResource1.Text").ToString()

    Label1.Text = Resources.Shared.MySharedKey

    TextBox1.Text = _
        GetAppResourceObject("Shared", "MySharedKey").ToString()

  End Sub
</script>
```

Extensibility

Sources for resource keys and their values are not limited to the file-based
.resx format. You can use ASP.NET 2.0's rich extensibility mechanisms to
store and retrieve the resource keys and their values from a database or
any custom file format. Using a database makes it easier to centralize the
resources for the application across many servers in a Web farm and to ensure central consistency.

Extensibility is supported in both the .NET Framework and Visual Studio
2005. You can write and read resource values from a custom source using the
ResourceProviderFactory and DesignTimeResourceProviderFactory
classes.

Web Resources

Along with their assemblies, control developers often have to supply additional static files, such as stylesheets and images. With ASP.NET 2.0's
new resources model, these static files can now be embedded into assemblies as resources. This is achieved through the addition of the
WebResourceAttribute (from System.Web.UI), as shown in the following
example:

```
<assembly:WebResource("MyImage.gif", "image/gif")>

Public Class MyControl
  ' control code here
End Class
```

This simply enables the image to be available as a Web resource. Within the control code, the resource can be accessed like this:

```
Protected Overrides Sub CreateChildControls()

  Controls.Clear()

  Dim img As New Image()

  img.ImageUrl = GetWebResourceUrl("MyImage.gif")

  Me.Controls.Add(img)

End Sub
```

At compile time the resource can be embedded into the assembly:

```
vbc /t:library /out:MyControl.dll
    /r:System.dll,System.web.dll
    /res:MyImage.gif,MyImage.gif
```

The Web resources feature is not limited just to images. For example, to embed JavaScript for client-side support, you could add

```
<assembly:WebResource("MyScript.js", "text/javascript", True)>

Public Class MyControl
  ' control code here
End Class
```

The third parameter for this attribute indicates that the Web resource parser should be invoked for the resource (which it isn't by default). This ensures that the embedded resource is parsed and will be correct when used by the client. You might notice that this technique is used for JavaScript by ASP.NET pages and certain controls, such as the `TreeView`.

Embedded Web resources can also be accessed from within ASP.NET pages. For example:

```
<script runat="server">
  Sub Page_Load()

    img1.Image = Page.GetWebResourceUrl(GetType(MyControl), _
                                       "MyImage.gif")

  End Sub
</script>
```

Note that this example uses a second form of `GetWebResourceUrl`, which applies to the `Page` object. Here the type of control for which the Web resource is being fetched is also required. Notice that the control type is the custom control, not `Image`, as the resource is part of the custom control itself.

SUMMARY

In this chapter we've looked at several topics that deal with ASP.NET pages. We first looked at cross-page posting and how some new properties have made it easy to use the standard postback architecture to post to another page and then from that other page to easily access the details of the previous page.

We then looked at improvements to validation, showing how the introduction of validation groups has enabled validation to be limited to selections of controls. This is particularly useful when dealing with wizards, which provide a simple way to create multistep pages. Because all of the controls exist on the same page, there's no problem about having to store the values from the previous step, and the validation groups allow each step to be validated as a whole but separately from the other steps.

We then looked at URL mapping, showing how virtual URLs can be mapped to real pages while preserving the original URL. This allows for easier site navigation without the work of constructing complex site hierarchies.

We then moved to the client-side features, first looking at simple improvements such as setting the default button and the focus of controls. This took us into improvements for registering client-side script blocks and then into the client callback architecture, which brings a powerful way to run server code without involving a postback.

We then looked at the form and page features, such as improvements to form and button focus, exposing more page features via properties (such as the page header and title), and how the controls now render xHTML output. We also covered the new and changed `page` directives and the page event life cycle, showing where the new events fit into the event order.

We then examined the site and page counters features, which allow simple tracking of page counts and site redirections. Although not an enterprise-level reporting tool, these features provide easy-to-use reporting capabilities.

Finally, we covered the topic of resources, first looking at localization and how the `Resources` directory can be used to store localized versions of text for pages. Through simple property settings, these localized strings can be automatically used on pages, providing an easy way to offer Web sites that support multiple cultures. The combination of implicit and explicit expressions, local- and application-level resources, the `<localize>` element, and extensibility provides a power-packed new functionality to handle multiple cultures in your Web pages and applications.

In closing, we looked at how other types of resources can be used within an application, allowing control creators to store local resources, such as images and client script, within their control.

Now it's time to take a look at the new controls within ASP.NET 2.0 and how to cater to mobile devices.

10

The New Browser and Mobile Device Controls

I N VERSION 1.X OF THE .NET FRAMEWORK, the core controls from the `WebControls` and `HtmlControls` namespaces were "hard-coded" to create HTML output. This makes sense because most ASP.NET pages are aimed at standard Web browsers that recognize only HTML (albeit different versions, such as HTML 3.2 or HTML 4.0).

However, the growth in the use of mobile devices that don't recognize HTML, such as cellular phones that connect to the network through the Wireless Access Protocol (WAP), means that Microsoft has had to consider how ASP.NET can support such devices. The result for version 1.0 of the Framework was the Microsoft Mobile Internet Toolkit (MMIT), which was released as a separate install that added the classes required to the Framework class library.

In version 1.1 of the Framework, the MMIT controls became the ASP.NET Mobile Controls and were integrated into the class library rather than being a separate install, but this still doesn't solve the real underlying issues. In particular, what is the best way to make it easier for developers to create pages that work on different types of client devices without having to learn new programming techniques and new APIs, as well as figure out the complex matrix of capabilities of the multitude of device types in use today?

The answer lies in a fundamental redesign of the underlying architecture of the whole ASP.NET control set to provide better device-specific support for all types of clients, without changing the way that the controls are used or their existing interfaces and declarative syntax.

And, of course, there are many new controls added in version 2.0 of ASP.NET. Several have already been discussed in earlier chapters; the rest are covered here. Enhanced features for existing controls are covered in Chapter 11.

This chapter covers the following topics:

- The issues of programming for different types of client devices
- The unified control and adapter architecture in ASP.NET 2.0
- An overview and listing of all the new controls in ASP.NET 2.0
- A detailed look at the new controls not covered elsewhere
- The controls and attributes specific to mobile devices

We'll start with a look at the whole issue of supporting different types of client devices.

Programming for Different Types of Devices

The main issue with trying to write pages that target multiple devices lies in knowing exactly what each device expects to receive. For example, most mobile phones expect the content to be Wireless Markup Language (WML), of which there are several versions in current use. The devices connect to the Internet through a telecom provider's WAP gateway, which takes the output from a Web site and compiles it into a special format to deliver over what is currently a very narrow bandwidth connection to the device. Then it does the converse with the page requests and any posted content from the client, converting that back into standard HTTP format to send to the server.

However, there are several versions of this gateway software in use with different telecom providers, and each version may treat the content slightly differently during the compilation and decompilation processes. Add to this the huge number of different phones and devices currently available (which support different versions or different implementations of WML or other languages, such as cHTML) and it soon becomes a real challenge to decide what output to send to each client.

The Microsoft Mobile Internet Toolkit

The MMIT went a long way toward solving these issues by including support for a large number of popular devices. You use the special controls that are part of the MMIT to build a page, and these controls interact with the page framework to detect the device type (and in some cases the gateway) and generate content that will produce the correct output in the current device. At the last count, over 200 device combinations were documented.

To understand how each of the controls in version 2.0 of ASP.NET generates the appropriate output, it's useful to see how the MMIT was designed. One way to change the output generated by a control is to hard-code within it the equivalent of one (or more) huge `case` statements. However, this is prone to errors and difficult to implement successfully, and it makes updating the control as new devices appear extremely cumbersome.

Device Adapters

Instead, the MMIT uses **device adapters** to generate the output. A set of device adapters (one for each markup language) is available, and all the controls can use these device adapters to generate output suitable for a particular device. The device adapter overrides some of the events in the life cycle of the control, in particular the `Render` event.

This allows the device adapter to generate the appropriate output when the page recursively calls the `Render` method of each control and its child controls. It means that the control doesn't have to worry about the output format, while the device adapter doesn't have to know what the control actually does.

Device adapters may also have to override other events to ensure that the device is properly supported. For example, they may have to carry out specific actions for the load or save events for the viewstate of the page. (Many mobile devices require special handling of the viewstate because limitations in the total size of the posted values prevent it from being stored in a hidden control within the page.) They may also have to handle special situations for a postback, including issues where redirection to another page is handled differently in mobile devices.

Microsoft has moved all the ASP.NET server controls to a new unified control and adapter architecture. This was part of the original intentions for ASP.NET, but it was not fully developed in time to be implemented in version 1.0.

The set of ASP.NET Mobile Controls available in version 1.1 is still in the Framework, so existing pages that use them will work just as before in version 2.0.

The Unified Control and Adapter Architecture

Effectively, the new page framework in version 2.0 works like the special MobilePage class that is used in the MMIT for version 1.x. It does so using a **page adapter** that exposes a full range of information about the capabilities of the current client. This information includes things like the device type and version, the kind of markup language it expects to receive, and more detailed data such as the screen size, support for scripts, cookies and frames, and much more.

Then, each control that will produce output tailored for the device uses a **control adapter** that generates the appropriate markup output to suit the current device. This process is often referred to as **adaptive rendering**. Externally, to the developer, very little changes other than the addition of a few extra properties on the controls and a change of the control name prefix for the mobile controls from mobile to asp. This unified architecture therefore provides several advantages.

- There is no longer any need to make an initial design time decision as to whether the page should support mobile devices (though other factors such as the physical size of the page must still be considered).
- The developer does not have to learn the API of different sets of controls for standard and mobile pages or install a separate toolkit.
- Existing MMIT (version 1.x) applications will run on ASP.NET version 2.0 without any reconfiguration or code changes because of the continued use of the ASP.NET Mobile Control classes instead of the new adaptive controls (i.e., they use the mobile namespace prefix rather than the asp namespace prefix).
- It makes it much easier to create development tools that can use and display the output of the controls for the various devices that are supported.
- The developer will generally have to write less code than with the MMIT controls in version 1.x because most of the new rich ("high-functionality") controls will work in pages targeted at mobile devices.

However, there is one issue to watch out for. Adaptive rendering requires that the ASP.NET controls are located on a server-side form (a `<form>` element with the `runat="server"` attribute) when accessed by a WML-enabled device. A `HyperLink`, for example, generates an error if not placed on a form, while a `Label` is ignored and not displayed in the page. Standard HTML browsers require a server-side form only if controls participate in a postback.

As an example of how adaptive rendering works, take a look at the ASP.NET code in Listing 10.1, which displays some text and uses a `Calendar` control to provide a date selection feature.

LISTING 10.1. Using an ASP.NET 2.0 Calendar Control

```
<%@ Page Language="VB" %>
<html>
<head>
  <style>
    .Normal {font-family:Arial; font-size:xsmall}
  </style>
</head>
<body>
  <form runat="server">
    <p class="Normal">
    Select a date:<br />
    <asp:Calendar id="MyCal" cssClass="MyStyle" runat="server" />
    </p>
  </form>
</body>
</html>
```

You can see that it uses only "ordinary" HTML, including the `<html>` and `<body>` elements, a style definition, and two ASP.NET server controls. There is the `Calendar` control itself plus a `<form>` control that the `Calendar` requires to perform postbacks when a date is selected or the month is changed. Both of these server controls are standard ASP.NET 2.0 controls.

When viewed in an ordinary HTML browser, the page generates standard HTML (see Listing 10.2). For clarity, we've removed some of the sections that are not pertinent to our discussion.

LISTING 10.2. The Output from the Calendar Control in Internet Explorer

```html
<html>
<head>
  <style>
    .Normal {font-family:Arial; font-size:xsmall}
  </style>
</head>
<body>
  <form method="post" action="calendar.aspx" id="_ctl0">
    ...
    <p class="Normal">
    Select a date:<br />
    <table id="MyCal" class="MyStyle" cellspacing="0" cellpadding="2"
    border="0" style="border-width:1px;border-style:solid;border-
    collapse:collapse;">
    <tr><td colspan="7" style="background-color:Silver;">
    <table class="MyStyle" cellspacing="0" border="0"
    style="width:100%;border-collapse:collapse;">
    <tr><td style="width:15%;">
    <a href="javascript:__doPostBack('MyCal','V1155')"
    style="color:Black">&lt;</a></td><td align="Center"
    style="width:70%;">April 2003</td><td align="Right"
    style="width:15%;">
    <a href="javascript:__doPostBack('MyCal','V1216')"
    style="color:Black">&gt;</a></td>
    ...
    </table>
    </p>
  </form>
</body>
</html>
```

Figure 10.1 shows that this gives the kind of output you would expect in Internet Explorer.

However, if you open the same page in a mobile device, WML output is generated. You'll see output like that shown in Figure 10.2 (depending on which emulator you are using). Selecting the [Calendar] link causes the control to provide a multistep menu for selecting a date.

The point to note is that while the original page was written as though we expected the client to accept HTML (e.g., we enclosed the page content in an <html> element and used the standard ASP.NET Form and Calendar server controls rather than those from the MMIT), the output has been converted automatically into the correct WML syntax for our mobile phone client. Listing 10.3 shows the actual WML sent to an emulator client.

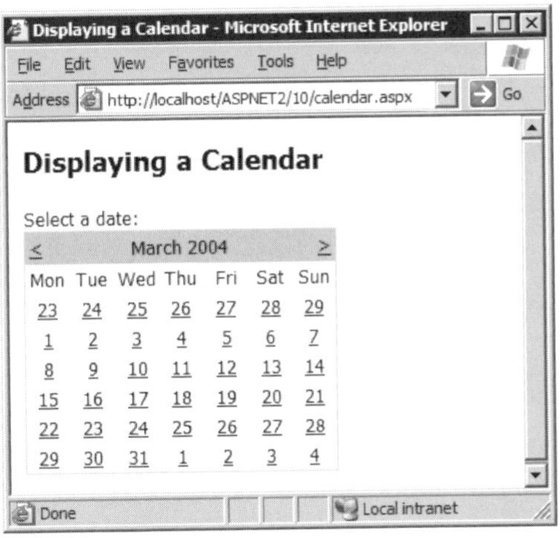

FIGURE 10.1. The Calendar control viewed in Internet Explorer

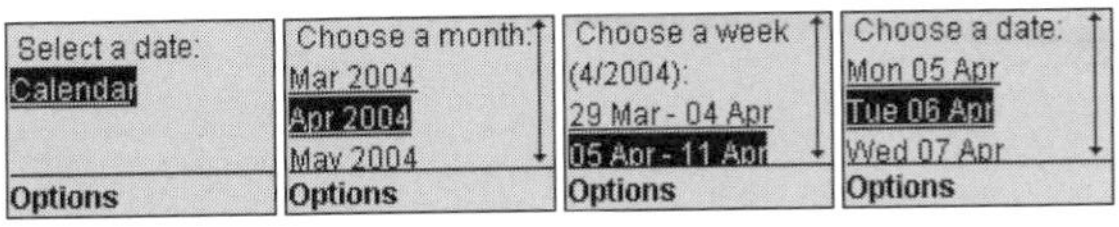

FIGURE 10.2. The Calendar control viewed in a mobile device

LISTING 10.3. The Output from the Calendar Control in a Mobile Device Emulator

```
<?xml version='1.0'?>
<!DOCTYPE wml PUBLIC '-//WAPFORUM//DTD WML 1.1//EN'
            'http://www.wapforum.org/DTD /wml_1.1.xml'>
<wml>
<head>
  <meta http-equiv="Cache-Control" content="max-age=0" forua="true"/>
</head>
<card>
  <onevent type="onenterforward">
    <refresh>
      <setvar name="mcsvt" value="" />
      <setvar name="mcsva" value="" />
    </refresh>
  </onevent>
  <onevent type="onenterbackward">
    <refresh>
      <setvar name="mcsvt" value="" />
      <setvar name="mcsva" value="" />
    </refresh>
  </onevent>
  <p>
  Select a date:<br/>
  <anchor title="Go">
    Calendar
```

continues

```
         <go href="/test/test2.aspx?__ufps=309633" method="post">
         <postfield name="__EVENTTARGET" value="MyCal" />
         <postfield name="__EVENTARGUMENT" value="1" />
         </go>
         </anchor>
         </p>
    </card>
    </wml>
```

It's clear that the controls, including the `Page` itself, have recognized the device and—through adaptive rendering—have generated the correct output to create the equivalent functionality in the mobile device. There is the correct `DOCTYPE` to identify the document type, and the `<html>` and `<body>` elements have been replaced by the appropriate `<wml>` and `<card>` elements. And the great thing is that it all happened automatically. There are no references to the MMIT in the source code for the page, no controls from the MMIT `mobile` namespace, and no code to tailor the output to suit this type of client.

This hugely powerful built-in feature of the page and control framework in ASP.NET 2.0 makes it a lot easier to create pages that work in different types of devices without having to explicitly design for this. For example, if you were using the MMIT in ASP.NET version 1.x, you would have to avoid using any HTML-specific elements that cause a syntax error in a WML device and use the specific MMIT controls instead of the ASP.NET core controls.

Browser Definitions

One of the issues discovered with the MMIT was that it added an extremely large section of browser definitions to the `machine.config` file. This could make working with `machine.config` cumbersome and also made simple updates to the definitions more complex than it really should be. In version 2.0, all browser definitions (including definitions for specific WAP gateways) have been moved to separate files that have the `.browser` file extension. They are stored in the `$windir\Microsoft.NET\Framework \[version]\Config\Browsers\` folder of the machine. These browser definition files follow the general format shown in Listing 10.4.

LISTING 10.4. The General Format of a Browser Definition File

```
<browsers>
  <browser id="device-name" parentID="family-type-to-inherit-from">
    <identification>
      <!-- Specifies how to identify this browser -->
    </identification>
```

```
<capture>
  <!-- Specifies additional HTTP header values to match -->
</capture>
<capabilities>
  <!-- Specifies capabilities values to set, for example -->
  <capability name="cookies" value="true" />
</capabilities>
<controlAdapters>
  <!-- Specifies control adapters to use for this browser -->
</controlAdapters>
  </browser>
</browsers>
```

A file named `Default.browser` defines the default values and capabilities for the base browser type and the more common manufacturer-specific values (such as Internet Explorer and Mozilla). These are referenced by the `id` and `parentID` attributes in each definition, creating a hierarchy of settings relevant to each browser.

All these files are compiled into a single compact representation when the Framework is installed. If a definition is updated, recompilation must be manually initiated by running the `aspnet_regbrowsers.exe` utility that is installed along with the Framework. An interesting possibility arising from this is that automated updates to browser definitions will be much easier to implement and might even become part of the Framework process in time.

> Any browser definitions within a `<browserCaps>` element in a `web.config` file are still recognized and are merged into the final set of definitions used by the Framework. However, any definitions in `machine.config` are ignored.

The BrowserCapabilities Class

Although the plumbing and implementation of the device detection system are different from version 1.0, its use is familiar in version 2.0. The current `Request` (`HttpRequest`) class exposes an instance of the `HttpBrowserCapabilities` class through its `Browser` property. This means that you can still write code that interrogates the browser capabilities properties, just as in version 1.0:

```
Dim sPlatform As String = Request.Browser("Platform")
```

Page Design and Device Support

Under the unified control and adapter architecture, all the ASP.NET standard server controls will change their behavior and the markup they generate depending on the type of device accessing the page. So does this mean that you can now build pages and even complete Web sites or applications that will work on any device? The answer is "yes," but—to a greater extent—you probably won't want to.

The reason has to do with the design of the page and how well it matches the devices it will be viewed on. Although the new 2.5G and 3G cellular phones are appearing, with increased bandwidth and screen size, the fundamental issues are related more to the actual rendered page versus available screen size, as well as the input devices available on the client.

For example, a common design for pages aimed at the traditional Web browser is multiple columns, separate navigation bars at the top or left, and a multitude of small text links or clickable images. This kind of page generally depends on the use of a mouse to navigate.

On the latest cellular phones there is generally no mouse, though there may be some kind of navigation pad. However, the majority of mobile phone devices use only simple text, perhaps up to 20 characters per line over six lines, and may not even be able to display images.

So, while a `Label`, `HyperLink`, or `Textbox` control can modify its behavior to suit the device and the markup language required, there is no real possibility of designing the layout of the entire page so that it "works" (in the usability sense) on all devices. And this is not the aim of the unified control and adapter architecture. Instead, it does allow you to build pages using the same techniques, tools, and programming model, but you will generally have to implement different versions of your Web applications to suit the different major categories of devices you want to support (probably one version for ordinary Web browsers and one version for mobile devices).

Device Filters

Even though the controls automatically tailor their output to suit the current device, it's useful to be able to adjust the output in specific ways to suit your own requirements. In version 2.0 of ASP.NET, this is accomplished by filtering on specific devices or on classes of devices. All you have to do is prefix a property or attribute within a control declaration with the device class or name.

For example, if there is a browser definition with `id="Nokia"` (which matches any Nokia device), you can change the text and display style of a

`Label` control for devices of this type simply by adding the device-specific attributes (see Listing 10.5).

LISTING 10.5. Using Device-Specific Attributes to Change Behavior

```
<asp:Label id="MyLabel" runat="server"
           Text="Welcome to our site"
           Nokia:Text="Time to upgrade your Nokia phone!"
           cssClass="StandardStyleClass"
           Nokia:cssClass="SpecialNokiaStyleClass" />
```

Device-Specific Templates

It's also possible to use the same approach to change the output from bound controls. A good example is where you want to display data in an HTML table. However, most mobile devices do not support tables, so the output has to be formatted in a different way for these devices. And, because of the limited screen area, you often need to provide more compact output, perhaps by omitting some of the columns.

The code in Listing 10.6 shows this concept in action. If for example, you have browser definitions for the device categories `HtmlBrowsers` and `WmlBrowsers`, you can use these to define different `HeaderTemplate`, `ItemTemplate`, and `FooterTemplate` sections for the `Repeater` control, depending on which of these categories the current device falls into.

LISTING 10.6. Using Device-Specific Templates to Change Behavior

```
<asp:Repeater runat="server" ...>

  <HtmlBrowsers:HeaderTemplate>
    <table>
      <tr><td>UserName</td><td>Address</td><td>Phone</td></tr>
  </HtmlBrowsers:HeaderTemplate>

  <HtmlBrowsers:ItemTemplate>
    <tr>
      <td><%# Container.DataItem("UserName") %></td>
      <td><%# Container.DataItem("Address") %></td>
      <td><%# Container.DataItem("Phone") %></td>
    </tr>
  </HtmlBrowsers:ItemTemplate>

  <WmlBrowsers:ItemTemplate>
    <asp:Panel runat="server">
      <%# Container.DataItem("UserName") %>
      <%# Container.DataItem("Phone") %>
    </asp:Panel>
  </WmlBrowsers:ItemTemplate>
```

continues

```
<HtmlBrowsers:FooterTemplate>
  </table>
</HtmlBrowsers:FooterTemplate>
```

```
</asp:Repeater>
```

When multiple browser definitions or device filters match the current client, the one that specifies the device with the most precision is chosen, though the settings specified in definitions from which this one inherits are also available if not overridden. For example, an Ericsson T86 phone will expose all the properties defined for a browser definition named `Ericsson T86` plus any that are not overridden here from a general definition aimed at all Ericsson devices, as well as any that are exposed from the `WmlBrowsers` definition.

Summary of the New Controls in ASP.NET 2.0

In addition to the switch to the unified control architecture, ASP.NET 2.0 provides many new controls. There are also enhancements to many of the existing controls, which we'll examine in detail in Chapter 11. This section summarizes all the controls that are completely new. We've divided them into six groups:

1. **Standard form- and page-based controls,** such as the bullet list and `FileUpload` controls
2. **Rich controls,** such as the `DynamicImage` control and the `Wizard` control
3. **Login and authentication controls,** used in conjunction with the ASP.NET authentication and access control features
4. **Navigation controls,** such as the tree view and site map controls, and **counters**
5. **Data access and display controls** designed to display relational data, XML data, and data held in other formats
6. **Mobile device controls,** such as the phone call and pagination controls

Standard Form- and Page-Based Controls

Several new controls are available for generating standard elements for use in a Web page, including some that generate elements for use in a `<form>` section.

- The `HtmlHead`, `HtmlTitle`, and `HtmlLink` controls can be used to generate server-side equivalents of the HTML `<head>`, `<title>`, and `<link>` elements while allowing server-side programming of their content.

- The `HtmlInputPassword`, `HtmlInputReset`, and `HtmlInputSubmit` controls make it easier to generate `<input>` elements that represent password boxes, Reset buttons, and Submit buttons.

- The `BulletedList` control creates either a `<ul>` or `<ol>` bullet list. It exposes properties that allow developers to specify the bullet type and the start number for numeric lists. It inherits from `ListControl`, so its use is familiar—including the ability to populate it using server-side data binding.

- The `FileUpload` control generates an `<input type="file">` element, allowing users to upload files to the server. On postback, it exposes properties that can be used to access the uploaded file stream.

- The `HiddenField` control generates an `<input type="hidden">` element and exposes its value on postback.

We look at all these controls in more detail later in this chapter.

Rich Controls

ASP.NET 1.0 contained several rich controls, and these proved to be a big hit with developers. We define a rich control as one that generates multiple different elements, and often client-side code as well, so as to create whole sections of UI or to provide features not supported by ordinary single HTML (or other) elements. A good example is the `Calendar` control, which generates a whole month of clickable dates and has navigation built in to scroll to other months. In ASP.NET 2.0, some exciting new rich controls are included in the Framework.

- The `DynamicImage` control automatically translates an image into the correct format for different devices. It can stream the bytes for an image from an external source via a `Byte` array, or use the Image Generation Service (described later in this chapter).

- The `ImageMap` control makes it easier to define client-side image maps and react to events that they raise.

- The `MultiView` and `View` controls provide the same kind of features seen in the Internet Explorer Web Controls pack that is available for ASP.NET 1.x. The new controls allow developers to create different blocks of UI and insert the appropriate one into the page at runtime.

- The `Wizard` control, which makes it easier to build multipage wizards that have the same look and feel as those encountered in non-Web applications.
- A range of Web Parts controls, which can be used to generate portal-style pages that can be customized by each visitor.

The Web Parts technology and the associated controls were covered in Chapter 8. We look at all the other controls listed above in more detail later in this chapter.

Login and Authentication Controls

ASP.NET introduced built-in authentication and access control features as part of the Framework. In ASP.NET 2.0, the way that you interact with the classes exposed by the Framework when creating secured pages or folders is much simpler. Instead of writing code, you can use the new login controls.

- The `Login` control presents the user with the customary Username and Password text boxes.
- The `LoginName` control displays the name of the currently authenticated user.
- The `LoginStatus` control displays the authentication status for the current user, such as Log In when not authenticated or Log Out when authenticated.
- The `LoginView` control provides two templates in which the UI for a section of the page is declared. The appropriate template content is displayed, depending on the authentication status of the current user.
- The `PasswordRecovery` control displays a three-step wizard that guides a user through the process of providing the details required to have a forgotten password sent to him or her.

All these controls were covered in detail in Chapter 6.

Navigation Controls and Counters

One area where there is no real support for developers in ASP.NET 1.x is when building effective navigation systems for a Web site or application. In ASP.NET 2.0, several new controls make it easier to build menus and other types of site navigation UIs. The new controls are listed below.

- The `TreeView` control generates a collapsible tree view in the browser.
- The `SiteMapDataSource` control exposes hierarchical XML data in a suitable format for data binding to navigation controls such as the `TreeView`.
- The `SiteMapPath` control displays the hierarchical path through the site's menu system to the current page and supports navigation between pages.
- The `Menu` control can be used to generate a range of interactive or static menu systems.

All these controls were covered in detail in Chapter 5.

Data Access and Display Controls

One of the major changes in the way pages that use separate sources of data are created in ASP.NET 2.0 is the provision of **data source controls.** This concept was originally pioneered in Web Matrix, which contained a simple data source control that makes server-side data binding much easier to achieve.

Web Matrix also included a new type of grid control, designed to make it easier to display the data exposed by a data source control. Several data source controls are included in version 2.0 of ASP.NET.

- The `SqlDataSource` control and `AccessDataSource` control provide read and update access to almost any type of relational database.
- The `ObjectDataSource` control provides access to data exposed through a strongly typed data layer, allowing *n*-tier techniques to be used.
- The `XmlDataSource` control exposes hierarchical formatted XML documents for data binding to controls that can display hierarchical data.
- The `DataSetDataSource` control exposes nonhierarchical ("flat") XML documents for data binding to grid and list controls.
- The `GridView`, `DetailsView`, and `FormView` controls can be data-bound to various data source controls and can display data in a range of ways. They automatically adapt their output to suit different types of browsers, mobile devices, or other user agents.

The data controls were covered in detail in Chapters 3 and 4.

Mobile Device Controls

Support for different types of client devices is now integrated into the `Page` framework, and all the controls from the `System.Web.UI.WebControls` namespace. However, some new controls are aimed primarily at particular types of devices, such as cellular phones.

- The `ContentPager` control works as part of the underlying page architecture to divide pages into separate sections for small-screen and mobile devices.
- The `PhoneLink` control can be used in phone-enabled devices to initiate a phone call to a specified number.

We look at these controls in more detail toward the end of this chapter.

The New Controls in Detail

With the exception of some specialist controls, such as the Web Parts controls, all the server controls in ASP.NET are implemented in two namespaces—`System.Web.UI.HtmlControls` and `System.Web.UI.WebControls`. The first of these contains the direct equivalents of the elements defined within HTML, and the properties of the controls mirror the attribute names for the elements.

The second set of controls, the ASP.NET Web Controls from the `WebControls` namespace, are task-centric controls whose class and property names reflect their purpose, rather than the more arbitrary and sometimes confusing set of properties in the classes from the `HtmlControls` namespace.

However, certain controls that you use on the vast majority of your Web pages are in the `HtmlControls` namespace, the perfect example being the `HtmlForm` control that generates a server-side `<form>` element. Although Microsoft has generally focused more on the controls from the `WebControls` namespace, where there are several exciting new controls in version 2.0, there are some new controls in the `HtmlControls` namespace as well.

We look at the new classes in the `HtmlControls` namespace in the next section, and then devote the remainder of the chapter to the new controls from the `WebControls` namespace.

New Controls within the HtmlControls Namespace

In ASP.NET 1.x, developers are often faced with the task of dynamically interacting with elements on a Web page that are not implemented as specific server controls. Examples are the `<body>`, `<head>`, and `<link>` elements. In version 2.0, new server controls within the `HtmlControls` namespace implement these elements.

The other types of controls used regularly in Web pages are the ubiquitous Reset and Submit buttons. Although these can be created using an ASP.NET `Button` control, many developers still prefer to use `HtmlInputButton` and specify the type. For example:

```
<input type="submit" value="Send" runat="server" />
<input type="reset" value="Clear" runat="server" />
```

In version 2.0, you can use specific classes instead. They expose properties that mirror the attributes of these types of `<input>` elements, but you no longer need to specify the `type` property or attribute. Finally, there is a new control to implement a password entry field (a text box that displays asterisks as you enter a value). Again, this does not require the `type` property or attribute to be specified.

Table 10.1 summarizes the six new `HtmlControl` classes, showing their control-specific properties. Because all descend from `Control` or `HtmlControl`, they also, of course, expose the standard set of properties, methods, and events of the base classes as well.

TABLE 10.1. New Controls in the HtmlControls Namespace

Control	Description
HtmlHead	Generates an HTML `<head>` element in a Web page. Descended from the `System.Web.UI.Control` class, so other elements can be inserted into its `Controls` collection. Adds the following six properties to the standard set of properties exposed by `Control`:

• `Attributes`: A reference to a collection of all the HTML attributes for this control.

• `Disabled`: A `Boolean` value that indicates whether the control is disabled.

• `Style`: A `String` that is rendered as the `style` attribute of the control.

• `TagName`: A `String` that is the HTML element name, in this case, `"head"`.

• `InnerHtml`: A `String` that is the entire content of the element and any child elements, including any HTML element tags.

• `InnerText`: A `String` that is the entire content of the element and any child elements, excluding any HTML element tags. |

continues

TABLE 10.1. New Controls in the HtmlControls Namespace (continued)

Control	Description
HtmlInputPassword	Generates an HTML `<input type="password">` element. Has the following properties, in addition to the standard set inherited from `Control`:

- `Attributes`: A reference to a collection of all the HTML attributes for this control.
- `Disabled`: A `Boolean` value that indicates whether the control is disabled.
- `Style`: A `String` that is rendered as the `style` attribute of the control.
- `TagName`: A `String` that is the HTML element name, in this case `"input"`.
- `Name`: A `String` that is used as the `id` and `name` attributes of the element.
- `Type`: A `String` that is used as the `type` attribute of the element, in this case, `"password"`.
- `Value`: A read-only `String` that is the value entered by the user following a postback. You cannot set the content of a password text box in server-side code.
- `MaxLength`: An `Integer` that is the maximum number of characters that can be typed into the control by the user, used to set the `maxlength` attribute.
- `Size`: An `Integer` that is the size of the control as displayed on the page, as a number of characters, used to set the `size` attribute.

The `HtmlInputPassword` control also exposes the same event added to the `TextBox` control in version 2.0:

- `ServerChange`: Raised on the server when a postback occurs and the value has been changed since the page was last created.

Control	Description
HtmlInputReset	Generates an HTML `<input type="reset">` element. Has the following properties, in addition to the standard set inherited from `Control`:

- `Attributes`: A reference to a collection of all the HTML attributes for this control.
- `Disabled`: A `Boolean` value that indicates whether the control is disabled.
- `Style`: A `String` that is rendered as the `style` attribute of the control.
- `TagName`: A `String` that is the HTML element name, in this case `"input"`.
- `Name`: A `String` that is used as the `id` and `name` attributes of the element.
- `Type`: A `String` that is used as the `type` attribute of the element, in this case `"reset"` (or, in the case of the `HtmlInputSubmit` control, `"submit"`).

TABLE 10.1. New Controls in the HtmlControls Namespace (continued)

Control	Description
`HtmlInputReset` (continued)	• `Value`: A `String` that is used as the caption of the button.
	• `CausesValidation`: A `Boolean` value that specifies whether activating this control will cause any validation controls in its validation group to check the value.
	• `ValidationGroup`: The validation group that this control is a member of. Validation groups are discussed in Chapter 9.
	The `HtmlInputReset` control also exposes the same event added to the other HTML button-type controls in version 2.0:
	• `ServerClick`: Raised on the server when the button is clicked.
`HtmlInputSubmit`	Generates an HTML `<input type="submit">` element. Has the same set of interface members as the `HtmlInputReset` control.
`HtmlLink`	Generates an HTML `<link>` element in a Web page. Has the following five properties:
	• `Attributes`: A reference to a collection of all the HTML attributes for this control.
	• `Disabled`: A `Boolean` value that indicates whether the control is disabled.
	• `Style`: A `String` that is rendered as the `style` attribute of the control.
	• `TagName`: A `String` that is the HTML element name, in this case `"link"`.
	• `Href`: A `String` that is the URL of the linked document or resource.
	Other attributes (such as `rel` and `type` for a stylesheet) must be set using the `Attributes` collection.
`HtmlTitle`	Generates an HTML `<title>` element in a Web page. Has the following five properties:
	• `Attributes`: A reference to a collection of all the HTML attributes for this control.
	• `Disabled`: A `Boolean` value that indicates whether the control is disabled.
	• `Style`: A `String` that is rendered as the `style` attribute of the control.
	• `TagName`: A `String` that is the HTML element name, in this case `"title"`.
	• `Text`: A `String` that is the text to be inserted into the `<title>` element.

Using the New HtmlHead, HtmlLink, and HtmlTitle Classes

In ASP.NET 1.x, you can declare an HTML `<head>`, `<link>`, or `<title>` element in a page and add the `runat="server"` attribute to have them generated as controls on the server and therefore be accessible in your server-side code. However, because there are no server controls specifically designed to implement these elements, in ASP.NET 1.x the `HtmlGenericControl` is used instead.

In ASP.NET 2.0, the new `HtmlHead`, `HtmlLink`, and `HtmlTitle` controls are automatically used instead of the `HtmlGenericControl`, and the task-specific properties of these new controls can be used to directly set the values of attributes for the elements when rendered to the client. You can also generate instances of these controls dynamically (usually in the `Page_Load` event) and insert them into the control tree as you would with any other ASP.NET server control.

Listing 10.7 shows how the `HtmlHead`, `HtmlLink`, and `HtmlTitle` controls can be used. In this case, the `<head>` and `<title>` elements are declared in the page with an `id` and the `runat="server"` attribute. There is no content declared within the `<title>` element. However, code in the `Page_Load` event can set the `Text` property of the `HtmlTitle` element at runtime, as shown in Listing 10.7.

LISTING 10.7. Using the New HtmlHead, HtmlLink, and HtmlTitle Controls

```
<html>
<head id="MyHead" runat="server">
<title id="MyTitle" runat="server" />
</head>
<body>
... rest of page here ...
</body>
</html>

<script runat="server">

Sub Page_Load()

  ' set Text property of HtmlTitle control already declared in page
  MyTitle.Text = "Using the New HtmlControls"

  ' add new HtmlLink to HtmlHead control already declared in page
  Dim oLink As New HtmlLink()
  oLink.Href = "style.css"
  MyHead.Controls.Add(oLink)

  ' have to add other attributes for a stylesheet link directly
  ' these are not exposed as properties for the control
```

```
oLink.Attributes.Add("rel", "stylesheet")
oLink.Attributes.Add("title", "Main Stylesheet")
oLink.Attributes.Add("type", "text/css")

</script>
```

The `HtmlHead` control that implements the `<head>` element is a container control and has a `Controls` collection. This means that you can add content to it either by generating new control instances and adding them to the `Controls` collection or by simply generating a `String` that contains the declarative HTML and content you want and then using it to set the `InnerHtml` property of the `HtmlHead` control.

The example code generates a new instance of an `HtmlLink` element and sets the `Href` property to the name of the stylesheet for this page. However, to add any other required attributes, you have to add them to the `Attributes` collection directly. The code in Listing 10.7 adds the `rel`, `title`, and `type` attributes and then inserts the new `HtmlLink` control instance into the page by adding it to the `Controls` collection of the `HtmlHead` control.

Listing 10.8 shows the resulting output that is generated from the `HtmlHead`, `HtmlLink`, and `HtmlTitle` controls (formatted with the addition of line breaks so that you can see it more easily).

LISTING 10.8. The Output Generated by the HtmlHead, HtmlLink, and HtmlTitle Controls

```
<html>
<head id="MyHead">
<link href="style.css" rel="stylesheet"
      title="Main Stylesheet" type="text/css">
<title>Using the New HtmlControls</title>
</head>
<body>
...
```

Using the New HtmlInputPassword, HtmlInputSubmit, and HtmlInputReset Classes

The new `HtmlInputPassword`, `HtmlInputSubmit`, and `HtmlInputReset` controls make it easy to generate password entry fields, Submit buttons, and Reset buttons, especially when generating instances of the controls dynamically in your server-side code. Listing 10.9 shows the entire `<form>` section of an ASP.NET page, containing a normal ASP.NET `TextBox` control, a `CheckBox` control, and a `Label` control that has viewstate disabled so that it can be used for interactive messages without retaining any previous text.

LISTING 10.9. A Form for Demonstrating the New HTML Input Controls

```
<form id="MyForm" runat="server">

  An ordinary text box:
  <asp:TextBox id="MyText" runat="server" /><p />
  <asp:CheckBox id="chkPostReset" Text="PostBack from Reset Button"
             AutoPostBack="True" runat="server" /><p />
  <asp:Label id="lblResult" EnableViewState="False"
             runat="server" /><p />

</form>
```

The Page_Load event handler can then add instances of the three new controls to the page, along with some extra formatting elements such as the caption for the password field and a <p /> element to keep the display looking tidy. Listing 10.10 shows the Page_Load event handler. You can see that each control is instantiated and relevant properties set before being added to the Controls collection of the <form> in the page. Server-side event handlers are also attached to the ServerChange event of the password field and the ServerClick event of the Submit button, specifying event handlers named PasswordChange and SubmitClick, respectively.

LISTING 10.10. The Page_Load Event Handler That Generates the Control Instances

```
Sub Page_Load()

  ' insert some formatting content into <form> section
  Dim oLiteral As New LiteralControl("HtmlInputPassword control: ")
  MyForm.Controls.Add(oLiteral)

  ' create new HtmlInputPassword control and set properties
  Dim oPassword As New HtmlInputPassword()
  oPassword.ID = "MyPassword"
  oPassword.Size = 10
  oPassword.MaxLength = 10
  MyForm.Controls.Add(oPassword)

  ' add server-side event handler
  AddHandler oPassword.ServerChange, _
          New EventHandler(AddressOf PasswordChange)

  ' insert some formatting content into <form> section
  oLiteral = New LiteralControl("<p />")
  MyForm.Controls.Add(oLiteral)

  ' create new HtmlInputSubmit control and set properties
  ' default for Value property is "Submit Query"
  Dim oSubmit As New HtmlInputSubmit()
```

```
oSubmit.ID = "MySubmit"
oSubmit.Value = "Submit"
MyForm.Controls.Add(oSubmit)

' add server-side event handler
AddHandler oSubmit.ServerClick, _
          New EventHandler (AddressOf SubmitClick)

' create new HtmlInputReset control and set properties
' default for Value property is "Reset"
Dim oReset As New HtmlInputReset()
oReset.ID = "MyReset"
MyForm.Controls.Add(oReset)

' only add server-side event handler if checkbox is set
If chkPostReset.Checked = "True" Then
  AddHandler oReset.ServerClick, _
          New EventHandler (AddressOf ResetClick)
End If

lblResult.Text &= "TextBox value is: '" & MyText.Text & "'<br />"

End Sub
```

The HtmlInputReset control is treated in a different way. The code adds
a server-side event handler only if the checkbox named chkPostReset is
checked. You'll see why shortly. Finally, the Page_Load event handler code
also displays the content of the TextBox control each time the page loads,
so that you can see what value it has when the page is posted back to the
server.

The remaining code within the page, shown in Listing 10.11, implements the event handlers for the password field, Submit, and Reset button
controls. For the password control, a message is displayed in the Label
control that contains the value entered into the password text box when
the page was submitted. For the Submit and Reset button controls, the message simply indicates that they were clicked. However, for the Reset button, the code also clears the contents of the text box named MyText (which
was declared in Listing 10.9) and displays another message to this effect.

LISTING 10.11. The Event Handlers for the Password Field and Button Controls

```
Sub PasswordChange(sender As Object, e As EventArgs)
   lblResult.Text &= "Password changed to: '" & sender.Value & "'<br />"
End Sub

Sub SubmitClick(sender As Object, e As EventArgs)
   lblResult.Text &= "Submit button was clicked<br />"
End Sub
```

continues

```
Sub ResetClick(sender As Object, e As EventArgs)
  lblResult.Text &= "Reset button was clicked<br />"
  MyText.Text = ""
  lblResult.Text &= "Deleted content of TextBox<br />"
End Sub
```

The Behavior of the HtmlInputReset Control

The way that the `HtmlInputReset` control behaves, and the reason why we added the checkbox and the extra code in the `ResetClick` event handler, provides an insight into how it can be used. If you add a server-side event handler to its `ServerClick` event, the `HtmlInputReset` control will cause a postback to the server (using the usual `doPostBack` client-side function) when clicked. What ASP.NET actually generates is

```
<input language="javascript" onclick="__doPostBack('MyReset','')"
      name="MyReset" type="reset" id="MyReset" />
```

This means that the postback will maintain the values in the controls using viewstate, and they are not cleared. For this reason, the code in the `ResetClick` event handler shown in Listing 10.11 clears the content of the control by setting the `Text` property to an empty string (there is no need to clear the password text box because it does not maintain viewstate).

However, if you do not specify a server-side event handler for the `ServerClick` event, the `HtmlInputReset` control will generate a standard `<input type="reset">` element, which does not cause a postback. Instead, it just sets the values of all the controls on the form to their initial states (this is standard browser behavior). Of course, any values that are maintained in the viewstate are classed as the initial values because they are present in the `value` attribute of the control.

Figure 10.3 shows what happens if the Submit button is clicked after entering some text into the text box and the password box. The values entered are available to the server-side code, but the password is not persisted in the viewstate, so the password box is empty following the postback.

If you now enter more text into the two controls and then click Reset, you'll see that the value in the text box goes back to the value it had during the last postback. This is the initial value as inserted into the `value` attribute by ASP.NET during the last postback. The password box is cleared because it cannot have an initial value.

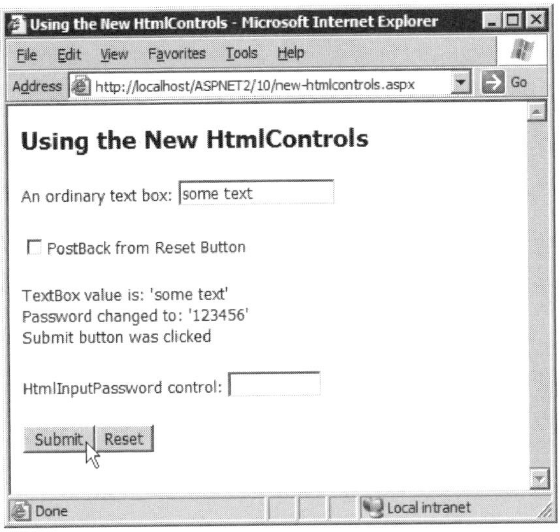

FIGURE 10.3. Testing the HtmlInputSubmit control

However, in Figure 10.4, you can see that the checkbox has been set so that the Reset button will now cause a postback to the server when clicked. In this case, the text box is cleared because the server-side event handler sets the Text property to an empty string. Notice that the values in the controls when the button was clicked are available on the server this time.

This means that you must choose whether to adopt the standard behavior of an HTML Reset button or use a server-side event handler to perform

FIGURE 10.4. Testing the HtmlInputReset control

the clearing of values. When there is no server-side event handler attached, the HtmlInputReset control sets the values of all the controls on the form back to their initial values (which could, of course, be empty if this is the first time the page has loaded or if the user did not enter a value before the previous postback). When there is an event handler attached, you must use the event to clear or reset the contents of controls yourself.

The BulletedList Control

We now move on to look at the new controls in the WebControls namespace, starting with the BulletedList control. This control provides an easy route to creating <ol> and <ul> lists in a page. Because it inherits from ListControl, the contents of the list can be created by declaring individual child ListItem controls, or through data binding. It also adds extra features; for example, you can display each item as a HyperLink or a LinkButton and then handle the OnClick event that the BulletedList control exposes to see which item was clicked.

The style of bullet used in the list is specified as the BulletStyle property, using values from the BulletStyle enumeration. These are fairly self-explanatory and consist of NotSet, Numbered, LowerAlpha, UpperAlpha, LowerRoman, UpperRoman, Disc, Circle, Square, and CustomImage. The default, if not specified, is a decimal numbered list. It is also possible to specify the starting number for the list by setting the FirstBulletNumber property. Listing 10.12 shows the simplest form of declaring a BulletedList control, followed by one that specifies a numeric list starting at 4.

LISTING 10.12. Using the BulletedList Control

```
<asp:BulletedList id="List1" runat="server">
  <asp:listitem>Item 1</asp:listitem>
  <asp:listitem>Item 2</asp:listitem>
  <asp:listitem>Item 3</asp:listitem>
</asp:BulletedList>

<asp:BulletedList id="List2" BulletStyle="Numbered"
    FirstBulletNumber="4" DisplayMode="Text" runat="server">
  <asp:ListItem>Numbered Item 1</asp:ListItem>
  <asp:ListItem>Numbered Item 2</asp:ListItem>
  <asp:ListItem>Numbered Item 3</asp:ListItem>
</asp:BulletedList>
```

The second BulletedList control shown in Listing 10.12 also specifies the DisplayMode property (or attribute), which is a value from the BulletedListDisplayMode enumeration. The default if not specified is

Text. The other two options for this property are HyperLink, which turns each item in the list into a hyperlink, and LinkButton, which renders each item with an attached JavaScript URL that runs client-side code to submit the form (it works just like a standard LinkButton).

Listing 10.13 shows these two options in use. The first sets the bullet style to a square and specifies that the list items should be displayed as hyperlinks. The Target property specifies the target attribute that will be added to each hyperlink in the list. The Value property of the ListItem control is used as the href attribute of the hyperlink. If the Value property is not declared (as in the third item), the Text property is used instead.

LISTING 10.13. A BulletedList Using HyperLink Controls

```
<asp:BulletedList id="List3" DisplayMode="HyperLink"
    BulletStyle="Square" Target="_blank" runat="server">
  <asp:ListItem Text="DaveAndAl" runat="server"
      Value="http://www.daveandal.net" />
  <asp:ListItem Text="ASP.NET" runat="server"
      Value="http://www.asp.net" />
  <asp:ListItem Text="http://localhost" runat="server" />
</asp:BulletedList>

<asp:BulletedList id="List4"  DisplayMode="LinkButton"
    BulletStyle="CustomImage" BulletImageUrl="bullet.gif"
    runat="server">
  <asp:ListItem Text="Value 1" runat="server" />
  <asp:ListItem Text="Value 2" runat="server" />
  <asp:ListItem Text="Value 3" runat="server" />
</asp:BulletedList>
```

The declaration of the fourth BulletedList control in our series of examples (i.e., the second control in Listing 10.13) shows the use of the value CustomImage for the BulletStyle property, with the URL of the image provided in the BulletImageUrl property. We've also specified LinkButton for the DisplayMode property, so each item will be rendered in the page as a link button (a hyperlink that uses a JavaScript URL to submit the form containing the control).

Data Binding to a BulletedList Control

The BulletedList class exposes the same properties, methods, and events as the ListControl and DataBoundControl classes from which it inherits, so we can use standard data binding techniques, just as we would with a DropDownList or ListBox control. First we declare the BulletedList with no content:

```
<asp:BulletedList id="List2" DisplayMode="Text"
    BulletStyle="Numbered" FirstBulletNumber="4" runat="server" />
```

Then we assign a suitable data source to the DataSource property of the control at runtime. In Listing 10.14, we use a simple routine that creates a String array and assign the array to the BulletedList during the Page_Load event.

LISTING 10.14. A Data-Bound BulletedList Control

```
Sub Page_Load()
  If Not Page.IsPostback Then
    List2.DataSource = GetListArray()
    Page.DataBind()
  End If
End Sub

Function GetListArray() As String()
  Dim aList(2) As String
  Dim iLoop As Integer
  For iLoop = 1 To 3
    aList(iLoop - 1) = "Bound item " & iLoop.ToString()
  Next
  Return aList
End Function
```

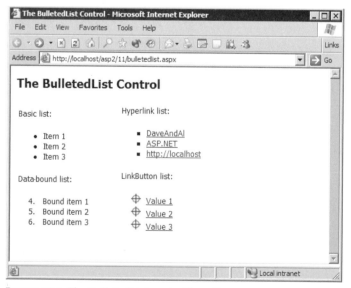

FIGURE 10.5. The BulletedList control in action

Figure 10.5 shows the four instances of the `BulletedList` control we've described so far, with the second one having the literal content replaced by data binding as demonstrated in Listing 10.14. You can see in the first "column" of the figure that the first `BulletedList` control displays a "normal" `<ul>` list, and the second displays a numeric `<ol>` ordered list starting at 4 and containing our data-bound values. The third instance, at the top of the second "column," displays hyperlinks, and the fourth uses link buttons (though the underlined text links for these two do, of course, look just the same in the page).

Detecting Which Item Was Clicked in a BulletedList Control

One reason for using `LinkButton` controls in the list is to cause a postback so that you can handle the user's selection (using `HyperLink` controls means that the user will navigate directly to the page specified in the list).

The `OnClick` attribute specifies the event handler that will be executed on a postback. This event handler accepts a `BulletedListEventArgs` object, which has the single property `Index` containing the index of the item that was clicked. The code shown in Listing 10.15 just displays that index in a `Label` control on the page.

LISTING 10.15. Specifying an OnClick Event Handler

```
<asp:BulletedList id="List4" DisplayMode="LinkButton"
    BulletStyle="CustomImage" BulletImageUrl="bullet.gif"
    OnClick="ShowItem" runat="server">
  <asp:ListItem Text="Value 1" runat="server" />
  <asp:ListItem Text="Value 2" runat="server" />
  <asp:ListItem Text="Value 3" runat="server" />
</asp:BulletedList>

<asp:Label id="lblResult" runat="server" />

<script runat="server">
Sub ShowItem(sender As Object, e As BulletedListEventArgs)
  lblResult.Text = "Selected item index is: " & e.Index
End Sub
</script>
```

The BulletedList Control Interface

The `BulletedList` control is descended from the `ListControl` class that is the base class for most of the simple list controls in ASP.NET. Therefore it exposes a similar set of properties as, for example, the `DropDownList` and

`ListBox` controls. Table 10.2 summarizes the properties and the single event that are most relevant when working with the `BulletedList` control.

TABLE 10.2. The BulletedList Control Members

Property/Attribute	Description
AutoPostBack	A `Boolean` value that specifies whether clicking an item in the list when the `DisplayMode` is set to `LinkButton` will cause an immediate postback.
BulletImageUrl	A `String` that is the URL of the image to display as the bullet when `BulletStyle` is set to `CustomImage`.
BulletStyle	A value from the `BulletStyle` enumeration that specifies the type of bullets, letters, or numbers that the bullets will display. Valid values are `NotSet` (the default), `Circle`, `Disc`, `Square`, `Numbered`, `LowerAlpha`, `UpperAlpha`, `LowerRoman`, `UpperRoman`, and `CustomImage`.
DisplayMode	A value from the `BulletedListDisplayMode` enumeration that specifies the way that the items in the list will be displayed. Valid values are `Text` (the default), `HyperLink`, and `LinkButton`.
FirstBulletNumber	An `Integer` that specifies the number of the first bullet when `BulletStyle` is set to `LowerRoman`, `Numbered`, or `UpperRoman`.
Items	A reference to a collection of all the `ListItem` instances that make up the list for this control.
SelectedIndex	An `Integer` that is the zero-based index of the item in the list that is currently selected, or `-1` if no item is selected. Set this property to select an item in the list.
SelectedItem	A reference to the currently selected item in the list as a `ListItem` instance.
Target	A `String` that is used to render the `target` attribute for each hyperlink in the list when `DisplayMode` is set to `HyperLink`.
ValidationGroup	A `String` that is the name of the validation group that this control belongs to, if validation groups are defined for the page.
Event	**Description**
Click	Raised when the `DisplayMode` is set to `HyperLink` or `LinkButton` and a postback is caused by one of the items in the list. Passes a `BulletListEventArgs` instance to the event handler, which exposes an extra property, `Index` (the `Integer` zero-based index of the item in the list that caused the postback).

The DynamicImage Control

The server controls in ASP.NET will automatically adapt their output to suit the markup language and features of different types of client devices, in particular for cellular phones. However, another issue arises with these kinds of devices in that many don't recognize the common image types used in HTML, such as the .gif, .png, and .jpg formats. To get around this problem, you can use a new control named DynamicImage.

The DynamicImage control uses the Image Generation Service, accessed via a special .axd HTTP handler (described in the upcoming Image Generation Service subsection), to dynamically generate a suitable stream of bytes for the image, rather than the more usual technique of specifying a file on the server as the src attribute of an <img> element. By providing the correct MIME type when it responds to the request for the image stream, the DynamicImage control ensures that the client can display the image just as it would an image file from disk.

The DynamicImage control can also accept as its image source an array of bytes that represents the image, or a reference to an ImageGenerator service that "contains" an image that has been created using drawing commands. You can create classes that inherit from ImageGenerator and that create an image, then use these as the input to the DynamicImage control.

To demonstrate the basic uses of the DynamicImage control, the following code declares two instances of the control. The first (see Listing 10.16) simply uses a disk file named car.gif, specifying that it is an image file on disk in the DynamicImageType property (attribute). The second of the control instances specifies ImageBytes for the DynamicImageType property, so the control will expect to receive a reference to a Byte array containing the data for the image.

LISTING 10.16. Declaring the DynamicImage Control

```
<form runat="server">

  From a file:<br />
  <asp:DynamicImage AutoSize="False" runat="server"
      DynamicImageType="ImageFile" ImageFile="car.gif" />

  From an array of bytes:<br />
  <asp:DynamicImage id="MyImage" runat="server"
      DynamicImageType="ImageBytes" />

</form>
```

This image data is generated in code and then assigned to the ImageBytes property at runtime. Listing 10.17 shows the code we used.

LISTING 10.17. Streaming Content into the DynamicImage Control

```
Sub Page_Load()

    Dim Stream = New FileStream(Server.MapPath("car.gif"), _
                    FileMode.Open, FileAccess.Read)
    Dim MyArray(oStream.Length - 1) As Byte
    Stream.Read(MyArray, 0, oStream.Length)
    Stream.Close()
    MyImage.ImageBytes = MyArray

End Sub
```

You can see that we are simply opening the image file on disk and reading it into the array as a stream. Of course, you would probably store the image data in a database instead and stream it from there into an array. The final line of code in the Page_Load event handler shown in Listing 10.17 then assigns the array to the ImageBytes property of the DynamicImage control. Figure 10.6 shows the output generated by these two DynamicImage controls.

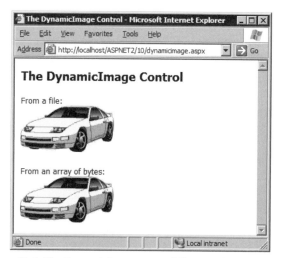

FIGURE 10.6. The DynamicImage control from a Windows browser

The DynamicImage control can also be used to convert images between different types. For example, consider the following, which converts logo.gif into a JPEG file.

```
<asp:DynamicImage runat="server"
     ImageType="Jpeg" ImageFile="logo.gif" />
```

Other useful features are the ability of the control to resize an image to suit the device or display window size. The `PercentScreenCover`, `ScaleMode`, `Width`, and `Height` properties can be set to specify the size of the image as seen on the client device. You can also set the `ResizeOnServer` property to specify that the image should be resized on the server, rather than just being delivered to the client where it will be displayed at the size specified by the `Width` and `Height` attributes. Server-side resizing can considerably reduce the amount of data sent over the wire and is also useful where the client device doesn't provide any support for resizing when displaying images.

Automatic Translation of Images for Other Devices

When a `DynamicImage` control is used in a page that is being served to a non-HTML device, such as a cellular phone, the Image Generation Service that is generating the image automatically converts the image into the correct representation for the device where possible. Opening a page that contains just the first instance of the `DynamicImage` control shown in Listing 10.16 to a mobile device results in the output shown in Listing 10.18 being sent to the client in response to the `GET` request for the image.

LISTING 10.18. The Output Generated by the DynamicImage Control for a Mobile Device

```
HTTP GET Request: HTTP://LOCALHOST/aspnet20/ch03/CachedImage
Service.axd?data=07ce61a2-b688-436a-9cb1-c94f91d582e4
---------------- DATA SIZE ----------------------
Uncompiled data from HTTP is 1373 bytes.
...found Content-Type: image/vnd.wap.wbmp.
Compiled WAP binary is 1458 bytes.
--------------------------------------------------
Measured image is 150 x 72
```

You can see that now it appears as a `.wbmp` file, with the content type `image/vnd.wap.wbmp`, and it looks like Figure 10.7.

FIGURE 10.7. The DynamicImage control from a phone browser

The DynamicImage Control Interface

Table 10.3 lists the properties and the single event that are most relevant when working with the DynamicImage control.

TABLE 10.3. The DynamicImage Control Members

Property/Attribute	Description
Image	A reference to an instance of the Image class to display in the control.
ImageType	A value from the ImageType enumeration that specifies the type of image that will be generated by the control. Valid values are Automatic (the same type as the source), Bmp, Gif, Jpeg, and Png.
ImageBytes	A reference to an array of type Byte that contains the data for the image.
ImageFile	A String that is the full path and name of the image file to display.
ImageGeneratorUrl	The URL of the Image Generation Service to use. The default service instance is used if no specific instance is specified. See the subsection on the Image Generation Service for details.
Parameters	A reference to a ParameterCollection instance containing the parameters to pass to the Image Generation Service.
ParameterMode	A value from the DynamicImageParameterMode enumeration that specifies how the parameters are to be persisted. Valid values are ImageGenerationStorage and QueryString.
Width	The width at which the image is to be displayed in pixels or as a Unit instance.
Height	The height at which the image is to be displayed in pixels or as a Unit instance.
PercentScreenCover	An Integer that specifies the percentage of the screen to use when displaying the image.
ScaleMode	A value from the System.Web.UI.Imaging.ImageScaleMode enumeration that specifies how the image should be resized to fit the available space. Valid values are FitBasedOnHeight, FitBasedOnWidth, ScaleBasedOnHeight, ScaleBasedOnWidth, and NoScaling.
ResizeOnServer	A Boolean value that specifies whether the image will be resized on the server before being sent to the client.

TABLE 10.3. The DynamicImage Control Members (continued)

Property/Attribute	Description
GenerateEmptyAlternateText	A Boolean value that specifies whether an empty alt attribute will be generated. This allows specialist page readers to ignore the image if it does not form a significant or meaningful part of the page content.

The Image Generation Service

ASP.NET 2.0 introduces several new file extensions for files that are part of the page architecture but are not actually ASP.NET pages. Examples already discussed in this book include theme, skin, and master page files. One other new file type is that used for the Image Generation Service, which uses files with the extension .asix.

It was possible to create images dynamically in ASP.NET 1.x, but there was no standard way to do it—you invariably used an ASP.NET page or a Web Service, created the image, and then saved it to the output stream. In ASP.NET 2.0, the Image Generation Service makes it easy to create images dynamically and have them automatically modified to suit the current client type and its capabilities. A base control named ImageGenerator provides much of this default behavior. All you need to do is inherit from this control and then perform the actual drawing. For example, Listing 10.19 shows how a .asix file could be used.

LISTING 10.19. Using the ImageGenerator Control

```
<%@ Image Class="Test" Language="VB" %>

Imports System
Imports System.Drawing

Public Class Test
  Inherits System.Web.UI.Imaging.ImageGenerator

    Protected Overrides Sub RenderImage(g As Graphics)

      g.FillRectangle(Brushes.Black, g.ClipBounds)

      Dim f As New Font("Ariel", 22)

      g.DrawString("Welcome", f, _
        Brushes.White, 0, 0)
      g.DrawString("to our site", f, _
        Brushes.White, 10, 30)

    End Sub
End Class
```

This simply draws a rectangle and then two lines of text, resulting in the image shown in Figure 10.8. The beauty of this method of image creation is its simplicity—all you have to do is concentrate on creating the image itself, letting the Framework handle how it is to be rendered to the browser.

FIGURE 10.8. The ImageGenerator control in action

Image Generation Service Configuration

The Image Generation Service can be configured by modifying the imageGeneration section in web.config or machine.config. The syntax is shown here:

```
<system.web>
    <imageGeneration
        storageType="[Cache|Disk]"
        storageExpiration="[Number]"
        storagePath="[String]" />
</system.web>
```

The storageType attribute determines where the images will be stored (the default is Cache), and the storageExpiration attribute specifies the number of seconds until the image expires (the default is 300). The storagePath attribute indicates the location for images if Disk storage is used. Note that an empty string (the default) will cause an exception if storageType is set to Disk.

The ImageMap Control

The `ImageMap` control provides a server implementation of the HTML `<map>` element and its child `<area>` elements, allowing sections of images to be used as clickable hot spots. There are three hot spot types:

- `RectangleHotSpot`, to define the bounds of a rectangular portion of the image
- `CircleHotSpot`, to define the bounds of a circular portion of the image
- `PolygonHotSpot`, to define the bounds of an irregular portion of the image

A simple example of the use of the `ImageMap` control is shown below:

```
<asp:ImageMap id="String" ImageUrl="String" runat="server"
            HotSpotMode="[Navigate|Postback]" />
```

Specifying Hot Spots

On its own the `ImageMap` control isn't much use because you need to specify the areas within the image that will act as hot spots, as well as what happens when those regions are clicked. For example, consider the page shown in Figure 10.9, which has two rectangular hot spot regions and one circular region. The code to implement this appears in Listing 10.20.

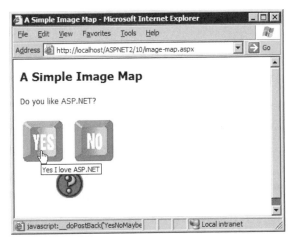

FIGURE 10.9. Sample ImageMap control

LISTING 10.20. Declaring the ImageMap Control

```
<asp:ImageMap id="YesNoMaybe"  runat="server"
     ImageUrl="YesNoMaybe.jpg" onClick="ImageClicked">

  <asp:RectangleHotSpot HotSpotMode="Postback" PostBackValue="Yes"
       Top="3" Left="3" Right="68" Bottom ="68"
       AlternateText="Yes I love ASP.NET"/>

  <asp:RectangleHotSpot HotSpotMode="Postback" PostBackValue="No"
       Top="3" Left="86" Right="149" Bottom ="68"
       AlternateText="No but I'll give it a try"/>

  <asp:CircleHotSpot HotSpotMode="Navigate"
       X="78" Y="104" Radius="22"
       NavigateUrl="http://www.asp.net" Target="_blank"
       AlternateText="Tell me more about ASP.NET" />

</asp:ImageMap>
```

The RectangleHotSpot has four properties to define its region—Top, Left, Right, and Bottom—which contain pixel values. The CircleHotSpot has three properties—x and y to define the center point and Radius to define the circle radius. Both types of controls have the AlternateText property that sets the tooltip text, as well as the HotSpotMode property that defines what action is to be taken when this image region is clicked. If the HotSpotMode is Navigate, the NavigateUrl is used as the URL to navigate to; if it is Postback, the PostBackValue is passed to the event procedure defined by the OnClick property of the ImageMap control. A suitable event handler is shown in Listing 10.21.

LISTING 10.21. Implementing the OnClick Event Handler for an ImageMap Control

```
Sub ImageClicked(sender As Object, e As ImageMapEventArgs)

  ' hide the image map control
  YesNoMaybe.Visible = False

  ' see which area was clicked
  Select Case e.PostBackValue
    Case "Yes"
      Message.Text = "Yes, they love it"
    Case "No"
      Message.Text = "No, but they are going to love it"
  End Select

End Sub
```

Irregular Hot Spots

Irregular hot spots are enabled by a `PolygonHotSpot` control that defines a series of x- and y-coordinates that define the bounds of the image region. For example, consider a map of the United Kingdom, perhaps used to pick sales regions, as shown in Figure 10.10. A section of the code to create the appropriate hot spots for the regions is shown in Listing 10.22.

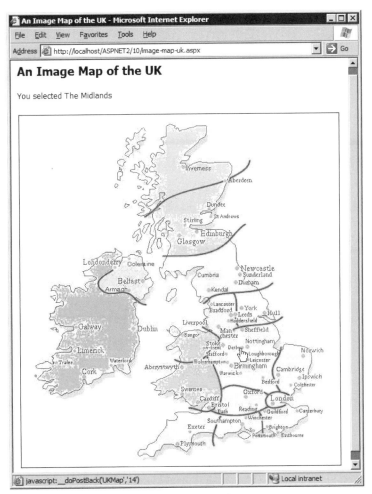

FIGURE 10.10. ImageMap of the United Kingdom

LISTING 10.22. Defining Irregular Hot Spots

```
<asp:ImageMap id="UKMap" HotSpotMode="Postback"
    ImageUrl="UKMap.jpg" onClick="MapClicked" runat="server">

  <asp:PolygonHotSpot Coordinates="205,17,328,38,...201,159"
      PostBackValue="Northern Scotland"/>
  <asp:PolygonHotSpot Coordinates="209,166,225,224,...335,112"
      PostBackValue="Southern Scotland"/>
  ...
  <asp:CircleHotSpot Value="London"
      X="411" Y="452" radius="11" />
  ...
</asp:ImageMap>
```

There is no real limit to the number of coordinates you put in—using more of them leads to a finer-grained and smoother polygon but takes more time to type. In reality you don't have to be 100% accurate to the area you are defining because users tend to click near the middle of a region anyway.

The ImageMap and Hot Spot Control Interfaces

The commonly used properties and single event of the ImageMap control are described in Table 10.4, and the properties of the different types of hot spot controls are listed in Tables 10.5 and 10.6.

TABLE 10.4. The ImageMap Control Members

Property/Attribute	Description
HotSpotMode	Sets or returns the mode in which hot spots work. This can be one of the HotSpotMode enumeration values: •Navigate: Indicates that navigation takes place when the hot spot is clicked. In this mode the NavigateUrl property of the hot spot should contain the URL of the target page. •PostBack: Indicates that a postback should take place when the hot spot is clicked. In this mode the contents of the hot spot's PostBackValue property are passed into the server-side event handler.
Target	Sets or returns a String value that is used to set the target attribute of the hyperlinks for the hot spots when the HotSpotMode is Navigate.
GenerateEmptyAlternateText	Sets or returns a Boolean value that specifies whether an empty alt attribute will be generated. This allows specialist page readers to ignore the image if it does not form a significant or meaningful part of the page content.

TABLE 10.4. The ImageMap Control Members (continued)

Property/Attribute	Description
HotSpots	Returns a `HotSpotCollection` containing all defined hot spot regions.
ImageUrl	Sets or returns the URL of the image to display.
Event	**Description**
Click	Raised when the user clicks on a hot spot and the page is submitted. Passes an `ImageMapEventArgs` instance to the event handler, which exposes an extra property, `Value` (a `String` that is the content of the `Value` property of the hot spot that was clicked).

In addition to these properties, the `ImageMap` control implements the Site Counters Service and therefore supports the standard set of properties described in Chapter 9. These are `CountClicks`, `CounterGroup`, `CounterName`, `RowsPerDay`, `TrackApplicationName`, `TrackNavigateUrl`, and `TrackPageUrl`. The three types of controls that implement the hot spots within an `ImageMap` all expose the properties shown in Table 10.5.

TABLE 10.5. The Properties Common to All Hot Spot Controls

Property/Attribute	Description
AlternateText	A `String` that is the text for the `alt` attribute generated for this hot spot.
HotSpotMode	A value from the `HotSpotMode` enumeration that defines what action will be taken when the hot spot is clicked. Valid values are `Default`, `PostBack`, `Navigate`, and `Inactive`.
NavigateUrl	A `String` value that is the URL to open when the user clicks this hot spot and the `HotSpotMode` is `Navigate`.
PostBackValue	A `String` value that is passed back to the server when the user clicks this hot spot and the `HotSpotMode` is `Postback`.
Target	A `String` value that is used to set the `target` attribute of the hyperlink for this specific hot spot when the `HotSpotMode` is `Navigate`. Overrides the setting of the `Target` property in the `ImageMap` control.

The hot spot controls also implement extra properties that are specific to the hot spot shape they generate. Table 10.6 lists these extra properties.

TABLE 10.6. The Class-Specific Properties of the Hot Spot Controls

Control	Properties
CircleHotSpot	Radius, X, Y
PolygonHotSpot	Coordinates
RectangleHotSpot	Top, Bottom, Left, Right

The FileUpload Control

Uploading files to the server in ASP.NET 1.x is accomplished by using the `HtmlInputFile` control from the `HtmlControls` namespace, as `<input type="file" runat="server">`. This involves setting the correct `enctype` for the form and accessing the uploaded file through an instance of the `PostedFile` class. In ASP.NET 2.0, a new `FileUpload` control simplifies the work required to upload files. It exposes a reference to the uploaded (or "posted" file) in the same way as the `HtmlInputFile` control but has additional properties that provide details about the file.

The `FileUpload` control must be placed on a server-side form, though there is no need to specify the `enctype` attribute for the form. When ASP.NET 2.0 detects that a form contains a `FileUpload` control, it automatically adds the attribute `enctype="multipart/form-data"` to the form. Listing 10.23 shows how easy it is to declare the control, together with the `AlternateText` that will be displayed if the current client's browser doesn't support file uploads.

LISTING 10.23. Declaring a FileUpload Control

```
<form runat="server">
<asp:FileUpload id="MyFile" runat="server"
     AlternateText="Sorry, cannot upload files" /><p/>
<asp:Button id="btnUpload" Text="Go" runat="server"
          OnClick="GetFile" /><p />
<asp:Label id="lblResult" runat="server" />
</form>
```

We've included a Button control to start the upload and a Label control that will display the results of the process. The Button control generates an HTML Submit button, which will cause the file that the user chooses in the FileUpload control to be posted to the server. However, the OnClick attribute of the button will also cause the event handler named GetFile to run when the postback occurs. The code in this event handler is responsible for collecting the file from the request and storing it on disk (see Listing 10.24).

LISTING 10.24. Processing the Uploaded File

```
Sub GetFile(Sender As Object, E As EventArgs)

  ' first see if a file was posted to the server
  If MyFile.HasFile Then
    Try

      ' display details about the file from the FileUpload control
      lblResult.Text = "Uploading file " & MyFile.FileName

      ' save the uploaded file to disk
      MyFile.SaveAs("C:\temp\uploaded_" & MyFile.FileName)

      ' display details about file using the PostedFile instance
      lblResult.Text &= "Received file " _
        & MyFile.PostedFile.FileName _
        & "Type: " & MyFile.PostedFile.ContentType _
        & "Length: " & MyFile.PostedFile.ContentLength.ToString() _
        & " bytes<br />" _
        & "Saved as: C:\temp\uploaded_" & MyFile.FileName

    Catch e As Exception
      lblResult.Text &= "Cannot save uploaded file " & e.Message
    End Try

  Else
    lblResult.Text &= "No file received"
  End If

End Sub
```

Figure 10.11 shows the results. You can see from the preceding code that the file was uploaded and stored in the C:\temp\ folder on the server. Note that a full path for the saved file must be specified or an exception is raised.

FIGURE 10.11. The FileUpload control in action

Remember that the account you are running ASP.NET under must have write permission for the folder where you are saving the up-loaded file. In Windows XP/2000 the account is named ASPNET. In Windows Server 2003 you should allocate permission to the IIS_WPG account group. Also note that the maximum size of a file that can be uploaded is governed by the maxRequestLength value in the <httpRuntime> section of machine.config. The default is 4096K. You can change it in machine.config to a larger or smaller value, or you can do the same in the web.config file for your application.

The FileUpload Control Interface

The commonly used properties of the FileUpload control are described in Table 10.7.

TABLE 10.7. The FileUpload Control Members

Property/Attribute	Description
AlternateText	A String containing the text to display if the client does not support file uploads and to act as the tooltip for the control.
FileContent	The instance of the Stream class used to upload the file.
FileName	A read-only String that contains the name of the file the user uploaded, without the path information.

TABLE 10.7. The FileUpload Control Members (continued)

Property/Attribute	Description
HasFile	A `Boolean` value that indicates whether a file was uploaded.
PostedFile	A reference to the file that was uploaded as an `HttpPostedFile` instance. The `HttpPostedFile` class exposes the following properties: •`ContentLength`: The size of the uploaded file in bytes. •`ContentType`: The MIME type of the posted file. •`FileName`: The full path and name of the file on the client machine. •`InputStream`: Returns a `Stream` instance pointing to the file after it has been uploaded.

Method	Description
SaveAs(*filename*)	Saves the posted file to disk using the specified path and filename.

The HiddenField Control

Hidden-type `<input>` elements are useful for storing values in a Web page, especially where you don't want to rely on using ASP.NET sessions. In ASP.NET 1.x, the only way to generate a hidden control is by using the `HtmlInputHidden` control from the `HtmlControls` namespace, as `<input type="hidden" runat="server">`. In ASP.NET 2.0, the new `HiddenField` control can be used instead.

One nice feature of this control is the ability to detect changes to the value after a postback. This is useful if the page uses hidden controls to submit values to the server because the `ValueChanged` event of the `HiddenField` control is raised on the server after a postback only when the value currently in the control is different from that when the page was sent to the client.

Listings 10.25 through 10.27 demonstrate this. The server-side form contains a `HiddenField` control, together with two buttons. The first is a simple HTML button that only runs a client-side script function named `ChangeValue`. The other is an ASP.NET `Button` control that submits the form to the server. Finally, there is a `Label` control to display the results.

LISTING 10.25. Declaring the HiddenField Control

```
<form runat="server">
  <asp:HiddenField id="MyField" Value="some value"
      OnValueChanged="ShowValue" runat="server" /><p/>
```

continues

```
<input type="button" Value="Change value"
       onclick="ChangeValue()">
<asp:Button Text="Submit" runat="server" /><p />
<asp:Label id="lblResult"
    Text="Field contains: 'some value'" runat="server" />
</form>
```

The client-side script function is shown in Listing 10.26. ASP.NET inserts the value of the `ClientID` property of the `HiddenField` control into this code section when creating the page, so that it contains the value of the `id` attribute of the `<input type="hidden">` element that is generated. Then the client-side code can access this element and change the value to include the current date and time, then display a confirmation message in an `alert` dialog.

LISTING 10.26. Accessing the HiddenField Content in Client Script

```
<script language="JavaScript">
// NB: this is client-side script
function ChangeValue() {
  var ctrlName = '<%=MyField.ClientID%>'
  var ctrl = document.getElementById(ctrlName);
  ctrl.value = 'Whoops, I changed it on ' + Date() + '!';
  alert('OK, I changed it');
}
</script>
```

The server-side code that runs when the Submit button is clicked is even simpler (see Listing 10.27). It just displays the value of the `HiddenField` control in the `Label` control on the page. `Value` is the only property exposed by the `HiddenField` control.

LISTING 10.27. Accessing the HiddenField Content in Server Script

```
Sub ShowValue(oSender As Object, oArgs As EventArgs)
   lblResult.Text = "New value is '" & MyField.Value & "'"
End Sub
```

Figure 10.12 shows the result. Clicking the Change value button updates the `HiddenField`, and then the Submit button posts the form containing the control to the server. If the value has been changed (by the client-side code), the `ValueChanged` event is raised and the new value is displayed.

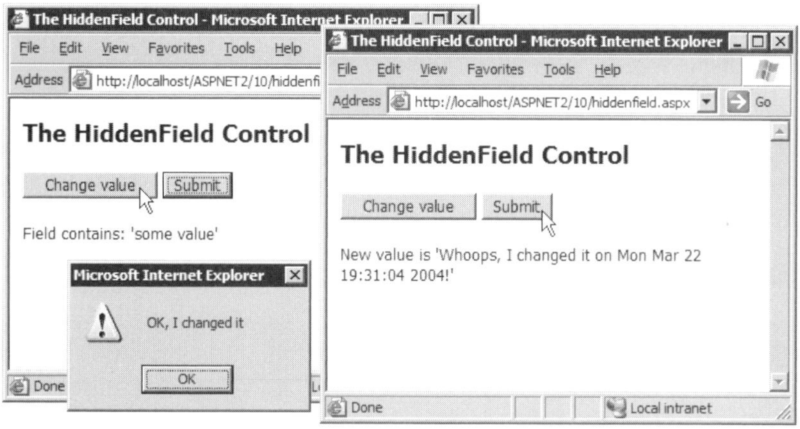

FIGURE 10.12. The HiddenField control in action

The HiddenField Control Interface

The commonly used members of the HiddenField control are described in Table 10.8.

TABLE 10.8. The HiddenField Control Members

Property/Attribute	Description
Value	A String that is the content of the hidden control, as represented in the page as its Value attribute.

Event	Description
ValueChanged	Raised during a postback when the value in the control has changed since the page was sent to the client.

The MultiView and View Controls

If you installed and played with the Internet Explorer Web Controls pack in ASP.NET 1.x, you were probably impressed with the way you can easily create quite complex effects that are common in executable applications in a Web page. One of the many useful controls in the Internet Explorer Web Controls pack is the MultiView control. This control allows you to declare several "screens" or "views," which are each separate sections of the UI for a page, and then display any one of them in the page on demand.

However, while the Internet Explorer Web Controls version can take advantage of some clever client-side code to provide these features in Internet Explorer without requiring a postback, the MultiView control in ASP.NET

2.0 works only with a postback to the server every time you want to change the screen or view displayed.

To declare a `MultiView` control and its content, you use the ASP.NET `MultiView` as the container and then place within it one or more `View` controls. Listing 10.28 shows a simple `MultiView` declaration containing two `View` controls. Each `View` contains just some text and a `Button` control.

LISTING 10.28. Declaring the MultiView Control

```
<asp:MultiView id="MyMulti" ActiveViewIndex="0" runat="server">

  <asp:View id="View1" runat="server">
    This is View 1<br />
    <asp:button id="btnView1Next" Text="Next" runat="server"
            CommandName="NextView" />
  </asp:View>

  <asp:View id="View2" runat="server">
    This is View 2<br />
    <asp:button id="btnView2Prev" Text="Previous" runat="server"
            CommandName="PrevView" />
  </asp:View>

</asp:MultiView>
```

The `MultiView` control chooses which `View` to display based on the value of the `ActiveViewIndex` property (indexed from 0). By default this property is set to `-1` (no `View` is shown), so when the page loads for the first time we specify that the first of the `View` controls should be displayed by setting the `ActiveViewIndex` attribute to `0`. We could alternatively set it in code in a `Page_Load` event handler.

Navigating Views Using Commands

Within the `View` controls in Listing 10.28, the buttons (captioned `Next` in the first view and `Previous` in the second view) have specific values set for their `CommandName` attributes. These automatically cause the `MultiView` to switch the `ActiveViewIndex` (and hence the view that is displayed) to the next or previous view when they cause a postback. This automatic navigation feature can be implemented using any control that supports the `CommandName` and `CommandArgument` properties, such as the `Button` and `LinkButton` controls.

There are also two other options you can use to automatically switch views. If the `CommandName` is set to `"SwitchViewByID"`, the `CommandArgument` can contain the `id` of the `View` to switch to, which happens automatically when the button is clicked. If the `CommandName` is set to `"SwitchViewByIndex"`, the `CommandArgument` can be set to the zero-based index of the `View` to switch to. The actual values that are valid for the `CommandName` property are specified in the four static fields of the `MultiView` control as shown in Table 10.9 (see the upcoming subsection on `MultiView` and `View` control interfaces). In Listing 10.29, we've added another button to each of the `View` controls to demonstrate the way that the `"Switch"` commands are declared in a `MultiView` control. The result is shown in Figure 10.13.

LISTING 10.29. Using the "Switch" Commands to Navigate in a MultiView Control

```
<asp:MultiView id="MyMulti" ActiveViewIndex="0" runat="server">

  <asp:View id="View1" runat="server">
    This is View 1<br />
    <asp:button id="btnView1Next" Text="Next" runat="server"
                CommandName="NextView" />
    <asp:button id="btnView1Switch" runat="server"
                Text="SwitchByIndex to Index=1"
                CommandName="SwitchViewByIndex"
                CommandArgument="1" />
  </asp:View>

  <asp:View id="View2" runat="server">
    This is View 2<br />
    <asp:button id="btnView2Prev" Text="Previous" runat="server"
                CommandName="PrevView" />
    <asp:button id="btnView2Switch" runat="server"
                Text="SwitchByID to ID=View1"
                CommandName="SwitchViewByID"
                CommandArgument="View1" />
  </asp:View>

</asp:MultiView>
```

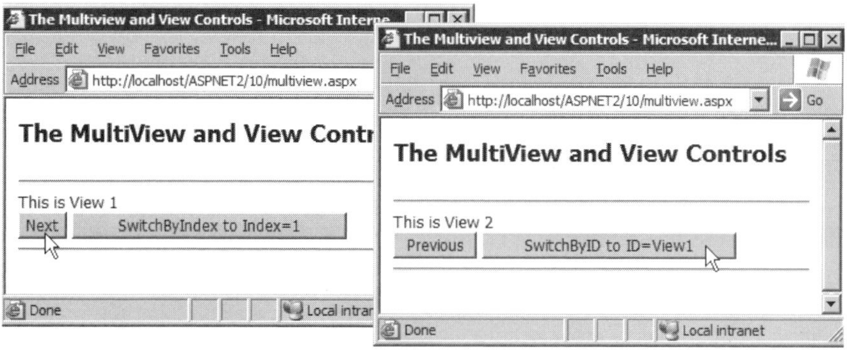

FIGURE 10.13. The MultiView control in action

Navigating Views Using Properties and Methods of the MultiView

The `ActiveViewIndex` property of the `MultiView` specifies the `Integer` zero-based index of the `View` that is displayed. It is a read/write property, so you can change the `View` that is displayed by setting it to the index of the `View` control you want to show. For example, Listing 10.30 shows two `Button` controls that are located on the page outside of the `MultiView` control declaration. When clicked, they execute an event handler named `ShowView`. So that the event handler can tell which button was clicked, each has the index of the view it will activate as the `CommandName`.

Listing 10.30 also shows the event handler. All it does is extract the value of the `CommandName` from the control that raised the event and set the `ActiveViewIndex` property. This causes the appropriate `View` instance to be displayed.

LISTING 10.30. Setting the ActiveViewIndex Property from a Button Control

```
<asp:Button id="btnActiveView0" Text="Set ActiveViewIndex to 0"
         OnClick="ShowView" CommandName="0" runat="server" /><br />
<asp:Button id="btnActiveView1" Text="Set ActiveViewIndex to 1"
         OnClick="ShowView" CommandName="1" runat="server" /><p />
. . .
Sub ShowView(sender As Object, e As EventArgs)
  MyMulti.ActiveViewIndex = Int32.Parse(sender.CommandName)
End Sub
```

Another alternative for switching between `View` instances is to use the `SetActiveView` method. This takes a reference to a `View` instance and makes it the current `View` for display. This might be useful if you access `View` instances through the `Views` property of the `MultiView` (which exposes a reference to a `ViewCollection`).

Handling Events for the MultiView and View Controls

Both the `MultiView` and `View` controls expose events that you can handle in your server-side code. The `MultiView` control raises the `ActiveViewChanged` event when the active `View` is changed, and the `View` control raises the `Activate` and `Deactivate` events when it is activated or deactivated, respectively. In Listing 10.31, the `OnActiveViewChanged` attribute has been added to the `MultiView` control, and the `OnActivate` and `OnDeactivate` attributes added to the first of the two `View` controls. We also added a `Label` control to the page, outside the declaration of the `MultiView` control, where interactive messages will be displayed.

LISTING 10.31. Specifying the Event Handler Attributes for MultiView and View Controls

```
<asp:MultiView id="MyMulti" ActiveViewIndex="0" runat="server"
    OnActiveViewChanged="ViewChanged">

  <asp:View id="View1" runat="server"
      OnDeactivate="ViewDeactivated"
      OnActivate="ViewActivated">
    This is View 1<br />
    <asp:button id="btnView1Next" Text="Next" runat="server"
              CommandName="NextView" />
  </asp:View>
  ...
  ...


</asp:MultiView>

<asp:Label id="lblStatus" EnableViewState="False" runat="server" />
```

Listing 10.32 shows the event handlers. When the `ActiveViewChanged` event is raised for the `MultiView` control, the `ViewChanged` event handler gets a reference to the current `View` using the `GetActiveView` method and displays the ID of this view in the `Label` control. When the `Activate` or `Deactivate` events are raised for the `View` control, the two remaining event handlers in Listing 10.32 display a text message to this effect in the `Label` control. Figure 10.14 shows the results.

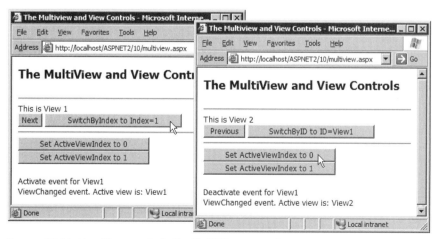

FIGURE 10.14. Handling events in the MultiView control

LISTING 10.32. The Event Handlers for the MultiView and View Controls

```
Sub ViewChanged(sender As Object, e As EventArgs)
   Dim oView As View = MyMulti.GetActiveView()
   lblStatus.Text &= "ViewChanged event. Active view is: " _
             & oView.ID & "<br />"
End Sub

Sub ViewActivated(sender As Object, e As EventArgs)
   lblStatus.Text &= "Activate event for View1<br />"
End Sub

Sub ViewDeactivated(sender As Object, e As EventArgs)
   lblStatus.Text &= "Deactivate event for View1<br />"
End Sub
```

Obviously you can include a lot more views or screens in a `MultiView` than we've shown in the preceding samples, and the handy thing is that all the controls declared in all the views are available to your server-side code, even when not included in the output sent to the client. They all maintain their values using the viewstate of the page, so it's easy to build tabbed dialogs or wizard-style pages using this control. However, if you really want to build wizards for your Web applications, the `Wizard` control (which we'll discuss soon) makes it even easier.

The MultiView and View Control Interfaces

The commonly used members of the `MultiView` control are described in Table 10.9, and those of the `View` control in Table 10.10.

TABLE 10.9. The Commonly Used Members of the MultiView Control

Property/Attribute	Description
Views	A reference to a `ViewCollection` instance that contains all the `View` controls defined for this `MultiView`. You can create `View` controls dynamically and add them to this collection or remove them in code.
ActiveViewIndex	A read/write `Integer` value that indicates which view will be displayed, as the zero-based index of that view in the `ViewCollection`.
NextViewCommandName	A `Static String` field containing the name of the command that moves to the next view. The default value is `NextView`.

TABLE 10.9. The Commonly Used Members of the MultiView Control (continued)

Property/Attribute	Description
PreviousViewCommandName	A Static String field containing the name of the command that moves to the previous view. The default value is PrevView.
SwitchViewByIDCommandName	A Static String field containing the name of the command that moves to the view whose ID is given in the CommandArgument property. The default value is SwitchViewByID.
SwitchViewByIndexCommandName	A Static String field containing the name of the command that moves to the view whose index is given in the CommandArgument property. The default value is SwitchViewByIndex.

Method	Description
GetActiveView()	Returns a reference to the currently displayed view as a View control instance.
SetActiveView(view)	Takes a reference to a View control instance and sets the ActiveViewIndex so that this View instance is displayed.

Event	Description
ActiveViewChanged	Raised when the active view is changed.

TABLE 10.10. The Commonly Used Members of the View Control

Property/Attribute	Description
Visible	A Boolean value that indicates whether this View control will be displayed.

Event	Description
Activate	Raised when the active view in the MultiView control changes so that this View is no longer displayed.
Deactivate	Raised when the active view in the MultiView control changes so that this View is displayed.

The Wizard Control

Modern applications increasingly use "wizards" to help users configure systems, provide information, or achieve some complex task that requires a number of selections to be made. Developers have found ways to build wizards in their Web applications, but ASP.NET 2.0 makes it easier than ever by providing a new `Wizard` control. The `Wizard` control has the following aims.

- Make it easy for developers to build wizards, and have the control automatically look after all the requirements other than the actual UI of each step. In other words, the `Wizard` control looks after things like maintaining values between postbacks, handling navigation, and so on.
- Provide both linear (step 1, step 2, step 3, and the reverse) and non-linear (from any step to any step) navigation. This allows a user to change his or her mind about the values in one step without having to go back through every step. It also allows navigation paths to be changed at runtime in response to selections made by the user.
- Provide opportunities to build the UI using styles, templates, and themes. Some parts of the UI that are auto-generated (such as the Previous, Next, and Finish buttons) can instead be overridden using templates in the same way as is possible in controls like the `DataGrid`.
- Provide support for User Controls, allowing reuse of certain UI and code sections throughout an application.
- Ensure that you don't have to create a page per step and create complex code to pass data or controls between those pages.

The `Wizard` control uses postbacks to the same page and does not support cross-page posting. The advantage is that all the controls, whether visible in the current step or not, are still part of the control tree of the page, have their values maintained through viewstate, and are available to code in the page.

From all this you will gather that the `Wizard` control is quite complex and exposes a great many properties and methods, plus some useful events. In this book we only have room for a description of the more useful basic properties; however, this will be enough for you to get started using the control. You can get a good idea of what the `Wizard` control provides by simply dragging one onto a page in Visual Studio 2005 (see Figure 10.15).

FIGURE 10.15. The Wizard control in Visual Studio 2005 design view

The Basic Structure of a Wizard

The following code shows the declaration of a very basic wizard. The `Wizard` control shown takes an attribute named `SideBarEnabled`, which determines whether or not the "sidebar" containing the navigation links between steps is shown at the left side of the page. Within the `Wizard` control element declaration is a `WizardSteps` element, and this in turn contains one or more `WizardStep` elements. Each `WizardStep` element defines one step, or one "screen" that will appear in the wizard (see Listing 10.33).

LISTING 10.33. The Basic Declaration of a Wizard Control

```
<asp:Wizard id="MyWizard" runat="server" SideBarEnabled="True">
  <WizardSteps>
    <asp:WizardStep id="WizardStep1" Title="First Step">
      This is step 1
      ... other step 1 content here ...
    </asp:WizardStep>
    <asp:WizardStep id="WizardStep2" Title="Second Step">
      This is step 2
      ... other step 2 content here ...
    </asp:WizardStep>
    ...
    ... more wizard steps here ...
    ...
  </WizardSteps>
</asp:Wizard>
```

Notice that there are no navigation instructions and no declarations of buttons or links. However, this declaration produces a fully functional (if not very useful) wizard, as shown in Figure 10.16.

FIGURE 10.16. A simple "no-code" Wizard in action

Each step is shown as a link in the left-hand side, and the appropriate Next, Previous, and Finish buttons appear in the right-hand side for each step. No code is required—it just works!

Specifying the Wizard Step Types

Each step (i.e., each `WizardStep` control) is automatically assigned a value from the `WizardStepType` enumeration for its `StepType` property. By default the value is `Auto`, and the order of the steps is determined by the order they are declared within the `Wizard` control.

However, you can assign specific values to the `StepType` property to change the default behavior. The first step should be `StepType="Start"` (which has only a Next button) and the last should be `StepType="Finish"` (which has Previous and Finish buttons). The intervening steps should be `StepType="Step"` (which has Previous and Next buttons). One exception is if you want a final "confirmation" page that contains no navigation features to appear as the last step. In this case, assign one of the steps the value `StepType="Complete"`, as shown here:

```
<asp:WizardStep id="Done" StepType="Complete">
  Finished! Your new software will now work faultlessly forever.
</asp:WizardStep>
```

Using Styles and Templates in a Wizard

While the basic `Wizard` control output is extremely plain and functional, it's possible to improve the appearance using styles or themes, or you can even replace the UI by defining templates. The style properties of the `Wizard` control are `HeaderStyle`, `NavigationButtonStyle`, `SideBarStyle`, and `StepStyle`. There are also individual style properties for each button type, including the buttons in the sidebar.

To change the caption of the buttons, set the `NextStepButtonText`, `PreviousStepButtonText`, `CancelButtonText`, and `FinishStepButtonText` properties to the text you want to display. You can even replace the standard buttons with `LinkButton` or `ImageButton` controls by setting the various `ButtonType` and `ButtonImageUrl` properties. Or, if you prefer to specify the content and the navigation controls yourself, you can use templates. The templates you can define are listed here.

- `HeaderTemplate` specifies the UI content, controls, and styles for the section at the top of each step, which is the same for every step.
- `SideBarTemplate` specifies the UI content, controls, and styles for the left-hand list of steps.
- `StartNavigationTemplate` specifies the UI content, controls, and styles for the bottom section of the first step (the one with `StepType="Start"` or the first step in the declaration of the control).
- `StepNavigationTemplate` specifies the UI content, controls, and styles for the bottom section of the intermediate steps (the ones with `StepType="Step"` or the steps other than the first and last ones in the declaration of the control).
- `FinishNavigationTemplate` specifies the UI content, controls, and styles for the bottom section of the final step (the one with `StepType="Finish"` or the last step in the declaration of the control).

Listing 10.34 shows in outline how these templates are used.

LISTING 10.34. Customizing the Wizard Control with Templates

```
<asp:Wizard id="MyWizard" runat="server">

  <HeaderTemplate>
    ... content for header goes here ...
  </HeaderTemplate>

  <SideBarTemplate>
    <asp:ImageButton OnClick="Wizard_Step" runat="server" />
  </SideBarTemplate>

  <StartNavigationTemplate>
    <asp:ImageButton OnClick="Wizard_Next" runat="server" />
  </StartNavigationTemplate>

  <StepNavigationTemplate>
    <asp:ImageButton OnClick="Wizard_Previous" runat="server" />
```

continues

```
    <asp:ImageButton OnClick="Wizard_Next" runat="server" />
  </StepNavigationTemplate>

  <FinishNavigationTemplate>
    <asp:ImageButton OnClick="Wizard_Previous" runat="server" />
    <asp:ImageButton OnClick="Wizard_Finish" runat="server" />
  </FinishNavigationTemplate>

  <WizardSteps>
    <asp:WizardStep id="Step1">
      ... visual content and controls go here ...
    </asp:WizardStep>
    ... more WizardStep declarations go here ...
  </WizardSteps >

</asp:Wizard>
```

Navigation Methods for a Wizard Control

The `Wizard` control exposes properties, methods, and events that you can use to change the default navigation path through the steps or react to events as the user interacts with the control. One useful feature is the `AllowReturn` property of the individual `WizardStep` controls, which prevents a user from returning to a step, so that he or she can view this step only once before finishing the wizard:

```
<asp:WizardStep id="Step2" Title="Second Step" AllowReturn="False">
  ...
</asp:WizardStep>
```

The `Wizard` control also exposes the `ActiveStep` and `ActiveStepIndex` properties. The `ActiveStep` property returns a reference to the current step as a `WizardStepBase` instance (the base class for `WizardStep`). The `ActiveStepIndex` property is read/write, so you can specify the step to be displayed in code by setting this to the zero-based `Integer` index of the required step.

Handling Events for a Wizard Control

The `Wizard` control exposes six events, as shown in Table 10.11. Note that there is no concept of a previous step because you are moving either forward or backward by way of the Next and Previous buttons. The `NextStepIndex` therefore indicates the index number irrespective of direction. Thus for consecutively numbered steps, moving backward from step 2 to step 1 would leave `NextStepIndex` as 1.

TABLE 10.11. The Events of the Wizard Control

Event	Description
ActiveViewChanged	Raised when the user moves from one step to another. Passes a standard `EventArgs` instance to the event handler.
NextButtonClick	Raised when the user clicks the Next button or link. Passes a `WizardNavigationEventArgs` instance to the event handler. This exposes three properties: • `CurrentStepIndex`: Returns the index of the current step. • `NextStepIndex`: Returns the index of the next step. Code can change this to display a different step if required. • `Cancel`: If set to `True` within the event procedure, the navigation event is canceled and the original step is shown again.
PreviousButtonClick	Raised when the user clicks the Previous button or link. Passes a `WizardNavigationEventArgs` instance to the event handler (see the `NextButtonClick` event).
CancelButtonClick	Raised when the user clicks the Cancel button or link. Passes a standard `EventArgs` instance to the event handler.
FinishButtonClick	Raised when the user clicks the Finish button or link. Passes a `WizardNavigationEventArgs` instance to the event handler (see the `NextButtonClick` event).
SideBarButtonClick	Raised when the user clicks one of the buttons or links on the sidebar. Passes a `WizardNavigationEventArgs` instance to the event handler (see the `NextButtonClick` event).

At any stage, you can access the individual steps and the content of each one through the `WizardSteps` property, which returns a reference to a `WizardStepCollection` that contains all the steps defined for the wizard. Methods of the `WizardStepCollection` can be used to add or remove steps from the wizard programmatically.

An Example of a Wizard Control

To demonstrate most of the features of the `Wizard` control, the following example creates a four-step wizard that allows text to be entered at each step, contains one step that you cannot return to, has a Cancel button in each step, and displays the step history and text box values when you click the Finish button.

Listing 10.35 shows the declaration of the `Wizard` control and the nested `WizardStep` controls. The `DisplayCancelButton` attribute forces the Cancel button to be shown, and event handlers are declared for the CancelButtonClick, FinishButtonClick, and ActiveViewChanged events. The background color of the wizard is also set in this declaration.

Nested within the Wizard control are the four steps, each having a Title specified and containing a standard ASP.NET TextBox control. Notice that the second step has the AllowReturn="False" attribute. Finally, in Listing 10.35, a Label control is declared (outside the Wizard control) to display status messages as the user interacts with the page.

LISTING 10.35. The Declaration of a Sample Wizard Control

```
<asp:Wizard id="MyWizard" Title="Simple Wizard" runat="server"
    SideBarEnabled="True" DisplayCancelButton="True"
    OnCancelButtonClick="WizardCancel"
    OnFinishButtonClick="WizardFinish"
    OnActiveViewChanged="ViewChanged"
    BackColor="LightBlue">
  <WizardSteps>
    <asp:WizardStep id="Step1" Title="First Step">
      This is step 1<br />
      <asp:TextBox id="txtStep1" Text="Step One Text" runat="server" />
    </asp:WizardStep>
    <asp:WizardStep id="Step2" Title="Second Step" AllowReturn="False">
      This is step 2<br />
      <asp:TextBox id="txtStep2" Text="Step Two Text" runat="server" />
    </asp:WizardStep>
    <asp:WizardStep id="Step3" Title="Third Step">
      This is step 3<br />
      <asp:TextBox id="txtStep3" Text="Step Three Text" runat="server" />
    </asp:WizardStep>
    <asp:WizardStep id="Step4" Title="Final Step">
      This is step 4<br />
      <asp:TextBox id="txtStep4" Text="Step Four Text" runat="server" />
    </asp:WizardStep>
  </WizardSteps>
</asp:Wizard>

<asp:Label id="lblMessage" EnableViewState="False" runat="server" />
```

As the user navigates through the steps, the ActiveViewChanged event is raised each time. Listing 10.36 shows the event handler named ViewChanged, which handles the ActiveViewChanged event. In the event handler, the code gets a reference to the active step that is currently displayed from the ActiveStep property. This property returns a WizardStep instance, and from it the code can extract and display the id and Title properties of the currently active step. Figure 10.17 shows the result.

LISTING 10.36. Handling the ActiveViewChanged and CancelButtonClick Events

```
Sub ViewChanged(sender As Object, e As EventArgs)

  ' display details of the current step
  Dim wstep As WizardStep = CType(MyWizard.ActiveStep, WizardStep)
  lblMessage.Text = "ActiveViewChanged event. ActiveStep is '" _
                 & wstep.id & "' - Title is '" & wstep.Title & "'"

End Sub

Sub WizardCancel(sender As Object, e As EventArgs)

  ' display message and hide wizard
  lblMessage.Text = "Canceled"
  MyWizard.Visible = False

End Sub
```

Notice in Figure 10.17 that a Cancel button is visible in each step. If the user clicks this button, the wizard will raise the `CancelButtonClick` event, which will call the `WizardCancel` event handler shown in Listing 10.36. This simply displays a message and hides the `Wizard` control by setting its `Visible` property to `False`.

FIGURE 10.17. Handling the ActiveViewChanged event to display step details

Handling the FinishButtonClick Event

The whole point of using a wizard is to be able to collect a range of information and then use it all to perform some process after the user clicks the Finish button. The example discussed here demonstrates how you can collect the values and the step history after the Finish button is clicked, by handling the `FinishButtonClick` event.

Listing 10.37 shows the `WizardFinish` event handler, which is executed when the `FinishButtonClick` event is raised. It uses the `GetHistory` method of the `Wizard` control to get an `ArrayList` of step instances (which are stored in reverse order). Then it can iterate through these, displaying the details of each one.

Next, the event handler extracts the values of all the `TextBox` controls that are declared on all the steps of the wizard. Even though only the last step is visible to the user, all the controls on all the steps are still part of the control tree of the page. Thus they will maintain their values in the view-state and can be accessed in your server-side code. Figure 10.18 shows the result of clicking the Finish button.

LISTING 10.37. Handling the FinishButtonClick Event

```
Sub WizardFinish(sender As Object, e As WizardNavigationEventArgs)

  ' display history of steps (stored in reverse order)
  lblMessage.Text = "<b>Step history:</b><br />"
  Dim steps As ICollection = MyWizard.GetHistory()
  For Each wstep As WizardStep In steps
    lblMessage.Text &= wstep.id & " Title: '" & wstep.Title & "'<br />"
  Next

  ' display values in text boxes
  lblMessage.Text &= "<b>Control values:</b><br />'" _
                  & txtStep1.Text & "'<br />'" _
                  & txtStep2.Text & "'<br />'" _
                  & txtStep3.Text & "'<br />'" _
                  & txtStep4.Text & "'<br />"

  ' hide the wizard
  MyWizard.Visible = False

End Sub
```

One point to note if you try this example is that on the third step, you get a Next button but no Previous button. This is because the declaration of the second step contains the attribute `AllowReturn="False"`. The first step still contains a Next button, and the second step still appears as a link in the sidebar, but clicking either of these has no effect. The control automatically cancels the navigation action to that step after it has been visited once.

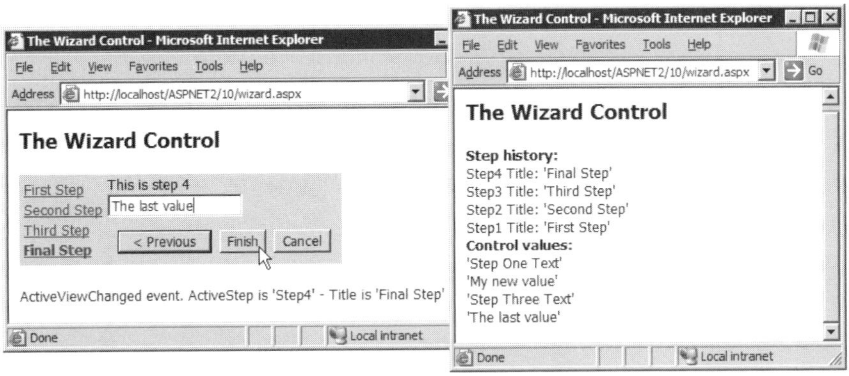

FIGURE 10.18. Displaying step history and control values when the Finish button is clicked

Controls and Attributes Specific to Mobile Devices

As you saw at the start of this chapter, most of the ASP.NET server controls within version 2.0 of the .NET Framework can modify their output to suit different types of devices. So the techniques for using the controls that you saw in this and earlier chapters are identical when building pages targeted at mobile devices. However, several controls are specific to mobile devices—in particular, devices that have built-in phone capabilities. These controls consist of

- The `ContentPager` control, which works as part of the underlying page architecture to divide pages into separate sections for small-screen and mobile devices
- The `PhoneLink` control, which can be used in phone-enabled devices to initiate a phone call to a specified number
- The `SoftKeyLabel` attribute, which is added to most of the controls to allow the developer to provide better soft-key support for mobile devices such as cellular phones

The `MultiView` and `View` controls were also originally designed to provide better small-screen device support, though they are often used in pages targeted at other types of browsers as well.

We'll look at each of these controls and attributes next to see what they do and how they are used. Also remember that some of the standard ASP.NET 2.0 controls from the `WebControls` namespace are specifically designed to better support mobile and WML-based devices such as cellular phones, in addition to the other new features they offer aimed at traditional client devices.

- The new `DynamicImage` control will automatically convert images into the correct `.wbmp` format for cellular phones.
- The `Table`, `GridView`, `FormView`, and `DataGrid` controls now automatically provide two different modes for viewing the content when sent to a mobile device: summary view and details view.

The ContentPager Control

Although the `ContentPager` control can be used in pages that target any type of browser or other client device, it is generally most useful for small-screen devices. These devices, particularly mobile phones, have extremely limited memory capacity and a slow bandwidth connection, so it is good practice to minimize the amount of content sent to the device for each "screen" (or page) displayed.

One way to minimize the content when there is a lot of information to display is to separate it into individual pages and provide Next and Previous buttons so that the user can navigate from one page to the next. However, this often involves considerable extra coding. In ASP.NET 2.0, the new `ContentPager` control can handle all the issues of creating the appearance of separate pages from a single source page.

The `ContentPager` control is placed within an ASP.NET page and its `ControlToPaginate` property set to the `id` of a container control on the page (which must have the `runat="server"` attribute). A common approach is to use the `ContentPager` control to paginate the contents of a `<form>`. In Listing 10.38, the `<form>` contains eight `<div>` controls. Each `<div>` contains one or more child controls.

LISTING 10.38. Using a ContentPager Control with a `<form>`

```
...
<form id="MyForm" runat="server">

  <div runat="server">
    <asp:Label Text="Name:" runat="server" />
    <asp:Textbox id="txtName" runat="server" />
  </div>
```

```
<div runat="server">
  <asp:Label Text="Phone:" runat="server" />
  <asp:Textbox id="txtPhone" runat="server" />
</div>
<div runat="server">
  <asp:Label Text="Email:" runat="server" />
  <asp:Textbox id="txtEmail" runat="server" />
</div>
<div runat="server">
  <asp:Label Text="Address:" runat="server" />
  <asp:Textbox id="txtAddress" runat="server" />
</div>
<div runat="server">
  <asp:Label Text="City:" runat="server" />
  <asp:Textbox id="txtCity" runat="server" />
</div>
<div runat="server">
  <asp:Label Text="State:" runat="server" />
  <asp:Textbox id="txtState" runat="server" />
</div>
<div runat="server">
  <asp:Label Text="Zip:" runat="server" />
  <asp:Textbox id="txtZip" runat="server" />
</div>
<div runat="server">
 <asp:Button Text="Submit" runat="server" />
</div>
<asp:ContentPager id="MyPager" ControlToPaginate="MyForm"
                  ItemsPerPage="3" runat="server" />

</form>
...
```

After the code for the Submit button comes the declaration of the ContentPager control. The ControlToPaginate attribute specifies the <form> as the container control, whose content (the controls that are direct children of the container being paginated) will be divided into separate pages. The number of controls that will appear on each page is controlled by the ItemsPerPage property, here set to 3 using the ItemsPerPage attribute.

That's all you need to do to provide pagination of the output. In a browser and in a mobile device, the output now consists of three separate screens, with the Next and Previous buttons displayed automatically at the appropriate times. Figure 10.19 shows the results in a mobile device emulator, and Figure 10.20 shows the same page viewed in Internet Explorer.

We see three screens because ItemsPerPage specifies the maximum number of top-level controls, within the pageable control, that are to be displayed for each screen or page. The <div> controls wrap the individual

Name: ▨	Address: ▨	Zip: ▨
Phone: [...]	City: [...]	Submit
Email: [...]	State: [...]	Prev
Next	Prev Next	
Options	Options	Options

FIGURE 10.19. The ContentPager control viewed in a mobile device emulator

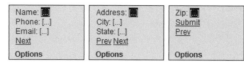

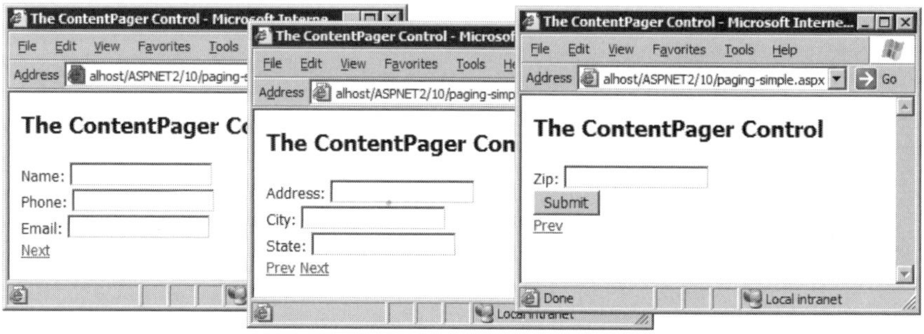

FIGURE 10.20. The ContentPager control viewed in Internet Explorer

Label, TextBox, and Button controls so that they are not individually paged. Therefore, we get three Label controls and three TextBox controls for screens 1 and 2, and a Label, TextBox, and Button for screen 3.

You can also put more than one ContentPager control on a page if you wish. This might be useful if you want the Next and Previous links to appear at the top and bottom of the list—you just insert them into the page at the points you want their output to appear. Note that you must set their ItemsPerPage attributes to the same value.

Displaying Numeric Navigation Links

Alternatively, you can force the ContentPager control to display a list of all the available page numbers as hyperlinks so that users can jump directly to any one of them. All that's required is to add the Mode attribute with the value NumericPages:

```
<asp:ContentPager id="MyPager" ... Mode="NumericPages" />
```

Figure 10.21 shows how this looks in Internet Explorer, and the result is much the same in a mobile device. As you can see from the screenshot, the page numbers show the "proper" values, indexed from 1.

To control how many page numbers are displayed in this mode, change the PageButtonCount property from its default of 10. The usual format of

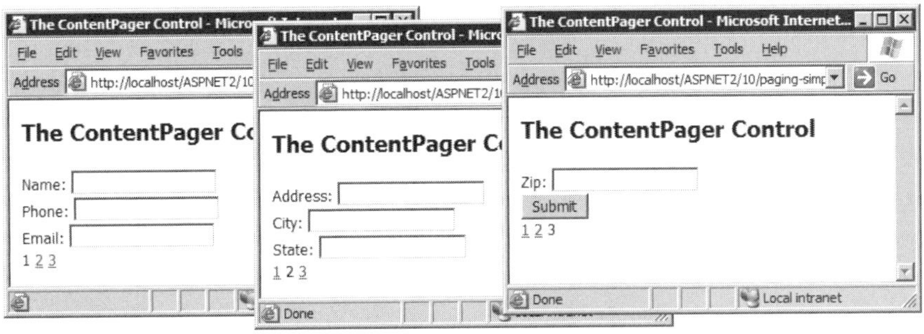

FIGURE 10.21. Displaying the page numbers as hyperlinks

three dots after the last page number shown (or before the first one) signifies that there are more pages available:

$$\underline{0}\ \underline{1}\ \underline{2}\ \underline{3}\ \underline{4}\ \underline{5}\ \underline{6}\ \dots \qquad \text{or} \qquad \dots\ \underline{7}\ \underline{8}\ \underline{9}\ \underline{10}\ \underline{11}\ \underline{12}$$

You can also set the `Mode` property at runtime to a value from the `PagerButtons` enumeration. The values available are `NextPrevious`, `NextPreviousFirstLast`, `Numeric`, and `NumericFirstLast` (which displays the text links First and Last with the individual page number links between them). You can also change the text of the links by setting the `FirstPageText`, `PreviousPageText`, `NextPageText`, and `LastPageText` attributes or properties to the required `String` values, or use your own images by setting the `FirstImageUrl`, `PreviousImageUrl`, `NextImageUrl`, and `LastImageUrl` attributes or properties. And, of course, you can style the output of the `ContentPager` control by using the `PageStyle`, `ButtonStyle`, and `CurrentPageStyle` properties.

Displaying Page Numbers

The `ContentPager` control exposes properties named `CurrentPage` and `PageCount` so you can easily indicate to users where they are in the set of pages by displaying these values. (The `PageCount` property is read-only, but you can set the `CurrentPage` property in code to force a specific page to be displayed.) The example in Listing 10.39 uses the `ContentPager` control to page the output from a `DataList` control. The `ContentPager` points to the `DataList` by using the `ControlToPaginate="MyList"` attribute and specifies there will be five items per page. Text links will be displayed, including the First and Last links. Finally, the `OnPaginated` attribute is included, specifying that the event handler named `ShowPage` will be executed when the `ContentPager` paginates the content of its associated control (`Paginated` is the only event exposed by the `ContentPager` control).

LISTING 10.39. Paging a DataList Control with a ContentPager Control

```
<asp:DataList id="MyList" runat="server">
  <ItemTemplate><%# Container.DataItem %></ItemTemplate>
</asp:DataList>

<asp:ContentPager id="MyPager" runat="server"
    ControlToPaginate="MyList" ItemsPerPage="5"
    Mode="NextPreviousFirstLast"
    OnPaginated="ShowPage" />

<asp:Label id="lblPageNum" EnableViewState="False" runat="server" />
```

Listing 10.40 shows the server-side code in this example page. The `Page_Load` event handler is responsible for populating the `DataList` with 21 entries when the page first loads. The `ShowPage` event handler, also shown in Listing 10.40, is responsible for displaying the page number and total number of pages as Page *x* of *x*. It does this by querying the `CurrentPage` and `PageCount` properties of the `ContentPager` control.

However, notice that the pages are numbered from 0—we add 1 to the value of the `CurrentPage` property in the code in Listing 10.40 so that it displays the page numbers as 1, 2, and 3 (which tends to be more intuitive for users). The screenshot in Figure 10.22 shows the result.

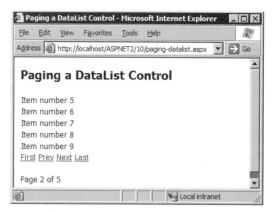

FIGURE 10.22. Displaying the page number and page count

LISTING 10.40. Populating the DataList and Handling the Paginated Event

```
Sub Page_Load()
  If Not Page.IsPostback Then
    Dim aValue As New ArrayList()
    Dim iLoop As Integer
    For iLoop = 0 To 20
      aValue.Add("Item number " & iLoop.ToString())
    Next
    MyList.DataSource = aValue
    MyList.DataBind()
  End If
End Sub

Sub ShowPage(sender As Object, e As EventArgs)
  lblPageNum.Text = "Page " & MyPager.CurrentPage + 1 _
                & " of " & MyPager.PageCount
End Sub
```

Custom Paging

You can also choose to abandon the built-in pagination features and instead create build routines and UIs to suit your own specific requirements using templates. This technique does require more effort but allows you to exert full control over the process. The ContentPager control accepts a <PagerTemplate> declaration and can be wired up to separate controls in the template that will activate the Next and Back operations. Any control that exposes the CommandName property (e.g., Button, LinkButton, or ImageButton) is an ideal candidate. Listing 10.41 shows an example of the technique.

LISTING 10.41. Custom Paging with a Pager Template

```
<asp:ContentPager ... runat="server">
  <PagerTemplate>
    <asp:Button Text="Previous" runat="server"
            CommandName="Previous" />
    <asp:Button Text="Next" runat="server"
            CommandName="Next" />
  </PagerTemplate>
</asp:ContentPager>
```

Simply set the CommandName attributes of the buttons to the same values as the NextPageCommandName and PreviousPageCommandName properties of the ContentPager control, and they will automatically cause the postback that moves to the next or previous page. The default values for the `NextPageCommandName` and `PreviousPageCommandName` properties of the `ContentPager` control are "`Next`" and "`Previous`", respectively, but you can change the values if you need to wire the buttons to different instances of the `ContentPager` control.

Page Weightings

So far, all the examples we've shown set a specific value for the `ItemsPerPage` property of the `ContentPager` control. This is fine if each item takes up roughly the same amount of vertical space on the page. However, if they don't, the lengths of the pages will vary even when each page contains the same number of items.

To get around this, the `ContentPager` control can use *weightings* to determine where the page breaks should occur. Page weightings are automatically used if you don't specify a value for the `ItemsPerPage` attribute when declaring the `ContentPager` control and don't set the `ItemsPerPage` property at runtime.

If the controls used within the container control implement the `IPaginationInfo` or `IItemPaginationInfo` interfaces, they can be assigned specific weightings for their `Weight` property. Otherwise, the `ContentPager` control uses the number of contained controls for each top-level item to work out the weightings. Then, taking into account the value of the container control's `MaximumWeight` property, the `ContentPager` control can calculate where to place the page breaks.

Keeping Child Controls Together

The `IPaginationInfo` interface exposes a property named `PaginateChildren`. When this is set to `True` (the default varies depending on the control type), the pagination process will break up the pages between the child controls of a top-level item. When set to `False`, all child controls are kept together for each top-level item in the container control that is being paginated. The `Panel` control is probably the most suitable server control to act as the parent container in this case. For plain HTML controls, the `<div>` control, as shown previously, also keeps child controls together.

The PhoneLink Control

One useful technique in voice-enabled devices such as mobile phones is to provide a link that dials a specified number when activated. A `PhoneLink` control to achieve this is part of the MMIT, and an equivalent is now part of the core control set in ASP.NET 2.0.

The `PhoneLink` control has a property named `PhoneNumber`, which specifies the number to be dialed when activated. It also supports the display and formatting properties that are standard for the controls that inherit from `WebControl`, plus the `SoftKeyLabel` attribute that we discuss in more detail in the next subsection.

```
<asp:PhoneLink id="Phone1" runat="server" SoftKeyLabel="Dial"
               PhoneNumber="123-456-7890" />
```

In a device that does not support voice calls, the control will usually just render the phone number in the page as text within an HTML anchor element:

```
<a id="Phone1" class="Normal">123-456-7890</a>
```

However, in a voice-enabled device, the output is a hyperlink that specifies the protocol `wtai:`, which initiates a voice call. Notice that the number in the `href` attribute below is prefixed with a special URL as well, which is used by the phone to make the connection, and the number has all non-numeric formatting characters removed:

```
<a href="wtai://wp/mc;1234567890">123-456-7890</a>
```

The result in a mobile device emulator is shown in Figure 10.23.

FIGURE 10.23. The PhoneLink control in a mobile device emulator

The SoftKeyLabel Attribute

Some of the interactive controls in the ASP.NET 2.0 `WebControls` namespace (mainly link and button controls) have the `SoftKeyLabel` attribute. This can be set programmatically or declaratively through the `SoftKeyLabel` attribute. The value is a `String` displayed by many mobile devices that have soft-key buttons (usually located just below the screen). It provides a useful hint to users about which button to press to activate or interact with the control.

As an example, the code in Listing 10.42 creates a page containing a `HyperLink` and a `PhoneLink` control. Both of these controls carry a definition of the `SoftKeyLabel` attribute.

LISTING 10.42. Using the SoftKeyLabel Attribute

```
<%@ Page Language="VB" %>
<html>
<head>
  <style>
    .Heading {font-family:Arial; font-size:xsmall; font-weight:bold}
    .Normal {font-family:Arial; font-size:xsmall}
  </style>
</head>
<body>
  <form runat="server">

    <asp:HyperLink cssClass="Normal" id="Link1" runat="server"
      Text="Next Page" NavigateUrl="nextpage.aspx"
      SoftKeyLabel="Next" />

    <br />

    <asp:PhoneLink cssClass="Normal" id="Call1" runat="server"
      PhoneNumber="123-456-7890" SoftKeyLabel="Dial" />

  </form>
</body>
</html>
```

When viewed in a cellular phone, the value of the SoftKeyLabel is displayed above the soft-key button as each control receives the focus, making it easy to see what each one does. You saw this demonstrated in Figure 10.23 when we discussed the PhoneLink control.

Mobile Browser Emulators

If you don't have a mobile device to test your pages, you can use one of several emulators to simulate a mobile phone, including the following:

- Mobile Phone Simulator from OpenWave, available at http://developer.openwave.com/
- R380 WAP Emulator from Symbian, available at http://www.symbian.com/developer/
- Nokia Mobile Browser from Nokia, available at http://forum.nokia.com/
- SmartPhone Emulator from Yospace, available at http://www.yospace.com/

Using one of these emulators allows you to easily test how well your pages work on a WML-enabled device. Mobile devices do, of course, include PDAs and phones based on Windows Pocket PC. Although these devices feature a version of Internet Explorer, you still face the problems of a small screen size, so your pages may need to be adjusted and tested accordingly. Find out more about Microsoft Mobile Support at http://www.microsoft.com/windowsmobile/.

SUMMARY

In this chapter we've looked at how the ASP.NET 2.0 server controls are implemented to take advantage of the new universal control architecture. The controls use device adapters to generate their output. The page framework automatically detects the client type and selects the appropriate adapter at runtime to provide the best possible support for that client. This makes building pages to suit different types of devices much easier and more intuitive than in earlier versions of ASP.NET and, in fact, in any other Web programming environment. You no longer have to decide what types of clients you want to support or write special code to suit each type of device.

After discussing the universal control architecture, the chapter presented an overview and breakdown of the new server controls provided with ASP.NET 2.0. Many of these controls have been described in earlier chapters, but in this chapter we covered in detail those that you haven't seen in earlier chapters. In addition, we looked at two new controls specific to mobile devices, including the `ContentPager` control, which makes it easy to break a page into separate screens, and the `PhoneLink` control, which can initiate a voice connection.

In the next chapter, we'll continue this look at server controls by examining how several of the existing controls have been enhanced to provide better usability, accessibility, programmability, or performance.

■ 11 ■

Enhancements to Existing Controls

T HROUGHOUT THIS BOOK you've seen many examples of the great new features of ASP.NET 2.0, including all of the new server controls. In this chapter we are going to focus on the enhancements to the existing version 1.x server controls. Many of the existing controls have gained new properties that extend their capabilities, as well as bringing them into line with the new features and services in ASP.NET version 2.0. For example, the various button and link controls now support validation groups and site counters. The `Table` and `DataGrid` controls now automatically support the details view on small-screen and mobile devices. Meanwhile, many controls have been enhanced to provide better usability or accessibility features.

To make it easier to see what has changed with the existing controls, this chapter takes three different approaches. It looks at the different types of new features, listing the controls to which they apply, and then lists the individual controls with a summary of the changes to the interface of each one. Finally, this chapter looks in more detail at those controls that have changed significantly, so that you can see how the new features are used. So, in this chapter you'll find the following:

- A summary of new features that have been added to the existing controls

- A full list of the changes to the existing control interfaces
- Examples of the ways the enhanced controls can be used

We start with a look at the new features introduced in version 2.0 and the controls to which they apply.

Summary of New Control Features

This section of the chapter summarizes the enhancements to the server controls that were originally provided with ASP.NET version 1.x, breaking them down into the new feature groups that are part of ASP.NET 2.0. For example, the section on accessibility improvements briefly describes the aims of this feature, the new properties that implement it, and the controls to which they apply.

Accessibility Improvements

Increasingly, Web developers must consider the needs of users of non-graphical Web browsers, such as text-only browsers, Braille output devices, aural page readers, and other specialist user agents. There are also issues to consider such as the use of colors and small text for users who have less than perfect vision. Many governments require that their Web sites conform to certain accessibility guides: In the United States, Section 508 of the Rehabilitation Act covers this; in Canada, the Treasury Board sets standards; and in Australia, there is a Disability Discrimination Act. Many other countries also require adherence to certain standards, so ASP.NET 2.0 controls improve the ease with which you can build accessible sites. While the controls can't provide all the solutions (only good page design and implementation can do that), they do provide some useful new features.

- The `Caption` property, and the associated `CaptionAlign` property, can be used to display a caption that describes a table. These properties apply to the `Calendar`, `DetailsView`, `FormView`, `GridView`, `Table`, `DataList`, and `DataGrid` controls.
- The `DescriptionUrl` property can be used to provide nonvisual page readers with the URL of a page that contains more details of an image, perhaps in text or aural form that can be presented to the user in a way that conveys what the image contains or represents. This property applies to the `Image` control.

- The `GenerateEmptyAlternateText` property instructs a control to add the attribute `alt=""` (an empty string) to the element(s) it generates. This attribute should be present on any image that does not contribute to the meaning or content of the page. Examples are graphical bullets, page divider images, or "blank" images used to align or position other elements. This property applies to the `Image`, `ImageButton`, and `ImageMap` controls.

- The `UseAccessibleHeader` property forces a control that displays a table to add the `scope` attribute to the header cells, which a nonvisual user agent can take advantage of to make it easier for the user to understand what the contents of a table mean. This property applies to the `Calendar`, `GridView`, `DataList`, and `DataGrid` controls.

- The `AssociatedHeaderCellID` property is an array of `String` values that link a table cell to one or more specific table header cells through their ID values. In tables that do not have a simple grid layout (i.e., tables that use column or row spans, or identify individual rows with row headers), this allows nonvisual user agents to relate the data in the table with the correct headers. This property applies to the `TableCell` control.

- The `AccessibleHeaderText` property is used to specify text that explains what each column header means in more detail, without being visible in the normal output (and therefore not disturbing the layout of the table). This property applies to the controls used to generate columns or rows in a `GridView` and `DetailsView` control, namely, `BoundField`, `AutoGeneratedField`, `ButtonField`, `CommandField`, `CheckBoxField`, `HyperlinkField`, `ImageField`, and `TemplateField`.

Input Control Enhancements

Several new features have been added to ASP.NET 2.0 to make it easier to build interactive Web forms that are intuitive for the user.

- The `AssociatedControlID` property is used to link a `Label` control to an interactive control such as a text box, checkbox, or list control. It allows a hot key to be defined that moves the input focus directly to that control. See the subsection on the `Label` control later in this chapter for details.

- The `AutoCompleteType` property is used to specify the field of a user's VCard that should be used to automatically populate a `TextBox` control.

- The InputAttributes and LabelAttributes properties are used with a CheckBox control to access the individual elements generated by a CheckBox control (i.e., the <span> and <input> elements), allowing specific or custom attributes to be added or removed.
- The PostBackUrl property is used with the Button, ImageButton, and LinkButton controls to force the page to be posted to a different URL, rather than using the ASP.NET postback architecture. See the Cross-Page Posting section in Chapter 9.
- The UseSubmitBehavior property is used with the Button, ImageButton, and LinkButton controls to specify whether the <form> should be submitted using a client-side JavaScript function (the default with a LinkButton) or the standard browser submit behavior (the default for a Button and ImageButton).

Changes to the Forms and Postback Architecture

Chapter 9 looked at the changes that have been made to the postback architecture to support new features such as setting and maintaining the input focus and specifying the default button for a page. To support these features there are three new properties, all of which apply only to the HtmlForm control that implements a server-side form.

- The DefaultButton property is used to specify the ID of the button-type control that will be clicked when the user presses the Return key.
- The DefaultFocus property is used to specify the control that will get the input focus by default when the page loads.
- The SubmitDisabledControls property is a Boolean value that indicates whether controls that have the disabled="disabled" attribute (or the Enabled property set to False) will submit their values when the form is posted to the server.

Validation Controls and Validation Groups

Chapter 9 also examined the addition of another feature to ASP.NET called **validation groups.** This feature allows multiple sections of the same page to be validated separately. There are also changes that make it easier to work with the validation controls.

- The ValidationGroup property specifies which validation group the control belongs to. It applies to all the validation controls; all of the

interactive form controls such as `TextBox` and `CheckBox`; the various
list controls such as `ListBox` and `DropDownList`; the button-type
controls such as `Button` and `HtmlInputButton`; and the field controls that are used in the `GridView` and `DetailsView` controls.

- The `SetFocusOnError` property can be used to force the input focus
  to a control that fails validation when a page is submitted. It applies
  to the `CompareValidator`, `CustomValidator`, `RangeValidator`,
  `RegularExpressionValidator`, and `RequiredFieldValidator`.

- The `CausesValidation` property, previously available on most
  button-type controls, allows a control to submit a page containing
  validation controls without the values being validated (useful, for
  example, for a Cancel button). This property has been added to the
  base class `ListControl` in ASP.NET 2.0, and so is now available for
  the `ListBox`, `DropDownList`, `CheckBoxList`, and `RadioButtonList`
  controls, as well as the new `BulletedList` control.

- The `ValidateEmptyText` property can be used to specify that a
  validation control should treat an empty value as a validation failure. The default is to ignore empty values. However, this applies
  only to the `CustomValidator` control.

Data Source Control Integration

Chapter 3 examined the new data source controls added to ASP.NET in version 2.0. To support the use of data source controls, all the existing controls
that support data binding now expose the `DataSourceID` property, which
specifies the ID of the data source control to which they are bound. As well
as the new grid-type controls in ASP.NET 2.0, this property also applies to
the existing `HtmlSelect`, `ListBox`, `DropDownList`, `CheckBoxList`,
`RadioButtonList`, `Repeater`, `DataList`, and `DataGrid` controls.

Mobile Device Support

Chapter 10 discussed the new features designed to integrate better support
for mobile devices into ASP.NET. The three main features are listed here.

- The new ability to display multiple views of a table and to navigate
  between them applies to the existing `DataGrid` and `Table` controls,
  as well as the new `GridView` and `DetailsView` controls.

- The `SoftKeyLabel` property provides easily accessible links in mobile devices such as cellular phones. This property applies to the

new `PhoneCall` control and the existing `Button`, `LinkButton`, `ImageButton`, and `HyperLink` controls.

- The `AllowPaginate` property specifies whether a control will allow its content to be broken into separate pages by a `ContentPager` control. This property applies only to the `Panel` control.

Site and Page Counter Integration

The site and page counters feature in ASP.NET 2.0 is described in Chapter 9. It adds a set of properties specific to counting page views and click-throughs:

CountClicks	CounterGroup	CounterName
CountViews	RowsPerDay	SiteCountersProvider
TrackApplicationName	TrackNavigateUrl	TrackPageUrl

These properties are supported by the `AdRotator`, `Button`, `LinkButton`, `ImageButton`, `HyperLink`, and `ImageMap` controls.

List Control Enhancements

Two new properties are useful when working with controls descended from the `ListControl` base class.

- The `AppendDataBoundItems` property instructs the control to add any items provided by a data source to which it is bound to those already in the list, rather than replacing them (the default behavior). Useful for adding a blank or "dummy" entry to the top of the list in the declaration of the control, rather than having to insert it dynamically after the control has been bound to and populated from its data source. This property applies to the `ListBox`, `DropDownList`, `CheckBoxList`, and `RadioButtonList` controls, as well as the new `BulletedList` control.
- The `Enabled` property has been added to the `ListItem` control used to implement individual items in a list control. It allows individual items to be removed from the list when displayed but remain in the `Items` collection of the list control within the server-side control tree.

Themes Integration

Chapter 7 described the theming features of ASP.NET. These involve two properties: `EnableTheming` and `SkinID`, which are added to the `WebControl` base class from which most controls in the `System.Web.UI.WebControls` namespace are descended.

Tables of Control Enhancements

As you saw in the previous section of this chapter, there has been an impressive series of updates to the existing controls to achieve improved usability, accessibility, and general performance of the existing server controls in ASP.NET. So that you can more easily see how each of the existing controls has changed, the following subsections list the controls individually, summarizing the interface changes to each one.

Enhancements to Existing Controls in the HtmlControls Namespace

Table 11.1 lists the changes to the controls in the `System.Web.UI.HtmlControls` namespace that were originally provided with ASP.NET version 1.x and have been enhanced or extended in version 2.0.

TABLE 11.1. Enhancements to Controls in the HtmlControls Namespace

Control	Description
HtmlSelect	Gains one new property: ●DataSourceID: The ID of a data source control that will provide the source data for this control.
HtmlButton	Gains one new property: ●ValidationGroup: The name of the validation group to which this control belongs.
HtmlInputButton	Gains one new property: ●ValidationGroup: The name of the validation group to which this control belongs.
HtmlInputImage	Gains one new property: ●ValidationGroup: The name of the validation group to which this control belongs.
HtmlForm	Gains three new properties designed to support the new features added to the ASP.NET page architecture in version 2.0. See Chapter 9 for more details. ●DefaultButton: The ID of the button-type control that will be clicked when the user presses the Return key. ●DefaultFocus: The control that will get the input focus when the page loads unless another control is specified declaratively or programmatically. ●SubmitDisabledControls: A Boolean value that indicates whether controls that have the disabled="disabled" attribute (or the Enabled property set to False) will submit their values when the form is posted to the server. The default value is False.

Enhancements to Existing Controls in the WebControls Namespace

Table 11.2 lists the changes to the controls in the `System.Web.UI.WebControls` namespace that were originally provided with ASP.NET version 1.x and have been enhanced or extended in version 2.0. The base classes for the majority of the controls in the `WebControls` namespace are listed first, followed by the remaining controls in alphabetical order.

TABLE 11.2. Enhancements to Controls in the WebControls Namespace

Control	Description
WebControl	This is the base class from which the majority of the controls in the `WebControls` namespace are descended. See Chapter 7 for details of the theming features. Three new properties are added to the `WebControl` class.
	• `EnableTheming`: A `Boolean` value that specifies whether any themes that set the style or behavior of the control will be applied. The default value is `True`.
	• `HasAttributes`: A `Boolean` value that indicates whether the control has any attributes.
	• `SkinID`: The ID of the specific skin within a themes file that will be applied to the control.
ListControl	This is the base class from which the list controls `BulletedList`, `CheckBoxList`, `RadioButtonList`, `ListBox`, and `DropDownList` inherit. See the subsection on the `List` and `ListItem` controls later in this chapter for more details. Four properties are added to all these classes.
	• `AppendDataBoundItems`: A `Boolean` value that indicates whether bound items will be added to any existing items in the `Items` collection of the list, rather than replacing them.
	• `CausesValidation`: A `Boolean` value that indicates whether this control will cause any attached validation controls to validate the values of the controls on the form when the form is submitted. Set this property to `False` to allow the form to be submitted without any validation taking place. The default value is `False`.
	• `DataSourceID`: The ID of a data source control that will provide the source data for this control.
	• `ValidationGroup`: The name of the validation group to which this control belongs.
BaseValidator	This is the base class from which all the validation controls (with the exception of the `ValidationSummary` control) are descended. See Chapter 9 for details of the validation control enhancements. All the descendant validation controls gain two new properties.
	• `SetFocusOnError`: A `Boolean` value that specifies whether the associated control should receive the input focus when the validation test on its value fails. The default value is `False`.
	• `ValidationGroup`: The name of the validation group to which this control belongs.

TABLE 11.2. Enhancements to Controls in the WebControls Namespace (continued)

Control	Description
AdRotator	A range of properties and one method are added to the `AdRotator` control. It is now descended from `DataBoundControl` (rather than `WebControl`) and so also supports ASP.NET server-side data binding. See the subsection on the `AdRotator` control later in this chapter for more details. The new properties are listed here.

- `AdType`: Indicates the type of advertisement, which can be one of the `AdType` enumeration values: `Banner` (the default) for a banner ad, `Popup` for a pop-up window containing the ad, and `PopUnder` for a window that appears behind the current window.

- `AlternateTextField`: Sets or returns the element name or database field from which the alternate text is returned. The default is `AlternateText`.

- `DataSource`: Sets or returns the data source to bind the `AdRotator` to.

- `DataMember`: Sets or returns the name of the table or individual data rowset in the data source if the data source supports more than one set of data items.

- `DataSourceID`: Sets or returns the ID of a data source control that will provide the source data for this control.

- `ImageUrlField`: Sets or returns the element name or database field from which the image URL is returned. The default is `ImageUrl`.

- `NavigateUrlField`: Sets or returns the element name or database field from which the navigation URL is returned. The default is `NavigateUrl`.

- `PopFrequency`: Sets or returns the frequency, as a percentage, with which to create pop-up or pop-under ads.

- `PopPositionLeft`: Sets or returns the screen position that defines the left side of the ad. If not defined, the advertisement is centered horizontally on the screen.

- `PopPositionTop`: Sets or returns the screen position that defines the top of the ad. If not defined, the advertisement is centered vertically on the screen.

The `AdRotator` control also supports the Site Counters Service and so exposes the standard set of properties required for this service. See the Site and Page Counters section in Chapter 9.

- `AdCreated` event: Raised when an advertisement is displayed. Exposes four properties that provide information about the event. `AdProperties` is a reference to an `IDictionary` instance that contains information specific to the extended properties in the current advertisements file. The other three properties are `AlternateText`, `ImageUrl`, and `NavigateUrl`, which contain the values of these properties for the current advertisement.

continues

TABLE 11.2. Enhancements to Controls in the WebControls Namespace (continued)

Control	Description
Button	Four new properties are added to the `Button` control. See the subsection on the `Button`, `LinkButton`, and `ImageButton` controls later in this chapter for more details.
	• `OnClientClick`: A `String` that is the name of the client-side function, or a code fragment, to be executed on the client when the button is clicked.
	• `PostBackUrl`: A `String` that is the URL to which the containing form will be posted. See the Cross-Page Posting section in Chapter 9.
	• `SoftKeyLabel`: The text to display in a small-screen or mobile device for the soft-key or shortcut key when this control has the focus.
	• `UseSubmitBehavior`: A `Boolean` value that specifies whether the containing form should be submitted using a client-side JavaScript function or the standard browser "submit" behavior. The default value is `True`.
	• `ValidationGroup`: The name of the validation group to which this control belongs.
Calendar	Four new properties are added to the `Calendar` control.
	• `CalendarEntryText`: The text displayed in a small-screen or mobile device when the calendar is first displayed in multistep mode. The default is `"Calendar"`.
	• `Caption`: The text caption to display above the calendar in the page.
	• `CaptionAlign`: A value from the `TableCaptionAlign` enumeration that indicates how the caption will be aligned with respect to the calendar. Valid values are `Bottom`, `Top`, `Left`, `Right`, and `NotSet`.
	• `UseAccessibleHeader`: Specifies whether the control should add the `scope` attribute to the cells in the header row to assist users of specialist browsers and page readers.
CheckBox	Three new properties are added to the `CheckBox` control. See the subsection on the **CheckBox** control later in this chapter for more details.
	• `InputAttributes` (read-only): A reference to the `Attributes` collection for the `<input type="radio">` element that is generated by the `CheckBox` control. It allows arbitrary attributes to be added to the element.
	• `LabelAttributes` (read-only): A reference to the `Attributes` collection for the `<span>` element that is generated by the `CheckBox` control for the caption text. It allows arbitrary attributes to be added to the element.
	• `ValidationGroup`: The name of the validation group to which this control belongs.

TABLE 11.2. Enhancements to Controls in the WebControls Namespace (continued)

Control	Description
CustomValidator	One new property is added to the CustomValidator control. See Chapter 9 for details of the validation control enhancements. • ValidateEmptyText: A Boolean value that indicates whether an empty value will be classed as being invalid (True) or not validated (False). The default value is False.
DataGrid	Support is added to the DataGrid control for multiple views in mobile devices, which works in much the same way as the GridView control (see Chapter 4) and the Table control (see the subsection on the DataGrid control later in this chapter). Several new properties have been added to the DataGrid control. • Caption: The text caption to display above the control in the page. • CaptionAlign: A value from the TableCaptionAlign enumeration that indicates how the caption will be aligned with respect to the control. Valid values are Bottom, Top, Left, Right, and NotSet. The default value is NotSet. • DataSourceID: The ID of a data source control that will provide the source data for this control. • DetailNextRowText: The text to display on a mobile device for the link to the next row when in details view. The default value is "Next Row". • DetailPreviousRowText: The text to display on a mobile device for the link to the previous row when in details view. The default value is "Previous Row". • DetailSummaryText: The text to display on a mobile device for the link back to summary view when in details view. The default value is "Summary View". • DetailLinkStyle: A reference to a Style instance that specifies the appearance of the text of the links when in details view. • DetailTitleStyle: A reference to a Style instance that specifies the appearance of the text displayed as the list title when in details view. • SummaryViewColumn: The name of the column that will be displayed on a mobile device when in summary view. • SummaryTitleStyle: A reference to a Style instance that specifies the appearance of the text displayed as the list title when in summary view. • UseAccessibleHeader: Specifies whether the control should add the scope attribute to the cells in the header row to assist users of specialist browsers and page readers. The default value is False.
DataList	Four new properties are added to the DataList control. • Caption: The text caption to display above the control in the page. • CaptionAlign: A value from the TableCaptionAlign enumeration that indicates how the caption will be aligned with respect to the control. Valid values are Bottom, Top, Left, Right, and NotSet. The default value is NotSet.

continues

TABLE 11.2. Enhancements to Controls in the WebControls Namespace (continued)

Control	Description
DataList (continued)	● DataSourceID: The ID of a data source control that will provide the source data for this control. ● UseAccessibleHeader: Specifies whether the control should add the scope attribute to the cells in the header row to assist users of specialist browsers and page readers. The default value is False.
HyperLink	One new property is added to the HyperLink control: ● SoftKeyLabel: The text to display in a small-screen or mobile device for the soft-key or shortcut key when this control has the focus.
Image	Two new properties are added to the Image control. See the subsection on the Image control later in this chapter for more details. ● DescriptionUrl: A String that is the URL to use in the longdesc attribute of the <img> element generated by this control. ● GenerateEmptyAlternateText: A Boolean value that indicates whether an empty alt attribute will be added to the <img> element. The default value is False.
ImageButton	Five new properties are added to the ImageButton control. See the subsection on the Button, LinkButton, and ImageButton controls later in this chapter for more details. ● GenerateEmptyAlternateText: A Boolean value that indicates whether an empty alt attribute will be added to the <img> element. The default value is False. ● OnClientClick: A String that is the name of the client-side function, or a code fragment, to be executed on the client when the button is clicked. ● PostBackUrl: A String that is the URL to which the containing form will be posted. See the Cross-Page Posting section in Chapter 9. ● SoftKeyLabel: The text to display in a small-screen or mobile device for the soft-key or shortcut key when this control has the focus. ● ValidationGroup: The name of the validation group to which this control belongs.
Label	One new property is added to the Label control. See the subsection on the Label control later in this chapter for more details. ● AssociatedControlID: The ID of a control to which the label applies. It allows a hot key to be defined that switches focus to the control and indicates to the user which control this text is associated with.
LinkButton	Four new properties are added to the LinkButton control. See the subsection on the Button, LinkButton, and ImageButton controls later in this chapter for more details. ● OnClientClick: A String that is the name of the client-side function, or a code fragment, to be executed on the client when the button is clicked. ● PostBackUrl: A String that is the URL to which the containing form will be posted. See the Cross-Page Posting section in Chapter 9.

TABLE 11.2. Enhancements to Controls in the WebControls Namespace (continued)

Control	Description
LinkButton (continued)	• SoftKeyLabel: The text to display in a small-screen or mobile device for the soft-key or shortcut key when this control has the focus. • ValidationGroup: The name of the validation group to which this control belongs.
ListItem	One new property is added to the ListItem control, which represents the individual items in the Items collection of a ListControl. See the subsection on the List and ListItem controls later in this chapter for more details. • Enabled: A Boolean value that indicates if this item will appear in the visible list generated on the client (as an <option> element). It will be present in the Items collection of the list control even when Enabled is False.
Literal	One new property is added to the Literal control. See the subsection on the Literal control later in this chapter for more details. • Mode: A value from the LiteralMode enumeration that defines how the content of the control will be processed before being sent to the client. Valid values are Transform, Passthrough, and Encode. The default value is Transform.
Panel	Three new properties are added to the Panel control. See the subsection on the Panel control later in this chapter for more details. • AllowPaginate: A Boolean value that indicates whether the controls inside the Panel will be paginated when a ContentPager is attached to the control, in other words, separated across pages or kept on the same page. The default value is True. • GroupingText: A String value that, when specified, forces the Panel control to generate a <fieldset> element instead of the usual <div> or <table> element. The GroupingText becomes the header text shown on the fieldset. • ScrollBars: When used in conjunction with the Width and/or Height properties, allows the content to be displayed in a fixed-size scrollable region on a Web page. The default value is None.
Repeater	One new property is added to the Repeater control. • DataSourceID: The ID of a data source control that will provide the source data for this control.
Table	Support is added to the Table control for multiple views in mobile devices. See the subsection on the Table, TableHeaderCell, and TableCell controls later in this chapter for more details. Several new properties are added as well. • Caption: The text caption to display above the table in the page. • CaptionAlign: A value from the TableCaptionAlign enumeration that indicates how the caption will be aligned with respect to the calendar. Valid values are Bottom, Top, Left, Right, and NotSet. The default value is NotSet.

continues

TABLE 11.2. Enhancements to Controls in the WebControls Namespace (continued)

Control	Description
Table (continued)	• CurrentRow: The zero-based index of the row currently being shown on a mobile device in details view, or -1 if no row is current. It can be set to change the current row. The default value is -1.
	• DetailHeaderRowIndex: The zero-based index of the column whose value will be displayed above the row values on a mobile device when in details view. The default value is -1.
	• DetailNextRowText: The text to display on a mobile device for the link to the next row when in details view. The default value is "Next Row".
	• DetailPreviousRowText: The text to display on a mobile device for the link to the previous row when in details view. The default is "Previous Row".
	• DetailSummaryText: The text to display on a mobile device for the link back to summary view when in details view. The default is "Summary View".
	• DetailLinkStyle: A reference to a Style instance that specifies the appearance of the text of the links when in details view.
	• DetailTitleStyle: A reference to a Style instance that specifies the appearance of the text displayed as the list title when in details view.
	• SummaryViewColumn: The name of the column that will be displayed on a mobile device when in summary view.
	• SummaryTitleStyle: A reference to a Style instance that specifies the appearance of the text displayed as the list title when in summary view.
	• SummaryViewColumnIndex: The zero-based index of the column that will be displayed on a mobile device when in summary view. The default value is 0.
	• ViewMode: A value from the TableViewMode enumeration that indicates which mode the table is being displayed in on a mobile device. Valid values are Summary and Details. It can be set to change the mode. The default value is Summary.
TableCell	One new property is added to the TableCell control. See the subsection on the Table, TableHeaderCell, and TableCell controls later in this chapter for more details.
	• AssociatedHeaderCellID: A String array that specifies the ID of the header cells that relate to this table cell.
TextBox	Three new properties are added to the TextBox control.
	• AutoCompleteType: A value from the AutoCompleteType enumeration that indicates the field in the user's VCard that should be used to populate the text box. Examples are BusinessPhone, HomeZipCode, and so on. The default value is None.
	• CausesValidation: A Boolean value that indicates whether this control will cause any attached validation controls to validate the values of the controls on the form when the form is submitted. Set this property to False to allow the form to be submitted with no validation occurring. The default value is False.
	• ValidationGroup: The name of the validation group to which this control belongs.

TABLE 11.2. Enhancements to Controls in the WebControls Namespace (continued)

Control	Description
ValidationSummary	• One new property is added to the `ValidationSummary` control. See Chapter 9 for details of the validation control enhancements. • `ValidationGroup`: The name of the validation group to which this control belongs.
Xml	• One new property is added to the `Xml` control. • `XPathNavigator`: A reference to an `XPathNavigator` instance that will be used to populate the control, overriding any existing settings of the `Document` and `DocumentSource` properties.

Details of Individual Control Enhancements

The unified control architecture implemented in ASP.NET 2.0 means that all the controls in the `System.Web.UI.WebControls` namespace have been updated in order to take advantage of control adapters and the new architecture. The good news is that, to maintain backward compatibility with existing code (and to make it easier for developers to move to ASP.NET 2.0), almost all of the controls expose the same interfaces as before, so they are declared and programmed against in just the same way as in ASP.NET 1.x.

However, as you've seen, many of the controls have also changed in other minor ways, allowing them to integrate with new features in other controls (such as the new validation groups feature and page/site counters), to provide enhanced features, or simply to fill in the "gaps" left when they were first implemented in version 1.0.

In this section we look at each of the following controls in turn:

- AdRotator
- Button, LinkButton, and ImageButton
- CheckBox
- DataGrid
- HyperLink
- Image

- Label
- List and ListItem
- Literal
- Panel
- Table, TableHeaderCell, and TableCell

The AdRotator Control

ASP.NET 1.0 shipped with an `AdRotator` control to randomly display banner advertisements, and in ASP.NET 2.0 it has been updated with support for

- Displaying advertisements in pop-up or pop-under windows
- Binding advertisement data from non-XML data sources
- Using site counters that track impressions and click-throughs
- Sending advertisements to mobile devices
- Displaying dynamic advertisements when the page is cached

The syntax for declaring an `AdRotator` control is shown in Listing 11.1.

LISTING 11.1. The AdRotator Control Syntax

```
<asp:AdRotator runat="server"
  AdType="[Banner|Popup|PopUnder]"
  AdvertisementFile="String"
  AlternateTextField="String"
  DataSource="String"
  DataMember="String"
  DataSourceId="String"
  Font="String"
  ImageUrlField="String"
  KeywordFilter="String"
  NavigateUrlField="String"
  PopFrequency="Integer"
  PopPositionLeft="Integer"
  PopPositionTop="Integer"
  Target="String" />
```

Some of these are the same as the properties used in the existing version of the control. The new properties are shown in Table 11.3.

TABLE 11.3. New Properties of the AdRotator Control

Property/Attribute	Description
`AdType`	Indicates the type of advertisement, which can be one of the `AdType` enumeration values: • `Banner`: For a banner ad. This is the default value. • `Popup`: For a pop-up ad. • `PopUnder`: For a pop-under ad.
`AlternateTextField`	Sets or returns the element name or database field from which the alternate text is returned. The default is `AlternateText`.
`DataSource`	Sets or returns the data source to bind the `AdRotator` to. `DataSource` and `AdvertisementFile` cannot be defined simultaneously.

TABLE 11.3. New Properties of the AdRotator Control (continued)

Property/Attribute	Description
DataSourceId	• Sets or returns the data source control to bind the AdRotator to. DataSourceId and AdvertisementFile cannot be defined simultaneously.
DataMember	• Sets or returns the name of the table or individual data rowset in the data source if the data source supports more than one set of data items (e.g., the table name in a DataSet).
ImageUrlField	• Sets or returns the element name or database field from which the image URL is returned. The default is ImageUrl.
NavigateUrlField	• Sets or returns the element name or database field from which the navigation URL is returned. The default is NavigateUrl.
PopFrequency	• Sets or returns the frequency, as a percentage, with which to create pop-up or pop-under ads. This applies only when the AdType property is Popup or PopUnder. The default is 100.
PopPositionLeft	• Sets or returns the screen position that defines the left side of the ad. If not defined, the advertisement is centered horizontally on the screen. This applies only when the AdType property is Popup or PopUnder.
PopPositionTop	• Sets or returns the screen position that defines the top of the ad. If not defined, the advertisement is centered vertically on the screen. This applies only when the AdType property is Popup or PopUnder.

In addition to these properties, the AdRotator control integrates with the Site Counters Service and therefore supports the following properties:

CountClicks	CounterGroup	CounterName
CountViews	RowsPerDay	SiteCountersProvider
TrackApplicationName	TrackNavigateUrl	TrackPageUrl

Pop-ups and Pop-unders

Support for pop-up advertisements is achieved by simply setting the AdType property. For example, a pop-up advertisement could be created like this:

```
<asp:AdRotator AdvertisementFile="adverts.xml" runat="server"
  PopPositionLeft="20" PopPositionTop="50" AdType="Popup" />
```

If no position is defined for the pop-up, it will be centered on the screen.

Tracking Banners

The addition of site counter support allows easy tracking of advertisement data. For example, a simple banner advertisement could be

```
<asp:AdRotator AdvertisementFile="adverts.xml" runat="server"
  CountClicks="True" CountViews="True"
  TrackNavigateUrl="True" />
```

Tracking details for these advertisements can be obtained either directly from the `SiteCounters` table or via the Site Counters API. Figure 11.1 shows an example of the available data. With this information it is easy to work out the hit percentages to see how effective ads are.

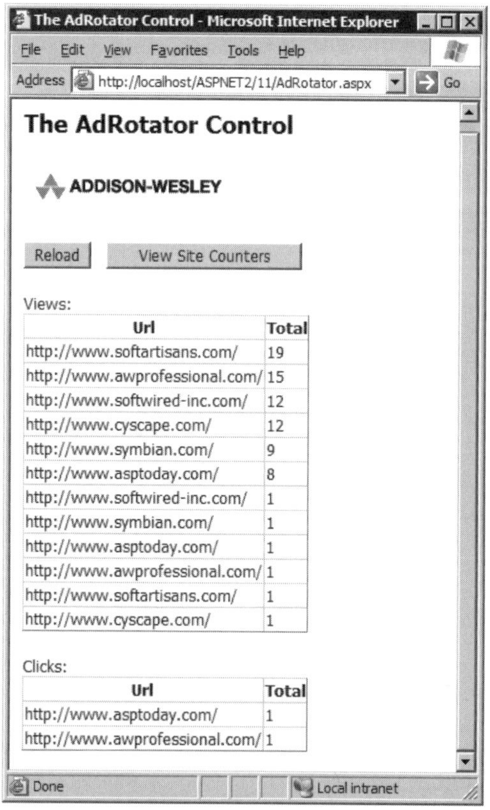

FIGURE 11.1. Banner advertisement views and clicks

XML Advertisements File

A number of new elements are supported in the XML advertisements file (see Table 11.4). Listing 11.2 shows an example of these in use.

TABLE 11.4. New Elements of the XML Advertisements File

Element	Description
CounterGroup	The site counter group to use when tracking this ad.
CounterName	The site counter name to use when tracking this ad.
Height	The height of the ad. If not supplied, the Height of the AdRotator control is used.
Width	The width of the ad. If not supplied, the Width of the AdRotator control is used.

LISTING 11.2. Sample Advertisements File

```
<Advertisements>
  <Ad>
    <ImageUrl>ads/awpro.gif</ImageUrl>
    <NavigateUrl>http://www.awprofessional.com/</NavigateUrl>
    <AlternateText>Addison-Wesley</AlternateText>
    <Impressions>20</Impressions>
    <Keyword>Books</Keyword>
    <Height>40</Height>
    <Width>160</Width>
    <CounterGroup>Publishers</CounterGroup>
    <CounterName>Addison-Wesley</CounterName>
  </Ad>
  <Ad>
    . . .
  </Ad>
</Advertisements>
```

Like previous versions, the advertisements file also supports custom fields, which are mapped to the AdProperties property of the AdCreatedEventArgs for the AdCreated event.

Support for Mobile Devices

Support for mobile devices has now been integrated into the AdRotator control. Support has also been added to the XML file, allowing device-specific elements. For example, consider an advertisement for a site that supports both standard browsers and WML browsers. The advertisement file could look like this:

```
<Ad>
  <ImageUrl>ads/awpro.gif</ImageUrl>
  <NavigateUrl>http://www.awpro.com/</NavigateUrl>
  <WmlImageUrl>ads/awpro.wbmp</WmlImageUrl>
  <WmlNavigateUrl>http://wml.awpro.com/mobile/</WmlNavigateUrl>
  <AlternateText>Addison-Wesley</AlternateText>
    ...
```

This specifies normal `ImageUrl` and `NavigateUrl` properties, as well as custom properties to a WML-specific image and navigation URL. Unlike standard custom properties, these can be mapped directly to device attributes by the `AdRotator` control. For example:

```
<asp:AdRotator runat="server"
  AdvertisementFile="adverts.xml"
  Wml:ImageUrl="WmlImageUrl"
  Wml:NavigateUrl="WmlNavigateUrl" />
```

This allows you to easily add support for custom devices without changing the infrastructure of your site.

Support for Data Binding

Data binding support has been added for both the existing data binding architecture and the new data source controls, as long as the underlying data matches the allowable schema. For example, Listing 11.3 shows binding the `AdRotator` to a `DataSet`, using the ASP.NET 1.x data binding syntax.

LISTING 11.3. Binding the AdRotator Control to a DataSet Control

```
<script runat="server">
Sub Page_Load(Sender As Object, E As EventArgs)
  Dim conn As New _
    SqlConnection(ConfigurationSettings.AppSettings("Ads"))
  Dim da As New SqlDataAdapter("select * from ads", conn)
  Dim ds As New DataSet()
  da.Fill(ds, "Ads")
  BannerAds.DataSource = ds
  BannerAds.DataBind()
End Sub
</script>

<form runat="server">
  <asp:AdRotator runat="server" id="BannerAds" />
</form>
```

This is also possible using the ASP.NET 2.0 data binding controls (see Listing 11.4).

LISTING 11.4. Binding the AdRotator Control to a SqlDataSource Control

```
<form runat="server">

  <asp:SqlDataSource id="AdData" runat="server"
    ConnectionString="..." />

  <asp:AdRotator id="ads" runat="server" DataSourceId="AdData" />

</form>
```

Adding data binding to the `AdRotator` means that advertisement data can be supplied by any data provider.

The Button, LinkButton, and ImageButton Controls

One issue discovered with the `WebForm` button-type controls in ASP.NET 1.x was how to arrange for the button to raise a client-side event as well as a server-side event. It's often useful to be able to run some client-side script when a button is clicked, before the page is submitted to the server. There is a workaround, of course, which involves adding the `OnClick` attribute to the control at runtime by using the `Attributes` collection. However, now you can simply set the `OnClientClick` property to the name of your client-side script function or specify it as the `OnClientClick` attribute when declaring your control:

```
<asp:Button Text="Click Me" runat="server"
            OnClick="MyServerSideCode"
            OnClientClick="MyClientSideFunction()"/>
```

The same approach works for the `LinkButton` and `ImageButton` controls.

The SoftKeyLabel Property

As we described in detail in Chapter 10, several button-type controls now carry the `SoftKeyLabel` property. This includes the `Button`, `LinkButton`, `ImageButton`, and `PhoneLink` controls. When the page is sent to a mobile device, the string specified for this property can (depending on the device) be displayed next to one of the "one-touch" buttons on the device. This property is usually implemented in devices such as cellular phones, where there is only limited input capability (basically a number keypad and a few soft-key buttons).

Support for Site and Page Counters

The three button-type controls are often used to process actions or navigate to other pages in situations where you want to track the movements of visitors. The site and page counters feature of ASP.NET is ideal for this, and the button-type controls (as well as the `HyperLink` control) have properties you can use to integrate them with this feature. These are described in the Site and Page Counters section in Chapter 9.

The CheckBox Control

In line with the way that browsers work, the `CheckBox` control does not provide a simple way to add a `value` attribute to the `<input type="checkbox">` element it generates. This is because a checkbox does not submit a value when the containing form is posted to the server. It simply submits the text `"on"` if it is checked, or nothing if it is not checked. However, because a `CheckBox` server control can be accessed on the server, developers often try to specify a value for it (there is a `Value` property, but it has no effect).

Another issue is that, like many controls, a `CheckBox` generates more than one element. What you actually get is a `<span>` that contains the `<input type="checkbox">` element and a `<label>` element that contains the caption (the value of the `Text` property). However, adding attributes to the `CheckBox` control adds them to the `<span>` element, not the `<input>` or `<label>` element.

In ASP.NET 2.0, the `CheckBox` control gains two new properties, named `InputAttributes` and `LabelAttributes`, that provide access to the `Attributes` collections of the `<input>` and `<label>` elements. The code in Listing 11.5 declares a `CheckBox` control and attempts to set the value to the string `"The Value"`. It also adds a custom attribute to the `CheckBox` control.

LISTING 11.5. The InputAttributes and LabelAttributes Properties of the CheckBox Control

```
<form runat="server">
  <asp:CheckBox id="MyCheck" runat="server"
      Text="CheckBox with Added Attributes"
      Value="The Value"
      MyImaginaryAttribute="MyAttrValue" />
</form>
...
Sub Page_Load()
  MyCheck.LabelAttributes.Add("MyNewLabelAttribute", _
                              "MyLabelAttrValue")
  MyCheck.InputAttributes.Add("MyNewInputAttribute", _
```

```
                              "MyInputAttrValue")
    MyCheck.InputAttributes.Add("value", "42")
End Sub
```

Then code in the `Page_Load` event handler (also shown in Listing 11.5) uses the `InputAttributes` and `LabelAttributes` properties to add two custom attributes directly to the `<input>` and `<label>` elements. It also adds a `value` attribute, though to extract this on the server following a postback, you have to access the `InputAttributes` collection again using something like sValue = MyCheck.Attributes("value").

To see what's actually happening, you can view the generated output within the browser by using the View | Source menu options. Listing 11.6 shows what you see (with carriage returns added to make it more obvious). Notice that the `<input>` element now has a `value` attribute, while the `<span>` element does not.

LISTING 11.6. The Result Generated by the InputAttributes and LabelAttributes
            Properties

```
<span MyImaginaryAttribute="MyAttrValue">
  <input id="MyCheck" type="checkbox" name="MyCheck"
         MyNewInputAttribute="MyInputAttrValue" value="42" />
  <label for="MyCheck" MyNewLabelAttribute="MyLabelAttrValue">
    CheckBox with Added Attributes
  </label>
</span>
```

The DataGrid Control

The `DataGrid` control in ASP.NET 2.0 takes advantage of the new device adapter and control adapter architecture to provide support for mobile and small-screen devices, in much the same way as the `GridView` control we examined in Chapter 4. It automatically displays the contents in summary view and details view, with links to select rows and switch from one mode to another. And, as with the `GridView` control, the `SummaryViewColumn` attribute is used to specify which column will be shown in summary view.

Listing 11.7 shows a simple declaration of a `DataGrid` control (the associated data source control is not shown here). The `SummaryViewColumn` is specified as the `ProductName` column in the data source, so this column is shown when the `DataGrid` is first displayed on a mobile device (see the first screen in Figure 11.2). Selecting an item in this column switches the display to details view, and all the columns from this row are then displayed,

FIGURE 11.2. The DataGrid control output in a mobile device

together with the links to the next and previous rows and back to summary view (as seen in the second and third screens in Figure 11.2).

LISTING 11.7. The SummaryViewColumn and UseAccessibleHeader Properties of the DataGrid Control

```
<asp:DataGrid id="MyGrid" DataSourceID="datasource1" runat="server"
            SummaryViewColumn="ProductName"
            UseAccessibleHeader="True" />
```

Listing 11.7 also shows the `UseAccessibleHeader` property in use. By simply adding this attribute or setting this property, the normal "grid" output generated in a Web browser (as an HTML table) will include the `scope` attributes in the header row, for example:

```
<th scope="col">ProductName</th>
```

This allows nonvisual user agents to figure out the structure of the table more easily, by knowing that the data is in columns and that each cell in the first row contains the description of the values in that column.

> If an HTML table uses the left-hand column for descriptions of the content of each row, something that the `DataGrid` cannot do by default, the attribute `scope="row"` will be used in these cells.

The HyperLink Control

The `HyperLink` control now exposes a `SoftKeyLabel` property, as described earlier for the three button-type controls. It also supports integration with site and page counters, again as described earlier for the button-type controls. However, because a hyperlink element causes a client-side action to take place (through the `href` value set by the `NavigateUrl` property), there is an extra property for the `HyperLink` control named `TrackNavigateUrl`, which is described in the Site and Page Counters section in Chapter 9.

The Image Control

HTML 4.0 and higher specifies an attribute named `longdesc` for the `<img>` element. This attribute is useful where the user might not be able to view the image for a variety of reasons (e.g., he or she may be using a text-only browser or one specially designed for blind or partly sighted users). The new `String` property named `DescriptionUrl` can be set to the URL of a page that contains a text or aural description of the image and will then be used to set the `longdesc` attribute. Specialist browsers and user agents should provide the user with the opportunity to retrieve this page instead of the image file.

> If you generate an image that is a chart or some graphical data representation, perhaps using the graphics capabilities in ASP.NET, you should consider building a separate page that displays the data in a format suitable for nonvisual user agents. A simple table will do, or even a series of text statements that describe the data. The same source data can be used to create this page, and you could add code to the existing page so that a simple query string or form value specifies which version of the output is generated from the same data. This value can then be included in the URL specified for the `DescriptionUrl` property.

Also remember that unimportant images, such as bullets and "blank" images that are used only to control the layout of the page content, should include the `alt=""` attribute. Simply add the `GenerateEmptyAlternateText="True"` attribute to the `Image` control. If there is a value specified for the `AlternateText` attribute or property, this is used and the setting of the `GenerateEmptyAlternateText` property is ignored.

The Label Control

One useful capability of HTML 4.0 and higher, when building pages that use the various interactive form controls (such as lists, buttons, checkboxes, and text boxes), is to associate a text label with a control. In most modern browsers, including Internet Explorer, you can define a hot key for the control and then display this hot key in the associated label to make the form more like a traditional Windows executable application.

In ASP.NET 2.0, the `Label` control gains a new property named `AssociatedControlID`. You set it to a `String` value that is the ID of the interactive control you want to associate the `Label` control with and then set the `AccessKey` property for the label to the key you want to act as the hot key. You can also indicate this key to the user by underlining it in the `Label` text:

```
<asp:Label id="MyLabel" Text="<u>N</u>ame" runat="server"
        AccessKey="N" AssociatedControlID="MyTextBox" />
<asp:TextBox id="MyTextBox" runat="server" />
```

Now, when the hot-key combination (in this case, ALT + N) is pressed, the focus moves to the `TextBox` control automatically (see Figure 11.3). However, you cannot use keys that are already defined for the various UI features of the browser. For example, ALT + T cannot be used in Internet Explorer because it activates the Tools menu.

FIGURE 11.3. Using the AssociatedControlID property to create hot keys

The List and ListItem Controls

Ever since version 4.0 of Internet Explorer, and now in most other recent browsers, it's possible to disable controls in a page by setting their client-side `disabled` attribute, for example:

```
<input type="text" disabled="disabled" />
```

In ASP.NET, you achieve the same effect by setting the `Enabled` property to `False` on the server, either in code or by adding the `Enabled="False"` attribute to the control declaration. However, for list controls such as a `ListBox` or `DropDownList`, you can enable or disable only the complete control, not specific items within the list. Most browsers do not actually support this feature anyway, so to provide something like the same functionality, ASP.NET 2.0 allows individual items in the list to be removed from the display but still exist server-side in the list.

In other words, if the `Items` collection of a list control contains five `ListItem` controls, but one has the `Enabled` property set to `False` (or carries the `Enabled="False"` attribute), this item will not be rendered in the

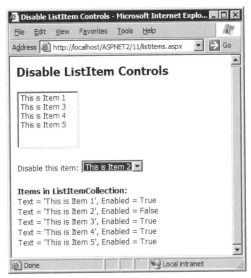

FIGURE 11.4. Enabling and disabling items in a list control

list client-side. However, it is still accessible in server-side code as part of the `Items` collection.

Figure 11.4 shows an example that demonstrates this feature. A `ListBox` control contains file `ListItem` elements, numbered from 1 to 5. A `DropDownList` control is used to select one of the items and automatically causes a postback when one is selected. Listing 11.8 shows the code that runs when an item is selected in the `DropDownList`.

LISTING 11.8. Changing the Enabled Property of a ListItem Control

```
Sub DoEnable(sender As Object, e As EventArgs)

   ' start by making all items visible
   For Each oItem As ListItem In MyList.Items
     oItem.Enabled = True
   Next

   ' disable selected item
   MyList.Items(MyDropDown.SelectedValue).Enabled = False

   ' display details of Items collection
   lblList.Text = "<b>Items in ListItemCollection:</b><br />"
   For Each oItem As ListItem In MyList.Items
     lblList.Text &= "Text = '" & oItem.Text & "', Enabled = " _
               & oItem.Enabled.ToString() & "<br />"
   Next

End Sub
```

The code starts by setting the `Enabled` property of all the `ListItem` objects in the `Items` collection of the `ListBox` control to `True`, then sets the `Enabled` property of the selected one to `False`. To show that they are all still present in the list, the code then outputs details of the complete `ListItemCollection` in a `Label` control on the page.

Appending Data-Bound Items to a List

A second new feature of the list controls in ASP.NET 2.0 is the addition of the `AppendDataBoundItems` property to the `ListControl` base class, from which the `BulletedList`, `CheckBoxList`, `RadioButtonList`, `ListBox`, and `DropDownList` controls are descended. Setting this property to `True` causes any existing `ListItem` instances within the `Items` collection to remain there, rather than being replaced as is the default behavior.

Figure 11.5 shows one situation where this is extremely useful. All four of the list controls (two `ListBox` and two `DropDownList` controls) are bound to a data source control that fetches a list of products from the Northwind sample database. They also all have a single `ListItem` included within their control declarations. For example:

```
<asp:DropDownList id="List1" runat="server" DataSourceID="ds1"
    DataTextField="ProductName" DataValueField="ProductID">
  <asp:ListItem Value="-1" Text="Select a product..." />
</asp:DropDownList>  
```

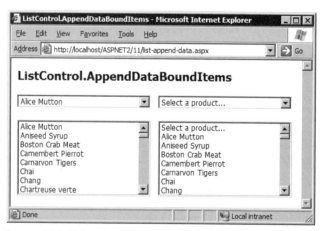

FIGURE 11.5. Using the AppendDataBoundItems property

However, the two controls on the right side of the page also have the `AppendDataBoundItems="True"` attribute, as shown here:

```
<asp:DropDownList id="List2" runat="server" DataSourceID="ds1"
    DataTextField="ProductName" DataValueField="ProductID"
    AppendDataBoundItems="True">
  <asp:ListItem Value="-1" Text="Select a product..." />
</asp:DropDownList>
```

The result is that the ListItem control that was added declaratively remains in the list, and you no longer need to insert these kinds of dummy entries into a list at runtime after the data binding process has completed.

The Literal Control

A common approach to inserting content into a page, without using a control that generates its own markup (e.g., a Label that generates a <span> element in the page) is to use the Literal control. You simply set the Text property to any String value, and that string is inserted into the page at the point where the Literal control is located.

In ASP.NET 2.0, a new property named Mode has been added to the Literal control, which allows you to control how the String assigned to the Text property value is processed before being sent to the client. The reason for this is simple: The page needs to be able to tailor its output to suit different types of device. For example, an <hr /> element in the String assigned to the Literal control will cause an error if sent to a device that expects to receive WML.

The Mode property can take one of the three values defined for the LiteralMode enumeration (see Table 11.5).

TABLE 11.5. The LiteralMode Enumeration Values

Value	Description
Transform	All markup not supported by the current client device is removed from the output generated by the control (e.g., <hr /> is removed for WML devices). If there is content within an unsupported element (e.g., <my-tag>Some text</mytag>), the tags are removed and the content is sent to the client. This is the default setting if not specified, meaning that backward compatibility is maximized for pages that don't specify a LiteralMode value and may be sent to a mobile device. If you use nonstandard markup in your pages, perhaps to interact with client-side code or special controls, you may have to change the LiteralMode property to PassThrough to ensure that it is delivered correctly.
PassThrough	The content of the Text property is sent to the client unchanged.
Encode	The content of the Text property is HTML-encoded before being sent to the client (e.g., <img> becomes <img>).

The Panel Control

One of the features that many developers have requested is a control that can be of fixed size and can display scroll bars when there is more content than will fit into an area of the specified size. In ASP.NET 2.0, the `Panel` control has been extended to provide these features. It has also been adapted to work better with pagination through a `ContentPager` control, allowing output to be broken up into separate "screens" for small-screen devices such as PDAs and cellular phones.

Figure 11.6 shows how the `Panel` control can now provide fixed-size scrollable regions in a page. The first and second panels have only a vertical scroll bar, while the third one has both horizontal and vertical scroll bars. The second panel also changes the layout direction, so the text is aligned to the right and the scroll bar appears on the left. (The control adds the HTML attribute `dir="RTL"` to the element in the page to achieve this.) Finally, the text in the third panel does not wrap like the other two because we set the `Wrap` property to `False` in the declaration of that `Panel` control.

Listing 11.9 shows the declaration of the first and third of the `Panel` controls shown in Figure 11.6. The first one includes the `Width` and `Height` attributes, and the `ScrollBars` attribute is set to `Vertical`. This value comes from the `ScrollBars` enumeration, which contains the four expected values (`Vertical`, `Horizontal`, `Both`, and `None`) plus `Auto` to automatically add scroll bars as needed.

To force right-to-left layout in the `Panel` control, as in the second example shown in Figure 11.6, you just have to add the `Direction="RightToLeft"` attribute to the declaration. The default for `Direction` depends on the language and international settings of your machine. Right-to-left is, of course, the default for some languages.

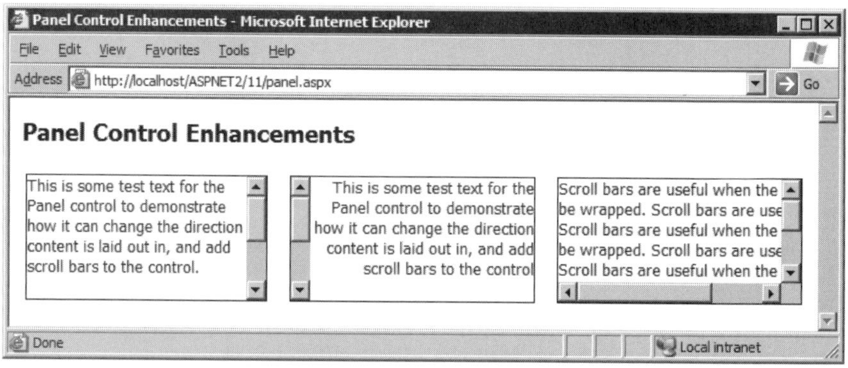

FIGURE 11.6. The Panel control with scroll bar variations

The third `Panel` control simply carries the `ScrollBars="Both"` attribute. To prevent the text in the control from wrapping, you add the `Wrap="False"` attribute to the declaration and use `<br />` elements in the text to break it into separate lines.

LISTING 11.9. The Declaration of the First and Third Panel Controls

```
<asp:Panel id="MyPanel1" BorderStyle="Solid" BorderWidth="1"
           Width="200" Height="100" ScrollBars="Vertical"
           runat="server">
  <asp:Label runat="server">This is some test text...</asp:Label>
  <p />
  <asp:Label runat="server">This is some test text...</asp:Label>
  <p />
</asp:Panel>
...
...
<asp:Panel id="MyPanel3" BorderStyle="Solid" BorderWidth="1"
           Width="200" Height="100" runat="server"
           ScrollBars="Both" Wrap="False">
  <asp:Label runat="server">
    Scroll bars are useful when the text
    cannot<br />be wrapped. Scroll bars are useful<br />
    Scroll bars are useful when the text cannot<br />...
  </asp:Label>
</asp:Panel>
```

Pagination in a Panel Control

We discussed the pagination features of ASP.NET 2.0 in detail in Chapter 10, where we looked at the `ContentPager` control. However, to integrate with the `ContentPager` control, the `Panel` control gains a new property named `AllowPaginate`. This `Boolean` value indicates whether the contents of the `Panel` control can be broken up across pages. When `True`, the `ContentPager` control can divide the content of the `Panel` control over more than one page or screen when displayed in a device that requires pagination. When `False` (the default), the content always appears together on the same page or screen.

Creating a FieldSet with a Panel Control

Since HTML 4.0 there has been a definition for the `<fieldset>` and `<legend>` elements, which are designed to be used to group together controls in interactive Web pages. Almost all recent browsers support these elements, and the ASP.NET `Panel` control has been extended to generate `<fieldset>` and `<legend>` elements in version 2.0.

All that's required is to specify a `String` value for the `GroupingText` attribute or property of the `Panel` control, as shown in Listing 11.10.

LISTING 11.10. The GroupingText Property of the Panel Control

```
<asp:Panel id="MyPanel1" Width="200" Height="100" runat="server"
    GroupingText="My Panel" Style="padding:10px"
    BorderStyle="Solid" BorderWidth="1">
  This is some test text for the <b>Panel</b> control to demonstrate
  how it can be used to generate a &lt;fieldset&gt; element
  instead of the usual &lt;div&gt; or &lt;table&gt; element.
</asp:Panel>
```

The value you provide for the `GroupingText` property is used for the `<legend>` element content, and this and the content of the `Panel` control (the value of the `Text` property) are displayed within the `<fieldset>` element when the control is rendered, as shown here:

```
<fieldset id="MyPanel1" style="...">
  <legend>My Panel</legend>
    ... content of Panel control here ...
</fieldset>
```

The appearance of the `<fieldset>` and `<legend>` elements in the browser is shown in Figure 11.7. Note that normally the text is placed right up against the borders of the `<fieldset>` element, as it would be in a `<textarea>` element. As we did for this example, you will probably want to add some padding to the control and make the border visible. In Listing 11.10, the following attributes are added to achieve this:

FIGURE 11.7. The Panel control generating <fieldset> and <legend> elements

```
Style="padding:10px" BorderStyle="Solid" BorderWidth="1"
```

The Table, TableHeaderCell, and TableCell Controls

ASP.NET 2.0 automatically adapts the output it generates to suit different types of clients, as you saw in Chapter 10. One specific issue is with devices that have only limited screen real estate—cellular phones are a prime example. If you want to display a table but the page may be delivered to a small-screen device, it's likely that device will not be able to display the information in any meaningful way.

The ideal approach for a small-screen device is to break up the table into individual rows and display these separately. But for the user to be able to grasp the whole picture, he or she needs to see how many rows there are and look at each one individually or choose one from the table. Conversely, in a normal Web browser, the user generally wants to see the whole table.

Three Views of the Content

To meet these requirements, the `Table` control automatically provides three views of the data in a table. For normal Web browsers, it outputs a standard HTML table. By taking advantage of the new header and footer rows features, you can generate a table that contains `<th>` elements as well as the usual `<td>` elements (see Figure 11.8).

However, the same page viewed in a cellular phone contains a table with the same number of rows but only one column. This view is called **summary view,** and the column shown is the **summary column**. Notice that each row (except for the header and footer) is a link that can be followed (see Figure 11.9).

Activating the link for any of the rows switches the page to **details view.** In this view, all the columns for the selected row are displayed (see Figure 11.10). At the bottom of the page are links that allow the user to go back to summary view or move to the next or previous row. So the user

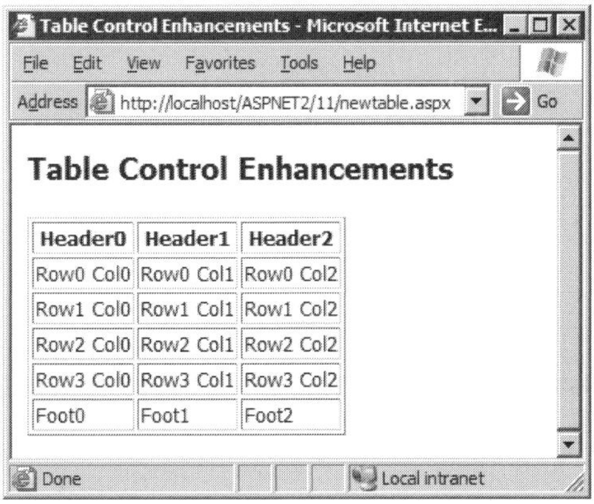

FIGURE 11.8. The Table control viewed in a Windows browser

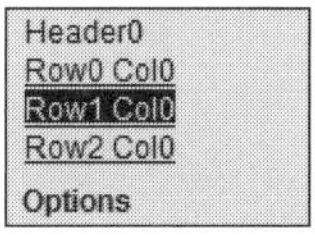

FIGURE 11.9. The Table control viewed in a phone browser

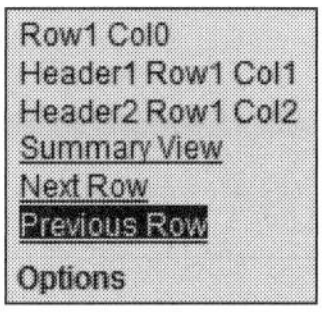

FIGURE 11.10. Paging a Table control

can easily browse the table, and the developer didn't have to do anything to make all this happen!

The Code to Build the Table

The page you've been looking at contains four rows of three columns, with each cell containing the row and column number so that you can see what's happening. The Table control itself is declared in the page, but with no rows defined. (Note that it has to be located on a server-side form.)

```
<form runat="server">
  <asp:Table id="MyTable" GridLines="Both" runat="server" />
</form>
```

The page also contains a subroutine named CreateTable that dynamically builds the rows for the table and adds them to the Table control (see Listing 11.11). The technique is the same as that used with the ASP.NET 1.x Table control, but here we're taking advantage of the new TableHeaderRow and TableFooterRow controls (as well as the existing TableHeaderCell and TableCell controls) to create the header and footer rows.

Listing 11.11. Creating a Table Control Dynamically

```
Sub CreateTable()
  Dim Rows As Integer = 4
  Dim Cols As Integer = 3
  Dim RowCount, ColCount As Integer
  Dim Row As TableRow
  Dim Cell As TableCell

  ' header row
  Row = New TableHeaderRow()
  For ColCount = 0 To Cols - 1
    Cell = New TableHeaderCell()
    Cell.Controls.Add( _
          New LiteralControl("Header" & ColCount))
    Row.Cells.Add(Cell)
  Next
  MyTable.Rows.Add(Row)

  ' data rows
  For RowCount = 0 To Rows - 1
    Row = New TableRow()
    For ColCount = 0 To Cols - 1
      Cell = New TableCell()
      Cell.Controls.Add( _
            New LiteralControl("Row" _
              & RowCount & " Col" & ColCount))
```

```
      oRow.Cells.Add(Cell)
    Next
    MyTable.Rows.Add(Row)
  Next

  ' footer row
  Row = New TableFooterRow()
  For ColCount = 0 To Cols - 1
    Cell = New TableCell()
    Cell.Controls.Add( _
          New LiteralControl("Foot" & ColCount))
    oRow.Cells.Add(Cell)
  Next
  MyTable.Rows.Add(Row)
End Sub
```

Then, in the `Page_Load` event, we can call this routine when the page loads each time:

```
Sub Page_Load()
  CreateTable()
End Sub
```

This is all that's required. Of course, we could simply declare each row of the table using the usual `<tr>`, `<th>`, and `<td>` elements, without building it at runtime using code. However, in that case, the header and footer rows will be treated as "ordinary rows" and will be selectable in summary view.

Programmatically Selecting the View Mode and Row

When the `Table` control is serving content to a small-screen device, the view mode can be selected by using the `ViewMode` property (the options from the `TableViewMode` enumeration are `Details` and Summary) or by adding the `ViewMode` attribute to the declaration of the `Table` control (see Listing 11.12). And when the table is in details view, the current row (the row actually being displayed) can be specified by using the `CurrentRow` property. Of course, you probably want to do this only when the page is first loaded, and not on a postback, or the user will not be able to browse from row to row or switch from one mode to the other.

LISTING 11.12. Setting the CurrentRow and ViewMode for a Table Control

```
Sub Page_Load()
  CreateTable()
  If Not Page.IsPostback Then
    MyTable.CurrentRow = 1
    MyTable.ViewMode = TableViewMode.Details
  End If
End Sub
```

By default the column displayed in summary view is the one at index 0 (the first column). However, you can change this by specifying the index of any other column in the table for the SummaryViewColumnIndex property or by adding the attribute SummaryViewColumnIndex="index" to the declaration of the Table control. And if the table has more than one header row, you can specify which one is used in details view with the DetailsHeaderRowIndex property.

You can also change the text displayed for the links below the row details in details view by setting the DetailNextRowText, DetailPreviousRowText, and DetailSummaryRowText properties or attributes to the String values you require. And there are style properties for each section of the table in both view modes as well.

Maximizing Accessibility with a Table Control

When an HTML table is rendered in a browser, comprehending the information it contains is generally a matter of scanning the rows and columns and mentally relating them with the header descriptions for each row. Often the table is like a spreadsheet in design, where each cell value in the body relates to the description for the column *and* the row where it resides.

For most users, this just involves looking at the header and the left-hand row to locate the desired descriptions, then scanning down and across to the cell where they meet. However, for users of nonvisual browsers and user agents, this is hard to do. Their browser will usually iterate through the table row by row, and it's easy to lose track of which header description each cell in the row relates to.

To assist such users, HTML 4.0 includes the headers attribute for a table cell, which should be set to a list of the header cell ID values for the header and row description that this cell relates to. This way, the browser can extract the header and row descriptions as it iterates through the cells in each row and present them to the user in a suitable manner.

To demonstrate this, we created the table shown in Figure 11.11. It contains descriptions in the headers of each column and in the left-hand cell of each row (these are called **row headers,** as opposed to column headers). They are created using the TableHeaderCell control, rather than the TableCell control used for the cells that contain the data.

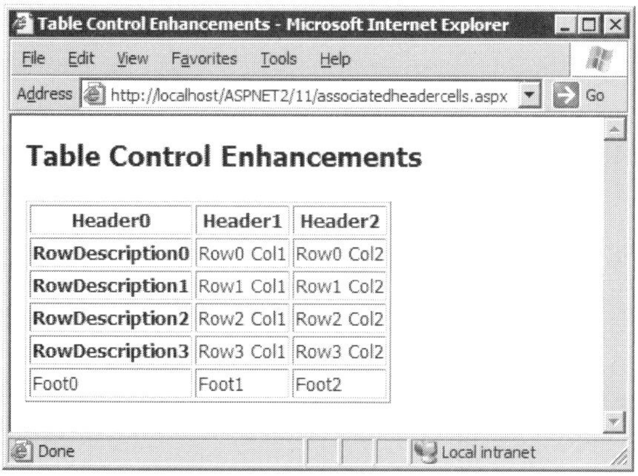

FIGURE 11.11. A Table control containing both row headers and column headers

The `TableHeaderCell` control generates a `<th>` element rather than a `<td>` element, which the browser will usually render differently (generally it is centered and in a bold font). However, more importantly, it is a different control type within the control tree of the page, which allows ASP.NET to verify that it is a true header cell, not a cell containing data.

Listing 11.13 shows the HTML that is rendered to display the table shown in Figure 11.11. You can see the column and row `<th>` elements and the `headers` attributes on each `<td>` element, which relates the cells to the appropriate row and column headers.

LISTING 11.13. The Rendered Output Containing the headers Attributes

```
<table id="MyTable" rules="all" border="1">
  <tr>
    <th id="Header0">Header0</th>
    <th id="Header1">Header1</th>
    <th id="Header2">Header2</th>
  </tr>
  <tr>
    <th id="RowDesc0">RowDescription0</th>
    <td headers="Header1,RowDesc0">Row0 Col1</td>
    <td headers="Header2,RowDesc0">Row0 Col2</td>
  </tr>
  <tr>
    <th id="RowDesc1">RowDescription1</th>
    <td headers="Header1,RowDesc1">Row1 Col1</td>
```

continues

```
    <td headers="Header2,RowDesc1">Row1 Col2</td>
  </tr>
  ... more rows here ...
  <tr>
    <td>Foot0</td>
    <td>Foot1</td>
    <td>Foot2</td>
  </tr>
</table>
```

To generate the output shown in Listing 11.13, you must be sure to use the correct cell type as you create each row in the table. Listing 11.14 shows the code used in the example, with the relevant parts set in bold. The technique is similar to that shown earlier (in Listing 11.11) to generate a "normal" table. However, this time you must add the ID attribute to each header cell and generate the first cell in each row as a header cell as well.

LISTING 11.14. Generating header Attributes with the AssociatedHeaderCellID Property

```
Sub CreateTable()
  Dim iRows As Integer = 4
  Dim iCols As Integer = 3
  Dim iRowCount, iColCount As Integer
  Dim oRow As TableRow
  Dim oCell As TableCell

  ' create header row, setting ID of each cell
  oRow = New TableHeaderRow()
  For iColCount = 0 To iCols - 1
    oCell = New TableHeaderCell()
    oCell.ID = "Header" & iColCount.ToString()
    oCell.Controls.Add(New LiteralControl("Header" _
                                    & iColCount.ToString()))
    oRow.Cells.Add(oCell)
  Next
  MyTable.Rows.Add(oRow)

  ' create data rows
  For iRowCount = 0 To iRows - 1
    oRow = New TableRow()

    ' first cell is a <th> "header" containing description of row
    oCell = New TableHeaderCell()
    'set ID for "header" cell
    oCell.ID = "RowDesc" & iRowCount.ToString()
    oCell.Controls.Add(New LiteralControl("RowDescription" _
                                    & iRowCount.ToString()))
    oRow.Cells.Add(oCell)

    ' remaining cells are data <td> elements
```

```
  For iColCount = 1 To iCols - 1
    oCell = New TableCell()
    oCell.Controls.Add(New LiteralControl("Row" _
      & iRowCount.ToString()& " Col" & iColCount.ToString()))

    ' add HTML "headers" attributes to cell
    oCell.AssociatedHeaderCellID = New String() {"Header" _
      & iColCount.ToString(), "RowDesc" & iRowCount.ToString()}
    oRow.Cells.Add(oCell)
  Next
  MyTable.Rows.Add(oRow)
Next

' create footer row
oRow = New TableFooterRow()
For iColCount = 0 To iCols - 1
  oCell = New TableCell()
  oCell.Controls.Add(New LiteralControl("Foot" _
                               & iColCount.ToString()))
  oRow.Cells.Add(oCell)
Next
MyTable.Rows.Add(oRow)
End Sub
```

Notice the use of the `AssociatedHeaderCellID` property for the cells containing the data in the table. This property accepts an array of `String` values. A suitable array can be generated by using the following syntax:

```
New String() {"string1", " string2"[, " string3"]}
```

Alternatively, if you specify the table declaratively, you can use a comma-delimited list of values:

```
<td runat="server"
    AssociatedHeaderCellID="String1,String2[,String3]">
  Cell contents
</td>
```

SUMMARY

In this chapter we looked at enhancements to the existing controls that were originally provided with ASP.NET 1.0. In general the changes are concentrated on the controls from the `System.Web.UI.WebControls` namespace. This follows from the new control architecture and adaptive rendering advances, and the few gaps left in the `WebControl` range have also been filled with new controls in that namespace (such as the file upload and hidden controls described in Chapter 10).

While we haven't covered every single change to every control, nor demonstrated all the possibilities of the new controls (mainly through lack of space), this chapter and the previous one have provided you with a good foundation to become familiar with using the new controls and the new architecture that supports them.

In the next chapter, we change tack completely to look at another important aspect of ASP.NET 2.0, namely, how the caching features have been vastly improved in this new version.

12

Caching

O NE OF THE MOST FREQUENTLY requested features for the
ASP.NET Cache is the ability to invalidate cached items from the
database. This capability, along with some changes to the underlying
plumbing such as disk-based output caching, has been added to the
ASP.NET 2.0 Cache infrastructure.

The caching features in ASP.NET are specifically designed to increase
throughput and decrease load on the server by keeping frequently accessed content in memory versus constantly running code. Of course this
also translates to amazing performance gains since common application
bottlenecks can be avoided. There are two primary uses of the `Cache`.

1. *Output caching* involves storing the response generated by an
   ASP.NET page, User Control, or Web Service in memory and using
   the cached response on subsequent requests rather than executing
   code. This is extremely fast since the server simply needs to copy
   the response from memory and is akin to static pages. A good example of this technique is a report. The contents used to render the
   report are generated once and stored in the output cache. Then the
   cached versions are used for subsequent requests, skipping all of
   the complex algorithms and data access required to initially generate the report.

2. *The* `Cache` *API* is a programmatic, dictionary-based API for accessing and storing frequently used application data. Unlike output caching, which caches the contents of the response, the `Cache` API is used within running code to cache frequently accessed data. For example, a `DataSet` used in 50% of the pages within an application could be cached so that each page that requires the data doesn't have to recalculate the data for every request.

Behind the scenes, pages marked for output caching are stored and retrieved through the `Cache` API. The `Cache` itself is simply a hashtable with enhanced capabilities.

- *Least recently used (LRU)*: When ASP.NET needs more memory, the `Cache` will automatically evict items by using an LRU algorithm to remove items that are accessed infrequently. Furthermore, this guarantees that the Cache cannot consume more memory than what is available on the system.
- *Cache dependencies*: Items added to the `Cache` can be made dependent on external conditions whereby they are removed. For example, ASP.NET 1.0 supported three dependencies: `Time`, `File`, and `Key`. Items could be expired at a point in time (by using the `Time` dependency), when a file changed (by using the `File` dependency), and when another item in the `Cache` changed (by using a `Key` dependency). This functionality is encapsulated in the `CacheDependency` class found in the `System.Web.Caching` namespace.

Caching is your best friend when it comes to building truly scalable applications. Don't scrimp on memory for the Web servers; an investment in memory will allow your applications to perform better because more data can remain cached.

While the `Cache` and its dependency features allowed complex applications to be built, the ASP.NET team soon realized that most cached data came from a database and there was not a dependency that allowed for invalidation when data in the database changed. Database change dependency is now possible in the ASP.NET 2.0 `Cache`.

Listing 12.1 demonstrates how this is used in a page by using the new `sqldependency` attribute of the `<%@ OutputCache %>` directive.

LISTING 12.1. SQL Server–Based Cache Dependency

```
<%@ Page Language="VB" %>
<%@ Import Namespace="System.Data" %>
<%@ Import Namespace="System.Data.SqlClient" %>
<%@ OutputCache duration="5555"
                varybyparam="none"
                sqldependency="Northwind:Products"  %>

<h1>Last update: <%=DateTime.Now.ToString("r")%></h1>
<hr>
<form runat="server">
    <asp:gridview id="GridView1"
                  datasourceid="SqlDataSource1"
                  runat="server" />

    <asp:sqldatasource id="SqlDataSource1"
         runat="server"
         selectcommand="SELECT * FROM dbo.[Products]"
         connectionstring="<%$ ConnectionStrings: nwind %>" />
</form>
```

Database cache invalidation allows for the removal of an item from the `Cache` when data stored in the database changes.

ASP.NET 2.0 adds support for database cache invalidation for Microsoft SQL Server 7, Microsoft SQL Server 2000, and the next version of Microsoft SQL Server 2005 (code-named "Yukon").

Although support for these three databases is built into ASP.NET, there are some significant differences.

- *Microsoft SQL Server 7 and Microsoft SQL Server 2000*: For these database products, only table-level changes are supported. For example, if you cached data from the Products table in the Northwind database and the table was updated, all cached data dependent on that table would be evicted from the `Cache`.

- *Microsoft SQL Server 2005*: Implicit support for invalidation is built directly into the database. Data can be invalidated from the `Cache` when the specific results of a request, such as a stored procedure, change.

The level of granularity between the databases is very relative. For example, if you output cached a page for each product in the Products table, you would output cache 77 pages. If you were using SQL Server 7 or SQL Server 2000, each of the 77 pages would be invalidated if the Products table were updated. However, with SQL Server 2005 you can be more selective about how items are invalidated; you can invalidate only output-cached pages that changed (e.g., the page displaying information for the product with ID 35).

We are not going to focus on the SQL Server 2005 caching capabilities in this book but will instead examine how to enable database cache invalidation from Microsoft SQL Server 7 and 2000. In order to use database cache invalidation on these databases, we first need to enable it.

Enabling Database Cache Invalidation

The command-line tool `aspnet_regsqlcache.exe` is used to configure databases for SQL cache invalidation, a combination command-line and GUI tool. The SQL Server database may also be configured using the new Web Site Administration Tool (see Chapter 6). Note that configuring the database for cache invalidation is only required to enable Microsoft SQL Server 7 and Microsoft SQL Server 2000 databases. Microsoft SQL Server 2005 has implicit support for database change notification.

> **IMPORTANT**
> You can also use the `SqlCacheDependencyAdmin` class in the `System.Web.Caching` namespace to enable the database and tables for Microsoft SQL Server 7 and 2000 databases. This functionality is not examined in this book.

To use `aspnet_regsqlcache.exe`, first open a command prompt window and navigate to the installation directory of the .NET Framework:

```
\Windows\Microsoft.NET\Framework\v2.0.XXXXX\
```

Next, type `aspnet_regsqlcache`, as shown in Figure 12.1.

The command-line tool options should be familiar if you have used command-line SQL tools such as `osqlw.exe`. Table 12.1 describes the various options in more detail. Note that the tool is case-sensitive.

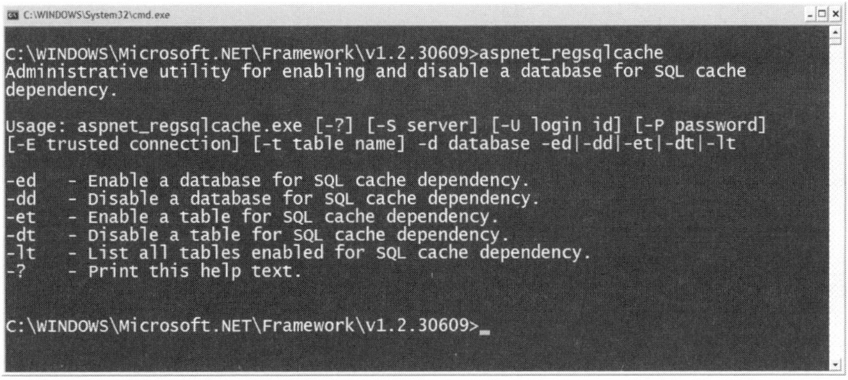

FIGURE 12.1. Use of aspnet_regsqlcache.exe

TABLE 12.1. Options for aspnet_regsqlcache.exe

Flag	Description
-?	Displays a help listing of the various flags supported by the tool.
-S	Names the SQL Server to connect to. This can be either the computer name or the IP address.
-U	Names the user to connect as when using SQL Server Authentication (e.g., the SQL Server administrator account, sa).
-P	Used in conjunction with the -U flag to specify the user's password.
-E	Connects to the SQL Server when using Windows Authentication and the current user has administrator capabilities on the database. The -U and -P flags are not needed when using -E.
-t	Specifies the table to apply necessary changes for SQL Server cache invalidation to.
-d	Specifies the database to apply changes for SQL Server cache invalidation to.
-ed	Enables a database for SQL cache dependency.
-dd	Disables a database for SQL cache dependency.
-et	Enables a table for SQL cache dependency.
-dt	Disables a table for SQL cache dependency.
-lt	Lists all tables enabled for SQL cache dependency.

The following subsections contain some sample sessions using `aspnet_regsqlcache.exe`.

Enabling a Database for SQL Cache Invalidation

Before a database table can participate in SQL cache invalidation, both the database and table must be enabled. To enable a database on the same machine, use this code:

```
aspnet_regsqlcache.exe -U [user] -P [password] -d [database] -ed
```

In Figure 12.2 we assume that SQL Server is running on the same machine, and we specify a user `sa` with the password `00password` on the Northwind database. This creates a new table named AspNet_SqlCacheTablesForChangeNotification.

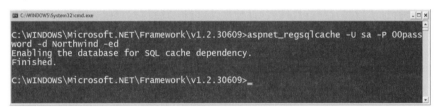

FIGURE 12.2. Enabling a database for SQL cache invalidation

This new table contains the columns shown in Table 12.2.

TABLE 12.2. Columns of AspNet_SqlCacheTablesForChangeNotification

Column	Description
tableName	Stores the name of all tables in the current database capable of participating in change notifications.
notificationCreated	Sets the timestamp indicating when the table was enabled for notifications.
changeId	Sets the numeric change ID incremented when a table is changed.

Now that the database is enabled for change notifications, we need to enlist tables that we wish to watch for changes.

Enabling a Table for SQL Cache Invalidation

After we enable the database for change notifications, we need to enlist selected tables for change notifications. For example, if we desire to enable the Customers, Employees, and Products tables in the Northwind database, we execute `aspnet_regsqlcache.exe` with the following parameters:

```
aspnet_regsqlcache.exe -U [user] -P [password]
                       -d [database] -t [table] -et
```

In Figure 12.3 we enable the Products table in the Northwind database. This creates a trigger `Products_AspNet_SqlCacheNotification_Trigger` on the Products table and also adds an entry into the AspNet _SqlCacheTablesForChangeNotification table for the Products table. Whenever data within the Products table is updated, inserted, or deleted, the trigger causes the `changeId` value stored in the AspNet_SqlCacheTablesForChangeNotification table to be incremented.

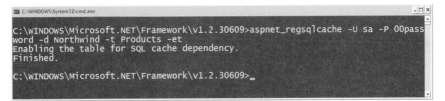

FIGURE 12.3. Enabling a table for SQL cache invalidation

We'll see how this all works in conjunction with ASP.NET shortly. Let's first look at how we list all the tables participating in change notifications for a database.

Listing Tables Enabled for SQL Cache Invalidation

To list tables for a particular database that are enabled for change notifications, use this code:

```
aspnet_regsqlcache.exe -U [user] -P [password] -d [database] -lt
```

In Figure 12.4 we use the `-lt` flag to retrieve a listing of all the tables in the Northwind database enabled for SQL cache invalidation.

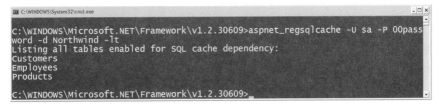

FIGURE 12.4. Listing tables enabled for SQL cache invalidation

Now that we've enabled the Northwind database and several tables to participate in SQL Server cache invalidation, let's see how we can use this in our ASP.NET application.

Invalidating the ASP.NET Cache

ASP.NET uses polling to retrieve change notifications for Microsoft SQL Server 7 and 2000. This polling occurs on a background thread apart from the threads used to service requests—a request will never be obstructed because of a polling operation. When there are no changes being monitored, the polling is stopped automatically; when a new `SqlCacheDependency` is created, the polling begins anew.

Configuration

The poll simply asks SQL for all of the records in the AspNet _SqlCacheTablesForChangeNotification table. The number of records in this table will not exceed the number of tables in the database. This is a fast operation because there are no joins or other complex SQL operations and the table is very small. The poll time can be configured for each application, but it defaults to once every 5 seconds.

Before we can create a `SqlCacheDependency`, we need to add some entries in the `web.config` file of our application (see Listing 12.2).

LISTING 12.2. SQL Server Cache Dependency Configuration

```
<configuration>
  <connectionStrings>
    <add name="Northwind"
        connectionString="server=localhost;
                          database=Northwind;
                          uid=sa;pwd=00password" />
  </connectionStrings>

  <system.web>
    <caching>
      <sqlCacheDependency enabled="true">
<databases>
      <add name="Northwind"
    connectionStringName="Northwind"
          pollTime="500" />
  </databases>
 </sqlCacheDependency>
    </caching>
  </system.web>
</configuration>
```

This configuration file adds an entry for the Northwind database in the `<connectionStrings/>` configuration section. The `<caching/>` section is a new entry for the `<system.web/>` configuration section group.

The `<sqlCacheDependency/>` section contains the elements and attributes shown in Table 12.3.

TABLE 12.3. The `<sqlCacheDependency/>` Configuration Section

Element	Description
sqlCacheDependency	Contains entries for individual connection strings that can be used for dependencies. This is the root element and allows for two attributes: • enabled: Controls whether or not the feature is enabled or disabled. • pollTime: If specified, sets a default pollTime for all entries added.
add	Adds a named entry for databases that support SQL change notification. The element allows for three attributes: • name: A string name used to identify the SQL database on the page. • connectionStringName: A reference to the `<connectionStrings/>` configuration section as to what connection string to use to connect to the database. • pollTime: The time interval between polls made to the database using the connection string to ask for changes.
remove	Removes an inherited entry. For example, if the Northwind entry has already been defined, the `<remove/>` element could be used to first remove it in a subapplication and then `<add/>` could be used to redefine it using a different connection string or pollTime. It supports a single attribute: • name: The string name used to identify the entry to remove.

Now that SQL cache invalidation is configured, we can begin using it in our ASP.NET application.

Invalidating Output-Cached Pages

There are two ways you can use SQL Server invalidation within pages: through directives or through the page output-cache APIs. The easiest way is to use the new `sqldependency` attribute of the `<%@ OutputCache %>` directive.

The `sqldependency` attribute accepts two types of values:

1. [name:table]: This value sets the cache entry and table name, where name represents the name of the entry from <sqlCacheDependency /> within the web.config file and table is the name of the table enabled for change notification.

2. CommandNotification: Used only by SQL Server 2005, this value instructs the ASP.NET page to make any and all SqlCommand instances needed to notify ASP.NET of changes.

The Syntax for SQL Server 7 and 2000

To use sqldependency for SQL Server 7 or 2000, here's the syntax:

```
<%@ OutputCache duration="9999"
                varybyparam="none"
                sqldependency="Northwind:Products" %>
```

You can also specify multiple dependencies by separating items with a semicolon. For example, if you also want the page dependent on the Pubs Authors table, use this syntax:

```
<%@ OutputCache duration="9999"
                varybyparam="none"
                sqldependency="Northwind:Products;Pubs:Authors" %>
```

The Syntax for SQL Server 2005

To use sqldependency for SQL Server 2005, here's the syntax:

```
<%@ OutputCache duration="9999"
                varybyparam="none"
                sqldependency="CommandNotification" %>
```

When the page is created, the page uses the value of the sqldependency attribute as parameters for the constructor of SqlCacheDependency. (We'll look at the SqlCacheDependency class shortly.)

Using Response.Cache API

An alternative to using the <%@ OutputCache %> directive is to use the Response.Cache API and create the SqlCacheDependency ourselves (see Listing 12.3).

LISTING 12.3. Using the Cache API for SQL Server Dependency

```
<%@ Page Language="VB" %>
<%@ Import Namespace="System.Data" %>
```

```
<%@ Import Namespace="System.Data.SqlClient" %>

<script runat="server">

  Public Sub Page_Load(ByVal sender As Object, ByVal e As EventArgs)

    ' Create the SqlCacheDependency
    Dim dp As New SqlCacheDependency("Northwind", "Products")

    ' Set up page output caching
    Response.Cache.SetExpires(DateTime.Now.AddSeconds(60))
    Response.Cache.SetCacheability(HttpCacheability.Public)
    Response.Cache.SetValidUntilExpires(True)

    ' Make this page dependent on the SqlCacheDependency
    Response.AddCacheDependency(dp)

    ' Can you guess the encrypted password?
    Dim connection As New SqlConnection( _
        "server=.; database=Northwind;uid=demo;pwd=mxddujbn")
    Dim command As New SqlCommand("SELECT * FROM Products", _
                                  connection)

    connection.Open()

    DataGrid1.DataSource = command.ExecuteReader()
    DataGrid1.DataBind()

    connection.Close()

  End Sub

</script>
<h1>Last update: <%=DateTime.Now.ToString("r")%></h1>
<hr>
<asp:DataGrid runat="server" id="DataGrid1" />
```

Immediately when SqlCacheDependency is created, polling begins.

How It Works

On the first poll, the list of notification-enabled tables is returned from the database. This list of tables is used to construct a cache entry for each table returned. Any dependencies requested through SqlCacheDependency are then made on this hidden cache entry. Thus, multiple SqlCacheDependency instances can be made for the same table, all dependent on one entry in the cache. When the table cache entry changes, it invalidates all dependent cache items.

Below is an example session (which assumes that the Northwind database and Products table are already configured for change notifications).

1. The user creates the page `default.aspx` and instructs the page to output to the cache and be dependent on the Northwind database's Products table.
2. The page is requested.
   a. `SqlCacheDependency` is created and polling begins.
   b. An entry in the cache is created for the Products table (e.g., `Products_Table`) by ASP.NET. This entry stores the `changeId` value returned from the database.
   c. The output-cached page is made dependent on the `Products_Table` cache entry.
3. The page is output cached, and subsequent requests draw the page from the cache.
4. A sales manager updates the Products table for a new Web site special sale.
   a. The Northwind Products table changes, and the `changeId` for this table is updated in the AspNet_SqlCacheTablesForChangeNotification table.
   b. The next poll by ASP.NET gets the new `changeId` value for the Products table.
   c. The `Products_Table` cache key is updated with the new `changeId` value, causing all dependent cache keys to be invalidated, including the `default.aspx` page.
5. The next request to the ASP.NET application causes the page to reexecute (because it is no longer in the output cache) and get added again.

Let's look at `SqlCacheDependency` in more detail.

The SqlCacheDependency Class

`SqlCacheDependency` is a new class in ASP.NET 2.0. It is found in the `System.Web.Caching` namespace and is used to create cache dependencies on Microsoft SQL Server 7, 2000, and 2005 databases.

The class inherits from `CacheDependency`, which has been unsealed for ASP.NET 2.0. Interaction with `SqlCacheDependency` can be achieved only through the two public constructors:

```
SqlCacheDependency (databaseEntry As String, tableName As String)


SqlCacheDependency (sqlCmd As SqlCommand)
```

Creating SQL Server 7 and 2000 Dependencies

The following constructor is used to create database dependencies on Microsoft SQL Server 7 and 2000 databases:

```
SqlCacheDependency (databaseEntry As String, tableName As String)
```

It requires that the web.config <sqlCacheDependency /> section is defined; the *databaseEntry* parameter matches the *name* value added in <sqlCacheDependency />. The *tableName* parameter is used to name a table in the database to monitor for changes. The named table must be enabled for change notifications. If the table name contains special characters or spaces, use brackets, as shown below:

```
Dim dp As New SqlCacheDependency("MyDatabase", "[Some Table]")
```

Creating SQL Server 2005 Dependencies

The following constructor can be used to create dependencies only for SQL Server 2005:

```
SqlCacheDependency (sqlCmd As SqlCommand)
```

Although not discussed in this book, a dependency created on a SQL Server 2005 database requires only the SqlCommand used when accessing the database (see Listing 12.4).

LISTING 12.4. Creating a SqlCacheDependency on a 2005 Database

```
<%@ Page Language="VB" %>
<%@ Import Namespace="System.Data" %>
<%@ Import Namespace="System.Data.SqlClient" %>


<script runat="server">

  Public Sub Page_Load(ByVal sender As Object, ByVal e As EventArgs)

    Dim connection As New SqlConnection( _
        "server=.;database=Northwind;uid=sa;pwd=00password")
    Dim command As New SqlCommand("SELECT * FROM Products", _
                                  connection)

    ' Create the SqlCacheDependency on a "Yukon" database
```

continues

```
Dim dp As New SqlCacheDependency(command)

' Set up page output caching

Response.Cache.SetExpires(DateTime.Now.AddSeconds(60))
Response.Cache.SetCacheability(HttpCacheability.Public)
Response.Cache.SetValidUntilExpires(True)

' Make this page dependent on the SqlCacheDependency

Response.AddCacheDependency(dp)

connection.Open()

DataGrid1.DataSource = command.ExecuteReader()
DataGrid1.DataBind()

connection.Close()

End Sub

</script>
<h1>Last update: <%=DateTime.Now.ToString("r")%></h1>
<hr>
<asp:DataGrid runat="server" id="DataGrid1" />
```

As mentioned above, `SqlCacheDependency` inherits from `CacheDependency`, which was a sealed class in ASP.NET 1.0. In ASP.NET 2.0 Microsoft has unsealed `CacheDependency`, added a default public constructor, and changed some of the internal plumbing of the class so that you can inherit from it and create your own cache dependencies.

Let's take a look at the changes to the `CacheDependency` class.

The CacheDependency Class

Version 1.0 of ASP.NET introduced the ASP.NET `Cache`, an application-specific hashtable used to store frequently accessed data. The structure and API of the `Cache` is very similar to two other structures, `Application` and `Session`, insofar as they all support similar APIs. `Application` is most similar to the `Cache` because it is global to the application, whereas `Session` is memory set aside for each user.

The biggest differentiator between `Application` and `Cache` is the `Cache`'s support of `Cache` dependencies. `Cache` dependencies allow developers to build solutions that can automatically remove cached items from the `Cache` on the occurrence of certain events. The support events are listed below.

- `Time`: After a specific duration of time, the item is removed from the `Cache`. This feature is most evident in the page output-caching features of ASP.NET.
- `File`: If a file or files change, the item is removed from the `Cache`.
- `Key`: If another `Cache` key changes, the item is removed from the `Cache`.

The above functionality is encapsulated in the `CacheDependency` class found in the `System.Web.Caching` namespace.

Although these three dependency features address a great number of the needs for most developers, people are constantly requesting the ability to add more. For example, the dependency feature most requested is database dependency—which Microsoft added to ASP.NET 2.0. Another common request is to generalize the `CacheDependency` class so that anyone can implement a `CacheDependency` (e.g., a cache dependency that relies on values returned from an XML Web Service).

Microsoft has unsealed the `CacheDependency` class and has done other work to make it possible for you to extend `CacheDependency`; in fact, this is just what was done for `SqlCacheDependency`!

SUMMARY

Although the ASP.NET team hasn't completed all of the feature work for the ASP.NET `Cache` (at the time of this writing there is yet another coding milestone currently in progress), the features that are available address two of the main requests most customers had: support for database change notifications and the ability to inherit from `CacheDependency`. The remaining work items will include new APIs for managing partial page caching as well as new configuration for managing the `Cache` at the application level.

Database cache invalidations are different for Microsoft SQL Server 7 and 2000 versus Microsoft SQL Server 2005. Microsoft SQL Server 7 and 2000 support only table-level change notifications. Microsoft SQL Server 2005 supports more granular notifications (e.g., the results of a stored procedure).

There are three ways to enable a Microsoft SQL Server 7 or 2000 database for change notifications: the `aspnet_regsqlcache.exe` tool, the

SqlCacheDependencyAdmin class, or the Web Site Administration Tool (see Chapter 6). In this chapter we looked at the aspnet_regsqlcache.exe tool and learned how to enable the database and tables, as well as return a listing of all tables within a database enabled for change notifications.

Enabling caching in your ASP.NET application is easy. You can either use the new sqldependency attribute of the <%@ OutputCache %> directive or create an instance of SqlCacheDependency directly. Either option will ensure that the page is dependent on the named database and table.

Finally, we learned about the changes to the CacheDependency class and how it is now designed so that you can inherit from it and create your own cache dependencies.

In the next chapter, we will look at the ASP.NET administration and configuration.

■ 13 ■

Configuration and Administration

YOU'VE SEEN THROUGHOUT THIS BOOK that building Web sites with ASP.NET is easier than ever. Not only have more features been added, but also there's much less code to write, with more use of declarative properties. However, when it comes to administration, the features are split—it's more complex because there are more features to configure, but at the same time it's easier because there is a Web-based administration tool and an API to support it.

For the last chapter in this look at the new ASP.NET features, we'll explore a variety of configuration and administration topics. We'll start by looking at the configuration files, seeing which sections have changed and what the new sections are. Some of this material has been covered elsewhere in the book in more detail, but this chapter provides the definitive reference for the changes in ASP.NET.

We'll then take a look at the Web Site Administration Tool before moving on to the Management API, which is the underlying set of classes that provide easy management and configuration. Having a consistent API means that it's easy to build custom configuration routines.

Application Configuration Files

The application configuration files (`web.config` and the site-wide `machine.config`) have had a number of changes, including new attributes added to existing elements as well as new elements to support the new features. The changed sections of the configuration files cover the topics listed below:

- Client targets
- Compilation
- Build providers
- Web proxy
- HTTP modules
- HTTP runtime

- HTTP handlers
- Globalization
- Pages
- Session state
- Web request modules

The new sections cover the following topics:

- Anonymous identification
- Code DOM
- Connection strings
- Data
- Caching
- Expression builders
- Hosting
- Image generation
- HTTP cookies
- Membership
- Site maps

- Site counters
- Personalization Profile
- Protocol bindings
- Role Manager
- Mail servers
- URL mappings
- Web Parts
- Web Site Administration Tool
- Protected data
- Health monitoring

Changed Sections

The text in this subsection details only the changes made to the configuration files and the changed attributes.

Client Targets

The `<clientTarget/>` section identifies browsers by their user agent string and provides a mapping to a simple alias. For the `downlevel` alias, the user agent has been changed from `Unknown` to `Generic Downlevel`, as shown here:

```
<clientTarget>
  <add alias="downlevel" userAgent="Generic Downlevel" />
</clientTarget>
```

Compilation

The `<compilation/>` section has been enhanced to allow for automatic compilation of source files and pre-compilation of applications. For this there is a new `<codeSubDirectories/>` element that indicates which directories contain code that should be automatically compiled. This section contains a collection of relative directory names where code is placed. The syntax is shown here:

```
<compilation
  urlLinePragmas="[true|false]"
  >
    <codeSubDirectories>
      <add directoryName="String" />
    </codeSubDirectories>
  </compilation>
```

A new `Boolean` attribute on the main compilation section, `urlLinePragmas`, indicates whether or not pragmas use URLs. The default is `false`, which means that pragmas use physical paths. The `<compilers/>` section has been moved to the new `<system.codedom/>` section, which is covered later in the chapter.

Build Providers

The `<buildProviders/>` section, within the `<compilation/>` section, identifies which files are part of the dynamic compilation process. This section has the following syntax:

```
<buildProviders>
  <add
    extension="String"
    appliesTo="String"
    type="String" />
</buildProviders>
```

The attributes are described in Table 13.1.

TABLE 13.1. buildProvider Attributes

Attribute	Description
extension	The file extension (e.g., .resx) of the file to be built.
appliesTo	The directory (e.g., Resources) where the files reside.
type	The type name of the build provider class used to invoke the compilation.

The `<buildProviders/>` section is for files that aren't part of the `<compilation/>` section (those files are automatically built). Compilation and build providers were covered in Chapter 2.

Web Proxy

The `<defaultProxy/>` section (under the `<system.net/>` section) defines how the System.Net classes access the Internet and has been enhanced to include the following settings:

```
<defaultProxy
  scriptDownloadInterval="Integer"
  scriptDownloadTimeout="Integer"
  useDefaultCredentialsForScriptDownload="[true|false]"
  />
```

The attributes are described in Table 13.2.

TABLE 13.2. defaultProxy Attributes

Attribute	Description
scriptDownloadInterval	Defines, in seconds, the time that elapses before the configuration script is refreshed.
scriptDownloadTimeout	Defines, in seconds, the time allowed for the configuration script to download.
useDefaultCredentialsForScriptDownload	Indicates whether or not default credentials are used when accessing the configuration script.

HTTP Modules

Several new HTTP modules have been added to the pipeline.

- `SessionID` allows generation of `Session` ID values to be factored out by programmers. This enables developers to easily provide their own `Session` ID values.
- `RoleManager` provides support for the Role Manager.
- `AnonymousIdentification` provides support for identification of anonymous visitors.
- `Profile` provides support for Personalization.
- `PageCountersModule` provides support for the page counters.
- `SqlBatchModule` provides support for batch SQL commands.

A full description of these is beyond the scope of this book, but details can be found in the SDK documentation.

HTTP Runtime

The `<httpRuntime/>` section has been enhanced to cater to application domain shutdowns and buffered uploads, with the new attributes shown in Listing 13.1.

LISTING 13.1. httpRuntime Syntax

```
<httpRuntime
   enable=" [true|false] "
   requestLengthDiskThreshold=" Integer "
   requireRootedSaveAsPath=" [true|false] "
   waitChangeNotification=" Integer "
   maxWaitChangeNotification=" Integer "
   compilationTempDirectory=" String "
   requestPriority=" [Normal|High|Critical] "
   />
```

The attributes are described in Table 13.3 on the next page.

The `enable` attribute allows an entire application domain to be disabled, perhaps in a hosting environment. Any requests to that application will result in a 404 error.

The addition of automatic shutdowns is useful for sites that are hit infrequently (such as personal sites, maybe a photo album), where keeping the application active wastes resources.

The `requestLengthDiskThreshold` and `requireRootedSaveAsPath` attributes are for file uploads. They define the maximum size of uploaded files and whether the upload path where files are saved must be rooted, respectively.

TABLE 13.3. httpRuntime Attributes

Attribute	Description
enable	Indicates whether or not the current application domain (and those below it) is enabled. The default value is `true`.
requestLengthDiskThreshold	Indicates the threshold, in kilobytes, for buffering the input stream; should not exceed the `MaxRequestLength` property. The default value is `256`.
requireRootedSaveAsPath	Indicates whether or not the path for Save As operations must be a rooted path. The default value is `true`.
waitChangeNotification	Indicates the time in seconds to wait for another file change notification before restarting the application domain.
maxWaitChangeNotification	Indicates the maximum time in seconds to wait from the first file change notification before restarting the application domain.
compilationTempDirectory	Indicates the directory for temporary files used during compilation.
requestPriority	Indicates the request priority.

HTTP Handlers

The `<httpHandlers/>` section has been enhanced to cater to the following new handlers:

- `WebAdmin.axd`, for the Web Site Administration Tool
- `WebResource.axd`, for Web resources
- `CachedImageService.axd`, for cached images
- `Counters.axd`, for site counters for URL redirection
- `Precompile.axd`, for site pre-compilation
- `WebPartExport.axd`, for exporting settings of Web Parts to an XML file

In addition, the following file suffixes are handled by the forbidden handler (`System.Web.HttpForbiddenHandler`), stopping them being served directly:

- `.asix`
- `.master`
- `.skin`
- `.browser`

- `.mdb`
- `.ldb`
- `.sitemap`
- `.mdw`

Globalization

The `<globalization/>` section has two new attributes, to allow automatic setting of culture depending on the browser.

```
<globalization
  responseHeaderEncoding="String"
  enableClientBasedCulture="[true|false]"
  />
```

The `responseHeaderEncoding` allows the encoding to be set for response headers. The default is `utf-8`.

The `enableClientBasedCulture` attribute indicates whether or not the `uiCulture` and `culture` will be based on the `accept-language` header sent by the client browser. This overrides culture settings in configuration files, unless the client cultures cannot be mapped to a specific culture. The default value is `false`.

Pages

The `<pages/>` section has been enhanced to add Personalization, master pages, and theme support. Additionally, a new subelement allows automatic addition of namespace references to each page (see Listing 13.2).

LISTING 13.2. pages Configuration Syntax

```
<pages
  compilationMode="[Auto|Never|Always]"
  maxPageStateFieldLength="Integer"
  masterPageFile="String"
  theme="String"
  stylesheetTheme="String"
  >
  <namespaces>
    <add namespace="String" />
  </namespaces>
</pages>
```

The attributes are described in Table 13.4. Both the `masterPageFile` and `theme` attributes can be overridden at the page level.

TABLE 13.4. pages Attributes

Attribute	Description
`compilationMode`	Indicates the mode of compilation. Can be `Always`, `Auto`, or `Never`. The default is `Always`.
`maxPageStateFieldLength`	Indicates the maximum length of the field used for `ViewState`. If set, the `VIEWSTATE` field is split into multiple fields (`VIEWSTATE`, `VIEWSTATE1`, `VIEWSTATE2`, and so on) so that each field does not exceed the maximum size as specified by this setting.
`masterPageFile`	Defines the site-wide master page. This allows a master page to be applied to all pages without adding the `masterPageFile` attribute to the `Page` directive.
`theme`	Defines the site-wide theme. This allows a theme to be applied to all pages without adding the `Theme` attribute to the `Page` directive.
`stylesheetTheme`	Defines the site-wide stylesheet theme. This allows a stylesheet theme to be applied to all pages without adding the `StylesheetTheme` attribute to the `Page` directive.

For the `namespaces` subelement, the namespace is the full namespace to be included as a reference. For example:

```
<namespaces>
  <add namespace="System" />
  <add namespace="System.Collections" />
</namespaces>
```

The following namespaces are included in `machine.config`:

* `System`
* `System.Collections`
* `System.Collections.Specialized`
* `System.ComponentModel`
* `System.Configuration`
* `System.Text`

- System.Text.RegularExpressions
- System.Web
- System.Web.Caching
- System.Web.SessionState
- System.Web.Security
- System.Web.Profile
- System.Web.UI
- System.Web.UI.Imaging
- System.Web.UI.WebControls
- System.Web.UI.WebControls.WebParts
- System.Web.UI.HtmlControls

In addition to globally defining namespaces, tag controls can also be defined through the use of a `controls` subelement, as shown in this example:

```
<controls>
  <add
    tagPrefix="asp"
    namespace="System.Web.UI.WebControls.WebParts"
    assembly="…" />
</controls>
```

Session State

There are several changes to the state handling mechanism, which are covered in detail later in the chapter. Here's the new syntax for the `<sessionState/>` section:

```
<sessionState
  mode="[Off|InProc|StateServer|SQLServer|Custom]"
  sqlCommandTimeout="Integer"
  customProvider="String"
  cookieName="String"
  allowCustomSqlDatabase="[true|false]"
  >
  <providers>
    <clear />
    <add
      Name="String"
      Type="String"
      [providerSpecificConfiguration] />
  </providers>
</sessionState>
```

The new attributes are described in Table 13.5.

TABLE 13.5. sessionState Attributes

Attribute	Description
mode	Indicates how session state is being managed. This has been enhanced to allow the new Custom value, which indicates that session state is stored in a custom manner.
sqlCommandTimeout	Indicates, in seconds, the timeout for a SQL command when the mode is SQLServer. The default value is 30.
customProvider	Indicates the name of the provider when the mode is Custom. The name attribute should match one of the provider names declared in the <Providers/> section.
cookieName	Defines the default cookie name used to store the session ID.
allowCustomSqlDatabase	Indicates whether or not a custom database name can be specified in the Initial Catalog attribute of the SQL Server connection string.

The addition of the <providers/> element brings session state handling inline with the standard provider model, allowing you to define custom providers.

In the Technology Preview release there was no <providers/> section. Instead only a single custom provider could be specified through the use of the customType attribute.

Mobile Devices State

In addition to the session state changes, there is also a <sessionPageState/> element, which details the number of pages of session state stored on the server:

```
<sessionPageState
  historySize="Integer"
  />
```

This works in a way similar to the session state management for mobile controls in the MMIT from ASP.NET 1.x. This is required because the session state is stored on the server, and without the history the session state could become out of sync with the displayed page. The default value is 9.

Web Request Modules

When using the `WebRequest` class to access Web resources, you have the option of using HTTP, HTTPS, or FILE as the protocols. The `<webRequestModules/>` section now has FTP added to provide file transfer support:

```
<add prefix="ftp"
  type="String"
  />
```

The `type` attribute identifies the full type of the class implementing the service.

New Sections

The configuration files contain many new sections to cater to the new features in ASP.NET 2.0. These new sections are described briefly in the next several pages.

Anonymous Identification

The `<anonymousIdentification/>` section deals with how identity is assigned to users who are not authenticated (see Listing 13.3). It is used by the Personalization services.

LISTING 13.3. anonymousIdentification Configuration Syntax

```
<anonymousIdentification
  enabled="[true|false]"
  cookieName="String"
  cookieTimeout="Integer"
  cookiePath="String"
  cookieRequireSSL="[true|false]"
  cookieSlidingExpiration="[true|false]"
  cookieProtection="[None|Validation|Encryption|All]"
  cookieless="[UseCookies|UseUri|AutoDetect|UseDeviceProfile]"
  />
```

The attributes are described in Table 13.6.

TABLE 13.6. anonymousIdentification Attributes

Attribute	Description
`enabled`	Indicates whether or not anonymous identification is enabled. The default value is `false`.
`cookieName`	Specifies the name of the cookie. The default value is `.ASPXANONYMOUS`.
`cookieTimeout`	Specifies the value, in minutes, before the cookie expires. This cannot be `0` or less. The default value is `100000`.
`cookiePath`	Specifies the path, which is case-sensitive, used to write the cookie. Using `'/'` allows applications within the same domain to access the cookie. The default is `'/'`.
`cookieRequireSSL`	Indicates whether or not the cookie requires an SSL connection in order to be written to the client. The default value is `false`.
`cookieSlidingExpiration`	Indicates whether the cookie timeout resets upon each request (a value of `true`) or expires at a fixed time (a value of `false`). The default value is `true`.
`cookieProtection`	Specifies the protection scheme used to store the cookie. Can be one of the `CookieProtection` enumerations (from `System.Web.Security`): • `None`: Indicates no protection is used. • `Validation`: Indicates that the cookie is hashed and validated. • `Encryption`: Indicates that the cookie is encrypted. • `All`: Indicates that both validation and encryption are used. The default value is `None`.
`cookieless`	Specifies the cookie scheme to use. Can be one of the following: • `UseCookies`: Forces the authentication ticket to be stored in the cookie (same as ASP.NET 1.x behavior). • `UseUri`: Forces the authentication ticket to be stored in the URL. • `AutoDetect`: Automatically detects whether the browser/device supports cookies. • `UseDeviceProfile`: Chooses to use cookies or not based on the device profile settings from `machine.config`. The default value is `UseDeviceProfile`.

Code DOM

The `<system.codedom/>` section has been introduced to centralize the configuration of compilation features across all aspects of the .NET Framework, rather than having them be part of the Web configuration. The `<compilers/>` element has been moved into this new section (see Listing 13.4).

LISTING 13.4. system.codedom Configuration Syntax

```
<system.codedom>
  <compilers>
    <compiler
      language="String"
      extensions="String"
      type="String"
      warningLevel="Integer"
      compilerOptions="String"
    />
  </compilers>
</system.codedom>
```

The attributes for each listed compiler are the same as the previous version, but with one addition, `compilerOptions`, which allows default compiler options to be set.

Connection Strings

The `<connectionStrings/>` section allows database connection strings to be stored. Previously these were often stored in the `<appSettings/>` section and thus used to get mixed in with general application settings. Now, however, they have a specific section, allowing database details to be stored either at the application level or for the entire machine. This also allows the connection string details to be protected (perhaps by encryption), thus keeping them secure.

```
<connectionStrings>
  <add name="String"
    connectionString="String"
    providerName="String"
  />
  <remove name="String" />
  <clear />
</connectionStrings>
```

The attributes are described in Table 13.7.

TABLE 13.7. connectionStrings Attributes

Attribute	Description
name	The name of the connection string.
connectionString	The full connection details. No validity checking is performed.
providerName	The name of the data provider, for example, "System.Data.SqlClient".

Like the application-specific settings, the connection strings are exposed through the ConfigurationSettings class. For example, we could define our database details as

```
<connectionStrings>
  <add
    name="MyData"
    connectionString="server=.;database=MyData;Uid=;Pwd=" />
</connectionStrings>
```

Then we could use these details in our page or class:

```
Dim cs As String
cs = ConfigurationSettings.ConnectionStrings("MyData").ConnectionString

Dim conn As New SqlConnection(cs)
```

Data

The <system.data/> section allows configuration of data provider factories, allowing for abstracted access to data stores (see Listing 13.5).

LISTING 13.5. system.data Configuration Syntax

```
<system.data>
  <DbProviderFactories>
    <add
      name="String"
      invariant="String"
      support="String"
      description="String"
      type="String"
      />
  </DbProviderFactories>
</system.data>
```

The attributes for <DbProviderFactories/> are described in Table 13.8.

TABLE 13.8. DbProviderFactories Attributes

Attribute	Description
name	The name of the data factory.
invariant	The namespace of the data factory.
support	The level of support supplied by the provider. Can be a combination of items in the DbProviderSupportedClasses enumeration.
description	The description of the data factory.
type	The full type of the class that handles the factory.

The supplied data factories are for:

- Odbc
- OleDb
- OracleClient
- SqlClient

Caching

Caching—already an area of ASP.NET that led to performance enhancements—has been greatly improved in ASP.NET 2.0, with new features and configuration of existing features. All of this is exposed underneath the <caching/> section, which has no attributes itself but contains the following subsections:

- <cache/>, for the cache API
- <outputCache/>, for disk caching
- <outputCacheSettings/>, to define cache profiles that can be used by pages
- <sqlCacheDependency/>, to configure SQL Server–based cache dependencies

The syntax for the <cache/> element is shown in Listing 13.6.

LISTING 13.6. cache Configuration Syntax

```
<cache
  cacheAPIEnabled="[true|false]"
  disableMemoryCollection="[true|false]"
  disableExpiration="[true|false]"
  />
```

The attributes for `<cache/>` are described in Table 13.9.

TABLE 13.9. cache Attributes

Attribute	Description
cacheAPIEnabled	Indicates whether or not the Cache API is enabled. If disabled, calls to the Cache API will have no effect. This does not affect ASP.NET internal usage of the Cache. The default value is true.
disableMemoryCollection	Indicates whether or not the cache memory collection is enabled. The default value is false.
disableExpiration	Indicates whether or not the expiration of items from the cache is enabled. The default value is true.

The syntax for the `<outputCache/>` element is shown in Listing 13.7.

LISTING 13.7. outputCache and diskCache Configuration Syntax

```
<outputCache enabled="[true|false]">
  <diskCache
    enabled="[true|false]"
    path="String"
    maxDiskPercentTotal="Integer"
    maxSizePerApp="Integer"
    />
</outputCache>
```

The attributes for `<outputCache/>` and `<diskCache/>` are described in Table 13.10.

TABLE 13.10. outputCache and diskCache Attributes

Attribute	Description
enabled	If used on the outputCache element, indicates whether or not the output cache is enabled. If used on the diskCache element, indicates whether or not disk-based persistent caching is enabled. The default in both cases is true.
path	Defines the location for disk-based persistent cache entries.
maxDiskPercentTotal	Indicates the maximum size, as a percentage of the disk size, of the disk cache. The default is 10.
maxSizePerApp	Indicates the maximum size, in megabytes, of the cache per application. The default is 5.

The `<outputCacheSettings/>` section has no attributes but has two subsections to allow configuration of the cache profiles (`<outputCacheProfiles/>`) and fragment cache profiles (`<fragmentCacheProfiles/>`). The syntax for these is the same, as shown in Listing 13.8.

LISTING 13.8. outputCacheProfiles and fragmentCacheProfiles Configuration Syntax

```
<outputCacheProfiles>
  <clear />
  <add
    name="String"
    enabled="[true|false]"
    diskCacheable="[true|false]"
    duration="Integer"
    location="String"
    shared="[true|false]"
    sqlDependency="String"
    varyByControl="String"
    varyByCustom="String"
    varyByHeader="String"
    varyByParam="String"
    noStore="[true|false]"
    />
</outputCacheProfiles>
```

The attributes for cache profiles are described in Table 13.11.

TABLE 13.11. outputCacheProfiles and fragmentCacheProfiles Attributes

Attribute	Description
name	Indicates the name of the profile, which can be referenced by the CacheProfile attribute of the OutputCache page directive.
enabled	Indicates whether or not caching for the profile is enabled.
diskCacheable	Indicates whether or not the profile caches to disk.
duration	Defines how long, in seconds, to cache the data.
location	Defines the location where the data is cached along the server/proxy/client path. The values can be •Any, allowing the output cache to be located anywhere •Client, to specify the output cache is located on the client •Downstream, to specify the cache can be stored in any HTTP 1.1 cache device •None, to disable the output cache

continues

TABLE 13.11. outputCacheProfiles and fragmentCacheProfiles Attributes (continued)

Attribute	Description
location (continued)	• `Server`, to specify the cache is located on the server where the request was processed • `ServerAndClient`, to specify the cache can be stored only on the processing server or the requesting client
shared	Applies only to user controls, and indicates whether a cached version of the control can be shared between pages. Sharing of cached user controls is not supported in beta release 1.
sqlDependency	Defines a SQL dependency string.
varyByControl	Defines the comma-separated list of controls to vary by.
varyByCustom	Defines the comma-separated list of custom strings to vary by.
varyByHeader	Defines the comma-separated list of headers to vary by.
varyByParam	Defines the comma-separated list of parameters to vary by.
noStore	Indicates whether or not a `Cache-Control:no-store` header is sent, to prevent caching on secondary cache servers.

The `<sqlCacheDependency/>` section defines dependencies on SQL Server tables. The syntax is shown in Listing 13.9.

LISTING 13.9. cache Configuration Syntax

```
<sqlCacheDependency
  enabled="[true|false]"
  pollTime="Integer"
  >
  <databases>
    <add
      name="String"
      connectionStringName="String"
      pollTime="Integer"
      />
    <remove
      name="String"
      />
  </databases>
</sqlCacheDependency>
```

The attributes for `<sqlCacheDependency/>` and `<databases/>` are described in Tables 13.12 and 13.13, respectively.

TABLE 13.12. sqlCacheDependency Attributes

Attribute	Description
enabled	Indicates whether or not the SQL cache dependency polling is enabled. The default value is `true`.
pollTime	Defines, in milliseconds, the poll time. The minimum value is `500`. The default value is `60000`.

TABLE 13.13. databases Attributes

Attribute	Description
name	Indicates the name of the database.
connectionStringName	Indicates the name of the connection string from the `<connectionStrings/>` configuration section.
pollTime	Defines the time, in milliseconds, between polls. If not specified, the `pollTime` from the parent element is used.

For more details on caching, please see Chapter 12. In the Technology Preview release only database caching was supported, under the `<cache/>` element.

Expression Builders

The `<expressionBuilders/>` section identifies inline expressions and the class used to evaluate them. The syntax for this section is shown here:

```
<expressionBuilders>
  <add
    expressionPrefix="String"
    type="String" />
</expressionBuilders>
```

The three configured expression builders are `Resources`, `Connection Strings`, and `AppSettings`, allowing dynamic binding that uses the following syntax:

```
<%$ ConnectionStrings: pubs %>
```

Hosting

The `<hostingEnvironment/>` section allows configuration of timeouts for hosted environments. Listing 13.10 shows the syntax.

LISTING 13.10. hostingEnvironment Configuration Syntax

```
<hostingEnvironment
  idleTimeout="Integer"
  shutdownTimeout="Integer"
  />
```

The attributes are described in Table 13.14.

TABLE 13.14. hostingEnvironment Attributes

Attribute	Description
idleTimeout	Indicates the time, in minutes, to unload the application.
shutdownTimeout	Indicates the time, in minutes, given for graceful shutdown of the application.

Image Generation

The `<imageGeneration/>` section allows configuration of the dynamic generation of images. The syntax is shown here:

```
<imageGeneration
  storageType="[Cache|Disk]"
  storagePath="String"
  storageExpiration="Integer"
  customErrorImageUrl="String"
  />
```

The attributes are described in Table 13.15.

TABLE 13.15. imageGeneration Attributes

Attribute	Description
storageType	The type of storage to be used. This can be one of the StorageType enumerations from System.Web.UI.Imaging: • Cache: Indicates storage in the cache. • Disk: Indicates storage on disk. The default value is Cache.

TABLE 13.15. imageGeneration Attributes (continued)

Attribute	Description
storagePath	If `Disk` storage is being used, this specifies the path where generated images will be stored. If not supplied, the `ASPNETImageStorage` directory is used, in the `Temp` directory of the ASPNET account.
storageExpiration	The default length of time, in seconds, before an image expires. The default value is `300`.
customErrorImageUrl	The URL to an image to display when an unhandled exception is thrown.

HTTP Cookies

The `<httpCookies/>` section controls whether certain HTTP headers are sent to the browser. This enables more secure storage of cookies and ensures that user-supplied code cannot access the cookies from the browser. Here's the syntax:

```
<httpCookies
  httpOnlyCookies="[true|false]"
  requireSSL="[true|false]"
  domain="String"
  />
```

The attributes are described in Table 13.16.

TABLE 13.16. httpCookies Attributes

Attribute	Description
httpOnlyCookies	Indicates whether or not the `HttpOnly` cookie attribute is added to the page, to ensure that cookies cannot be accessed client side.
requireSSL	Indicates whether or not the secure cookie attribute is added to the page.
domain	Defines the domain to which the cookie applies, which sets the `domain` cookie attribute for the page.

Membership

The <membership/> section defines the configuration for the supplied Membership schemes. It follows the standard providers pattern, allowing custom providers to be supplied (see Listing 13.11).

LISTING 13.11. membership Configuration Syntax

```
<membership
  defaultProvider="String"
  userIsOnlineTimeWindow="Integer">
  <providers>
    <add name="String"
      type="String"
      [providerSpecificSettings]
      />
    <remove name="String"
     />
    <clear />
  </providers>
</membership>
```

The membership and providers attributes are described in Tables 13.17 and 13.18, respectively.

TABLE 13.17. membership Attributes

Attribute	Description
defaultProvider	The name of the default provider. There is no default value.
userIsOnlineTimeWindow	The time, in minutes, since the last activity when the user was deemed to be online. The default value is 15.

TABLE 13.18. providers Attributes

Attribute	Description
name	The name of the membership provider. The default value is AspNetAccessProvider.
type	A string containing the full .NET type of the provider.
providerSpecificSettings	A name/value collection detailing provider-specific settings.

SQL Server and Access Membership Providers

Two providers are supplied with this release, giving support for SQL Server and Access databases. These are named `AspNetSqlProvider` and `AspNetAccessProvider`, respectively, and both have the same syntax for the provider-specific section:

```
connectionStringName="String"
enablePasswordRetrieval="[true|false]"
enablePasswordReset="[true|false]"
requiresQuestionAndAnswer="[true|false]"
applicationName="String"
requiresUniqueEmail="[true|false]"
passwordFormat="[Clear|Hashed|Encrypted]"
description="String"
```

The attributes are described in Table 13.19.

TABLE 13.19. SQL Server and Access Membership Provider-Specific Attributes

Attribute	Description
`connectionStringName`	Specifies the name of the connection string, from the `<connectionStrings/>` section.
`enablePasswordRetrieval`	Indicates whether or not the provider will allow retrieval of passwords. The default value is `false`.
`enablePasswordReset`	Indicates whether or not the provider will allow passwords to be reset. The default value is `true`.
`requiresQuestionAndAnswer`	Indicates whether or not the provider enforces a question-and-answer method for retrieving forgotten passwords. The default value is `false`. Valid only when the `passwordFormat` setting is not `Hashed` and `enablePasswordRetrieval` is true.
`applicationName`	Defines the scope of the application. The default value is `/`.
`requiresUniqueEmail`	Indicates whether or not the provider enforces unique e-mail addresses. The default value is `false`.
`passwordFormat`	Defines how the passwords should be stored. Values can be one of the following: • `Clear`: For clear text passwords. • `Hashed`: For hashed passwords. • `Encrypted`: For encrypted passwords. The default value is `Hashed`.
`description`	Defines the description of the provider.

Membership is covered in detail in Chapter 6.

Site Maps

The `<siteMap/>` section allows configuration of site map providers, providing menuing and navigation features (see Listing 13.12).

LISTING 13.12. sitemap Configuration Syntax

```
<siteMap
    defaultProvider="String"
    enabled="[true|false]">
  <providers>
    <add
      name="String"
      type="String"
      securitytrimmingEnabled="[true|false]"
      [providerSpecificSettings]
      />
    <remove name="String"
      />
    <clear />
  </providers>
</siteMap>
```

The `siteMap` and `siteMap providers` attributes are described in Tables 13.20 and 13.21, respectively.

TABLE 13.20. siteMap Attributes

Attribute	Description
defaultProvider	The name of the default provider. This should match one of the names supplied in the `providers` section. The default value is `AspNetXmlSiteMapProvider`.
enabled	A `Boolean` value indicating whether or not site maps are enabled. The default value is `true`.

TABLE 13.21. siteMap providers Attributes

Attribute	Description
name	The name of the site map provider.
type	A string containing the full .NET type of the provider.

TABLE 13.21. siteMap providers Attributes (continued)

Attribute	Description
securityTrimmingEnabled	Indicates whether or not security trimming is enabled, allowing the nodes to be filtered by selected roles. The default value is false.
providerSpecificSettings	The provider-specific settings.

AspNetXmlSiteMapProvider

The supplied site provider is for XML files and has a single attribute, siteMapFile, which defines the name of the site map file. The default value for this is app.SiteMap.

Site Counters

The <siteCounters/> section defines the configuration for the Site Counters Service, allowing tracking of navigation from server controls (see Listing 13.13).

LISTING 13.13. siteCounters Configuration Syntax

```
<siteCounters
  enabled="[true|false]"
  defaultProvider="String"
  handlerPath="String"
  handlerType="String"
  rowsPerDay="Integer"
  >
    <providers>
      <add
        name="String"
        type="String"
        [providerSpecificSettings]
        />
      <remove
        name="String" />
      <clear/>
    </providers>

    <pageCounters
      enabled="[true|false]"
      defaultProvider="String"
      rowsPerDay="Integer"
      trackApplicationName="[true|false]"
      trackPageUrl="[true|false]"
      counterGroup="String"
      counterName="String">
```

continues

```
        <pagesToCount>
          <add path="String" />
          <remove path="String" />
          <clear/>
        </pagesToCount>
      </pageCounters>
    </siteCounters>
```

The attributes are described in Table 13.22.

TABLE 13.22. siteCounters Attributes

Attribute	Description
enabled	Indicates whether or not the service is enabled. The default value is `true`.
defaultProvider	Indicates the provider to use if no explicit provider is named. The default value is `AspNetAccessProvider`. If no default provider is specified, the first provider in the collection is used as the default.
handlerPath	Indicates the URL used to handle click-throughs. The default is `~/counters.axd`, which is an `HttpHandler` that intercepts page clicks and tracks the data.
handlerType	Defines the full name of the class that handles the site counter data. The shortened default is `System.Web.Handlers.SiteCountersHandler`. Full class details can be found in the configuration file.
rowsPerDay	Defines the granularity with which data is logged to the provider. The maximum value is `1440` (1 row per minute). The default value is `1`.

The two supplied providers for site counters, `AspNetAccessProvider` and `AspNetSqlProvider`, both have the same provider-specific attributes, as shown in Table 13.23.

TABLE 13.23. Access and SQL Server Site Counters Attributes

Attribute	Description
name	The name of the provider.
type	The full class name of the provider.

TABLE 13.23. Access and SQL Server Site Counters Attributes (continued)

Attribute	Description
connectionStringName	The name of the connection string, from the `<connectionStrings/>` configuration elements, that defines the connection details for the tracking database. This property is specific to Access and SQL Server.
description	A description of the provider.
commitInterval	The interval, in seconds, between flushes of the in-memory counters to the database. The default is 90.
commitTimeout	The time, in seconds, to wait before aborting the database command that writes the counters. The default is 60.

The `<pageCounters/>` section allows configuration of how pages are tracked as part of the Site Counters Service. The attributes are shown in Table 13.24.

TABLE 13.24. pageCounters Attributes

Attribute	Description
enabled	Indicates whether or not page tracking is enabled. This is ignored if site counters are disabled. The default value is `false`.
defaultProvider	Specifies the default provider to use for tracking pages.
rowsPerDay	Defines the granularity with which data is logged to the provider. The maximum value is 1440 (1 row per minute). The default value is 1.
trackApplicationName	Indicates whether or not the application name is tracked with the site counter details. The default value is `true`.
trackPageUrl	Indicates whether or not the URL of the current page is tracked with the site counter details. The default value is `true`.
counterGroup	Defines the group name to use for tracked pages. The default is `PageCounters`.
counterName	Defines the counter name to use for tracked pages.

The `<pagesToCount/>` element contains a collection of page names, meaning that the `add` and `remove` elements do not behave like ordinary `add` and `remove` elements that have a key. For the `add` element, the default value for the `path` attribute is `*`, which indicates that all pages recursively are included. Under default conditions, therefore, the `remove` element indicates the pages to exclude.

Personalization Profile

The `<profile/>` section allows configuration of the Personalization Profile service (see Listing 13.14).

LISTING 13.14. profile Configuration Syntax

```
<profile
  enabled="[true|false]"
  defaultProvider="String">
  <providers>
    <add name="String"
      type="String"
      [providerSpecificSettings]
      />
    <remove name="String"
      />
    <clear />

  <properties>
    <add
      name="String"
      readOnly="[true|false]"
      serializeAs="[String|Xml|Binary|ProviderSpecific]"
      provider="String"
      defaultValue="String"
      type="String"
      allowAnonymous="[true|false]"
      />
    <remove
      name="String"
      />
    <clear />
    <group name="String">
      <add
        name="String"
        readOnly="[true|false]"
        serializeAs="[String|Xml|Binary|ProviderSpecific]"
        provider="String"
        defaultValue="String"
        type="String"
        allowAnonymous="[true|false]"
```

```
      />
    <remove
      name="String"
      />
    </group>
  </properties>
</profile>
```

The `profile` and `profile providers` attributes are described in Tables 13.25 and 13.26, respectively.

TABLE 13.25. profile Attributes

Attribute	Description
enabled	A `Boolean` value indicating whether or not the profile is enabled. The default value is `true`.
defaultProvider	The name of the default provider. This should match one of the names supplied in the `providers` section. The default value is `AspNetAccessProvider`.

TABLE 13.26. profile providers Attributes

Attribute	Description
name	The name of the profile provider.
type	A string containing the full .NET type of the provider.
providerSpecificSettings	The provider-specific settings.

The `<properties/>` section allows definition of profile properties, including custom types such as a shopping cart, that can be stored with the profile details.

Table 13.27 shows the attributes of an individual property, as configured by the `<add/>` section. Only the `name` attribute is required—all others are optional.

TABLE 13.27. Individual Profile Property Attributes

Attribute	Description
name	Specifies the name of the profile.
readOnly	Indicates whether or not the property is read-only. The default value is false.
serializeAs	Defines how the property is serialized. Can be one of the items from the SettingsSerializeAs enumeration (from System.Configuration.Settings): • String: Indicates the property is serialized as a string. • Xml: Indicates the property is serialized as XML. • Binary: Indicates the property is serialized in a binary format. • ProviderSpecific: Indicates the property is serialized in a provider-specific way. The default value is ProviderSpecific.
provider	Defines the name of the property.
defaultValue	Defines the default value for the property.
type	Defines the type of the property.
allowAnonymous	Indicates whether or not values can be stored for anonymous users.

The <group/> section allows profile properties to be grouped into logical units. Each group is given a name, and within that group you can add properties, taking the same attributes as those in the <properties/> section.

Protocol Bindings

The <httpProtocolBindings/> section allows file types to be mapped to different HTTP pipelines in IIS. This will be used by Indigo to map the .svc file type to the appropriate pipeline. Listing 13.15 shows the syntax.

LISTING 13.15. httpProtocolBindings Configuration Syntax

```
<httpProtocolBindings defaultType="String">
  <add
    extension="String"
    type="String"
    validate="[true|false]"
  <clear />
</httpProtocolBindings>
```

The `defaultType` identifies the default type to be used and defaults to `System.Web.Hosting.AspNetHttpWorkerRequestHandler`. The attributes for added types (which map to the `HttpProtocolBinding` class) are shown in Table 13.28.

TABLE 13.28. httpProtocolBindings Attributes

Attribute	Description
extension	Indicates the file extension to be mapped to the handler.
type	Defines the type used to handle the protocol.
validate	Indicates whether or not the type is validated.

Role Manager

The `<roleManager/>` section allows configuration of roles for use in authorization (see Listing 13.16).

LISTING 13.16. roleManager Configuration Syntax

```
<roleManager
  defaultProvider="String"
  enabled="[true|false]"
  cacheRolesInCookie="[true|false]"
  cookieName="String"
  cookieTimeout="Integer"
  cookiePath="String"
  cookieRequireSSL="[true|false]"
  cookieSlidingExpiration="[true|false]"
  cookieProtection="[None|Validation|Encryption|All]"
  >
  <providers>
    <add name="String"
      type="String"
      [providerSpecificSettings]
      />
    <remove name="String"
      />
    <clear />
  </providers>
</roleManager>
```

The attributes for the `<roleManager/>` section are described in Table 13.29.

TABLE 13.29. roleManager Attributes

Attribute	Description
defaultProvider	Indicates the name of the default role provider. The default value is `AspNetAccessProvider`.
enabled	Indicates whether or not the Role Manager is enabled. The default value is `false`.
cacheRolesInCookie	Indicates whether or not cookies are used to store role information. The default value is `true`.
cookieName	Specifies the name of the cookie. The default value is `.ASPROLES`.
cookieTimeout	Specifies the time, in minutes, before the cookie expires. This cannot be `0` or less. The default value is `100000`.
cookiePath	Specifies the path, which is case-sensitive, used to write the cookie. Using `'/'` allows applications within the same domain to access the cookie. The default is `'/'`.
cookieRequireSSL	Indicates whether or not the cookie requires an SSL connection in order to be written to the client. The default value is `false`.
cookieSlidingExpiration	Indicates whether the cookie timeout resets on each request (a value of `true`) or expires at a fixed time (a value of `false`). The default value is `true`.
cookieProtection	Specifies the protection scheme used to store the cookie. Can be one of the `CookieProtection` enumeration values (from `System.Web.Security`): • `None`: Indicates no protection is used. • `Validation`: Indicates that the cookie is hashed and validated. • `Encryption`: Indicates that the cookie is encrypted. • `All`: Indicates that both validation and encryption are used. The default value is `None`.

Role Manager Providers

There are four supplied Role Manager providers:

- `AspNetSqlProvider`, which uses SQL Server to store and retrieve role information
- `AspNetAccessProvider`, which uses Access to store and retrieve role information

- `AuthorizationStoreRoleProvider`, which uses the Authorization Manager
- `WindowsToken`, which retrieves role information from the Windows authenticated token

The SQL Server and Access providers have the following attributes:

- `connectionStringName`, which defines the name of the connection string in the `<connectionStrings/>` configuration section
- `applicationName`, which defines the application to which the provider has scope

The Authorization Manager provider has the following attributes:

- `connectionStringName`, which defines the name of the connection string in the `<connectionStrings/>` configuration section
- `applicationName`, which defines the application to which the provider has scope
- `scopeName`, which indicates the scope (role information) within the application to which the authorization applies

All four providers also have `description` and `type` attributes.

Mail Servers

The `<smtpMail/>` section allows configuration of a mail server for use with the SMTP `Mail` class (see Listing 13.17).

LISTING 13.17. smtpMail Configuration Syntax

```
<smtpMail
  serverName="String"
  serverPort="Integer"
  from="String">
  <fields>
    <add name="String"
      value="String"
      typeName="String"
      />
    <remove name="String"
      />
    <clear />
  </fields>
</smtpMail>
```

The attributes are described in Table 13.30.

TABLE 13.30. smtpMail Attributes

Attribute	Description
serverName	Defines the name of the SMTP server. The default value is localhost.
serverPort	Defines the port used to send mail. This must be a positive number; the default value is 25.
from	Defines the from tag to use when sending mail.

Field Settings

The `<fields/>` section allows definition of custom fields for the SMTP mail server. The attributes are described in Table 13.31.

TABLE 13.31. smtpMail fields Attributes

Attribute	Description
name	Defines the name of the field.
value	Defines the value of the field.
typeName	Defines the data type of the field. The default value is String.

URL Mappings

The `<urlMappings/>` section allows configuration of URLs that will be rewritten, thus allowing the actual URL to be hidden. Here's the syntax:

```
<urlMappings
   enabled="[true|false]">
  <add
    url="String"
    mappedUrl="String"
    />
  <remove name="String"
    />
</urlMappings>
```

The attributes are detailed in Table 13.32. For removal, the url attribute must contain a relative URL starting with ~/.

TABLE 13.32. urlMappings Attributes

Attribute	Description
enabled	Indicates whether or not the URL mappings service is enabled. The default is true.
url	Specifies the displayed URL. This must be a relative URL starting with ~/.
mappedUrl	Specifies the actual URL. This must be a relative URL starting with ~/.

Web Parts

The `<webParts/>` section allows for configuration of Web Part personalization and data transformation. The configuration syntax is shown in Listing 13.18.

LISTING 13.18. webParts Configuration Syntax

```
<webParts>
  <personalization defaultProvider="String">
    <providers>
      <add
        name="String"
        type="String"
        />
      <remove name="String" />
      <clear />
    </providers>

    <authorization />

  </personalization>

  <transformers>
    <add
      name="String"
      type="String"
      />
    <remove name="String" />
    <clear />
  </transformers>
</webParts>
```

The `<providers/>` section follows the standard provider pattern, allowing personalization providers to be added or removed. The `<authorization/>` section follows the same format as for setting application authorization.

The `<transformers/>` section allows definition of data transformers, which convert data exposed by one Web Part into data accepted by another. This follows the standard provider pattern, allowing declaration of a transformer by its name and data type. There are three default transformers to convert Web Parts that implement the IRow interface into other forms:

- `RowToFieldTransformer`, to convert a row into a field
- `RowToFilterTransformer`, to convert a row into a filter
- `RowToParameterTransformer`, to convert a row into parameters

Web Parts are covered in Chapter 8.

Web Site Administration Tool

The Web Site Administration Tool is configured with the `<webSiteAdministrationTool/>` section (see Listing 13.19).

LISTING 13.19. webSiteAdministrationTool Configuration Syntax

```
<webSiteAdministrationTool
  defaultUrl="String"
  enabled="[true|false]"
  errorPage="String"
  localOnly="[true|false]"
  requireSSL="[true|false]"
  >
  <authorization>
    <allow
      [users|roles]="String"
      applicationPath="String"
      />
    <deny
      [users|roles]="String"
      applicationPath="String"
      />
  </authorization>
  <categories>
    <category
      title="String"
      navigateUrl="String"
      />
  </categories>
</webSiteAdministrationTool>
```

The attributes are described in Table 13.33.

TABLE 13.33. webSiteAdministrationTool Attributes

Attribute	Description
defaultUrl	Defines the URL of the Web Site Administration Tool and is used by the HttpHandler to redirect requests to WebAdmin.axd to the correct URL. The default value is /aspnet_webadmin/default.aspx.
enabled	Indicates whether or not the Web Site Administration Tool is enabled. The default value is true.
errorPage	Defines the page to use for displaying errors.
localOnly	Indicates whether or not the tool can be used only from the local machine (i.e., http://localhost).
requireSSL	Indicates whether or not the tool requires a secure channel.

Authorization Settings

The <authorization/> section allows configuration of which users or roles are allowed access to which parts of the administration interface. The attributes are described in Table 13.34.

TABLE 13.34. authorization Attributes

Attribute	Description
users/roles	Specifies the collection of users or roles defining who is allowed or denied access to the Web Site Administration Tool.
applicationPath	Defines the application that the users or roles are allowed or not allowed to administer.

The default value for the <authorization/> section is to allow all users from all application paths.

Categories

The <categories/> section defines the categories that appear on the main administration page, under which there are <category/> elements. Table 13.35 shows the attributes for these elements.

TABLE 13.35. category Attributes

Attribute	Description
title	Defines the category title.
navigateUrl	Defines the relative or absolute URL that will be requested for this category.

The default categories are:

* Home
* Security
* Profile
* Application
* Provider

Use of the tool is covered later in this chapter under the Web Site Administration Tool section.

Protected Data

Encryption of items within the configuration file (web.config) is now supported by the <protectedData/> section, the syntax of which is shown in Listing 13.20.

LISTING 13.20. protectedData Configuration Syntax

```
<protectedData defaultProvider="String">
  <providers>
    <add
      name="String"
      type="String"
      description="String"
      [providerSpecificConfiguration]
      />
  </providers>
  <protectedDataSections>
    <add
      name="String"
      Provider="String"
      />
  </protectedDataSections>
</protectedData>
```

This follows the standard provider pattern, and two providers are configured by default: `RSAProtectedConfigurationProvider` (the default) and `DataProtectionConfigurationProvider`, both implemented in `System.Configuration`.

The properties for the `RSAProtectedConfigurationProvider` are detailed in Table 13.36.

TABLE 13.36. RSAProtectedConfigurationProvider Attributes

Attribute	Description
cspProviderName	Specifies the name of the configuration section provider.
keyContainerName	Specifies the name of the key container used to store the key. Valid names are determined by the configuration section provider.
keyName	Specifies the name of the key.
RSAPublicKey	Specifies the RSA public key that corresponds to the key container.
useMachineContainer	Specifies whether or not a machine key container is used. The default value is `true`.
useOAEP	Specifies whether or not to use the optimal asymmetric encryption padding (OAEP) algorithm when writing the configuration. The default value is `false`.

The properties for the `DataProtectionConfigurationProvider` are detailed in Table 13.37.

TABLE 13.37. DataProtectionConfigurationProvider Attributes

Attribute	Description
doNotShowUI	Indicates whether or not to suppress the access user interface if the encryption is called from the client configuration system. The default value is `true`.
keyEntropy	Specifies the optional entropy for encryption and decryption.
keyName	Specifies the name of the key.
useMachineProtection	Indicates whether to use the per-machine mode of the API.

Sections within the configuration file are defined by use of the `<protectedDataSections/>` element, like so:

```
<protectedDataSections>
  <add name="connectionStrings"
       provider="RSAProtectedConfurationProvider" />
  <add name="appSettings"
       provider="RSAProtectedConfurationProvider" />
  <add name="system.web/identity"
       provider="RSAProtectedConfurationProvider" />
</protectedDataSections>
```

The section name should be in XPath syntax.

Sections Not Supported by Encryption

Several sections cannot be encrypted because they are not handled by section handlers, or they are consumed by the CLR by native code or XML parsers. These sections are listed here:

* `<processModel/>`
* `<runtime/>`
* `<mscorlib/>`
* `<startup/>`
* `<system.runtime.remoting/>`
* `<protectedData/>`
* `<satelliteAssemblies/>`
* `<cryptographySettings/>`
* `<cryptoNameMapping/>`
* `<cryptoClasses/>`

Section Encryption Tool

The `aspnet_regiis.exe` tool, which has been enhanced with the switches shown in Table 13.38, is used to manage protected sections of the configuration file. A separate tool for this may be provided in the future.

Table 13.39 shows the syntax for using these switches.

TABLE 13.38. Encryption Tool Switches

Switch	Operation
-pe	Encrypt.
-pd	Decrypt.
-pc	Create key.
-pz	Delete key.
-pi	Import key.
-px	Export key.
-pa	Add ACE.
-pr	Remove ACE.
-csp	Use this configuration section provider for the operation.
-pku	Use the keystore for the current user. By default the machine store is used.
-prov	Specify the provider to use for the operation.
-app	Treat the following virtual path as an application file. By default `machine.config` is used.

TABLE 13.39. Syntax for Encryption Tool Switches

Action	Switches
Encryption	`-pe configurationXPath [-prov provider] [-app virtualPath]`
Decryption	`-pd configurationXPath [-app virtualPath]`
Create key	`-pc ContainerName [-csp csp] [-pku] [-exp] [-size sizeSpecifier]`
Delete key	`-pz ContainerName [-csp csp] -pkm|-pku`
Import key	`-pi ContainerName InputFile [-csp] [-pku] [-exp]`
Export key	`-px ContainerName ExportFile [-csp] [-pku] [-pri]`
Add ACE	`-pa ContainerName Account [-csp] [-pku] [-full]`
Remove ACE	`-pr ContainerName Account [-csp] [-pku]`

For example, to encrypt a section you first create a public key:

```
aspnet_regiis -pc MySecretKeys -pku -exp -size 1024
```

The encryption can then be done by using this code:

```
aspnet_regiis -pe connectionStrings -app MyApplicationName
```

In shared environments it may be necessary to export keys so that a centrally stored encrypted configuration file (e.g., one stored in a source code control system) can be checked out and used by developers. The keys can be exported from the server like so:

```
aspnet_regiis -px MySecretKeys myKeys.xml –pri
```

The developer can then import them into the local Web Server:

```
aspnet_regiis –pi MySecretKeys myKeys.xml
```

> Encryption of configuration sections was not supported in the Technology Preview release.

Health Monitoring

The `<healthMonitoring/>` section allows configuration of the ASP.NET Windows monitoring data, allowing it to be written to a variety of data stores such as SQL Server or Windows Management Instrumentation (WMI). This data can be consumed by products such as HealthMon. Listing 13.21 shows the syntax for this section.

LISTING 13.21. healthMonitoring Configuration Syntax

```
<healthMonitoring
    enabled=" [true|false] "
    heartBeatInterval="Integer">

    <bufferModes>
      <add name="String"
        maxBufferSize="Integer"
        maxFlushSize="Integer"
        urgentFlushThreshold="Integer"
        regularFlushInterval=" [Infinite|Integer] "
        urgentFlushInterval="TimeSpan"
        maxBufferThreads="Integer"
```

```
          />
      </bufferModes>

      <providers>
        <add
          name="String"
          type="String"
          [providerSpecificProperties]
          />
      <clear />
      </providers>

      <eventMappings>
        <add
          name="String"
          type="String"
          startEventCode="Integer"
          endEventCode="Integer"
          />
        <clear />
      </eventMappings>

      <profiles>
        <add name="String"
          minInstances="Integer"
          maxLimit="[Infinite|Integer]"
          minInterval="TimeSpan"
          custom="String"
          />
        <clear />
      </profiles>

      <rules>
        <add name="String"
          eventName="String"
          provider="String"
          profile="String"
          minInterval="TimeSpan"
          minInstances="Integer"
          maxLimit="[Infinite|Integer]"
          custom="String"
          />
        <clear />
        <remove
          name="String" />
      </rules>

</healthMonitoring>
```

For the root `<healthMonitoring/>` element the attributes allow health monitoring to be enabled or disabled and the `heartBeatInterval` set, which specifies how often, in seconds, the `WebHeartBeatEvent` is raised. The default is `0`, which means the event is never raised.

Buffer Modes

Buffer modes define the number of events that are buffered and how often the buffer is flushed. The properties for the `<bufferModes/>` section are shown in Table 13.40.

TABLE 13.40. bufferModes Attributes

Attribute	Description
name	The name of the buffer mode setting.
maxBufferSize	The maximum number of events that can be buffered at one time.
maxFlushSize	The number of events flushed in a single flush.
urgentFlushThreshold	The number of events accumulated in the buffer before it is flushed.
regularFlushInterval	The time between attempted buffer flushes.
urgentFlushInterval	The minimum time that must pass between flushes.
maxBufferThreads	The maximum number of threads used for buffering.

TABLE 13.41. Configured Buffer Modes

Attribute	Value	Value	Value	Value
name	Critical Notification	Notification	Analysis	Logging
maxBufferSize	100	300	1000	1000
maxFlushSize	20	20	100	200
urgentFlushThreshold	1	1	100	800
regularFlushInterval	Infinite	Infinite	00:05:00	00:30:00
urgentFlushInterval	00:01:00	00:01:00	00:01:00	00:05:00
maxBufferThreads	1	1	1	1

Four buffer modes are configured by default (`Critical Notification`, `Notification`, `Analysis`, and `Logging`); their properties are shown in Table 13.41.

Providers

The health monitoring `<providers/>` section defines the providers used to write WMI events. There are only two mandatory properties, `name` and `type`, which follow the standard conventions for providers, giving the name and full type of the provider class. Each provider can then implement specific properties as required. Three providers are configured by default:

- `EventLogProvider`, which writes events to the Event Log
- `SqlWebEventProvider`, which writes events to SQL Server
- `WmiWebEventProvider`, which writes to the WMI event sink

Only the SQL Server provider has additional attributes, which are described in Table 13.42.

TABLE 13.42. SqlWebEventProvider Attributes

Attribute	Description
connectionStringName	The name of the connection string. The default value is `LocalSqlServer`.
maxEventDetailsLength	The maximum length for event details. The default is `1073741823`.
buffer	Indicates whether or not events are buffered. The default value is `false`.
bufferMode	The name (as shown in Table 13.41) of the buffer mode to use if buffering is enabled. The default value is `Notification`.

Event Mappings

The `<eventMappings/>` section maps event codes to event classes. The attributes are shown in Table 13.43.

TABLE 13.43. eventMappings Attributes

Attribute	Description
name	The name of the event class.
type	The type of the event class.
startEventCode	The starting event code range. The default is 0.
endEventCode	The ending event code range. The default is the maximum size for an integer (Int32.MaxValue).

By default the following events are mapped, all using the default values for the event codes:

- System.Web.Management.WebBaseEvent
- System.Web.Management.WebHeartBeatEvent
- System.Web.Management.WebApplicationLifetimeEvent
- System.Web.Management.WebRequestEvent
- System.Web.Management.WebBaseErrorEvent
- System.Web.Management.WebErrorEvent
- System.Web.Management.WebRequestErrorEvent
- System.Web.Management.WebAuditEvent
- System.Web.Management.WebFailureAuditEvent
- System.Web.Management.WebSuccessAuditEvent

Profiles

The `<profiles/>` section allows profiles to be defined for health events. The attributes are shown in Table 13.44.

Two profiles, named Default and Critical, are configured by default, both with minInstances set to 1 and maxLimit set to Infinite. For Default the minInterval is 1 minute (00:01:00), and for Critical it is 0 (00:00:00).

TABLE 13.44. profiles Attributes

Attribute	Description
name	The name of the profile.
minInstances	The minimum number of occurrences of the event before it is fired. The default value is 1.
maxLimit	The maximum number of occurrences of the event, after which it stops being fired. The default value is Infinite.
minInterval	The minimum time between two events of the same type being fired. The default value is 0.
custom	The full type of a class that implements IWebEventCustomEvaluator.

Rules

The `<rules/>` section defines the mappings between event types, providers, and associated profiles. They dictate which event is sent to which provider and which throttling parameters are applied. Table 13.45 shows the attributes.

TABLE 13.45. rules Attributes

Attribute	Description
name	The name of the rule.
eventName	The name of the event type, as specified in the `<eventMappings/>` section.
provider	The name of the provider.
profile	The name of the profile for the event type, as specified in the `<profiles/>` section.

In addition, the `<rules/>` section supports the same attributes supported by the `<profiles/>` section (shown in Table 13.44), allowing those profile attributes to be overridden for rules.

Two rules (All Errors Default and Failure Audits Default) are configured by default, as shown in Table 13.46.

TABLE 13.46. Default Rules

Attribute	Value	Value
name	All Errors Default	Failure Audits Default
eventName	All Errors	Failure Audits
provider	EventLogProvider	EventLogProvider
profile	Default	Default
minInterval	00:01:00	00:01:00

Health monitoring was not supported in the Technology Preview release.

State Management

Because Web applications are transmitted via HTTP, we have to carefully ensure that any state we require is kept between postbacks to the server. In ASP most state was handled by the SessionState dictionary, but in ASP.NET controls intrinsically handled their own state via the viewstate mechanism. However, the problem with this is that viewstate can become large, especially when dealing with grids.

One of the goals of ASP.NET 2.0 is to add flexibility by introducing three new state handling mechanisms:

- **Control state,** allowing controls to store specific state that they require between round-trips
- **Page state,** where a history of state is kept, ensuring that state for mobile browsers is synchronized with the state held on the server
- **Session state plugability,** allowing custom state modules to replace the existing session state module

As part of this support for session bases, state persistence is also supported. This allows state to be stored server-side when dealing with mobile browsers, where large pages can be a limiting factor for both memory and bandwidth reasons.

Control State

In ASP.NET 1.x, controls save state as part of the viewstate. However, viewstate is really intended to store state set by the application, not individual controls. Additionally, if viewstate is turned off at the page level, several controls break (e.g., the current view of a multiview or the sort order of a sortable data grid). The only solution is to reset the properties on every request, which is not always practical because the controls themselves decide what state they need.

To solve this problem, a new state has been created, called control state, to store control-specific state. Control state is stored in a hidden field (called __CONTROLSTATE) in the same way as viewstate, but it is completely separate from viewstate and thus works when viewstate is turned off. For example, consider a ContentPager control:

```
<asp:ContentPager runat="server" />
```

This would normally require viewstate, but under the new model its viewstate is 0 and the control state is 12 bytes. This can be found by looking at a new column when tracing is enabled, as shown in Figure 13.1.

Control Tree				
Control UniqueID	Type	Render Size Bytes (including children)	Viewstate Size Bytes (excluding children)	Controlstate Size Bytes (excluding children)
__Page	ASP.paging_datalist_aspx	2543	0	0
_ctl1	System.Web.UI.LiteralControl	22	0	0
_ctl2	System.Web.UI.ResourceBasedLiteralControl	329	0	0
_ctl3	System.Web.UI.LiteralControl	117	0	0
_ctl0	System.Web.UI.HtmlControls.HtmlForm	2055	0	0
_ctl4	System.Web.UI.LiteralControl	7	0	0
MyPager	System.Web.UI.WebControls.ContentPager	162	0	12
MyPager$_ctl0	System.Web.UI.WebControls.LinkButton	0	0	0
MyPager$_ctl1	System.Web.UI.WebControls.ImageButton	0	0	0
MyPager$_ctl8	System.Web.UI.LiteralControl	0	0	0
MyPager$_ctl2	System.Web.UI.WebControls.LinkButton	0	0	0
MyPager$_ctl3	System.Web.UI.WebControls.ImageButton	0	0	0
MyPager$_ctl9	System.Web.UI.LiteralControl	0	0	0
MyPager$_ctl4	System.Web.UI.WebControls.LinkButton	62	0	0

FIGURE 13.1. Page trace showing control state

Implementing Control State in Custom Controls

When creating custom controls, control state can be implemented by the following three steps:

1. Calling Page.RegisterRequiresControlState()
2. Overriding SaveControlState() and returning the control state
3. Overriding LoadControlState() and processing the control state

Listing 13.22 shows an example.

LISTING 13.22. Implementing Control State

```
Public Class MyControl
    Inherits WebControl

  Private _myProperty As Integer

  Protected Overrides Sub OnInit(E As EventArgs)
    Page.RegisterRequiresControlState(Me)
    MyBase.OnInit(E)
  End  Sub

  Protected Overrides Function SaveControlState() As Object
    Return CType(_MyProperty, Object)
  End Function

  Protected Overrides Sub LoadControlState(State As Object)
    If State <> Nothing Then
      _myProperty = Convert.ToInt32(state)
    End If
  End Sub

End Class
```

It is important to remember that control state is designed for critical private storage of state, so storage should be kept to a minimum.

Page State Persistence

ASP.NET 1.x persisted all viewstate to a hidden control on a page. As mentioned earlier, this can be inconvenient for some devices (such as phones), where the reduced bandwidth means slower loading speeds and reduced memory means a limited page size. Under these circumstances it's sensible to store state on the server.

In ASP.NET 2.0 the page adapter architecture allows for page state to be implemented by an object that inherits from a page state persister. This lets the page abstract the storage of state into a separate class, which the adapter can implement, allowing different state mechanisms to be implemented depending on the adapter.

The framework supplies two page state persisters:

* `HiddenFieldPageStatePersister`, which stores server-side hidden form controls, such as viewstate and control state
* `SessionPageStatePersister`, which keeps a history of viewstates and control states in session state

The latter of these is implemented in a way similar to the viewstate persistence in the MMIT from version 1.x.

Session State Plugability

By default there are three ways to store session state:

- In-Process, stored within the ASP.NET worker process
- State Server, stored in the Windows State Server service
- SQL Server, stored within a SQL Server database

These provide most users with what they need, but session state handling in version 1.x isn't extensible. ASP.NET 2.0 allows session state to be completely unplugged and replaced with a custom module. In addition, there is a new Session State ID module, allowing just the creation of IDs for session state to be replaced. Both of these allow custom data stores or even just custom handling of the session data.

There are two ways to provide custom session state handling. The first is to author a completely new session state module; the other is to just replace portions of the existing system. The first of these is the most flexible solution but also the most complex, whereas the second is simpler because you can replace only those bits that need to be changed. For example, you could just implement an Oracle session provider.

To replace the session state system, you can do any of the following:

- Replace the `SessionStateModule` class with one that implements `IHttpModule`.
- Replace the `HttpSessionStateProvider` class with one that implements `IHttpSessionState`.
- Replace the `SessionIDModule` class with one that implements `ISessionIDModule`.

Only the first of these is required to implement your own method of handling session state. Optionally you can implement your own `HttpSessionStateProvider` to provide your own storage mechanism for session state or implement `SessionIDModule` to provide creation of session IDs. As mentioned, you don't need to implement these—there's no requirement for a custom session state module to implement ID handling at all. In fact, you don't even need an `HttpSessionStateProvider`, although your custom class has to return an object that implements `IHttpSessionState`.

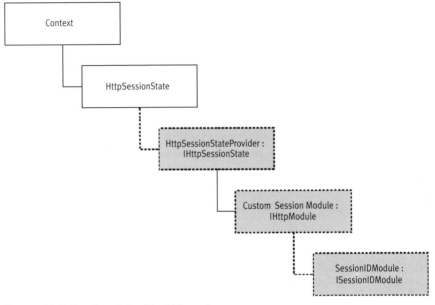

FIGURE 13.2. Session state object hierarchy

Together the three of these provide a complete implementation of session state. Figure 13.2 shows the hierarchy of objects.

Once session state is implemented, you can simply replace the existing module with the new custom module by editing the `<httpModules/>` configuration section (see Listing 13.23).

LISTING 13.23. Configuring Your Own Session State

```
<configuration>
  <system.web>
    <httpModules>
      <remove name="Session" />
      <add name="Session"
          type="AW.MyStateModule, MyStateModule" />
    </httpModules>
  </system.web>
</configuration>
```

The second approach to customizing session state is to use the existing session state module but to replace portions of it, such as

- `ISessionDictionary`, which is the interface for the class that manages the session data

- `SessionStateStoreItem`, which represents the data retrieved from the session data store
- `SessionIDModule`, which represents the handling of IDs for the session
- `ISessionStateStore`, which is the interface for the class that provides the interface to the actual data store

Only the session state store (`ISessionStateStore`) is required to customize session state—replacing other classes is optional, allowing the existing functionality to be preserved while customizing just selected sections. The hierarchy of these items is shown in Figure 13.3.

If implementing a custom state provider class, this can be configured by modifying the `<sessionState/>` section of the configuration file:

```
<configuration>
  <system.web>
    <sessionState mode="Custom"
      customType="AW.MyStateModule, StateModule"
      />
  </system.web>
</configuration>
```

A more detailed explanation of customizing session state is beyond the scope of this book.

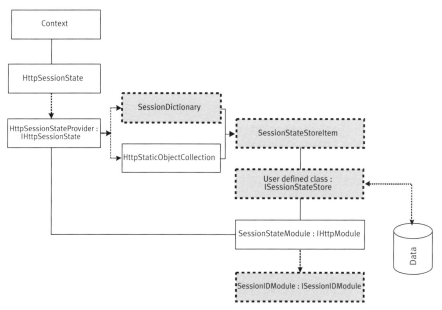

FIGURE 13.3. Session state customization

The Web Site Administration Tool

The Web Site Administration Tool provides Web-based configuration for selected application options. It is accessed through a special HTTP handler, `WebAdmin.axd`, accessed from the root of the application. For example, to access the Web Site Administration Tool for a virtual application called `MySite` on the local machine you would use the following URL:

```
http://localhost/MySite/WebAdmin.axd
```

Upon accessing this URL you see the administration Home page, as shown in Figure 13.4.

The first section is Security, as shown in Figure 13.5. This section, which allows configuration of the security provider, users, and roles, was covered in Chapter 6.

The third section, Profile, covers the Personalization Profile, allowing the enablement of personalization and whether personalization can be applied for anonymous users. Also allowed is the configuration of Profile properties, as shown in Figure 13.6. You also have the option to delete profile property values, thus allowing you to expunge stale data from the data store.

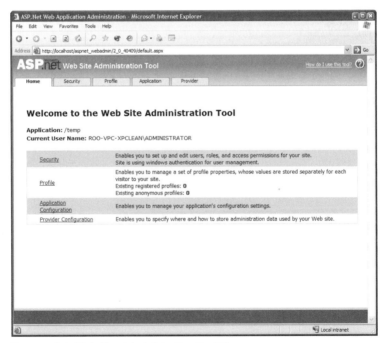

FIGURE 13.4. Web Site Administration Tool Home page

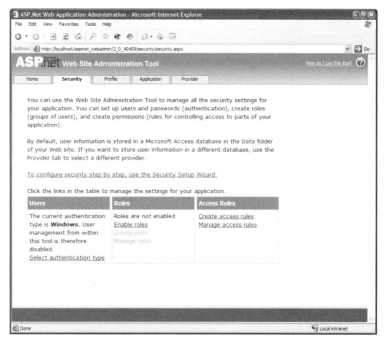

FIGURE 13.5. Configuring security

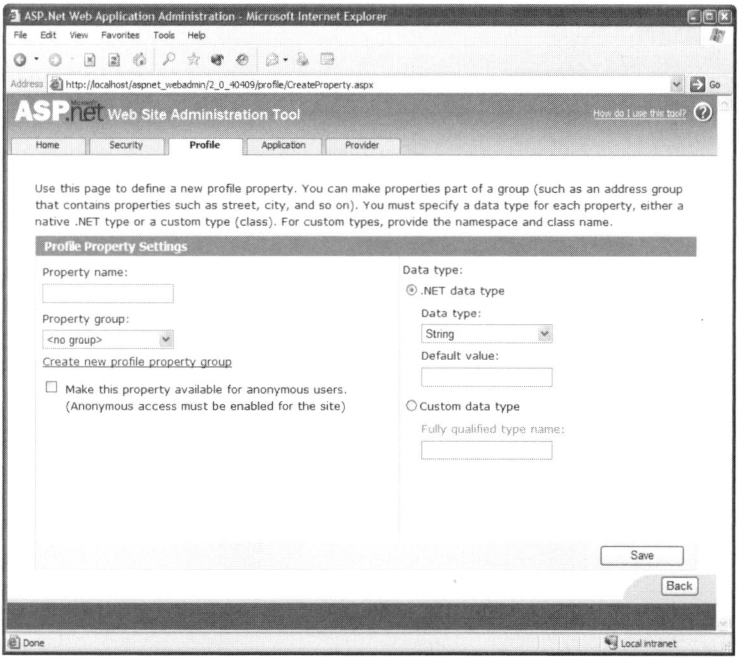

FIGURE 13.6. Configuring the Profile

The Application section deals with four areas:

- Application Settings, where the `<appSettings/>` configuration section can be modified
- Site Statistics, where site and page counters can be configured
- SMTP Settings, to allow an SMTP mail server to be set
- Debugging and Tracing, to enable debugging, tracing, and configuration of an error page

Most of these are simple, but the Site Statistics part not only covers configuration of site and page counters but also includes reports. Figure 13.7 shows the options allowed for site and page counters, such as whether to enable counting for individual pages and how often to aggregate the counters. Figure 13.8 shows how you can select individual pages, on which site counters will be enabled, and Figure 13.9 shows the reports for those pages that have counters enabled.

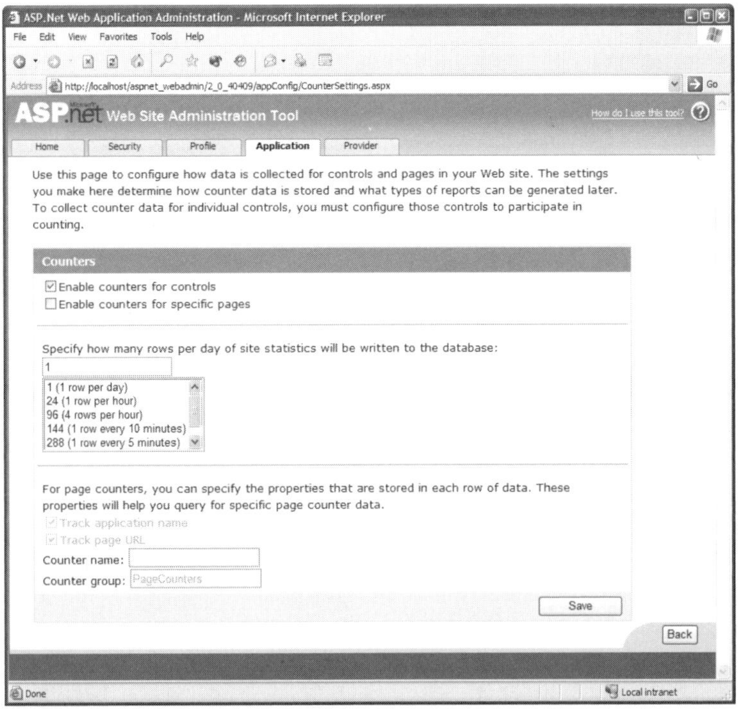

FIGURE 13.7. Configuring site and page counters

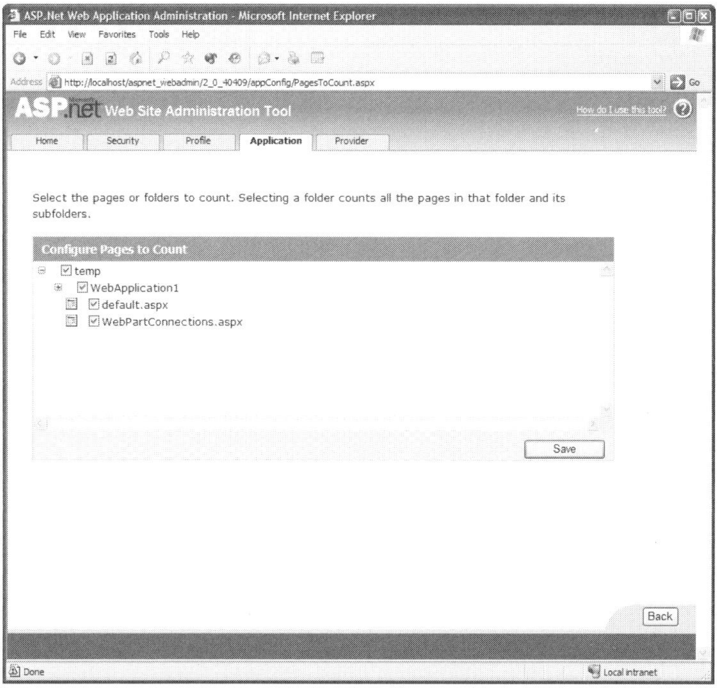

FIGURE 13.8. Configuring which pages to include in the page counters

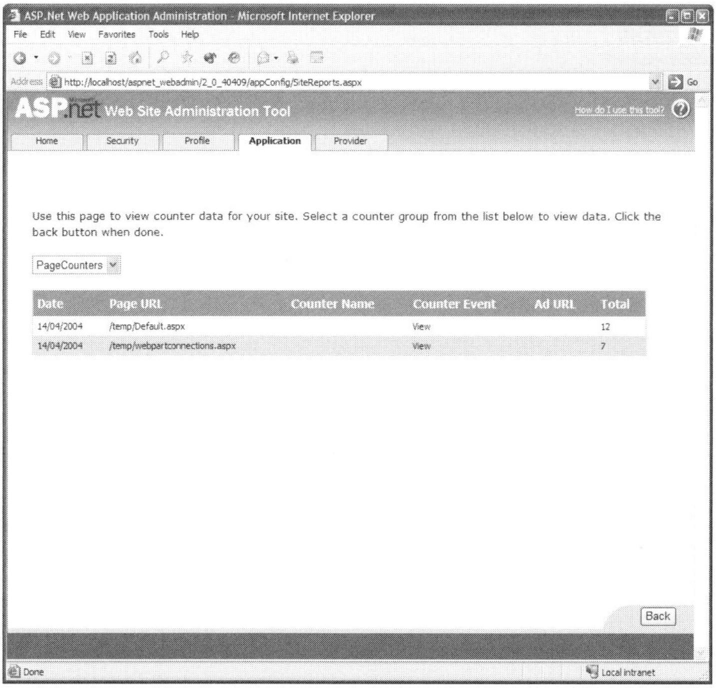

FIGURE 13.9. Viewing page counter reports

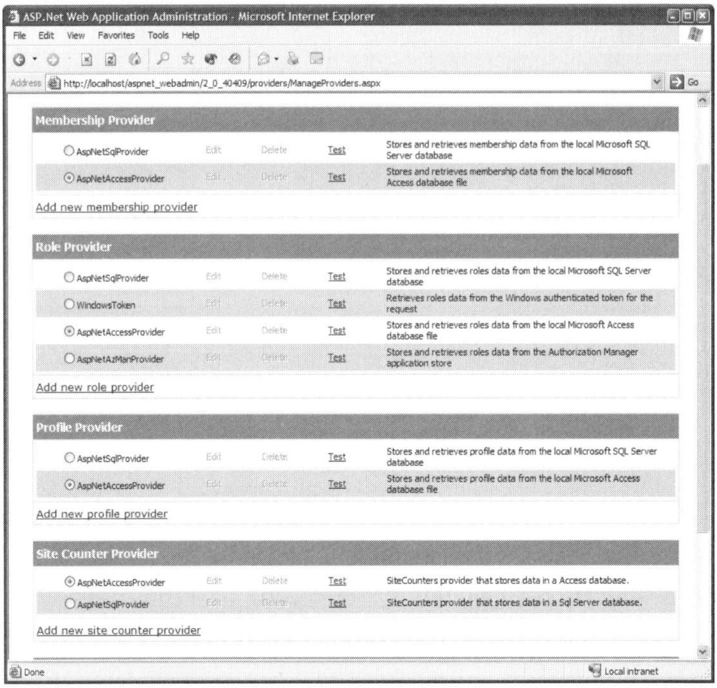

FIGURE 13.10. Configuring application providers

The final section of the Web Site Administration Tool, Provider, allows setting the providers. This can either be a single provider for the application or individual providers, as shown in Figure 13.10.

The Management API

There's no doubt that the Web Site Administration Tool is a great utility to help administer an application, but some administrative tasks either aren't suited to a Web interface or need to be run before the application is created (or as part of the application).

ASP.NET 2.0 provides a comprehensive Management API, which allows complete manipulation of the XML configuration files as well as integration with IIS. In particular, the following configuration tasks are supported.

- View configuration data merged from all levels of an application hierarchy.
- Allow configuration changes to specific configuration files.
- Import and export configuration sections.
- Create new configuration sections.

These features allow you to set up and configure not only local machines but also remote machines.

IIS Integration

The Management API has been integrated into the IIS Management Console, so when you view the properties of a site or virtual directory, you now see an additional ASP.NET tab, as shown in Figure 13.11.

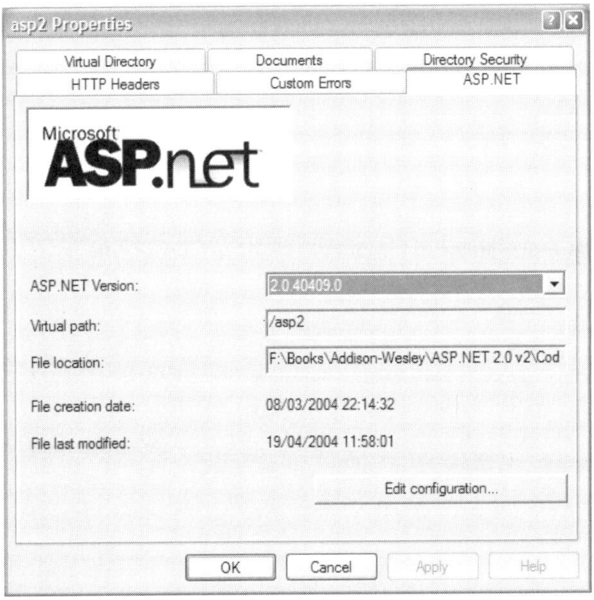

FIGURE 13.11. IIS ASP.NET configuration

On this screen you can see the current ASP.NET version, with a drop-down list allowing you to select other versions to use for this application (if other versions are installed). You can also see the full path to the application and the dates and times the configuration file was created and changed.

Figure 13.12 shows the screen that appears when the Edit configuration button is selected. Here you can see tabs for the major configuration sections. We won't go through them in detail because they just map the properties from the XML file. Any settings that don't appear to have a tab themselves are on other tabs—Membership and Roles are on the Authentication tab, and things like Tracing, Compilation, HTTP Handlers, and so on are on the Advanced tab.

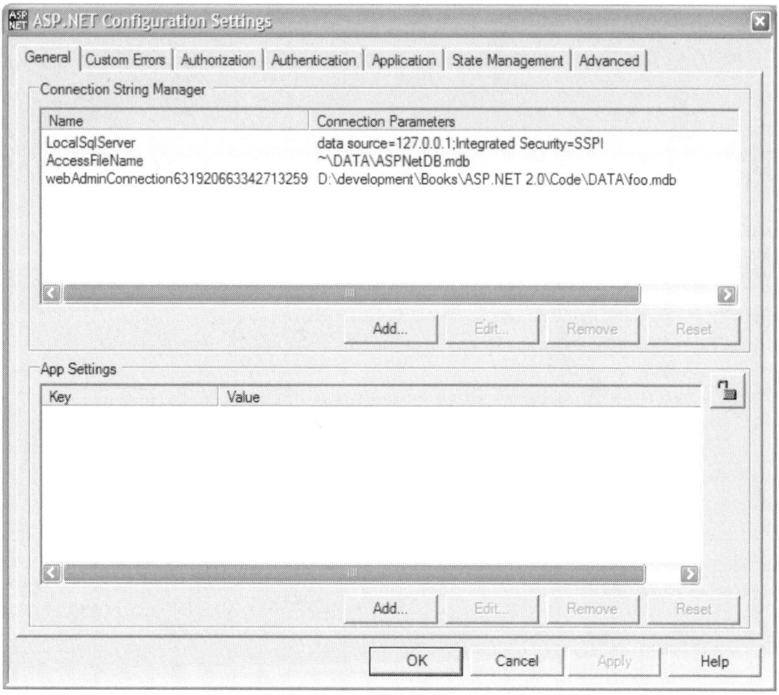

FIGURE 13.12. ASP.NET Configuration Settings window

There are two things to note about this interface.

- It shows a merged view of the settings and thus includes settings from all levels of the hierarchy.
- Sections can be locked, thus preventing any changes at a lower level in the application hierarchy. When locking a section is allowed, you'll see a padlock icon next to the section.

Management Classes

The management classes reside in the System.Configuration and System.Web.Configuration namespaces, and provide access to configuration files at both the machine and application levels. There are too many classes to detail here, but the examples shown should give you a good start in seeing what's possible with the API.

At the root of everything is the Configuration object from System.Configuration. This provides properties such as AppSettings and ConnectionStrings to access their equivalent sections in the configuration file. There are also methods such as GetMachineConfiguration to access the machine-level configuration file, and GetWebConfiguration for the application configuration file. For sections within the `<system.web/>` configuration section the classes live in `System.Web.Configuration`, which contains classes such as `AuthorizationSection`, `OutputCacheSection`, and `ProfileSection` to provide strongly typed access to the configuration. For example, Listing 13.24 shows how to access the `<profile/>` configuration section.

LISTING 13.24. Accessing the Profile Configuration Section

```
Dim cfg As System.Configuration.Configuration
Dim profSection As System.Web.Configuration.ProfileSection

Sub Page_Load(ByVal sender As Object, ByVal e As System.EventArgs)

cfg = Configuration.GetWebConfiguration("/temp")
profSection = CType(cfg.GetSection("system.web/profile"), _
                    System.Web.Configuration.ProfileSection)
```

The properties of the `<profile/>` configuration section are held as a collection, accessed via the `PropertySettings` method, allowing them to be bound to grids, accessed directly, and added to, as shown in Listing 13.25. The `Update` method must be called for changes to any configuration value to be flushed to the file.

LISTING 13.25. Updating the Profile Configuration Section

```
Dim propSettings As New System.Web.Configuration.ProfilePropertySet-
tings()
propSettings.Name = PropertyName.Text
propSettings.Type = PropertyType.Text

profSection.PropertySettings.Add(propSettings)
cfg.Update()
```

A good way to understand more about how the `Configuration` API works is to examine the code for the Web Site Administration Tool, which can be found under `InetPub\wwwroot\aspnet_webadmin`.

> Note that the ASP.NET process needs write permissions on both the `web.config` file and the application directory. This is because a copy of `web.config` is created during the update process and removed once the update is complete.

SUMMARY

Although left to the end of the book, this chapter certainly doesn't contain the least useful material. In fact, in many ways it contains some of the most useful information because the increased administration facilities reduce the time (and potential for errors) that inevitably get tied up with administrative work. Simplifying the tasks required, adding an API to allow custom administration, and providing a Web-based administration tool make our jobs much easier.

That may not seem so important, but consider what the bulk of this chapter has been about—documenting the changes to the configuration files. There are many changes and new sections, so anything that enables us to administer them more easily is a boon.

Now it's time for you to come to grips with all of the new and exciting features. Install the .NET Framework and start playing. You'll soon be wondering how you lived without the new features that ASP.NET 2.0 offers.

Index

Microsoft .NET Development Series

.NET Framework
Standard Library
Annotated Reference

Volume 1:

Microsoft .NET Framework
Class Libraries Team
Brad Abrams, Editor

0321154894

.NET Web Services
Architecture and Implementation

Keith Ballinger

0321113594

A First Look at
SQL Server 2005
for Developers

Bob Beauchemin
Niels Berglund
Dan Sullivan

0321180593

Essential .NET
Volume 1
The Common Language Runtime

Don Box
with Chris Sells

0201734117

Graphics
Programming
with GDI+

Mahesh Chand

0321160770

The C#
Programming
Language

Anders Hejlsberg
Scott Wiltamuth
Peter Golde

0321154916

A First Look at
ADO.NET and
System Xml v 2.0

Alex Homer
Dave Sussman
Mark Fussell

0321228391

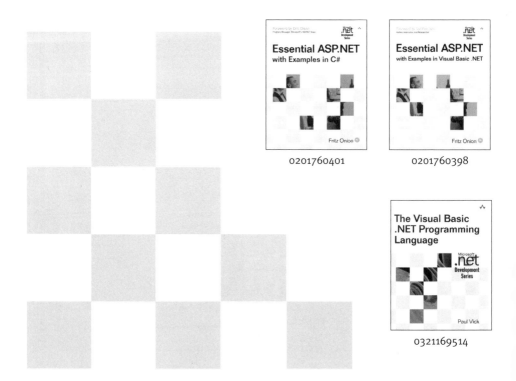

Essential ASP.NET
with Examples in C#

Fritz Onion

0201760401

Essential ASP.NET
with Examples in Visual Basic .NET

Fritz Onion

0201760398

The Visual Basic
.NET Programming
Language

Paul Vick

0321169514

For more information go to
www.awprofessional.com/msdotnetseries/

A First Look at
ASP.NET v.2.0

Alex Homer
Dave Sussman
Rob Howard

0321228960

The
Common Language
Infrastructure
Annotated Standard

James S. Miller
Susann Ragsdale

0321154932

Building Applications
and Components with
Visual Basic .NET

Ted Pattison
with Dr. Joe Hummel

0201734958

Windows Forms
Programming in C#

Chris Sells

0321116208

Windows Forms
Programming in
Visual Basic .NET

Chris Sells
Justin Gehtland

0321125193

Programming
in the .NET
Environment

Damien Watkins
Mark Hammond
Brad Abrams

0201770180

Pragmatic ADO.NET
Data Access for the Internet World

Shawn Wildermuth

0201745682

.NET Compact
Framework Programming
with C#

Paul Yao
David Durant

0321174038

.NET Compact
Framework Programming
with Visual Basic .NET

Paul Yao
David Durant

0321174046